OBJECTS, ABSTRACTION, DATA STRUCTURES AND DESIGN USING C++

ELLIOT B. KOFFMAN
Temple University

PAUL A. T. WOLFGANG
Temple University

WILEY

John Wiley & Sons, Inc.

ASSOCIATE PUBLISHER	Dan Sayre
ACQUISITIONS EDITOR	Paul Crockett / Bill Zobrist
PROJECT MANAGER	Cindy Johnson, Publishing Services
SENIOR EDITORIAL ASSISTANT	Bridget Morrisey
SENIOR PRODUCTION EDITOR	Ken Santor
MARKETING MANAGER	Phyllis Diaz Cerys
PRODUCT MANAGER	Catherine Shultz
SENIOR DESIGNER	Kevin Murphy
COVER DESIGNER	Howard Grossman
TEXT DESIGN AND COMPOSITION	Greg Johnson, Art Directions
MEDIA EDITOR	Stefanie Liebman
FRONT COVER PHOTO	© Michael Powers/Image State
BACK COVER PHOTO	© Philip and Karen Smith/Image State

This book was set in 10 point Sabon, and printed and bound by R.R. Donnelley–Crawfordsville. The cover was printed by Phoenix Color Corporation.

This book is printed on acid free paper.

CREDITS: Figure 1.2, page 67, Booch, Jacobson, Rumbaugh, *Unified Modeling Language User Guide* (AW Object Tech Series), pg. 451, ©1999 by Addison Wesley Longman, Inc. Reprinted by permission of Pearson Education, Inc., publishing as Pearson Addison Wesley. Figure 6.1, page 358, Photodisc/Punchstock.

To order books or for customer service please, call 1-800-CALL WILEY (225-5945).

Library of Congress Cataloging-in-Publication Data

Koffman, Elliot B.
  Objects, abstraction, data structures, and design : using C++ / Elliot B.
Koffman, Paul A.T. Wolfgang.
    p. cm.
  Includes bibliographical references and index.
  ISBN-13: 978-0-471-46755-7 (pbk.)
  ISBN-10: 0-471-46755-3 (pbk.)
  1. Object-oriented programming (Computer science) 2. Data structures
(Computer science) 3. Application program interfaces (Computer software)
4. C++ (Computer program language) I. Wolfgang, Paul A. T. II. Title.
  QA76.64.K63 2005
  005.1'17--dc22
                        2005021403

ISBN-13 978-0-471-46755-7
ISBN-10 0-471-46755-3

Printed in the United States of America
10 9 8 7 6 5 4 3 2 1

Preface

Our goal in writing this book was to combine a strong emphasis on problem solving and software design with the study of data structures. To this end, we discuss applications of each data structure to motivate its study. After providing the specification (a header file) and the implementation of an abstract data type, we cover case studies that use the data structure to solve a significant problem. Examples include a phone directory using an array and a list, postfix expression evaluation using a stack, simulation of an airline ticket counter using a queue, and Huffman coding using a binary tree and a priority queue. In the implementation of each data structure and in the solutions of the case studies, we reinforce the message "Think, then code" by performing a thorough analysis of the problem and then carefully designing a solution (using pseudocode and UML class diagrams) before the implementation. We also provide a performance analysis when appropriate. Readers gain an understanding of why different data structures are needed, the applications they are suited for, and the advantages and disadvantages of their possible implementations.

The text is designed for the second course in programming, especially those that apply object-oriented design (OOD) to the study of data structures and algorithms. The text could carry over to the third course in algorithms and data structures for schools with a three-course sequence. In addition to the coverage of the basic data structures and algorithms (lists, stacks, queues, trees, recursion, sorting), there are chapters on sets and maps, balanced binary search trees, and graphs. Although we expect that most readers will have completed a first programming course in C++, there is an extensive review chapter for those who may have taken a first programming course in a different object-oriented language, or for those who need a refresher in C++.

Think, Then Code To help readers "Think, then code," we provide the appropriate software design tools and background in the first two chapters before they begin their formal study of data structures. The first chapter discusses two different models for the software life cycle and for object-oriented design (OOD), the use of the Uniform Modeling Language™ (UML) to document an OOD, and the use of interfaces to specify abstract data types and to facilitate contract programming. We develop the solution to an extensive case study to illustrate these principles. The second chapter focuses on program correctness and efficiency by discussing exceptions and exception handling, different kinds of testing and testing strategies, debugging with and without a debugger, reasoning about programs, and using big-O notation. As part of our emphasis on OOD, we introduce two design patterns in Chapter 3, the object factory and delegation. We make use of them where appropriate in the textbook.

Case Studies As mentioned earlier, we apply these concepts to design and implement the new data structures and to solve approximately 20 case studies. Case studies follow a five-step process (problem specification, analysis, design, implementation, and testing). As is done in industry, we sometimes perform these steps in an iterative fashion rather than in strict sequence. Several case studies have extensive discussions of testing and include methods that automate the testing process. Some case studies are revisited in later chapters, and solutions involving different data structures are compared.

Data Structures in the C++ Standard Library Each data structure that we introduce faithfully follows the C++ Standard Library (commonly called the STL) for that data structure (if it exists) and readers are encouraged throughout the text to use the STL as a resource for their programming. We begin the study of a new data structure by specifying an abstract data type as an interface, which we adapt from the C++ STL. Therefore, our expectation is that readers who complete this book will be familiar with the data structures available in the C++ STL and will be able to use them immediately and in their future programming. They will also know "what is under the hood" so they will have the ability to implement these data structures. The degree to which instructors cover the implementation of the data structures will vary, but we provide ample material for those who want to study it thoroughly.

We use modern C++ programming practices to a greater extent than most other data structures textbooks. Because this book was written after object-oriented programming became widely used and was based on our earlier Java book, it incorporates advances in C++ programming as well as lessons learned from Java. The programs in the text have been tested using the g++ versions 3.4.3 and 4.0.0 compilers and the Microsoft Visual Studio .NET 2003 C++ compiler.

Intended Audience

This book was written for anyone with a curiosity or need to know about data structures, those essential elements of good programs and reliable software. We hope that the text will be useful to readers with either professional or educational interest. In developing this text, we paid careful attention to the ACM's Computing Curricula 2001, in particular, the curriculum for the second ($CS102_o$ – Objects and Data Abstraction) and third ($CS103_o$ – Algorithms and Data Structures) introductory courses in programming in the three-course, "objects-first" sequence. The book is also suitable for $CS112_o$ – Object Oriented Design and Methodology, the second course in the two-course "objects-first" sequence. Further, although the book follows the object-oriented approach, it could be used after a first course that does not, because the principles of object-oriented programming are introduced and motivated in Chapters 1, 3, and the C++ *Primer* (Chapter P). Consequently it could be used for the following courses: $CS102_I$ (The Object-Oriented Paradigm), $CS103_I$ (Data Structures and Algorithms), and $CS112_I$ (Data Abstraction) in the "imperative-first" approach or $CS112_F$ (Objects and Algorithms) in the "functional-first" approach.

Prerequisites

Our expectation is that the reader will be familiar with the C++ primitive data types including `int`, `bool`, `char`, and `double`; control structures including `if`, `switch`, `while`, and `for`; the `string` class; the one-dimensional array; and input/output using text streams. For those readers who lack some of the concepts or who need some review, we provide complete coverage of these topics in the C++ *Primer*. This chapter provides full coverage of the background topics and has all the pedagogical features of the other chapters (discussed below). We expect most readers will have some experience with C++ programming, but someone who knows another high-level language should be able to undertake the book after careful study of the C++ *Primer*. We do not require prior knowledge of inheritance or vectors as we introduce them in Chapters 3 and 4.

Pedagogy

The book contains the following pedagogical features to assist inexperienced programmers in learning the material.

- Learning Objectives at the beginning of each chapter tell readers what skills they should develop.
- Introductions for each chapter help set the stage for what the chapter will cover and tie the chapter contents to other material that they have learned.
- Case Studies emphasize problem solving and provide complete and detailed solutions to real-world problems using the data structures studied in the chapter.
- Chapter Summaries review the contents of the chapter.
- Boxed Features emphasize and call attention to material designed to help readers become better programmers.

   Pitfall boxes help readers with common problems and how to avoid them.

  Design Concept boxes illuminate programming design decisions and tradeoffs.

  Program Style boxes discuss program features that illustrate good programming style and provide tips for writing clear and effective code.

  Syntax boxes are a quick reference to the C++ language structures being introduced.

- Self-Check and Programming Exercises at the end of each section provide immediate feedback and practice for readers as they work through the chapter.
- Quick-Check, Review Exercises, and Programming Projects in each chapter give readers a variety of skill-building activities, including longer projects that integrate chapter concepts as they exercise the use of the data structures.

Theoretical Rigor

Chapter 2 discusses algorithm correctness and algorithm efficiency. We use the concepts discussed in this chapter throughout the book. However, we have tried to strike a balance between pure "hand waving" and extreme rigor when determining the efficiency of algorithms. Rather than provide several paragraphs of formulas, we have provided simplified derivations of algorithm efficiency using big-O notation. We feel this will give readers an appreciation of the performance of various algorithms and methods and the process one follows to determine algorithm efficiency without bogging them down in unnecessary detail.

Overview of the Book

Object-oriented software design is introduced in Chapter 1, as are UML class and sequence diagrams. We use UML sequence diagrams to describe several use cases of a simple problem: maintaining a phone number directory. We decompose the problem into two subproblems, the design of the user interface and the design of the phone directory itself. We emphasize the role of an interface (or header file) as a contract between the developer and client and its contribution to good software design.

The next two chapters concentrate on software design topics. Following the introduction to software design in Chapter 1, the topics of throwing and catching exceptions, debugging, testing, and algorithm efficiency are introduced in Chapter 2. Chapter 3 provides a thorough discussion of inheritance, class hierarchies, abstract classes, and an introduction to object factories.

Chapters 4 through 6 introduce the Standard Library (STL) as the foundation for the traditional data structures: sequences (including vector and list classes), stacks, queues, and deques. Each new data structure is introduced as an abstract data type (ADT) and its specification is written in the form of an interface. We carefully follow the C++ STL specification (when available), so that readers will know how to use the standard data structures that are supplied by C++, and we show one or two simple applications of the data structure. Next, we show how to implement the data structure as a class that implements the interface. Finally, we study additional applications of the data structure by solving sample problems and case studies.

Chapter 7 covers recursion so that readers are prepared for the study of trees, a recursive data structure. As discussed below, this chapter could be studied earlier.

Chapter 8 discusses binary trees, including binary search trees, heaps, priority queues, and Huffman trees.

Chapter 9 covers sets, multisets, maps, and multimaps. Although the STL uses a binary search tree to implement these data structures, this chapter also discusses hashing and hash tables and shows how a hash table can be used in an implementation of these data structures. The Huffman Tree case study is completed in this chapter.

Chapter 10 covers selection sort, bubble sort, insertion sort, Shell sort, merge sort, heapsort, and quicksort. We compare the performance of the various sorting algorithms and discuss their memory requirements. Unlike most textbooks, we have chosen to show how to implement the sorting algorithms as they are implemented in the C++ algorithm library using iterators to define the range of the sequence being sorted, so they can be used to sort vectors and deques as well as arrays.

Chapters 11 and 12 cover self-balancing search trees and graphs, focusing on algorithms for manipulating them. Included are AVL and Red-Black trees, 2-3 trees, 2-3-4 trees, B-trees and B+ trees. We provide several well-known algorithms for graphs including Dijkstra's shortest path algorithm and Prim's minimum spanning tree algorithm. In most Computer Science programs of study, the last two or three chapters would be covered in the second course of a two-course sequence in data structures.

Pathways Through the Book

Figure 1 shows the dependencies among chapters in the book. Most readers will start with Chapters 1, 2, and 3, which provide fundamental background on software design, exceptions, testing, debugging, big-O analysis, class hierarchies, and inheritance. In a course that emphasizes software design, these foundation chapters should be studied carefully. Readers with knowledge of this material from a prior course in programming may want to read these chapters quickly, focusing on material that is new to them. Similarly, those interested primarily in data structures should study Chapter 2 carefully, but they can read Chapters 1 and 3 quickly.

The basic data structures, lists (Chapter 4), stacks (Chapter 5), and queues (Chapter 6), should be covered by all. Recursion (Chapter 7) can be covered any time after stacks. The chapter on trees (Chapter 8) follows recursion. Chapter 9 covers sets and maps and hash tables. Although this chapter follows the chapter on trees, it can be studied anytime after stacks if the case study on Huffman trees is omitted. Similarly, Chapter 10 on sorting can be studied anytime after recursion, provided the section on heapsort is omitted (heaps are introduced in Chapter 8). Chapter 11 (Self-Balancing Search Trees) and Chapter 12 (Graphs) would generally be covered at the end of the second programming course if time permits, or in the third course of a three-course sequence.

Readers with limited knowledge of C++ should begin with the C++ *Primer* (Chapter P). An overview of UML is covered in Appendix B; however, features of UML are introduced and explained as needed in the text.

These paths can be modified depending on interests and abilities. (See Figure 1 on the next page.)

Supplements and Companion Web Sites

The following supplementary materials are available on the Instructor's Companion Web Site for this textbook at www.wiley.com/college/koffman. Items marked for students are accessible on the Student Companion Web Site at the same address. Navigate to either site by clicking the appropriate companion buttons for this text.

- Additional homework problems with solutions
- Source code for all classes in the book
- Solutions to end of section odd-numbered self-check and programming exercises (for students)
- Solutions to all exercises for instructors
- Solutions to chapter-review exercises for instructors
- Sample programming project solutions for instructors
- PowerPoint slides
- Electronic test bank for instructors

FIGURE 1
Chapter Dependencies

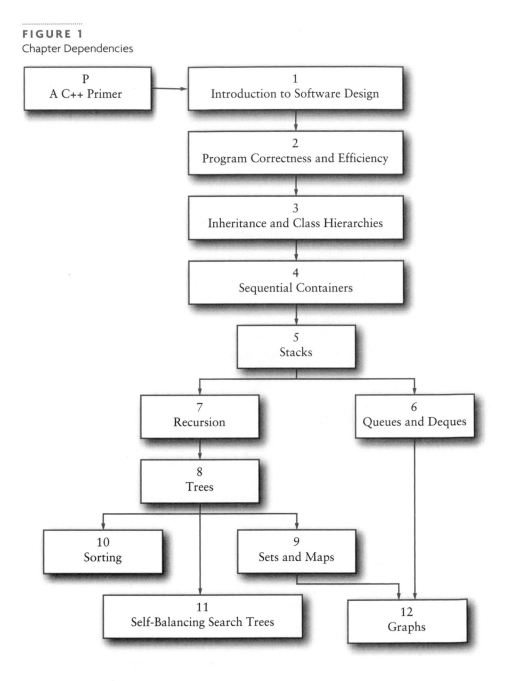

Acknowledgments

Many individuals helped us with the preparation of this book and improved it greatly. We are grateful to all of them. We would like to thank Anthony Hughes, James Korsh, and Rolf Lakaemper, colleagues at Temple University, who used the Java version of this book in their classes.

We are especially grateful to reviewers of this book and the Java version who provided invaluable comments that helped us correct errors and helped us set our revision goals for the next version. The individuals who reviewed this book and its Java predecessor are listed below.

C++ Reviewers

Prithviraj Dasgupta, *University of Nebraska–Omaha*
Michelle McElvany Hugue, *University of Maryland*
Kurt Schmidt, *Drexel University*
David J. Trombley
Alan Verbanec, *Pennsylvania State University*

Java Reviewers

Sheikh Iqbal Ahamed, *Marquette University*
Justin Beck, *Oklahoma State University*
John Bowles, *University of South Carolina*
Tom Cortina, *SUNY Stony Brook*
Chris Dovolis, *University of Minnesota*
Vladimir Drobot, *San Jose State University*
Ralph Grayson, *Oklahoma State University*
Chris Ingram, *University of Waterloo*
Gregory Kesden, *Carnegie Mellon University*
Sarah Matzko, *Clemson University*
Ron Metoyer, *Oregon State University*
Michael Olan, *Richard Stockton College*
Rich Pattis, *Carnegie Mellon University*
Sally Peterson, *University of Wisconsin–Madison*
J.P. Pretti, *University of Waterloo*
Mike Scott, *University of Texas–Austin*
Mark Stehlik, *Carnegie Mellon University*
Ralph Tomlinson, *Iowa State University*
Frank Tompa, *University of Waterloo*
Renee Turban, *Arizona State University*
Paul Tymann, *Rochester Institute of Technology*
Karen Ward, *University of Texas–El Paso*
Jim Weir, *Marist College*
Lee Wittenberg, *Kean University*
Martin Zhao, *Mercer University*

Besides the principal reviewers, there were a number of faculty members who reviewed the page proofs and made valuable comments and criticisms of its content. We would like to thank those individuals, listed below.

C++ Pages Reviewers

Tim H. Lin, *California State Polytechnic University, Pomona*
Kurt Schmidt, *Drexel University*

Java Pages Reviewers

Razvan Andonie, *Central Washington University*
Ziya Arnavut, *SUNY Fredonia*
Antonia Boadi, *California State University–Dominguez Hills*
Christine Bouamalay, *Golden Gate University*
Amy Briggs, *Middlebury College*
Mikhail Brikman, *Salem State College*
Gerald Burgess, *Wilmington College*
Robert Burton, *Brigham Young University*
Debra Calliss, *Mesa Community College*
Tat Chan, *Methodist College*
Chakib Chraibi, *Barry University*
Teresa Cole, *Boise State University*
Jose Cordova, *University of Louisiana Monroe*
Joyce Crowell, *Belmont University*
Vladimir Drobot, *San Jose State University*
Francisco Fernandez, *University of Texas–El Paso*
Michael Floeser, *Rochester Institute of Technology*
Robert Franks, *Central College*
Barbara Gannod, *Arizona State University East*
Wayne Goddard, *Clemson University*
Simon Gray, *College of Wooster*
Bruce Hillam, *California State University–Pomona*
Wei Hu, *Houghton College*
Jerry Humphrey, *Tulsa Community College*
Edward Kovach, *Franciscan University of Steubenville*
Richard Martin, *Southwest Missouri State University*
Bob McGlinn, *Southern Illinois University*
Sandeep Mitra, *SUNY Brockport*
Saeed Monemi, *California Polytechnic and State University*
Lakshmi Narasimhan, *University of Newcastle, Australia*
Robert Noonan, *College of William and Mary*
Kathleen O'Brien, *Foothill College*
Michael Olan, *Richard Stockton College*
Peter Patton, *University of St. Thomas*
Eugen Radian, *North Dakota State University*
Rathika Rajaravivarma, *Central Connecticut State University*
Sam Rhoads, *Honolulu Community College*
Jeff Rufinus, *Widener University*
Rassul Saeedipour, *Johnson County Community College*
Vijayakumar Shanmugasundaram, *Concordia College Moorhead*
Gene Sheppard, *Georgia Perimeter College*
Linda Sherrell, *University of Memphis*
Meena Srinivasan, *Mary Washington College*
David Weaver, *Shepherd University*
Stephen Weiss, *University of North Carolina–Chapel Hill*
Glenn Wiggins, *Mississippi College*

Finally, we want to acknowledge the participants in focus groups for the second programming course organized by John Wiley and Sons at the Annual Meeting of the SIGCSE Symposium, in March, 2004. Thank you to those listed below who reviewed the preface, table of contents, and sample chapters and also provided valuable input on the book and future directions of the course:

Jay M. Anderson, *Franklin & Marshall University*
Claude Anderson, *Rose-Hulman Institute*
John Avitabile, *College of Saint Rose*
Cathy Bishop-Clark, *Miami University–Middletown*
Debra Burhans, *Canisius College*
Michael Clancy, *University of California–Berkeley*
Nina Cooper, *University of Nevada–Las Vegas*
Kossi Edoh, *Montclair State University*
Robert Franks, *Central College*
Evan Golub, *University of Maryland*
Graciela Gonzalez, *Sam Houston State University*
Scott Grissom, *Grand Valley State University*
Jim Huggins, *Kettering University*
Lester McCann, *University of Wisconsin–Parkside*
Briana Morrison, *Southern Polytechnic State University*
Judy Mullins, *University of Missouri–Kansas City*
Roy Pargas, *Clemson University*
J.P. Pretti, *University of Waterloo*
Reza Sanati, *Utah Valley State College*
Barbara Smith, *University of Dayton*
Suzanne Smith, *East Tennessee State University*
Michael Stiber, *University of Washington, Bothell*
Jorge Vasconcelos, *University of Mexico (UNAM)*
Lee Wittenberg, *Kean University*

We would also like to acknowledge the team at John Wiley and Sons who were responsible for the inception and production of this book. Our editors, Paul Crockett and Bill Zobrist, were intimately involved in every detail of this book, from its origination to the final product. We are grateful to them for their confidence in us and for all the support and resources they provided to help us accomplish our goal and to keep us on track. Bridget Morrisey was the editorial assistant who provided us with additional help when needed. We would also like to thank Phyllis Cerys for her many contributions to marketing and sales of the book.

Cindy Johnson, the developmental editor and production coordinator, worked very closely with us during all stages of the manuscript development and production. We are very grateful to her for her tireless efforts on our behalf and for her excellent ideas and suggestions.

Greg Johnson was the compositor for the book, and he did an excellent job in preparing it for printing.

We would like to acknowledge the help and support of our colleague Frank Friedman, who read an early draft of this textbook and offered suggestions for improvement. Frank and Elliot began writing textbooks together almost thirty years ago and Frank's substantial influence on the format and content of these books is still present. Frank also encouraged Paul to begin his teaching career as an adjunct faculty member, then full-time when he retired from industry. Paul is grateful for his continued support.

Finally, we would like to thank our wives who provided us with comfort and support through the creative process. We very much appreciate their understanding and the sacrifices that enabled us to focus on this book, often during time we would normally be spending with them. In particular Elliot Koffman would like to thank

Caryn Koffman

and Paul Wolfgang would like to thank

Sharon Wolfgang.

Contents

A C++ Primer

This chapter reviews object-oriented programming in C++. It assumes the reader has prior experience programming in C++ or another language and is, therefore, familiar with control statements for selection and repetition, basic data types, arrays, and functions. If your first course was in C++, you can skim this chapter for review or just use it as a reference as needed. However, you should read it more carefully if your C++ course did not emphasize object-oriented design.

If your first course was not in C++, you should read this chapter carefully. If your first course followed an object-oriented approach but was in another language, you should concentrate on the differences between C++ syntax and that of the language that you know. If you have programmed only in a language that was not object-oriented, you will need to concentrate on aspects of object-oriented programming and classes as well as C++ syntax.

We begin the chapter with an introduction to the C++ environment and the run-time system. Control structures and statements are then discussed, followed by a discussion of functions.

Next we cover the basic data types of C++, called primitive data types. Then we introduce classes and objects. Because C++ uses pointers to reference objects, we discuss how to declare and use pointer variables.

The C++ standard library provides a rich collection of classes that simplify programming in C++. The first C++ class that we cover is the `string` class. The `string` class provides several functions and an operator + (concatenation) that process sequences of characters (strings).

We also review arrays in C++. We cover both one- and two-dimensional arrays and C-strings, which are arrays of characters.

Finally we discuss input/output. We also show how to use streams and the console for input/output and how to write functions that let us use the stream input/output operations on objects.

A C++ Primer

P.1 The C++ Environment

Before we talk about the C++ language, we will briefly discuss the C++ environment and how C++ programs are executed. C++ was developed by Bjarne Stroustrup as an extension to the C programming language by adding object-oriented capabilities. Since its original development, C++ has undergone significant evolution and refinement. In 1998 the definition of the language was standardized. Like its predecessor C, C++ has proven to be a popular language for implementing a variety of applications across different platforms. There are C++ compilers available for most computers. Some of the concepts and features of C++ have been implemented in other languages, including Java.

An extensive collection of classes and functions is available to a C++ program. This collection is known as the *standard library*. We will discuss numerous capabilities provided by this library in this textbook. Among them are classes and functions to perform input and output and classes that can serve as containers for values.

Include Files

A C++ program is *compiled* into a form that is directly executed by the computer. (This form is called *machine language*.) A C++ program does not have to be compiled all at once. Generally, individual functions, or a set of related functions, or a class definition are placed in separate source files that are compiled individually.

For a C++ program to reference a function, class, or variable, the compiler must have seen a *declaration* of that function, class, or variable. Thus, if you write a function, class, or variable that you want to be referenced by other C++ functions, you need to make a declaration of it available. Instead of rewriting all such declarations in every file that uses those functions, classes, or variables, you would place the declarations in a separate file to be included by any program file that uses them. Such a file is called an *include file*. The declarations of classes and functions in the standard library are also placed in include files.

The Preprocessor

The include files that a program uses are merged into the source file by a part of the compiler program known as the *preprocessor*. The preprocessor also performs some other functions, which are discussed in subsequent paragraphs.

The result of the preprocessing is that when the compiler goes to translate the C++ statements into machine instructions, it sees a modified version of the input source file. This can occasionally result in some incomprehensible errors. For example, a missing } in an include file can result in error messages about a subsequent include file that actually has no errors and may even be part of the standard library.

The C++ Compiler

The C++ compiler translates the source program (in file *sourceFile*.cpp) into an intermediate form known as *object code*. This intermediate form is similar to machine language except that references to external functions and variables are in a format that can't be processed directly by the compiler but must be resolved by the linker (discussed next).

The Linker

Once all of the source code files associated with a program have been compiled by the compiler, the object code files need to be linked together along with the object code files that implement the functions declared in the standard library. This task is performed by a program known as the *linker*, which produces a file that can be loaded into memory by the operating system and executed. The relationship among the library, preprocessor, compiler, and linker is shown in Figure P.1.

Functions, Classes, and Objects

In C++ the fundamental programming unit is the *function*. The *class* is also a programming unit. Every program is written as a collection of functions and classes. Functions may either be stand-alone or belong to a class. In C++, function and class

FIGURE P.1

Compiling and Executing a C++ Program

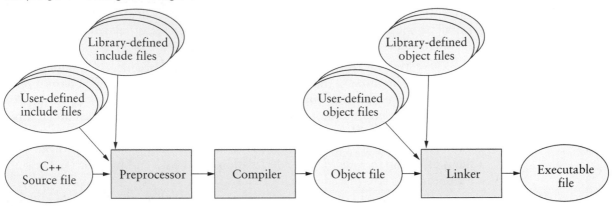

declarations are stored in include files, also known as *headers*, that have the extension .h. Function and class *definitions* are stored in files with the extension .cpp. (Other conventions are sometimes used: include files may also use the extension .hpp or .H, and definition files may use the extension .cc or .C.)

A class is a named description for a group of entities called *objects*, or *instances* of the class, that all have the same kinds of information (known as *attributes*, *data fields*, or *instance variables*) and can participate in the same operations (functions). The attributes and the functions are *members* of the class—not to be confused with the instances or objects in the class. The functions are referred to as *member functions*.

If you are new to object-oriented design, you may be confused about the differences between a class, an object or instance, and a member. A class is a general description of a group of entities that all have the same characteristics—that is, they can all perform or undergo the same kinds of actions, and the same pieces of information are meaningful for all of them. The individual entities are the objects or instances, whereas the characteristics are the members. For example, the class House would describe a collection of entities that each have a number of bedrooms, a number of bathrooms, a kind of roof, and so on (but not a horsepower rating or mileage); they can all be built, remodeled, assessed for property tax, and so on (but not have their transmission fluid changed). The house where you live and the house where your best friend lives can be represented by two objects, or instances, of class House. The numbers of bedrooms and bathrooms and the actions of building and assessing the house would be represented by members of the class House.

Classes extend C++ by providing additional data types. For example, the class string is a predefined class that enables the programmer to process sequences of characters easily. We will discuss the string class in detail in Section P.8.

The #include Directive

Next, we show a sample C++ source file (HelloWorld.cpp) that contains an application program. Our goal in the rest of this section is to give you an overview of the process of creating and executing an application program. The statements in this program will be covered in more detail later in this chapter.

```cpp
#include <iostream>
#include <string>

using namespace std;

int main()
{
  cout << "Enter your name\n";
  string name;
  getline(cin, name);
  cout << "Hello " << name
       << " - welcome to C++\n";
  return 0;
}
```

The C++ source file begins with the directives

```cpp
#include <iostream>
#include <string>
```

These tell the C++ preprocessor to include the definitions from the library headers `iostream` and `string` into the program. The header `iostream` declares objects associated with the standard input/output streams such as `cin` and `cout` and functions for processing input/output streams.

The using Statement and namespace std

The line

```cpp
using namespace std;
```

tells the compiler to make all the names in the predefined namespace `std` (for standard) available to our program. A *namespace* is a collection of names or identifiers that are defined together. Because the C++ standard library is defined in the standard namespace `std`, a program containing this line will be able to access all functions and identifiers declared in the standard library.

Although this is the easiest way to get access to all names defined in the standard namespace, as we will discuss further in Chapter 3, including all of the names from `namespace std` can lead to problems in larger programs. As an alternative, we can list each name that we will actually need from a particular namespace in a separate statement of the form:

```cpp
using namespace::name;
```

For the `main` function in the previous section, the four statements:

```cpp
using std::cin;
using std::cout;
using std::string;
using std::getline;
```

tell the compiler to make just the names `cin`, `cout`, `string`, and `getline` from the standard namespace available to our program.

Even without **using** statements, you can reference names declared in a namespace by specifying the actual namespace before each use of a name from that namespace. For example, we can use std::cout to reference name cout.

Function main

The line

```
int main()
```

identifies the start of the definition for function main. This is the place where the operating system begins the execution of the program. The word **int** tells the compiler that main will return an **int** value to the operating system. A return value of 0 (through execution of the statement return 0;) indicates that the program exited normally, and a nonzero value indicates that there was an error. This information can be used by the operating system to determine whether to execute the next program in a script.

The function main contains two statements that invoke the insertion operator (<<) on the standard output stream cout. The first displays the following prompt message (or prompt) to the user:

```
Enter your name
```

Next the function getline is called. This function reads a line from the specified input stream (cin) and places the result into the specified string, name.

Then the insertion operator is invoked on cout to output the strings

```
Hello
```
the entered line

and

```
- welcome to C++
```

as a single line of output. For example, if the characters John Doe are typed in, the output would be

```
Hello John Doe - welcome to C++
```

Finally the statement

```
return 0;
```

is executed, indicating normal completion.

Execution of a C++ Program

You can compile, link, and run HelloWorld using an Integrated Development Environment (IDE) or a command-line compiler. If you are using an IDE, you may need to create a project first. Then type this program into the edit window for file HelloWorld.cpp and select Run. If you are not using an IDE, you must create this file using an editor program and save it as file HelloWorld.cpp. Then you can use a command that invokes the compiler and linker/loader. This command depends on the compiler you are using. For example, if you are using the gcc compiler, the command to compile and link the program would be

```
g++ -o HelloWorld HelloWorld.cpp
```

whereas if you are using the Microsoft C++ compiler, the command to compile and link the program would be

```
cl /EHsc HelloWorld.cpp
```

The `/EHsc` in the command line sets a compiler switch that enables exception handling (discussed in Chapter 2). The command

```
HelloWorld
```

tells the operating system to load and execute the program.

EXERCISES FOR SECTION P.1

SELF-CHECK

1. What is the C++ standard library? How does its role differ from that of the C++ compiler?
2. What is the role of the preprocessor?
3. Explain the relationship between a class and an object. Which is general and which is specific?

P.2 Preprocessor Directives and Macros

Before your program is processed by the compiler, the preprocessor transforms it into a form that the compiler can work with. Among the steps performed by the preprocessor are the following:

- Remove comments and replace them by a single space.
- Split the input file into tokens.
- Carry out preprocessing directives.
- Expand macros.

Removing Comments

There are two forms of comments:

Any characters between the character pairs `/*` and `*/` are treated as a comment. Note that you cannot nest comments. A comment that begins with a `/*` is terminated by the first `*/`. These comments may extend over more than one line.

Any characters that follow the character pair `//` until the end of the current line are treated as a comment. If you have a comment that takes more than one line, you should either use the `/* ... */` form or start each new line with its own `//`.

Also note that if a `/*` or `*/` appears after a `//`, the slash and asterisk are ignored, and if a `//` appears within a `/* ... */`, the double slash is ignored.

Macros

A macro is similar to a function in that a single instruction in the source file results in multiple instructions being executed by the computer. The macro, however, is expanded by the preprocessor when the program is compiled rather than being called by the program at run time, and the macro operates only on tokens, which are sequences of letters and numbers, or operator symbols. The C programming language relies on macros, and because C++ is a superset of the C language, C++ includes them as well. In its simplest form, we use a macro definition to associate a name with a constant value:

```
#define PI 3.14159
```

This macro definition directs the preprocessor to replace every occurrence of the name PI with the sequence of characters 3.14159.

SYNTAX **The define Preprocessor Directive**

FORM:

#define *macro-name macro-definition*
#define *macro-name(parameter-list) macro-definition*

EXAMPLES:

#define NULL 0
#define MAX(x, y) ((x) > (y) ? (x) : (y))

MEANING:

Subsequent to the definition, whenever the symbol *macro-name* is encountered, the preprocessor will replace it with the *macro-definition*. The *macro-definition* begins with the first nonspace character after the *macro-name* and ends with the last nonspace character on the same line as the #define directive. If there are parameters following the *macro-name* (for example, x and y in MAX(x, y)), they are replaced in the *macro-definition* with the corresponding actual arguments.

EXAMPLE P.1 Assume that NULL is defined as shown in the syntax box. Then, wherever NULL appears in the program, it is replaced by 0. Thus, when you write

```
if (ptr == NULL)
```

the compiler will see

```
if (ptr == 0)
```

Macros are used in the C language for functions such as MAX shown in the syntax example because the function can be applied to different types. Such functions are known as *generic functions*. As we will discuss in the text, C++ uses templates to define generic functions and classes.

There are two cases where macros are useful in C++. One is the use of the # macro operator, which converts a macro parameter into a string literal, and the other is to prevent multiple inclusion of include files.

The # Operator

If you place a # before a macro parameter, then the preprocessor replaces it with a string literal of the corresponding argument. This can be useful for placing debugging information into a program. For example, an assertion macro is used to verify that a condition that should be true at a certain point in a program is in fact true. It can be defined as follows:

```
#define kw_assert(x)\
if (!(x)) {\
  std::cerr << "Assertion " << #x << " failed\n";\
  std::cerr << "Line " << __LINE__ << " in file " << __FILE__\
            << "\n";\
  exit(1);\
}
```

Macro definitions must appear on a single line. The preprocessor provides a way around this limitation. Any line that ends with the backslash character (\) is treated as if the following line were part of the same line.

For example, if we write

```
kw_assert(length > 5)
```

the preprocessor will transform this line into

```
if (!(length > 5)) {\
  std::cerr << "Assertion " << "length > 5" << " failed\n";\
  std::cerr << "Line " << current line number << " in file "\
            << current file name << "\n";\
  exit(1);\
}
```

If the assertion length > 5 is true, this statement does nothing. If it is false, an error message is output that gives the assertion and the place in the program where it is tested, and the program then terminates. The macros __LINE__ and __FILE__ are predefined to be replaced by the line number and file name of the source file that the preprocessor is currently processing. The function exit, as its name implies, exits the program immediately. Its argument is the return value that is passed back to the operating system; a value of 1 indicates an error.

Conditional Compilation

The preprocessor directives #ifdef, #ifndef, #else, and #endif tell the preprocessor to include or exclude selected lines of code in the output passed to the compiler.

 **SYNTAX** **The #ifdef, #ifndef, #else, and #endif Preprocessor Directives**

FORM:

```
#ifdef macro-name
code to be included if macro-name is defined
#else
code to be included if macro-name is not defined
#endif
```

or

```
#ifndef macro-name
code to be included if macro-name is not defined
#else
code to be included if macro-name is defined
#endif
```

The #else is optional, but there must be an #endif to correspond to the #ifdef or #ifndef.

EXAMPLE:

```
#ifdef __cplusplus
extern "C" {
   ...
}
#endif
```

MEANING:

Indicates what to include if the *macro-name* is defined or not defined. If the *macro-name* is defined, include all the lines of code between the #ifdef and the #else (if present), or between the #ifdef and the #endif if there is no #else. If the *macro-name* is not defined, include all the lines between the #else and the #endif (if any). The opposite happens if the first line begins with #ifndef.

In the example shown in the syntax display, the macro __cplusplus is defined by the compiler if it is processing a C++ program. The declaration

```
extern "C" {
   ...
}
```

tells the compiler that all functions declared inside the brackets (not shown, but indicated by ...) are C functions and not C++ functions. This declaration is used in header files that are shared by both C and C++.

More on the #include Directive

The #include directive has one of two forms:

```
#include <header>
```

and

```
#include "file-name"
```

The form

```
#include <header>
```

is reserved to include definitions that are defined in the standard library and the form

    `#include "`*file-name*`"`

is used to include a user-defined include file.

✓ PROGRAM STYLE

Using Preprocessor Directives to Prevent Multiple Inclusion of an Include File

We use include files to package function and class declarations. It is possible that a function or class uses other functions or classes that are defined in other include files. However, it is an error if the same function declaration or class declaration is presented to the compiler more than once. When you write an include file, you do not know when it is going to be used or by what programs, so each include file should be guarded using preprocessor directives to ensure that it is included only one time. The way this is done is to begin the include file with two directives of the form:

`#ifndef` *unique-name*
`#define` *unique-name*

where *unique-name*, as the place holder implies, is a unique name. Generally the file name is converted to uppercase, the period that separates the name from the extension is replaced by an underscore, and a trailing underscore is added. Thus the include file `myfile.h` would use `MYFILE_H_` as the unique name. You may see other conventions. The last line of the include file is an `#endif` directive.

The first time the preprocessor sees the `#ifndef` directive, the *unique-name* will not be defined. Thus the lines that follow will be processed by the preprocessor and passed on to the compiler. The `#define` directive will define *unique-name* so that the next time the preprocessor sees the include file, the `#ifndef` will be false and the file will be skipped. Note again that the last line of the file should be `#endif`.

EXERCISES FOR SECTION P.2

SELF-CHECK

1. What does the preprocessor do with the following:
   ```
   #define MIN(x,y) \
   ((x) < (y)) ? (x) : (y)
   ```

2. Given the macro definition
   ```
   #define ECHO(x) #x << ": " << (x)
   ```

   What does the compiler see after the preprocessor processes the statement
   ```
   cout << ECHO(a) << ECHO(b) << ECHO(a + b) << '\n';
   cout << ECHO(sum) << ECHO(sum << 2) << '\n';
   ```

3. What if we omit the second set of parentheses in the definition given in question 2?

P.3 C++ Control Statements

The control statements of a programming language determine the flow of execution through a program. They fall into three categories: sequence, selection, and repetition.

Sequence and Compound Statements

A group of statements that is executed in sequence is written as a compound statement delimited (enclosed) by braces. The statements execute in the order in which they are listed.

EXAMPLE P.2   The following statements constitute a compound statement:

```
{
    double x = 3.45;
    double y = 2 * x;
    int i = int(y);
    i++;
}
```

Selection and Repetition Control

Table P.1 shows the C++ control statements for selection and repetition. (C++ uses the same basic syntax for control structures as C and Java do.) We assume that you are familiar with basic programming control structures from your first course, so we won't dwell on them here.

In Table P.1, each condition is a **bool** expression in parentheses. Type **bool** expressions often involve comparisons written using equality (==, !=) and relational operators (<, <=, >, >=). For example, the condition (x + y > x - y) is true if the sum of the two variables shown is larger than their difference. The logical operators ! (not, or complement), && (and), and || (or) are used to combine **bool** expressions. For example, the condition (n >= 0 && n <= 10) is true if n has a value between zero and 10, inclusive.

C++ uses short-circuit evaluation, which means that evaluation of a **bool** expression terminates when its value can be determined. For example, if in the expression bool1 || bool2, bool1 is true, the expression must be true, so bool2 is not evaluated. Similarly, in the expression bool3 && bool4, if bool3 is false, the expression must be false, so bool4 is not evaluated.

EXAMPLE P.3   In the condition

```
    (num != 0 && sum / num)
```

if num is 0, the expression following && is not evaluated. This prevents a division by zero.

....
TABLE P.1
C++ Control Statements

Control Structure	Purpose	Syntax

`if ... else`	Used to write a decision with *condition* that selects the alternative to be executed. Executes the first (second) alternative if the condition is true (false).	`if (condition) {`
		`   ...`
		`} else {`
		`   ...`
		`}`

`switch`	Used to write a decision with scalar values (integers, characters) that select the alternative to be executed. Executes the *statements* following the *label* that is the *selector* value. Execution falls through to the next **case** if there is no **return** or **break**. Executes the statements following **default** if the selector value does not match any *label*.	`switch (selector) {`
		`   case label : statements;`
		`      break;`
		`   case label : statements;`
		`      break;`
		`   ...`
		`   default : statements;`
		`}`

`while`	Used to write a loop that specifies the repetition *condition* in the loop header. The *condition* is tested before each iteration of the loop and, if it is true, the loop body executes; otherwise, the loop is exited.	`while (condition) {`
		`   ...`
		`}`

`do ... while`	Used to write a loop that executes at least once. The repetition *condition* is at the end of the loop. The *condition* is tested after each iteration of the loop, and if it is true, the loop body executes again; otherwise the loop is exited.	`do {`
		`   ...`
		`} while (condition);`

`for`	Used to write a loop that specifies the *initialization*, repetition *condition*, and *update* steps in the loop header. The *initialization* statements execute before the loop repetition begins; the *condition* is tested before each iteration of the loop and, if it is true, the loop body executes; otherwise, the loop is exited. The *update* statements execute after each iteration.	`for (initialization;`
		`     condition;`
		`     update) {`
		`   ...`
		`}`

EXAMPLE P.4 Below we use a **for** statement and a **while** statement to write loops with the same behavior. Each loop accumulates the sum of even integers from 1 to MAX_VAL in variable sum (initial value 0) and they store the product of the odd integers in variable prod (initial value 1). The operator % in the condition (next_int % 2 == 0) gives the remainder after an integer division, so the condition is true if next_int is an even number. Generally the **for** statement implementation will be more efficient because some compilers will be able to optimize the compiled code.

```
for (int next_int = 1;              int next_int = 1;
     next_int <= MAX_VAL;           while (next_int <= MAX_VAL) {
     next_int++) {                     if (next_int % 2 == 0) {
  if (next_int % 2 == 0) {              sum += next_int;
    sum += next_int;                  } else {
  } else {                             prod *= next_int;
    prod *= next_int;                }
  }                                  next_int++;
}                                  }
```

> ## ☑ PROGRAM STYLE
>
> ### Braces and Indentation in Control Statements
>
> C++ programmers often place the opening brace { on the same line as the control statement header. The closing brace } aligns with the first word in the control statement header. We will always indent the statements inside a control structure to clarify the meaning of the control statement.
>
> Although we write the symbols } **else** { on one line, another popular style convention is to place the word **else** under the symbol } and aligned with **if**:
>
> ```
> if (next_int % 2 == 0) {
>   sum += next_int;
> }
> else {
>   prod *= next_int;
> }
> ```
>
> Some programmers omit the braces when a true task or false task or a loop body consists of a single statement. Others prefer to include them always, both for clarity and because having the braces will permit them to insert additional statements later if needed.

Nested if Statements

You can write **if** statements that select among more than two alternatives by nesting one **if** statement inside another. Often each inner **if** statement will follow the keyword **else** of its corresponding outer **if** statement.

EXAMPLE P.5   The following nested **if** statement has four alternatives. The conditions are evaluated in sequence until one evaluates to **true**. The compound statement following the first true condition then executes.

```
if (operator == '+') {
  result = x + y;
  add_op++;
}
else
  if (operator == '-') {
    result = x - y;
    subtract_op++;
  }
  else
    if (operator == '*') {
      result = x * y;
      multiply_op++;
    }
    else
      if (operator == '/') {
        result = x / y;
        divide_op++;
      }
```

⊘ PITFALL

Omitting Braces Around a Compound Statement

The braces in the preceding example delimit compound statements. Each compound statement consists of two statements. If you omit a brace, you will get the syntax error `'else' without 'if'`.

☑ PROGRAM STYLE

Writing `if` Statements with Multiple Alternatives

C++ programmers often write nested **if** statements like those in the preceding example without indenting each nested **if**. The following multiple-alternative decision has the same meaning but is easier to write and read.

```
if (operator == '+') {
  result = x + y;
  add_op++;
} else if (operator == '-') {
  result = x - y;
  subtract_op++;
} else if (operator == '*') {
  result = x * y;
  multiply_op++;
} else if (operator == '/') {
  result = x / y;
  divide_op++;
}
```

The `switch` Statement

The **if** statement in Example P.5 could also be written as the following **switch** statement. Each **case** label (for example, '+') indicates a possible value of the selector expression operator. The statements that follow a particular label execute if the selector has that value. The **break** statements cause an exit from the **switch** statement. Without them, execution would continue on to the statements in the next case. The last case, with label **default**, executes if the selector value doesn't match any **case** label. (Note that the compound statements for each case are not surrounded by braces.) Using the **switch** statement (instead of nested **if**s) reduces extra branches and can result in safer code.

```
switch (operator) {
  case '+':
    result = x + y;
    add_op++;
    break;
```

```
      case '-':
        result = x - y;
        subtract_op++;
        break;
      case '*':
        result = x * y;
        multiply_op++;
        break;
      case '/':
        result = x / y;
        divide_op++;
        break;
      default:
        // Do nothing
    }
```

EXERCISES FOR SECTION P.3

SELF-CHECK

1. What is the purpose of the **break** statement in the preceding **switch** statement? List the statements that would execute when operator is '-' with the **break** statements in place and if they were removed.

2. What is the difference between a **while** loop and a **do ... while** loop? What is the minimum number of repetitions of the loop body you can have with each kind of loop?

PROGRAMMING

1. Rewrite the **for** statement in Example P.4 using a **do ... while** loop.

P.4 Primitive Data Types and Class Types

C++ distinguishes between data of many different *types*. The type of a data item determines what values it can have and what can be done with it. For example, a character cannot have the value –2.718, and a floating-point real number cannot be converted to uppercase. Types may be *primitive types* (numbers, characters) and *class types*. The primitive types are defined by the computer on which the program is being executed and are built into the language. The class types are defined in terms of the primitive types. In C++ you can define a class type so that it behaves as if it were a primitive type. For example, the library class std::string has many of the characteristics of a primitive data type. You will begin to learn how to define class types in Chapter 1.

Primitive Data Types

The primitive data types in C++ represent numbers, characters, and Boolean values (**true, false**) (see Table P.2). Integers are represented by data types **short, int,** and

TABLE P.2
C++ Primitive Data Types in Increasing Order of Range

Data Type	Range of Values for the Intel x86 architecture
`short`	−32,768 through 32,767
`unsigned short`	0 through 65,535
`int`	−2,147,483,648 through 2,147,483,647
`unsigned int, size_t`	0 through 4,294,967,295
`long`	−2,147,483,648 through 2,147,483,647
`unsigned long`	0 through 4,294,967,295
`float`	Approximately $\pm 10^{-38}$ through $\pm 10^{38}$ and 0 with 7 digits precision
`double`	Approximately $\pm 10^{-308}$ through $\pm 10^{308}$ and 0 with 15 digits precision
`long double`	Approximately $\pm 10^{-4932}$ through $\pm 10^{4932}$ and 0 with 18 digits precision
`char`	The 7-bit ASCII characters
`signed char`	−128 through 127
`unsigned char`	0 through 255
`wchar_t`	The Unicode characters
`bool`	`true, false`

`long`; integers may be either signed or unsigned. The real numbers are represented by **float, double,** and **long double.** The keyword **double** is short for "double precision," implying that values of this type have a wider range and can be specified to many more decimal places than the "single-precision" **float** values. However, the actual range of values for each data type is implementation defined. That is, they depend on the compiler and the target computer. We list the ranges for the 32-bit Intel x86 architecture (such as the Intel Pentium processors and the AMD Athlon processors) in Table P.2. Observe that the range for **int** and **long** are the same. The only requirements of the standard for integers are that the range of **short** be less than or equal to that of **int** and that the range of **int** be less than or equal to that of **long.** Similarly, the standard requires that the range and precision provided by **float** be less than or equal to that provided by **double** and that the range and precision provided by **double** be less than or equal to that provided by **long double.**

Type `size_t` is used to represent an unsigned integer, or an integer whose value is always positive. Some functions in the C++ standard library return results that are type `size_t`.

Type **char** is used in C++ to represent the characters. C++ uses the 7-bit ASCII (American Standard Code for Information Interchange) characters. The types **unsigned char** and **signed char** are effectively eight-bit integers. Table P.3 shows the ASCII characters. These include the control characters and the Basic Latin alphabet.

The code for each character, expressed as a hexadecimal number, consists of the single-digit column number (0 through 7) followed by the row number (0 through F). For example, the code for the letter Q is 51, and the code for the letter q is 71. The characters in the first two columns of Table P.3 and the code character 7F (delete) are control characters. The hexadecimal digits A through F are equivalent to the decimal values 10 through 15. The hexadecimal number 7F is equivalent to the decimal number $7 \times 16 + 15$.

The type **wchar_t** is defined to support the larger international character set known as Unicode. When first published, the Unicode character set required a 16-bit representation. However, this has proven inadequate to represent all of the possible characters and symbols defined by the standard, so some implementations now use a 32-bit value for **wchar_t**. The first 128 characters in the Unicode character set correspond to the ASCII characters.

C++ uses type **bool** to represent logical data. The **bool** data type has only two values: **true** and **false**. C++ performs automatic conversion between **bool** and integral types. The **bool** value **true** is converted to 1 and **false** is converted to 0. Converting the other way, a zero is converted to **false**, and a nonzero value is converted to **true**.

TABLE P.3
The Seven-Bit ASCII Characters

	0	1	2	3	4	5	6	7
0	Null		Space	0	@	P	`	p
1			!	1	A	Q	a	q
2			"	2	B	R	b	r
3			#	3	C	S	c	s
4			$	4	D	T	d	t
5			%	5	E	U	e	u
6			&	6	F	V	f	v
7	Bell		'	7	G	W	g	w
8	Backspace		(	8	H	X	h	x
9	Tab		)	9	I	Y	I	y
A	Line feed		*	:	J	Z	j	z
B		Escape	+	;	K	[	k	{
C	Form feed		,	<	L	\	l	|
D	Return		–	=	M	]	m	}
E			.	>	N	^	n	~
F			/	?	O	_	o	delete

TABLE P.4

Functions Defined in `numeric_limits<`*type-name*`>`

Function	Result
`min()`	The minimum value
`max()`	The maximum value
`epsilon()`	The difference between 1.0 and the next larger value; defined only for floating-point types.
`infinity()`	The representation for infinity, defined only for floating-point types.

Numeric Limits

You can obtain the data shown in Table P.2 from the template class `numeric_limits`, which is defined in the header file `<limits>`. This class defines several static functions, some of which are shown in Table P.4. Versions of these functions are defined for each of the primitive types listed in Table P.2. Thus, to obtain information about a given type *type-name*, you reference the class `numeric_limits<`*type-name*`>`. For example, to obtain the maximum value of an **int**, you make the function call

```
numeric_limits<int>::max()
```

Primitive-Type Variables

C++ uses declaration statements to declare and initialize primitive-type variables.

```
int count_items;
double sum = 0.0;
char star = '*';
boolean more_data;
```

The second and third of these statements initialize variables `sum` and `star` to the values after the operator =. As shown, you can use primitive-type values (such as `0.0` and `'*'`) as *literals* in C++ statements. A literal is a constant value that appears directly in a statement.

Identifiers, such as variable names in C++, must consist of some combination of letters, digits, and the underscore character, beginning with a letter. Identifiers cannot begin with a digit. Although identifiers can begin with an underscore, these identifiers are reserved for use by the standard library, and they should not be used in programs you write.

Operators

Table P.5 shows the C++ operators in decreasing precedence. We will not use any of the bitwise operators, shifting operators, or conditional operator. The arithmetic operators (*, /, +, -) and the increment (++) and decrement (--) operators can be used with any of the primitive numeric types or type **char**. The remainder operator (%) is only defined for integer types including **char**. All operators with the same rank have the same associativity.

TABLE P.5
Operator Precedence

Rank	Operator	Operation	Associativity
1	[]	Array subscript	Left
	()	Function call	
	.	Member access	
	->	Member access	
2	++	Pre- or postfix increment	Right
	--	Pre- or postfix decrement	
	+ -	Unary plus or minus	
	!	Complement	
	~	Bitwise complement	
	new	Object creation	
3	*, /, %	Multiply, divide, remainder	Left
4	+	Addition or string concatenation	Left
	-	Subtraction	
5	<<	Signed bit shift left	Left
	>>	Signed bit shift right	
6	<, <=	Less than, less than or equal	Left
	>, >=	Greater than, greater than or equal	
7	==	Equal to	Left
	!=	Not equal to	
8	&	Bitwise and	Left
9	^	Bitwise exclusive or	Left
10	|	Bitwise or	Left
11	&&	Logical and	Left
12	||	Logical or	Left
13	?:	Conditional	Left
14	=	Assignment	Right
	*=, /=, %=, +=, -=, <<=, >>=, >>=, &=, |=	Compound assignment	

> ☑ **PROGRAM STYLE**
>
> ### C++ Convention for Identifiers
>
> Many C++ programmers use lowercase words or phrases for variable names. Words are separated using the underscore character. For classes it is common to use a word or words that begin with an initial uppercase letter. However, the C++ standard uses lowercase for both variable and class names. Identifiers that are in all uppercase are used for macros.
>
> Another convention that is becoming popular is "camel notation" for variable names. All letters are in lowercase except for identifiers that are made up of more than one word. The first letter of each word, starting with the second word, is in uppercase (for example, thisLongIdentifier). Camel notation gets its name from the appearance of the identifier, with the uppercase letters in the interior forming "humps."

Postfix and Prefix Increment

In C++ you can write statements such as

    i = i + 1;

using the increment operator:

    i++;

This form is the postfix increment. You can also use the prefix increment

    ++i;

but the postfix increment (or decrement) is more common.

When the postfix form is used in an expression (for example, x * i++), the variable i is evaluated and then incremented. When the prefix form is used in an expression (for example, x * ++i), the variable i is incremented before it is evaluated.

EXAMPLE P.6   In the assignment

    z = i++;

i is incremented, but z gets the value i had before it was incremented. So if i is 3 before the assignment statement, z would be 3 and i would be 4 after the assignment. In the assignment statement

    z = ++i;

i is incremented and z gets its new value, so if i is 3 before the assignment, z and i would both be 4 after the assignment statement.

⊘ **PITFALL**

Using Increment and Decrement in Expressions with Other Operators

In the preceding example, the increment operator is used with the assignment operator in the same statement. Similarly, the expression x * i++ uses the multiplication and postfix increment operators. In this expression, the variable i is evaluated and then incremented. When the prefix form is used in an expression (for example, x * ++i), the variable i is incremented before it is evaluated. However, you should avoid writing expressions like these, which could easily be interpreted incorrectly by the human reader.

Type Compatibility and Conversion

In operations involving mixed-type operands, the numeric type of the smaller range is converted to the numeric type of the larger range. This means that if an operation involves a type **int** and a type **double** operand, the type **int** operand is automatically converted to type **double**. This is called a *widening conversion*.

In an assignment operation, a numeric type of a smaller range can be assigned to a numeric type of a larger range; for example, a type **int** expression can be assigned to a type **float** or **double** variable. C++ performs the widening conversion automatically.

```
int item = 25;
double real_item = item;    // Valid - automatic widening
```

The converse is also true, but the compiler will probably issue a warning message.

```
double y = -6.375;
int x = y;    // May cause a warning message
```

This statement is valid, but it attempts to store a real value in an integer variable. It could cause display of a warning message such as initialization to 'int' from 'double'. This means that a type **int** expression is required for the assignment. You can use explicit type conversion operations to perform such a *narrowing conversion* and ensure that the assignment statement will be valid. In the following statement, the expression int(y) instructs the compiler to convert the value of y to type **int** before assigning the integer value to x.

```
int x = int(y);    // Convert to int before assignment
```

You can also convert back and forth between an unsigned integer (type **unsigned int**) and an **int**. You will get a warning if you attempt to compare a signed and unsigned value.

The Conditional Operator

The conditional operator takes three operands. Its form is

boolean-expression ? *value1* : *value2*

If the *boolean-expression* is evaluated to be **true**, then the result is *value1*, otherwise the result is *value2*. In most cases the same effect can be achieved using the **if** statement (discussed in Section P.3).

EXERCISES FOR SECTION P.4

SELF-CHECK

1. For the following assignment statement, assume that x, y are type **double** and m, n are type **int**. List the order in which the operations would be performed. Include any widening and narrowing conversions that would occur.

   m = (int) (x * y + m / n / y * (m + x));

2. What is the value assigned to m in Exercise 1 when m is 5, n is 3, x is 2.5, and y is 2.0?

P.5 Objects, Pointers, and References

In this section we describe objects and how they are referenced. In C++ an *object* is fundamentally an area of the computer's memory containing data of some kind. What kind of data is indicated by the object's *type*, which may be either a built-in type, as described in Section P.4, or a class type. In this respect C++ is different from other programming languages such as Java, where an object is always an instance of a class and primitive-type values are not considered objects. Objects may be contained inside other objects. This is especially true of the class-type objects, which are composed of other class-type objects or primitive-type objects.

Object Lifetimes

Objects are created when they are declared. The declaration may optionally include an initialization expression. When an object declaration is executed, space is allocated for the object, and it is (optionally) initialized to a specified value.

SYNTAX **Object Declaration**

FORM:
type-name name ;
type-name name = initial-value ;
type-name name (*parameter-list*) ;

EXAMPLE:
```
int i;
string s = "hello";
double x = 5.5;
double y(6.7);
point p(x, y);
```

MEANING:

The specified *name* is declared to reference an object of the specified *type-name*. Memory for this object is allocated and initialized to the specified value. In the first example, the name i refers to an **int** object, with an unspecified initial value. In the third and fourth examples the names x and y refer to **double** objects with the initial values 5.5 and 6.7, respectively. Note that the two forms used to initialize x and y are equivalent. In the final example p refers to an object of type point (a class type) with the initial value (x, y).

Object declarations may be either inside or outside the scope of a function or class. Objects that are declared outside the scope of a function or class are called *global objects*. Global objects are created before the function main is called and are destroyed after the function main is exited. Generally, declaring global objects is not a good practice and should be avoided.

Objects declared within a function are created when the declaration is executed and are destroyed when the block in which they are declared is exited. Objects declared in a class are created when the object (the class instance) containing them is created; they are destroyed when the object containing them is destroyed.

Pointers

A *pointer* is an object that refers to another object. A pointer object contains the memory *address* of the object it points to. For example, if x is an object of type **double**, then the declaration:

```
double* px;
```

will declare an object, px, of type **double***—that is, type pointer-to-**double**. The statements

```
double x = 5.1234;
px = &x;
```

declare and initialize a type-**double** variable x (value is 5.1234) and set pointer variable px to *reference* x (or point to x). The prefix operator & is known as the *address-of operator*, and it gives the memory location (address) of the object that follows it.

In this book we will frequently use diagrams to illustrate objects and the relationships between them. In these diagrams we will represent a pointer as a box with an arrow pointing to the referenced object.

The prefix operator * is the *dereferencing* operator. When it is applied to a pointer value, it converts that value to a reference to the object that is pointed to. Using the foregoing example the expression *px gives a reference to the object pointed to by px, which is the object x. Therefore, the statement

```
*px = 1.2345;
```

changes the value of the object referenced by px (the variable x) to 1.2345.

Note that the values of pointers can be changed. Thus, after the statement

    px = &y;

executes, the value stored in pointer px is the address of object y, so pointer px now points to the object y.

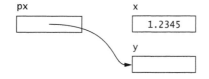

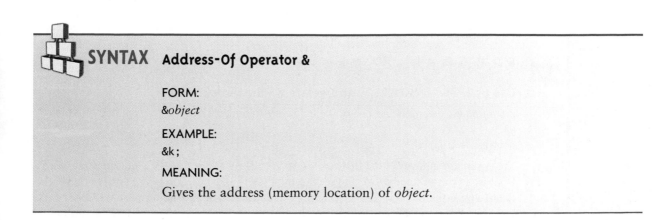

SYNTAX   **Pointer Declaration**

FORM:
type-name * *pointer-variable*;
type-name * *pointer-variable* = &*object*;

EXAMPLE:
int* k;
int* k = &count;

MEANING:
The value of the *pointer-variable* will be a memory address. If the initial value begins with the prefix &, as in &*object*, the *pointer-variable* is initialized to the memory address of *object*.

SYNTAX   **Address-Of Operator &**

FORM:
&*object*

EXAMPLE:
&k;

MEANING:
Gives the address (memory location) of *object*.

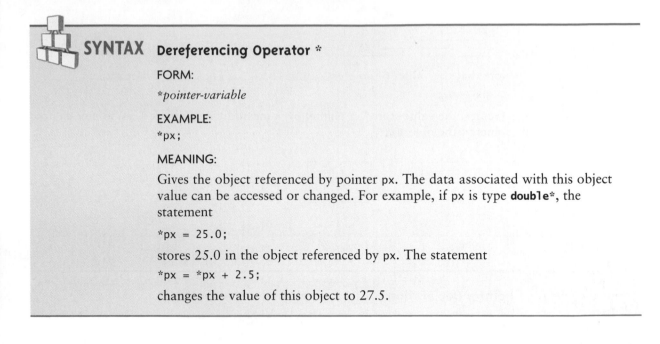

SYNTAX **Dereferencing Operator ***

FORM:

pointer-variable

EXAMPLE:

`*px;`

MEANING:

Gives the object referenced by pointer px. The data associated with this object value can be accessed or changed. For example, if px is type **double***, the statement

`*px = 25.0;`

stores 25.0 in the object referenced by px. The statement

`*px = *px + 2.5;`

changes the value of this object to 27.5.

EXAMPLE P.7   Consider the following sequence of statements:

```
double x = 5.5;
double* px = &x;
cout << *px << '\n';     // Outputs 5.5
*px = 10.0;              // Stores 10.0 in x
cout << x << '\n';       // Outputs 10.0
```

The first two statements declare the variables x and px and initialize x to the value 5.5 and px to the address of x. The value of *px is the same as the value of x, which is 5.5. If we assign 10.0 to *px, we are assigning 10.0 to x. Thus, the last statement will result in an output of 10.0.

✓ PROGRAM STYLE

Use of T* v versus T *v to Declare a Pointer Variable

Programmers generally use one of the following statements to declare a pointer variable.

```
double* px;
double *px;
```

The argument in favor of the first form is that it clearly states that px is of type **double*** (that is, a pointer to **double**). The second form states that the expression *px is of type **double** (and therefore px is of type pointer to **double**). The second form is technically more correct, since this is how the compiler interprets it. Which one you use is a matter of personal taste as long as you declare each variable individually.

🚫 **PITFALL**

Declaring Multiple Pointer Variables in One Declaration

You may also declare multiple variables of the same type in one declaration statement. In that case you must remember that the compiler binds the * to the variable and not the type. Thus the declaration

```
double* px, py;
```

declares that px is a pointer to **double**, but that py is a **double**! To declare both px and py to be pointers we need to use the declaration

```
double *px, *py;
```

The Null Pointer

There is a special pointer value that does not point to any object. This is called the *null pointer*. In most implementations the value 0 is used to represent the null pointer, but this is not required. The header <cstddef> contains a macro definition for NULL that can be used as a null pointer constant. It is defined with the following preprocessor directive:

```
#define NULL 0
```

☑ **PROGRAM STYLE**

Use of NULL versus 0

The choice of using NULL or 0 to represent the null pointer is the subject of much discussion among C++ programmers. The C++ standards committee is currently working on a revision to the C++ standard. One of the proposed changes is to define a true null pointer constant as a new reserved word in the language.

Dynamically Created Objects

In C++ programs we generally do not initialize pointers using the address-of operator. Instead, pointers are used to refer to dynamically created objects. A dynamically created object is created using the **new** operator and is destroyed using the **delete** operator. For example, the first of the following statements,

```
double* px = new double;
*px = 5.1234;
```

allocates a new unnamed object of type **double** and initializes px to point to it.

px

The second statement stores the indicated value in the object pointed to by px.

The statement

```
delete px;
```

destroys the object pointed to by px and returns the memory to the free memory area.

SYNTAX   The new Operator

FORM:

new *type-name*
new *type-name*(*initial-value*)
new *class-name*(*parameters*)

EXAMPLE:

```
new double;
new double(1.23456);
new std::string(line, 5, 10)
```

MEANING:

Memory is allocated for an object of type *type-name*. If an *initial-value* or list of *parameters* is provided, those values are placed in the new object. (In the case of an object of class type, these actions are carried out by a call to the constructor for the class that takes these parameters. Constructors will be discussed in Chapter 1.) A pointer to the created object is returned. The first of the foregoing examples creates a **double** object and returns a pointer to it. The second example creates a **double** object, initializes its value to 1.23456, and returns a pointer to it. The third example creates a new string object and initializes it to the substring of the string line that begins at the fifth character and has a length of 10 characters.

SYNTAX   The delete Operator

FORM:

delete *pointer-variable*;

EXAMPLE:

```
delete px;
```

MEANING:

The memory occupied by the object pointed to by px is returned to the free memory pool. (If the object is of class type, the destructor function for the class is called first; destructors will be discussed in Chapter 1.) Note that the pointer variable must point to an object that was created via the **new** operator.

References

In C++ the term *reference* is the subject of some potential confusion. A *reference variable* is used to give a name to an object. For example, the declaration

```
double& rx = x;
```

declares rx to be a reference variable that refers to the same object as x. Note that rx itself is not an object. For example, if you apply the address-of operator & to rx, you will obtain the same value (an address) as if you applied it to x.

Also, once it is declared, a reference variable cannot be changed to reference a different object. The statement

```
rx = y
```

will change the value of x to be the same as y. In other words, rx will still reference x, but now x must store the same value as y. The same effect is achieved by the statement

```
x = y;
```

Where references get confused with pointers is in their use as function parameters. We discuss reference parameters in the next section.

EXERCISES FOR SECTION P.5

SELF-CHECK

1. What is the value of the variables after each statement is executed?

```
string welcome = "hello";
string greeting("ciao");
point p(1.5, 3.7);
double x = 5.5;
double y = 10.2;
double z;
double *px = &x;
double& ry = y;
*px = 3.14;
z = ry;
double &r = *px;
r = 99.44;
px = &z;
ry = *px;
```

P.6 Functions

C++ programmers can use functions to define a group of statements that perform a particular operation. The C++ function min_char that follows returns the character with the smaller value. The statements beginning with keyword **return** cause an exit from the function; the expression following **return** is the function result.

```
char min_char(char ch1, char ch2) {
  if (ch1 <= ch2)
    return ch1;
  else
    return ch2;
}
```

The identifiers ch1 and ch2 are the *parameters* of function min_char. Whenever min_char is called, the calling program must supply values for these parameters:

```
lesser_char = min_char('p', 's');
```

These supplied values, known as *arguments*, may be literals, identifiers, or expressions.

Function Declarations

In order for the compiler to compile a function call, it must first see a declaration of that function. The declaration of a function specifies the name, return type, and parameter types of a function. The declaration of the function min_char defined previously would have the form:

```
char min_char(char, char);
```

Observe that only the parameter types are given, not parameter names, and that there is a trailing semicolon instead of the function body. Parameter names may be included in a function declaration, but they are ignored. Function declarations normally appear before the main function in a program, but they can also be placed in include files.

Call by Value Versus Call by Reference

In C++, function parameters are either *call-by-value* or *call-by-reference*. Call by value means that the argument's value—that is, a copy of the object named by the argument—is passed to the function, so that even if the function modifies the parameter value, the modification will not remain after the return from the function. This is true whether the argument is a primitive type or a class type. You declare that an argument is to be passed by value by merely declaring the type of the argument. The arguments of function min_char just shown are passed by value.

With call by reference, a reference to the argument object is passed to the function. If the function modifies the parameter value, this modification is made to the original object named by the argument. You declare that a parameter is to be passed by reference by declaring the parameter to be a reference type. For example, the function swap is defined as follows:

```
void swap(int& x, int& y) {
  int temp = x;
  x = y;
  y = temp;
}
```

The function swap would have the declaration

```
void swap(int&, int&);
```

When this function is called with the statement

```
swap(i, j);
```

the value of i is changed to the value of j and the value of j is changed to the value of i. If the parameters were given as type **int** (instead of type **int&**), local copies of parameters x and y would be exchanged by the function execution, but i and j would retain their original value after the function call.

Call by Constant Reference

As we will see later, objects of class types can occupy several locations in memory. For example, a string object occupies the storage necessary to hold the several characters that are included in the string. When they are passed by value, a copy of the object is made. It is more efficient, therefore, to pass class objects by reference. However, the caller may not want the value of the argument to be changed. As the author of a function we can guarantee that the argument will not change by declaring the parameter to be a constant reference, as shown in the following example.

EXAMPLE P.8   The function count_occurrences takes a string and a char argument and returns the number of times the char argument occurs in the string. The char argument is passed by value, but the string argument is passed as a constant reference. The function count_occurrences cannot modify the string parameter (any attempt causes a syntax error), and any modifications to the char parameter will not change the original.

```
int count_occurrences(char c, const string& s) {
   int count = 0;
   for (int i = 0; i < s.size(); i++) {
     if (c == s[i])
        count++;
   }
   return count;
}
```

Operator Functions

C++ allows us to define class types so that they behave as if they were primitive types. Thus you can define the operators such as +, -, *, and / to operate on objects of class types. For example, if s1 and s2 are strings, then s1 + s2 is the string consisting of the characters of s1 followed by the characters of s2.

Operators are functions. In C++ the name of the function that corresponds to the operator designated by the symbol (say, @) is operator@. For example, operator+ represents the + function that performs addition, and operator- represents the function that performs subtraction. Note that at least one parameter of these functions must be a class type. You cannot redefine the operators that operate on the built-in types. All of the operators, with a few exceptions, that are listed in Table P.5 can be defined to operate on a class type. The exceptions are the member access operator (.), the scope resolution operator (::), and the conditional operator (?...:).

The `string operator+` is declared as follows:

```
string operator+(const string&, const string&);
```

Class Member Functions and Implicit Parameters

When a function is declared as a member function of a class, it can be applied to an object of that class by writing the identifier for the object, followed by the member access operator (`.`), followed by the name of the function. A pointer to that object is passed to the function as an *implicit parameter*. We use the term implicit parameter because it is not declared in the parameter list; it does not have to be, because its type is already known—a pointer to the class to which the function belongs. The implicit parameter is passed as a pointer so that the function can make permanent changes to the object.

For example, as will be shown in Section P.8, the `string` class contains a member function `length`, which returns the length of the implicit parameter. If `first_name` is a `string` object containing `"Elliot"`, then

```
first_name.length()
```

returns 6. This notation for applying a member function to an object is called *dot notation*. Writing these functions is discussed further in Chapter 1.

EXERCISES FOR SECTION P.6

SELF-CHECK

1. Explain the difference between call by value, call by reference, and call by constant reference.
2. For each of the following, indicate the kind of parameter you would declare:
   a. a value that is going to be used in a computation by the function
   b. a parameter that is going to return a value computed in the function
   c. an object that is going to be modified by a function
   d. an object with information that will be used by the function but should not be modified

PROGRAMMING

1. Show the declarations and the definition for a function named `get_min` that returns the smaller of its three **int** arguments.
2. Show the declarations and the definition for a function named `rotate` that has three parameters and returns the first parameter through its second parameter, its second parameter through its third parameter, and its third parameter through its first parameter. For example, if x is 10, y is 5, and z is 8, after `rotate(x, y, z)`, x will be 8, y will be 10, and z will be 5.

P.7 Arrays and C Strings

In C++, an array is also an object. The elements of an array are indexed and are referenced using a subscripted variable of the form:

array-name[*subscript*]

Next, we show some different ways to declare arrays and allocate storage for arrays.

EXAMPLE P.9   The following statement declares a variable scores that references a new array object that can store five type **int** values (subscripts 0 through 4) as shown. The contents are undefined.

```
int scores[5];   // An array with 5 type int values
```

EXAMPLE P.10   The first of the following statements declares a variable names that references a new array object that can store four type string objects. The values stored are specified in the initializer list enclosed in braces. The **for** statement displays each element of array names on a separate line.

```
string names[] = {"Sally", "Jill", "Hal", "Rick"};
for (int i = 0; i < 4; i++)
   cout << names[i] << endl;
```

```
           names
    [0]  │   Sally   │
    [1]  │   Jill    │
    [2]  │   Hal     │
    [3]  │   Rick    │
```

⊘ PITFALL

Out-of-Bounds Subscripts

C++ allows you to use an array subscript that is outside of the array bounds. For example, if you attempt to reference scores[5], a C or C++ compiler would access the first memory cell following the array scores. This is considered an error, but it is not detected by the run-time system and will probably lead to another error that will be detected further down the road (before it does too much damage, you hope).

EXAMPLE P.11   The following statements declare an array `students` for storing `N` (a constant) type `string` objects. Storage is allocated for the array object and for the `string` objects. Each array element can contain a type `string` object, but initially each element has the value of the default `string`.

```
// Defines N as a constant.
const int N = 10;
// Declare students as an array of strings.
string students[N];
```

We can create some `string` objects and store them in the array. The following statements store two `string` objects in array `students`.

```
students[0] = "Tom Jones";
students[1] = "Sally Smith";
```

Array-Pointer Equivalence

C++ performs an automatic conversion from an array type to a pointer type. The resulting pointer is a pointer to the first element of the array. Therefore, you can use either

```
students[0]
```

or

```
*students
```

to reference the first element of array `students`.

Array indexing is related to pointer dereferencing by the following equivalence:

`a[i]` *is equivalent to* `*(a + i)`

and

`&a[i]` *is equivalent to* `(a + i)`

For this reason, pointer variables can be used like arrays. However, caution must be used when doing this. The expression

```
*(p + i)
```

where `p` is a pointer and `i` is an **int**, is meaningful only if `p` points to an element of an array and `p + i` is within the size of the array. That is, if `a` is an array of size `n` and `p = &a[j]`, then `*(p + i)` is within the array bounds only if `j + i < n`.

Dynamically Allocated Arrays

The **new** operator can be used to allocate an array of objects. The expression

```
new T[n]
```

allocates an array of objects of type `T` of size `n` and returns a pointer to the first element of the array. This value can then be stored in a pointer variable. The pointer variable can be used like an array name. Dynamic allocation of arrays enables the program user to specify the array size at run time.

EXAMPLE P.12   The following sequence allocates an array of size num_students of type string, where num_students is entered by the user.

```
cout << "Enter the number of students: ";
cin >> num_students;
string* students = new string[num_students];
```

The elements of array students can be referenced using subscript notation in the normal way.

All dynamically allocated objects must be deleted when the program no longer needs them. This is important to avoid running out of dynamic storage. To delete a dynamically allocated array, use the statement:

```
delete[] pointer;
```

where *pointer* is a pointer to the first element of a dynamically allocated array.

After the program has finished processing students, or before a new array of string objects is allocated, the current array should be deleted using the statement

```
delete[] students;
```

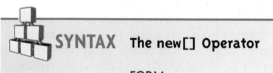

SYNTAX   **The new[] Operator**

FORM:
new *type-name*[*expression*]

EXAMPLE:
new string[n]

MEANING:
Space is allocated for an array of *type-name* objects of length *expression*. A pointer to the first element of this array is returned.

SYNTAX   **The delete[] Operator**

FORM:
delete[] *pointer*;

EXAMPLE:
delete[] students;

MEANING:
The dynamically allocated array whose first element is pointed to by *pointer* is deleted and returned to the free storage pool. Note that the array must have been allocated using the new[] operator.

Array Arguments

When an array is passed as an argument to a function, it is passed as a pointer to its first element. Array parameters can be declared either as pointers or as arrays. For example, the following two function declarations are equivalent:

```
int find(int x[], int n, int target);
int find(int* x, int n, int target);
```

You can call this function by passing either an array or a pointer to an element of an array. Suppose that `scores` is an array of size 10. Then the following are valid calls to the function `find` with 50 passed to `target`.

```
int loc = find(scores, 10, 50);
int loc = find(scores + 5, 5, 50);
```

The first call asks `find` to search the whole array `scores`. The second call asks find to search the sub-array `scores[5]` . . . `scores[9]`.

String Literals and C Strings

The C programming language uses an array of characters to represent a string. The end of the string is indicated by a *null character*, which has a code value of zero in seven-bit ASCII (written `'\0'` in C++, not to be confused with a printable zero character, `'0'`). Since C++ is (almost) a superset of C, C++ uses this convention for string literals as well. A string literal is stored internally as an array of constant characters. This array is one longer than the number of characters in the literal (not counting the enclosing quotes). The last position is occupied by the null character. Although C++ programmers can use character arrays for strings, C++ provides the `string` class, which is easier to use and less error prone. The `string` class provides functions for converting from character arrays into `string` objects, so using the `string` class with string literals is transparent. Since the operating system interface is defined to work with C, it is occasionally necessary to convert from a string back into a zero-terminated array of characters. The `string` class provides a function to do this. We discuss the `string` class in Section P.8.

Multidimensional Arrays

You can also declare arrays with multiple dimensions in C++. For example, the statement

```
int[2][4] my_stuff = {{1, 5, 3, 9},
                      {2, 8, 22, 8}};
```

declares a two-dimensional array with two rows and four columns. The optional initializer list initializes the first row to an array of odd numbers and initializes the second row to an array of even numbers. You reference the element in row i, column j using the expression `my_stuff[i][j]`. In the following diagram, element `my_stuff[1][3]` is highlighted.

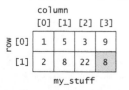

my_stuff

When you use a multidimensional array as a function parameter, the size of each dimension, except the first, must be specified in the parameter declaration. In the following function sum_each_row, the first parameter is a two-dimensional array (with 4 columns in each row) and the second parameter is the number of rows. This function returns a one-dimensional array; each element stores the sum of values in that row of the array argument. For example, result[0] stores the sum of the elements in row 0 of the argument array.

```
/*  Returns an array that contains the sum of elements in each row of a
    two-dimensional array with four columns and num_rows rows.
*/
int* sum_each_row(int x[][4], int num_rows) {
  // Allocate storage for the array of sums.
  int* result = new int[num_rows];
  for (int r = 0; r < num_rows; r++) {
    result[r] = 0;
    // Add the value in each column of row r to result[r]
    for (int c = 0; c < 4; c++) {
      result[r] += x[r][c];
    }
  }
  return result;
}
```

The statement

```
int* result = new int[num_rows];
```

dynamically allocates storage for a one-dimensional array of the required size (num_rows). The statement

```
result[r] += x[r][c];
```

adds the element at row r, column c to the sum for row r.

You can use the statement

```
int* sums = sum_each_row(my_stuff, 2);
```

to determine the row sums for array my_stuff. Array sums will reference the array returned by this function. The array elements are sums[0] (value will be 18) and sums[1] (value will be 40).

EXERCISES FOR SECTION P.7

SELF-CHECK

1. What is the output of the following sample code fragment?

```
int* x;
int* y;
int* z;
x = new int[20];
x[10] = 0;
y = x;
x[10] = 5;
cout << x[10] << ", " << y[10] << endl;
```

```
x[10] = 15;
z = new int[10];
for (int i = 0, i < 10; i++)
  z[i] = x[i];
x[10] = 25;
cout << x[10] << ", " << y[10] << ", " << z[10] << endl;
```

PROGRAMMING

1. Write code for a function
   ```
   bool same_elements(int a[], int b[], int n)
   ```
   that checks whether two arrays have the same elements with the same multiplicities. For example, two arrays

   | 121 | 144 | 19 | 161 | 19 | 144 | 19 | 11 |

   and

   | 11 | 121 | 144 | 19 | 161 | 19 | 144 | 19 |

   would be considered to have the same elements because 19 appears 3 times in each array, 144 appears twice in each array, and all other elements appear once in each array.

P.8 The string Class

The string class defines a data type that is used to store a sequence of characters. In this section we describe the C++ string class. This class is easier to use and less error-prone than using arrays of characters. The string class is intended to be used like a primitive type, where appropriate operator functions are defined.

You have already encountered strings and string operators. The following statements use the concatenation operator (+) with string variables last_name and first_name, the assignment operator (=), and then the insertion operator (<<).

```
string whole_name = last_name + ", " + first_name;
cout << whole_name;
```

Table P.6 describes some string class member functions. The first column shows the result type for each function followed by its signature. For example, for the function at, the first column shows that the function returns a type **char&** (a reference to a **char**) result and has a type size_t argument. The second column describes what the function does. The phrase "this string" means the implicit parameter; that is, the string to which the function is applied by the dot notation. Where there are functions that have similar behavior, they are grouped so that there are multiple signature forms with one description.

Some of the function parameters are described using the form *type-name parameter = default*. This means that the parameter is optional. If it is not provided, its value will be the specified *default*. For example, size_t pos = 0 means that the pos parameter is optional and 0 will be used if it is omitted. If a function signature ends with const, it means that the function can't modify the string object.

TABLE P.6

Functions in string

Function	Behavior
Constructors/Destructor	
`string()`	Constructs a default, empty string.
`string(const string& str);` `string(const string& str, size_t pos, size_t n)`	Makes a copy of a string. The second form makes a copy of a substring of the parameter starting at position pos and n characters long.
`string(const char*)`	Constructs a string from a null-terminated array of characters.
`~string()`	Destroys a string.
Assignment Operators	

`string& operator=(const string& str);`
`string& operator=(const char*);`
`string& operator=(const char)`
	Assigns one string to another;
	assigns a C string to a string;
	assigns a single character to a string.

Query Operators	
`size_t size();` `size_t length()`	Returns the current size of this string.
Element Access	

`char& operator[](size_t index);`
`const char& operator[](size_t index) const;`
`char& at(size_t index);`
`const char& at(size_t index) const`
	Returns a reference to a character at the specified index of this string. The function operator[] allows the use of a string as if it was an array. The function at validates the index and indicates an error if it is out of range. The forms ending with const are automatically called when the expression is on the right-hand side of an assignment, and the other form is automatically called when the expression is on the left-hand side of an assignment.

Concatenation	

`string& operator+=(const string&);`
`string& operator+=(const char*);`
`string& operator+=(const char)`
	Appends the argument string to this string.

`string operator+(const string&, const& string);`
`string operator+(const string&, const char*);`
`string operator+(const string&, const char);`
`string operator+(const char*, const string&);`
`string operator+(const char, const string&)`
	Creates a new string that is the concatenation of two strings. One of the operands must be a string object, but the other one can be a null-terminated character array or a single character.

TABLE P.6 (cont.)

Function	Behavior
Search	

`size_t find(const string& str, size_t pos) const;`
`size_t find(const char* s, size_t pos) const;`
`size_t find(const char c, size_t pos) const`
	Returns the index of where the target first occurs in this string, starting the search at pos. If the target is not found the value `string::npos` is returned.

`size_t rfind(const string& str, size_t pos)`
`   const;`
`size_t rfind(const char* s, size_t pos) const;`
`size_t rfind(const char, size_t pos) const`
	Returns the index of where the target last occurs in this string, starting the search at pos. If the target is not found, the value `string::npos` is returned.

`size_t find_first_of(const string& str,`
`   size_t pos = 0) const;`
`size_t find_first_of(const char* s,`
`   size_t pos = 0) const;`
`size_t find_first_of(const char* s,`
`   size_t pos, size_t n) const;`
`size_t find_first_of(char c, size_t pos) const`
	Returns the index of where any character in the target first occurs in this string, starting the search at pos. If such a character is not found, the value `string::npos` is returned. If the parameter pos is not specified, 0 is the default. The parameter n indicates the length of the character array pointed to by s. If it is omitted, the character array s is null terminated.

`size_t find_first_not_of(const string& str,`
`   size_t pos = 0) const;`
`size_t find_first_not_of(const char* s,`
`   size_t pos = 0);`
`size_t find_first_not_of(const char* s,`
`   size_t pos, size_t n) const;`
`find first_not_of(char c, size_t pos = 0) const`
	Returns the index of where any character that is not in the target first occurs in this string, starting the search at pos. If such a character is not found, the value `string::npos` is returned. If the parameter pos is not specified, 0 is the default. The parameter n indicates the length of the character array pointed to by s. If it is omitted, the character array s is null terminated.

Substring	
`string substr(size_t pos, size_t n =` `   string::npos) const`	Returns a copy of the substring of this string starting at pos that is n characters long. If the parameter n is omitted, the characters starting at pos through the end of the string are used.
Comparisons	
`size_t compare(const string& other)`	Returns 0 if other is equal to this string, −1 if this string is less than the other string, and +1 if this string is greater than the other string.

`bool operator==(const string&, const string&);`
`bool operator!=(const string&, const string&);`
`bool operator<(const string&, const string&);`
`bool operator<=(const string&, const string&);`
`bool operator>=(const string&, const string&);`
`bool operator>(const string&, const string&)`
	All of the infix comparisons are defined.

Conversion to C String	
`const char* c_str()`	Returns a pointer to a null-terminated array of characters that contain the same data as this string.
`const char* data()`	Returns a pointer to an array of characters that contain the data contained in this string. This array is at least `size()` characters long and is not necessarily null-terminated.

The Value `string::npos`

As described in Table P.6, the search functions return the value `string::npos` to indicate that a target was not found. What is this, and why is it necessary? The functions cannot use zero for this purpose, because zero is a valid string position in C++. They cannot use a negative value such as −1 either, because the value returned is of type `size_t`, which is unsigned. Therefore the maximum value for a `size_t` is specified as `string::npos`. You may happen to know what that number is (for your intended target computer, anyway), but it is good practice to use the symbolically defined value rather than a "magic number" such as 4294967295 in writing your programs. A future revision of the standard could change this definition.

EXAMPLE P.13   Assume that `keyboard` (type `string`) contains "qwerty". We evaluate several expressions:

- `keyboard.at(0)` is `'q'`.
- `keyboard.length()` is 6.
- `keyboard.find('o')` is `string::npos`.
- `keyboard.find('y')` is 5.

Finally, the expression

```
keyboard.at(keyboard.length() - 1)
```

applies two member functions to `keyboard`. The inner call, to function `length`, returns the value 6; the outer call, to function `at`, returns y, the last character in the string (at position 5).

The function `substr` returns a new string containing a portion of the `string` object to which it is applied. The first argument is the start position, and the second is the number of characters in the substring. If the number of characters requested is larger than the number available, the remainder of the string starting at `pos` is returned. If the second parameter is omitted, the contents of the returned string will be all characters from `pos` to the end.

EXAMPLE P.14   The expression

```
keyboard.substr(0, keyboard.size() - 1)
```

returns a new string "qwert" consisting of all characters except for the last character in the string referenced by `keyboard`. The contents of `keyboard` are unchanged.

The function `find` searches for a character or a substring within a string. Using our same example, the expression

```
keyboard.find("er")
```

would return 2, the index of the substring "er" within "qwerty".

The function `find_first_of` is different from `find`. It searches the string for the *first* occurrence of *any* character that is contained in the string parameter. Although the parameter is a string itself, it serves in this function as a *set* of target characters. The function `find_first_not_of` searches for the first character that is not contained in the parameter string.

EXAMPLE P.15   Assume that we define a word to be a sequence of letters. Spaces and the punctuation characters (, . ! ?) are not part of a word. Assume that the string `line` contains the following:

    Look! Look!

The statement

    int start = line.find_first_not_of(".,!? ");

will set `start` to 0, the index of the first character that is not a space or a punctuation mark. The statement

    int end = line.find_first_of(".,!? ", start);

will set `end` to 4, the index of the first !

Splitting a String into Tokens

Often we want to process individual pieces, or *tokens*, in a string. For example, in the string `"Doe, John 5/15/65"`, we are likely to be interested in one or more of the particular pieces `"Doe"`, `"John"`, `"5"`, `"15"`, and `"65"`. These pieces would have to be extracted from the string as tokens. Beginnings and ends of tokens are marked by characters, referred to as *delimiters*, that cannot be part of the tokens they separate. In this example, slashes make good delimiters for the date components because they are not parts of numbers. You can divide a string into tokens in C++ using the `find_first_of` and `find_first_not_of` functions combined with the `substr` function.

EXAMPLE P.16   Assume that the string `the_source` contains a set of tokens, and the string `the_delim` contains the delimiters. Our goal is to set **int** variable `start` to the position of the first character in each token and to set **int** variable `end` to the position of the delimiter for that token. We initially set `end` to 0. The beginning of a token is found using the statement

    start = the_source.find_first_not_of(the_delim, end);

This will search the string `the_source` starting at `end` looking for a character that is not in the string `the_delim`. We save this value in `start`. Then the end of the token is found by the statement

    end = the_source.find_first_of(the_delim, start);

This searches for a character that is in the string `the_delim` starting at the beginning of the token just found. Then the statement

```
string token = the_source.substr(start, end - start);
```

will extract the token from `the_source`. The start of the next token can then be found by repeating the statement

```
start = the_source.find_first_not_of(the_delim, end);
```

EXAMPLE P.17 In Section P.7 we said that it is sometimes convenient to convert a C++ string into a C-style string. You can use function `c_str` to do this. This will enable you to use C-string functions that may not have counterparts in the C++ `string` class. For example, if `year_string` contains a string of digit characters only, the statement

```
int year = atoi(year_string.c_str());
```

will store the numeric value of `year_string` in year. The function `atoi` is defined in the header `<cstdlib>`, and it returns the **int** equivalent of its C-string argument (a string of digit characters).

Strings Are Really Templates

Table P.6 is not the way the `string` class is defined in the standard. Instead the `string` class is defined as:

```
typedef basic_string<char, char_traits<char>, allocator<char> > string;
```

Normally, you would not need to worry about this. However, if you make a syntax error in your program and misuse the `string` class, you will get an error message that complains about `std::basic_string<char, std::char_traits<char>, std::allocator<char> >` instead of complaining about `string`. In Chapter 4 we will introduce you to templates and to the `vector` and `list` classes. We will also revisit the `string` class as a template and explain a bit more about what this means.

☑ PROGRAM STYLE

Use of at Versus the Subscript Operators

If names is a `string`, you can reference the character at position `index` using either `names.at(index)` or `names[index]`. The use of at has the advantage that if the index is not valid, the program is aborted as a result of an exception being thrown. (Exceptions are discussed in Chapter 2.) However, despite this advantage, C++ programmers generally prefer to use the latter form because it is simpler.

EXERCISES FOR SECTION P.8

SELF-CHECK

1. Evaluate each of these expressions.
```
string happy = "Happy birthday to you";
happy == "Happy birthday to you ";
"Happy birthday to you" == happy;
string un_happy == happy[0] + string("Happy birthday to you").substr(1);
"happy" < "Happy"
"happy" < happy
int p1 = happy.find_first_of(" ,.!", 1);
int p2 = happy. find_first_of(" ,.!", p1 + 1);
string what = happy.substr(p1 + 1, p2 - p1 -1);
```

PROGRAMMING

1. Write statements to extract the individual tokens in a string of the form "Doe, John 5/15/65". Use the find_first_of and find_first_not_of functions to find the space, comma, and the symbol / and use the substr member function to extract the substrings between these delimiters.

P.9 Input/Output Using Streams

In this section we will show you the basics of using streams for I/O in C++. An *input stream* is a sequence of characters representing data to be used by the program. An *output stream* is a sequence of characters representing program output. There is a stream associated with the console, cin. When the user types data characters at the console keyboard, they are appended to cin. The console window is associated with cout, the standard output stream. We have used the *insertion operator* (<<) to write information to this stream.

Besides using the console for I/O, you can create a text file (using a word processor or editor), save it to disk, and then use it as an input stream for a program. Similarly, a program can write characters to an output stream and save it as a disk file.

Console Input/Output

To use the standard input and output streams you need to include the header <iostream>. This header declares the input stream (istream) object cin and the output stream (ostream) objects cout and cerr. By default, cin is associated with console input, and cout and cerr are associated with console output. Normally, error messages are sent to stream cerr.

Console input/output is generally buffered. This means that characters are collected in a memory area (the buffer), and all the characters in the buffer are transferred as a unit from/to the keyboard/screen, rather than each individual character being transferred as it is typed at the keyboard or displayed on the screen. Thus, when you request input from cin and cin is empty, your program stops execution temporarily, all of the characters typed (up to a newline character) are transferred from the input buffer for cin, and your program then resumes. If there is more input than that requested by the call to the *extraction operator* (>>), the next call to the extraction operator will use the remaining input.

EXAMPLE P.18 Assume that your program has the following sequence of statements:

```
cout << "Enter your favorite pet ";
cin >> first_choice;
cout << "Enter your second favorite pet ";
cin >> second_choice;
```

Now assume that when the first call to cin >> is executed, you type

```
cat dog
```

The string "cat" is stored in first_choice. Then, when the second call to cin >> is executed, the computer will not pause but immediately set second_choice to "dog".

Input Streams

An input stream is a sequence of characters. These can be characters typed on the input console, read from an input file, or read from a network socket. The istream class works the same regardless of the input source. The class istream defines the extraction operator (>>) for the primitive types. This operator breaks the input into groups of characters separated by spaces. If the current group can be converted to the primitive type of the operand, it is converted, and the value is stored in that operand. Otherwise an error flag is set, and the stream freezes.

The processing for each type is shown in Table P.7.

TABLE P.7
Extraction Operator Processing of Primitive Types and Strings

Type of Operand	Processing
char	The first nonspace character is read.
string	Starting with the first nonspace character, characters are read up to the next space.
int short long	If the first nonspace character is a digit, characters are read until a nondigit is encountered. The sequence of digits is then converted to an integer value of the specified type.
float double long double	If the first nonspace character is a digit, characters are read as long as they match the syntax of a floating-point literal. The sequence of digits is then converted to a floating-point value of the specified type.

EXAMPLE P.19   Assume that the input buffer for `cin` contains the following:

```
cat dog 123 1.4 1e4x
```

Assume that c1 and c2 are **char** variables, s1 and s2 are `string` variables, i is an **int** variable, and d1 and d2 are **double** variables. Then the statement

```
cin >> c1;
```

will skip the spaces before "cat" and read the character c into c1.

Next the statement

```
cin >> s1;
```

will read the characters up to the next space and place them into s1. The result is that s1 is "at".

Next the statement

```
cin >> s2;
```

will read "dog" into s2;

Then

```
cin >> i;
```

will read the value 123 into i, and

```
cin >> d1;
```

will read the value 1.4 into d1. Then the statement

```
cin >> d2;
```

will read `1e4` as a valid **double** literal and store the value 10000.0 into d2.

Finally the statement

```
cin >> c2;
```

will read the x into c2. You could, of course, get the same effect by placing multiple extraction operators in a statement:

```
cin >> c1 >> s1 >> s2;
cin >> i >> d1 >> d2 >> c2;
```

Reading a Whole Line

When the extraction operator is used to read strings, it breaks the input into sequences of characters separated by spaces. (Spaces include the newline and tab characters in addition to the space character.) But what if you want to read a whole line, spaces included? The function `getline` can be used for this. The function `getline` is defined in the header `<string>` and has the following declaration:

```
istream& getline(istream&, string&, char delim = '\n');
```

This extracts characters from the `istream` and appends them to the `string` until the `delim` character is reached or until the end of file is reached. The delimiter character is extracted but not appended to the string. The newline character is the default delimiter.

> ## 🚫 PITFALL
>
> If you extract the last value on a data line using the extraction operator >> and then use
> `getline`, you will get a surprising result. There will still be an unprocessed \n character
> at the end of the data line, so the function call
>
> `getline(cin, name, '\n');`
>
> would extract just the '\n' character, and an empty string would be stored in name.
> Consequently, you must first skip over the '\n' character (using function `ignore`)
> before calling `getline` to read the characters typed in on the next line.
>
> ```
> // Skip all characters through the first '\n'
> cin.ignore(numeric_limits<int>::max(), '\n');
> getline(cin, name, '\n');
> ```

The function `getline` is defined in the `<string>` header and is described in Table P.8.
The function `ignore` is a member of the `istream` class and is described in Table P.9.
The function `numeric_limits<int>::max` returns the largest **int** value (see Table P.4).

Detecting Errors on Input

Input errors are fairly common. Fortunately, C++ provides several member functions that can be used to determine whether there are errors on an input stream (see Table P.10).

TABLE P.8
The Function `getline`

Function	Behavior
`istream& getline(istream& is, string& str, char delim);` `istream& getline(istream& is, string& str)`	Reads characters from `is` and appends them to the string `str`. Reading stops when the character `delim` is encountered or when end-of-file is reached. The `delim` character is extracted from the stream, but it is not appended to the string. If the `delim` parameter is omitted, it is assumed to be a newline character, '\n'.

TABLE P.9
The Function `ignore`

Function	Behavior
`istream& ignore(int n, int delim);` `istream& ignore(int n)`	Characters are skipped from the input stream until n characters are read or until the `delim` character is read or until end-of-file is reached. If n is equal to `numeric_limits<int>::max()`, there is no limit on the number of characters skipped. If the `delim` parameter is omitted, then n characters are skipped unless end-of-file is reached first.

TABLE P.10
Error-Reporting Member Functions

Member Function	Behavior
`bool eof() const`	Returns **true** if there is no more input data available on this input stream and there was an attempt to read past the end.
`bool fail() const`	Returns **true** if the input data on this input stream did not match the expected format or if there is an unrecoverable error.
`bool bad() const`	Returns **true** if there is an unrecoverable error on this input stream.
`bool operator!() const`	Returns `fail()`. This function allows the use of an `istream` variable as a logical variable. By applying the logical operator ! to `cin`, you get the result of `cin.fail()`
`operator void*() const`	Returns a null pointer if `fail()` returns **true**, otherwise returns a non-null pointer. This function allows the use of an `istream` variable as a logical variable.

Under most circumstances you should rely on the result of the `fail` function to indicate whether input was successful. Function `eof` indicates whether the end of the input file was reached during the last extraction operation. If `fail` is true and `eof` is also true, then the extraction operation failed because all the input data was read (a good situation). If `fail` is true and `eof` is false, then an error occurred before the last item was read (a bad situation). If `fail` is true and `bad` is true, an unrecoverable error occurred.

The last two function operators listed in the table make it easy to test the result of `fail` by allowing you to treat the `istream` variable as a logical variable. For example, the expression `cin >> i` returns a reference to `istream` variable `cin`. If the last extraction operation was successful, `fail` will be false and (`cin >> i`) will be true. If the extraction operation failed, `fail` will be true and (`cin >> i`) will be false. This is illustrated in the following example.

EXAMPLE P.20   The following loop will read a sequence of numbers from `cin` into variable `i`. The loop terminates when `cin` enters the fail state (that is, no data was read into `i`).

```
int n = 0;
int sum = 0;
int i;
while (cin >> i) {
  n++;
  sum += i;
}
```

By using the expression `cin >> i` as the **while**-loop condition we are effectively testing the result of the `fail` function after each input operation. If the `fail` function returns **false**, the condition (`cin >> i`) is true, and the **while** loop repeats. Loop exit occurs when `fail` returns **true**, making the repetition condition false. The function `fail` can return **true** under three conditions: an end of file is reached, there is an unrecoverable I/O error, or a non-number was entered. The end of file is the expected terminating condition, but the others are errors. We can distinguish them by placing the following **if** statement after the loop.

```
if (cin.eof()) {
  cout << "End of file reached\n";
  cout << "You entered " << n << " numbers\n";
  cout << "Their sum is " << sum << endl;
} else if (cin.bad()) {
  cout << "Unrecoverable i/o error on cin\n";
  return 1;
} else {
  cout << "The last entry was not a valid number\n";
  return 1;
}
```

Output Streams

An output stream is a sequence of characters. These characters can be displayed on the console, written to an output file, or written to a network socket. The ostream class works the same regardless of the output destination. The class ostream defines the insertion operator (<<) for the primitive types. This operator converts the data to a sequence of characters and inserts them into the stream.

The processing for each type is shown in Table P.11.

TABLE P.11
Insertion Operator Processing of Primitive Types and Strings

Type of Operand	Processing
`char`	The character is output.
`string`	The sequence of characters in the string is output.

`int`
`short`
`long`
	The integer value is converted to decimal and the characters are output. Leading zeros are not output unless the value is zero, in which case a single zero is output. If the value is negative, the output is preceded by a minus sign.

`float`
`double`
`long double`
	The floating-point value is converted to a decimal representation and output. By default a maximum of six digits is output. If the absolute value of the number is between 10^{-4} and 10^6, the output is in fixed format, otherwise it is in scientific format.

EXAMPLE P.21   The following sequence of code:

```
char c = 'A';
string s = "Hello";
int i = 12345;
float f = 123.45;
float b = 10e6;
float d = 1.234e-6;
cout << "c = " << c << endl;
cout << "s = " << s << endl;
cout << "i = " << i << endl;
cout << "f = " << f << endl;
```

```
cout << "b = " << b << endl;
cout << "d = " << d << endl;
```

will produce the following output:

```
c = A
s = Hello
i = 12345
f = 123.45
b = 1e+007
d = 1.234e-006
```

Formatting Output Using I/O Manipulators

I/O manipulators are special objects that are used to set the formatting and other flags that control the input and output streams. To use an I/O manipulator you insert it into the output stream or extract into it from an input stream. Some I/O manipulators are simple identifiers. These are defined in the header <iostream> or in headers automatically included by it. Table P.12 lists the I/O manipulators defined by including <iostream>. The default settings are indicated in the second column.

Other I/O manipulators are functions that take parameters. These I/O manipulators are defined in the header <iomanip>. Table P.13 lists the I/O manipulators defined by including <iomanip>.

TABLE P.12
I/O Manipulators Defined by `<iostream>`

I/O Manipulator	Default	Behavior
noshowpoint	yes	Suppresses the decimal point. If a floating-point value is a whole number, the decimal point is not shown. However, it is shown for other floating-point values.
showpoint	no	Shows the decimal point. The decimal point is always shown for floating-point output.
skipws	yes	Sets the format flag so that on input, white space (space, newline, tab) characters are skipped.
noskipws	no	Clears the format flag so that on input, white space characters are not skipped.
right	yes	On output, the value is right-justified.
left	no	On output, the value is left-justified.
dec	yes	The input/output base is set to decimal.
hex	no	The input/output base is set to hexadecimal.
fixed	no	Floating-point output is in fixed format.
scientific	no	Floating-point output is in scientific format.
ws	no	On input, white space is skipped. This is a one-time action; it does not clear the flag that is cleared by noskipws.
endl	no	On output, a newline character is output and the output buffer is flushed.

....
TABLE P.13

I/O Manipulators Defined by `<iomanip>`

I/O Manipulator	Behavior
`setw(int)`	Sets the minimum width of the next output.
`setprecision(int)`	Sets the precision. Depending on the output format, the precision is the total number of digits or the number of fraction digits.
`setfill(char)`	Sets the fill character. The default fill character is the space.
`resetiosflags(ios_base::fmtflags)`	Clears the format flags set in the parameter.
`setiosflags(ios_base::fmtflags)`	Sets the format flags set in the parameter.

EXAMPLE P.22   The following program illustrates the effect of some of these manipulators.

```
/* Program to demonstrate the effect of some I/O manipulators. */

#include <iostream>
#include <iomanip>
using namespace std;

int main()
{
  // showpoint
  cout << "Using showpoint the number 12345.0 "
       << " is output as " << showpoint << 12345.0
       << "\nand using noshowpoint it is output as "
       << noshowpoint << 12345.0 << endl;

  // setw
  cout << "Using setw(10) the number 12345 appears as "
       << setw(10) << 12345 << endl;

  // setfill and setw
  cout << "Using setfill('0') and setw(10) 12345 appears as "
       << setfill('0') << setw(10) << 12345 << endl;
  // Reset to blank fill (the default)
  cout << setfill(' ');

  // left, setfill and setw
  cout << "Using left, setfill('*') and setw(10) 12345 appears as "
       << left << setfill('*') << setw(10) << 12345 << endl;
  // Reset to right justification and blank fill (the defaults)
  cout << right << setfill(' ');
}
```

This program produces the following output:

```
Command Prompt                                                  _|□|×

F:\C++Book\programs\APXA>manipulator_example
Using showpoint the number 12345.0  is output as 12345.0
and using noshowpoint it is output as 12345
Using setw(10) the number 12345 appears as       12345
Using setfill('0') and setw(10) 12345 appears as 0000012345
Using left, setfill('*') and setw(10) 12345 appears as 12345*****
```

TABLE P.14
The Effect of Different Formats

Format	Example	Description
Fixed	123.456789	Output is of the form ddd.ffffff where the number of digits following the decimal point is controlled by the value of precision.
Scientific	1.234568e+002	Output is of the form d.fffff+ennn where the number of digits following the decimal point is controlled by the value of precision. (On some systems, only two digits for the exponent are displayed.)
General	1.23457e+006 123457 123.457 1.23457e-005	A combination of fixed and scientific. If the absolute value is between 10^{-4} and 10^6, output is in fixed format; otherwise it is in scientific format. The number of significant digits is controlled by the value of precision.

Floating-Point Formats and Precision

There are three floating-point formats: general, fixed, and scientific. These formats are described in Table P.14. The general format is the default. To get the fixed format, you can use the manipulator fixed or the manipulator setiosflags(ios_base::fixed). To get the scientific format you can use either the manipulator scientific or the manipulator setiosflags(ios_base::scientific). To get the general format after setting the fixed or scientific, you must turn off both flags using the manipulator resetiosflags(ios_base::fixed | ios_base::scientific).

EXAMPLE P.23 The following program illustrates the different floating-point output formats.

```
/* Program to demonstrate different floating-point output formats */

#include <iostream>
#include <iomanip>
using namespace std;

int main()
{
  double d = 1234567890.0;
  // Display the column headers
  cout << setw(18) << "general" << setw(18) << "fixed"
       << setw(18) << "scientific\n";
  for (int i = 0; i < 20; i++) {
    // Set the format to general
    cout << resetiosflags(ios_base::fixed | ios_base::scientific);
    cout << setw(18) << d;
    // Set the format to fixed
    cout << fixed << setw(18) << d;
    // Set the format to scientific
    cout << scientific << setw(18) << d << endl;
    d /= 10;
  }
}
```

This program produces the following output.

```
Command Prompt                                                          _ □ ×

F:\C++Book\programs\APXA>format_demo
        general            fixed              scientific
     1.23457e+009  1234567890.000000      1.234568e+009
     1.23457e+008   123456789.000000      1.234568e+008
     1.23457e+007    12345678.900000      1.234568e+007
     1.23457e+006     1234567.890000      1.234568e+006
           123457      123456.789000      1.234568e+005
          12345.7       12345.678900      1.234568e+004
          1234.57        1234.567890      1.234568e+003
          123.457         123.456789      1.234568e+002
          12.3457          12.345679      1.234568e+001
          1.23457           1.234568      1.234568e+000
         0.123457           0.123457      1.234568e-001
        0.0123457           0.012346      1.234568e-002
       0.00123457           0.001235      1.234568e-003
      0.000123457           0.000123      1.234568e-004
     1.23457e-005           0.000012      1.234568e-005
     1.23457e-006           0.000001      1.234568e-006
     1.23457e-007           0.000000      1.234568e-007
     1.23457e-008           0.000000      1.234568e-008
     1.23457e-009           0.000000      1.234568e-009
     1.23457e-010           0.000000      1.234568e-010
```

As shown in the previous example, the default precision is 6. The next example
shows the effect of precision.

EXAMPLE P.24   The following program shows the effect of precision on the different floating-point
formats.

```cpp
/* Program to demonstrate the effect of precision on different
   floating-point output formats. */

#include <iostream>
#include <iomanip>
using namespace std;

int main()
{
  double d = 12345.6789;
  // Display the column headers
  cout << setw(10) << "precision" << setw(18) << "general" << setw(18)
       << "fixed" << setw(18) << "scientific\n";
  for (int i = 10; i >= 0; i--) {
    // Set the precision
    cout << setprecision(i);
    cout << setw(10) << i;
    // Set the format to general
    cout << resetiosflags(ios_base::fixed | ios_base::scientific);
    cout << setw(18) << d;
    // Set the format to fixed
    cout << fixed << setw(18) << d;
    // Set the format to scientific
    cout << scientific << setw(18) << d << endl;
  }
}
```

This program produces the following output.

```
Command Prompt                                                            _ □ ×
F:\C++Book\programs\APXA>precision_demo
precision           general           fixed        scientific
       10       12345.6789   12345.6789000000  1.2345678900e+004
        9       12345.6789   12345.678900000   1.234567890e+004
        8       12345.679    12345.67890000    1.23456789e+004
        7       12345.68     12345.6789000     1.2345679e+004
        6       12345.7      12345.678900      1.234568e+004
        5       12346        12345.67890       1.23457e+004
        4       1.235e+004   12345.6789        1.2346e+004
        3       1.23e+004    12345.679         1.235e+004
        2       1.2e+004     12345.68          1.23e+004
        1       1e+004       12345.7           1.2e+004
        0       12345.7      12346             1.234568e+004
```

File Streams

The header <fstream> defines the classes ifstream, ofstream, and fstream. These classes extend the istream, ostream and iostream classes. The class iostream is a combination of the classes istream and ostream that supports both input and output. We will discuss the concept of one class extending another in Chapter 3. Simply put, the classes ifstream and ofstream have all of the member functions of the classes istream and ostream and also have member functions that support input and output using files.

Associating a File with a Stream

Just as for console input/output, you use the extraction operator (>>) to read from a file and the insertion operator (<<) to write to a file. However, to read from or write to a file you first must associate it with an ifstream or ofstream. There are two ways to do this: through the constructor or via the open member function. The form for these is described in Table P.15. If the open function fails, then the fail function will return **true**. Note that the file name is a C string and not a string. If you want to open a file whose name is contained in a string object, you must use the c_str member function to convert it to a C string.

openmode

When a file stream is associated with a file, you have the option of setting the open-mode flags. By default, ifstreams have the in flag set, ofstreams have the out flag set, and fstreams have both in and out set. These flags are described in Table P.16.

EXAMPLE P.25   The following creates an ofstream out, to append data to the existing file whose name is in the string file_name.

```
ofstream out(file_name.c_str(), ios_base::out | ios_base::app);
```

A Complete File-Processing Application

We put all these pieces together in the next example. In Listing P.1, the main function creates an ifstream and an ofstream associated with the input and output file

TABLE P.15
Constructors and **open** Member Function

Function	Behavior
`ifstream()`	Constructs an `ifstream` that is not associated with a file.
`ifstream(const char* file_name,` `  ios_base::openmode mode = ios_base::in)`	Constructs an `ifstream` and associate it with the named file. By default, the file is opened for input.
`ofstream()`	Constructs an `ofstream` that is not associated with a file.
`ofstream(const char* file_name,` `  ios_base::openmode mode = ios_base::out)`	Constructs an `ofstream` and associate it with the named file. By default, the file is opened for output.
`fstream()`	Constructs an `fstream` that is not associated with a file

`fstream(const char* file_name,`
`  ios_base::openmode mode =`
`  ios_base::in | ios_base::out)`
	Constructs an `fstream` that is associated with the named file. By default, the file is opened for both input and output.

`void open(const char* file_name,` `  ios_base::openmode)`	Associates an `ifstream` or `ofstream` with the named file. When opening an `ifstream` the default `openmode` is input (`ios_base::in`), and when opening an `ofstream` the default `openmode` is output (`ios_base::out`).

TABLE P.16
Definition of **openmode** Flags (in `<ios_base>`)

openmode	Meaning
`in`	The file is open for input.
`out`	The file is open for output.
`binary`	No translation is made between internal and external character representation.
`trunc`	The existing file is discarded and a new file is written. This is the default, and applies only to output.
`app`	Data is appended to the existing file. Applies only to output.

names specified on the command line. These names are stored in the array argument argv in index positions 1 and 2. The value of argv[0] is the name of the file containing the executable program. Note that the main function heading

```
int main(int argc, char* argv[])
```

indicates that parameter argv represents an array of C-style strings; the parameter argc is the number of elements in this array.

The **while** loop invokes the extraction operator to read strings from stream ins, storing the information read in the string object first. By using the call to the extraction operator as a **while** condition, we implicitly are checking the results of the `fail` function each time data is extracted. If the extraction does not fail (the normal situation when data is read), the user sees a console prompt asking for more data. The data entered by the user is read into the `string` object `second`.

```
cout << "Type a word to follow " << first << ": ";
cin >> second;
```

Next, the contents of `second` are appended to `first`, and the new string is written to the output file.

```
outs << first << ", " << second << endl;
```

This process continues until the end of the data file is reached, loop exit occurs, and the files are closed.

LISTING P.1
File_Test.cpp

```cpp
/* File_Test is an application that illustrates stream operations. */

#include <iostream>
#include <fstream>
#include <string>

using namespace std;

/* Reads a line from an input file and a line from the console.
   Concatenates the two lines and writes them to an output file.
   Does this until all input lines have been read.
   For the array pointed to by argv, argv[1] is the input file name
   and argv[2] is the output file name. argc is the number of
   elements in this array.
*/
int main(int argc, char* argv[]) {

  // Validate the number of arguments
  if (argc < 3) {
    cerr << "Usage file_test <input file> <output file>\n";
    return 1;
  }

  // Define the input file stream
  ifstream ins(argv[1]);
  if (!ins) {
    cerr << "Failed to open " << argv[1] << " for input\n";
    return 1;
  }

  // Define the output file stream
  ofstream outs(argv[2]);
  if (!outs) {
    cerr << "Failed to open " << argv[2] << " for output\n";
    return 1;
  }
```

```
// Reads words and writes them to the output file until done.
string first;
string second;
while (ins >> first) {
  cout << "Type a word to follow " << first << ": ";
  cin >> second;
  outs << first << ", " << second << endl;
}
// Close files
ins.close();
outs.close();
return 0;
}
```

Figure P.2 shows a sample run. The input file contains the three lines

```
apple
cat
John
```

and the output file contains three lines consisting of a word read from the data file, a comma, and a word typed in at the console.

```
apple, butter
cat, dog
John, Doe
```

String Streams

The header <sstream> defines the classes istringstream and ostringstream. These classes extend istream and ostream to extract from or insert into a string. You can use the istringstream to convert a string that represents a number into the equivalent integer or floating-point value. You can use the ostringstream to format an integer or floating-point value as a string. Table P.17 shows the constructors and member functions for these classes.

We illustrate the use of the istringstream and ostringstream in the following examples.

FIGURE P.2
Sample Run of Program
File_Test

```
F:\C++Book\programs\APXA>file_test input.txt output.txt
Type a word to follow apple: butter
Type a word to follow cat: dog
Type a word to follow John: Doe
```

TABLE P.17
The Classes istringstream and ostringstream

Constructors	Behavior
explicit istringstream(const string&)	Construct an istringstream to extract from the given string.
explicit ostringstream(string&)	Construct an ostringstream to insert into the given string.
ostringstream()	Construct an ostringstream to insert into an internal string.
Member Function	**Result**
string str() const	Returns a copy of the string that is the source or destination of the istringstream or ostringstream.

EXAMPLE P.26   Given the string person_data that contains the following:

    "Doe, John 5/15/65"

we can use the extraction operator to remove the individual tokens ("Doe", "John", and so on). First, associate this string with an istringstream using the declaration

    istringstream in(person_data);

Next we can read the family_name and given_name using the following statement:

    in >> family_name >> given_name;

This will set family_name to "Doe," and given_name to "John". Note that the comma is included in the family name because the extraction stops at the first space character. Next we can read the month, day, and year as **int** values using the following sequence of statements. The first two extractions stop at the character '/'.

```
in >> month;        // Read the month as an int
in >> c;            // Read the '/' character
in >> day;          // Read the day as an int
in >> c;            // Read the '/' character
in >> year;         // Read the year as an int
```

EXAMPLE P.27   We can use an ostringstream to create a person_data string from the individual data items family_name, given_name, month, day, and year as follows:

```
ostringstream out;
out << family_name << ", " << given_name << ' ' << month << '/'
    << day << '/' << year;
string person_data3 = out.str();
```

EXERCISES FOR SECTION P.9

SELF-CHECK

1. What would happen if the output file name matched the name of a file already saved on disk?
2. What lines are displayed by the following fragment?
```
double d = 53.12345;
cout << setprecision(3);
cout << general << setw(15) << d;
cout << fixed << setw(12) << d;
cout << scientific << setw(15) << d;
```

PROGRAMMING

1. Write a main function that reads a set of lines each containing three **int** values from an input file and writes the three numbers and their sum to an output file. If a line does not contain exactly three integers, write the message "**** invalid data line, line number " followed by the number of the data line to the file. At

the end, write the message "Number of lines processed is " followed by the count of lines, and write the message "Number of invalid lines is " followed by the count of invalid data lines.

2. Write a main function that reads all the data for a collection of books from an input stream. Each line of the input stream has the year of publication, the price, the title, and author's name. There is a slash character between the title and author's name. Write each line to an output file that has the form: author's name, title, year and price, with three asterisks between items.

Chapter Review

♦ C++ defines a set of primitive data types that are used to represent numbers (**int, double, float,** and so on), characters (**char**), and Boolean data (**bool**). Characters are represented using ASCII. Variables can be used to store either primitive types or class types.

♦ The control structures of C++ are similar to those found in other languages: sequence (a compound statement), selection (**if** and **switch**), and repetition (**while, for, do ... while**).

♦ Pointer variables are used to reference or point to objects and are declared using a statement of the form:

  type-name* pointer-variable;

To refer to the object that is pointed to by a *pointer-variable,* use the expression **pointer-variable,* where the symbol * is called the dereferencing operator.

♦ Parameters for a C++ function may be call by value, call by reference, or call by constant reference. A parameter declared as *type-name parameter-name* is call-by-value. When the function is called, a copy of the argument is made and is passed to the function. An actual argument that corresponds to a call-by-value parameter remains unchanged even if the function changes the parameter.

♦ A parameter declared as *type-name& parameter-name* is call by reference. When the function is called, the address of the actual argument is passed to the parameter and the actual argument is processed by the function. Therefore, the actual argument retains any new value computed for it by the function.

♦ A parameter declared as const *type-name& parameter-name* is call by constant reference. When the function is called, the address of the actual argument is passed to the parameter, but the actual argument value cannot be changed by the function. Any attempt to do this will cause a syntax error. This kind of parameter combines the safety of call by value (it can't be changed) with the efficiency of call by reference (the actual argument is not copied).

◆ Elements of an array can be referenced using normal subscript notation (*array-name*[*subscript*]) or through a pointer *(*array-name* + *offset*). You can reference the first element of array x as x[0] or *x and the last element of an array with N items as x[N - 1] or *(x + N - 1).

◆ Arrays can be dynamically allocated. A dynamically allocated array is allocated using a statement of the form

    type-name *pointer* = new *type-name*[*size*];

where *size* is an **int** expression. You can reference the elements of this array using either subscript notation or pointer dereferencing. When you are finished with this array, you must deallocate storage for it using the statement

    delete[] *pointer*;

◆ Strings can be represented using either C++ strings (defined in header <string>) or C-style strings, which are arrays of characters. The C++ **string** class has operators for referencing individual characters (the indexing operator []), string assignment (=), concatenation (+), and string comparison (==, !=, <, <=, >, >=). The stream classes have operators for inserting strings in an output stream (<<) and for extracting strings from an input stream (>>). Included in the member functions of the **string** class are operators for referencing substrings and for converting to a C-style string.

◆ The console is represented by input stream **cin** and output stream **cout**. You can declare your own input (output) streams as type **ifstream** (**ofstream**) objects. These streams must be associated with a disk file whose name is specified as the first argument (a C-style string) in an **open** function. Output files can be formatted using I/O manipulators.

Quick-Check Exercises

1. List the operations performed by the C++ preprocessor.
2. What is the effect of the following fragment?
```
double *px;
px = new double(2.5);
*px = 2 * (*px);
cout << *px << endl;
```
3. What kind of parameter would you use for each of the following? Show the parameter declaration.
   a. A parameter array_size that indicates the number of elements in the array.
   b. A parameter small that will return the smallest **int** after function execution.
   c. A parameter that references a string. The first token in this string is returned as the function result. The string argument is unchanged.
   d. A parameter that references a string whose first token is removed from the string argument as a result of function execution.
4. Does the following function swap swap the values of the array elements that are selected by its second and third parameters if they are in bounds, or do they retain their values? What if the second parameter is out of bounds?

```
void swap(int x[], int a, int b) {
  int temp = x[a];
  x[a] = x[b];
  x[b] = temp;
}
```

5. Does your answer to Question 4 change if the array is declared as int* x? What if the array is declared as const int x[]?

6. If a two-dimensional array is used as a function parameter, do you need to specify the number of rows or the number of columns in the array parameter declaration?

7. Write a function that counts the number of occurrences of target (**int**) in a two-dimensional array of integers with six columns.

8. What is displayed by the following:

```
cout << setw(10) << left << "Jane Doe" << right << setw(8) << fixed
     << setprecision(2) << 123.45678;
```

9. Answer Question 8 if fixed is replaced by scientific and left by right.

Answers to Quick-Check Exercises

1. Remove comments and replace them by a single space; split the input file into tokens; carry out preprocessing directives; expand macros.

2. It doubles the value in the memory cell referenced by pointer variable px and displays 5.

3. **a.** call by value, int array_size
   b. call by reference, int& min_value
   c. call by constant reference, const string& str
   d. call by reference, string& str

4. Yes, the values are swapped. If the second parameter is out of bounds, the array element selected by the third parameter would be swapped with a value outside the array and an execution error could occur.

5. The result is the same if the array is declared as int* x. However, if it is declared as const int x[], there would be a syntax error at the statement x[a] = x[b]; .

6. You need to specify the number of columns in each row.

7.
```
int count(int x[][6], int target, int rows) {
  int result = 0;
  for (int r = 0; r < rows ; r++)
    for (int c = 0; c < 6; c++)
      if (x[r][c] == target)
        result++;
  return result;
}
```

8. Jane Doe****123.46 (the *'s indicate spaces)

9. **JaneDoe1.23e+02 (the *'s indicate spaces)

Review Questions

1. Discuss how a C++ source file is processed prior to execution.

2. Draw diagrams that illustrate the effect of each of the following statements.

```
string s1 = "woops";
string* s2 = new string(s1);
string s3 = s1;
s1 = "Oops!";
```

What are the values of s1 == s2, s1 == s3, and s2 == s3?

3. Write a `main` function that reads two `string` objects. Concatenate them and display the result. Also, display each substring of the result, starting with the one that begins at position 1 and goes to the end, then the one that begins at position 2 and goes to the end, and so on.

4. Answer Review Question 3 assuming the two strings are stored in data file `twostrings.txt`. Write the output to file `substrings.txt`.

5. Write a function that returns the sum of all elements on the major diagonal of a square matrix. The major diagonal has the elements at `[0][0]` and at `[size-1][size-1]` as its endpoints.

6. Write a function that determines the sum of all elements on the minor diagonal of a square matrix. The minor diagonal has the elements at `[0][size-1]` and at `[size-1][0]` as its endpoints.

7. Write a function that returns the sum of all elements below the major diagonal.

8. Write a function that returns the sum of all elements above the major diagonal.

Programming Projects

1. Write a `main` function together with a collection of functions that operates on a two-dimensional matrix (a global variable) with `ROW_SIZE` rows and `COL_SIZE` columns. The main function should provide calls to each of the functions and display the results. The functions should have the following declarations:

```
void set_row(int row, double[] row_vals);    // Stores the array of
                                             // row_vals in row
double* get_row(int row);                    // Returns the specified row
void set_element(int row, int col, int val); // Sets the specified
                                             // element
double get_element(int row, int col);  // Returns the specified element

double sum();        // Returns sum of the values in the array
double find_max();   // Returns the largest value in the array
double find_min();   // Returns the smallest value in the array
string to_string();  // Returns a string representing the matrix
```

2. Write a program that stores a collection of exam scores in an array. Provide functions to find the average score, to assign a letter grade based on a standard scale, to sort the scores so they are in increasing order, and to display the scores. Test these functions.

3. Write a program that reads the following from each data line of an input file: a person's name, the number of exam scores, followed by all the exam scores. Write the following functions to process this data.

   • Read each data line from a text file.
   • Write all information stored to an output file.
   • Write each student's data, average exam score, and letter grade to an output line.

4. Modify Programming Project 3 so that all students have the same number of exam scores. The number of students and number of scores should be data items. Store the exam scores in a two-dimensional array. The row subscript should be the student number and the column subscript should be the exam number. Calculate and write the average score for all students on each exam to the output file. Write each student's name to the output file followed by the student's score and grade on each exam. Use the average score for each exam to calculate and display the student's grade for that exam. If the student's score is within + or – 5 points of the average, give a grade of C. If the grade is more than 5 points above (below) the average, give a grade of B (D). If the grade is more than 15 points above (below) the average give a grade of A (F).

Chapter 1

Introduction to Software Design

Chapter Objectives

- ◆ To become familiar with the software challenge and the software life cycle
- ◆ To understand what activities take place in each phase of the software life cycle
- ◆ To learn how to use top-down design and object-oriented design
- ◆ To learn to use data abstraction, procedural abstraction, and information hiding to manage complexity
- ◆ To learn how to design your own classes
- ◆ To learn how to draw class diagrams, which document the interaction between classes
- ◆ To learn the role of abstract data types in building models of computer systems and how to implement them using classes and interfaces
- ◆ To become familiar with use cases as a tool to document a system's interaction with the user
- ◆ To understand the software design process by following the design and implementation of an array-based telephone directory
- ◆ To become familiar with sequence diagrams as a tool for documenting the interaction between multiple classes used in a program

This chapter discusses software design and introduces tools and techniques used by professional programmers to facilitate the design and maintenance (upkeep) of large-scale programs. You will see how software designers use abstraction to create models of computer systems and how they use abstract data types to encapsulate data elements and operators. You will learn how to specify the behavior of an abstract data type (ADT) using an interface and how to implement it using classes. The use of interfaces enables programmers to develop systems with a high degree of flexibility and also enables a programmer to code program systems that have interchangeable parts.

You will see how interfaces, preconditions, and postconditions serve as contracts between system designers and programmers. They also serve as a contract between application programmers who use an API (Application Programming Interface) to develop applications software and those who design and implement the classes that are part of the API.

Through examination of a large case study, you will learn how to follow a five-step software development process to design and implement new software applications. These steps include problem specification, analysis, design, implementation, and testing. You will see how to employ use cases to specify the interaction between the system and its users during problem specification and analysis. You will see how to use sequence diagrams and procedural abstraction to develop the algorithms for the class member functions during the design phase. Carefully following the software development process will lead to more efficient implementations with fewer errors, making it easier to test and debug the completed system.

Introduction to Software Design

1.1 The Software Life Cycle

The goal of a college programming assignment is to give you some experience with a particular concept, thus reinforcing your mastery of it. The resulting program is used briefly to demonstrate to the instructor that you have mastered the assignment. The only users of the program are you (its author) and perhaps the instructor.

In industry, on the other hand, a software product is expected to be used for an extended period of time by someone who did not write the program and who is not intimately familiar with its internal design. The impetus for a software project comes from users of an existing software product or potential users of a new software product. The users see a need for improving the operation of an existing product or for computerizing an operation that is currently done without the use of computers. This need is communicated to the individual(s) responsible for developing new software products in the organization (normally called *system analysts*). A team of system analysts and programmers are responsible for guiding the development of a new software system from its inception to its completion. We discuss this process next.

A software product goes through several stages as it matures from an initial concept to a finished product in regular use. This series of stages could be compared to the stages that an insect goes through as it develops from egg, to larva, to pupa, to adult. This sequence of stages is known as the life cycle; thus, we speak of a *software life cycle*.

Software products can require years to develop and require the efforts of many individuals. A successful software product will be used for many years after it is first released. During the term of its use, new or updated versions may be released that contain changes to fit new situations or that fix errors that were previously undetected. For this reason, it is important to design and document software in an organized way so that it can be easily understood and maintained after its initial release. This is especially important because the person who maintains the software may not have been involved in its original design.

Software Life Cycle Models

Many different views of the software life cycle have been proposed over the years and are in use today. There are also many different ways of organizing the activities that transform the software from one stage to another. The simplest version is the waterfall model, in which the activities are performed in sequence and the result of one flows into the next (indicated by downward-pointing arrows in Figure 1.1), much like water flowing down a cascading waterfall.

Table 1.1 describes the activities that are performed in each of the five phases of the waterfall model. We will provide more details later in this section.

TABLE 1.1
Waterfall Model of the Software Life Cycle

1. Requirements	The requirements for the software system are determined.
2. Analysis	The requirements are studied and clarified, and the overall architecture of the solution is determined. Each major subsystem is analyzed, and its component classes are determined. Also, any interaction between components is determined.
3. Design	Functions and data fields are defined for classes. Detailed algorithms for the functions are defined.
4. Implementation	The individual classes and functions are coded in the target programming language.
5. Testing	The functions of each class are tested in isolation and as a class (unit testing). The functions and classes are tested together (integration testing) to verify that they work together and meet the requirements.

FIGURE 1.1
The Waterfall Software
Life Cycle Model

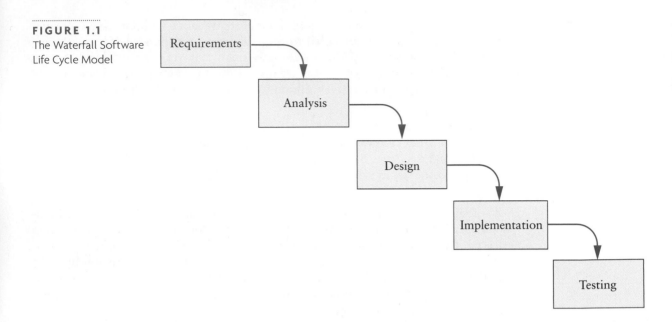

Although simple in concept, the waterfall model has proved to be unworkable in practice. The fundamental flaw in this model is the assumption that each stage can and must be completed before the next one starts. That is rarely the case in actual practice. For example, system designers may identify incomplete or inconsistent requirements during the design process, or programmers may find during the implementation phase that there are areas of the design that are incomplete or inconsistent. Sometimes it is not until the product is finished and the user first sees it that the user's requirements are "specified" in the form of the complaint, "That's not what I meant!"

Various alternatives have been proposed. The common theme is to develop a software product in stages or cycles. Each cycle is a mini-version of the waterfall, with varying amounts of emphasis on the different activities for the particular cycles. At the end of each cycle there is a review with the users to obtain feedback, which will be taken into account in the next cycle.

One example of such a model is the Unified Model, shown in Figure 1.2. The cycles, called *phases* and *iterations*, are shown along the horizontal axis, and the activities, called *workflows*, are shown down the vertical axis. The four phases are *inception*, *elaboration*, *construction*, and *transition* (switching over to the new system). Time moves across the horizontal axis from iteration 1 to iteration *n*, and each iteration is a mini-waterfall. The five activities are the same as in the simple waterfall model. The shaded areas under the curves next to each activity are intended to show the relative amount of effort spent on that activity during each iteration. For example, during the inception phase (iterations 1 and 2), most effort is spent on specifying requirements. In fact, requirements specification is the only activity performed during iteration 1. During iteration 2, some effort is also spent on analysis, with a tiny amount on design and implementation. As the software developers move into the

FIGURE 1.2
The Unified Software
Life Cycle Model

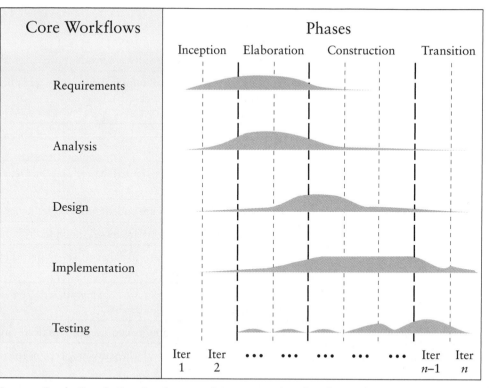

Source: Grady Booch, Ivar Jacobson, and James Rumbaugh, *The Unified Software Development Process* (Addison Wesley, 1999)

elaboration phase, they continue to work on requirements and analysis but also start to spend more time on design and implementation, particularly toward the end of the elaboration phase. In the construction phase, the requirements specification and analysis activities are completed, and most effort is spent on design and implementation. The diagram also shows that some time is spent on testing during all phases after inception, but more time is spent on testing during the construction and transition phases. We will discuss testing in more detail in Chapter 2.

Software Life Cycle Activities

Independently of how they are organized, there is general consensus that the activities shown in Table 1.2 are essential for the development of a software product. We will consider activities 1 through 5 in the rest of this chapter; activities 6 through 8 will be the subject of the next chapter.

Because our case studies are relatively small compared to a commercial software project, we generally follow the simple waterfall model. However, we do revisit some case study solutions in later chapters and iterate through the five activities, much as in the Unified Model.

TABLE 1.2
Software Life Cycle Activities

1. Requirements specification	The requirements for the software product are determined and documented.
2. Architectural design	The architecture of the solution is determined. This breaks the solution into different components, which are allocated to one or more processing resources.
3. Component design	For each component, classes are identified, with specified roles and responsibilities.
4. Detailed design	Functions and data fields are defined for classes. Detailed algorithms for the functions are defined.
5. Implementation	The individual functions are coded in the target programming language.
6. Unit test	Each class and its functions are tested individually.
7. Integration test	Groups of classes are tested together to verify that they work together and meet the requirements.
8. Acceptance test	The product as a whole is tested against its requirements to demonstrate that the product meets its requirements.
9. Installation	The product is installed in its end-use (production) environment.
10. Maintenance	Based upon experience with the software, enhancements and corrections are made to the product.

Requirements Specification

Because the potential users of a new system are often naïve as to what can be accomplished, the initial specification for a software product may be incomplete or ambiguous. The specification is clarified through extensive interaction between the users of the software and the system analyst. Through this interaction, the system analyst determines precisely what the users want the proposed software to do, and the users learn what to expect from the software product. This way there are no surprises in the end.

Although it may seem like common sense to proceed in this way, very often a software product does not perform as its users expected. The reason is usually a communication gap between those responsible for the product's design and its eventual users; generally, both parties are at fault when the software fails to meet expectations. To avoid this possibility, it is imperative that a complete, written description of the requirements—a *requirements specification*—for a new software product be generated at the beginning of the project and that both users and designers review and approve the document.

The system analyst works with the software users to clarify the detailed system requirements. Some of the questions that need to be answered deal with the format of the input data, the desired form of any output screens or printed forms, and the need for data validation. You often need to mimic this process by interrogating your instructor or teaching assistant to determine the precise details of a programming assignment.

For example, assume that your instructor has given you the following incomplete specification of a programming assignment.

> *Problem:* Write an interactive telephone directory program that will contain a collection of names and telephone numbers. You should be able to insert new entries in the directory, retrieve an entry in the directory, or change a directory entry.

Some of the questions that come to mind and might require clarification are the following:

- Is there an initial list of names and numbers to be stored in the directory beforehand, or are all entries inserted at the same time?
- If there is an initial list, is it stored in a file, or should it be entered interactively?
- If the initial directory is stored in a file, is the file a text file (file of characters) or a binary file (file of binary values)?
- If the file is a text file, are there any formatting conventions (for example, the name starts in column 1 and the phone number starts in column 20). Are the name and number on the same data line or on separate lines? How are the names stored (for example, last, first or first last)?
- Is it possible for there to be more than one telephone number associated with a particular name? If so, should the first number be retrieved, the last number, or all numbers?
- Is it possible to change a person's name as well as the person's phone number?
- When a number is retrieved, should both the person's name and number be displayed or just the number? What form should this display take?
- What action should be taken if a "new" entry has the same name as a person already in the directory? Should this be flagged as an error?

As you can see, there are plenty of questions left unanswered by the initial problem statement. To complete the requirements specification, you should answer these questions and more. Many of the questions deal with details of input data, handling of potential errors in input data, and formats of input data and output lists.

Analysis

Once the system requirements are specified, the *analysis* stage begins. Before you can embark on the design of a program solution, you should make sure that you completely understand the problem. If the requirements specification has been carefully done, this will be easy. If there are any questions remaining, they should be cleared up at this time.

The next step is to evaluate different approaches to the program design. In industry, the system analyst and users may consider whether there are commercial software packages that can be purchased to satisfy their requirements (as an alternative to developing the software in-house). They must also determine the impact of the new software product on existing computer systems and what new hardware or software will be needed to develop and run the new system. They determine the feasibility of each approach by estimating its cost and anticipated benefits. The analysis stage culminates with the selection of what appears to be the best design approach.

In your coursework, you do not have this flexibility. You must design and implement each program. During the analysis, your goal is to carefully determine the input/output requirements for the system and its interaction with the user. You will also find it helpful to break your system up into a set of small and manageable components, which you can then design and code separately. To do so, you need to identify the modules or components that will constitute the system and specify the interactions between them. You complete this process in the *design* phase, which we discuss next.

Design

Once you understand the problem and have selected the overall approach, it is time to develop a high-level design of the system. Professional software engineers make use of several design approaches in their work. The top-down approach, in which a system is broken into a set of smaller subsystems, each of those subsystems is broken into smaller components, and so forth until components are small and simple enough to be coded easily, has been used successfully for many years. More recently, the object-oriented approach, in which the developer identifies a set of objects and specifies their interaction, has been increasingly used. In this text we will utilize both the top-down and object-oriented approaches to software design.

Top-Down Design

The *top-down* approach to software design (also called *stepwise refinement*) instructs you to start at the top level (the original problem) and divide it into subproblems. For each subproblem, identify a subsystem with the responsibility of solving that subproblem. You can use a *structure chart* to indicate the relationship between the subproblems (and subsystems). For example, a structure chart for the telephone directory problem is shown in Figure 1.3.

Figure 1.3 shows the two top levels of the structure chart, which include the original problem and its major subproblems. Each of these subproblems may be further refined and divided into still smaller subproblems. Figure 1.4 shows that to solve the subproblem "Read the initial directory" you must be able to "Read an entry from file" and "Store an entry in the directory". Figure 1.5 shows that to solve the subproblem "Retrieve and display an entry" you must be able to "read a name", "find

FIGURE 1.3
Structure Chart for
Telephone Directory
Problem

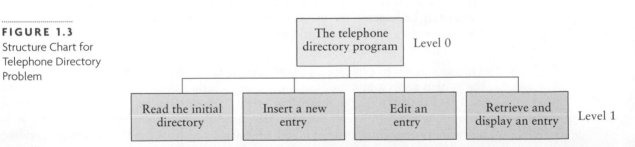

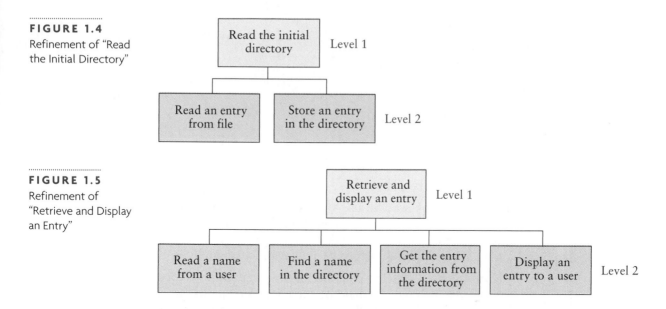

a name in the directory", "get the entry information from the directory", and "display an entry".

Figure 1.3 indicates that you can solve the original problem (level 0) by providing solutions to four level 1 subproblems. Figures 1.4 and 1.5 represent the solutions to two level 1 subproblems in terms of six level 2 subproblems.

Object-Oriented Design

Top-down design is process-oriented in that it focuses on the actions that are needed rather than the data structures. In contrast, *object-oriented design* (OOD) focuses on the data elements that are needed and operations to be performed on those data elements. In OOD, you first identify the objects that participate in your problem, and then you identify how they interact to form a solution. The common characteristics of a collection of similar objects define a class, and the interactions are identified as *messages* that one object sends to another. For an object to receive a message, its class must provide an *operator* (usually a function) to process that message. Looking at the nouns in the problem statement can help you identify objects, and looking at the verbs can point to the operators. We will discuss how to write C++ classes later in this chapter.

In looking at the phone directory problem statement, we have ascertained that there is a directory and that the directory contains entries. An entry consists of a name and a number. There is also a user, and there is a data file that contains entries. The user is external to the program and is called an *actor* in object-oriented terminology. The user selects the operations that will be performed on the directory and data file.

Object-oriented design incorporates some of the elements of top-down design. It also incorporates some of the elements of *bottom-up design*, which focuses on the design of individual system components. So OOD is a combination of both of these earlier techniques.

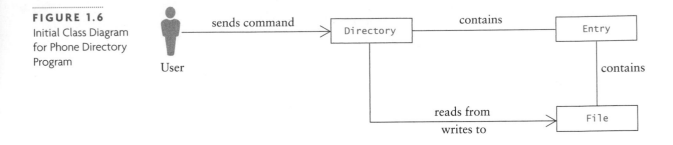

UML as a Design Tool

In this textbook we will use Unified Modeling Language™ (UML) diagrams as a design tool to illustrate the interaction between classes and between classes and external entities (users). We will introduce several features of UML in this textbook on an as-needed basis. Appendix B provides a summary of UML diagrams.

Figure 1.6 is a UML class diagram for the telephone directory program, showing the classes that are used and their interaction and relationships. The classes (Directory, Entry, and File) are identified by rectangles, whereas lines show the interaction and relationships. The lines ending with an arrow indicate an interaction between classes. For example, the class Directory has functions that read or write information from class File. External entities, called actors, are represented by small figures. This seems to imply that the external entity is a person, but that is not necessarily the case. So far, our class diagrams have no detail, because we have not yet identified their data elements and functions; we are focusing here on the interaction between classes.

UML diagrams are a standard means of documenting class relationships that is widely used in industry. We recommend that you use UML diagrams to describe the classes that you develop in solving your programming assignments.

EXERCISES FOR SECTION 1.1

SELF-CHECK

1. What are the advantages of the Unified Model over the waterfall model of the software life cycle?
2. What are the five activities in the software development life cycle followed in this book?
3. Name the four phases of the Unified Model. Name the five activities in the Unified Model.
4. Draw a structure chart showing the refinement of the subproblem "Insert a new entry".
5. Draw a structure chart showing the refinement of the subproblem "Edit an entry".

1.2 Using Abstraction to Manage Complexity

Abstraction is a powerful technique that helps programmers (or problem solvers) deal with complex issues in a piecemeal fashion. An abstraction is a model of a physical entity or activity. In this book, we use abstraction to develop models of entities (objects and classes) and also of the operations performed on these objects. One example of abstraction is the use of a program variable (for example, `name` or `number`) to denote a storage location in memory for a data value. You need not be concerned with the details of the physical structure of memory or the actual bits (binary digits) that are used to represent the value of a variable; you don't need to know those things to use variables in programming. This is analogous to driving a car. You need to know how to use a key to start the engine, how to use the accelerator and brake pedals to control speed, and how to use the steering wheel to control direction. However, you don't need to know details of the car's electrical system, drive train, braking system, or steering mechanism.

Procedural Abstraction

Procedural abstraction is the philosophy that procedure development should separate the concern of what is to be achieved by a procedure (a C++ function) from the details of how it is to be achieved. In other words, you can specify what you expect a function to do, then use that function in the design of a problem solution before you know how to implement the function. As an example of procedural abstraction, suppose you have functions available to perform all the Level 2 steps in Figure 1.5. You can then write the following C++ fragment to retrieve an entry from the directory using these functions.

```
name = read_name();          // Reads a name
number = directory.get(name); // Gets number associated with name
if (number != "")
  // Display name and number.
  cout << "Phone number for " << name
       << " is " << number << endl;
else
  // Display message that name is not in directory.
  cout << name << " is not in directory\n";
```

Data Abstraction

In this course we will also use another type of abstraction: *data abstraction*. The idea of data abstraction is to specify the data objects for a problem and the operations to be performed on these data objects without being overly concerned with how they (the data objects) will be represented and stored in memory. You can describe what information is stored in the data object without being specific as to how the information is organized and represented. This is the *logical view* of the data object, as opposed to the *physical view*, its actual internal representation in memory. Once you understand the logical view, you can use the data object and its operators in your programs; however, you (or someone else) will eventually have to implement the data object and its operators before you can run any program that uses them. In C++, the operators are called *member functions*, so we will use these terms interchangeably.

As an example, you have already practiced data abstraction in that you have used the `string` data type to represent sequences of characters without knowing how a character sequence is actually stored in memory. The C++ `string` is an abstraction for a sequence of characters. You can use `string` objects and their operators (`length`, `at`, and so on) without knowing the details of their implementation.

Information Hiding

One advantage of procedural abstraction and data abstraction is that they enable the designer to make implementation decisions in a piecemeal fashion. The designer can postpone making decisions regarding the actual internal representation of the data objects and the implementation of its operators. At the top levels of the design the designer focuses on how to use a data object and its operators; at the lower levels of design the designer (or perhaps a different designer or programmer on the team) works out the implementation details. In this way, the designer can control or reduce the overall complexity of the problem.

If the details of a data object's implementation are not known when the higher-level module (a C++ class) is designed, the higher-level class can access the data object only through its member functions. From a software design viewpoint, this is an advantage rather than a limitation. It allows the designer of each class to make changes at a later date, such as to accommodate new government regulations or to implement a function in a more efficient way. If the higher-level classes reference a data object only through its functions, the higher-level class will not have to be rewritten. The process of "hiding" the details of a class's implementation from users of the class is called *information hiding*.

As an example of how information hiding works, let's see how you might access the name part of a new entry (called `my_entry`) for the phone directory. If you assume that `my_entry` is an object with a field called `name`, you could use the qualified identifier

        my_entry.name

As implementation proceeds, you might change your mind and decide to use an array `data` to hold each entry's name and telephone number instead of separate data fields. In this case, you would have to go back and change the preceding reference (and all similar references) to

        my_entry.data[0]

It is much cleaner to hide the structure of an entry and instead use a function to retrieve the name string. If `get_name` is a function that extracts the name string from an `Entry` object, the statement

        a_name = my_entry.get_name();

will return the name string stored in `my_entry` and assign it to `a_name` regardless of the internal representation chosen for an entry. If you decide to change the internal representation, you only have to change the body of function `get_name`. You will not need to change any of the higher-level modules that call `get_name`.

The rest of this chapter assumes that you are familiar with array processing and I/O fundamentals in C++. If you are not, you can learn about them in the first chapter, *A C++ Primer*. We next discuss C++ classes and show you how to define your own classes.

EXERCISES FOR SECTION 1.2

SELF-CHECK

1. How is information hiding related to data abstraction?
2. How does information hiding relate to procedural abstraction?
3. How does the logical view of a data object differ from its physical view?
4. Explain why type **int** is an abstraction for integers in mathematics.

1.3 Defining C++ Classes

A C++ program is a collection of functions and classes; consequently, when you write a C++ program, you will develop one or more classes. We will show you how to write a C++ class next.

A class represents a set of objects that have common properties. A class can be thought of as a template for specifying or creating objects. A class also represents a type. As discussed in *A C++ Primer*, a type determines what set of values an item of data can have and the operations that can be performed on it. In C++ there are two kinds of types: the primitive or built-in types and the user-defined or class types.

To define a class completely, we must provide two things: a *class definition* and a *class implementation*. The class definition describes the class to its users—the names of the operations and the internal data contents. The class implementation provides the implementation of the operations.

Class Definition

A class consists of members (not to be confused with the objects, or instances, of the class). Members can be either *data members* (also called data fields or attributes) or member functions (also called operators, functions, or methods). Data members are sometimes called *instance variables* because each class instance (object) has its own storage for them. The data members may be either primitive types or class types. As we discussed earlier, we want the operations to be visible to the users of the class, but we want to keep the implementation details hidden. Therefore, we specify that the member functions are *public* and the data members are *private*. Before getting into the formal syntax of a class definition, let us examine a simple example.

TABLE 1.3
The Clock Member Functions

Function	Behavior
void set_clock(int hr, int min, int sec)	Sets the clock to the specified values.
int get_hours()	Gets the number of hours since midnight or noon.
int get_minutes()	Gets the number of minutes in the current hour.
int get_seconds()	Gets the number of seconds in the current minute.
void tick()	Advances the clock by one second.

EXAMPLE 1.1   The class Clock describes a group of objects, each of which represents the time using a 12-hour clock. Operations that we want to perform on Clock objects are setting the time, determining the value of hours, minutes, and seconds, and advancing the clock by one second. These operations are described in Table 1.3.

So that a class can be used by other classes or functions, which become the class's *clients*, we place the class definition into a header file. Listing 1.1 shows the header file Clock.h for the class Clock.

LISTING 1.1
Clock.h

```
#ifndef CLOCK_H_
#define CLOCK_H_

/** The class Clock represents the time of day. */
class Clock {

    public:
        // The interface is defined here
        /** Set the clock. */
        void set_clock(int hr, int min, int sec);

        /** Get the current hour. */
        int get_hours() const;

        /** Get the current minute. */
        int get_minutes() const;

        /** Get the current second. */
        int get_seconds() const;

        /** Advance the clock by one second. */
        void tick();
```

```
    private:
        // The implementation details are defined here
    };
```

```
#endif
```

This header file consists of only the member function declarations (the name and parameters). The implementation of these functions is provided separately—part of the hidden information. Notice that the definition for class `Clock` is enclosed in braces (`{`, `}`) and there is a semicolon after the closing brace.

Notice that the comments above each function declaration are introduced by `/**` rather than simply `/*` as described in the *C++ Primer*. The reason is discussed at the end of this section.

Preprocessor Directives in `Clock.h`

The preprocessor directives `#ifndef`, `#define`, and `#endif` are used to prevent multiple definitions of the identifiers in file `Clock.h`, which could happen if it were included more than once (as when it is included in two different files that are both included by a third file). The first directive,

```
    #ifndef CLOCK_H_
```

tests to see whether the identifier `CLOCK_H_` is not defined. If it is defined, the preprocessor skips the lines in the source file through the directive

```
    #endif
```

If `CLOCK_H_` is not defined, the preprocessor reads the second directive,

```
    #define CLOCK_H_
```

and it defines the identifier `CLOCK_H_`, giving it the value of the empty string. Consequently, this directive and the lines that constitute the definition for class `Clock` will be processed just one time, so the identifiers declared in this class cannot be multiply defined.

The identifier, `CLOCK_H_`, used in these directives was chosen arbitrarily; any identifier can be used. However, it is a common convention to use the file name in uppercase, replacing the period with an underscore and appending a trailing underscore.

The **public** and **private** Parts

The keywords **public** and **private** are known as *access specifiers*. Members declared in the public part of the class definition can be accessed by any other class. Members declared in the private part can be accessed directly only within class `Clock`. So far, our class definition is incomplete, because we have shown only the public part. Although the implementation details are hidden within the private part of the class definition, we still must provide them. Thus, when we talk about information hiding, we do not mean that the *client programmer* (that is, the programmer who uses this class) cannot see this information; we mean that the client programmer cannot take advantage of this information, because this data is not directly accessible in the client program.

In our `Clock` class we have at least two choices for how to store the time. We can provide data fields for the hours, minutes, and seconds separately, or we can provide a data field that contains the number of seconds since midnight. We will choose the former because it simplifies the implementation of the member functions, except for `tick`. Thus, after the keyword **private** in Listing 1.1, we would have the following:

```
/** The hours since midnight or noon. */
int hours;
/** The minutes within the current hour. */
int minutes;
/** The seconds within the current minute. */
int seconds;
```

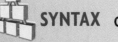

SYNTAX   Class Definition

FORM:
```
class name {
  public:
    member declarations
  private:
    member declarations
};
```

EXAMPLE:

See Listing 1.1.

MEANING:

The class *name* is defined to have the members listed. Members may be either data members (also called data fields), member functions (also called functions), or nested classes. Members that are declared following the access specifier **public:** are accessible by functions outside of the class, while those following the access specifier **private:** are accessible only by functions that are members of the class or are declared to be friends of the class. There may be multiple public and private regions, but generally all public members are declared together, followed by all private members. Also, declarations that precede the first access specifier are considered to be private.

Private Data Fields, Public Functions

The access specifier **private** sets the visibility of each declaration that follows it to private visibility. This means that whatever is declared after **private:** can be accessed only within the class definition. All the data members for the `Clock` class are private. Ordinarily, only class members with public visibility can be accessed outside of the class. The access specifier **public** sets the visibility of each declaration that follows it to public. In Listing 1.1, all the members declared after **public:** and before **private:** are member functions.

The reason for having private visibility for data fields is to control access to an object's data and to prevent improper use and processing of an object's data. If a data field is private, it can be processed outside of the class only by invoking one of the public member functions that are part of the class. Therefore, the programmer who writes the public member functions controls how the data field is processed. Also, the details of how the private data is represented and stored can be changed at a later time by the programmer who implements the class; the other programs that use the class (called the class's clients) will not need to be changed.

Constant Member Functions

The declarations for the functions get_hours, get_minutes, and get_seconds in Listing 1.1 each have the keyword **const** immediately preceding the semicolon. This tells the users and the compiler that these functions will not modify the object on which they operate. This serves three purposes: First, it documents for the user that calling this function will not change its value, and second, it permits the compiler to incorporate certain optimizations when it generates the machine language code. Also, if you declare a member function to be **const**, the compiler will enforce this intention by flagging as an error any operation that could potentially modify the object. Therefore, you should declare as constant a member function that is not supposed to modify an object.

Class Implementation

Member function definitions are the same as regular function definitions except that the class name is placed in front of the function name, separated from the name by a pair of colons. Thus, we can implement the get_hours function in our clock class as

```
int Clock::get_hours() const {
  return hours;
}
```

SYNTAX   **Member Function Definition**

FORM:
return-type class-name::*function-name*(*parameter list*) const*opt* { *body* }

EXAMPLE:
int Clock::get_hours() const { return hours; }

MEANING:
The function *function-name* that is a member of the class *class-name* is defined by the sequence of statements provided in the *body*. The declaration portion of the definition must be the same as that given in the class definition with respect to the return type, function name, types of parameters, and **const** specifier. The subscript *opt* following the **const** specifier indicates that it is optional. However, if it is present in the function declaration, it must also be present in the corresponding function definition. If these do not match, the compiler will report an error such as "*function-name* is not a member of *class-name*."

Usually all of the member function definitions for a class are grouped into a single source (.cpp) file. Listing 1.2 shows the implementation for the Clock class. The source file must begin with the line

```
#include "Clock.h"
```

which includes the header file for class Clock, thereby defining the class members. Notice that the header file name is surrounded by quotes, not angle brackets (<>). Angle brackets are used only with system-defined classes.

LISTING 1.2
Clock.cpp

```
// Implementation of the Clock class.
#include "Clock.h"

/** Set the clock. */
void Clock::set_clock(int hr, int min, int sec) {
  hours = hr;
  minutes = min;
  seconds = sec;
}

/** Get the current hour. */
int Clock::get_hours() const {
  return hours;
}

/** Get the current minute. */
int Clock::get_minutes() const {
  return minutes;
}

/** Get the current second. */
int Clock::get_seconds() const {
  return seconds;
}

/** Advance the clock by one second. */
void Clock::tick() {
  seconds++;
  if (seconds >= 60) {
    minutes++;
    seconds -= 60;
  }
  if (minutes >= 60) {
    hours++;
    minutes -= 60;
  }
  if (hours > 12) {
    hours -= 12;
  }
}
```

Using Class Clock

Let's consider how class Clock might be used. The program in Listing 1.3 first includes the header file for class Clock. The main function begins by declaring an object c of type Clock. The remaining statements use dot notation to apply one of the Clock member functions to object c. First, the clock is set to 12:59:58 (12 hours, 59 minutes, and 58 seconds). Next, the clock is advanced by four seconds, and the updated time is displayed. The output line displayed should be

```
The new time is 01:00:02
```

···
LISTING 1.3
Test_Clock.cpp

```
/** Program to test the Clock class. */
#include "Clock.h"
#include <iostream>
#include <iomanip>
using namespace std;

int main() {
  Clock c;
  c.set_clock(12, 59, 58);
  c.tick();
  c.tick();
  c.tick();
  c.tick();
  cout << setfill('0');
  cout << "The new time is "
       << setw(2) << c.get_hours() << ':'
       << setw(2) << c.get_minutes() << ':'
       << setw(2) << c.get_seconds() << '\n';
  return 0;
}
```

The Class Person

We now consider a more complicated example of a class definition and implementation. A class Person might describe a group of objects, each of which is a particular human being. For example, instances of class Person would be yourself, your mother, and your father. A Person object could store the following data:

- Given name
- Family name
- ID number
- Year of birth

The following are a few of the operations that can be performed on a Person object:

- Calculate the person's age
- Test whether two Person objects refer to the same person
- Determine whether the person is old enough to vote

- Determine whether the person is a senior citizen
- Get one or more of the data fields for the Person object
- Set one or more of the data fields for the Person object

Figure 1.7 shows a diagram of class Person. This figure uses the Unified Modeling Language (UML) to represent the class. UML diagrams are a standard way of documenting class relationships that is widely used in industry. The class is represented by a box. The top compartment of the box contains the class name. The data fields (data members or instance variables) are shown in the middle compartment, and some of the functions are shown in the bottom compartment. We discuss UML further in Appendix B.

Figure 1.8 shows how two objects or instances of the class Person (author1 and author2) are represented in UML. Each object is represented by a box in which the top compartment contains the class name (Person), underlined, followed by the object name (author1 or author2), also underlined, and the bottom compartment contains the data fields and their values.

Listing 1.4 shows class Person and the member functions for this class.

We declare four data fields and two constants (all uppercase letters) after the functions (although some C++ programmers prefer to declare member functions after data fields). In the constant declarations, the modifier **const** indicates that the constant value may not be changed. The modifier **static** indicates that the constant is being defined for the class and does not have to be replicated in each instance. In other words, storage for the constant VOTE_AGE is allocated once, regardless of how many instances of Person are created.

The file Person.h contains the class declaration. As with the Clock class, the member functions are declared in this file, but, in several cases, they are also implemented. We discuss the reason for this next.

FIGURE 1.7
Class Diagram for
Person

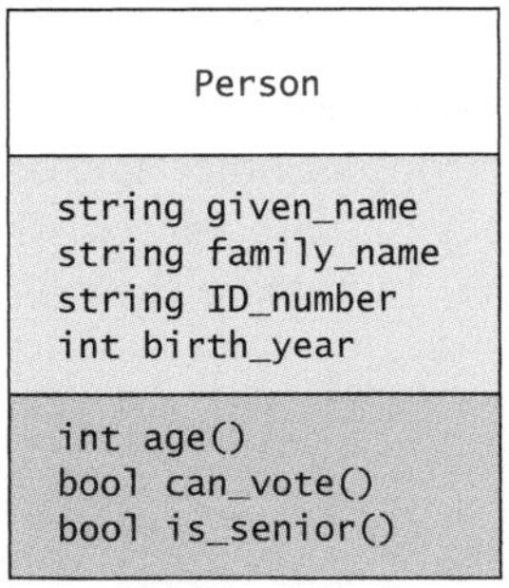

```
              Person
  ┌──────────────────────────┐
  │ string given_name        │
  │ string family_name       │
  │ string ID_number         │
  │ int birth_year           │
  ├──────────────────────────┤
  │ int age()                │
  │ bool can_vote()          │
  │ bool is_senior()         │
  └──────────────────────────┘
```

FIGURE 1.8
Object Diagram of Two
Instances of **Person**

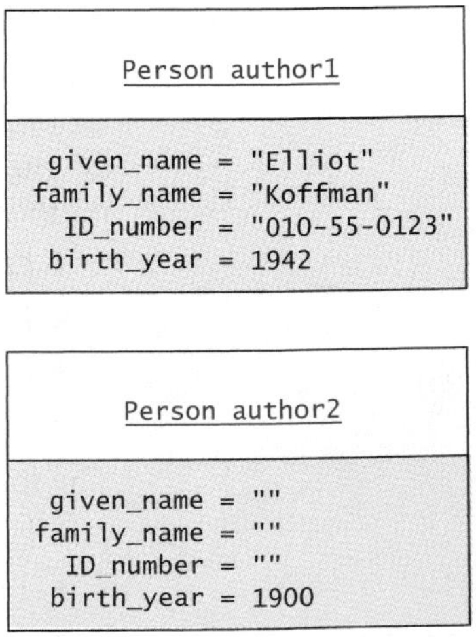

```
          Person author1
  ┌────────────────────────────────────┐
  │ given_name  = "Elliot"             │
  │ family_name = "Koffman"            │
  │  ID_number  = "010-55-0123"        │
  │ birth_year  = 1942                 │
  └────────────────────────────────────┘


          Person author2
  ┌────────────────────────────────────┐
  │ given_name  = ""                   │
  │ family_name = ""                   │
  │  ID_number  = ""                   │
  │ birth_year  = 1900                 │
  └────────────────────────────────────┘
```

....

LISTING 1.4
Person.h

```cpp
#ifndef PERSON_H_
#define PERSON_H_
#include <string>
#include <iostream>

/** Person is a class that represents a human being. */
class Person {
  public:
    // Constructors
    /** Construct a person with given values.
        @param first The given name
        @param family The family name
        @param ID The ID number
        @param birth The birth year
    */
    Person(std::string first, std::string family,
           std::string ID, int birth) :
      given_name(first), family_name(family), ID_number(ID),
      birth_year(birth) { }

    /** Construct a default person. */
    Person() : given_name(""), family_name(""), ID_number(""),
      birth_year(1900) { }

    // Modifier Functions
    /** Sets the given_name field.
        @param given The given name
    */
    void set_given_name(std::string given) {
      given_name = given;
    }

    /** Sets the family_name field.
        @param family The family name
    */
    void set_family_name(std::string family) {
      family_name = family;
    }

    /** Sets the birth_year field.
        @param birth The year of birth
    */
    void set_birth_year(int birth) {
      birth_year = birth;
    }

    // Accessor Functions
    /** Gets the person's given name.
        @return the given name as a string
    */
    std::string get_given_name() const { return given_name; }
```

```
/** Gets the person's family name.
    @return the family name as a string
*/
std::string get_family_name() const { return family_name; }

/** Gets the person's ID number.
    @return the ID number as a string
*/
std::string get_ID_number() const { return ID_number; }

/** Gets the person's year of birth.
    @return the year of birth as an int value
*/
int get_birth_year() const { return birth_year; }

// Other Functions
/** Calculates a person's age at this year's birthday.
    @param year The current year
    @return the year minus the birth year
*/
int age(int year) const;

/** Determines whether a person can vote.
    @param year The current year
    @return true if the person's age is greater than or
               equal to the voting age
*/
bool can_vote(int year) const;

/** Determines whether a person is a senior citizen.
    @param year the current year
    @return true if person's age is greater than or
               equal to the age at which a person is
               considered to be a senior citizen
*/
bool is_senior(int year) const;

/** Compares two Person objects for equality.
    @param per The second Person object
    @return true if the Person objects have the same
               ID number; false if they don't
*/
bool operator==(const Person& per) const;

/** Compares two Person objects for inequality.
    @param per The second Person object
    @return the negation of the equals operator
*/
bool operator!=(const Person& per) const;

/** Declaration of the stream insertion operator for Person.
    @param os The target ostream
    @param per The Person object being output
    @return The updated output stream
*/
friend std::ostream& operator<<(std::ostream& os, const Person& per);
```

```
    private:
      // Data Fields
      /** The given name. */
      std::string given_name;
      /** The family name. */
      std::string family_name;
      /** The ID number. */
      std::string ID_number;
      /** The birth year. */
      int birth_year;

      // Constants
      /** The age at which a person can vote. */
      static const int VOTE_AGE = 18;
      /** The age at which a person is considered a senior citizen. */
      static const int SENIOR_AGE = 65;
};

#endif
```

✓ PROGRAM STYLE

Explicit Namespace Qualification in Include Files

You will notice that the include file included the standard headers `<string>` and
`<iostream>`, but it did not contain a **using** directive such as
`using namespace std;`

Instead we specifically qualified the classes `string` and `ostream` with the prefix `std::`.
This is because we do not know whether the client program will include the **using** directive. In Chapter 3 we will see reasons why this may not be desirable. It is considered
good program style to always use explicit namespace qualification in header files.

Constructors

In Listing 1.4, there are two constructors that begin with `Person`. Exactly one of
these is invoked automatically when a new class instance is created. The constructor with four parameters is called if the values of all data fields are known before
the object is created. For example, the statement

```
    Person author1("Elliot", "Koffman", "010-55-0123", 1942);
```

creates the first object shown in Figure 1.8, initializing its data fields to the values
passed as arguments. Note that a constructor differs from a member function in that
it has no return type.

SYNTAX Constructor Definition

FORM:

class-name(*parameters*) : *initialization-expressions* { *body* }

EXAMPLES:

```
Person(std::string first, std::string family, std::string ID, int birth) :
  given_name(first), family_name(family), ID_number(ID),
  birth_year(birth) { }
Person() : given_name(""), family_name(""), ID_number(""),
  birth_year(1900) { }
```

MEANING:

A constructor has the same name as its class and has no return type. A constructor is called automatically when an object is created. Its purpose is to initialize the memory allocated to the object to initial values. Constructors may have parameters, and constructors having different parameter lists may be defined. The *initialization-expressions* are of the form *data-field-name*(*initial-value*). As the object is constructed, the named data fields are set to the given initial values. After the object is constructed, the body of the constructor is then executed.

✓ PROGRAM STYLE

Use of Initialization Expressions in Constructors

It is preferable to use initialization expressions to initialize data fields rather than using assignment statements in the body. Initialization expressions have the form

data-member(*initial-value-expression*)

An initialization expression such as

```
given_name(first)
```

is evaluated as the object is being constructed. If there is no initialization expression for a class data field, it may be initialized to a default value. The body is executed after the object is constructed. Thus, if you initialize a class data field in the body using an assignment statement

```
given_name = first;
```

you are effectively initializing it twice. While this does not matter for the built-in types because they have no default initialization, it is significant for class types, which may have several data fields of their own to initialize.

The second constructor, the no-parameter constructor, is called when the data field values are not known at the time the object is created.

```
Person author2;
```

In this case, the data fields are initialized to the default values given (for example, 1900 for birth_year). The three string data fields are initialized to the empty string. You can use modifier functions (discussed next) at a later time to set or modify the values of the data fields.

The no-parameter constructor is sometimes called the *default constructor* because C++ automatically defines this constructor for a class that has no constructor definitions. Therefore, the following constructor was automatically defined for class Clock.

```
/** Default constructor for class Clock. */
public Clock::clock() { }
```

However, if you define one or more constructors for a class, you must also explicitly define the no-parameter constructor, or it will be undefined for that class.

Modifier and Accessor Member Functions

Because the data fields have private visibility, we need to provide public member functions to access them. Normally, we want to be able to get or retrieve the value of a data field, so each data field in class Person has an *accessor* member function (also called a *getter*) that begins with the word get and ends with the name of the data field (for example, get_family_name). If we want to allow a class user to update or modify the value of a data field, we provide a *modifier* function (also called a *mutator* or *setter*) beginning with the word set and ending with the name of the data field (for example, set_given_name). Currently, there is an accessor for each data field in this example. However, there is no set_ID_number member function because it would not be a good practice to allow a user program to modify a person's ID number. It might also be a good practice to have get_ID_number return just a portion of the value stored in data field ID_number (say, the last four digits) rather than the whole string.

The modifier member functions are type **void** because they are executed for their effect (to update a data field), not to return a value. In the member function set_birth_year,

```
void set_birth_year(int birth) {
  birth_year = birth;
}
```

the assignment statement stores the integer value passed as an argument in data field birth_year.

The accessor function for data field given_name,

```
std::string get_given_name() const { return given_name; }
```

is type std::string because it returns a copy of the string object given_name. The **const** in the function declaration indicates that this function will not change the value of the object on which it is called.

> ☑ **PROGRAM STYLE**
>
> ### Inline Definition of Constructors, Accessors, and Modifiers
>
> It is a good programming practice to separate the declarations of the member functions from their definitions. The public portion of a class definition is its interface. This is how clients view the class. If the function definition is included in the class definition, the client programs include the function definition into their own code. Then, if we want to change a function's implementation, we force the client programs to change. There are two reasons for making an exception for constructors, accessors, and modifiers. First of all, if a function definition is included in a class definition, the compiler treats this function as an *inline* function. That is, the compiler replaces a call to that function with the code contained in the function body. Such code executes faster. Second, constructors, accessors, and modifiers generally are very simple and are unlikely to change. Constructors generally consist only of initialization expressions; accessors generally consist of a **return** statement, and modifiers generally consist of a single assignment statement. Although we did not insert the accessor function definitions for class Clock in the public part of file Clock.h; it would have been permissible, and even desirable, to do this.

Operators

In addition to the functions defined in class Person, we declare the operators == and !=.

```
bool operator==(const Person& per) const;
bool operator!=(const Person& per) const;
```

Declaring and defining these operators in class Person enables us to use them with operands of type Person. For example, we can write the Boolean expressions author1 == author2 and author1 != author2 to compare two Person objects. The word operator precedes the operator symbol being defined. The left-hand operand is the current object; the right-hand operand is declared in parentheses following the operator symbol. We say that C++ permits us to *overload* these operators so that they can be used with operands other than the primitive types.

⬛ **SYNTAX**   **Operator Declaration**

FORM:
return-type operator *operator-symbol*(*parameter*) const;

EXAMPLES:
```
bool operator==(const Person& per) const;
bool operator!=(const Person& per) const;
```

MEANING:
The operator specified by *operator-symbol* is defined for this class. The left-hand operand is the current object; the right-hand operand is specified by *parameter* in the same way as a function parameter. If the word **const** appears at the end of the declaration, the left-hand operand is not changed by the operator.

Friends

The insertion operator that you have been using to output data to an ostream, such as cout, is really an overloading of the left shift operator. The class ostream contains several overloaded member functions named operator<< that each take a primitive type as the parameter. Each operator<< function formats its primitive type and outputs the resulting string to the ostream. To output a class type, we must define this operator for that class. Class Person has the following declaration:

```cpp
friend std::ostream& operator<<(std::ostream&, const Person&);
```

This function is not a member of either the class ostream or the class Person. It is a stand-alone function that takes as its left-hand operand an object of type ostream and as its right-hand operand an object of type Person (for example, cout << author1). It returns a reference to the output stream that has been modified. This declaration appears within the class definition prefixed with the keyword **friend**. Declaring it a *friend* gives it the same rights as member functions, so it can access the private members of the class.

Implementing the Person Class

The implementation file for the Person class (file Person.cpp) is given in Listing 1.5. We define all the functions that were declared in Listing 1.4 but were not written as inline functions.

LISTING 1.5
Person.cpp

```cpp
/** Implementation file for the class Person. */
#include "Person.h"
#include <ostream>
using std::ostream;

/** Calculates a person's age at this year's birthday.
    @param year The current year
    @return the year minus the birth year
*/
int Person::age(int year) const {
  return year - birth_year;
}

/** Determines whether a person can vote.
    @param year The current year
    @return true if the person's age is greater than or
            equal to the voting age
*/
bool Person::can_vote(int year) const {
  int the_age = age(year);
  return the_age >= VOTE_AGE;
}

/** Determines whether a person is a senior citizen.
    @param year the current year
    @return true if person's age is greater than or
            equal to the age at which a person is
            considered to be a senior citizen
```

```
*/
bool Person::is_senior(int year) const {
  return age(year) >= SENIOR_AGE;
}

/** Compares two Person objects for equality.
    @param per The second Person object
    @return true if the Person objects have same
            ID number; false if they don't
*/
bool Person::operator==(const Person& per) const {
  return ID_number == per.ID_number;
}

/** Compares two Person objects for inequality.
    @param per The second Person object
    @return The opposite of the equality operator
*/
bool Person::operator!=(const Person& per) const {
  return !(*this == per);
}

/** Retrieves the information in a Person object
    and formats it for output. The result is
    then inserted into the target ostream.
    @param os The target ostream
    @param per The source Person
    @return The modified ostream after the data has
            been inserted
*/
ostream& operator<<(ostream& os, const Person& per) {
  os << "Given name: " << per.given_name << '\n'
     << "Family name: " << per.family_name << '\n'
     << "ID number: " << per.ID_number << '\n'
     << "Year of birth: " << per.birth_year << '\n';
  return os;
}
```

Declaring Local Variables in Class **Person**

Functions age, can_vote, and is_senior are all passed the current year as an argument. Function can_vote calls member function age to determine the person's age. The result is stored in local variable the_age. The result of calling function can_vote is the value of the Boolean expression following the keyword **return**.

```
bool Person::can_vote(int year) const {
  int the_age = age(year);
  return the_age >= VOTE_AGE;
}
```

It really was not necessary to introduce local variable the_age; the call to member function age could have been placed directly in the **return** statement (as it is in function is_senior). We wanted, however, to show you how to declare local variables in a C++ function. The scope of the local variable the_age and the parameter year is the body of member function can_vote.

Implementing the Operators

We will assume that two Persons are the same if they have the same ID number. This leads to the following definition for operator ==.

```
bool Person::operator==(const Person& per) const {
   return ID_number == per.ID_number;
}
```

Notice that we can look at parameter per's private `ID_number` because per references an object of this class (type `Person`). Because `ID_number` is type `string`, the equality operator of class `string` is invoked with the `ID_number` of the second object as an argument. If the two `ID_number` data fields have the same contents, the `string` operator== function will return **true**; otherwise, it will return **false**. The Person operator== member function returns the result of the `string` operator== function.

Because we want `operator!=` to return the opposite of what `operator==` returns, we define it as follows:

```
bool Person::operator!=(const Person& per) const {
   return !(*this == per);
}
```

The **this** Parameter

Each member function has an implicit parameter named **this** whose value is a pointer to the object for which the member function was called. Normally in writing a member function you do not need to use the **this** parameter, because references to members are implicitly understood to be to the object for which the member function was called. However, in the case of `operator!=` we want to apply the == operator between the object on which the function was called and the other object, per. Since **this** is a pointer to the object we are interested in, the expression *this is a reference to that object. Thus the expression *this == per does what we want. We could also have written `operator!=` this way:

```
bool Person::operator!=(const Person& per) const {
   return !(operator==(per));
}
```

☑ PROGRAM STYLE

Returning a Boolean Value

Some programmers unnecessarily write **if** statements to return a Boolean value. For example, instead of writing

```
return ID_number == per.ID_number;
```

they write

```
if (ID_number == per.ID_number)
    return true;
else
    return false;
```

Resist this temptation. The **return** statement by itself returns the value of the **if** statement condition, which must be **true** or **false**. It does this in a clear and succinct manner using one line instead of four.

> ⊘ **PITFALL**
>
> **Referencing a Data Field or Parameter Hidden by a Local Declaration**
>
> If you happen to declare a local variable (or parameter) with the same name as a data field, the local declaration hides the data field declaration, so the C++ compiler will translate the use of that name as meaning the local variable (or parameter), not the data field. So, if `birth_year` was also declared locally in class `Person`, the statement
> `birth_year++;`
> would increment the local variable, but the data field value would not change.

Defining the Extraction Operator

In the following definition for `operator<<`, the function body outputs data field values to output stream os. It then returns a reference to its output stream parameter.

```
ostream& operator<<(ostream& os, const Person& per) {
  os << "Given name: " << per.given_name << '\n'
     << "Family name: " << per.family_name << '\n'
     << "ID number: " << per.ID_number << '\n'
     << "Year of birth: " << per.birth_year << '\n';
  return os;
}
```

If author1 is the first type `Person` object in Fig. 1.8, the statement

```
cout << author1;
```

would display the following.

```
Given name: Elliot
Family name: Koffman
ID number: 010-55-0123
Year of birth: 1942
```

An Application That Uses Class Person

To test class `Person` we need to write a C++ application program that consists of a main function. The main function should create one or more instances of class `Person` and display the results of applying the class functions. Listing 1.6 shows the program `Test_Person` that does this. To execute the main function, you must compile `Test_Person.cpp` and `Person.cpp` and link them. Figure 1.9 shows a sample run.

A main function that is written primarily to test another class is often called a *driver program*. A test that demonstrates that certain requirements of a particular class are met is called a *unit test*. We will have more to say about testing in Chapter 2.

······································
LISTING 1.6
Test_Person.cpp

```cpp
/** Test_Person is an application that tests class Person. */
#include <iostream>
#include "Person.h"
using std::cout;
using std::endl;

int main() {
  Person p1("Sam", "Jones", "1234", 1930);
  cout << "p1: " << p1 << endl;
  Person p2("Jane", "Jones", "5678", 1990);
  cout << "p2: " << p2 << endl;

  cout << "Age of " << p1.get_given_name()
       << " is " << p1.age(2004) << endl;
  if (p1.is_senior(2004))
    cout << p1.get_given_name() << " can ride the subway for free\n";
  else
    cout << p1.get_given_name() << " must pay to ride the subway\n";
  if (p2.can_vote(2004))
    cout << p2.get_given_name() << " can vote\n";
  else
    cout << p2.get_given_name() << " can't vote\n";
  // Make Sam younger
  p1.set_birth_year(1950);
  // Now see whether he has to pay to ride the subway.
  cout << "Age of " << p1.get_given_name()
       << " is " << p1.age(2004) << endl;
  if (p1.is_senior(2004))
    cout << p1.get_given_name() << " can ride the subway for free\n";
  else
    cout << p1.get_given_name() << " must pay to ride the subway\n";
}
```

······································
FIGURE 1.9
Sample Run of Class Test_Person

```
F:\C++Book\programs\CH01>Test_Person
p1: Given name: Sam
Family name: Jones
ID number: 1234
Year of birth: 1930

p2: Given name: Jane
Family name: Jones
ID number: 5678
Year of birth: 1990

Age of Sam is 74
Sam can ride the subway for free
Jane can't vote
Age of Sam is 54
Sam must pay to ride the subway
```

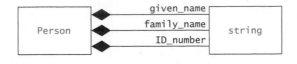

Classes as Components of Other Classes

Class `Person` has three data fields that are type `string`, so `string` objects are components of a `Person` object. In Figure 1.10 this component relationship is indicated by the solid diamond symbol at the end of the lines drawn from the box representing class `string` to the box representing class `Person`. The names `given_name`, `family_name`, and `ID_number` above the lines and near the box representing the `string` class correspond to the data member names within the `Person` class. Figure 1.10 is a UML diagram, this one showing the relationships between classes. We will follow UML's set of conventions for documenting class relationships in this book.

Array Data Fields

It is very common in C++ to encapsulate an array, together with the functions that process it, within a class. Rather than allocate storage for a fixed-size array, we would like the client to be able to specify the array size when an object is created. Therefore, we should define a constructor with the array size as a parameter and have the constructor allocate storage for the array. Class `Company` in Listing 1.7 has a data field `employees` that references an array of `Person` objects. Both constructors allocate storage for a new array when a `Company` object is created. The client of this class can specify the size of the array by passing a type `int` value to the constructor parameter `size`. If no argument is passed, the no-parameter constructor sets the array size to `DEFAULT_SIZE`.

LISTING 1.7
Company.h

```cpp
#ifndef COMPANY_H_
#define COMPANY_H_

#include "Person.h"  // Definition of the Person class
#include <iostream>  // Declaration of I/O classes

/** Company is a class that represents a company.
    The data field employees provides storage for
    an array of Person objects.
*/
class Company {
  public:
    // Constructors
    /** Creates a new array of Person objects.
        @param size The size of array employees
    */
    Company(int size) :
      num_employees(size), employees(new Person[size]) {}
```

```
      Company() :
        num_employees(DEFAULT_SIZE), employees(new Person[DEFAULT_SIZE]) {}

      // Functions

      /** Sets an element of employees.
          @param index The position of the employee
          @param emp The employee
      */
      void set_employee(int index, Person emp);

      /** Gets an employee.
          @param index The position of the employee
          @return the employee object or if not defined
                  a default Person object
      */
      Person get_employee(int index);

      /** Builds and outputs a string consisting of all employees'
          data, with newline characters between employees.
          @param os The destination ostream
          @param company The company object to be output
          @return The updated ostream object
      */
      friend std::ostream& operator<<(std::ostream& os,
                                      const Company& company);

  private:
    // Data Fields
    /** The number of employees. */
    int num_employees;
    /** The array of employees. */
    Person* employees;

    /** The default size of the array. */
    static const int DEFAULT_SIZE = 100;
};

#endif
```

·······························
LISTING 1.8
Company.cpp

```
#include "Company.h"
#include <ostream>
using std::ostream;
using std::endl;

/** Sets an element of employees.
    @param index The position of the employee
    @param emp The employee
*/
void Company::set_employee(int index, Person emp) {
  if (index >= 0 && index < num_employees)
    employees[index] = emp;
}
```

```
/** Gets an employee.
    @param index The position of the employee
    @return The employee object or if not defined
            return a default Person object
*/
Person Company::get_employee(int index) {
  if (index >= 0 && index < num_employees)
    return employees[index];
  else
    return Person();
}

/** Builds and inserts a string consisting of all employees'
    data, with newline characters between employees.
    @param os The destination ostream
    @param company The Company object to be output
    @return The updated ostream
*/
ostream& operator<<(ostream& os, const Company& company) {
  for (int i = 0; i < company.num_employees; i++)
    os << company.employees[i] << endl;
  return os;
}
```

There are modifier and accessor functions that process individual elements of array Company (set_employee and get_employee). Function get_employee returns the type Person object at position index, or a default Person object if the value of index is out of bounds.

The ostream insertion operator << creates a string representing the contents of array employees. The **for** loop calls the ostream insertion operator for each Person object in the array.

The following main function illustrates the use of class Company and displays the state of object comp. It stores two Person objects in the array and then displays the contents of the array.

```
#include "Company.h"
#include <iostream>
using std::cout;

int main() {
  Company comp(2);
  comp.set_employee(0, Person("Elliot", "K", "123", 1942));
  comp.set_employee(1, Person("Paul", "W", "234", 1945));
  cout << comp;
  return 0;
}
```

Documentation Style for Classes and Functions

In this book we write documentation comments for classes, member functions, and data members in a standard format that was originally developed for the Java language. The Java software developer's kit contains a program called Javadoc that reads a Java program file and writes neatly formatted HTML documentation pages if the program contains documentation comments in the standard form. Using Javadoc

······················

TABLE 1.4
Documentation Comment Tags

Tag and Example of Use	Purpose
@param given *The given name*	Identifies a function parameter
@return *The person's age*	Identifies a function return value

forces the programmer to describe the function in an orderly manner. As a result, that format has gained popularity for documenting programs in other languages, such as C++, as well. You can run a variety of programs on your C++ files to generate a set of HTML pages describing each class and its data fields and functions as Javadoc does for Java. Two such programs that are freely available are DOC++ and Doxygen.

These programs focus on text that is enclosed within the delimiters /** and */. The introductory comment that describes the class is displayed on the HTML page exactly as it is written, so you should write that carefully. The lines that begin with the symbol @ are tags. They are described in Table 1.4. We will use one @param tag for each function parameter. We will not use a @return tag for **void** functions. The first line of the comment for each function appears in the function summary part of the HTML page. The information provided in the tags will appear in the function detail part. Figure 1.11 shows part of the documentation generated by running Doxygen for class Person.

······················

FIGURE 1.11
Generated Documentation for Class Person

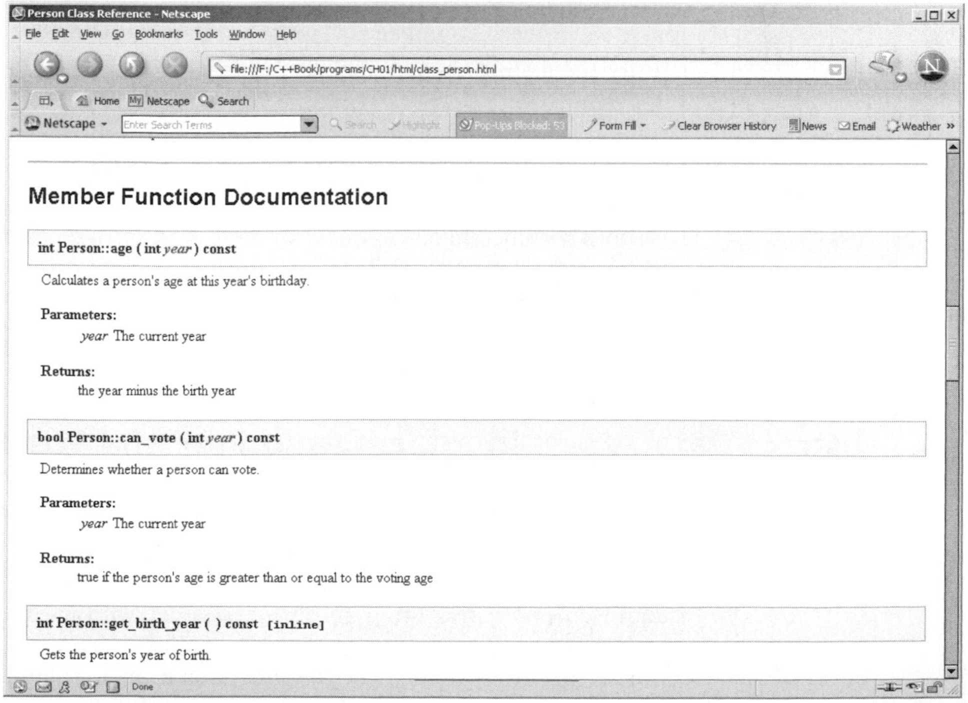

EXERCISES FOR SECTION 1.3

SELF-CHECK

1. Explain why member functions have public visibility but data fields have private visibility.

2. Trace the execution of the following statements.
   ```
   Person p1("Adam", "Jones", "wxyz", 0);
   p1.set_birth_year(1990);
   Person p2;
   p2.set_given_name("Eve");
   p2.set_family_name(p1.get_family_name());
   p2.set_birth_year(p1.get_birth_year() + 10);
   if (p1 == p2)
     cout << p1 << " is the same person as " << p2 << endl;
   else
     cout << p1 << " is not the same person as " << p2 << endl;
   ```

PROGRAMMING

1. Overload the `ostream` insertion operator for the `Clock` class to output the time in the form `hh:mm:ss`.

2. Write a member function `get_initials` that returns a string representing a `Person` object's initials. There should be a period after each initial. Write documentation comments for the function.

3. Add a data field `mother_maiden_name` to `Person`. Write an accessor and a modifier function for this data field. Modify the `ostream` insertion operator and the equality operator to include this data field. Assume two `Person` objects are equal if they have the same ID number and mother's maiden name.

4. Write the member functions `operator<`, `operator>`, `operator<=`, and `operator>=` that compare two `Person` objects and return an appropriate result based on a comparison of the ID numbers. For `operator<`, if the ID number of the object that the operator is applied to is less than the ID number of the argument object, the result should be true. Write documentation comments for the member functions.

5. Write a member function `switch_names` that exchanges a `Person` object's given and family names. Write documentation comments for the member function.

1.4 Abstract Data Types, Interfaces, and Pre- and Postconditions

One of the goals of object-oriented programming is to write *reusable code*, which is code that can be reused in many different applications, preferably without having to be recompiled. One way to make code reusable is to *encapsulate* or combine a group of data elements representing an object together with its operations (functions and operators) in a separate program module (a class). As we discussed in the previous section, a new program can use the functions to manipulate the data without being

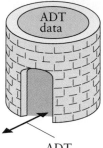

ADT
operations

concerned about details of the data representation and the implementation of its operations. In this way, the class can be used as a building block to construct new application programs. The combination of data together with its operations is called an *abstract data type* (ADT).

Figure 1.12 shows a diagram of an abstract data type. The data values stored in the ADT are hidden inside the circular wall. The bricks around this wall are used to indicate that these data values cannot be accessed except by going through the ADT's operations.

A class provides one way to implement an ADT in C++. If the data fields are private, they can be accessed only through public functions. Therefore, the functions control access to the data and determine the manner in which the data is manipulated.

A primary goal of this text is to show you how to write and use ADTs in programming. As you progress through this book, you will create a large collection of ADT implementations (classes) in your own program library. Because each ADT implementation in your library will already have been coded, debugged, and tested, using them would make it much easier for you to design and implement new application programs.

Also, the C++ Standard Library provides a rich collection of ADT implementations. You will be introduced to many of these ADTs and their implementations as you progress through this book. Many of the classes you study will implement these ADTs in whole or in part.

Abstract Data Types (ADTs) and Interfaces

The public part of a class definition is a way to specify (but not implement) an ADT. The public part of a class definition specifies the names, parameters, and return values of the ADT operations without specifying how the operations are performed and without specifying how the data is internally represented. The public part of a class definition defines the *interface* for that class. (If you are familiar with the Java programming language, take note that C++ does not have Java's syntactic element called an interface).

The classes that declare the data fields and code member functions that perform the operations are said to *implement* the ADT. There may be more than one way to implement the operations; hence, there may be more than one class that implements the ADT. Therefore, an ADT describes a set of classes that perform the operations and define the internal data.

Each class that implements an ADT must provide the complete definition (implementation) of all operations declared in the ADT. In addition, it may declare data fields and define other member functions.

An ADT for a Telephone Directory Class

There are many different ways to represent a telephone directory. One of our goals in this course is to show you several ways to do this task and to compare their performance. Consequently, rather than provide a single class of type Phone_Directory, we will define an ADT that specifies the operations required of all classes that are

TABLE 1.5
Specification of the `Phone_Directory` ADT

Function	Behavior
`void load_data(const string& source_name)`	Load the data file containing the directory, or establish a connection with the data source.
`string lookup_entry(const string& name)`	Look up an entry in the directory. If there is no such entry, return an empty string.
`string add_or_change_entry(const string& name, const string& number)`	Changes the number associated with the given name to the new value. Returns the previous value or an empty string if this is a new entry.
`string remove_entry(const string& name)`	Removes the entry with the specified name from the directory. Returns the name or an empty string if the name was not in the directory.
`void save()`	Writes the directory to the data file.

intended to implement this ADT. This will enable other programmers (including ourselves) to invoke the telephone directory operations without knowing exactly how the directory is represented or how its operations are implemented. We describe this ADT in Table 1.5.

Contracts and ADTs

An ADT is a contract between the ADT designer and the programmer who codes a class that implements the ADT. This programmer must code functions that perform the operations specified in the ADT. Therefore, any programmer who uses a class that implements the ADT knows exactly what functions are available in that class and what operations they will perform. This allows that programmer to proceed to write application programs without needing to coordinate with the person who is coding classes that implement the ADT. Similarly, the programmer who is coding a class that implements the ADT can proceed independently of what the application programmers are doing.

There may be several classes that implement the ADT, and each class can code the data and the functions in a different way. One class may be more efficient than another class at performing certain kinds of operations. For example, one class may be more efficient at retrieving information from a directory, so that class will be used if retrieval operations are more likely in a particular application.

Preconditions and Postconditions

At a lower level, we communicate the intent of an operation through its *preconditions* and *postconditions*, which are part of the behavior description provided in the specification. A precondition is a statement of any assumptions or constraints on the operation's data (input parameters) that are expected to apply before the operation is performed. A postcondition is a statement that describes the result of performing an operation. An operation's preconditions and postconditions serve as a contract between a function caller (who requires the operation to be performed) and the function programmer (who implements the operation); if a caller satisfies the precondition, the function result will satisfy the postcondition. If the precondition is not satisfied, there is no guarantee that the function will do what is expected, and it may even fail. We discuss this further in Chapter 2. The preconditions and postconditions allow a function user and function implementor both to proceed without further coordination. When implementing an ADT, we document the preconditions and postconditions in the multiline documentation comments associated with the class and each function.

Although some programmers write preconditions and postconditions for every function that they write, we will use them only when they provide additional information that is not readily apparent. If an operation has specific requirements for its arguments (for example, an argument must be positive), we will express these requirements through a precondition. We will use postconditions to describe the change in object state caused by executing a mutator operation. As a general rule, you should write a postcondition comment for operations that change an object's state. (In C++ these operations are generally implemented by functions that have a **void** return type.) If an operation returns a value, you do not usually need a postcondition because the @return tag describes the effect of performing the operation.

EXAMPLE 1.2   A class Bank_Account might define the following function process_deposit. The precondition (after pre:) shows that the deposit amount must be positive. The postcondition (after post:) shows that data field balance is increased by the value of amount. The words pre: and post: are not part of the language recognized by Javadoc or Doxygen, so these comments are not processed by the comment-processing program.

```
/** Processes a deposit in a bank account.
    pre: amount is positive.
    post: Adds the specified amount to balance.
*/
public void process_deposit(double amount) {
  balance = balance + amount;
}
```

EXERCISES FOR SECTION 1.4

SELF-CHECK

1. What are the two parts of an ADT? Which part is accessible to a user and which is not? Explain the relationships between an ADT and a class.
2. What are two different uses of the term *interface* in programming?

PROGRAMMING

1. Write a documentation comment for the following member function of a class Person. Assume that class Person has two string data fields last_name and first_name with the obvious meanings. Provide preconditions and postconditions if needed.

```
bool operator<(const Person& per) {
  if (last_name == per.last_name)
    return first_name < per.last_name;
  else
    return last_name < per.last_name;
}
```

2. Write a documentation comment for the following member function of a class Person. Provide preconditions and postconditions if needed.

```
void change_last_name(bool just_married, string new_last) {
  if (just_married)
    last_name = new_last;
}
```

1.5 Requirements Analysis, Use Cases, and Sequence Diagrams

In this section, we will illustrate how to solve a programming problem similar to the telephone directory assignment introduced earlier. The solution will have multiple classes and interfaces. Our goal in this case study is to show you the process that would be followed in the software design and implementation. Don't be concerned at this point if you do not understand all the details of the final program. In this section, we show the requirements specification and analysis and introduce two new tools: the use case and sequence diagram.

CASE STUDY   Designing a Telephone Directory Program

Problem   You have a client who wants to store a simple telephone directory in her computer that she can use for storage and retrieval of names and numbers. She has a data file that contains the names and numbers of her friends. She wants to be able to insert new names and numbers, change the number for an entry, and retrieve selected telephone numbers. She also wants to save any changes in her data file.

Input/Output Requirements

Earlier we discussed some questions that would have to be answered in order to complete the specification of the requirements for the phone directory problem. Most of the questions dealt with input and output considerations. We will list some answers to these questions next.

INPUTS

Initial phone directory	Each name and number will be read from separate lines of a text file. The entries will be read in sequence until all entries are read.
Additional entries	Each entry is typed by the user at the keyboard when requested.

OUTPUTS

Names and phone numbers	The name and number of each person selected by the program user are displayed on separate output lines.
Updated phone directory	Each name and number will be written to separate lines of a text file. The entries will be written in sequence until all entries are written.

Analysis The first step in the analysis is to study the problem input and output requirements carefully to make sure that they are understood and make sense. You can use a tool called a *use case* to help you refine the system requirements.

Use Cases

A use case is a list of the user actions and system responses for a particular sub-problem in the order that they are likely to occur.

The following four subproblems were identified for the telephone directory program:

- Read the initial directory from an existing file
- Insert a new entry
- Edit an existing entry
- Retrieve and display an entry

The use case (Table 1.6) for the first subproblem ("Read the initial directory") shows that the user issues a single command and the system responds either by reading a directory from a file or by creating an empty directory if there is no file. The second use case (Table 1.7) is for the subproblems "Insert a new entry" and "Edit

TABLE 1.6
Use Case for Reading the Initial Directory

Step	User's Action	System's Response
1.	User issues a command to the operating system to load and run the Phone Directory program, specifying the name of the file that contains the directory.	
2.		The Phone Directory program is started, and the directory contents initialized from the data file. If the data file does not exist, an initially empty directory is created.

an existing entry". Because the names in the directory must be unique, inserting a new entry and editing an existing entry require a search to determine whether the name is already present. Thus, from the user's point of view, the insert and edit processes are the same. The last use case (Table 1.8) shows the user interaction for the last subproblem ("Retrieve and display an entry").

The steps shown in each use case flesh out the user interaction with the program. The use cases should be reviewed by the client to make sure that your intentions are the same as hers. For most of the problems we study in this book, the user interaction is straightforward enough that use cases will not be required.

TABLE 1.7
Use Case for Inserting a New Entry or Editing an Existing Entry

Step	User's Action	System's Response
1.	User issues the command to insert or change an entry.	
2.		System prompts for the name.
3.	User enters name.	If user cancels entry of name, process terminates.
4.		System prompts for the number.
5.	User enters number.	If user cancels entry of number, process terminates.
6.		The directory is updated to contain the new name and number. If the name was not already in the directory, the user is notified that a new name was entered. If the name already exists, the user is notified that the number was changed and is shown both the old and new numbers.

TABLE 1.8
Use Case for Retrieving and Displaying an Entry

Step	User's Action	System's Response
1.	User issues the command to retrieve and display an entry.	
2.		System prompts for the name.
3.	User enters name.	If user cancels entry of name, process terminates.
4.		The system retrieves the entry from the directory. If found, the name and number are displayed; otherwise, a message is displayed indicating that the name is not in the directory.

Refinement of Initial Class Diagram

Earlier we used the top-down design approach to identify the subproblems to be solved (see Figures 1.3 through 1.5) and came up with the list of level 1 subproblems shown in the previous section. As discussed, you can combine the second and

FIGURE 1.13

Phone Directory Application Class Diagram: Revision 1

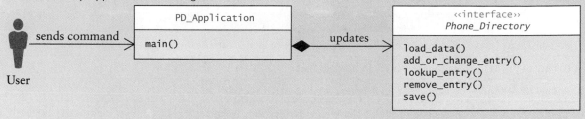

third subproblems ("Insert a new entry", "Edit an existing entry") and add a sub-problem to save the directory. The modified list follows:

- Read the initial directory from an existing file.
- Insert a new entry or edit an existing entry.
- Retrieve and display an entry.
- Save the modified directory back to the file.

The directory should be saved whenever the program is exited. The phone directory has limited usefulness if updates to the directory cannot be saved from one run to the next.

There is another way to split this problem into subproblems. Overall, we want a phone directory application that combines a *user interface* as the *front end* and a *persistent* (permanent) *storage* of data as the *back end*. Thus, Figure 1.6 can be refined as shown in Figure 1.13. The black diamond in Figure 1.13 indicates that a PD_Application object has an object of type Phone_Directory as its component and that it is created by the PD_Application object. The arrowhead shows that PD_Application updates the Phone_Directory object.

We have identified the abstract data type: the Phone_Directory. It is shown in the class diagram as an interface. (UML does not have a notation for ADTs, but its notation for *interface* is equivalent.) In Section 1.6 a class that implements this ADT will be designed. By splitting the design between the user interface (PD_Application) and the directory, we can work on them independently. As long as the requirements defined by the interfaces are met, the front-end user interface does not care which back end it is dealing with, and the back-end directory does not care which front end it is dealing with.

Design   Overview of Classes and Their Interaction

Next, we identify all classes that will be part of the problem solution and describe their interaction. Besides the class that implements the interface shown in Figure 1.13, classes from the C++ standard library will be used to perform input/output.

Note that the PD_Application class is artificial. In C++ the main function is a stand-alone function—that is, it is not a member function of any class—and all programs must have a main function. UML, however, does not have a notation for stand-alone functions. Thus, we show the main function encapsulated in a class that represents the program PD_Application. Table 1.9 shows a summary of some of the classes and interfaces that will be used in our solution.

TABLE 1.9
Summary of Classes and Objects Used in Phone Directory Solution

Class/Interface	Description
PD_Application	Contains the main function that provides the user interface.
Directory_Entry	Contains a name-number pair.
Phone_Directory	Class that implements the Phone_Directory ADT.
ifstream	A class in the C++ standard library that breaks a stream of input characters from a file into lines or data values.
istream cin	An object in the C++ standard library that breaks a stream of input characters from the console into lines or data values.
ofstream	A class in the C++ standard library that formats objects for output to a file.
ostream cout	An object in the C++ standard library that formats objects for output to the console.

From the use case in Table 1.6, we know that this function must create the Phone_Directory object and read in the initial directory. It then reads and executes the user's commands.

The following algorithm for the main function is written in *pseudocode*, a combination of English and C++ language constructs.

Algorithm for main Function

1.   Send the Phone_Directory a message to read the initial directory data from a file.
2.   Read a command from the user.
3.   **do**
4.   Prompt the user for a command
5.   Read the command
6.   Send the appropriate message to the Phone_Directory to execute the command
7.   Report the result to the user
8.   **while** the command is not exit.

Next we show the UML *sequence diagram* for the main function. A sequence diagram (see Appendix B) is an OOD tool that documents the interaction between the objects in a program. Sequence diagrams are used to show the flow of information through the program and to identify the messages that are passed from one object to another.

Sequence Diagram for **main** Function

The sequence diagram for the main function is shown in Figure 1.14. The first (and only) parameter for main will be the name of the file containing the directory data. We show this event in the sequence diagram as the user issuing the message

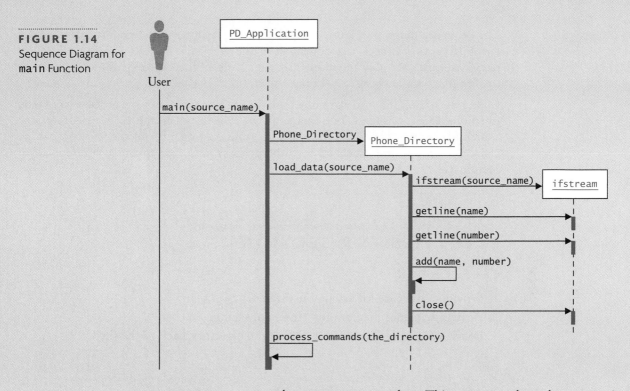

FIGURE 1.14
Sequence Diagram for
`main` Function

`main(source_name)` to the `PD_Application` class. This corresponds to the user typing the command

    PD_Application source_name

on the command line.

The sequence diagram shows all the objects involved in this use case across the horizontal axis, with each object's type underlined. Time is shown along the vertical axis. There is a dashed line coming down from each object that represents the object's *life line*. When a function of this object is called, the dashed line becomes a solid line indicating that the function is executing. All interaction with an object is indicated by a horizontal line that terminates at the object's life line.

For purposes of the diagram, we show the `PD_Application` object as being created when the application begins execution. Tracing down its life line, you can see that the `main` function first sends the `Phone_Directory` message to a class that implements the `Phone_Directory` ADT. This corresponds to the declaration statement

    Phone_Directory the_directory;

that creates a new `Phone_Directory` object. Next, `main` sends that object the `load_data` message. Looking at the life line for this `Phone_Directory` object, you see that function `load_data` creates a new `ifstream` object and sends it two `getline` messages. Next, `load_data` sends the `add` message to the `Phone_Directory` object. (Note that `add` is a new function that was not identified earlier.) This is the same object as the one that received the `load_data` message, so this `add` message is known as a *message to self*. Although the sequence diagram cannot show looping, the process of reading lines and adding entries continues until there are no remaining entries.

The sequence diagram (Figure 1.14) shows that member function load_data of the Phone_Directory object performs most of the work for the "Read initial directory data" use case. Member function load_data calls all the functions shown after it on the life line for the Phone_Directory object.

Upon return from the load_data function, the main function calls the process_commands function. This is a stand-alone function that is included in the PD_Application.cpp source file, so we show it on the UML diagram as a member of the PD_Application class. Design and implementation of the process_commands function is discussed in Section 1.8.

EXERCISES FOR SECTION 1.5

SELF-CHECK

1. Provide a use case for saving the directory to a file.
2. Draw a sequence diagram for "Insert or change an entry".
3. Draw a sequence diagram for "Write the directory back to the file".

1.6 Design of an Array-Based Phone Directory

The case study continues with the design, implementation, and testing of class Directory_Entry and a class that implements the Phone_Directory ADT. We will identify data fields for these classes and provide algorithms for their member functions. As we design the member functions of each class, we will identify new functions needed for that class. The design, implementation, and testing of these classes are discussed in the remaining sections of this chapter.

CASE STUDY   Designing a Telephone Directory Program (cont.)

Design   Design of Data Structures for the Phone Directory

Next, we consider the actual data elements that will be involved in the telephone directory problem. We will define a class Directory_Entry, which will contain the name-number pairs, and a class Array_Based_PD, which implements the Phone_Directory ADT. This class will contain an array of Directory_Entrys. In later chapters we will show alternative designs that use classes that are part of the C++ standard library (for example, class vector).

Our new class diagram is shown in Figure 1.15. The line from Array_Based_PD to Directory_Entry indicates that Directory_Entry objects are components of

Array_Based_PD objects, but they can also be associated with other objects (for example, the data file). For class Directory_Entry, we show data fields (attributes) in the light-color screen and member functions in the darker-color screen. Next, we discuss the two actual classes shown in this diagram: Directory_Entry and Array_Based_PD.

SYNTAX   UML Syntax

In UML class diagrams, the + sign next to the function names indicate that these functions are public. The − sign next to the attributes name and number indicate that they are private. For the class Directory_Entry we show the types of the attributes, and the parameter types and return types of the member functions. Showing this information on the diagram is optional. We will generally show this information in separate tables such as Table 1.9. Appendix B provides a summary of UML.

FIGURE 1.15
Phone Directory Application Class Diagram: Revision 2

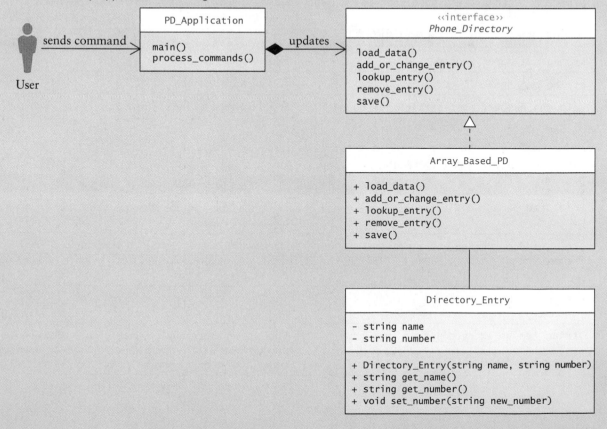

Design of the `Directory_Entry` Class

The `Directory_Entry` objects will contain the name-and-number pairs. The name is immutable; that is, it cannot be changed. For the purposes of your design, if you need to change the name of a person in your directory, you must remove the old entry and create a new one. The number, however, can be changed. Thus a straight-forward design consists of

- Two data fields: `name` and `number`
- A constructor that sets both `name` and `number`
- Accessor functions for both `name` and `number`
- A mutator function for `number`

This design is shown in Table 1.10.

TABLE 1.10
Design of the `Directory_Entry` Class

Data Field	Attribute
`string name`	The name of the individual represented in the entry.
`string number`	The phone number for this individual.
Constructor	**Behavior**
`Directory_Entry(string name, string number)`	Creates a new `Directory_Entry` with the specified `name` and `number`.
Function	**Behavior**
`string get_name() const`	Retrieves the name.
`string get_number() const`	Retrieves the `number`.
`void set_number(const string& new_number)`	Sets the `number` to the specified value.

TABLE 1.11
Functions Declared in ADT `Phone_Directory`

Function	Behavior
`void load_data(const string& source_name)`	Loads the data from the data file whose name is given by `source_name`.
`string add_or_change_entry(const string& name, const string& number)`	Changes the `number` associated with the given `name` to the new value, or adds a new entry with this `name` and `number`.
`string lookup_entry (const string& name) const`	Searches the directory for the given `name`.
`string remove_entry(const string& name)`	Removes the entry with the specified name from the directory and returns that person's number or an empty string if not in the directory (left as an exercise).
`void save()`	Writes the contents of the array of directory entries to the data file.

Design of the **Array_Based_PD** Class

The Array_Based_PD class implements the Phone_Directory ADT. We showed a portion of this ADT earlier (Table 1.5); Table 1.11 shows the functions for the ADT.

Class Array_Based_PD must implement these functions. It must also declare a data field for storage of the phone directory. Table 1.12 describes the data fields of class Array_Based_PD. In addition to the array of directory entries, the class includes data fields to help keep track of the array size and capacity and whether it has been modified. The functions will be designed in the next section.

Design of **Array_Based_PD** Member Functions

In this section you will complete the design of the Array_Based_PD class. At this stage you need to specify the function algorithms. First, we will develop pseudocode descriptions of the algorithms.

Function **load_data**

Function load_data is used to read the initial directory from a data file. The file name is passed as an argument to load_data when it is called.

Algorithm for Function **load_data**

1. Create an ifstream for the input file.
2. Read the name of the data file.
3. **while** the ifstream is not in the fail state
4.   Read the number.
5.   **if** the ifstream is not in the fail state
6.   Add a new entry using function add.
7.   Read the name.

Note that we have identified a new member function, add, for class Array_Based_PD.

Function **add_or_change_entry**

Function add_or_change_entry is used to either add a new entry to the directory or change an existing entry if the name is already in the directory. The name and number are passed as arguments to add_or_change_entry.

TABLE 1.12
Data Fields of Class Array_Based_PD

Data Field	Attribute
static const int INITIAL_CAPACITY	The initial capacity of the array to hold the directory entries.
int capacity	The current capacity of the array to hold the directory entries.
int size	The number of directory entries currently stored in the array.
Directory_Entry* the_directory	The array of directory entries.
string source_name	The name of the data file.
bool modified	A **bool** variable to indicate whether the contents of the array have been modified since they were last loaded or saved.

Algorithm for Function add_or_change_entry

1.   Call function find to see whether the name is in the directory.
2.   **if** the name is in the directory
3.   Change the number using the set_number function of the Directory_Entry.
4.   Return the previous value of the number.
    else
5.   Add a new entry using function add.
6.   Return an empty string.

Note that we have identified another new function, find, for class Array_Based_PD.

Function lookup_entry

Function lookup_entry is passed a person's name as an argument. It retrieves the person's number if the name is found and an empty string if the name is not found.

Algorithm for lookup_entry

1.   Call function find to see whether the name is in the directory..
2.   **if** the entry is found
3.   Directory_Entry's get_number function retrieves the number, which is returned to the caller.
    else
4.   The empty string is returned.

Function save

Function save creates an output file and then writes all information stored in the array to this file. The file name is stored in data field source_name. The algorithm for the save function follows.

Algorithm for save

1.   Create an ofstream object associated with the file.
2.   **for** each entry in the array
3.   Call get_name to get the name from the entry.
4.   Write the name on a line.
5.   Call get_number to get the number from the entry.
6.   Write the number on a line.
7.   Close the ofstream object.

Figure 1.16 shows the final class diagram with the additional functions.

FIGURE 1.16
Phone Directory Application Class Diagram: Revision 3

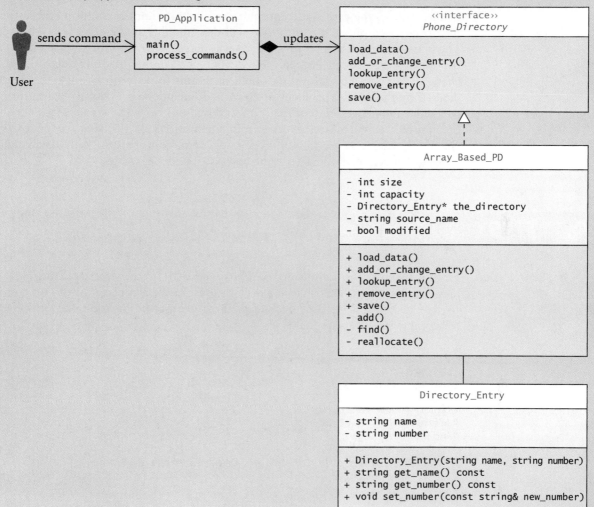

EXERCISES FOR SECTION 1.6

SELF-CHECK

1. Write the algorithm for the use case "Remove entry".

PROGRAMMING

1. Code class `Directory_Entry`.

1.7 Implementing and Testing the Array-Based Phone Directory

In this section, the case study continues to illustrate implementation and testing of the array-based phone directory. We will describe this as the class `Array_Based_PD`. The class definition will be in the file `Array_Based_PD.h` and the implementation in the file `Array_Based_PD.cpp`. However, the name of the class will be `Phone_Directory`. This allows the client programs to be written to use the interface defined by the ADT. The client program will include `Array_Based_PD.h` to use this particular implementation of the ADT and will link with the `Array_Based_PD` object file. Later we will describe other implementations of the `Phone_Directory`. To change the client to use the different implementation, we need only to change the #include directive and link with the correct object file.

CASE STUDY   Designing a Telephone Directory Program (cont.)

Implementation   First we show the definition of class `Phone_Directory` (See Listing 1.9, file `Array_Based_PD.h`). The data field declarations for the class are shown in the private part of Listing 1.9. As previously described, we use the Javadoc or Doxygen style for commenting the data fields.

LISTING 1.9
Array_Based_PD.h

```
#ifndef ARRAY_BASED_PD_H_
#define ARRAY_BASED_PD_H_
#include <string>

/** Specification file for the array-based phone directory. */
class Phone_Directory {

  public:
    /** Construct an empty phone directory. */
    Phone_Directory();

    /** Destroy the phone directory when it is no longer needed. */
    ~Phone_Directory();

    /** Load the data file containing the directory, or
        establish a connection with the data source.
        @param source_name The name of the file (data source)
                            with the phone directory entries.
    */
    void load_data(const std::string& source_name);
```

```cpp
/** Look up an entry.
    @param name The name of the person to look up
    @return The number associated with that person
            or an empty string if name is not in
            the directory
*/
std::string lookup_entry(const std::string& name) const;

/** Changes the number associated with the given name to
    the new value, or adds a new entry with this name and
    number.
    @param name The name of the person
    @param number The new number
    @return The old value of number or an empty string
            if this is a new entry
*/
std::string add_or_change_entry(const std::string& name,
                                const std::string& number);

/** Removes the entry with the specified name from the directory.
    @param name The name of the person
    @return The person's name or an empty string if not in
            the directory
*/
std::string remove_entry(const std::string& name);

/** Writes the contents of the directory to the data file. */
void save();

private:
    // Insert the definition of the Directory_Entry class here.

    // Private Functions
    /** Searches the array of directory entries for the name.
        @param name The name to be found
        @return The index of the entry containing the name, or size
                if the name is not found
    */
    int find(const std::string& name) const;

    /** Adds a new entry with the given name and number to the array
        of directory entries.
        @param name The name to be added
        @param number The number to be added
    */
    void add(const std::string& name, const std::string& number);

    /** Removes the entry at the given index.
        @param index The index of the entry to be removed
    */
    void remove_entry(int index);

    /** Creates a new array of directory entries with twice the
        capacity of the current one.
    */
    void reallocate();
```

```
/** The number of entries in the directory. */
int size;
/** The current capacity of the array. */
int capacity;
/** Pointer to the array containing the directory data. */
Directory_Entry* the_directory;
/** The name of the data file that contains the directory data. */
std::string source_name;
/** Boolean flag to indicate whether the directory was
      modified since it was either loaded or saved. */
bool modified;
};

#endif
```

Coding the Functions in the Implementation File

Table 1.13 reviews the private functions defined in file class `Array_Based_PD.cpp`. They are private because they were not declared in the `Phone_Directory` interface and should not be called by a client. Two of these, `add` and `find`, were discussed previously. Function `reallocate` will be discussed later in this section. Function `remove_entry` is left as an exercise.

TABLE 1.13
Private Functions of `Array_Based_PD` Class

Private Function	Behavior
`int find(string& name) const`	Searches the array of directory entries for the `name`.
`void add(const string& name, string& number)`	Adds a new entry with the given `name` and `number` to the array of directory entries.
`void remove_entry(int index)`	Removes the entry at the given `index` from the directory array.
`void reallocate()`	Creates a new array of directory entries with twice the capacity of the current one.

The `load_data` Function

The `load_data` function (Listing 1.10) is called by the `main` function to read the initial directory data from an input file (parameter `source_name`). The data entry process takes place in the `while` loop. The `while` loop implements Steps 4 through 6 of the algorithm for `load_data` shown earlier. This function reads each name and number from two consecutive data lines and adds that entry to the array.

LISTING 1.10
Function `load_data` from `Array_Based_PD.cpp`

```
/** Function to load the data file.
    pre:  The directory storage has been created and it is empty.
          If the file exists, it consists of the name-number pairs
          on adjacent lines.
    post: The data from the file is loaded into the directory.
    @param source_name The name of the data file
```

```
*/
void Phone_Directory::load_data(const string& source_name)
{
  // Remember the source name for use by save.
  this->source_name = source_name;
  // Create an input stream for this file.
  ifstream in(source_name.c_str());
  if (in) { // Stream exists.
    string name;
    string number;
    while (getline(in, name)) {
      if (getline(in, number)) {
        add(name, number);
      }
    }
    // Close the file.
    in.close();
  }
}
```

The getline function reads a line from an istream and returns it in a string object. The istream is the returned value. If there is no more data to be read, the istream is returned in the fail state, so we exit the **while** loop. Note that we combined the call to getline and an implicit call to fail in the **while** statement condition

```
while (getline(in, name)) {...}
```

Similarly we combined the call to getline and fail when reading the number in the **if** condition

```
if (getline(in, number))
```

Therefore, we also exit the loop if a name was read but a number was not. If both a name and number are read, then a new entry is added to the directory and we continue reading and adding entries.

If a file with name source_name is not found, we immediately return (no data to read). (Later, we will write the new directory to file source_name.)

The **add_or_change_entry** Function

This function calls the internal function find to locate the name in the array. Function find will either return the index of the entry, or return –1 (minus 1) to indicate that the entry is not in the array. If the entry is in the array, that entry's set_number function is called to change the number; otherwise a new entry is added by calling the add function:

```
/** Add an entry or change an existing entry.
    @param name The name of the person being added or changed
    @param number The new number to be assigned
    @return The old number or, if a new entry, an empty string
*/
string Phone_Directory::add_or_change_entry(const string& name,
                                            const string& number)
```

```
{
  string old_number = "";
  int index = find(name);
  if (index != -1) {
    old_number = the_directory[index].get_number();
    the_directory[index].set_number(number);
  } else {
    add(name, number);
  }
  modified = true;
  return old_number;
}
```

The `lookup_entry` Function

This function also uses the internal `find` function to locate the entry in the array. If the entry is located, it is returned; otherwise the empty string is returned.

```
/** Look up an entry.
    @param name The name of the person
    @return The number. If not in the directory, an empty string
*/
string Phone_Directory::lookup_entry(const string& name) const {
  int index = find(name);
  if (index != -1) {
    return the_directory[index].get_number();
  } else {
    return "";
  }
}
```

The **save** Function

If the directory has not been modified, function save does nothing. Otherwise it creates an `ofstream` object and writes all phone directory entries to it. The output file name is the same as the input file name (source_name), so an existing directory file will be overwritten. The **for** statement writes the entries.

```
/** Function to save the directory.
    pre:  The directory has been loaded with data
    post: Contents of directory written back to the file in the
          form of name-number pairs on adjacent lines.
          modified is reset to false.
*/
void Phone_Directory::save() {
  if (modified) {  // If not modified, do nothing
    // Create an output stream.
    ofstream out(source_name.c_str());
    for (int i = 0; i < size; i++) {
      out << the_directory[i].get_name() << endl;
      out << the_directory[i].get_number() << endl;
    }
    // Close the output stream.
    out.close();
    modified = false;
  }
}
```

The **find** Function

The find function uses a **for** loop to search the array for the requested name. If located, its index is returned; otherwise –1 is returned.

```
/** Search the array for a given name.
    @param name The name to be found
    @return The index of the entry containing this name
            or -1 if the name is not present
*/
int Phone_Directory::find(const string& name) const {
  for (int i = 0; i < size; i++) {
    if (the_directory[i].get_name() == name)
      return i;
  }
  return -1;
}
```

The **add** Function

The add function checks to see whether there is room in the array by comparing the size to the capacity. If the size is less than the capacity, the new entry is stored at the end of the array and size is incremented by one after the entry is stored (size++). If the size is greater than or equal to the capacity, then the reallocate function is called to increase the size of the array before the new item is inserted.

```
/** Add a new name-number pair to the directory.
    @param name The name to be added
    @param number The number to be added
*/
void Phone_Directory::add(const string& name,
                          const string& number) {
  if (size == capacity) // If no room, reallocate.
    reallocate();
  // Increment size and add new entry.
  the_directory[size] = Directory_Entry(name, number);
  size++;
}
```

Ⓧ PITFALL

Returning –1 (Failure) Before Examining All Array Elements

A common logic error is to code the search loop for function find as follows:

```
for (int i = 0; i < size; i++) {
  if (the_directory[i].get_name() == name) {
    return i;
  } else {
    return -1;  // Incorrect! - tests only one element.
  }
}
```

This loop incorrectly returns a result after testing just the first element.

The `reallocate` Function

This function allocates a new array whose size is twice the current array. We use a **for** loop to copy the old array to the new array, and the_directory is changed to point to the new array. The storage allocated to the old array is then returned to the free-memory pool via the delete[] operator.

By doubling the size each time that a reallocation is necessary, we reduce the number of times we need to do this. Surprisingly, if we do this only fourteen times, we can store over 1 million entries.

```
/** Create a new array of directory entries with twice the capacity
    of the current one.
*/
void Phone_Directory::reallocate() {
  // Double the capacity.
  capacity *= 2;
  // Create a new directory array.
  Directory_Entry* new_directory = new Directory_Entry[capacity];
  // Copy the old to the new
  for (int i = 0; i < size; i++) {
    new_directory[i] = the_directory[i];
  }
  // Return the memory occupied by the old directory.
  delete[] the_directory;
  // Set the_directory to point to the new directory.
  the_directory = new_directory;
}
```

Using a Storage Structure Without Reallocation

In Chapter 4, you will study the vector data structure, which will enable you to store a directory of increasing size without needing to reallocate storage. You will see that we can change to a different data structure for storing the directory with very little effort, because the problem solution has been so carefully designed. We will only need to code the functions declared in the Phone_Directory ADT so that they perform the same operations on a vector.

PITFALL

Failure to Delete Dynamically Allocated Arrays

If we do not return the storage allocated to the old array to the free-memory pool, this memory is lost. This is known as a *memory-leak*. Although modern computers seem to have infinite memory, there is in fact only a finite supply. Furthermore, programs that leak memory can impact other programs running on the same computer. A program that routinely leaks memory can eventually require you to reboot your computer.

Testing   Class **Array_Based_PD**

To test this class, you should run it with data files that are empty or that contain a single name-and-number pair. You should also run it with data files that contain an odd number of lines (ending with a name but no number). You should see what happens when the array is completely filled and you try to add a new entry. Does function `reallocate` properly double the array's size? When you do a retrieval or an edit operation, make sure you try to retrieve names that are not in the directory as well as names that are in the directory. If an entry has been changed, verify that the new number is retrieved. Finally, check that all new and edited entries are written correctly to the output file. We will discuss testing further in the next chapter.

EXERCISES FOR SECTION 1.7

PROGRAMMING

1. Code the `remove_entry` function.

1.8 Completing the Phone Directory Application

So far we have described the `main` function and the `Phone_Directory` ADT. The `main` function creates a `Phone_Directory` object, calls its `load_data` function, and then calls the `process_commands` function.

CASE STUDY   Designing a Telephone Directory Program (cont.)

Analysis   The `process_commmands` function is declared as follows:

```
void process_commands(Phone_Directory the_directory);
```

The interface enables clients to use function `process_commands` without knowing the details of its implementation (information hiding). We will introduce additional functions that are called by `process_commands` to perform its tasks.

The function `process_commands` should present a menu of choices to the user:

- Add or Change an Entry
- Look Up an Entry
- Remove an Entry
- Save the Directory Data
- Exit the Program

Design   The function process_commands will use a "menu-driven" loop to control the interaction with the user. After each command is processed, the menu of choices is displayed again. This process continues until the user selects "Exit".

```
do {
  // Get the action to perform from the user.
  // The user's choice will be a number from 0 through 4.
  ...
  switch (choice) {
    case 0: do_add_change_entry(); break;
    case 1: do_lookup_entry(); break;
    case 2: do_remove_entry(); break;
    case 3: do_save(); break;
    case 4: do_save(); break;
  }
} while (choice < NUM_COMMANDS - 1);
```

The function process_commands calls a function shown in the foregoing **switch** statement to perform the user's choice. Note that function do_save is called by the last two cases. We discuss the design and coding of these functions next.

Implementation   Listing 1.11 shows the code for the PD_Application. This program uses cout to display the menu of choices and results. It also uses cin to read data from the user. It begins with forward definitions of the functions that are called in the **switch** statement. C++ functions must be declared in a function prototype that appears before the first use of the function. The prototype consists of the heading of the function only.

Function **process_commands**

The function process_commands begins by displaying the menu:

```
Select: 0 Add/Change Entry
Select: 1 Look Up Entry
Select: 2 Remove Entry
Select: 3 Save Directory
Select: 4 Exit
```

The first statement below

```
cin >> choice;
cin.ignore(numeric_limits<int>::max(), '\n');
```

reads the user's choice (an integer) from the console. The second statements skips over the newline character that follows the integer.

Function **do_add_change_entry**

The do_add_change_entry function requests the name followed by the number. The Phone_Directory.add_or_change_entry function is called after values are entered for the name and number. A return value of an empty string indicates that this is a new entry, and a confirmation dialog is displayed as follows

```
Enter name: Quincy
Enter number: 555-111-3333
Quincy has been added to the directory
```

If the name was already in the directory, the previous value of the number is returned, and the confirmation shows both the old and new number as follows:

```
Enter name: Tom
Enter number: 123-456-7890
Tom has been changed in the directory
Old number was 444-555-6666
```

Function do_lookup_entry

The do_lookup_entry function uses the same prompt as do_add_change_entry to request the name. The number is looked up by calling the Phone_Directory.lookup_entry function, and the result is displayed. If the name is not in the directory, a message is displayed. Examples of both cases follow:

```
Enter name: Tom
The number for Tom is 123-456-7890

Enter name: Dick
Dick is not in the directory
```

Function do_save

The do_save function calls the save function of the Phone_Directory.

LISTING 1.11
PD_Application.cpp

```cpp
/** Phone directory application that uses console I/O. */
#include "Array_Based_PD.h"
#include <iostream>
#include <istream>
#include <ostream>
#include <limits>
using namespace std;

// Forward declaration of functions
void process_commands(Phone_Directory&);
void do_add_change_entry(Phone_Directory&);
void do_lookup_entry(Phone_Directory&);
void do_remove_entry(Phone_Directory&);
void do_save(Phone_Directory&);

int main(int argc, char* argv[]) {
  if (argc < 2) {
    cerr << "Must specify the name of the data file"
         << " that contains the directory\n";
    return 1;
  }
  Phone_Directory the_directory;
  the_directory.load_data(argv[1]);
  process_commands(the_directory);
}
```

```cpp
void process_commands(Phone_Directory& the_directory) {
  string commands[] = {
    "Add/Change Entry",
    "Look Up Entry",
    "Remove Entry",
    "Save Directory",
    "Exit" };
  const int NUM_COMMANDS = 5;
  int choice = NUM_COMMANDS - 1;
  do {
    for (int i = 0; i < NUM_COMMANDS; i++) {
      cout << "Select: " << i << " " << commands[i] << "\n";
    }
    cin >> choice;
    cin.ignore(numeric_limits<int>::max(), '\n');
    switch (choice) {
      case 0: do_add_change_entry(the_directory); break;
      case 1: do_lookup_entry(the_directory); break;
      case 2: do_remove_entry(the_directory); break;
      case 3: do_save(the_directory); break;
      case 4: do_save(the_directory); break;
    }
  } while (choice < NUM_COMMANDS - 1);
}

void do_add_change_entry(Phone_Directory& the_directory) {
  string name;
  string number;
  cout << "Enter name: ";
  getline(cin, name);
  cout << "Enter number: ";
  getline(cin, number);
  string old_number =
    the_directory.add_or_change_entry(name, number);
  if (old_number != "") {
    cout << name << " has been changed in the directory\n";
    cout << "Old number was " << old_number << "\n";
  } else {
    cout << name << " has been added to the directory\n";
  }
}

void do_lookup_entry(Phone_Directory& the_directory) {
  string name;
  cout << "Enter name: ";
  getline(cin, name);
  string number = the_directory.lookup_entry(name);
  if (number != "") {
    cout << "The number for " << name << " is " << number << "\n";
  } else {
    cout << name << " is not in the directory\n";
  }
}

void do_remove_entry(Phone_Directory& the_directory) {
  // Exercise
}

void do_save(Phone_Directory& the_directory) {
  the_directory.save();
}
```

EXERCISES FOR SECTION 1.8

PROGRAMMING

1. Code the do_remove_entry function.

Chapter Review

- ◆ We discussed the software engineering process. We introduced two software life cycle models (waterfall and Unified) and discussed the activities performed in each stage of these models. In this text we will use a simplified five-step process for developing software:

  1. Requirements
  2. Analysis
  3. Design
  4. Implementation
  5. Testing

- ◆ Although these steps are shown in sequence, in reality there is quite a bit of inter-action between them. During the design phase, you may need to go back and redo the requirements and analysis steps. Of course, this is provided for in the full Unified Model.

- ◆ Procedural abstraction, data abstraction, and information hiding are tools for managing program complexity, so that progams can be designed as a collection of separate but interacting classes. Procedural abstraction focuses on the operations to be performed; data abstraction focuses on the data elements and their operations; information hiding means that users of a class or function need to know only how to use the class or function, not how it is implemented.

- ◆ An Abstract Data Type (ADT) defines a set of objects and the operations that can be performed on them. An ADT can have several classes that implement it (define its data and operations).

- ◆ Use cases summarize the interaction between the user and the system during requirements specification and analysis.

- ◆ UML class diagrams are used during the analysis and design phases to document the interaction of classes with each other and with the user.

- ◆ Sequence diagrams and pseudocode can be used to describe the sequence of actions performed by a program that is implemented as a collection of multiple interacting classes. Sequence diagrams are employed during the design phase of the software life cycle.

Quick-Check Exercises

1. The disadvantage of the _____ model is that it assumes that the software life cycle stages are performed in sequence and not revisited once completed. The Unified Model consists of _____ and _____, and the system designer can work on more than one _____ during each iteration.
2. Procedural abstraction enables a system designer to model _____; data abstraction focuses on the _____ and _____.
3. An ADT specifies a contract between the _____ and _____; a _____ implements the ADT.
4. An ADT can be implemented by multiple classes (True/False).
5. A _____ is a statement that must be true before a _____ executes, and a _____ represents the _____ of executing a _____.
6. A _____ specifies the interaction between an external entity and a system.
7. _____ means that a class _____ does not need to know its implementation details.
8. _____ is a mixture of English and _____ used to specify an algorithm.

Answers to Quick-Check Exercises

1. The disadvantage of the *waterfall* model is that it assumes that the software life cycle stages are perfromed in sequence and not revisited once completed. The Unified Model consists of *activities/workflows* and *phases*, and the system designer can work on more than one *activity* during each iteration.
2. Procedural abstraction enables a system designer to model *processes/operations*; data abstraction focuses on the *data elements* and *operations on that data*.
3. An ADT specifies a contract between the *developer* and *user*; a *class* implements the ADT.
4. True.
5. A *precondition* is a statement that must be true before a *function* executes, and a *postcondition* represents the *result* of executing a *function*.
6. A *use case* specifies the interaction between an external entity and a system.
7. *Information hiding* means that a class *user* does not need to know its implementation details.
8. *Pseudocode* is a mixture of English and *programming language* used to specify an algorithm.

Review Questions

1. Explain why the principle of information hiding is important to the software designer.
2. Discuss the differences between the waterfall model and Unified Model of the software life cycle.
3. Define the terms *procedural abstraction* and *data abstraction*.
4. Explain the role of function preconditions and postconditions.
5. What is the advantage of specifying an abstract data type instead of just going ahead and implementing a class?
6. Define an ADT Money that has operations for arithmetic operations (addition, subtraction, multiplication, and division) on real numbers having exactly two digits to the right

of the decimal point, as well as functions for representing a `Money` object as a string and as a real number. Also include the operators == and < for this ADT.

7. Answer Review Question 6 for an ADT `Complex` that has operations for arithmetic operations on a complex number (a number with a real and imaginary part). Assume that the same operations (+, −, *, /) are supported. Also define the == and != operators and overload the `ostream` extraction operator.

Programming Projects

1. Modify the telephone directory project in this chapter so that it could be used by a company. Each employee's information should contain a name, job description, telephone number, and room number. Assume that the information for each person is available on a single line of a data file in the form last name, first name, job description, phone number, room number with commas as separators between data items. Provide a submenu for the edit operation that allows the user to edit any of the person's data fields. After using the directory and updating it, save the data file in the same format as before.

2. Follow the software development model illustrated in this chapter to design and implement an array-based program application that manages a collection of DVDs. The data for each DVD will consist of a title, a category, running time, year of release, and price. Use a file to save the collection after it has been updated. The user should be able to add new DVDs to the collection, remove a DVD, edit the information stored for a DVD, list all DVDs in a specified category, and retrieve and display the information saved for a DVD given its title. Also, the user should be able to sort the collection of DVDs by year or by title.

3. Follow the software development model illustrated in this chapter to design and implement an array-based program application that manages your personal library. The data for each book will consist of a title, author, number of pages, year of publication, price, and the name of the person who has borrowed it (if any). Use a file to save the collection after it has been updated. The user should be able to add new books to the collection, remove a book, edit the information stored for a book, list all books by a specified author, list all books loaned to a particular person, and retrieve and display the information saved for a book given its title. Also, the user should be able to sort the collection of books by author or by title.

4. Assume that you have decided to loan DVDs in your DVD collection to friends (see Project 2) but just one DVD at a time to each friend. Assume that you also have a collection of friends. For each friend, you need to store the friend's name and phone number and the number of the DVD your friend has borrowed (−1 if none). Besides managing your DVD collection as in Project 2, you should also be able to manage your list of friends (add friend, edit friend, and so on). One of the edit operations should allow your friend to return a DVD or to exchange it for another. You should also be able to display each friend and the name of the DVD that the friend currently has (if any). Draw UML class diagrams before you start to code the program.

5. Develop a program that could be used to determine election results for a town. Assume that the town is divided into a number of precincts (an input item) and that the number of candidates is variable (an input item). The votes received for each candidate by precinct should be stored in a two-dimensional array that is part of class `Vote_Tabulation`. Your program should allow its user to issue any of the following instructions:

- Load the vote data from a file
- Load the vote data interactively
- Edit the vote data interactively to account for absentee ballots just received
- Request a table showing the raw vote results by precinct and candidate
- Request a table showing the percentage of votes by precinct and candidate
- Request a table showing the raw vote results by candidate and precinct
- Request a table showing the precentage of votes by candidate and precinct
- Display the top n vote getters for the township and their results in decreasing order, where n is a data item

6. Develop a program that could be used as a point-of-order inventory system. Read in a database from a file that represents the store inventory. Each item consists of an ID, a description, a price, a quantity on hand, and a reorder point. Assume that the database can be updated at a terminal by the operator when a customer purchases an item. The quantity purchased for an item is deducted from that item's quantity (if sufficient) and a register receipt is displayed after all purchases are entered. An operator can also process the return of an item by adding the quantity returned to the inventory. A register receipt should also be displayed for a return. Finally, the operator can process new items received from a supplier by adding the items to the database. It should also be possible for an operator to update the price of an item, provided the operator enters the correct security key. Also, the operator should be able to display a list of all items whose quantity on hand is less than the reorder point for that item.

7. Develop a sales-tracking program that enables a company to keep track of its sales force's performance by quarter. The program should read in each person's name and the past performance of that salesperson for the last n quarters, where n is a data item. The operator should be able to enter the results for each person for the current quarter interactively. The operator should be able to add a new salesperson to the system (past performances set to 0) and edit the information stored for a salesperson. The operator should be able to request any of the following tables:

- Total sales by quarter (for all quarters or for a specified quarter)
- Sales for each person by quarter (for all quarters or for a specified quarter)
- Rank of each person by quarter (for all quarters or for a specified quarter)
- A list of salespeople and amounts in decreasing order by quarter (for all quarters or for a specified quarter)

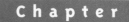

Chapter 2

Program Correctness and Efficiency

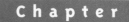

Chapter Objectives

- To understand the differences between the three categories of program errors
- To understand what it means to throw an exception and how to throw an exception in a function
- To understand the effect of an uncaught exception and why you should catch exceptions
- To learn how to catch and process exceptions
- To understand different testing strategies and when and how they are performed
- To learn how to write special functions to test other functions and classes
- To become familiar with debugging techniques and debugger programs
- To be introduced to the process of program verification and the use of assertions and loop invariants
- To understand the meaning of big-**O** notation and how it is used to analyze an algorithm's efficiency

This chapter discusses program correctness and efficiency. You will learn about program defects and how to avoid them in your programs: through careful program design and by using other members of your programming team to help detect errors in logic before they become part of the code. As in all other situations in life, early detection leads to the best results.

You will study the different kinds of errors that can occur in programs: syntax errors, run-time errors or exceptions, and logic errors. You will learn about the different kinds of exceptions in C++, how to handle exceptions in programs, and the benefit of doing so.

The chapter discusses program testing in some detail. You will learn how to generate a proper test plan and the differences between unit and integration testing as they apply to an object-oriented design. You will also learn how to use drivers and stubs, special functions that are written to test other functions and classes.

You will learn how to detect errors during debugging and techniques for generating diagnostic information to help in debugging. You will also see what features are available in debugger programs to help with this process.

You will also see how formal verification can be used to help you reason about a program. We don't expect you to write a program like a mathematical proof, but you can use these ideas to help in the design and documentation of your programs and to increase your confidence that critical parts of programs operate as intended.

Finally, you will learn about algorithm efficiency and how to characterize the efficiency of an algorithm. You will learn about big-O notation, which you can use to compare the relative efficiency of different algorithms.

Program Correctness and Efficiency

2.1 Program Defects and "Bugs"

This chapter is about program errors or defects and how to avoid them. It does not matter much whether a program runs efficiently if it does not do what it is supposed to do. Very often, defects appear in a software product after it is delivered, sometimes with disastrous results. Some notable software defects have caused power brownouts, telephone network saturation, space flight delays, loss of spacecraft, and even loss of life.

One way to show that a program is correct is by thorough testing, but it is difficult to determine how much testing needs to be done. In fact, testing can never demonstrate the complete absence of defects. Furthermore, in some situations it is very difficult to test a software product completely in the environment in which it is used, such as software that controls a missile or prevents a meltdown in a nuclear power plant.

You may also hear the term "bug" used to refer to a software defect. "Debugging" is a commonly used term for removing defects, and a debugger is a commonly used testing tool that helps find defects, as we discuss in Section 2.4. Because of society's ever-increasing dependence on computer systems, however, many software professionals have come to believe that calling software defects "bugs" tends to trivialize their serious consequences.

Careful design and careful testing can reduce program defects. Obviously, it is much easier to eliminate defects by design rather than by removing them later through testing.

There are three kinds of defects or errors that you might encounter:

- Syntax errors
- Run-time errors or exceptions
- Logic errors

Syntax Errors

Syntax errors are mistakes in your use of the grammar (or syntax) of the C++ language (for example, omitting a closing }). The C++ compiler will detect most syntax errors during compilation and will require you to correct them before it can successfully compile your program. The following are some other common syntax errors:

- Omitting or misplacing braces that bracket compound statements
- Invoking a member function that is not defined for the object it is applied to
- Not declaring a variable before using it
- Providing multiple declarations of a variable
- Not assigning a value to a local variable before referencing it
- Not returning a value from a function whose result type is not **void**

Some syntax errors are the result of typographical errors (for example, using = where you intended to use ==, misspelling a variable name, or typing { instead of } or [).

The compiler does not detect all typographical errors. For example, using = where you intended to use == is generally still valid syntax, but not what you intended. This will result in the computer performing a different operation from the one intended (assignment instead of comparison). Because a syntactically correct program can contain errors, careful review and testing are essential.

Run-time Errors

Run-time errors occur during program execution. A run-time error occurs when the computer or the C++ run-time library detects an operation that it knows to be incorrect. Table 2.1 shows some examples of common run-time errors. Most run-time errors will cause the operating system or run-time library to issue an error message and halt your program. The behavior will be different for different computers, operating systems, and compilers. This is a "good news, bad news" situation. The good news is that the error has been detected. The bad news is that your program is no longer executing. We will discuss exceptions in more detail in Sections 2.2 and 2.3 and show how to prevent the bad-news situation from occurring. Following are brief discussions and examples of some of the errors listed in the table.

Division by Zero

The C++ standard states that the result of division by zero is undefined. This is the standard's way of saying that something is an error but that the compiler and run-

TABLE 2.1

Common Run-time Errors in C++

Run-Time Error	Cause
Division by zero	Integer division by zero.
Array index out of bounds	Attempt to access an array with an index value that is greater than the array's length (not detected by C++).
Null pointer reference	Attempt to dereference a pointer whose value is NULL.

time system are not required to detect it. The behavior will depend on the computer, operating system, and compiler being used.

When using an Intel x68 family of computers, if count represents the number of items being processed and it is possible for count to be zero, then the assignment statement

```
average = sum / count;
```

will cause a division-by-zero error. Under the Windows operating system this error is indicated by a dialog box as follows:

Under the Linux operating system, you merely get the message:

```
Floating point exception
```

You can easily guard against such a division with an **if** statement so that the division operation will not be performed when count is zero:

```
if (count == 0)
   average = 0.0;
else
   average = sum / count;
```

Normally you would compute an average as a **double** value, so you could cast an **int** value in sum to type **double** before doing the division.

```
average = double(sum) / count;
```

On the Intel x86 this is not an error if count is 0. Instead, average is assigned a special value, representing either positive or negative infinity, depending on the sign of sum.

Array Index Out of Bounds

C++ does not check the validity of array subscripts. Accessing or modifying an array element using a subscript that is negative or greater than or equal to the array's length is another one of these conditions that the standard says is undefined.

> ☑ **PROGRAM STYLE**
>
> **Type Casting in C++ Versus C or Java**
>
> In the type cast
>
> double(sum)
>
> the target data type is used as an operator, and the expression being cast is enclosed in parentheses. You could also use the C or Java form for type casting:
>
> (double) sum
>
> but it is not the preferred form.

EXAMPLE 2.1   Suppose we define the array scores as follows:

    int scores[500];

The subscripted variable scores[i] uses i (type **int**) as the array index. If i is less than zero or greater than 499, a location outside of the array will be accessed or modified. What happens is that some location in memory that is not part of the array is either accessed or modified. If the location happens to be a location that is not accessible to the program, then an error may be reported. Otherwise the program may appear to work just fine. Or the program may exhibit strange behavior at some point far removed from the location of the error.

Incorrect loop control parameters can cause array-index-out-of-bounds errors. Carefully check the boundary values for an index that is also a loop control variable. A common error is using the array size as the upper limit rather than the array size minus 1.

EXAMPLE 2.2   If X_SIZE is the size of array x, the following loop would cause an array-index-out-of-bounds error during the last pass, when i is equal to X_SIZE.

    for (int i = 0; i <= X_SIZE; i++)
      x[i] = i * i;

You should replace the loop header with one of the following:.

    for (int i = 0; i < X_SIZE; i++)
    for (int i = 0; i <= X_SIZE - 1; i++)
    for (int i = 0; i != X_SIZE; i++)

If an array index is passed as a function argument, the function should validate the argument before using it as an array subscript. The next example shows one way to guard against this type of error.

EXAMPLE 2.3   Function set_element_of_x stores its second argument (val) in the element of array x (a type **int[]** data field) selected by its first argument (index). The **if** statement validates that index is in bounds before the assignment. The function returns a **bool** value indicating whether or not the array element was changed. If the function did not validate that index is in bounds, an out-of-bounds error could occur.

```
/** Stores val in the element of array x with subscript index.
    @param index The subscript of element to be changed
    @param val The value to be stored
    @return true if val is stored; otherwise, false
*/
bool set_element_of_x(int index, int val) {
  if (index >= 0 && index < X_SIZE) {
    x[index] = val;
    return true;
  } else {
    return false;
  }
}
```

EXAMPLE 2.4   A common technique for communicating the name of a data file to a program is to pass the file name as a parameter to function main. If you are running from the console window, you can do this by listing the file name on the command line that initiates program execution. If you are using an integrated deveopment environment (IDE), you can enter parameters in a special window. When the main function executes, any parameters are stored as strings in array argv. The name of the executable file is stored in argv[0] followed by the arguments starting at argv[1]. The value of the first parameter, argc, specifies the number of elements in array argv.

The following main function expects the second string to be the input file name, so it contains an **if** statement that validates that at least two strings were passed to array argv before the function attempts to store argv[1] in input_file_name. If a parameter is not supplied, then we use the string "Phone.dat" as the default name of the input file. Without the **if** statement, there would be an out-of-bounds error when argv[1] was referenced and no parameters were passed.

```
int main(int argc, char* argv[]) {
  string input_file_name;
  if (argc > 1)
    input_file_name = argv[1];
  else
    input_file_name = "Phone.dat";
  ...
```

✓ PROGRAM STYLE

Using a bool Result to Indicate Success or Failure

What is gained by returning a **bool** value when we execute function set_element_of_x? The caller of the function can use this result to display an error message to the program user if desired. The following **if** statement applies function set_element_of_x to array x and writes an error message to stream cerr:

```
if (!set_element_of_x(index, val))
   cerr << "*** ERROR - index value " << index
        << " is out of bounds. ***\n";
```

⊘ PITFALL

Buffer Overruns Cause Security Holes

Many of the security holes in programs are due to buffer overruns, which are a type of array-index-out-of-bounds error. A malicious program sends a large input stream to a program that does not check to see that the data fits into the array allocated to receive it. By modifying data outside of the allocated array, the malicious program is able to take over control of the target computer.

Null Pointer

If you attempt to de-reference a null pointer, the operating system will generally issue an error message and terminate the program. Under Windows the message is a dialog box similar to the following:

Under Linux the typical message is

```
Segmentation fault
```

You can avoid this error by ensuring that pointers are not null before dereferencing them.

EXAMPLE 2.5   The first of the following statements declares p to be a pointer variable that references a type **double** value, and it initializes p to NULL. The second statement attempts to store 15.5 in this variable by using the operator * to dereference p. Because p is NULL, this will lead to a run-time error.

```
double *p = NULL;
*p = 15.5;            // Invalid assignment - p is NULL
```

Before making the assignment, you must reset p to reference a memory cell that can be used to store a type **double** value:

```
double *p = NULL;
p = new double;
*p = 15.5;
```

Logic Errors

Logic errors are the final category of error. A logic error occurs when the programmer/analyst has made a mistake in the design of a class or a class function or has implemented an algorithm incorrectly. In either case, even if the C++ code compiles and runs, it will not meet the specification for that function—that is, it will produce incorrect results. If the user is fortunate, a logic error may cause a run-time error in another function that relies on the results generated by the faulty function, but this may not happen. Most logic errors do not cause syntax or run-time errors and, consequently, are difficult to find. Some examples are given in the Pitfalls in this chapter.

Sometimes logic errors are found during testing by careful comparison of the actual program output with the expected results. This can happen only if the tester provides *test cases* that cause execution of the incorrect portion of the algorithm. Also, the tester must determine beforehand the output that should be generated, so that the expected output can be compared with the actual output.

A worse scenario is when logic errors are encountered during real-world operation of a program. There are many examples in which logic errors have made the popular news. The original Mars Lander spacecraft crashed because of inconsistent calculations (feet versus meters). Billing programs have sent out bills for exorbitant

---

✓ PROGRAM STYLE

Initialize Pointers to NULL

Although your program crashes if it attempts to dereference a null pointer, this is much better than having an error go unreported. C++ does not assign default values automatically to pointers when they are allocated. Until a pointer is assigned a value, it may point to anything at all. For this reason, it is a good practice to initialize a pointer to NULL when you first declare it. This way, if you attempt to dereference such a pointer before it is given an initial value, you will know about it.

amounts of money. Logic errors in automatic teller machine (ATM) programs or off-track betting programs have caused machine owners to lose significant amounts of money. Many popular operating systems have been released with logic errors that have enabled hackers to access computers easily. One popular word processor, when integrated with any document management system, frequently would "eat" the document off the server and leave an empty file in its place. In the 1980s several patients died after errors in the software that controlled therapeutic radiation machines gave them massive overdoses. In August 2004, two of the four automobile recalls listed in *Consumer Reports* were due to software errors: an automatic braking system and an ignition control system. Both errors could lead to fatal accidents. To avoid these kinds of catastrophes, software professionals must be very diligent about detecting and correcting logic errors.

In Section 2.5 we show you how to reduce logic errors by carefully checking the program design. We also show how to detect logic errors through testing.

EXERCISES FOR SECTION 2.1

SELF-CHECK

1. Explain and correct any syntax errors in the following `main` function.
   ```
   int main() {
      int x = 3.45;
      double w = x / 2;
      char ch = 'a' + 'b';
      if (x = y) {
         int z = x++;
      else
         int z = y++;
      }
      cout << z << "***" << sqrt(z) << endl;
   }
   ```

2. Identify any of the following statements that would result in a run-time error.
   ```
   const int X_SIZE = 10;
   int x[X_SIZE];
   x[X_SIZE] = 5;
   x[X_SIZE - 1] = -95;
   x[0] = 7;
   int n = 0;
   x[n] = 10 / n;
   ```

PROGRAMMING

1. Write a member function `get_element_of_x` that returns a type **int** value stored in an array data field `x` of type `int[]`. The function argument is the subscript of the value to be retrieved. Validate the argument to prevent an array-out-of-bounds error. Return `numeric_limits<int>::min()` (defined in `<limits>`) if the subscript is not valid.

2.2 Exceptions

Ways to Indicate an Error

There are many ways to indicate an error. Some examples are:

- Return a special value.
- Use a **bool** return value to indicate success or failure.
- Set a global variable.
- Print an error message.
- Print an error message and exit the program.
- Put an input or output stream in a fail state.

The first three allow you, as a user of the function that detects the error, the ability to respond to the error. We illustrated how to use a **bool** return value in Example 2.3. We next show an example of returning a special value.

EXAMPLE 2.6 Assume function get_element_of_x(int index) returns the value of array element x[index] if index is in bounds and returns numeric_limits<int>::min() (defined in <limits>) if the argument is not valid. In the following fragment, we test the value returned and attempt to recover from the error if it is numeric_limits<int>::min().

```
int value = get_element_of_x(i);
if (value > numeric_limits<int>::min()) {
  // Do something with value
  ...
}
else {
  // Recover from the error
  ...
}
// Continue normal processing
```

However, if there are several possible errors, this approach can result in a program in which the main thread of execution is hard to follow. An alternative way to indicate an error is through the use of exceptions. *Exceptions* are used to signal that an error has occurred. You can insert code in your program that *throws an exception* when a particular kind of error occurs. When an exception is thrown, the normal flow of execution is interrupted. If there is no exception handler, then the program terminates. In this case, throwing an exception is equivalent to printing an error message and calling the exit function. However, by throwing an exception you give the user of the function the opportunity to *catch* or *handle* the exception and perhaps recover from the error. Next, we will discuss throwing and handling exceptions.

The throw Statement

In the following version of function get_element_of_x, the **throw** statement executes when the value of index is out of bounds. It throws an out_of_range exception, creating an instance of this class. The message passed to the constructor gives the cause

SYNTAX   The throw Statement

FORM:

throw *expression*;

EXAMPLES:

```
throw "The value of index is out of range";
throw std::out_of_range("The value of index is out of range");
```

MEANING:

The normal sequence of execution is interrupted, and control is transferred to the nearest exception handler whose parameter type matches the type of the *expression*. An exception handler is like a function, and the rules for matching an exception handler are the same as the rules for matching an overloaded function. If the current function body contains no such handler, then control is returned to the calling function, and a search is made from the point of the call. This process is repeated until the corresponding exception handler is found or until the main function is reached. If no exception handler is found, then the program terminates.

of the exception and is stored in the exception object. It can be retrieved and displayed by the exception. Control is then passed to the *exception handler* for this type of exception (discussed later) if one is available.

```
/** Gets the value in the element of array x with subscript index.
    @param index The subscript of the element to be retrieved
    @return the value stored at x[index] if index is in range
    @throws a std::out_of_range exception if index is not in range
*/
int get_element_of_x(int index) {
  if (index < 0 || index >= X_SIZE) {
    throw std::out_of_range(
      "In get_element_of_x, the value of index is out of range");
  }
  return x[index];
}
```

As is shown in the syntax box, the exception object can be of any type—for example, a string literal (of type const char*) or a class instance (std::out_of_range). The standard library includes classes that can be used to indicate exceptions. We discuss these later in this section. It is recommended that you use one of the standard exceptions or a class derived from one of the standard exceptions.

Uncaught Exceptions

When an exception occurs that is not caught, the program stops and an error message is displayed. This message is compiler- and operating-system dependent and generally not very informative. The g++ compiler under Linux merely gives the message

```
Aborted
```

and the Microsoft .NET C++ compiler gives the message

```
This application has requested the Runtime to terminate it in an
unusual way.
Please contact the application's support team for more information.
```

In the next few subsections you will see how to avoid the default behavior when an exception is thrown. You will also see why it is advantageous to do this.

Catching and Handling Exceptions with try and catch Blocks

To avoid uncaught exceptions you write a **try** *block* that can throw an exception and follow it with a **catch** *block* that actually catches an exception and handles it.

```
try {
  val = get_element_of_x(10);
}
catch (std::out_of_range& ex) {
  std::cerr << "Out of range exception occurred\n";
  std::cerr << ex.what() << endl;  // Display string stored in ex.
  std::abort();      // Exit with an error indication.
}
```

If all statements in the **try** block body execute without error, the exception handler is skipped. If an out_of_range exception is thrown, the **try** block body is exited and the exception handler (the **catch** block) executes. The **try** block in the preceding example will throw an exception if the argument, 10, in the function call get_element_of_x(10) is out of range.

The heading for the **catch** block,

```
catch (std::out_of_range& ex) {
```

is similar to a function declaration. The parameter, ex, has the type std::out_of_range. If an exception of this type is thrown in the **try** block, then the exception object will be copied into the parameter ex, and the code in the body of the exception handler will be executed.

This exception handler simply displays an error message and then exits with an error indication. The line

```
std::cerr << ex.what() << endl;  // Display string stored in ex
```

writes to the standard error stream cerr the string passed to object ex when it was thrown by get_element_of_x: "In get_element_of_x, the value of index is out of range". Note that the exception object is actually thrown (created) inside function get_element_of_x but is handled by the **catch** block in the caller of get_element_of_x.

Following a **try** block, there can be more than one **catch** block, each handling a different kind of exception. If so, they are checked in the order in which they appear.

Although the earlier **catch** block handles the exception, it basically duplicates the default behavior for uncaught exceptions with a slightly more informative error message. Next, we show you how to use the **catch** block to recover from errors and continue execution of your program.

SYNTAX   **The try Block**

FORM:
```
try {
    code that may throw an exception
}
catch (type-1 parameter-1) {
    statements to process type-1
}
catch (type-2 parameter-2) {
    statements to process type-2
}
...
catch (type-n parameter-n)
    statements to process type-n
}
```

EXAMPLE:
```
try {
    val = get_element_of_x(10);
}
catch (std::out_of_range& ex) {
    cerr << "Out of range exception occurred\n";
    cerr << ex.what() << endl;
    abort();     // Exit with an error indication.
}
```

MEANING:

The statements in the **try** block execute through to completion unless an exception is thrown. If there is an exception handler for the exception, its body executes to completion. If there is no exception handler that matches the exception, then the exception is passed up the call chain until either it is caught by some other function in the call chain or it is processed by the run-time library as an uncaught exception. If there are multiple **catch** blocks, they are checked in the order in which they appear.

Standard Exceptions

The C++ library defines several standard exception classes, which it uses to report errors. These are listed in Table 2.2. Other than ios_base::failure, these exception classes are defined in the header <stdexcept>. The ios_base::failure class is defined in the header <ios> inside the class ios_base.

Table 2.2 shows each exception class, the function(s) or operator(s) that throws each class of exception (the third column), and the reason it is thrown. Not all of these exceptions are used by the language or the library. The errors domain_error and range_error are indicated by the C mathematics functions (which C++ includes) by setting a global variable. In a function with calls to these functions, the programmer could report errors to higher-level functions by throwing these exceptions. The overflow_error and underflow_error are reported by the floating-point operators in most implementations. The function to detect them varies by implementation.

....
TABLE 2.2
Standard Exceptions

Standard Exception	Reason Thrown	Thrown by
bad_alloc	Memory is not available.	The **new** operator.
bad_cast	Attempt to cast a reference that is not of the target type.	The dynamic_cast operator.
bad_typeid	Attempt to obtain the typeid of a null pointer or of the default typeid object.	The typeid operator.
domain_error	Function not defined for the input value (for example, attempting to take the square root of a negative number).	Not thrown by a C++ operator or standard library function.
invalid_argument	Invalid function argument.	The bitset constructor takes a string argument. This string should contain only the characters 1 or 0. If any other characters appear, the invalid_argument exception will be thrown.
length_error	Attempt to create a string or vector that is larger than the maximum allowed size.	The string and vector classes.
out_of_range	Index that is either negative or larger than size().	The at member function for the string, vector, and deque classes. Also thrown by other string functions such as substr that take an index parameter. It is *not* thrown by the subscript operator (operator[]).
ios_base::failure	An error flag being set that matches one set earlier by a call to the exceptions function.	Input/output stream objects after erroneous input/output operations.
range_error	Output of a function that is larger or smaller than can be represented by the output data type.	Not thrown by a C++ operator or standard library function.
overflow_error	Result that is larger than can be represented by the output data type.	If the bit string contained in a bitset is larger than the value of an **unsigned long**, then the overflow_error exception will be thrown by the ulong member function.
underflow_error	Result that is smaller than can be represented by the output data type.	Not thrown by a C++ operator or standard library function.

EXAMPLE 2.7   The string function substr extracts a substring from the string object it is applied to starting at the index pos. If pos is greater than the length of the string, the out_of_range exception is thrown. The **catch** block in the following program handles this exception.

```
/** Program to demonstrate the out_of_range exception thrown
    by the string.substr function if the start index is greater
    than the length of the string.
*/
#include <string>
#include <stdexcept>
#include <iostream>

using namespace std;

int main() {
  // Enter a string and substring start index.
  string a_string;
  int start_pos;
  cout << "Type in a string: ";
  getline(cin, a_string);
  cout << "Enter start position of a substring: ";
  cin >> start_pos;

  try {
    cout << "The substring is "
         << a_string.substr(start_pos) << endl;
    return 0;
  } catch (out_of_range& ex) {
    cerr << "*** Out_of_range exception thrown for start position "
         << start_pos << "\n"
         << ex.what() << endl;
    return 1;
  }
}
```

The user is asked to enter a string and then the starting index of a substring. If the starting positon is valid, the substring is displayed:

```
Type in a string: unnecessary roughness
Enter start position of a substring: 2
The substring is necessary roughness
```

If the starting position is not valid, an error message is displayed and an error return occurs:

```
Type in a string: unnecessary roughness
Enter start position of a substring: 30
*** Out_of_range exception thrown for start position 30
basic_string::substr
```

Handling Exceptions to Recover from Errors

In addition to reporting errors, exceptions provide us with the opportunity to recover from errors. One common source of errors is user input. When you read a value using the istream extraction operator, if the input is not in the correct format, the stream is placed in the fail state. For example, we can use the following sequence to verify that input was read correctly.

```
if (cin >> i) {
  // Input of i was successful - process i
} else {
  // Problem reading i - attempt to recover
}
```

If the attempt to read a value into variable i is unsuccessful, the input stream cin is placed in the fail state and the condition (cin >> i) is false. However, this approach requires you to test the state of the input stream after each input operation.

Another approach is to have the istream object throw the exception std::ios_base::failure when an input error occurs. This is done by calling the istream member function exceptions and passing it the error flags that will cause an exception to be thrown when they are set by a failed input operation. The call

```
cin.exceptions(ios_base::failbit);
```

will cause the istream cin to throw the ios_base::failure exception when the error flag ios_base::failbit is set. This happens when the stream enters the fail state as a result of incorrectly formatted input.

EXAMPLE 2.8   Function read_int (Listing 2.1) returns the integer value that was typed into the console by the program user. The function argument is the prompt string.

The **while** loop repetition condition (**true**) ensures that the **try** block will execute "forever" or until the user enters a correct data item. The statements

```
cout << prompt;
cin >> num;
```

display the prompt string and read the input into the variable num, if the input contains only digit characters. If not, an ios_base::failure exception is thrown, which is handled by the exception handler. The exception handler displays an error message. The user then has another opportunity to enter a valid numeric string. The statement

```
cin.clear();
```

clears the error flags. The statement

```
cin.ignore(numeric_limits<int>::max(), '\n');
```

skips over the rest of the data on the current data line. The user then has another opportunity to enter a valid numeric string.

....
LISTING 2.1
Function **read_int**

```
#include <string>
#include <iostream>
#include <stdexcept>
#include <limits>
#include <ios>

using namespace std;

/** Function to return an integer data value in response
    to a prompt. If a non-number is entered (as when the
    first character is not a digit) the function will
    prompt for another input after discarding the
    erroneous input.
    @param prompt Message to be displayed
    @return The first valid data value
```

```
  */
  int read_int(const string& prompt) {
    cin.exceptions(ios_base::failbit);
    int num = 0;
    while (true) { // Loop until valid input
      try {
        cout << prompt;
        cin >> num;
        return num;
      } catch (ios_base::failure& ex) {
        cout << "Bad numeric string -- try again\n";
        // Reset the error flag
        cin.clear();
        // Skip current input line
        cin.ignore(numeric_limits<int>::max(), '\n');
      }
    }
  }
```

The Exception Class Hierarchy

As we will discuss in Chapter 3, one class may be derived from another. Such a class inherits the member functions of the class from which it is derived. The standard exception classes listed in Table 2.2 are all derived from the class exception, which has a member function named what. All of the exception classes have a constructor that takes a C-string argument. The value of this argument is saved in the exception object and can be retrieved by calling member function what as shown earlier in Example 2.7.

EXAMPLE 2.9   std::ios_base::failure is a class derived from std::exception. The two exception handlers in the following code must appear in the sequence shown to avoid a warning message. The first exception handler handles a std::ios_base::failure, which occurs when the format of the input is not correct. This exception handler sets the value of age to DEFAULT_AGE, and the program continues. The second exception handler processes any other standard exception, which indicates an unexpected error condition. It outputs an error message, then the string passed to the exception object (ex.what()), and then exits the program with an error indication (abort()).

```
    try {
      // Enter a value for age
      age = read_int("Enter your age  ");
    } catch (std::ios_base::failure& f) {
      cerr << "Invalid number format input\n";
      age = DEFAULT_AGE;
    } catch (std::exception& ex) {
      cerr << "Fatal error occurred in read_int\n";
      cerr << ex.what() << endl;
      abort();
    }
```

⊘ PITFALL

Unreachable Exception Handler

Note that only the first exception handler (**catch** block) that has an appropriate exception type executes. All other exception handlers are skipped. If an exception handler's parameter type is derived from the class in an earlier exception handler, the earlier handler will match that type as well, and the later exception handler cannot execute. In this case the C++ compiler will issue a warning message. To correct this error, switch the order of the exception handlers so that the exception handler for the derived class type comes first.

☑ PROGRAM STYLE

Using Exceptions to Enable Straightforward Code

In computer languages that did not provide exceptions, programmers had to incorporate error-checking logic throughout their code to check for many possibilities, some of which were of low probability. The result was sometimes messy, as follows:

```
Step A
if (Step A successful) {
   Step B
   if (Step B successful) {
      Step C
   } else {
      Report error in Step B
      Clean up after Step A
   }
} else {
   Report error in Step A
}
```

With exceptions this becomes much cleaner, as follows:

```
try {
   Step A
   Step B
   Step C
} catch (exception indicating Step B failed) {
   Report error in Step B
   Clean up after Step A
} catch (exception indicating Step A failed) {
   Report error in Step A
}
```

Catching All Exceptions

Exceptions may be of any type. Although it is recommended that all exceptions be derived from the `std::exception` class, there is no guarantee for this. Thus, even though you include an exception handler for `std::exception`, you might still have an uncaught exception. C++ allows you to define an exception handler that will catch *all* exceptions by using ... as the exception handler parameter. Unfortunately, in that case C++ does not provide a way to determine what exception was caught. Thus, to catch all possible exceptions, we add an additional **catch** clause to the code in Example 2.9:

```
try {
  // Enter a value for age
  age = read_int("Enter your age  ");
} catch (std::ios_base::failure& f) {
  cerr << "Invalid number format input\n";
  age = DEFAULT_AGE;
} catch (std::exception& ex) {
  cerr << "Fatal error occurred in read_int\n";
  cerr << ex.what() << '\n';
  abort();
} catch (...) {
  cerr << "Undefined exception occurred in read_int\n";
  abort();
}
```

EXERCISES FOR SECTION 2.2

SELF-CHECK

1. For each of the following errors, what kind of exception should be thrown?
   a. A subscript value that is equal to the number of elements in the array
   b. An index for a string that is less than 0
   c. A function return value that is too small to be represented
   d. A function return value that is too large to be represented
   e. An input operation that reads an invalid numeric string
   f. Attempting to open an input stream whose associated disk file cannot be found
   g. Attempting to allocate storage for a dynamic array when there is not sufficient memory available

PROGRAMMING

1. Rewrite function `set_element_of_x` in Example 2.3 to throw an exception if the argument passed to `index` is out of range.
2. Write a `read_int` function with three parameters, where the first parameter in the prompt string, the second parameter is the smallest acceptable integer, and the third parameter is the largest acceptable integer. Function `read_int` should return

the first data value that is within the range specified by its second and third parameters. It should throw a `std::invalid_argument` exception if the range of integer values is empty. It should throw a `std::ios_base::failure` exception if the input stream enters a bad state (unrecoverable error) or if the end of file is encountered. If the input is not in a valid format (input stream enters a fail state), the stream should be reset, the current input line discarded, and the user prompted to try again.

3. Write **try-catch** blocks that call function `read_int` from Programming Exercise 2 and handle any exceptions that may be thrown.

2.3 Testing Programs

After you have removed all syntax errors and run-time errors, a program will execute through to normal completion. That is no guarantee that the program does not contain logic errors, however. Because logic errors do not usually cause an error message to be displayed, they frequently go undetected.

Logic errors can be difficult to detect and isolate. If the logic error occurs in a part of the program that always executes, then each run of the program may generate incorrect results. Although this sounds bad, it is actually the best situation, because the error is more likely to be detected if it occurs frequently. If the value that is being computed incorrectly is always displayed, it will be easier to find the logic error. However, if this value is part of a computation and is not displayed, it will be very difficult to track down the error and the section of code that caused it.

The worst kind of logic error is one that occurs in a relatively obscure part of the code that is infrequently executed. If the test data set does not exercise this section of code, the error will not occur during normal program testing. Therefore, the software product will be delivered to its users with a hidden defect. Once that happens, it becomes much more difficult to detect and correct the problem.

Structured Walkthroughs

Most logic errors arise during the design phase and are the result of an incorrect algorithm. They can, however, also result from typographical errors during coding that do not cause syntax or run-time errors. One form of testing that does not involve execution of the program is checking the algorithm carefully before implementing it and checking that the program implements the algorithm. This can be done by hand-tracing the algorithm or program, carefully simulating the execution of each step, and comparing its execution result to one that is calculated by hand.

Hand-tracing an algorithm or program is complicated by the fact that the designer often anticipates what a step should do. Because the designer knows the purpose of each step, it requires quite a bit of discipline to simulate each individual step carefully. For this reason, programmers often work in teams. The designer must explain the algorithm or program to the other team members and simulate its execution with the other team members looking on (called a *structured walkthrough*). Industrial experience has shown that the use of structured walkthroughs is effective in detecting errors and removing defects.

Levels and Types of Testing

Testing is the process of exercising a program (or part of a program) under controlled conditions and verifying that the results are as expected. The purpose of testing is to detect program defects after all syntax errrors have been removed and the program compiles successfully. The more thorough the testing, the greater the likelihood that the defects will be found. However, no amount of testing can guarantee the absence of defects in sufficiently complex programs. The number of test cases required to test all possible inputs and states in which each function may execute can quickly become prohibitively large. That is one reason why commercial software products have successive versions or patches that the user must install. Version n usually corrects the errors that were discovered in version $n - 1$.

Testing is generally done at the following levels:

- *Unit testing* refers to testing the smallest testable piece of the software. In object-oriented design (OOD), the unit will be either a function or a class. The complexity of a function determines whether it should be tested as a separate unit or whether it can be tested as part of its class.
- *Integration testing* involves testing the interactions among units. If the unit is the function, then integration testing includes testing interactions among functions within a class. However, generally it involves testing interactions among several classes.
- *System testing* is the testing of the whole program in the context in which it will be used. A program is generally part of a collection of other programs and hardware, called a system. Sometimes a program will work correctly until some other software is loaded onto the system, and then it will fail for no apparent reason.
- *Acceptance testing* is system testing designed to show that the program meets its functional requirements. It generally involves use of the system in the real environment or as close to the real environment as possible.

There are two types of testing:

- *Black-box testing* tests the item (function, class, or program) based on its interfaces and functional requirements. This is also called *closed-box testing* or *functional testing*. For testing a function, the input parameters are varied over their allowed range and the results compared against independently calculated results. In addition, values outside the allowed range are tested to ensure that the function responds as specified (for example, throws an exception or computes a nominal value). Also, the inputs to a function are not only the explicit parameters of the function but also the values of the data fields of the implicit parameter and any global variables that the function accesses.
- *White-box testing* tests the software element (function, class, or program) using knowledge of its internal structure. Other terms used for this type of testing are *glass-box testing*, *open-box testing*, and *coverage testing*. The goal is to exer-

cise as many of the possible paths through the element as is practical. There are various degrees of coverage. The simplest is *statement coverage*; full statement coverage ensures that each statement is executed at least once. Full *branch coverage* ensures that each choice of each branch (**if** statements, **switch** statements, and loops) is taken. For example, if there are only **if** statements, and they are not nested, then each **if** statement is tried with its condition true and with its condition false. This could possibly be done with two test cases: one with all of the **if** conditions true and one with them all false. Full *path coverage* tests each path through a function. If there are n **if** statements and the **if** statements are not nested, each condition has two possible values, so there could be 2^n possible paths, so full path coverage could require 2^n test cases.

EXAMPLE 2.10 Function `test_function` has a nested **if** statement and displays one of four messages, `Path 1` through `Path 4`, depending on which path is followed. The values passed as its arguments determine the path.

```cpp
#include <iostream>
using std::cout;

void test_function(char a, char b) {
  if (a < 'M') {
    if (b < 'X') {
      cout << "Path 1\n";
    } else {
      cout << "Path 2\n";
    }
  } else {
    if (b < 'C') {
      cout << "Path 3\n";
    } else {
      cout << "Path 4\n";
    }
  }
}
```

To test this function, we need to pass it argument values that cause it to follow all of the different paths. Table 2.3 shows some possible values and the corresponding paths:

TABLE 2.3
Testing All Paths of `test_function`

a	b	Message
'A'	'A'	Path 1
'A'	'Z'	Path 2
'Z'	'A'	Path 3
'Z'	'Z'	Path 4

The values chosen for a and b in Table 2.3 are the smallest and largest uppercase letters. For a more thorough test, you should see what happens when a and b are passed values that are between A and Z. For example, what happens if the value of a changes from L to M? We pick those values because the condition (a < 'M') has different values for each of them.

Also, what happens when a and b are not uppercase letters? For example, if a and b are both digit characters (for example, '2'), the Path 1 message should be displayed because the digit characters precede the uppercase letters (see *A C++ Primer*, Table P.3). If a and b are both lowercase letters, the Path 4 message should be displayed. (Why?) If a is a digit and b is a lowercase letter, the Path 2 message should be displayed. (Why?) As you can see, the number of test cases required to test even a simple function like test_function thoroughly can become quite large.

Preparations for Testing

Although testing is usually done after each unit of the software is coded, a test plan should be developed early in the design stage. Some aspects of a test plan include deciding how the software will be tested, when the tests will occur, who will do the testing, and what test data will be used. If the test plan is developed early in the design stage, testing can take place concurrently with the design and coding. Again, the earlier an error is detected, the easier and less expensive it is to correct it.

Another advantage of deciding on the test plan early is that this will encourage programmers to prepare for testing as they write their code. A good programmer will practice defensive programming and include code that detects unexpected or invalid data values. For example, if a function has the precondition

    pre: n greater than zero.

you can place the assert statement

    assert (n > 0);

at the beginning of the function. The assert macro will provide a diagnostic message and terminate the program in the event that the argument passed to the function is invalid.

Similarly, if a data value being read from the keyboard is supposed to be between 0 and 40, a defensive programmer might read this value using a modified version of the read_int function that has three parameters instead of one (see Programming Exercise 2, Section 2.2). The first parameter would be the prompt string, the second parameter would be the lower limit, and the third parameter would be the upper limit.

    int read_int(string prompt, int low, int high) { ... }

If an integer was read without error, the revised function would verify that this value was in the desired range low to high before returning it. If not, the user would be asked to enter a new number. The following function call could be used to read a data value read between 0 and 40.

    hours = read_int("Enter number of hours worked ", 0, 40);

Testing Tips for Program Systems

Most of the time, you will be testing program systems that contain collections of classes, each with several functions. We provide a list of testing tips to follow in writing these functions next.

1. If the function implements an interface, the interface specification should document the input parameters and the expected results.
2. Carefully document each function parameter and class attribute using comments as you write the code. Also describe the function operation using documentation comments, following the conventions discussed in Section 1.3.
3. Leave a trace of execution by displaying the function name as you enter it.
4. Display the values of all input parameters upon entry to a function. Also display the values of any class attributes that are accessed by this function. Check that these values make sense.
5. Display the values of all function outputs after returning from a function. Also, display any class attributes that are modified by this function. Verify that these values are correct by hand computation.

You should plan for testing as you write each module rather than after the fact. Include the output statements required for Steps 2 through 4 in the original C++ code for the function. When you are satisfied that the function works as desired, you can "remove" the testing statements. One efficient way to remove them is to enclose them in an **if** (TESTING) block as follows:

```
if (TESTING) {
  // Code that you wish to "remove"
  ...
}
```

You would then define TESTING at the beginning of the class as **true** to enable testing,

```
static const bool TESTING = true;
```

or as **false** to disable testing,

```
static const bool TESTING = false;
```

If you need to, you can define different **bool** flags for different kinds of tests.

In Section 2.4 we discuss how to perform testing and debugging using a modern debugger. You will be able to view the effect of each statement's execution without adding output statements to your code.

Developing the Test Data

The test data should be specified during the analysis and design phases. This should be done for the different levels of testing: unit, integration, and system. In black-box testing, we are concerned with the relationship between the unit inputs and outputs. There should be test data to check for all expected inputs as well as unanticipated data. The test plan should also specify the expected unit behavior and outputs for each set of input data.

In white-box testing we are concerned with exercising alternative paths through the code. Thus the test data should be designed to ensure that all **if** statement conditions will evaluate to both **true** and **false**. For nested **if** statements, test different combinations of **true** and **false** values. For **switch** statements, make sure that the selector variable can take on all values listed as case labels and some that are not.

For loops, verify that the result is correct if an immediate exit occurs (zero repetitions). Also verify that the result is correct if only one iteraton is performed and if the maximum number of iterations is performed. Finally, verify that loop repetition can always terminate.

Testing Boundary Conditions

When hand-tracing through an algorithm or performing white-box testing, you must exercise all paths through the algorithm. It is also important to check special cases, called *boundary conditions*, to make sure that the algorithm works for these cases as well as the more common ones. For example, if you are testing a function that searches for a particular target element in an array, the code may contain a search loop such as

```
for (int i = 0; i < x_length; i++) {
  if (x[i] == target)
    return i;
}
```

Testing the boundary conditions means that you should make sure that the function works for all the cases in the following list. The first four test the boundary conditions for the loop and would be required in white-box testing. However, a program tester using black-box testing should also test these four cases. The next case (target in the middle) is not a boundary case, but it is a typical situation that should also be tested. The rest are boundary conditions for an array search that should be tested in either white-box or black-box testing.

- The target element is the first array element (x[0] == target is true).
- The target element is only in the last array element (x[x_length - 1] == target is true).
- The target element is not in the array (x[i] == target is always false).
- There are multiple occurrences of the target element (x[i] == target is true for more than one value of i).
- The target element is somewhere in the middle of the array.
- The array has only one element.
- The array has no elements.

To carry out the test, you can write a main function that creates an array to be searched. The easiest way to create such an array is to declare it using an initializer list. Listing 2.2 shows an array search function, and Listing 2.3 shows a main function that tests all the listed cases for it. In function search, the array to be searched is the first parameter, and the target of the search is the second parameter. The function either returns the subscript of the first occurrence of the target, or −1 if the target is not present. The value −1 is chosen because array subscripts are all greater than or equal to 0.

The function verify is passed the array to be searched, the array length, the target value, and the expected return value. It calls the search function and then prints the actual and expected results.

```
int actual = search(x, x_length, target);
cout << "search(x, " << target << ") is "
     << actual << ", expected " << expected;
```

It then prints either ":   Pass\n" or ":   ****Fail\n" depending on whether or not the expected value is equal to the actual value.

```
if (actual == expected)
  cout << ":   Pass\n";
else
  cout << ":   ****Fail\n";
```

There are calls to verify for each one of the test cases in the list. For example, the first call,

```
verify(x, x_length, 5, 0);
```

searches array x for a target 5, which is expected to be at x[0]. (The fourth argument is therefore 0). The line displayed should be:

```
search(x, 5) is 0, expected 0:   Pass
```

Figure 2.1 shows the result of a sample run. To verify that function search is correct, check for Pass at the end of each output line. For large-scale testing, you could write a program to do this.

In test_array_search, the line

```
const int x_length = sizeof(x) / sizeof(int);
```

computes the number of items in the test array. The compile time function sizeof returns the size of its argument in bytes. Therefore, sizeof(int) returns the size, in bytes, of an **int**, and sizeof(x) returns the size of the array x. The quotient is the number of items in array x.

LISTING 2.2
array_search.cpp

```
/** Searches an array to find the first occurrence of a target.
    @param x Array to search
    @param x_length The length of the array
    @param target Target to search for
    @return The subscript of first occurrence if found;
            otherwise, return -1.
*/
int search(int x[], int x_length, int target) {
  for (int i = 0; i < x_length; i++) {
    if (x[i] == target)
      return i;
  }

  // target not found
  return -1;
}
```

....
LISTING 2.3
test_array_search.cpp

```cpp
#include <iostream>
using std::cout;

// Declare function to be tested.
int search(int[], int, int);

// Declare verify function.
void verify(int[], int, int, int);

/** main function.   */
int main() {
  int x[] = {5, 12, 15, 4, 8, 12, 7};    // Array to search.
  // Compute length of array.
  const int x_length = sizeof(x) / sizeof(int);

  // Test for target as first element.
  verify(x, x_length, 5, 0);
  // Test for target as last element.
  verify(x, x_length, 7, 6);
  // Test for target not in array.
  verify(x, x_length, -5, -1);
  // Test for multiple occurrences of target.
  verify(x, x_length, 12, 1);
  // Test for target somewhere in middle.
  verify(x, x_length, 4, 3);

  // Test for 1-element array.
  int y[1] = {10};
  const int y_length = 1;
  verify(y, y_length, 10, 0);
  verify(y, y_length, -10, -1);

  // Test for an empty array.
  int* z = NULL;
  verify(z, 0, 10, -1);
}

/** Call the search function with the specified parameters and
    verify the expected result.
    @param x The array to be searched
    @param x_length The length of the array to be searched
    @param target The target to be found
    @param expected The expected result
*/
void verify(int x[], int x_length, int target, int expected) {
  int actual = search(x, x_length, target);
  cout << "search(x, " << target << ") is "
       << actual << ", expected " << expected;
  if (actual == expected)
    cout << ":  Pass\n";
  else
    cout << ":   ****Fail\n";
}
```

FIGURE 2.1

Testing Function `search`

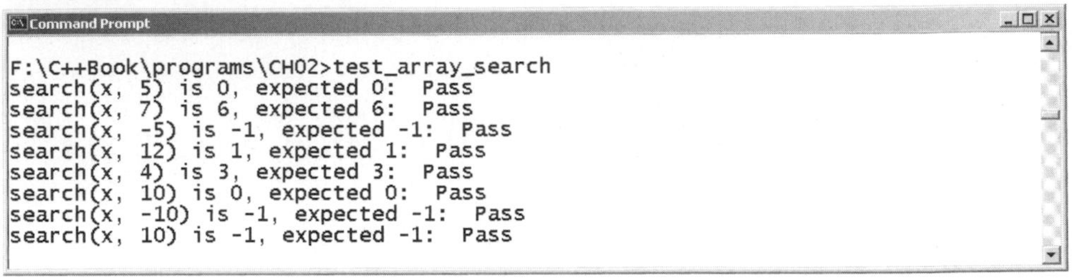

```
Command Prompt                                                    _ |□| x|

F:\C++Book\programs\CH02>test_array_search
search(x, 5) is 0, expected 0:  Pass
search(x, 7) is 6, expected 6:  Pass
search(x, -5) is -1, expected -1:  Pass
search(x, 12) is 1, expected 1:  Pass
search(x, 4) is 3, expected 3:  Pass
search(x, 10) is 0, expected 0:  Pass
search(x, -10) is -1, expected -1:  Pass
search(x, 10) is -1, expected -1:  Pass
```

Who Does the Testing?

Normally testing is done by the programmer, by other members of the software team who did not code the module being tested, and by the final users of the software product. It is extremely important not to rely only on the programmers who coded a module for testing it, because programmers are often blind to their own oversights. If they neglected to account for a possible error in the design, they are also likely to neglect testing for it. Some companies have special testing groups who are experts at finding defects in other programmers' code.

The reason for involving future users is to determine whether they have difficulty in interpreting prompts for data. Because they are not as knowledgeable about coding, users are more likely to make data entry errors than members of the programming or testing teams are.

Companies also have quality assurance (QA) organizations that verify that the testing process is performed correctly. Members of the QA organization typically do not do the testing themselves, but they independently review the test plans, witness the conduct of the tests, and independently verify the results.

Generally the programmer who wrote the unit does unit testing, while a separate test team does integration testing and system testing. However, many organizations are finding that having other members of the programming team do unit testing is very effective. There is one methodology (called *Extreme Programming*) in which programmers work in pairs; one writes the code and the other writes the tests. The tester also observes the coder while the code is being written. They take turns so that each team member is involved in both coding and testing. The units are kept small so that they can be coded and tested quickly.

Stubs

Although we want to do unit testing as soon as possible, it may be difficult to test a function or a class that interacts with other functions or classes. The problem is that not all functions and not all classes will be completed at the same time. So if a function in class A calls a function defined in class B (not yet written), the unit test for class A cannot be performed without the help of a replacement function for the one in class B. The replacement for a function that has not yet been implemented or tested is called a *stub*. A stub has the same header as the function it replaces, but its body only displays a message indicating that the stub was called.

EXAMPLE 2.11   The following function is a stub for a **void** function save. The stub will enable a function that calls save to be tested even though the real function save has not been written.

```
/** Function to save the directory.
    pre:  The directory has been loaded with data.
    post: The directory contents have been written back to the
          file as name-number pairs on adjacent lines.
          modified is reset to false.
*/
void save() {
  cout << "Stub for save has been called\n";
  modified = false;
}
```

Besides displaying an identification message, a stub can print out the values of the inputs and can assign predictable values (such as 0 or 1) to any outputs to prevent execution errors caused by undefined values. Also, if a function is supposed to change the state of a data field, the stub can do so (modified is set to **false** by the stub in this example). If a client program calls one or more stubs, the message printed by each stub when it is executed provides a trace of the call sequence and enables the programmer to determine whether the flow of control within the client program is correct.

Drivers

Another testing tool for a function is a driver program. A *driver program* declares any necessary object instances and variables, assigns values to any of the function's inputs (as specified in the function's preconditions), calls the function, and displays the values of any outputs returned by the function. When you run a C++ program, execution begins at the main function in the class you designate as the one to execute. The main function shown in Listing 2.3 is a driver program to test function search.

Testing a Class

In Section 1.6 we specified the Directory_Entry class. The coding of this class was left as an exercise. Below we show a test driver as a main function for this class. The test driver contains several test cases.

When main executes, two Directory_Entry objects are created and then displayed on the console. Both the name and number attributes are displayed. We can use these test cases to verify that the constructor and functions get_name and get_number perform as expected.

```
// Create some directory entries.
Directory_Entry tom("Tom", "123-555-4567");
Directory_Entry dick("Dick", "321-555-9876");
// Display the entries.
cout << "tom -- name: " << tom.get_name()
     << " number: " << tom.get_number() << '\n';
cout << "dick -- name: " << dick.get_name()
     << " number: " << dick.get_number() << '\n';
```

Next we test the == operator. Because the two objects have different name fields, we expect that they are not equal.

```
// See if they are equal.
if (tom == dick)
  cout << "FAILURE -- tom and dick are equal\n";
else
  cout << "SUCCESS -- tom and dick are not equal\n";
if (dick == tom)
  cout << "FAILURE -- tom and dick are equal\n";
else
  cout << "SUCCESS -- tom and dick are not equal\n";
```

Then we create a third Directory_Entry object with the same name as one of the others. We expect this to be equal to the one with the same name.

```
// Create another directory entry.
Directory_Entry tom2("Tom", "888-555-9999");
cout << "tom2 -- name: " << tom2.get_name()
     << " number: " << tom2.get_number() << '\n';
// See whether the two toms are equal.
if (tom == tom2)
  cout << "SUCCESS -- tom and tom2 are equal\n";
else
  cout << "FAILURE -- tom and tom2 are not equal\n";
if (tom2 == tom)
  cout << "SUCCESS -- tom and tom2 are equal\n";
else
  cout << "FAILURE -- tom and tom2 are not equal\n";
```

Finally we test the set_number function by changing the number of one of the objects and displaying it.

```
dick.set_number(tom.get_number());
// Dick and Tom should have the same number
cout << "dick -- name: " << dick.get_name()
     << " dick -- number: " << dick.get_number() << '\n';
```

Figure 2.2 shows the results of testing the Directory_Entry class.

Using a Test Framework

The test driver for the Directory_Entry class relied on visual verification of the output. In some instances the user needed to know the expected result, and in others we displayed a success/failure indication. We could have added code to verify the expected result for all of the tests, but that would have made our test code much longer.

FIGURE 2.2

FIGURE 2.2
Test of `Directory_Entry` Class

```
Command Prompt                                                      _□×
D:\C++Book\programs\CH02>test_directory_entry
tom -- name: Tom number: 123-555-4567
dick -- name: Dick number: 321-555-9876
SUCCESS -- tom and dick are not equal
SUCCESS -- tom and dick are not equal
tom2 -- name: Tom number: 888-555-9999
SUCCESS -- tom and tom2 are equal
SUCCESS -- tom and tom2 are equal
dick -- name: Dick dick -- number: 123-555-4567
```

This test driver contained several test cases. A test case is an individual test. A collection of test cases is known as a *test suite*. A program that executes a series of tests and reports the results is known as a *test harness*. Thus the test driver for the `Directory_Entry` class was both a test harness and a test suite.

A *test framework* is a software product that facilitates writing test cases, organizing the test cases into test suites, running the test suites, and reporting the results. One test framework often used for C++ projects is CppUnit, an open-source product that can be used in a stand-alone mode and is available from `cppunit.sourceforge.net`. We describe its usage in Appendix C.

Regression Testing

The test plan, test suite (stubs and drivers), and test results should be saved. Whenever a change is made to a function, class, or program, the tests can and should be rerun to determine that the change did not cause an unintended consequence. This rerunning of tests and verifying that nothing changed is called *regression testing*.

Integration Testing

Another aspect of testing a system is called integration testing. In integration testing, the program tester must determine whether the individual components of the system, which have been separately tested, can be integrated with other components. (In this context the word *component* is used to represent a function, a class, or a collection of classes.)

Each phase of integration testing deals with larger components, progressing from individual units, such as functions or classes, and ending with the entire system. For example, after two units are completed, integration testing must determine whether the two units can work together. Once the entire system is completed, integration testing must determine whether that system is compatible with other systems in the computing environment in which it will be used.

If you have prepared UML diagrams as system documentation, you can use these diagrams to determine the expected interaction between units in your program system. Then, as you add a new unit to your system, you can validate its interaction with other units.

EXERCISES FOR SECTION 2.3

SELF-CHECK

1. Why is it a good idea to use the structured walkthrough approach when hand-tracing an algorithm?
2. List two boundary conditions that should be checked when testing function read_int with three parameters (Programming Exercise 2, Section 2.2) where the first parameter is the prompt string, the second parameter is the smallest acceptable integer, and the third parameter is the largest acceptable integer. Function read_int should return the first data value that is within the range specified by its second and third parameters.
3. Explain why a function that does not match its declaration in the interface would not be discovered during white-box testing.
4. Devise a set of data to test the function read_int with three parameters using:
   a. White-box testing
   b. Black-box testing
5. During which phase of testing would each of the following tests be performed?
   a. Testing whether a function worked properly at all its boundary conditions
   b. Testing whether class A can use class B as a component
   c. Testing whether a phone directory application and a word-processing application can run simultaneously on a PC
   d. Testing whether function search can search an array that was returned by function build_array
   e. Testing whether a class with an array data field can use static function search in class Array_Search

PROGRAMMING

1. Write a driver program to test function read_int described in Self-Check Exercise 2.
2. Write a stub to use in place of function read_int.
3. Write a search function with four parameters: the search array, the target, the start subscript, and the finish subscript. The last two parameters indicate the part of the array that should be searched. Your function should catch or throw exceptions where warranted. Write a driver program to test this function.

2.4 Debugging a Program

In this section we will discuss the process of *debugging* (removing errors), both with and without the use of a debugger program. Debugging is the major activity performed by programmers during the testing phase. Testing determines whether you have an error; during debugging you determine the cause of run-time and logic errors and correct them, without introducing new ones. If you have followed the suggestions for testing described in the previous section, you will be well prepared to debug your program.

Debugging is like detective work. To debug a program, you must carefully inspect the information displayed by your program, starting at the beginning, to determine whether what you see is what you expect. For example, if the result returned by a function is incorrect but the arguments (if any) passed to the function had the correct values, then there is a problem inside the function. You can try to trace through the function to see whether you can find the source of the error and correct it. If you can't, you may need more information. One way to get that information is to insert additional diagnostic output statements in the function. For example, if the function contains a loop, you may want to display the values of loop control variables during loop execution.

EXAMPLE 2.12   The function read_int in Listing 2.4 does not seem to recognize that a value is outside of the specified range. Instead it appears to accept any input value.

LISTING 2.4
The Function read_int

```cpp
#include <string>
#include <iostream>
#include <stdexcept>
#include <limits>

using namespace std;

/** Function to return an integer data value between two
    specified end points.
    pre: min_n <= max_n
    @param prompt Message to be displayed
    @param min_n Smallest value in range
    @param max_n Largest value in range
    @throws invalid_argument if min_n > max_n
    @return The first data value that is in range
*/
int read_int(const string& prompt, int min_n, int max_n) {
  if (min_n > max_n)
    throw invalid_argument("In read_int, min_n not <= max_n");
  bool in_range = false;
  int num = 0;
  while (!in_range) {
    cout << prompt;
    if (cin >> num) {
      in_range = min_n <= num <= max_n;
    } else {
      cout << "Bad numeric string -- try again\n";
      // Reset the error flag.
      cin.clear();
      // Skip current input line.
      cin.ignore(numeric_limits<int>::max(), '\n');
    }
  }
  return num;
}
```

To determine the source of the problem, you should insert a diagnostic output statement that displays the value of min_n, max_n, n, and in_range. You could insert the statement

```
cout << "min_n:" << min_n << " max_n:" << max_n << " num:" << num
    << " in_range:" << in_range << '\n';
```

after the statement:

```
in_range = min_n <= num <= max_n;
```

This will show that min_n, max_n, and num all have the expected values, but that in_range is not correct! Therefore, there must be something wrong with the assignment to in_range. This is an example of valid syntax that does not mean what you may think. It is common in mathematics to use the expression $x_{low} \leq x \leq x_{high}$. However, in C++ the expression min_n <= n <= max_n first evaluates min_n <= n. The resulting **bool** value is then converted to an **int** value, 0 for **false** and 1 for **true**, and then compared to max_n. If max_n is greater than or equal to 1, the expression is always true. You need to change the calculation of in_range to

```
in_range = min_n <= num && num <= max_n;
```

Using a Debugger

Debugger programs were available long before IDEs, and they can still be used from the command line. If you are using an IDE, you will generally have a built-in debugger program. A debugger can execute your program incrementally rather than all at once. After each increment of the program executes, the debugger pauses, and you can view the contents of variables to determine whether the statement(s) executed as expected. You can inspect all the program variables without needing to insert diagnostic output statements. When you have finished examining the program variables, you direct the debugger to execute the next increment.

You can choose to execute in increments as small as one program statement (called *single-step execution*) to see the effect of each statement's execution. Another possibility is to set *breakpoints* in your program to divide it into sections. The debugger can execute all the statements from one breakpoint to the next as a group. For example, if you wanted to see the effects of a loop's execution but did not want to step through every iteration, you could set breakpoints at the statements just before and just after the loop.

When your program pauses, if the next statement contains a call to a function, you can select single-step execution in the function being called (that is, *step into* the function). Alternatively, you can execute all the function statements as a group and pause after the return from the function execution (that is, *step over* the function).

The actual mechanics of using a debugger depend on the IDE that you are using. However, the process that you follow is similar among IDEs, and if you understand the process for one, you should be able to use any debugger. In this section we demonstrate how to use the debugger in the Eclipse Platform. The Eclipse Platform is an open-source project available from www.eclipse.org. This platform was originally developed for Java, but there is a configuration option (called a plug-in) that supports C++.

Figure 2.3 is the display produced by this debugger at the beginning of debugging the read_int function. The source editor window displays the test program. The Run pull-down menu shows the options for executing the code. To start the debugger we select Debug. Figure 2.4 shows the display after the debugger has started. The source window (at the bottom left) shows that the statement:

```
int i = read_int("Enter a number between 1 and 10: ", 1, 10);
```

is the next to be executed. We select Step Into, a common technique for starting single-step execution, by selecting the icon with the curved yellow arrow pointing between the two dots (where the cursor arrow appears in Fig. 2.4). A window (such as the Variables window at the upper right) typically shows the values of data fields and local variables. In this case there is one local variable for function main: the **int** variable i, which currently has an undefined value. (The actual number displayed is whatever happens to have been in the memory location when the object containing this variable was created.) The arrow to the left of the highlighted line in the source editor window indicates the next step to execute (the call to function read_int). Select Step Into again to execute the individual statements of function read_int.

FIGURE 2.3
Starting the Debugger in Eclipse

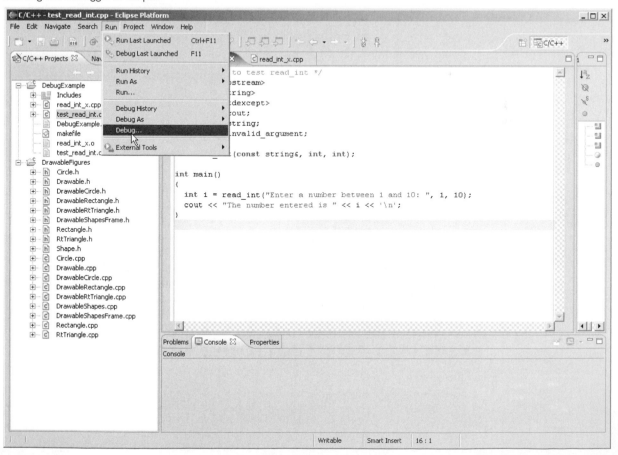

FIGURE 2.4

Using the Debugger in Eclipse

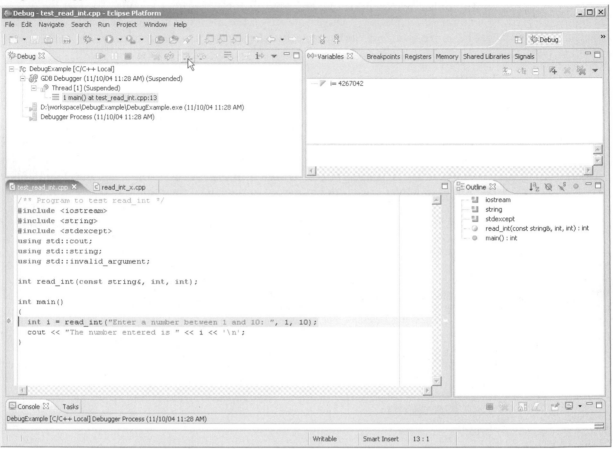

Figure 2.5 shows the editor and Local Variables windows after we have entered 11 and executed the statement

```
in_range = min_n <= num <= max_n;
```

The contents of num is 11, the value of in_range is true! The next statement to execute is highlighted. It is the loop header, which tests the loop repetition condition. Although we expect the condition to be false, it is true (why?).

EXERCISES FOR SECTION 2.4

SELF-CHECK

1. The following function does not appear to be working properly. Explain where you would add diagnostic output statements to debug it, and give an example of each statement. Write a driver program and test the function.

FIGURE 2.5

The Editor and Debugging Windows in Eclipse

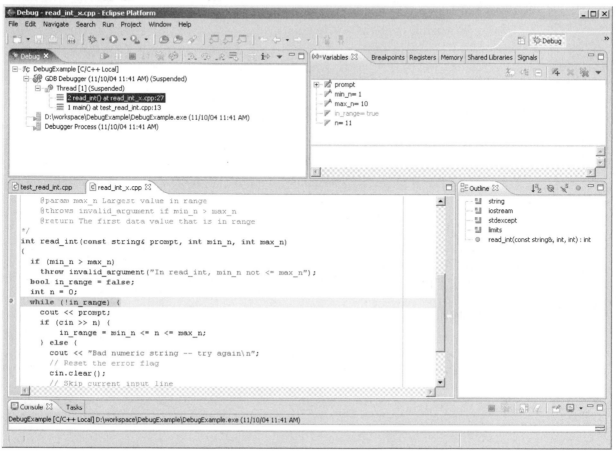

```cpp
/** Finds the largest value in array elements x[start] through x[last].
    pre: first <= last.
    @param x Array whose largest value is found
    @param start First subscript in range
    @param last Last subscript in range
    @return The largest value of x[start] through x[last]
*/
int find_max(int x[], int start, int last) {
  if (start > last)
    throw invalid_argument("Empty range");
  int max_so_far = 0;
  for (int i = start; i < last; i++) {
    if (x[i] > max_so_far)
      max_so_far = i;
  }
  return max_so_far;
}
```

2. Explain the difference between selecting Step Into and Step Over during debugging.

1. After debugging, provide a corrected version of the function in Self-Check Exercise 1. Leave the debugging statements in, but execute them only when the global constant TESTING is **true**.

2.5 Reasoning about Programs: Assertions and Loop Invariants

In Section 2.3 we discussed some aspects of program and system testing. In this section we describe some formal concepts that are intended to help a programmer prove that a program or function is correct. We will focus on using assertions and loop invariants to help you reason about an algorithm. Our goal is just to introduce the concepts and give you a feel for what can be done. Although it would be very desirable to be able to prove the correctness of a program, we usually cannot do this. In practice, formal verification is used more as a documentation tool and to enable a programmer to reason about a program than as a strict proof of correctness. Formal verification of programs is an active area of computer science research.

Assertions

An important part of formal verification is to document a program using *assertions*: logical statements about the program that are "asserted" to be true. An assertion is generally written as a comment, and it describes what is supposed to be true about the program variables at that point. Preconditions and postconditions are assertion statements. A precondition is an assertion about the state of the program (generally the input parameters) before a function is executed, and a postcondition is an assertion about the state when the function finishes.

EXAMPLE 2.13   We rewrite function search, shown earlier, with an assertion comment following loop exit.

```
int search(int x[], int x_length, int target) {
  for (int i = 0; i < x_length; i++) {
    if (x[i] == target)
      return i;
  }

  // assert: all elements were tested and target not found.
  return -1;
}
```

The assertion states what we know to be true at this point: All elements were tested and the target was not found, because, if it had been, we would have executed the **return** statement in the loop.

Loop Invariants

We stated earlier that loops are a very common source of program errors. It is often difficult to determine that a loop body executes exactly the right number of times or that loop execution causes the desired change in program variables. Programmers can use a special type of assertion, called a *loop invariant*, to help prove that a loop meets its specification. A loop invariant is a statement (a Boolean expression) that is true before loop execution begins, at the beginning of each repetition of the loop body, and just after loop exit. It is called an invariant because it is a relationship that remains true at all times as loop execution progresses; that is, the execution of the loop body preserves the invariant. If we can determine the loop invariant for the process that we want a loop to perform and then verify that the execution of a C++ loop preserves the invariant, then we can be quite confident that the C++ loop is correct.

A proposed invariant for a search loop that finds the first occurrence of a target value might be the following: If i is the subscript of the array element we are testing in the loop,

```
for all k, such that 0 <= k < i, x[k] != target
```

In English, this means "For all nonnegative integer values of k less than i, the kth element of x is not equal to the `target`." Let's verify that this is an invariant.

- *The invariant must be true before loop execution begins:* Before loop execution begins, i would be 0 and there is no nonnegative integer less than 0, so there are no possible values of k and thus no value of k such that x[k] is equal to `target`, so the invariant must be true.

- *The invariant must be true at the beginning of each repetition of the loop:* During loop repetition, we should compare x[i] to the `target` and exit the loop if the target is found. However, if x[k] was equal to `target` for a value of k < i, we would have already found the `target`, exited the loop, and not started the present repetition, so the invariant must be true.

- *The invariant must be true after loop exit:* We exit the loop after testing all array elements and finding that x[k] != `target` for all k < x_length, so the invariant must be true.

Now that we have the invariant, we must write a C++ loop that preserves it. Of course, we already have one, but let's pretend that we don't.

```
int i = 0;
// invariant: for all k, such that 0 <= k < i, x[k] != target
while (i < x_length) {
  if (x[i] == target)
    return i;    // target found at i
  i++;           // Test next element
}

// assert: for all k, such that 0 <= k < i, x[k] != target
//         and i >= x_length
return -1;       // target not found
```

Let's show that this loop preserves the invariant. Variable i is initially 0, so the invariant is certainly true before loop repetition begins. Prior to each loop repetition, the invariant must be true for the current value of i, or we would have executed the **return** statement with a value of k less than i. Loop exit occurs when the loop repetition condition fails (i is x_length), and because this occurs only if we did not find the target, x[k] != target must be true for all k < x_length (the current value of i), so the loop invariant is still true. When the loop ends, the invariant is still true, but the loop repetition condition is now false. We can therefore combine the loop invariant and the negation of the loop repetition condition to create the assertion that follows the loop.

This discussion used the loop invariant as a guide to writing a loop that preserved the invariant. A topic of computer science research is proving that a loop is correct by writing an assertion that is a loop precondition and an assertion that is a loop postcondition (an assertion that "ANDs" the loop invariant and the negation of the loop repetition condition), and then proving that the postcondition assertion follows from the precondition assertion. This would be a proof that the loop is correct.

The C++ assert Macro

Assertions written as comments are valuable for understanding a program, but the programmer must check the actual code manually. C++ allows us to give an assertion "teeth" by writing it using the C++ assert macro. This macro is defined in the header <cassert> and described in the syntax box. Generally the assert macro

---

✳ DESIGN CONCEPT

Loop Invariants as a Design Tool

You can write the loop invariant as a specification for a loop and use that specification to help determine the loop initialization, the loop repetition condition, and the loop body. For example, we can write the following loop invariant to describe a summation loop that adds *n* data items:

```
// invariant: sum is the sum of all the data read so far, and the
// count of data items read is less than or equal to n.
```

From the loop invariant we can determine that

- The loop initialization is
```
sum = 0.0;
count = 0;
```

- The loop repetition test is
```
count < n
```

- The loop body is
```
cout << "Enter next number: ";
cin >> next;
sum = sum + next;
count = count + 1;
```

Given all this information, it becomes a simple task to write the summation loop (see Programming Exercise 2).

SYNTAX   Assertion Statement

FORM:

assert(*expression*);

EXAMPLE:

assert(x == 5);

INTERPRETATION:

If the *expression* evaluates to **false**, then the program writes an error message and aborts. The error message includes the expression that failed, the source file name, and the line number of the assertion statement.

---

defined in the standard library implementation calls an internally defined function to print an error message and terminate the program if the condition asserted is not true. This internal function is passed the string representation of the assertion and the file name and line number as parameters.

The actual definition of this macro varies with different implementations. A functionally equivalent macro is the following:

```
#define kw_assert(x)\
if (!(x)) {\
  std::cerr << "Assertion " << #x << " failed\n";\
  std::cerr << "Line " << __LINE__ << " in file " << __FILE__ << "\n";\
  exit(1);\
}
```

EXERCISES FOR SECTION 2.5

SELF-CHECK

1. Write the loop invariant and the assertion following the **while** loop in function read_int.

PROGRAMMING

1. Write a function that returns the number of digits in an arbitrary integer (number). Your solution should include a **while** loop for which the following is a valid loop invariant:

    ```
    // invariant:
    // count >= 0 and number has been
    // divided by 10 count times.
    ```

    and the following assertion would be valid after exit from the loop:

    ```
    // assert: count is the number of digits.
    ```

2. Write a program fragment that implements the loop whose invariant is described in the Design Concept discussion "Loop Invariants as a Design Tool."

2.6 Efficiency of Algorithms

You can't easily measure the amount of time it takes to run a program with modern computers. When you issue the command

```
my_program
```

(or click the Run button of your IDE), the operating system first loads your program. Much of the time taken to execute the program is taken up by this step. If you run your program a second time immediately after the first, it may seem to take less time. This is because the operating system may have kept the files in a local memory area called a cache. However, if you have a large enough or complicated enough problem, then the actual running time of your program will dominate the time required to load it.

Because it is very difficult to get a precise measure of the performance of an algorithm or program, we normally try to approximate the effect of a *change* in the number of data items, *n*, that an algorithm processes. In this way, we can see how an algorithm's execution time increases with respect to *n*, so we can compare two algorithms by examining their growth rates.

For many problems there are algorithms that are relatively obvious but inefficient. Although computers are getting faster, with larger memories, every day, there are algorithms whose growth rate is so large that no computer, no matter how fast or with how much memory, can solve the problem above a certain size. Furthermore, if a problem that has been too large to be solved can now be solved with the latest, biggest, and fastest supercomputer, adding a few more inputs may make the problem impractical, if not impossible, again. Therefore, it is important to have some idea of the relative efficiency of different algorithms. Next, we see how we might obtain such an idea by examining three functions in the following examples.

EXAMPLE 2.14   Consider the following function, which searches an array for a value:

```
int search(int x[], int x_length, int target) {
  for (int i = 0; i < x_length; i++) {
    if (x[i] == target)
      return i;
  }

  // target not found
  return -1;
}
```

If the target is not present in the array, then the **for** loop body will be executed x_length times. If the target is present, it could be anywhere. If we consider the average over all cases where the target is present, then the loop body will execute x_length/2 times. Therefore the total execution time is directly proportional to x_length. If we doubled the size of the array, we would expect the time to double (not counting the overhead discussed earlier).

EXAMPLE 2.15   Now let us consider another problem. We want to find out whether two arrays have no common elements. We can use our search function to search one array for values that are in the other.

```
/** Determine whether two arrays have no common elements.
    @param x One array
    @param x_length The length of the x array
    @param y The other array
    @param y_length The length of the y array
    @return true if there are no common elements
*/
bool are_different(int x[], int x_length, int y[], int y_length) {
  for (int i = 0; i < x_length; i++) {
    if (search(y, y_length, x[i]) != -1)
      return false;
  }
  return true;
}
```

The loop body will execute x_length times. But it will call search, whose loop body will execute y_length times for each of the x_length times it is called. Therefore, the total execution time would be proportional to the product of x_length and y_length.

EXAMPLE 2.16   Let us consider the problem of determining whether each item in an array is unique. We could write the following function.

```
/** Determine whether the contents of an array are all unique.
    @param x The array
    @param x_length The length of the array
    @return true if all elements of x are unique
*/
bool are_unique(int x[], int x_length) {
  for (int i = 0; i < x_length; i++) {
    for (int j = 0; j < x_length; j++) {
      if (i != j && x[i] == x[j])
        return false;
    }
  }
  return true;
}
```

If all values are unique, the **for** loop with i as its index will execute x_length times. Inside this loop the **for** loop with j as its index will also execute x_length times. Thus the total number of times the loop body of the innermost loop will execute is $(x\_length)^2$.

EXAMPLE 2.17   The function we showed in Example 2.16 is very inefficient. We do twice as many tests as necessary. We can rewrite it as follows:

```
/** Determine whether the contents of an array are all unique.
    @param x The array
    @param x_length The length of the array
    @return true if all elements of x are unique
*/
bool are_unique(int x[], int x_length) {
  for (int i = 0; i < x_length; i++) {
    for (int j = i + 1; j < x_length; j++) {
      if (x[i] == x[j])
        return false;
    }
  }
  return true;
}
```

The first time the **for** loop with the j index will execute x_length - 1 times. The second time it will execute x_length - 2 times, and so on. The last time it will execute just once. The total number of times it will execute is:

x_length - 1 + x_length - 2 + · · · + 2 + 1

The series $1 + 2 + 3 + \cdots + (n - 1)$ is a well-known series that has a value of

$$\frac{n \times (n - 1)}{2}$$

Therefore, this sum is

x_length × (x_length - 1)/2 *or* $0.5 \times (x\_length)^2 - 0.5 \times x\_length$.

Big-O Notation

Today, the type of analysis just illustrated is more important to the development of efficient software than measuring the milliseconds in which a program runs on a particular computer. Understanding how the execution time (and memory requirements) of an algorithm grow as a function of increasing input size gives programmers a tool for comparing various algorithms and how they will perform. Computer scientists have developed useful terminology and notation for investigating and describing the relationship between input size and execution time. For example, if the time is approximately doubled when the number of inputs, n, is doubled, then the algorithm grows at a linear rate. Thus we say that the growth rate has an order of n. On the other hand, if the time is approximately quadrupled when the number of inputs is doubled, then the algorithm grows at a quadratic rate. In this case we say that the growth rate has an order of n^2.

In the previous section we looked at four functions: one whose execution time was related to x_length, another whose execution time was related to x_length times y_length, one whose execution time was related to $(x\_length)^2$, and one whose execution time was related to $(x\_length)^2$ and x_length. Computer scientists use the notation $O(n)$ to represent the first case, $O(n \times m)$ to represent the second, and $O(n^2)$ to represent the third and fourth, where n is x_length and m is y_length. The symbol O (which you will see in a variety of type faces and styles in computer science literature) can be thought of as an abbreviation for "order of magnitude". This notation is called *big-O notation*.

A simple way to determine the big-O of an algorithm or program is to look at the loops and to see whether the loops are nested. Assuming that the loop body consists only of simple statements, a single loop is $O(n)$, a nested loop is $O(n^2)$, a nested loop in a nested loop is $O(n^3)$, and so on. However, you also must examine the number of times the loop executes.

Consider the following:

```
for (int i = 1; i < x_length; i *= 2) {
   Do something with x[i]
}
```

The loop body will execute $k - 1$ times with i having the following values: 1, 2, 4, 8, 16, 32, . . . , 2^k until 2^k is greater than x_length. Since $2^{k-1} \leq$ x_length $< 2^k$ and $\log_2 2^k$ is k, we know that $k - 1 \leq \log_2($x_length$) < k$. Thus we say that this loop is $O(\log n)$. The logarithm function grows slowly. The log to the base 2 of 1,000,000 is approximately 20. Typically, in analyzing the running time of algorithms, we use logarithms to the base 2.

Formal Definition of Big-O

Consider a program that is structured as follows:

```
for (int i = 0; i < n; i++) {
   for (int j = 0; j < n; j++) {
      Simple Statement
   }
}
for (int k = 0; i < n; k++) {
   Simple Statement 1
   Simple Statement 2
   Simple Statement 3
   Simple Statement 4
   Simple Statement 5
}
Simple Statement 6
Simple Statement 7
. . .
Simple Statement 30
```

Let us assume that each *Simple Statement* takes one unit of time and that the **for** statements are free. The nested loop executes a *Simple Statement* n^2 times. Then 5 *Simple Statements* are executed n times. Finally, 25 *Simple Statements* are executed. We would then conclude that the expression

$$T(n) = n^2 + 5n + 25$$

expresses the relationship between processing time and n (the number of data items processed in the loop), where $T(n)$ represents the processing time as a function of n.

In terms of $T(n)$, formally, the big-O notation

$$T(n) = O(f(n))$$

means that there exist two constants, n_0 and c greater than zero, and a function, $f(n)$, such that for all $n > n_0$, $cf(n) \geq T(n)$. In other words, as n gets sufficiently large (larger than n_0), there is some constant c for which the processing time will always be less than or equal to $cf(n)$, so $cf(n)$ is an upper bound on the performance. The performance will never be worse than $cf(n)$ and may be better.

If we can determine how the value of $f(n)$ increases with n, we know how the processing time will increase with n. Often the growth rate of $f(n)$ will be determined by the growth rate of the fastest-growing term (the one with the largest exponent), which in this case is the n^2 term. This means that the algorithm in this example is an $O(n^2)$ algorithm rather than an $O(n^2 + 5n + 25)$ algorithm. In general, it is safe to ignore all constants and drop the lower-order terms when determining the order of magnitude for an algorithm.

EXAMPLE 2.18

Given $T(n) = n^2 + 5n + 25$, we want to show that this is indeed $O(n^2)$. Thus we want to show that there are constants n_0 and c such that for all $n > n_0$, $cn^2 > n^2 + 5n + 25$.

To solve this we need to find a point where

$$cn^2 = n^2 + 5n + 25$$

If we let n be n_0 and solve for c, we get

$$c = 1 + 5/n_0 + 25/n_0^2$$

For an n_0 of 5, this gives us a c of 3. So $3n^2 > n^2 + 5n + 25$ for all n greater than 5, as shown in Figure 2.6.

FIGURE 2.6

$3n^2$ versus $n^2 + 5n + 25$

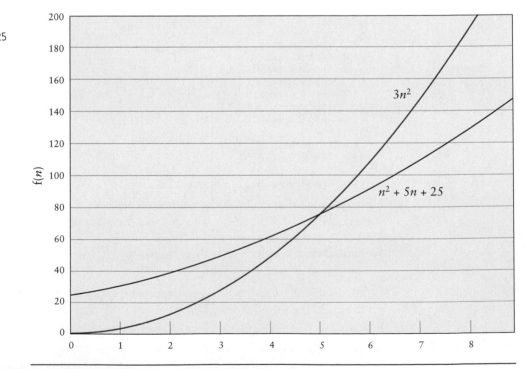

EXAMPLE 2.19   Consider the following program loop:

```
for (int i = 0; i < n - 1; i++) {
  for (int j = i + 1; j < n; j++) {
    3 simple statements
  }
}
```

The first time through the outer loop, the inner loop is executed $n - 1$ times; the next time $n - 2$, and the last time once. The outer loop is executed $n - 1$ times. So we get the following expression for $T(n)$:

$$3(n - 1) + 3(n - 2) + \cdots + 3$$

We can factor out the 3 to get

$$3(n - 1 + n - 2 + n + \cdots + 1)$$

The sum $1 + 2 + \cdots + n - 1$ (the factor in parentheses) is equal to

$$\frac{n \times (n - 1)}{2}$$

Thus our final $T(n)$ is

$$T(n) = 1.5n^2 - 1.5n$$

This polynomial is zero when n is 1. For values greater than 1, $1.5n^2$ is always greater than $1.5n^2 - 1.5n$. Therefore we can use 1 for n_0 and 1.5 for c to conclude that our $T(n)$ is $O(n^2)$ (see Figure 2.7).

FIGURE 2.7

$1.5n^2$ versus $1.5n^2 - 1.5n$

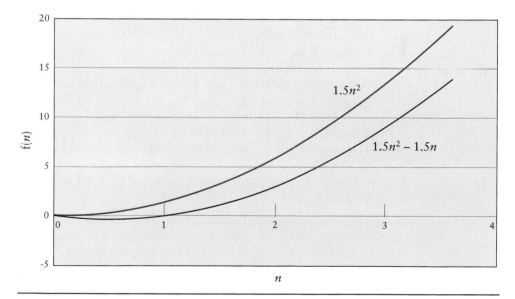

If $T(n)$ is the form of a polynomial of degree d (the highest exponent), then it is $O(n^d)$. A mathematically rigorous proof of this is beyond the scope of this text. An intuitive proof of this is demonstrated in the previous two examples. If the remaining terms have positive coefficients, find a value of n where the first term is equal to the remaining terms. As n gets bigger than this value, the n^d term will always be bigger.

···········

TABLE 2.4

Symbols Used in Quantifying Software Performance

$T(n)$	The time that a function or program takes as a function of the number of inputs, n. We may not be able to measure or determine this exactly.
$f(n)$	Any function of n. Generally $f(n)$ will represent a simpler function than $T(n)$, for example, n^2 rather than $1.5n^2 - 1.5n$.
$O(f(n))$	Order of magnitude. $O(f(n))$ is the set of functions that grow no faster than $f(n)$. We say that $T(n) = O(f(n))$ to indicate that the growth of $T(n)$ is bounded by the growth of $f(n)$.

We use the expression $O(1)$ to represent a constant growth rate. This is a value that doesn't change with the number of inputs. The simple steps all represent $O(1)$. Any finite number of $O(1)$ steps is still considered $O(1)$; that is, their aggregate time is not affected by the size of the problem.

Summary of Notation

In this section we have used the symbols $T(n)$, $f(n)$, and $O(f(n))$. Their meaning is summarized in Table 2.4.

Comparing Performance

Throughout this text, as we discuss various algorithms, we will discuss how their execution time or storage requirements grow as a function of the problem size using this big-O notation. There are several common growth rates that will be encountered. These are summarized in Table 2.5.

Figure 2.8 shows the growth rates of a logarithmic, a linear, a log-linear, a quadratic, a cubic, and an exponential function by plotting $f(n)$ for each function. Notice that for small values of n the exponential function is smaller than all of the others. As shown, it is not until n reaches 20 that the linear function is smaller than the quadratic. This illustrates two points. For small values of n, the less efficient algorithm may be actually more efficient. If you know that you are going to process only a limited amount of data, an $O(n^2)$ algorithm may be much more appropriate than an $O(n \log n)$ algorithm that has a large constant factor. On the other hand, algorithms with exponential growth rates can start out small but very quickly grow to be quite large.

The raw numbers in Figure 2.8 can be deceiving. Part of the reason is that big-O notation ignores all constants. An algorithm with a logarithmic growth rate $O(\log n)$ may be more complicated to program, so it may actually take more time per data item than an algorithm with a linear growth rate $O(n)$. For example, at $n = 25$, Figure 2.8 shows that the processing time is approximately 1800 units for an algorithm with a logarithmic growth rate and 2500 units for an algorithm with a linear growth rate. Comparisons of this sort are pretty meaningless. The logarithmic algorithm may actually take more time to execute than the linear algorithm for this relatively small data set. Again, what is important is the growth rate of each of these two kinds of algorithms, which tells you how performance of each kind of algorithm changes with n.

TABLE 2.5
Common Growth Rates

Big-O	Name
$O(1)$	Constant
$O(\log n)$	Logarithmic
$O(n)$	Linear
$O(n \log n)$	Log-linear
$O(n^2)$	Quadratic
$O(n^3)$	Cubic
$O(2^n)$	Exponential
$O(n!)$	Factorial

FIGURE 2.8
Different Growth Rates

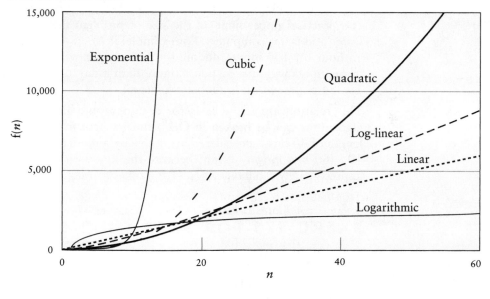

EXAMPLE 2.20   Let's look at how growth rates change as we double the value of n (say, from $n = 50$ to $n = 100$). The results are shown in Table 2.6. The third column gives the ratio of processing times for the two different data sizes. For example, it shows that it will take 2.35 times as long to process 100 numbers as it would to process 50 numbers with an $O(n \log n)$ algorithm.

TABLE 2.6
Effects of Different Growth Rates

O($f(n)$)	$f(50)$	$f(100)$	$f(100)/f(50)$
O(1)	1	1	1
O($\log n$)	5.64	6.64	1.18
O(n)	50	100	2
O($n \log n$)	282	664	2.35
O(n^2)	2500	10,000	4
O(n^3)	12,500	100,000	8
O(2^n)	1.126×10^{15}	1.27×10^{30}	1.126×10^{15}
O($n!$)	3.0×10^{64}	9.3×10^{157}	3.1×10^{93}

Algorithms with Exponential and Factorial Growth Rates

Algorithms with exponential and factorial (even faster) growth rates have an effective practical upper limit on the size of problem they can be used for, even with faster and faster computers. For example, if we have an O(2^n) algorithm that takes an hour for 100 inputs, adding the 101st input will take a second hour, adding 5 more inputs will take 32 hours (more than a day!), and adding 14 inputs will take 16,384 hours, which is almost two years!

This relationship is the basis for cryptographic algorithms. Some cryptographic algorithms can be broken in O(2^n) time, where n is the length of the key. A key length of 40 bits is considered breakable by a modern computer, but a key length of 100 (60 bits longer) is not, because the key with a length of 100 bits will take approximately a billion billion (10^{18}) times as long as the 40-bit key to crack.

EXERCISES FOR SECTION 2.6

SELF-CHECK

1. Determine how many times the output statement is displayed in each of the following fragments. Indicate whether the fragment execution time is O(n) or O(n^2).

   a. ```
   for (int i = 0; i < n; i++)
     for (int j = 0; j < n; j++)
       cout << i << "   " << j << endl;
   ```
   b. ```
   for (int i = 0; i < n; i++)
     for (int j = 0; j < 2; j++)
       cout << i << "   " << j << endl;
   ```
   c. ```
   for (int i = 0; i < n; i++)
     for (int j = n - 1; j >= i; j--)
       cout << i << "   " << j << endl;
   ```
   ```

d.
```
for (int i = 1; i < n; i++)
    for (int j = 0; j < i; j++)
        if (j % i == 0)
            cout << i << "  " << j << endl;
```

2. For the following $T(n)$ find values of n_0 and c such that cn^3 is larger than $T(n)$ for all n larger than n_0.

$$T(n) = n^3 - 5n^2 + 20n - 10$$

3. How does the performance grow as n goes from 2000 to 4000 for the following? Answer the same question as n goes from 4000 to 8000. Provide tables similar to Table 2.6.

   a. $O(\log n)$

   b. $O(n)$

   c. $O(n \log n)$

   d. $O(n^2)$

   e. $O(n^3)$

4. According to the plots in Figure 2.8, what are the processing times at $n = 20$ and at $n = 40$ for each of the growth rates shown?

PROGRAMMING

1. Write a program that compares the values of y1 and y2 in the following expressions for values of n up to 100 in increments of 10. Does the result surprise you?

```
y1 = 100 * n + 10
y2 = 5 * n * n + 2
```

Chapter Review

- There are three kinds of defects ("bugs") that can occur in programs. Syntax errors, which prevent your program from compiling, are generally the simplest to detect and fix. These are generally due to a typographical error or a misunderstanding of the language syntax. However, not all typographical errors result in syntax errors.

- Run-time errors are those errors that arise during the execution of your program and are generally indicated by exceptions. You can reduce the occurrence of run-time errors by using **if** statements to test the validity of variables before executing statements that can throw run-time exceptions.

- Logic errors occur when your program does not produce the correct result. Some logic errors are easy to find because the program always produces the wrong result. Other logic errors are difficult to find, because they occur only under special cases that are sometimes difficult to reproduce.

◆ You can throw an exception when you detect that an error will occur. The exception that is thrown will cause your program to stop if it is not caught or handled. If you throw an exception inside a **try** block, you can provide a **catch** block that handles that type of exception object. The **catch** block can either display an appropriate error message and terminate your program or attempt to recover from the error and continue execution.

◆ The C++ standard library defines a hierarchy of standard exceptions that it uses to indicate some errors. For example, if the index of a substring is greater than the size of the string, the exception out_of_range is thrown. Programmers should also use these standard exceptions or define their own exceptions as extensions of a standard exception.

◆ Program testing is done at several levels starting with the smallest testable piece of the program, called a unit. A unit is either a function or a class, depending on the complexity.

◆ Once units are individually tested, they can then be tested together; this level is called integration testing.

◆ Once the whole program is put together, it is tested as a whole; this level is called system testing.

◆ Finally, the program is tested in an operational manner demonstrating its functionality; this level is called acceptance testing.

◆ Black-box (also called closed-box) testing tests the item (unit or system) based on its functional requirements without using any knowledge of the internal structure.

◆ White-box (also called glass-box or open-box) testing tests the item using knowledge of its internal structure. One of the goals of white-box testing is to achieve test coverage. This can range from testing every statement at least once, to testing each branch condition (**if** statements, **switch** statements, and loops) for each path, to testing each possible path through the program.

◆ Test drivers and stubs are tools used in testing. A test driver exercises a function or class and drives the testing. A stub stands in for a function that the unit being tested calls. This can be used to provide a test result, and it can be used to enable a caller of that function to be tested when the function being called is not yet coded.

◆ We described the debugging process and showed an example of how a debugger can be used to obtain information about a program's state.

◆ We discussed formal verification of programs and how assertions and loop invariants can help in the design and verification of our programs.

◆ Computer scientists are interested in comparing the efficiency of different algorithms. We introduced big-O notation and showed how to determine it by examining the loops in a program. We will use this notation throughout the text to describe the relative efficiency of different data structures and algorithms that act on them.

Quick-Check Exercises

1. What are the three broad categories of program defects discussed in this chapter?
2. What is the purpose of a structured walkthrough of an algorithm?
3. _____ testing requires the use of test data that exercise each statement in a module.
4. _____ testing focuses on testing the functional characteristics of a module.
5. _____ determines whether a program has an error; _____ determines the _____ of the error and helps you _____ it.
6. Assume you have the following **catch** clauses following a **try** block. List the sequence in which they must occur:

```
catch(std::ios_base::failure& ex)
catch(...)
catch(std::exception& ex)
catch(std::out_of_range& ex)
```

7. Indicate which of the following may be false: loop invariant, **while** condition, assertion.
8. Write a loop invariant for the following code segment:

```
product = 1;
counter = 2;
while (counter < 5) {
   product *= counter;
   counter++;
}
```

9. Determine the order of magnitude (big-O) for an algorithm whose running time is given by the equation $T(n) = 3n^4 - 2n^2 + 100n + 37$.
10. If a loop processes n items and n changes from 1024 to 2048, how does that affect the running time of a loop that is $O(n^2)$? How about a loop that is $O(\log n)$? How about a loop that is $O(n \log n)$?

Answers to Quick-Check Exercises

1. Syntax errors, run-time errors, logic errors.
2. To increase the likelihood of finding program logic errors.
3. *White-box* testing requires the use of test data that exercise each statement in a module.
4. *Black-box* testing focuses on testing the functional characteristics of a module.
5. *Testing* determines whether a program has an error; *debugging* determines the cause of the error and helps you *correct* it.
6. The **catch** clauses for std::ios_base::failure and std::out_of_range& ex must be the first, followed by the **catch** clause for std::exception and then the **catch** clause catch(...).
7. A **while** condition
8. invariant: product *contains product of all positive integers < counter and counter is between 2 and 5, inclusive.*
9. $O(n^4)$
10. The running time quadruples for the $O(n^2)$ loop; it increases by a factor of 1.1 for the $O(\log n)$ loop (11/10); it increases by a factor of 2.2 for the $O(n \log n)$ algorithm $((2048 \times 11)/(1024 \times 10))$.

Review Questions

1. Describe a technique for preventing a run-time error caused by the user typing a bad character while entering a numeric value.
2. Describe the differences between stubs and drivers.
3. Briefly describe a test plan for the telephone directory program described in Chapter 1. Assume that integration testing is used.
4. Indicate in which stage of testing (unit, system, integration) each of the following kinds of errors should be detected:
   a. An array index is out of bounds.
   b. An `ios_base::failure` exception is thrown.
   c. An incorrect value of withholding tax is being computed under some circumstances.
5. Which of the following statements is incorrect?
   a. Loop invariants are used in loop verification.
   b. Loop invariants are used in loop design.
   c. A loop invariant is always an assertion.
   d. An assertion is always a loop invariant.
6. Write a function that counts the number of adjacent data items out of place in an array (assume increasing order is desired). Include loop invariants and any other assertions necessary to verify that the procedure is correct.
7. Write big-O expressions for the following loops.

   a.
   ```
   for (int i = 1; i <= n; i++)
      for (int j = 1; j <= n; j++)
         for (int k = n; k >= 1; k--) {
            sum = i + j + k;
            cout << sum << endl;
         }
   ```
   b.
   ```
   for (int i = 0; i < n; i++)
      for (int j = 0; j < i * i; j++)
         cout << j << endl;
   ```
   c.
   ```
   for (int i = n; i >= 0; i -= 2)
      cout << i << endl;
   ```
   d.
   ```
   for (int i = 0; i < n; i++)
      for (int j = i; j > 0; j /= 2)
         cout << j << endl;
   ```

Programming Projects

1. Write a program that determines the average number of array locations that were examined in successful searches to locate an integer in an array of 100 unordered integers using sequential search. Your program should also compute the average number of array calculations that were examined for a failed search in the same array. Your average calculations should be based on trials involving searching for at least 50 different numbers.
2. Redo Project 1 using an array of integers sorted in ascending order. Modify the sequential search algorithm to halt a search as soon as the array values are larger than the target value being sought.
3. Write a program that allows you to examine the effects of array size and initial data order when your favorite sort operates on an array of integers. Test three different array sizes ($n = 100$, $n = 1,000$, and $n = 10,000$) and three different array orderings (ascending

order, inverse order, and random order). This should produce nine test results. The C++ function rand() may be helpful in building the randomly ordered arrays. If you don't have a favorite sort, use function sort defined in the header <algorithm>.

4. Write a set of stub functions for the Array_Based_PD class (Section 1.6) that could be used to test the logic of a main function.

5. Design and program a white-box test for a class that computes the sine and cosine functions in a specialized manner. This class is going to be part of an embedded system running on a processor that does not support floating-point arithmetic. The class to be tested is shown in Listing 2.5. Your job is to test the functions sin and cos; you are to assume that the functions sin0to45 and sin45to90 have already been tested.

You need to design a set of test data that will exercise each of the **if** statements. To do this, look at the boundary conditions and pick values that are

- Exactly on the boundary
- Close to the boundary
- Between boundaries

LISTING 2.5
sin_cos.cpp

```
/** These functions compute the sine and cosine of an angle
    expressed in degrees. The result will be
    an integer representing the sine or cosine as
    ten-thousandths. For example, a result of 7071 represents
    7071e-4 or 0.7071.
*/

// Forward declarations
int sin0to45(int);
int sin45to90(int);
int polyEval(int, int[], int);

/** Compute the sine of an angle in degrees.
    @param x The angle in degrees
    @return The sine of x
*/
int sin(int x) {
  if (x < 0) {
    x = -x;
  }
  x = x % 360;
  if (0 <= x && x <= 45) {
    return sin0to45(x);
  }
  else if (45 <= x && x <= 90) {
    return sin45to90(x);
  }
  else if (90 <= x && x <= 180) {
    return sin(180 - x);
  }
  else {
    return -sin(x - 180);
  }
}
```

```
/** Compute the cosine of an angle in degrees.
    @param x The angle in degrees
    @return The cosine of x
*/
int cos(int x) {
  return sin(x + 90);
}

/** Compute the sine of an angle in degrees
    between 0 and 45.
    pre: 0 <= x < 45
    @param x The angle
    @return The sine of x
*/
int sin0to45(int x) {
  // Code to compute sin(x) for x between 0 and 45 degrees
  ...
}

/** Compute the sine of an angle in degrees
    between 45 and 90.
    pre: 45 <= x <= 90
    @param x The angle
    @return The sine of x
*/
int sin45to90(int x) {
  // Code to compute sin(x) for x between 45 and 90 degrees
  ...
}

...
```

6. Develop a test plan and test drivers/stubs as required to test Programming Project 2 in Chapter 1.

7. Update the test plan and test drivers/stubs to test the modified version of the DVD collection project described in Programming Project 4 in Chapter 1.

8. Develop a test plan and test drivers/stubs as required to test Programming Project 5 in Chapter 1.

9. Develop a test plan and test drivers/stubs as required to test Programming Project 6 in Chapter 1.

Inheritance and Class Hierarchies

Chapter Objectives

- ◆ To understand inheritance and how it facilitates code reuse
- ◆ To understand how C++ determines which member function to execute when there are multiple member functions with the same name in a class hierarchy
- ◆ To learn how to define and use abstract classes as base classes in a hierarchy
- ◆ To understand how to create namespaces and to learn more about visibility
- ◆ To learn about multiple inheritance and how to use it effectively
- ◆ To become familiar with a class hierarchy for geometric shapes

This chapter describes important features of C++ that can make your code more reusable. Object-oriented languages allow you to build and exploit hierarchies of classes to group common features and member functions in your program designs. You will learn how to extend an existing C++ class to define a new class that inherits all the attributes of the original, as well as having additional attributes of its own. Because there may be many versions of the same member function in a class hierarchy, we show how polymorphism enables C++ to determine which version to execute at any given time. We will also introduce multiple inheritance and show how desirable features of multiple inheritance can be exploited in C++.

You will learn how to create namespaces in C++ and how to use the different kinds of visibility for instance variables (data fields) and member functions.

3.1 Introduction to Inheritance and Class Hierarchies

A major reason for the popularity of object-oriented programming (OOP) is that it enables programmers to reuse previously written code saved as classes, reducing the time required to code new applications. Because previously written code has already been tested and debugged, the new applications should also be more reliable and therefore easier to test and debug. The C++ Standard Library gives the C++ programmer a head start in developing new applications. C++ programmers can also build and reuse their own individual libraries of classes.

However, OOP provides additional capabilities beyond the reuse of existing classes. If an application needs a new class that is similar to an existing class, the programmer can create it by *extending* the existing class, rather than rewriting the original class. The new class (called the *derived class*) can have additional data fields and member functions for increased functionality. Its objects also *inherit* the data fields and member functions of the original class (called the *base class*). You may also see the term *subclass* used for derived class and the term *superclass* used for base class. These terms are used generally in object-oriented programming and in discussion of other object-oriented programming languages such as Java. C++, however, uses the terms derived class and base class.

Classes can be arranged in a hierarchy, with a top-level base class. Figure 3.1 shows the input/output stream class hierarchy. The entities farther down the hierarchy inherit data fields (attributes) and functions from those farther up, but not vice versa. Because all I/O stream classes are derived classes of `ios_base` (the top-level base class), they can all use the functions and data fields that are defined in class `ios_base`. For example, the function `clear` which sets and resets the error flags, is a member of `ios_base`, so there is no need to define it in the lower-level classes such as `ifstream` and `ofstream`.

Inheritance in OOP is analogous to inheritance in humans. We all inherit genetic traits from our parents. If we are fortunate, we may even have some ancestors who have left us an inheritance of monetary value. As we grow up, we benefit from our ancestors' resources, knowledge, and experiences, but our experiences will not

FIGURE 3.1
Input/Output Stream
Class Hierarchy

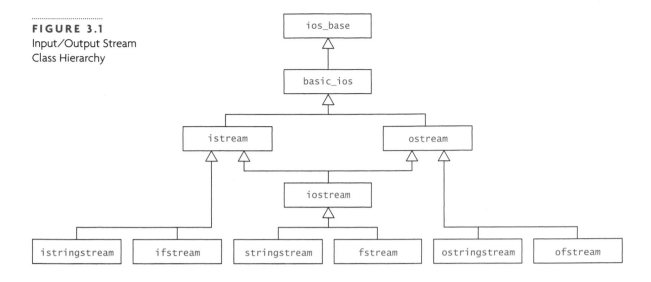

affect how our parents or ancestors developed. Although we have two parents to inherit from, C++ classes usually have only one parent, but may have multiple parents. We will discuss multiple parents in Section 3.4.

Inheritance and hierarchical organization allow you to capture the idea that one thing may be a refinement or extension of another. For example, an object that is an `Hourly_Employee` is also an `Employee`. This means that an object of type `Hourly_Employee` has all the data fields and functions defined by class `Employee`, but it may also have more. Objects further down the hierarchy are more complex and less general than those further up. For this reason an object that is an `Hourly_Employee` is an `Employee`, but the converse is not true, because an `Employee` object does not necessarily have the additional properties defined by class `Hourly_Employee`.

Is-a Versus *Has-a* Relationships

One misuse of inheritance is confusing the *has-a relationship* with the *is-a relationship*. The *is-a* relationship between classes means that every instance of one class is also an instance of the other class (but not the other way around). A jet airplane is an airplane, but not all airplanes are jets. The *is-a* relationship is represented in object-oriented programming by extending a class. For example, to say that a jet plane *is an* airplane means that the jet plane class is a derived class of the airplane class.

The *has-a* relationship between classes means that every instance of one class is or may be associated with one or more instances of the other class (but not necessarily the other way around). For example, a jet plane has a jet engine. The *has-a* relationship is represented by declaring in the one class a data field whose type is the other class.

We can combine is-a and has-a relationships. For example, a jet plane is an airplane, and it has a jet engine. Also, an airplane has a tail, so a jet plane does too because it is an airplane.

C++ allows you to capture both the inheritance (is-a) relationship and the has-a relationship. For example, a class `Jet_Plane` might be declared as:

```
class Jet_Plane : public Airplane {
  private:
    int num_engines;
    Jet_Engine jets[4]; // Jet planes have up to 4 engines.
  // ...
};
```

The part of the class heading following the colon specifies that `Jet_Plane` is a derived class of `Airplane`. The data field `jets` (type `Jet_Engine[4]`) stores information for up to 4 jet engines for a `Jet_Plane` object.

A Base Class and a Derived Class

FIGURE 3.2

Classes `Lap_Top` and `Computer`

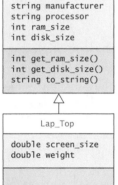

To illustrate the concepts of inheritance and class hierarchies, let's consider a simple case of two classes: `Computer` and `Lap_Top`. A computer has a manufacturer, processor, RAM, and disk. A laptop computer is a kind of computer, so it has all the properties of a computer plus some additional features (screen size and weight). Therefore, we can define class `Lap_Top` as a derived class of class `Computer`. Figure 3.2 shows the class hierarchy.

Class **Computer**

Listing 3.1 shows the definition file for the class `Computer` (`Computer.h`), and Listing 3.2 shows the implementation (`Computer.cpp`).

Notice that we refer to the standard `string` class using the fully qualified name `std::string` in file `Computer.h`, but we use the abbreviated name `string` in file `Computer.cpp`. We can do this in file `Computer.cpp` because it contains the statement `using string::std;`. The reason we did not put the `using` statement in file `Computer.h` is discussed in Section 3.5.

LISTING 3.1
Computer.h

```
#ifndef COMPUTER_H_
#define COMPUTER_H_

#include <string>

/** Class that represents a computer. */
class Computer {
  // Data Fields
  private:
    std::string manufacturer;
    std::string processor;
    int ram_size;
    int disk_size;
```

```
public:
  // Functions
  /** Initializes a Computer object with all properties specified.
      @param man The computer manufacturer
      @param proc The processor type
      @param ram The RAM size
      @param disk The disk size
  */
  Computer(const std::string& man,
           const std::string proc,
           int ram, int disk) :
    manufacturer(man), processor(proc),
    ram_size(ram), disk_size(disk) {}

  int get_ram_size() const { return ram_size; }

  int get_disk_size() const { return disk_size; }

  // Insert other accessor and modifier functions here.
  // ...
  std::string to_string() const;
};

#endif
```

....

LISTING 3.2
Computer.cpp

```
/** Implementation of the class Computer. */
#include "Computer.h"
#include <sstream>
using std::ostringstream;
using std::string;

string Computer::to_string() const {
  ostringstream sb;
  sb << "Manufacturer: " << manufacturer
     << "\nCPU: " << processor
     << "\nRAM: " << ram_size << " megabytes"
     << "\nDisk: " << disk_size << " gigabytes";
  return sb.str();
}
```

Class **Lap_Top**

In the Lap_Top class diagram in Figure 3.2, we show just the data fields declared in class Lap_Top; however, Lap_Top objects also have the data fields that are inherited from class Computer (processor, ram_size, and so forth). The first line in class Lap_Top,

```
class Lap_Top : public Computer {
```

indicates that class Lap_Top is derived from class Computer and inherits its data and member functions. The rest of the definition of class Lap_Top defines any additional data fields and functions for this class in the normal way.

SYNTAX Defining a Derived Class

FORM:

class *derived-class* : public *base-class* { ... }

EXAMPLE:

class Lap_Top : public Computer { ... }

MEANING:

The class *derived-class* inherits the member functions and data fields from the class *base-class*.

PITFALL

Neglecting the Keyword public When Declaring a Derived Class

If we omit the keyword **public** when we declare a derived class, we will declare a derived class with private inheritance. This means that the derived class will inherit the data fields and functions of the base class, but they will not be visible to client classes. Effectively, the derived class contains a private data field that contains a base-class object. This is another way to represent the has-a relationship.

Initializing Data Fields in a Derived Class

The constructor for class Lap_Top must begin by initializing the four data fields inherited from class Computer. Because those data fields are private to the base class, C++ requires that they be initialized by a base class constructor. Therefore, a Computer constructor must be invoked as the first data initialization expression in the Lap_Top constructor. We indicate this by inserting a call to this constructor as the first initialization expression (following the ":") for the Lap_Top constructor.

```
Lap_Top(const std::string& man, const std::string& proc,
        int ram, int disk, double screen, double wei) :
    Computer(man, proc, ram, disk), screen_size(screen), weight(wei) {}
```

The initialization expression Computer(man, proc, ram, disk) invokes the base class constructor with the signature Computer(const string&, const string&, int, int), passing it the four arguments listed. (A function *signature* consists of the function's name followed by its parameter types.) Next, the Lap_Top constructor initializes the data fields that are not inherited (screen_size to size and weight to wei). Listing 3.3 shows the class definition file for Lap_Top (Lap_Top.h).

LISTING 3.3
Lap_Top.h

```
#ifndef LAP_TOP_H_
#define LAP_TOP_H_

#include "Computer.h"
```

```
/** Class to represent a laptop computer. */
class Lap_Top : public Computer {
  private:
    // Data Fields
    double screen_size;
    double weight;

  public:
    // Functions
    /** Construct a Lap_Top object.
        @param man The manufacturer
        @param proc The processor
        @param ram The RAM size
        @param disk The disk size
        @param screen The screen size
        @param wei The weight
    */
    Lap_Top(const std::string& man, const std::string& proc,
            int ram, int disk, double screen, double wei) :
      Computer(man, proc, ram, disk), screen_size(screen), weight(wei) {}
};
#endif
```

The No-Parameter Constructor

If the execution of any constructor in a derived class does not invoke a base class constructor, C++ automatically invokes the no-parameter constructor for the base class. C++ does this to initialize that part of the object inherited from the base class before the derived class starts to initialize its part of the object. Otherwise, the part of the object that is inherited would remain uninitialized.

 PITFALL

Not Defining the No-Parameter Constructor

If no constructors are defined for a class, the no-parameter constructor for that class will be provided by default. However, if any constructors are defined, the no-parameter constructor must also be defined explicitly if it needs to be invoked. C++ does not provide it automatically in this case, because it may make no sense to create a new object of that type without providing initial data field values. (It was not defined in class Lap_Top or Computer because we want the client to specify some information about a Computer object when that object is created.) If the no-parameter constructor is defined in a derived class but is not defined in the base class, you will get a syntax error. For example, the g++ compiler displays an error such as

no matching function call to *class_name*::*class_name*()

You can also get this error if a derived-class constructor does not explicitly call a base-class constructor. There will be an implicit call to the no-parameter base-class constructor, so it must be defined.

Protected Visibility for Base-Class Data Fields

The data fields inherited from class `Computer` have private visibility. Therefore, they can be accessed only within class `Computer`, so the following assignment statement would not be valid in class `Lap_Top`:

```
manufacturer = man;
```

Because it is fairly common for a derived-class member function to reference data fields declared in its base class, C++ provides a less restrictive form of visibility called *protected visibility*. A data field (or member function) with protected visibility can be accessed in either the class defining it or any derived class of that class.

Therefore, if class `Computer` had the declaration

```
protected:
    string manufacturer;
```

the earlier assignment statement would be valid in class `Lap_Top`.

We will use protected visibility on occasion when we are writing a class that we intend to extend. However, in general, it is better to use private visibility, because derived classes may be written by different programmers, and it is always a good practice to restrict and control access to the base-class data fields. We discuss visibility further in Section 3.5.

EXERCISES FOR SECTION 3.1

SELF-CHECK

1. Explain the effect of each valid statement in the following fragment. Indicate any invalid statements.

```
Computer c1;
Computer c2("Ace", "AMD Athlon 2000", 512, 60);
Lap_Top c3("Ace", "AMD Athlon 2000", 512, 60);
Lap_Top c4("Ace", "AMD Athlon 2000", 512, 60, 15.5, 7.5);
cout << c2.manufacturer << ", " << c2.processor << endl;
cout << c2.get_disk_size() << ", " << c4.get_ram_size() << endl;
cout << c2.to_string() << '\n' << c4.to_string() << endl;
```

2. Indicate where in the hierarchy you might want to add data fields for the following and the kind of data field you would add.

   Cost
   The battery identification
   Time before battery discharges
   Number of expansion slots
   Has integrated wireless Internet

3. Can you add the following constructor to class `Lap_Top`? If so, what would you need to do to class `Computer`?

   ```
   Lap_Top() {}
   ```

PROGRAMMING

1. Write accessor and modifier member functions for class `Computer`.
2. Write accessor and modifier member functions for class `Lap_Top`.

3.2 Member Function Overriding, Member Function Overloading, and Polymorphism

In the preceding section we discussed inherited data fields. We found that we could not access an inherited data field in a derived-class object if its visibility was private. Next, we consider inherited member functions. Member functions generally have public visibility, so we should be able to access a member function that is inherited. However, what if there are multiple member functions with the same name in a class hierarchy? How does C++ determine which one to invoke? We answer this question next.

Member Function Overriding

Let's use the following main function to test our class hierarchy.

```
/** Tests classes Computer and Lap_Top. Creates an object of each and
    displays them.
*/
int main() {
  Computer my_computer("Acme", "Intel P4 2.4", 512, 60);
  Lap_Top your_computer("DellGate", "AMD Athlon 2000", 256, 40,
                        15.0, 7.5);
  cout << "My computer is :\n" << my_computer.to_string() << endl;
  cout << "\nYour computer is :\n" << your_computer.to_string()
       << endl;
}
```

In the second output statement, the function call

```
your_computer.to_string()
```

applies the function to_string to object your_computer (type Lap_Top). Because class Lap_Top doesn't define its own to_string member function, class Lap_Top inherits the to_string member function defined in class Computer. Executing this program displays the following output lines:

```
My computer is:
Manufacturer: Acme
CPU: Intel P4 2.4
RAM: 512 megabytes
Disk: 60 gigabytes

Your computer is:
Manufacturer: DellGate
CPU: AMD Athlon 2000
RAM: 256 megabytes
Disk: 40 gigabytes
```

Unfortunately, this output doesn't show the complete state of object your_computer. To show the state of a laptop computer, complete with screen size and weight, we need to define a to_string member function for class Lap_Top. If class Lap_Top has its own to_string member function, it will *override* the inherited member function and will be invoked by the member function call your_computer.to_string(). To show the complete state of the laptop, this function must access the Computer data fields, but because they are private, the overriding `to_string` function in class `Lap_Top` cannot access them. Class `Computer` does have a member function to output that information: `to_string`, the very function we are overriding. The `to_string` function for a `Lap_Top` needs a way to call the `to_string` function for the `Computer` that the laptop is. We define member function `to_string` for class `Lap_Top` next.

```
string Lap_Top::to_string() const {
  ostringstream sb;
  sb << Computer::to_string()
     << "\nScreen Size: " << screen_size
     << "\nWeight: " << weight;
  return sb.str();
}
```

This member function, `Lap_Top::to_string`, returns a string representation of the state of a `Lap_Top` object. The expression

```
Computer::to_string()
```

invokes the `to_string` function of the base class to get the string representation of the four data fields that are inherited from the base class. The next two lines append the data fields defined in class `Lap_Top` to this string.

Member Function Overloading

Let's assume we have decided to standardize and purchase our laptop computers from only one manufacturer. We could then introduce a new constructor with one less parameter for class `Lap_Top`.

```
Lap_Top(const std::string& proc, int ram, int disk,
        double screen, double wei) :
    Computer(DEFAULT_LT_MAN, proc, ram, disk), screen_size(screen),
            weight(wei) {}
```

We now have two constructors with different signatures in class `Lap_Top`. Having multiple member functions with the same name but different signatures in a class is called member function *overloading*. The operator overloading described in Chapter 1 is an example.

SYNTAX **Calling Base-Class Functions**

FORM:
base-class::*function-name*()
base-class::*function-name*(*argument-list*)

EXAMPLE:
`Computer::to_string()`

MEANING:
Using the prefix *base-class*:: in a call to function *function-name* calls the function with that name defined in the base class of the current class.

Now we have two ways to create new Lap_Top objects. Both of the following statements are valid:

```
Lap_Top ltp1("Intel P4 2.8", 256, 40, 14, 6.5);
Lap_Top ltp2("MicroSys", "AMD Athlon 2000", 256, 40, 15, 7.5);
```

Because the manufacturer string is not specified for ltp1, its manufacturer is DEFAULT_LT_MAN.

Listing 3.4 shows the revised Lap_Top class definition (Lap_Top.h), and Listing 3.5 shows the implementation file (Lap_Top.cpp). Figure 3.3 shows the UML diagram, revised to show that Lap_Top has a to_string member function and a constant data field.

LISTING 3.4
Lap_Top.h

```cpp
#ifndef LAP_TOP_H_
#define LAP_TOP_H_

#include "Computer.h"

/** Class to represent a laptop computer. */

class Lap_Top : public Computer {
  public:
    // Functions
    /** Construct a Lap_Top object.
        @param man The manufacturer
        @param proc The processor
        @param ram The RAM size
        @param disk The disk size
        @param screen The screen size
        @param wei The weight
    */
    Lap_Top(const std::string& man, const std::string& proc,
            int ram, int disk, double screen, double wei) :
      Computer(man, proc, ram, disk), screen_size(screen), weight(wei) {}

    /** Construct a Lap_Top object with a default manufacturer. */
    Lap_Top(const std::string& proc, int ram, int disk,
            double screen, double wei) :
      Computer(DEFAULT_LT_MAN, proc, ram, disk), screen_size(screen),
                weight(wei) {}

    /** Generate a string representation of a Lap_Top object. */
    std::string to_string() const;

  private:
    // Data Fields
    static const char* DEFAULT_LT_MAN;
    double screen_size;
    double weight;
};

#endif
```

LISTING 3.5
Lap_Top.cpp

```
/** Implementation of the Lap_Top class. */
#include "Lap_Top.h"
#include <sstream>

using std::string;
using std::ostringstream;

string Lap_Top::to_string() const {
  ostringstream sb;
  sb << Computer::to_string()
     << "\nScreen Size: " << screen_size
     << "\nWeight: " << weight;
  return sb.str();
}

const char* Lap_Top::DEFAULT_LT_MAN = "MyBrand";
```

Virtual Functions and Polymorphism

Suppose you are not sure whether a computer referenced in a program will be a laptop or a regular computer. Because of your uncertainty, you can't declare a variable of either type to store the data for that computer. However, if you declare the pointer variable

```
Computer* the_computer;
```

you can use it to reference an object of either type, because a type Lap_Top object can be referenced by a type Computer* variable. In C++ a pointer variable of a base-class type (general) can point to an object of a derived-class type (specific). Lap_Top objects are Computer objects with more features.

Now suppose you have purchased a laptop computer. What happens when the following statements are executed?

```
the_computer = new Lap_Top("Bravo", "Intel P4 2.4", 256, 40, 15.0, 7.5);
cout << the_computer->to_string() << endl;
```

Will the function call the_computer->to_string() return a string with all six data fields for a Lap_Top object (using Lap_Top::to_string) or just the four data fields defined for a Computer object (using Computer::to_string)? The answer is a string with just the four data fields because the_computer is type pointer-to-Computer. This is not what we want!

What we want is for the type of the object receiving the to_string message to determine which to_string member function is called. We can tell C++ that this is what we want by changing the declaration of the function to_string in the class Computer (in Computer.h) to a *virtual function*:

```
virtual std::string to_string() const;
```

If a member function is declared **virtual**, then when it is called through a pointer (or reference) variable the actual member function will be determined at run time and based on the type of the object pointed to (or referenced). For example, if the variable the_computer points to a Lap_Top object, then the expression

```
the_computer->to_string()
```

will call the member function to_string that is defined by the Lap_Top class.

The fact that the `to_string` member function invoked depends on the type of the object pointed to, and not the type of the pointer variable (`the_computer` is type pointer-to-`Computer`), is a very important feature of object-oriented programming languages. This feature is called *polymorphism*, which means "the quality of having many forms or many shapes." Polymorphism enables the program to determine which member function to invoke at run time. At compile time, the C++ compiler cannot determine what type of object `the_computer` will point to (type `Computer` or its derived type `Lap_Top`), but at run time the program knows the type of the object that receives the `to_string` message and can call the appropriate `to_string` function.

The following displays describe the C++ syntax for using pointer variables to reference objects.

SYNTAX   Declaring a Pointer Type

FORM:
type-name* *variable-name*;

EXAMPLE:
`Computer* the_computer;`

MEANING:
The variable *variable-name* is declared to be of type pointer-to-*type-name*. As discussed in the *C++ Primer*, a pointer is an object that contains the address of another object. To reference the object pointed to by a pointer variable, use either the dereferencing operator * (for example, `*the_computer`) or the pointer class member access operator -> (for example, `the_computer->`). Pointers are initialized using either the address-of operator (&) or the **new** operator.

SYNTAX   Creating New Objects Using the new Operator

FORM:
new *type-name*;
new *type-name*(*argument-list*);

EXAMPLE:
`new Computer("Acme", "Intel P4 2.4", 512, 60);`

MEANING:
Memory is dynamically allocated for a new object of type *type-name* and the constructor is then called to initialize the object. A pointer to the newly created object is the value of this expression.

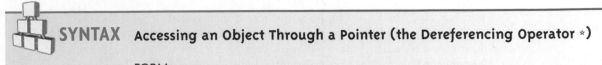

SYNTAX   **Accessing an Object Through a Pointer (the Dereferencing Operator *)**

FORM:

pointer-variable

EXAMPLE:

`*the_computer`

MEANING:

The expression *pointer-variable* is a reference to the object pointed to by *pointer-variable*. When used on the right-hand side of an assignment, it is the value of the object:

`Computer my_computer = *the_computer;`

Now, `my_computer` contains a copy of the `Computer` object referenced by the pointer variable `the_computer`.

When used on the left-hand side of an assignment

`*the_computer = your_computer;`

then the referenced object is assigned the value of the right-hand side.

SYNTAX   **Accessing a Class Member through the Class Member Access Operator**

FORM:

pointer-variable->member-name

EXAMPLE:

```
the_computer->to_string()
my_ram = the_computer->ram_size;
the_computer->ram_size = 1024;
```

MEANING:

The expression *pointer-variable->member-name* is a reference to the member of the object pointed to by *pointer-variable*. If *member-name* is a function, then that function is called. If *member-name* is a data field, then when the expression is used on the right-hand side of an assignment, it is the value of the data field. When the expression is used on the left-hand side of an assignment, then the referenced data field is assigned the value of the right-hand side.

The expression *pointer-variable->member-name* is equivalent to

(*pointer-variable) .member-name

but the -> operator is considered easier to read. Also, the -> operator can be overloaded, but the dot operator cannot.

✓ PROGRAM STYLE

When to Reference an Object through a Pointer Variable

You have seen two different ways to create and reference Computer objects:

```
Computer my_computer("Acme", "Intel P4 2.4", 512, 60);
Computer* my_computer = new Computer("Acme", "Intel P4 2.4", 512, 60);
```

What is the difference between these two statements? The first creates a type Computer object and references it through variable my_computer (for example, my_computer.to_string()). The second creates a Computer object and references it through a pointer to a Computer variable (for example, my_computer->to_string()). Use the first approach when you want the variable my_computer always to reference an object that is type Computer. Use the second approach when you want flexibility; it allows my_computer to reference an object of type Computer or any of its derived classes.

SYNTAX   Virtual Function Definition

FORM:

virtual *function-declaration*;
virtual *function-declaration* { *function-body* }

EXAMPLE:

virtual std::string to_string() const;

MEANING:

If the function declared by *function-declaration* is overridden in a derived class, and if this function is called through a pointer to (or reference to) the base class, then the function body associated with the actual object pointed to (or referenced) will be executed. If a function is declared virtual in a base class, it continues to be virtual in all derived classes. It is, however, a good practice to include the **virtual** declaration in the derived classes too, for documentation purposes.

⊘ PITFALL

Failure to Declare a Member Function virtual in a Base Class

Generally, when we override a function, we intend to use polymorphism to reference objects of it and its derived classes. However, if we omit the keyword **virtual**, then the C++ compiler will determine the function to be called at compile time, based on the type of the pointer and not on the type of the object pointed to.

⊘ PITFALL

Overridden Member Functions Must Have the Same Return Type

If you write a member function in a derived class that has the same signature as one in the base class but a different return type, you will get an error message.

☑ PROGRAM STYLE

Declaring a virtual Destructor

A class's destructor is called when an object of that class is deleted or goes out of scope. Its purpose is to release any resources (such as dynamically allocated memory for class-type data members) that the class owns. Suppose a derived-class object is created using the **new** operator, and the pointer to it is stored in a pointer to the base-class variable. If the destructor is not **virtual**, then only the base-class destructor will be called when the **delete** operator is invoked through the pointer. Therefore, when you declare a member function to be **virtual** in a class, you should always declare the destructor **virtual** even if the destructor does nothing. In our Computer class example we should include the following:

```
virtual ~Computer() {}
```

This declares a virtual destructor that performs no operation.

Some compilers will issue a warning message if the **virtual** destructor is omitted.

EXAMPLE 3.1 If we declare the array lab_computers as follows:

```
Computer* lab_computers[10];
```

we can store pointers to 10 Computer or Lap_Top objects in array lab_computers. Later we can use the following loop to display the information about each object in the array.

```
for (int i = 0; i < 10; i++)
   cout << lab_computers[i]->to_string() << endl;
```

The subscripted variable lab_computers[i] can point to either a Computer object or a Lap_Top object. Because of polymorphism, the actual type of the object pointed to by lab_computers[i] determines which to_string member function will execute (Computer::to_string or Lap_Top::to_string) for each value of subscript i.

EXAMPLE 3.2   We can define the ostream extraction operator for the Computer class as follows:

```
ostream& operator<<(ostream& os, const Computer& comp) {
   return os << comp.to_string;
}
```

Because comp is a reference to Computer, when this function is called with a Lap_Top object, the Lap_Top::to_string member function will be called, and when it is called with a Computer object, the Computer::to_string member function will be called.

EXERCISES FOR SECTION 3.2

SELF-CHECK

1. Indicate whether member functions with each of the following signatures and return types (if any) would be allowed and in what classes they would be allowed. Explain your answers.

```
Computer()
Lap_Top()
int to_string()
double get_ram_size()
string get_ram_size()
string get_ram_size(string)
string get_processor()
double get_screen_size()
```

2. For the loop body in the following fragment, indicate which member function is invoked for each value of i. What is printed?

```
Computer* comp[3];
comp[0] = new Computer("Ace", "AMD Athlon 2500", 512, 60);
comp[1] = new Lap_Top("Intel P4 2.4", 256, 40, 15.5, 7.5);
comp[2] = comp[1];
for (int i = 0; i < 3; i++) {
   cout << comp[i]->get_ram_size() <<  "\n"
        << comp[i]->to_string() << "\n";
}
```

3. When does C++ determine which to_string member function to execute for each value of i in the **for** statement in the preceding question: at compile time or at run time? Explain your answer.

PROGRAMMING

1. Write constructors for the Lap_Top and Computer classes that allow you to specify only the processor, RAM size, and disk size.
2. Complete the accessor and modifier member functions for class Computer.
3. Complete the accessor and modifier member functions for class Lap_Top.

3.3 Abstract Classes, Assignment, and Casting in a Hierarchy

In this section we introduce another kind of class called an *abstract class*. An abstract class differs from an actual class (sometimes called a concrete class) in two respects:

- An abstract class cannot be instantiated.
- An abstract class declares at least one abstract member function, which must be defined in its derived classes.

An *abstract function* is a virtual function that is declared but for which no body (definition) is provided. We introduce an abstract class in a class hierarchy when we need a base class for two or more actual classes that share some attributes. We may want to declare some of the attributes and define some of the functions that are common to these base classes. However, we may also want to require that the actual derived classes implement certain functions. We can accomplish this by declaring these functions abstract, which would make the base class abstract as well.

EXAMPLE 3.3   The Food Guide Pyramid provides a recommendation of what to eat each day based on established dietary guidelines. There are six categories of foods in the pyramid: fats, oils, and sweets; meats, poultry, fish, and nuts; milk, yogurt, and cheese; vegetables; fruits; and bread, cereal, and pasta. If we wanted to model the Food Guide Pyramid, we might have each of these as actual derived classes of an abstract class called Food as shown in Listing 3.6.

LISTING 3.6
Food.h

```
#ifndef FOOD_H_
#define FOOD_H_

/** Abstract class that models a kind of food. */
class Food {
  // Data Field
  private:
    double calories;

  public:
    // Abstract Functions
    /** Calculates the percent of protein in a Food object. */
    virtual double percent_protein() const = 0;
    /** Calculates the percent of fat in a Food object. */
    virtual double percent_fat() const = 0;
    /** Calculates the percent of carbohydrates in a Food object. */
    virtual double percent_carbohydrates() const = 0;

    // Functions
    double get_calories() const { return calories; }
    void set_calories(double cal) {
      calories = cal;
    }
};

#endif
```

The three abstract member function declarations,

```
virtual double percent_protein() const = 0;
virtual double percent_fat() const = 0;
virtual double percent_carbohydrates() const = 0;
```

impose the requirement that all actual derived classes implement these three functions. We would expect a different function definition for each kind of food.

SYNTAX   Abstract Function Definition

FORM:
virtual *function-declaration* = 0;

EXAMPLE:
virtual double percent_protein() const = 0;

INTERPRETATION:
The function declared by *function-declaration* is declared to be an abstract function. The expression = 0; is given in place of the function body and must be specified in the class declaration. You may also see the term *pure virtual function* to refer to an abstract function.

PITFALL

Omitting the Definition of an Abstract Function in a Derived Class

If you write class Vegetable and forget to define member function percent_protein, the class Vegetable will also be abstract. If you subsequently attempt to declare an object of type Vegetable, you will get a syntax error.

Referencing Actual Objects

Because class Food is abstract, you can't create type Food objects. Therefore, the statement

```
Food my_snack();    // Not valid - can't declare an object of an
                    // abstract class
```

is not valid. However, you can use a type Food pointer variable to point to an actual object that belongs to a class derived from Food. For example, if Vegetable is a derived class of Food, an object of type Vegetable can be pointed to by a Food pointer variable because a Vegetable object is also a Food object.

EXAMPLE 3.4 The following statement creates a `Vegetable` object that is referenced by variable `my_snack` (type pointer-to-Food).

```
Food* my_snack = new Vegetable("carrot sticks");
```

Summary of Features of Actual Classes and Abstract Classes

Students often get confused between abstract classes and actual classes (concrete classes). Table 3.1 summarizes some important points about these constructs. Notice that you cannot create instances of an abstract class type; however, you can use a pointer to an abstract type to reference an actual object that is a subclass of that abstract type.

Assignments in a Class Hierarchy

C++ is what is known as a *strongly typed language*. This means that each operand has a type and that operations can be performed only on operands of the same or compatible types. This includes the assignment operation: the left operand (the variable to the left of =) of an assignment operation is known as an *l-value*, and the right operand is known as an *r-value*. For the built-in types the r-value must be of the same type as the l-value or there must be a conversion defined to convert the r-value into a value that is the same type as the l-value. For class types, the assignment operator may be overridden and overloaded. This is discussed in the following section.

There is an exception to this rule for pointer types. A pointer variable (l-value) that is of type pointer-to-*base class* may point to a derived object (r-value). However, the opposite is not the case.

```
Computer* a_computer = new Lap_Top( ... ); // Legal
Lap_Top* a_laptop = new Computer( ... );   // Incompatible types
```

TABLE 3.1
Comparison of Actual Classes and Abstract Classes

Property	Actual Class	Abstract Class
Instances (objects) of this type can be created	Yes	No
This can define instance variables and functions	Yes	Yes
This can define constants	Yes	Yes
The number of these a class can extend	Any number	Any number
This can extend another class	Yes	Yes
This can declare abstract member functions	No	Yes
Pointers to this type can be declared	Yes	Yes
References of this type can be declared	Yes	Yes

DESIGN CONCEPT

The Importance of Strong Typing

Suppose C++ did not check the expression type and simply performed the assignment

```
Lap_Top* a_laptop = new Computer( ... );    // Incompatible types
```

Further down the line, we might attempt to apply a Lap_Top function to the object referenced by a_laptop. Because a_laptop is type Lap_Top*, the compiler would permit this. If a_laptop were pointing to a type Lap_Top object, then performing this operation would do no harm. But if a_laptop were pointing to an object that was not type Lap_Top, performing this operation would cause either a run-time error or an undetected logic error. It is much better to have the compiler tell us that the assignment is invalid.

Casting in a Class Hierarchy

C++ provides a mechanism, *dynamic casting*, that enables us to process the object referenced by a_computer through a pointer variable of its actual type, instead of through a type pointer-to-Computer. The expression

```
dynamic_cast<Lap_Top*>(a_computer)
```

casts the type of the object pointed to by a_computer (type Computer) to type Lap_Top. The casting operation will succeed only if the object referenced by a_computer is, in fact, type Lap_Top; if not, the result is the null pointer.

What is the advantage of performing the cast? Casting gives us a type Lap_Top pointer to the object that can be processed just like any other type Lap_Top pointer. The expression

```
dynamic_cast<Lap_Top*>(a_computer)->get_weight()
```

will compile because now get_weight is applied to a type Lap_Top reference. Similarly, the assignment statement

```
Lap_Top* a_laptop = dynamic_cast<Lap_Top*>(a_computer);
```

is valid because a type Lap_Top pointer is being assigned to a_laptop (type Lap_Top*).

Keep in mind that the casting operation does not change the object pointed to by a_computer; instead, it creates a type Lap_Top pointer to it. (This is called an *anonymous* or *unnamed pointer*.) Using the type Lap_Top pointer, we can invoke any member function of class Lap_Top and process the object just like any other type Lap_Top object.

The cast

```
dynamic_cast<Lap_Top*>(a_computer)
```

is called a *downcast* because we are casting from a higher type in the inheritance hierarchy (Computer) to a lower type (Lap_Top). Microsoft compilers require you to set a compiler switch to use dynamic_cast (see the Pitfall on this topic).

SYNTAX   Dynamic Cast

FORM:

dynamic_cast<*class-name**>(*object-name*)

EXAMPLE:

dynamic_cast<Lap_Top*>(a_computer)

INTERPRETATION:

A pointer of type *class-name* is created to object *object-name*, provided that *object-name* is an actual object of type *class-name* (or a derived class of *class-name*). If *object-name* is not type *class-name*, the result is a null pointer.

⊘ PITFALL

Run-time Type Identification Not Enabled

If you are using a Microsoft compiler, you may get a warning message that Run-time Type Identification is needed. You must set a compiler switch (/GR) to enable this or dynamic_cast will cause a run-time error.

CASE STUDY   Displaying Addresses for Different Countries

Problem   Different countries use different conventions when addressing mail. We want to write a program that will display the address in the correct format depending on the destination. Specifically, we want to distinguish between addresses in Germany and in the United States and Canada. In Germany the building number follows the street name (line 1 below), and the postal code (equivalent to the U.S. ZIP code) is placed before the municipality name (line 2 below). This is the opposite of the convention used in the United States and Canada. For example, a typical German address would read

```
Bahnhofstr 345
D-99999 Jedenstadt
```

while a typical U.S. and Canadian address would read

```
123 Main St
Somecity ZZ  99999-9999
```

However, the Canadian postal code is in a different format.

Analysis   There are several components that make up an address, and there are numerous variations between countries as to how to arrange them. One simple approach would be to ignore these variations and merely record complete address lines as strings. However, this approach does not allow us to analyze or validate addresses easily. By parsing the addresses into their components, we can validate addresses against databases provided by the national postal authorities and generate address labels that conform to national postal authority standards. There are several commercial software packages and databases that do this.

The number of components in an address and their names vary among countries. We are going to simplify this situation for the purposes of this case study. An address consists of the following data elements:

- The house number
- The street name
- The municipality

- The state or province
- The postal code

A German address is organized as follows:

```
<street name><house number>
<postal code><municipality>
```

A U.S./Canadian address, on the other hand, is organized this way:

```
<house number><street name>
<municipality><state or province><postal code>
```

Because we are originating the mail from the United States, the German address will have the additional requirement that the name of the destination country (Germany) be placed on a third line below the line containing the postal code and municipality.

Design We will create an abstract class, `Address`, that will contain the data elements. This class will also have the abstract function `to_string`, which will organize the elements into a format required for the destination country. The derived classes `German_Address` and `US_Address` will then implement the `to_string` function. Figure 3.4 shows the UML diagram. The # next to an attribute indicates that it has **protected** visibility.

Implementation Listing 3.7 shows the declarations of the classes `Address`, `US_Address`, and `German_Address` in a single file (`Address.h`). Although we have always defined a single class in each `.h` file, it is possible to define multiple classes in the same `.h` file.

FIGURE 3.4
Abstract Class **Address** and Two Derived Classes

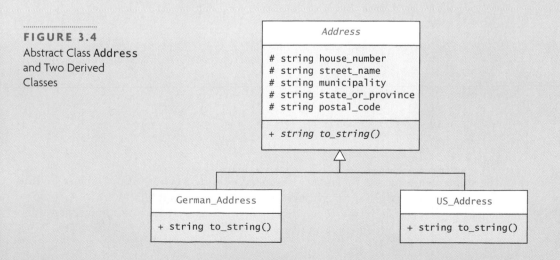

The Address class declares five data fields to store the address components. It also has a constructor to initialize them. The classes US_Address and German_Address are derived from Address. In addition to the declaration of the to_string function, they contain a constructor to initialize the address components. These constructors pass the data to the Address constructor.

LISTING 3.7
Address.h

```cpp
#ifndef ADDRESS_H_
#define ADDRESS_H_

#include <string>

/** Declaration of the abstract class Address. */
class Address {
  public:
    // Functions
    Address(const std::string& hn, const std::string& str,
            const std::string muni, const std::string& stpro,
            const std::string& pc) :
      house_number(hn), street_name(str), municipality(muni),
        state_or_province(stpro), postal_code(pc) {}

    virtual std::string to_string() const = 0;

    virtual ~Address() {}

    void set_house_number(std::string new_house_number) {
      house_number = new_house_number;
    }

  protected:
    // Data Fields
    std::string house_number;
    std::string street_name;
    std::string municipality;
    std::string state_or_province;
    std::string postal_code;
};

/** Declaration of the class German_Address. */
class German_Address : public Address {
  public:
    German_Address(const std::string& hn, const std::string& str,
                   const std::string& muni, const std::string& pc) :
      Address(hn, str, muni, "", pc) {}

    std::string to_string() const;
};

/** Declaration of the class US_Address. */
// Exercise

#endif
```

The implementation of the to_string member functions for the US_Address and German_Address classes is straightforward. They each assemble the address components into the appropriate order, adding the necessary spaces and line separators. Listing 3.8 is the implementation of the German_Address to_string function. Note that we can write this in its own file even though there is no separate header file for class German_Address. Definition and implementation of the US_Address class is left as an exercise.

LISTING 3.8
German_Address.cpp

```
/** Implementation file for the class German_Address */
#include "Address.h"
#include <sstream>
using std::string;
using std::ostringstream;

string German_Address::to_string() const {
  ostringstream result;
  result << street_name << " " << house_number << "\n"
         << postal_code << " " << municipality << "\n"
         << "Germany\n";
  return result.str();
}
```

Testing   We can test these classes by simply creating instances and displaying the results of their to_string functions. This is done with the following program:

```
#include "Address.h"
#include <iostream>
using std::cout;

int main() {
  Address* add1 = new US_Address("123", "Main St", "Somecity",
                                 "ZZ", "99999-9999");
  Address* add2 = new German_Address("345", "Bahnhofstr",
                                     "Jedenstadt", "D-99999");
  cout << add1->to_string() << "\n\n";
  cout << add2->to_string() << "\n\n";
}
```

EXERCISES FOR SECTION 3.3

SELF-CHECK

1. What are two important differences between an abstract class and an actual class? What are the similarities?

PROGRAMMING

1. Write class Vegetable. Assume that a vegetable has three **double** constants: VEG_PROTEIN_CAL, VEG_FAT_CAL, and VEG_CARBO_CAL. Compute the fat percentage as VEG_FAT_CAL divided by the sum of all the constants. Compute the protein and carbohydrate percentages in a similar manner.

2. We discussed a `Computer` class with a `Lap_Top` class as its only derived class. However, there are many different kinds of computers. An organization may have servers, mainframes, desktop PCs, and laptops. There are also personal data assistants (PDAs) and game computers. So it may be more appropriate to declare class `Computer` as an abstract class that has an actual derived class for each category of computer. Write an abstract class `Computer` that defines all the member functions shown earlier and declares an abstract member function with the signature `cost_benefit()` that returns the cost-benefit ratio (type **double**) for each category of computer.

3. Implement the `US_Address` class discussed in the case study.

3.4 Multiple Inheritance

The ability of a class to extend more than one class, found in C++, is called *multiple inheritance*. Multiple inheritance can be a useful concept in some class hierarchies. For example, you could have a class `Student` and also a class `Employee`. A university would have many students who are full-time students and many employees who are full-time employees, but there would also be some student workers who are both students and employees. This suggests the hierarchy in Figure 3.5. In this diagram, the data fields for the derived class are all inherited from its base classes.

Multiple inheritance is a language feature that can lead to ambiguity. If a class extends two classes, and each declares the same data field (for example, `name` in `Student` and `Employee`), which one does the derived class inherit? In C++, the answer is both. We will show how C++ handles this next. Because of the ambiguity problem, the programming language Java does not support multiple inheritance.

FIGURE 3.5
Class `Student_Worker` Extends `Student` and `Employee`

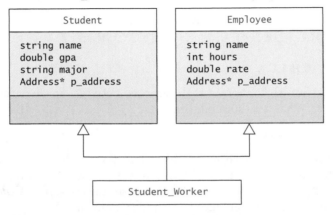

LISTING 3.9
Student_Worker.h

```cpp
#ifndef STUDENT_WORKER_H_
#define STUDENT_WORKER_H_

#include "Employee.h"
#include "Student.h"

class Student_Worker : public Employee, public Student {
  public:
    /** Construct a new Student_Worker.
        @param the_name The Student_Worker's name
        @param the_address Pointer to the address
        @param the_rate The hourly rate
        @param the_major The student's major
    */
    Student_Worker(const std::string& the_name,
                   Address* the_address,
                   double the_rate,
                   const std::string& the_major) :
      Employee(the_name, the_address, the_rate),
      Student(the_name, the_address, the_major) {}

    /** Return a string representation of a student worker. */
    std::string to_string() const;
};

#endif
```

LISTING 3.10
Student_Worker.cpp

```cpp
/** Return string representation of Student_Worker. */
std::string Student_Worker::to_string() const {
  std::ostringstream result;
  result << name << '\n'
         << p_address->to_string()
         << "\nMajor: " << major
         << " GPA: " << gpa
         << " rate: " << rate
         << " hours: " << hours;
  return result.str();
}
```

Definition of **Student_Worker**

Listings 3.9 and 3.10 show the declaration and implementation of the class Student_Worker. In Listing 3.9, the heading

```cpp
class Student_Worker : public Employee, public Student
```

shows that class Student_Worker extends class Employee and class Student. The constructor:

```
Student_Worker(const std::string& the_name,
               Address* the_address,
               double the_rate,
               const std::string& the_major) :
  Employee(the_name, the_address, the_rate),
  Student(the_name, the_address, the_major) {}
```

contains two initialization expressions separated by commas. The first initializes the Employee part and the second initializes the Student part. There is no argument given for data fields hours or gpa, so they are initialized to default values. This is similar to how we initialized the Computer part of the Lap_Top class (see Listing 3.3).

Unfortunately, when we attempt to compile Student_Worker.cpp, we receive an error message that says that the references to name and p_address are ambiguous. We can fix this as follows:

```
#include "Student_Worker.h"
#include <sstream>

/** Return a string representation of a Student_Worker. */
std::string Student_Worker::to_string() const {
  std::ostringstream result;
  result << Student::name << '\n'
         << Student::p_address->to_string()
         << "\nMajor: " << major
         << " GPA: " << gpa
         << " rate: " << rate
         << " hours: " << hours;
  return result.str();
}
```

We resolved the ambiguity by specifying which name and which p_address we want to use. However, this is not a very good solution. We still effectively have two name data fields and two p_address data fields, even though the constructor sets them both to the same value. Because the two p_address fields are the same, you may get a run-time error when the destructor for Student_Worker is called.

Refactoring the Employee and Student Classes

A better solution is to recognize that both Employees and Students have common data fields. These common data fields and their associated member functions could be collected into a separate class, which will become a common base class Person. This process is known as *refactoring* and is often used in object-oriented design. However, it leads to similar problems, because there are two Person components in the Student_Worker class: one inherited from Employee and the other inherited from Student. A workable solution to this problem is beyond the scope of this text; however, the interested reader can find this solution in Appendix A.

EXERCISES FOR SECTION 3.4

SELF-CHECK

1. Explain the basic problem involved in implementing multiple inheritance.
2. Draw the class hierarchy diagram that would result from refactoring the Employee and Student classes.

3.5 Namespaces and Visibility

Namespaces

You have already seen a namespace. The entire C++ standard library is contained in the namespace `std`. Namespaces are used to group collections of declarations into a functional unit. In this way clashes between duplicate names are avoided. For example, you may be writing an adventure game program and define the class `map` to represent the area where the action takes place. The standard library also defines a class called `map`, which associates values with keys. You may even want to use this class `std::map` as part of the implementation of your `map`. By prefixing the namespace name before the class name, you can distinguish between `std::map` and `map` (the class defined for your game program).

EXAMPLE 3.5   The following shows the declaration of a class map that uses the standard map as a component.

```
#include <map>  // Get the definition of the standard map.

class map {
  private:
    std::map the_map;  // Declare a component.
    ...
};
```

Declaring a Namespace

We could make the distinction even clearer by defining our own namespace `game` and placing all the definitions associated with this program into this namespace. Then we would have `std::map` versus `game::map`, thus making the two usages of the word "map" clear.

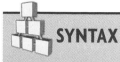

SYNTAX   Namespace Declaration

FORM:

namespace *name* { ... }

EXAMPLE:

namespace game { ... }

INTERPRETATION:

All identifiers (e.g., functions, variables, etc.) defined within the block following the *name* are within that namespace. Namespaces are open; this means that you may have more than one namespace declaration with the same name in your program. The identifiers defined within the different declarations are merged.

EXAMPLE 3.6   The following declares the namespace game and defines the class map inside of it.

```
namespace game {
  class map { ... };
}
```

Then the following declarations declare objects of different classes:

```
std::map a_std_map;   // A standard map
game::map a_game_map;
```

The Global Namespace

Namespaces are nested. At the top level there is the global namespace, whose name is effectively the null string. Thus, in Example 3.5 the distinction is between std::map and ::map. Since the reference to ::map is made within the default namespace, the leading prefix :: (the scope resolution operator) is not required. However, if we defined the namespace game but did not define the map class inside of it, code within the scope of namespace game that referenced class map, defined in the global namespace, would still require the :: qualifier, e.g., ::map.

EXAMPLE 3.7   The fragment below declares a class map in the global namespace and one in the game namespace.

```
class map { ... };   // Defined in the global namespace

namespace game {
  class map { ... }; // Defined in the game namespace
}
```

The statement

```
map map1;
```

in the global namespace will declare an object map1 of type ::map (that is, the map defined in the global namespace).

The statement

```
game::map map2
```

in the global namespace will declare an object map2 of type game::map (that is the map defined in namespace game).

The statements

```
namespace game {
    map map4;        // map4 is the map defined in the game namespace.
    ::map map5;      // map5 is the map defined in the global namespace.
}
```

are in the game namespace. The object map4 is of the map class that is declared in the game namespace, and the object map5 is of the type map defined in the global namespace.

The using Declaration and using Directive

The **using** *declaration* takes a name from the namespace in which it was declared and places it into the namespace where the **using** declaration appears.

The **using** *directive* takes all of the names from a given namespace and places them into the namespace where the **using** directive appears.

SYNTAX using Declaration

FORM:
using *namespace*::*name*;

EXAMPLE:
using std::cout;

MEANING:

The qualified *name* is now a member of the namespace in which the **using** declaration appears. In this example, we can now use the name cout without prefixing the namespace qualifier std:: in front of it.

SYNTAX using Directive

FORM:
using namespace *namespace-name*;

EXAMPLE:
using namespace std;

MEANING:

All of the names defined in *namespace-name* are now defined as such within the current namespace.

☑ **PROGRAM STYLE**

A using Declaration Versus a using Directive

You are probably in the habit of beginning your programs as follows:

```
#include <iostream>
// Other include directives
using namespace std;
...
```

As long as your programs are small, this generally does not cause a problem. But you should recognize that the standard library is quite large and defines a very large number of names. In many implementations the include directive

```
#include <iostream>
```

brings in a large number of other headers. Many of these headers you would expect, such as <istream> and <ostream>, but it also may include some headers that you never heard of, such as <locale>, and others you may not expect, such as <string>. Therefore, if your program is going to access only cout, then a **using** declaration is preferred:

```
#include <iostream>
// Other include directives
using std::cout;
...
```

☑ **PROGRAM STYLE**

using Declarations and using Directives in Header Files

Our definition of the class Person included a component of the class string from the standard library. You may be wondering why we didn't write the header file as:

```
#ifndef PERSON_H_
#define PERSON_H_
#include <string>
using namespace std;
class Person {
  ...
  string name;
};
```

Now assume that you start to write the game program we discussed in Example 3.6 and define your own class map. You decide that you need a Person class in your game program and use this revised header. Because class Person brings in all the names from namespace std, the game program will not compile, because there is now a name clash between your map and the standard map! Therefore, you should never place a **using** declaration or **using** directive inside a header file. Instead you should always explicitly qualify all names that are defined in a namespace with their namespace name; for example, std::cout.

....

TABLE 3.2
Summary of Kinds of Visibility

Visibility	Applied to Class Members
private	Visible only within this class
protected	Visible to classes that extend this class
public	Visible to all classes and functions

Using Visibility to Support Encapsulation

The rules for visibility control how encapsulation occurs in a C++ program. Table 3.2 summarizes the rules in order of decreasing protection.

Notice that private visibility is for members of a class that should not be accessible to anyone but the class, not even classes that extend it.

Use of protected visibility allows the class developer to give control to other programmers who want to extend classes. Protected data fields are typically essential to an object. Similarly, protected member functions are those that are essential to an extending class.

Table 3.2 shows that public members are universally visible.

The friend Declaration

Sometimes you need to define a function external to a class that has the ability to access the private members of that class. For example, the ostream extraction operator may need to access the private data fields. The **friend** declaration gives the functions and classes it specifies access to the private and protected members of the class in which the **friend** declaration appears. This effectively makes the named function or class a member of the declaring class. Note that the class itself must declare who its friends are. Also, friendship is not inherited and is not transitive. This means that if a base class is a friend of a particular class, its derived classes are not automatically friends too. They must be declared to be friends.

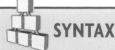

SYNTAX **friend Declaration**

FORM:

friend *function-name*;
friend class *class-name*;

EXAMPLE:

friend foo;

MEANING:

The named function or class is granted access to the private and protected members of the class in which the **friend** declaration appears.

EXAMPLE 3.8 The following shows that private data fields of a class can be referenced only in its friend classes.

```
class A {
  private:
    int x;
  friend foo;
}

void foo() {
  A a;
  // . . .
  a.x = 10;  // Valid, foo is a friend of A.
}

void bar() {
  A a;
  // . . .
  a.x = 10;  // Not valid, x is not visible to bar.
}
```

EXAMPLE 3.9 The following shows how friendship is not transitive.

```
class A {
  private:
    int x;
  friend class B;
};

class B {
  private:
    int y;
    void foo() {
      A a;
      a.x = 10;  // Legal, B is a friend of A.
    }
  friend class C;
};

class C {
  void bar() {
    A a;
    B b;
    b.y = 10; // Legal, C is a friend of B.
    a.x = 10; // Not valid, C is not a friend of A.
  }
};
```

EXERCISES FOR SECTION 3.5

SELF-CHECK

1. For class B, which is a friend of class A, is the statement

   a.x = 10;   // *Valid or not valid???*

   a valid statement? Why or why not? Answer the same questions for this statement in class C, which extends class B.

```
class A {
  private:
    int x;
  friend class B;
};

class B {
  void foo() {
    A a;
    a.x = 10;   // Valid or not valid???
  }
};

class C : public B {
  void bar() {
    A a;
    a.x = 10;   // Valid or not valid???
  }
};
```

3.6 A Shape Class Hierarchy

In this section we provide a case study that illustrates many of the principles in this chapter.

CASE STUDY Processing Geometric Shapes

Problem We would like to process some standard geometric shapes. Each figure object will be one of three standard shapes (rectangle, circle, right triangle). We would like to be able to do standard computations, such as finding the area and perimeter, for any of these shapes.

Analysis For each of the shapes we can process, we need a class that represents the shape and knows how to perform the standard computations on it (that is, find its area and perimeter). These classes will be Rectangle, Circle, and Rt_Triangle. To ensure that these shape classes all define the required computational functions, we will require them to implement an abstract class, Shape. If a class does not have the required functions, we will get a syntax error when we attempt to use it. Figure 3.6 shows the class hierarchy.

Design We will discuss the design of the Rectangle class here. The design of the other classes is similar and is left as an exercise. Table 3.3 shows class Rectangle. Class Rectangle has data fields width and height. It has functions to compute area and perimeter, to read in the attributes of a rectangular object (read_shape_data), and a to_string function.

FIGURE 3.6
Class **Shape** and
Three Implementors

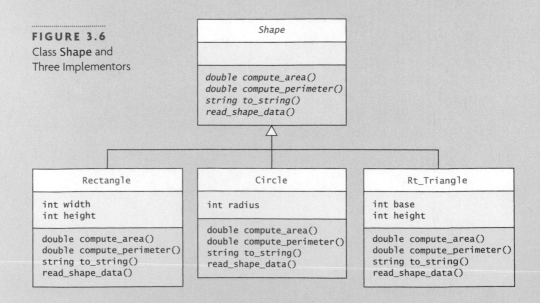

TABLE 3.3
Class Rectangle

Data Field	Attribute
`int width`	Width of a rectangle.
`int height`	Height of a rectangle.
Function	**Behavior**
`double compute_area() const`	Computes the rectangle area (width × height).
`double compute_perimeter() const`	Computes the rectangle perimeter (2 × width + 2 × height).
`void read_shape_data()`	Reads the width and height.
`string to_string() const`	Returns a string representing the state.

Implementation   Listing 3.11 shows class Shape.

LISTING 3.11
Shape.h

```
#ifndef SHAPE_H_
#define SHAPE_H_

#include <string>

/** Declaration file for the abstract class Shape. */
class Shape {
  public:
    virtual double compute_area() const = 0;
    virtual double compute_perimeter() const = 0;
    virtual void read_shape_data() = 0;
    virtual std::string to_string() const = 0;
};

#endif
```

Listings 3.12 and 3.13 show class Rectangle.

LISTING 3.12
Rectangle.h

```
#ifndef RECTANGLE_H_
#define RECTANGLE_H_

#include "Shape.h"
```

```
/** Definition file for the class Rectangle. */
class Rectangle : public virtual Shape {
  public:
    Rectangle() : width(0), height(0) {}
    Rectangle(int the_width, int the_height) :
      width(the_width), height(the_height) {}
    int get_width() { return width; }
    int get_height() { return height; }
    double compute_area() const;
    double compute_perimeter() const;
    void read_shape_data();
    std::string to_string() const;
  protected:
    int width;
    int height;
};

#endif
```

LISTING 3.13
Rectangle.cpp

```
/** Implementation of Rectangle class. */
#include "Rectangle.h"

#include <sstream>
#include <iostream>
#include <istream>
#include <ostream>

using std::string;
using std::ostringstream;
using std::cin;
using std::cout;

double Rectangle::compute_area() const {
  return width * height;
}

double Rectangle::compute_perimeter() const {
  return 2 * width + 2 * height;
}

void Rectangle::read_shape_data() {
  cout << "Enter the width of the rectangle: ";
  cin >> width;
  cout << "Enter the height of the rectangle: ";
  cin >> height;
}
```

```
string Rectangle::to_string() const {
  ostringstream result;
  result << "Rectangle: width is " << width
         << ", height is " << height;
  return result.str();
}
```

Testing

To test the shape hierarchy, we will write a program that will prompt for what kind of figure, read the parameters for that figure, and display the results. The code for Compute_Area_And_Perim is shown in Listing 3.14. The main function is very straightforward, and so is display_result. The main function first calls get_shape, which constructs a list of available shapes and prompts the user for the choice. The reply is expected to be a single character. The nested **if** statement determines which shape instance to return. For example, if the user's choice is C (for Circle), the statement

```
    return new Circle();
```

returns a pointer to a new Circle object.

After the new shape instance is returned to my_shape in main, the statement

```
    my_shape->read_shape_data();
```

uses polymorphism to invoke the correct member function read_shape_data to read the shape object's parameter(s). This member function must be declared a virtual function in class Shape and defined in each class. The member functions compute_area and compute_perimeter are then called to obtain the values of the area and perimeter. Finally, display_result is called to display the result.

The function get_shape is an example of a *factory function* because it creates a new object and returns a pointer to it. The author of the main function has no awareness of the individual kinds of shapes. Knowledge of the available shapes is confined to the get_shape function. This function must present a list of available shapes to the user and decode the user's response to return an instance of the desired shape.

LISTING 3.14
Compute_Area_And_Perim.cpp

```
/** Program to compute the area and perimeter of geometric shapes. */

#include "Rectangle.h"
#include "Rt_Triangle.h"
#include "Circle.h"

#include <iostream>
#include <istream>
#include <ostream>
#include <cctype>

using std::cout;
using std::cin;
using std::endl;
```

```
Shape* get_shape() {
  char fig_type;
  cout << "Enter C for circle\nEnter R for rectangle"
       << "\nEnter T for right triangle\n";
  cin >> fig_type;
  fig_type = tolower(fig_type);
  if (fig_type == 'c') {
    return new Circle();
  } else if (fig_type == 't') {
    return new Rt_Triangle();
  } else if (fig_type == 'r') {
    return new Rectangle();
  } else {
    return NULL;
  }
}

void display_result(double area, double perim) {
  cout << "The area is " << area
       << "\nThe perimeter is " << perim
       << endl;
}

int main() {
  Shape* my_shape;
  double perimeter;
  double area;
  my_shape = get_shape();
  my_shape->read_shape_data();
  perimeter = my_shape->compute_perimeter();
  area = my_shape->compute_area();
  display_result(area, perimeter);
  delete my_shape;
  return 0;
}
```

EXERCISES FOR SECTION 3.6

PROGRAMMING

1. Write class Circle.
2. Write class Rt_Triangle.

Chapter Review

◆ Inheritance and class hierarchies enable you to capture the idea that one thing may be a refinement or extension of another. For example, a plant is a living thing. Such is-a relationships create the right balance between too much and too little structure. Think of inheritance as a means of creating a refinement of an abstraction. The entities farther down the hierarchy are more complex and less general than those higher up. The entities farther down the hierarchy may inherit data members (attributes) and member functions from those farther up, but not vice versa. A class that inherits from another class is a derived class; the class from which it inherits is a base class.

◆ Encapsulation and inheritance impose structure on object abstractions. Polymorphism provides a degree of flexibility in defining member functions. It loosens the structure a bit in order to make member functions more accessible and useful. Polymorphism means "the ability to have many forms." It captures the idea that member functions may take on a variety of forms to suit different purposes.

◆ The keyword `virtual` defines a function that can be overridden by a corresponding function in a derived class. If a virtual function declaration is followed by = 0, this function is a pure virtual function or abstract function. An abstract class is a class that contains at least one abstract function. Abstract classes can also have data fields and actual functions. You use an abstract class as the base class for a group of derived classes in a hierarchy.

◆ You cannot declare an object of an abstract class, but you can declare a pointer (or a reference) to an abstract class. A pointer (or reference) to an abstract class must point to (refer to) an object of a concrete class that is derived from the abstract class.

Quick-Check Exercises

1. What does polymorphism mean, and how is it used? What is function overriding? Function overloading?
2. What is a function signature? Describe how it is used in function overloading.
3. When would you use an abstract class, and what should it contain?
4. Can a class extend more than one class?
5. Describe the difference between is-a and has-a relationships.
6. Which can have more data fields and member functions: the base class or the derived class?
7. You can point to an object of a _____ type through a variable of a _____ type.
8. You cast an object referenced by a _____ type to an object of a _____ type in order to apply member functions of the _____ type to the object. This is called a _____.
9. The three kinds of visibility in order of decreasing visibility are: _____, _____, and _____.

Answers to Quick-Check Exercises

1. Polymorphism means "the ability to have many forms." Function overriding means that the same function appears in a derived class and a base class. Function overloading means that the same function appears with different signatures in the same class.

2. A signature is the form of a function determined by its name and arguments. For example, do_it(int, double) is the signature for a function do_it that has one type **int** parameter and one type **double** parameter. If several functions in a class have the same name (function overloading), C++ invokes the one with the same signature as the function call.

3. An abstract class is used as a base class for a collection of related derived classes. An abstract class cannot be instantiated. The abstract functions (identified by **virtual** and by = 0 for the function body) defined in the abstract class act as placeholders for the actual functions. The abstract class should also contain the definitions of data fields that are common to all the derived classes. An abstract class can have actual functions as well as abstract functions.

4. A class can extend multiple classes; this capability is known as multiple inheritance.

5. An is-a relationship between classes means that one class is a derived class of a base class. A has-a relationship means that one class has data members (components) of the second class type.

6. The derived class.

7. You can point to an object of a *derived-class* type through a variable of *pointer-to-base-class* type.

8. You cast an object referenced by a *base-class* type to an object of a *derived-class* type in order to apply member functions of the *derived-class* type to the object. This is called a *downcast*.

9. The three kinds of visibility in order of decreasing visibility are *public*, *protected*, and *private*.

Review Questions

1. Which member function is invoked in a particular class when a member function definition is overridden in several classes that are part of an inheritance hierarchy? Answer the question for the case in which the class has a definition for the member function and also for the case where it doesn't.

2. Like a rectangle, a parallelogram has opposite sides that are parallel, but it has a corner angle, theta (Θ), that is less than 90 degrees. Discuss how you would add parallelograms to the class hierarchy for geometric shapes (see Figure 3.6). Write a definition for class Parallelogram.

3. Explain what multiple inheritance means and what problem it introduces.

4. Explain how assignments can be made within a class hierarchy and the role of casting in a class hierarchy. What is strong typing? Why is it an important language feature?

5. If C++ encounters a member function call of the following form:
   base_class_ptr->function_name()
   where base_class_ptr is a pointer to a base class that points to an object whose type is a derived class, what is necessary for this statement to compile? During run time, will function function_name from the class that is the type of base_class_ptr always be invoked, or is it possible that a different function function_name will be invoked? Explain your answer.

6. Assume the situation in Question 5, except that function `function_name` is not defined in the class that is the type of `base_class` but it is defined in the derived-class type. Rewrite the function call so that it will compile.

7. Explain the process of initializing an object that is a derived-class type in the derived-class constructor. What part of the object must be initialized first? How is this done?

8. Discuss when abstract classes are used. How do they differ from actual classes?

Programming Projects

1. A veterinary office wants to store information regarding the kinds of animals it treats. Data includes diet, whether the animal is nocturnal or not, whether its bite is poisonous (as for some snakes), whether it flies, and so on. Use a base class `Pet` with abstract functions and create appropriate derived classes to support about 10 animals of your choice.

2. A student is a person, and so is an employee. Create a class `Person` that has the data attributes common to both students and employees (name, social security number, age, gender, address, and telephone number) and appropriate member function definitions. A student has a grade-point average (GPA), major, and year of graduation. An employee has a department, job title, and year of hire. In addition, there are hourly employees (hourly rate, hours worked, and union dues) and salaried employees (annual salary). Define a class hierarchy and write an application class that you can use to first store the data for an array of people and then display that information in a meaningful way.

3. Create a pricing system for a company that makes individualized computers, such as you might see on a Web site. There are two kinds of computers: laptops and desktop computers. The customer can select the processor speed, the amount of memory, and the size of the disk drive. The customer can also choose a CD drive (CD ROM, CD-RW), a DVD drive, or both. For laptops, there is a choice of screen size. Other options are a modem, a network card, or wireless network. You should have an abstract class `Computer` and derived classes `Desk_Top` and `Lap_Top`. Each derived class should have member functions for calculating the price of a computer given the base price plus the cost of the different options. You should have member functions for calculating memory price, hard drive price, and so on. There should be a member function to calculate shipping cost.

4. Write a banking program that simulates the operation of your local bank. You should declare the following collection of classes.

   Class `Account`
   - Data fields: `customer` (type `Customer`), `balance`, `account_number`, `transactions` array (type `transaction*`)
   - Member functions: `get_balance()`, `get_customer()`, `to_string()`, `set_customer()`, `set_balance()`

   Class `Savings_Account` extends `Account`
   - Member functions: `deposit()`, `withdraw()`, `add_interest()`

   Class `Checking_Account` extends `Account`
   - Member functions: `deposit()`, `withdraw()`, `add_interest()`

   Class `Customer`
   - Data fields: `name`, `address`, `age`, `telephone_number`, `customer_number`
   - Member functions: Accessors and modifiers for data fields

Classes Senior, Adult, Student, all of which extend class Customer

- Each has constant data fields, SAVINGS_INTEREST, CHECK_INTEREST, CHECK_CHARGE, and OVERDRAFT_PENALTY, that define these values for customers of that type.

Class Bank

- Data field: array accounts (type Account*)
- Member functions: add_account(), make_deposit(), make_withdrawal(), get_account()

Class Transaction

- Data fields: customer_number, transaction_type, amount, fees (a string describing unusual fees)
- Member functions: process_tran()

You need to write all these classes and an application class that interacts with the user. In the application, you should first open several accounts and then enter several transactions.

5. You have a sizeable collection of music and videos and want to develop a database for storing and processing information about this collection. You need to develop a class hierarchy for your media collection that will be helpful in designing the database. Try the class hierarchy shown in Figure 3.7, where Audio and Video are media categories. Then CDs and cassette tapes would be derived classes of Audio, and DVDs and VHS tapes would be derived classes of Video.

If you go to the video store to get a movie, you can rent or purchase only movies that are recorded on VHS tapes or DVDs. For this reason, class Video (and also classes Media and Audio) should be abstract classes, because there are no actual objects of these types. However, they are useful classes to help define the hierarchy.

Class Media should have data fields and member functions common to all classes in the hierarchy. Every media object has a title, major artist, distributor, playing time, price, and so on. Class Video should have additional data fields for information describing movies recorded on DVDs and video tapes. This would include information about the supporting actors, the producer, the director, and the movie's rating. Class DVD would have specific information about DVD movies only, such as the format of the picture, special features on the disk, and so on. Figure 3.8 shows a possible class diagram for Media, Video, and derived classes of Video.

....
FIGURE 3.7
Media Class Hierarchy

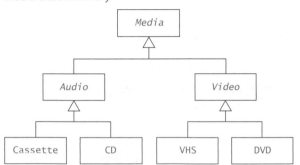

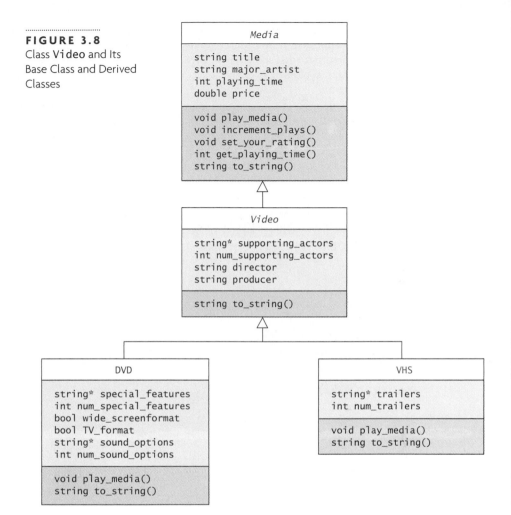

FIGURE 3.8
Class **Video** and Its
Base Class and Derived
Classes

Provide member functions to load the media collection from a file and write it back out to a file. Also provide a member function to retrieve the information for a particular item identified by its title and a member function to retrieve all your items for a particular artist.

6. Add shape classes `Square and Equilateral_Triangle` to the figures hierarchy in Section 3.6. Modify program `Compute_Area_And_Perim` (Listing 3.14) to compute the area and perimeter of these new figure types.

7. Complete the `Food` class hierarchy in Section 3.3. Read and store a list of your favorite foods. Show the total calories for these foods and the overall percentages of fat, protein, and carbohydrates for this list. To find the overall percentage, if an item has 200 calories and 10 percent is fat calories, then that item contributes 20 fat calories. You need to find the totals for fat calories, protein calories, and carbohydrate calories, and then calculate the percentages.

8. A hospital has different kinds of patients who require different procedures for billing and approval of procedures. Some patients have insurance and some do not. Of the insured patients, some are on Medicare, some are in HMOs, and some have other health insurance plans. Develop a collection of classes to model these different kinds of patients.

9. A company has two different kinds of employees: professional and nonprofessional. Generally, professional employees have a monthly salary, whereas nonprofessional employees are paid an hourly rate. Similarly, professional employees have a certain number of days of vacation, whereas nonprofessional employees receive vacation hours based on the number of hours they have worked. The amount contributed for health insurance is also different for each kind of employee. Use an abstract class `Employee` to store information common to all employees and to declare member functions for calculating weekly salary and computing health care contributions and vacation days earned that week. Define derived classes `Professional` and `Non_Professional`. Test your class hierarchy.

Sequential Containers

Chapter Objectives

- To become familiar with the Standard Template Library (STL) and template classes
- To understand how to use a vector class and how to implement it using an array for storage
- To understand the difference between a shallow and deep copy
- To introduce linked lists and study the differences between single-, double-, and circular linked list data structures
- To introduce **structs**
- To understand the iterator
- To learn how to implement the STL list class
- To learn how to implement the iterator for a linked list
- To learn how to declare aliases and use delegation
- To become familiar with the STL sequential containers
- To introduce the functions in the algorithm header

So far we have one data structure that you can use in your programming—the array. Giving a programmer an array and asking her to develop software systems is like giving a carpenter a hammer and asking him to build a house. In both cases, more tools are needed. The C++ developers attempted to supply those tools by providing a rich set of data structures written as C++ template classes. The classes are all part of the Standard Template Library (STL). We will discuss classes from this library in the rest of the book, starting in this chapter with the classes that are considered *sequences*.

A sequence has the property that elements can be inserted or removed anywhere in the sequence, not just at the beginning or at the end. Some sequences are indexed, which means their elements can be accessed in arbitrary order (called *random access*) using a subscript to select an element. For other sequences you must always start at the beginning and process the elements in sequence. We will also discuss iterators and their role in facilitating *sequential access* and random access.

In this chapter we will discuss the `vector` and `list` (linked list) classes and their similarities and differences. We will show that these classes implement the common interface requirements for sequential containers.

Sequential Containers

4.1 Template Classes and the Vector

Before studying our first data structure in the STL, we want to introduce the concept of a *template class*. A template class is a class that stores and processes a collection of information. The data type of this information is a parameter that is specified when the template class is instantiated. For example, in the declaration

```
template<typename T>
  class some_container { ... }
```

`some_container` is declared to be a template class. The parameter `T` is a placeholder for the actual data type of the information to be stored in `some_container`. The statements

```
some_container<int> call_lengths;
some_container<Person> people;
```

create two instances of `some_container`. The first, `call_lengths`, stores a collection of **int** values, and the second, `people`, stores a collection of `Person` objects. The same operations can be performed on both instances. At compile time, the actual data type is substituted for the parameter `T` to create the desired instantiation of `some_container`.

SYNTAX Instantiating a Template Class

FORM:

template-class-name<argument-list> object-name;

EXAMPLE:

```
some_container<int> call_lengths;
some_container<Person> people;
```

MEANING:

If one doesn't already exist, a distinct copy of the template class is created by substituting the arguments for the parameters. This is very similar to what happens when a function is called, except that this substitution occurs when the program is being compiled. Generally the arguments are types (either built-in or class types). In this example, two versions of the template class `some_container` are created: one to hold **int**s and the other to hold `People` objects. The classes `some_container<int>` and `some_container<People>` are distinct classes.

Vector

The first template class we will study is the `vector`, which is an enhancement of the C++ array. The `vector` uses an array as its basic storage structure. An array is an indexed data structure, which means you can select its elements in arbitrary order as determined by the subscript value. You can also access the elements in sequence using a loop that increments the subscript. However, you can't do the following with an array:

- Increase or decrease its length, which is fixed
- Insert an element at a specified position without writing code to shift the other elements to make room
- Remove an element at a specified position without writing code to shift the other elements to fill in the resulting gap

A *vector* is an improvement over an array in that it supports all of these operations. Vectors are used most often when a programmer wants to be able to add new elements to the end of a list but still needs the capability to access the elements stored in the list in arbitrary order. These are the features we needed for our telephone directory application: New entries were added at the end, and we also needed to find numbers for entries already in the directory. The size of a vector automatically increases as new elements are added to it, and the size decreases as elements are removed.

If an insertion is not at the end of the vector, the existing entries in the vector are automatically shifted to make room for the entry being inserted. Similarly, if an element other than the last one is removed, the other entries are automatically shifted to close up the space that was vacated.

A vector has a size, which is the number of elements it currently contains. This quantity is returned by the member function `size`. Each vector object also has a capacity, which is the number of elements it can store. When a vector's size is equal to its capacity, the capacity is automatically increased.

`vector` is a template class, so you can declare `vector` objects to hold objects of any other type. To declare `my_vector` to be a vector containing `string`s, you would use the declaration

```
vector<string> my_vector;
```

EXAMPLE 4.1   The statement

```
vector<string> my_vector;
```

allocates storage for a `vector` object `my_vector` whose elements are `string` objects. Initially `my_vector` is empty. The statements

```
my_vector.push_back("Bashful");
my_vector.push_back("Awful");
my_vector.push_back("Jumpy");
my_vector.push_back("Happy");
```

add four strings as shown in the top diagram of Figure 4.1. The final value of `my_vector.size()` is 4.

The middle diagram of Figure 4.1 shows vector `my_vector` after the insertion of `"Doc"` at the element with subscript 2:

```
my_vector.insert(2, "Doc");
```

The new size is 5. The strings formerly referenced with subscripts 2 and 3 are now referenced by the subscripts 3 and 4. This is the same as what happens when someone cuts into a line of people waiting to buy tickets; everyone following the person who cuts in moves back one position in the line.

FIGURE 4.1
Insertion into a **vector** Object

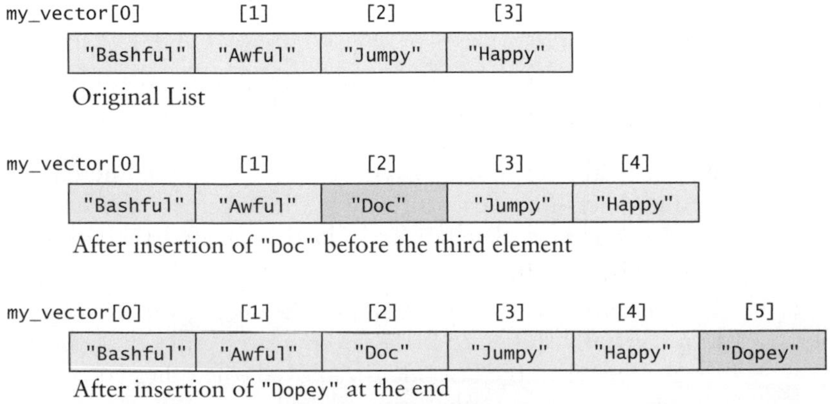

Original List

After insertion of "Doc" before the third element

After insertion of "Dopey" at the end

The last diagram in Figure 4.1 shows the effect of the statement

```
my_vector.push_back("Dopey");
```

which adds "Dopey" at the end of the vector. The size of my_vector is now 6.

Similarly, if you remove an element from a vector object, the size automatically decreases, and the elements following the one removed shift over to fill the vacated space. This is the same as when someone leaves a ticket line; the people in back all move forward. Here is object my_vector after using the statement

```
my_vector.erase(1);
```

to remove the element with subscript 1. Notice that the strings formerly referenced by subscripts 2 through 5 are now referenced by subscripts 1 through 4 (in the darker color), and the size has decreased by 1.

my_vector[0]	[1]	[2]	[3]	[4]
"Bashful"	"Doc"	"Jumpy"	"Happy"	"Dopey"

After removal of "Awful"

A vector is an indexed container; you can access its elements using a subscript. For example, the statement

```
string dwarf = my_vector[2];
```

stores the string object "Jumpy" in variable dwarf, without changing my_vector.

You would use the statement

```
my_vector[2] = "Sneezy";
```

to replace the string "Jumpy" in my_vector with the string "Sneezy". However, variable dwarf would still contain the string "Jumpy".

my_vector[0]	[1]	[2]	[3]	[4]
"Bashful"	"Doc"	"Sneezy"	"Happy"	"Dopey"

After replacing "Jumpy" with "Sneezy"

Specification of the vector Class

The vector class is part of the standard library and is specified in the header <vector>. Because it is a template class, the parameter Item_Type represents the actual type of the objects to be stored in the vector. As shown above, the actual item type is specified when a template class is instantiated. In the C++ standard library there is a second template parameter, called the *allocator*. The library provides a default value for this parameter that is adequate for most purposes. We will discuss the use of the allocator in Appendix A.

Table 4.1 shows a subset of the functions defined in the vector class. Because Item_Type is determined when the vector is created, the actual argument types and return types for these functions may be different for different instantiations of the vector class. Recall that the size_t type is an unsigned **int**. We use it here because all vector indexes must be nonnegative.

TABLE 4.1
Member Functions of Class `vector`

Member Function	Behavior
`const Item_Type& operator[](size_t index) const`	Returns a reference to the element at position `index` that can be used on the right-hand side of an assignment.
`Item_Type& operator[](size_t index)`	Returns a reference to the element at position `index` that can be used as the target of an assignment.
`const Item_Type& at(size_t index) const;` `Item_Type& at(size_t index)`	The same as `operator[]` except that the index is validated. If the index is not valid, the `out_of_range` exception is thrown.
`bool empty() const`	Returns **true** if the `vector` is empty.
`size_t size() const`	Returns the number of items stored in the `vector`.
`void resize(size_t new_size)`	Changes the size of the vector to `new_size`. If `new_size` is smaller than the current size, then items are removed from the end. If `new_size` is larger than the current size, then default-valued items are added to the end. The default-valued item is the value returned by the default (no-argument) constructor. For built-in types the default value is zero.
`void swap(vector<Item_Type>& other)`	Exchanges the contents of this vector with the contents of the `other` vector.
`void push_back(const Item_Type& the_value)`	Adds a copy of `the_value` at the end of this `vector`.
`void insert(size_t index, const Item_Type& the_value)`	Adds a copy of `the_value`, inserting it before the item at position `index`. Note this is not the form of the function as defined by the standard library. We will describe the actual form of this function in a later section.
`void erase(size_t index)`	Removes the item at position `index` and shifts the items that follow it to fill the vacated space. Note that this is not the form of the function as defined by the standard library. We will describe the actual form of this function in a later section.
`void pop_back()`	Removes the last item from the vector.

The functions `insert` and `erase` are defined differently in the standard library, but the form shown is what we will implement in Section 4.3. At the end of this chapter we will briefly revisit the vector and discuss how to modify our sample implementation to be like the standard one.

Function at and the Subscripting Operator

There are two entries in Table 4.1 for the subscripting operator `[]` and two for the member function `at`. The first entry for each returns the value of the specified vector element (indicated by the keyword **const** at the beginning and end of these entries); this value can't be changed. The second entry for each is a reference to an element of the vector; its value can be changed.

EXAMPLE 4.2   Both of the following statements retrieve and display the value of element 2 of vector<int> v.

```
cout << v[2];
cout << v.at(2);
```

Both of the following statements add 6 to the value of element 2 of vector v and assign that sum to element 3 of vector v.

```
v[3] = v[2] + 6;
v.at(3) = v.at(2) + 6;
```

In these statements, the reference to element 2 retrieves a value of vector v that is not changed. In contrast, both references to element 3 change its value.

☑ PROGRAM STYLE

Use of operator[] versus at

As discussed in Chapter 2, the fact that C++ does not perform range checking on array bounds has led to many problems, including many security holes in modern operating systems. Unlike function at, the standard vector subscripting operator does not perform range checking, leaving the door open for these problems. Although the subscripting operator is more error prone, it is also more convenient to use, so most programmers use it rather than member function at. In the next section, we show how you to redefine the subscripting operator to perform range checking.

EXERCISES FOR SECTION 4.1

SELF-CHECK

1. Describe the effect of each of the following operations on object my_vector as shown at the bottom of Figure 4.1. What is the value of my_vector.size() after each operation? Assume that function find returns the index of its second argument in the vector that is passed as the first argument. Assume that the function to_upper returns a string that converts each letter in its argument to uppercase but leaves other characters unchanged.

```
my_vector.push_back("Pokey");
my_vector.push_back("Campy");
int i = find(my_vector, "Happy");
my_vector[i] = "Bouncy";
my_vector.erase(my_vector.size() - 2);
string temp = my_vector[1];
my_vector[1] = to_upper(temp);
```

PROGRAMMING

1. Write the following function:

   ```
   /** Finds the first occurrence of target in a_vector.
       @return The index of the first occurrence of the target
               or size if the target is not found
   */
   int find(const vector<string>& a_vector,
            const string& target);
   ```

2. Write the following function:

   ```
   /** Replaces each occurrence of old_item in a_vector
       with new_item.
   */
   void replace(vector<string>& a_vector,
                const string& old_item,
                const string& new_item);
   ```

3. Write the following function:

   ```
   /** Deletes the first occurrence of target in a_vector. */
   template<typename Item_Type>
     void delete(vector<Item_Type>& a_vector,
                 const Item_Type& target);
   ```

4.2 Applications of vector

We illustrate some applications of vectors next.

EXAMPLE 4.3   The following statements store a collection of **int** values in vector some_ints.

```
vector<int> some_ints;
int nums[] = {5, 7, 2, 15};
for (int i = 0; i < 4; i++)
  some_ints.push_back(nums[i]);
```

After the loop finishes, vector element some_ints[i] and array element nums[i] (for all i in range) will contain the same value. The following fragment finds and displays the sum of the **int** values in some_ints.

```
int sum = 0;
for (size_t i = 0; i < some_ints.size(); i++) {
  sum += some_ints[i];
}
cout << "sum is " << sum << endl;
```

Although it may seem wasteful to carry out these operations when you already have an array of **int**s, the purpose of this example is to illustrate the steps needed to process a collection of **int** values in a vector.

The Phone Directory Application Revisited

In Chapter 1 we introduced a phone directory case study. Our solution involved building an array of phone directory entries that expanded as new directory entries were added. Basically we constructed an expandable array that was a data field of class Phone_Directory (see Listing 1.9, Array_Based_PD.h, and the implementations that follow it). We could accomplish the same operations much more easily using a vector to store the phone directory:

```
vector<Directory_Entry> the_directory;
```

We used function add to insert a new entry at the end of the array. If the array was full, this function called the reallocate function. By using a vector we merely need to create a new Directory_Entry object and then call push_back to insert it into the vector.

LISTING 4.1
Function add

```
/** Adds a new entry.
    @param name The name of the person being added
    @param new_number The new number to be assigned
*/
void add(string name, string new_number) {
  Directory_Entry new_entry(name, new_number);
  the_directory.push_back(new_entry);
}
```

EXERCISES FOR SECTION 4.2

SELF-CHECK

1. What does the following code fragment do?

```
vector<double> my_vector;
my_vector.push_back(3.456);
my_vector.push_back(5);
double result = my_vector[1] + my_vector[0];
cout << "Result is " << result;
```

PROGRAMMING

1. Write the lookup_entry function of the Array_Based_PD.cpp class to use vector the_directory.
2. Write the remove_entry function of Array_Based_PD.cpp class to use vector the_directory.
3. Write the save function of Array_Based_PD.cpp class to use vector the_directory.

4.3 Implementation of a vector Class

We will implement a simplified version of the vector class, which we will encapsulate in the namespace KW; thus our vector will be called KW::vector to distinguish it from the standard vector, std::vector. We use a C++ array internally to contain the data of a KW::vector, as shown in Figure 4.2. The physical size of the array is indicated by the data field current_capacity (type **size_t** because it must be non-negative). The number of data items stored is indicated by the data field num_items. The elements between num_items and current_capacity are available for the storage of new items.

```
namespace KW {

  template<typename Item_Type>
    class vector {

      private:
        // Data fields

        /** The initial capacity of the array */
        static const size_t INITIAL_CAPACITY = 10;

        /** The current capacity of the array */
        size_t current_capacity;

        /** The current num_items of the array */
        size_t num_items;

        /** The array to contain the data */
        Item_Type* the_data;

      public:
        // Member Functions
        ...
    };
};
```

The Default Constructor

Next, we discuss how to implement the constructors and member functions for the vector class. Because this is a template class, all of the code must be in the header or in a file included by the header. Constructors should be defined inline using initialization expressions.

The default constructor initializes the values of num_items and current_capacity and allocates the initial data array.

```
/** Constructs an empty vector with the default
    initial capacity.
*/
vector<Item_Type>() : current_capacity(INITIAL_CAPACITY),
  the_data(new Item_Type[INITIAL_CAPACITY]), num_items(0) { }
```

FIGURE 4.2
Internal Structure of vector

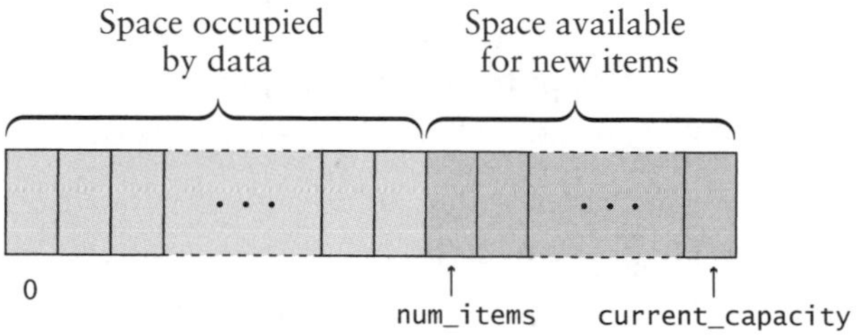

Defining a Template Class

FORM:

template*<formal-parameter-list>* class *class-name* { ... }

EXAMPLE:

```
template<typename Item_Type> class vector { ... }
template<class Item_Type> class bag { ... }
template<typename Item_Type, size_t MAX_SIZE> class bounded_list {
    ...
}
```

MEANING:

The class *class-name* is defined to take one or more template parameters. A template parameter follows the same syntax as a function parameter.

type-name parameter-name

where *type-name* is the name of the parameter's type, and *parameter-name* is the identifier that is used to designate this parameter. Generally you use the keyword **typename** or the keyword **class** for *type-name*. This indicates that the *parameter-name* is to be treated as a type within the body of the template class. You can also declare additional parameters for the template class that are built-in types or previously defined class types (see the last example above).

Note: The original C++ syntax used **class** to designate either classes or built-in types as template parameters, but the C++ standard introduced the alternative usage of **typename** as being a more accurate term. While **typename** is the preferred usage for new applications, the C++ standard uses **class**.

The swap Function

The swap function exchanges the value of this vector object with another vector object. It does this by swapping the values of the data fields using the standard template function swap. The details of how the swap function works are discussed in a later section.

```
/** Exchanges the contents of this vector with another.
    @param other The other vector
*/
void swap(vector<Item_Type>& other) {
  std::swap(num_items, other.num_items);
  std::swap(current_capacity, other.current_capacity);
  std::swap(the_data, other.the_data);
}
```

The Subscripting Operator

As discussed earlier, two forms of the subscripting operator are provided: one to return a modifiable reference to an item in the vector, and the other to return a non-modifiable reference. The declaration for the former is:

```
Item_Type& operator[](size_t index) {
```

and the declaration for the latter is:

```
const Item_Type& operator[](size_t index) const {
```

In the second form, notice that the modifier **const** appears both before the return type and after the function signature. The first **const** tells the compiler that the return value is a constant reference to an Item_Type, and the second **const** tells the compiler that invoking this function will not change the value of the vector object to which it is applied. The compiler will invoke the **const** version whenever the subscripting operator is applied on the right-hand side of an assignment operation, and it will invoke the non-**const** version when the subscripting operator is applied on the left-hand side of an assignment. The body of the code for both forms of the function is identical:

```
Item_Type& operator[](size_t index) {
  // Verify that the index is legal.
  if (index < 0 || index >= num_items) {
    throw std::out_of_range
      ("index to operator[] is out of range");
  }
  return the_data[index];
}
```

Also, observe that in our implementation we validate the value of the index, index. In the standard vector, the subscripting operator does not do this. Our implementation is equivalent to the standard vector function at.

Bjarne Stroustrup, the inventor of C++, suggests in his book, *The C++ Programming Language, 3rd Edition*, that programmers can easily define their own vector class that overcomes this limitation as follows.

```
template<typename Item_Type>
  class my_vector : public std::vector<Item_Type> {
    Item_Type& operator[](int index) {return at(index);}
    const Item_Type& operator[](int index) const {
      return at(index);}
  }
}
```

The new template class my_vector is defined as an extension of the standard vector class. The subscript operators in the standard class are overridden with ones that apply function at.

FIGURE 4.3
Adding an Element to the End of a vector

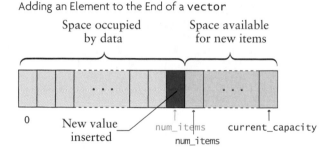

Space occupied by data

Space available for new items

0

New value inserted

num_items

num_items

current_capacity

The push_back Function

The push_back function appends an item to the end of a vector. If num_items is less than current_capacity, then, to append a new item:

a. Insert the new item at the position indicated by the value of num_items.

b. Increment the value of num_items.

This sequence of operations is illustrated in Figure 4.3. The old value of num_items is in gray; its new value is in color.

If num_items is already equal to current_capacity, we must first allocate a new array to hold the data and then copy the data to this new array. The member function reserve (explained shortly) does this. The code for the push_back member function follows.

```
void push_back(const Item_Type& the_value) {
  // Make sure there is space for the new item.
  if (num_items == current_capacity) {
    reserve(2 * current_capacity);    // Allocate an expanded array
  }
  // Insert the new item.
  the_data[num_items] = the_value;
  num_items++;
}
```

✓ PROGRAM STYLE

Using the Postfix (or Prefix) Operator with a Subscript

Some programmers prefer to combine the last two statements in the push_back function and write them as

```
the_data[num_items++] = the_value;
```

This is perfectly valid. C++ uses the current value of num_items as the subscript for array access and then increments it. The only difficulty is the fact that two operations are written in one statement and are carried out in a predetermined order. If you are unsure of the order, you might select prefix increment when you needed postfix increment, or vice versa.

FIGURE 4.4
Making Room to Insert an Item into an Array

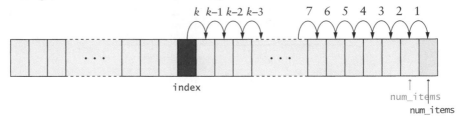

The `insert` Function

To insert an item into the middle of the array (anywhere but the end), the values that are at the insertion point and beyond must be shifted over to make room. In Figure 4.4, the arrow with label 1 shows the first element moved, the arrow with label 2 shows the next element moved, and so on. This data move is done using the following loop:

```
for (size_t i = num_items; i > index; i--) {
  the_data[i] = the_data[i - 1];
}
```

Notice that the array subscript starts at `num_items` and moves toward the beginning of the array (down to `index + 1`). If we had started the subscript at `index + 1` instead, we would copy the value at `index` into each element of the array with a larger subscript. Before we execute this loop, we need to be sure that `num_items` is not equal to `current_capacity`. If it is, we must call `reserve`.

After increasing the capacity (if necessary) and moving the other elements, we can then add the new item. The complete code is as follows:

```
void insert(size_t index, const Item_Type& the_value) {
  // Validate index.
  if (index > num_items) {
    throw std::out_of_range
      ("index to insert is out of range");
  }
  // Ensure that there is space for the new item.
  if (num_items == current_capacity) {
    reserve(2 * current_capacity);   // Allocate an expanded array
  }
  // Move data from index to num_items - 1 down.
  for (size_t i = num_items; i > index; i--) {
    the_data[i] = the_data[i - 1];
  }
  // Insert the new item.
  the_data[index] = the_value;
  num_items++;
}
```

The `erase` Function

To remove an item, the items that follow it must be moved forward to close up the space. In Figure 4.5, the arrow with label 1 shows the first element moved, the

FIGURE 4.5
Removing an Item from an Array

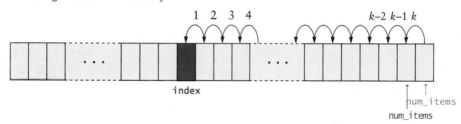

arrow with label 2 shows the next element moved, and so on. This data move is done using the following loop:

```
for (size_t i = index + 1; i < num_items; i++) {
  the_data[i - 1] = the_data[i];
}
```

The complete code for the erase function follows.

```
void erase(size_t index) {
  // Validate index.
  if (index > num_items) {
    throw std::out_of_range
      ("index to insert is out of range");
  }
  // Move items below the removed one up.
  for (size_t i = index + 1; i < num_items; i++) {
    the_data[i - 1] = the_data[i];
  }
  num_items--;
}
```

The reserve Function

The reserve function creates a new array that is at least twice the size of the current array and then copies the contents of the current array into the new one. The pointer variable the_data is then set to point to this new array. The code is as follows:

```
void reserve(size_t new_capacity) {
  if (new_capacity > current_capacity) {
    if (new_capacity > 2 * current_capacity)
      current_capacity = new_capacity;
    else
      current_capacity *= 2;  // Double the capacity.
    Item_Type* new_data = new Item_Type[current_capacity];
    // Copy the data over.
    for (size_t i = 0; i < num_items; i++)
      new_data[i] = the_data[i];
    // Free the memory occupied by the old copy.
    delete[] the_data;
    // Now point to the new data.
    the_data = new_data;
  }
}
```

The statement

```
delete[] the_data;
```

releases the memory allocated to the array pointed to by the_data. The reason we do this is to prevent memory leaks.

The reason for doubling is to spread out the cost of copying. Doubling an array of size n allows us to add n more items before we need to do another array copy. Therefore, we can add n new items after we have copied over n existing items. Although each reallocation is O(n), we only have to do a reallocation after n items are added. This averages out to 1 copy per add, so reallocation is effectively an O(1) operation. Another way of saying this is that insertion is performed in *amortized constant time*. Recall that it will take only about 20 reserve operations to create an array that can store over a million references (2^{20} is greater than 1,000,000).

Performance of the KW::vector

The functions operator[] and at are each a few lines of code and contain no loops. Thus we say that these functions execute in constant time, or O(1).

If we insert into (or remove from) the middle of a KW::vector, then at most n items have to be shifted. Therefore, the cost of inserting or removing an element is O(n).

What if we have to reallocate before we can insert? Recall that we spread out the cost of copying so that effectively it is an O(1) operation, so the insertion is still O(n). Even if we don't spread out the cost of copying, the copy operation would still be O(n), so the worst case would just double the cost.

EXERCISES FOR SECTION 4.3

SELF-CHECK

1. Trace the execution of the following:
   ```
   int an_array[] = {0, 1, 2, 3, 4, 5, 6, 7};
   for (int i = 3; i < 7; i++)
     an_array[i + 1] = an_array[i];
   ```
   and the following:
   ```
   int an_array[] = {0, 1, 2, 3, 4, 5, 6, 7};
   for (int i = 7; i > 3; i--)
     an_array[i] = an_array[i - 1];
   ```
   What are the contents of an_array after the execution of each loop?

2. Write statements to remove the middle object from a vector and place it at the end.

PROGRAMMING

1. Provide a constructor for class KW::vector that accepts a size_t argument, which represents the initial array size, and an initial value. Fill the array with copies of this value.

4.4 The Copy Constructor, Assignment Operator, and Destructor

Copying Objects and the Copy Constructor

Often, we need to make a copy of an object. When we do this, both the original and the copy will initially store the same information. We want the copy to be an *independent copy*, which means we should be able to modify one of the objects without affecting the other.

Copying of primitive types is straightforward—the values are duplicated and placed in the target location. For class types, copying is done by what is appropriately known as the *copy constructor*. Every class has a default copy constructor with the following signature:

> *class-name*(const *class-name*&);

The purpose of the copy constructor is to create an independent copy of an object. It is automatically invoked:

1. When an object is passed to a function by value
2. When an object is returned from a function
3. When an object is initialized with another object of the same class

Shallow Copy versus Deep Copy

In Section 4.3 we defined the KW::vector class as follows:

```
namespace KW {

    template<typename Item_Type>
      class vector {

        private:
          // Data fields

          /** The initial capacity of the array */
          static const size_t INITIAL_CAPACITY = 10;

          /** The current capacity of the array */
          size_t current_capacity;

          /** The current num_items of the array  */
          size_t num_items;

          /** The array to contain the data */
          Item_Type* the_data;

        public:
          // Member Functions
          ...
      };
};
```

EXAMPLE 4.4   In the statement

```
vector<int> v2(v1);
```

vector v1 is passed as a **const** reference argument to the vector copy constructor, so v1 can't be changed, and the variable v2 is then initialized to a copy of the vector v1. Each data field will be copied, and any changes made later to v2 should not affect v1.

The default copy constructor will make a copy of each data field's value. This is fine for the type **size_t** fields current_capacity and num_items. However, it is not what we want for the pointer variable the_data. When the value in v1.the_data is copied over, both v1.the_data and v2.the_data will point to the same array (see Figure 4.6).

Because v1.the_data and v2.the_data point to the same object, the statement

```
v1[2] = 10;
```

also changes v2[2] as shown in Figure 4.7. For this reason, v2 is considered a *shallow copy* of v1.

The statement

```
v1.push_back(20);
```

will insert 20 into v1[5] and will change v1.num_items to 6, but will not change v2.num_items. as shown in Figure 4.8. As you can see, some changes to v1 will be reflected in v2, but others will not.

What we need to do is create an independent copy of the underlying array so that both v1.the_data and v2.the_data point to different arrays (see Figure 4.9). Because it is now an independent copy, the resulting vector v2 is a *deep copy* of vector v1.

The following code fragment shows a copy constructor that accomplishes this. The constructor initializes the two **size_t** data fields by copying over the corresponding values from vector parameter other. A new array is allocated and pointed to by data field the_data. Next, the **for** statement copies each array element value from the original array (other.the_data[i]) to the new array (the_data[i]).

FIGURE 4.6
Shallow Copy of a Vector

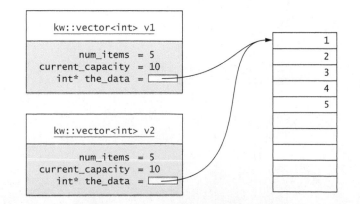

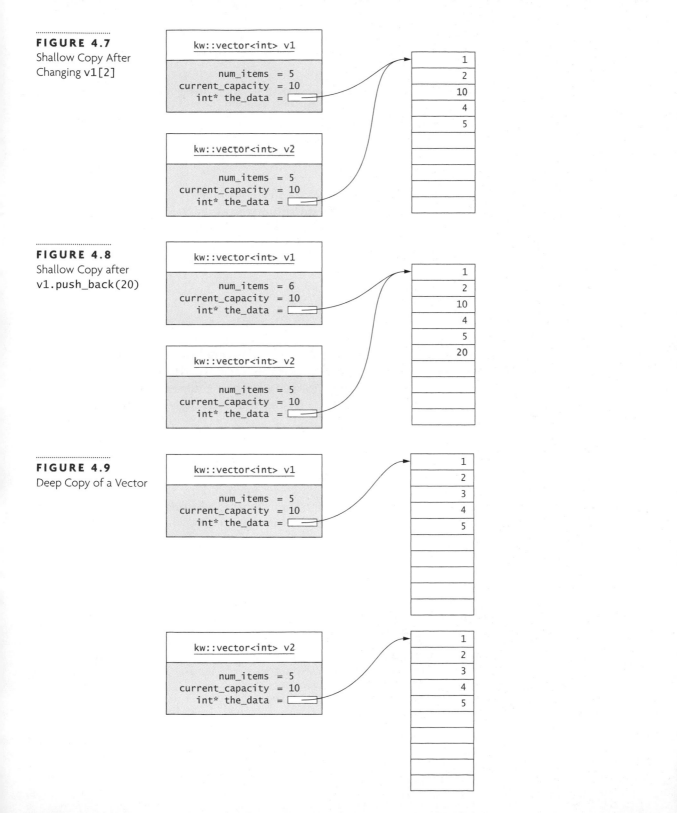

FIGURE 4.7
Shallow Copy After Changing v1[2]

FIGURE 4.8
Shallow Copy after v1.push_back(20)

FIGURE 4.9
Deep Copy of a Vector

```
/** Make a copy of a vector.
    @param other The vector to be copied
*/
vector<Item_Type>(const vector<Item_Type>& other) :
  current_capacity(other.capacity), num_items(other.num_items),
      the_data(new Item_Type[other.current_capacity]) {
  for (size_t i = 0; i < num_items; i++)
    the_data[i] = other.the_data[i];
}
```

Assignment Operator

The purpose of assignment is also to create an independent copy of an object. Assignment of primitive types is straightforward—the values are duplicated and placed in the target location (the variable on the left hand side of the assignment). For class types, assignment is done by what is appropriately known as the *assignment operator*. Thus, if v1 and v2 are vector objects, the statement

```
v2 = v1;
```

is executed as if it were written

```
v2.operator=(v1);
```

Every class has a default assignment operator. The default assignment operator makes a copy of each data field of the source object (v1 above) and places it into the corresponding data field of the target object (v2 above). If the data field is a class type, that class's assignment operator is used. The default assignment operator will make a shallow copy of an object, so we must override it if we want truly independent copies.

As we have shown so far, we have a function in our vector class that makes a copy of a vector object: the copy constructor. It is generally a poor design practice to have two functions that do very similar things, because they may do them differently by mistake. Therefore, we take the following approach: First we copy the source data (parameter other) into a temporary object (the_copy) using the copy constructor. Then we swap the target value and the temporary object value, and return the modified target (*this). Upon return, the destructor for the temporary object is automatically invoked by the compiler, thus deleting the old data. We will describe function swap in Section 4.11 and discuss the destructor next.

```
/** Assign the contents of one vector to another.
    @param other The vector to be assigned to this vector
    @return This vector with a copy of the other vector's
            contents
*/
vector<Item_Type>& operator=(const vector<Item_Type>& other) {
  // Make a copy of the other vector.
  vector<Item_Type> the_copy(other);
  // Swap contents of self with the copy.
  swap(the_copy);
  // Return -- upon return the copy will be destroyed.
  return *this;
}
```

The variable **this** is a pointer to the object to which a member function is applied. Normally we do not need to use it inside a member function, since the current object's data fields and member functions are implicitly referenced. The semantics for the assignment operator are such that the result of the assignment has the value of the modified target object. This is obtained by dereferencing the pointer using the * operator. Thus we exit the assignment operator using the strange-looking statement

```
return *this;
```

The **return** by reference does not use the copy constructor.

The Destructor

The purpose of the destructor is to undo what the constructor does. The constructor takes a block of uninitialized memory and sets it to a known state, thus creating an object. When the destructor is finished, the object is no longer considered to be in a valid state, and the memory it occupies can be reused for creating other objects. Unless this is done properly, the program will have memory leaks.

There is a default destructor, which effectively invokes the destructor for each data field. For primitive types, the destructor does nothing, and this is fine. However, a pointer is a primitive type that stores a memory address as its "value." Thus, if a class contains a pointer, the default destructor does not do anything with it either. However, if the pointer references a dynamically allocated object (such as the array referenced by pointer the_data), the memory allocated to that object must be freed as well. Therefore, we need to provide a destructor that does this when the object is destroyed.

The destructor for the vector class is defined as

```
~vector() {
  delete[] the_data;
}
```

The symbol ~ indicates that a destructor is being defined. The destructor body releases the memory occupied by the dynamically allocated array.

SYNTAX   Defining the Destructor

FORM:

~*class-name*() {*body*}

EXAMPLE:

~vector() {delete[] the_data;}

INTERPRETATION:

The function named ~*class-name* is the destructor for the class *class-name*. The purpose of the destructor is to supplement any actions taken by the default destructor. Specifically, it is to release any resources owned by the object, such as dynamically allocated memory.

◯ PITFALL

Failure to Define the Assignment Operator, Copy Constructor, and Destructor

If a class dynamically allocates a resource such as dynamically allocated memory, then it must define the assignment operator, copy constructor, and destructor. This is known are the "rule of three." Generally, if you define one of these three functions in a class, you must define all three of them, since they have to work consistently. If you define the assignment operator and not the copy constructor, then copies made by one may not be the same as copies made by the other. For example, the default copy constructor and assignment operator make shallow copies. If you define only a copy constructor that makes a deep copy, it will not work consistently with the default assignment operator. If you omit the destructor, then there is a potential for a memory leak.

EXERCISES FOR SECTION 4.4

SELF-CHECK

1. What is the difference between a shallow copy and a deep copy?
2. Why is it not a problem to have a shallow copy of a primitive-type data field?
3. Show what happens in Figure 4.6 (shallow copy) when the following statement executes:
   ```
   v2.pop_back();
   ```
4. Answer Exercise 3 for Figure 4.9 (deep copy).

4.5 Single-Linked Lists and Double-Linked Lists

The vector has the limitation that the insert and erase functions operate in linear ($O(n)$) time, because they require a loop to shift elements in the underlying array. In this section we introduce a data structure, the linked list, that overcomes this limitation by providing the ability to add or remove items anywhere in the list in constant ($O(1)$) time. A linked list is useful when you need to insert and remove elements at arbitrary locations (not just at the end) and when you will do frequent insertions and removals.

One example would be maintaining an alphabetized list of students in a course at the beginning of a semester while students are adding and dropping courses. If you were using a vector, you would have to shift all names that follow the new person's name down one position before you could insert a new student's name. Figure 4.10

FIGURE 4.10
Inserting a Student
into a Class List

Before adding Browniten, Barbara

Abidoye, Olandunni
Boado, Annabelle
Butler, James
Chee, Yong-Han
Debaggis, Tarra
⋮

After adding Browniten, Barbara

Abidoye, Olandunni
Boado, Annabelle
Browniten, Barbara
Butler, James
Chee, Yong-Han
Debaggis, Tarra
⋮

FIGURE 4.10
Inserting a Student
into a Class List

FIGURE 4.11
Removing a Student
Who Dropped

Before dropping Boado, Annabelle

Abidoye, Olandunni
Boado, Annabelle
Browniten, Barbara
Butler, James
Chee, Yong-Han
Debaggis, Tarra
⋮

After dropping Boado, Annabelle

Abidoye, Olandunni
Browniten, Barbara
Butler, James
Chee, Yong-Han
Debaggis, Tarra
⋮

FIGURE 4.12
Inserting into a
Numbered List of
Students Waiting to
Register

Before inserting Alice at position 1

0. Warner, Emily
1. Dang, Phong
2. Feldman, Anna
3. Barnes, Aaron
4. Torres, Kristopher
⋮

After inserting Alice at position 1

0. Warner, Emily
1. Franklin, Alice
2. Dang, Phong
3. Feldman, Anna
4. Barnes, Aaron
5. Torres, Kristopher
⋮

shows this process. The names in gray were all shifted down when Barbara added the course. Similarly, if a student drops the course, the names of all students after the one who dropped (in gray in Figure 4.11) would be shifted up one position to close up the space.

Another example would be maintaining a list of students who are waiting to register for a course. Instead of having the students waiting in an actual line, you can give each student a number, which is the student's position in the line. If someone drops out of the line, everyone with a higher number gets a new number that is 1 lower than before. If someone cuts into the line because they "need the course to graduate," everyone after this person gets a new number that is 1 higher than before. The person maintaining the list is responsible for giving everyone their new number after a change. Figure 4.12 illustrates what happens when Alice is inserted and given the number 1: Everyone whose number is ≥ 1 gets a new number. This process is analogous to maintaining the names in a vector; each person's number is that person's position in the list, and some names in the list are shifted after every change.

A better way to do this would be to give each person the name of the next person in line, instead of his or her own position in the line (which can change frequently). To start the registration process, the person who is registering students calls the person who is at the head of the line. After she finishes registration, the person at the head of the line calls the next person, and so on. Now what if person A lets person

B cut into the line before him? Because B has taken A's position in line, A will register after B, so person B must have A's name. Also, the person in front of the new person must know to call B instead of A. Figure 4.13 illustrates what happens when Alice is inserted in the list. Only the two entries shown in color need to be changed (Emily must call Alice instead of Phong, and Alice must call Phong). Although Alice is shown at the bottom of Figure 4.13, she is really the second student in the list. The first four students in the list are Emily Warner, Alice Franklin, Phong Dang, and Anna Feldman.

What happens if someone drops out of our line? In this case, the name of the person who follows the one that drops out must be given to the person who comes before the one who drops out. Figure 4.14 illustrates this. If Aaron drops out, only one entry needs to be changed (Anna must call Kristopher instead of Aaron).

Using a linked list is analogous to the process just discussed and illustrated in Figures 4.13 and 4.14 for storing our list of student names. Insertion and removal are done in constant time, and no shifts are required. Each element in a linked list, called a *node*, stores information and a link to the next node in the list. For example, for our list of students in Figure 4.14, the information "Warner, Emily" would be stored in the first node, and the link to the next node would reference a node whose information part was "Franklin, Alice". Here are the first three nodes of this list:

"Warner, Emily" ⟶ "Franklin, Alice" ⟶ "Dang, Phong"

We discuss how to represent and manipulate a linked list next.

FIGURE 4.13
Inserting into a Numbered List Where Each Student Knows Who Is Next

Before inserting Alice		After inserting Alice	
Person in line	*Person to call*	*Person in line*	*Person to call*
Warner, Emily	Dang, Phong	Warner, Emily	Franklin, Alice
Dang, Phong	Feldman, Anna	Dang, Phong	Feldman, Anna
Feldman, Anna	Barnes, Aaron	Feldman, Anna	Barnes, Aaron
Barnes, Aaron	Torres, Kristopher	Barnes, Aaron	Torres, Kristopher
Torres, Kristopher	...	Torres, Kristopher	...
⋮	⋮	⋮	⋮
		Franklin, Alice	Dang, Phong

FIGURE 4.14
Removing a Student from a List Where Each Student Knows Who Is Next

Before dropping Aaron		After dropping Aaron	
Person in line	*Person to call*	*Person in line*	*Person to call*
Warner, Emily	Franklin, Alice	Warner, Emily	Franklin, Alice
Dang, Phong	Feldman, Anna	Dang, Phong	Feldman, Anna
Feldman, Anna	Barnes, Aaron	Feldman, Anna	Torres, Kristopher
Barnes, Aaron	Torres, Kristopher	Barnes, Aaron	Torres, Kristopher
Torres, Kristopher	...	Torres, Kristopher	...
⋮	⋮	⋮	⋮
Franklin, Alice	Dang, Phong	Franklin, Alice	Dang, Phong

FIGURE 4.15
Node and Link

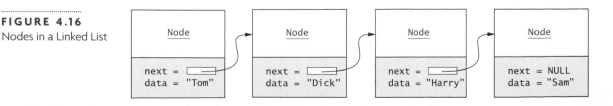

A List Node

A node is a data structure that contains a data item and one or more *links*. A link is a pointer to a node. A UML diagram of this relationship is shown in Figure 4.15. This shows that a Node contains a data field named data of type Item_Type and a pointer to a Node. The name of the pointer is next, as shown on the line from the Node to itself. Figure 4.16 shows four Nodes linked together to form the list [Tom, Dick, Harry, Sam]. In this figure Item_Type is string.

We can define a Node as a C++ **struct**. (A **struct** is a data structure that contains data fields and possibly constructors. It is like a class, except that it has no operators.) The definition of the **struct** Node is shown in Listing 4.2.

LISTING 4.2
Node.h

```
#ifndef NODE_H_
#define NODE_H_

/** A Node is the building block for a single-linked list. */
struct Node {
  // Data Fields
  /** The data */
  Item_Type data;
  /** The pointer to the next node. */
  Node* next;

  // Constructor
  /** Creates a new Node that points to another Node.
      @param data_item The data stored
      @param next_ptr Pointer to the Node that is
                      pointed to by the new Node
  */
  Node(const Item_Type& data_item, Node* next_ptr = NULL) :
    data(data_item), next(next_ptr) {}
};
#endif
```

A Node is defined inside of a class, making it an inner class. The outer class is a template class that has the template parameter Item_Type.

The Node will be defined in the private part of the outer class, thus keeping the details private from the outer class's clients. The reason for defining it as a **struct** is that a **struct**'s data members are public by default, thus accessible to the functions of the outer class.

The constructor initializes the values of data and next. We provide **NULL** as a default value for next.

FIGURE 4.16
Nodes in a Linked List

Node	Node	Node	Node
next = □	next = □	next = □	next = NULL
data = "Tom"	data = "Dick"	data = "Harry"	data = "Sam"

PROGRAM STYLE

Use of struct

The keywords **class** and **struct** are effectively synonymous in C++. The only difference is that members of classes are private by default, whereas members of **struct**s are public by default. Most C++ programmers have adopted the practice of using **struct** only to define a grouping of data that is to be publicly accessible. The only member functions defined are simple constructors that initialize the data. Such **struct**s are known as "Plain Old Data" (POD) and can be used as function parameters to functions written in other programming languages such as C.

Connecting Nodes

We can construct the list shown in Figure 4.16 using the following sequence of statements:

```
Node* tom = new Node("Tom");
Node* dick = new Node("Dick");
Node* harry = new Node("Harry");
Node* sam = new Node("Sam");
tom->next = dick;
dick->next = harry;
harry->next = sam;
```

The statement

```
tom->next = dick;
```

stores a pointer (link) to the node with data "Dick" in the data field next of the node pointed to by tom.

Generally we do not have individual pointers to each of the nodes. Instead, we have a pointer to the first node in the list and work from there. Thus we could build the list shown in Figure 4.16 as follows:

```
Node* head = new Node("Tom");
head->next = new Node("Dick");
head->next->next = new Node("Harry");
head->next->next->next = new Node("Sam");
```

In the foregoing fragment, we grew the list by adding each new node to the end of the list so far. The node referenced by head was always the first node in the list (data is "Tom"). We can also grow a list by adding nodes to the front of the list. The following fragment creates the same list, but each new node is added to the front of the list so far. After each addition, head references a different node. The first node referenced by head (data is "Sam") will be the last node in the final list.

```
Node* head = new Node("Sam");
head = new Node("Harry", head);
head = new Node("Dick", head);
head = new Node("Tom", head);
```

Each statement of the form

```
head = new Node(a_name, head);
```

creates a new node, whose data component is *a_name* and whose next component is the list so far. Then head is reset to point to this new node. This has the effect of adding the new node to the front of the existing list.

Inserting a Node in a List

We can insert a new node, "Bob", into the list after "Harry" as follows:

```
Node* bob = new Node("Bob");
bob->next = harry->next;    // Step 1
harry->next = bob;          // Step 2
```

The linked list now is as shown in Figure 4.17. We show the number of the step that created each link alongside it.

Removing a Node

If we have a pointer, tom, to the node that contains "Tom", we can remove the node that follows "Tom":

```
Node* ptr = tom->next;      // Pointer to Node to be deleted
tom->next = tom->next->next; // Remove Node from list
delete ptr;                 // Delete Node to free storage
```

The list is now as shown in Figure 4.18. Notice that we did not start with a pointer to "Dick" but instead started with a pointer to "Tom". To remove a node, we need to point to the node that precedes it, not the node being removed. (Recall from our registration list example that the person in front of the one dropping out of line must be told to call the person who follows the one who is dropping out.) Note that we use the statement

```
delete ptr;
```

to release the memory allocated to the node we removed. We do this to avoid memory leaks.

FIGURE 4.17
After Inserting "Bob"

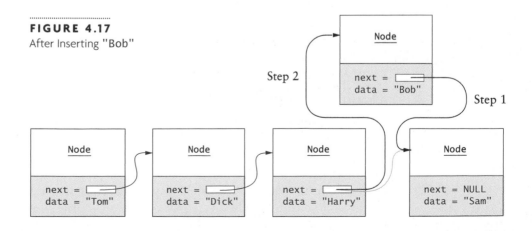

FIGURE 4.18

After Removing Node Following "Tom"

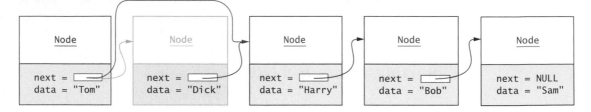

Traversing a Linked List

Traversing a linked list is a fairly simple process.

1.   Set node_ptr to point to the first node.
2.   **while** node_ptr is not **NULL**
3.   Do something with node pointed to by node_ptr.
4.   Set node_ptr to node_ptr->next.

This is illustrated by the following fragment, which displays the information in our example linked list:

```
node_ptr = tom;    // tom points to the first node
while (node_ptr != NULL) {
  cout << node_ptr->data;
  if (node_ptr->next != NULL) {
    cout << " ==> ";
  }
  node_ptr = node_ptr->next;
}
cout << endl;
```

As new values are assigned to variable node_ptr by the statement

```
node_ptr = node_ptr->next;
```

node_ptr walks down the list, pointing to each of the list nodes in turn. The value of node_ptr is **NULL** when the traversal is finished.

Traversing the list shown in Figure 4.18, the loop produces the following output:

```
Tom ==> Harry ==> Bob ==> Sam
```

Double-Linked Lists

Our single-linked list data structure has some limitations:

- We can insert a node only after a node we have a pointer to. For example, to insert "Bob" to arrive at Figure 4.17 we needed a pointer to the node containing "Harry". If we wanted to insert "Bob" before "Sam" but did not have a pointer to "Harry", we would have to start at the beginning of the list and search until we found a node whose next node was "Sam".

🚫 **PITFALL**

Falling Off the End of a List

If node_ptr is at the last list element and you execute the statement

node_ptr = node_ptr->next;

node_ptr will be set to **NULL**, and you will have fallen off the end of the list. This is not an error. However, if you execute this statement again, you will probably get a run-time error. The exact error message is operating system dependent, as discussed in Chapter 2.

- We can remove a node only if we have a pointer to its predecessor node. For example, to remove "Dick" to arrive at Figure 4.18 we needed a pointer to the node containing "Tom". If we wanted to remove "Dick" without having this pointer, we would have to start at the beginning of the list and search until we found a node whose next node was "Dick".

- We can traverse the list only in the forward direction, whereas with a vector we can move forward (or backward) by incrementing (or decrementing) the index.

We can overcome these limitations by adding a pointer prev to each node as shown in the UML class diagram in Figure 4.19. The lines indicate that both prev and next are pointers whose values can be changed. Our new, double-linked list is shown in Figure 4.20.

FIGURE 4.19
Double-Linked List
Node UML Diagram

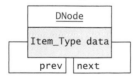

FIGURE 4.20
A Double-Linked List

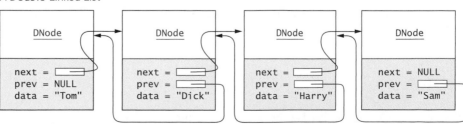

The **DNode** Class

The DNode class for a double-linked list has references to the data and to the next and previous nodes. Listing 4.3 shows the declaration of this class (as a **struct**).

....
LISTING 4.3
DNode.h

```
#ifndef DNODE_H_
#define DNODE_H_

/** A DNode is the building block for a double-linked list. */
struct DNode {
  /** A copy of the data */
  Item_Type data;
  /** A pointer to the next DNode */
  DNode* next;
  /** A pointer to the previous DNode */
  DNode* prev;
  DNode(const Item_Type& the_data,
        DNode* prev_val = NULL, DNode* next_val = NULL) :
    data(the_data), next(next_val), prev(prev_val) {}
};
#endif
```

Inserting into a Double-Linked List

If sam is a pointer to the node containing "Sam", we can insert a new node containing "Sharon" into the list before "Sam" using the following statements. Before the insertion, we can refer to the predecessor of sam as sam->prev. After the insertion, this node will be pointed to by sharon->prev.

```
DNode* sharon = new DNode("Sharon");
// Link new DNode to its neighbors.
sharon->next = sam;        // Step 1
sharon->prev = sam->prev;  // Step 2
// Link old predecessor of sam to new predecessor.
sam->prev->next = sharon;  // Step 3
// Link to new predecessor.
sam->prev = sharon;        // Step 4
```

The three DNodes affected by the insertion are shown in Figures 4.21 and 4.22. The old links are shown in gray, and the new links are shown in color. Next to each link we show the number of the step that creates it. Figure 4.21 shows the links after Steps 1 and 2, and Figure 4.22 shows the links after Steps 3 and 4.

Removing from a Double-Linked List

If we have a pointer, harry, to the node that contains "Harry", we can remove that node without having a named pointer to its predecessor:

```
harry->prev->next = harry->next; // Step 1
harry->next->prev = harry->prev; // Step 2
delete harry;
```

The list is now as shown in Figure 4.23.

FIGURE 4.21
Steps 1 and 2 in
Inserting sharon

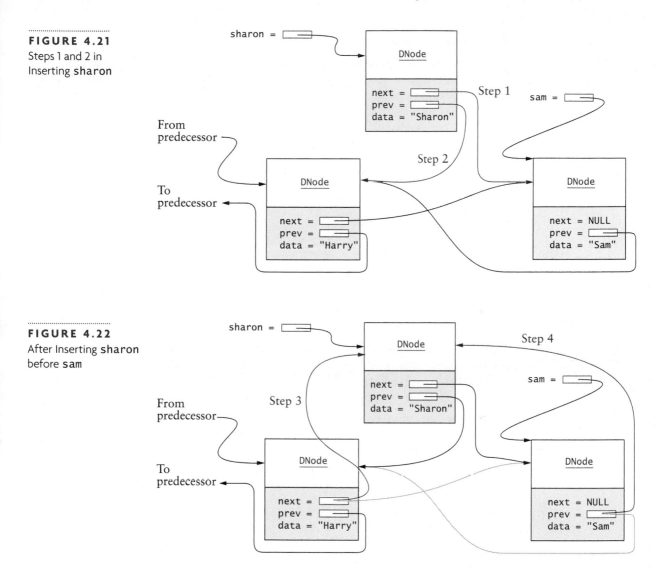

FIGURE 4.22
After Inserting sharon
before sam

FIGURE 4.23
Removing harry from a Double-Linked List

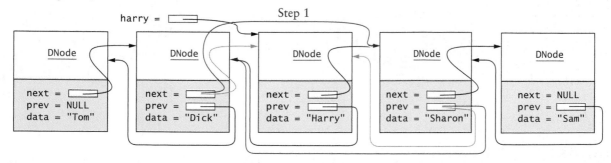

FIGURE 4.24
A Double-Linked
List Object

```
          list

   head = [    ]
   tail = [    ]
   num_items =
```

Creating a Double-Linked List Object

So far we have shown just the internal DNodes for a linked list. A double-linked list object would consist of a separate object with data fields head (a pointer to the first list DNode), tail (a pointer to the last list DNode), and num_items (the number of internal DNodes). See Figure 4.24.

Circular Lists

We can carry the development of the single-linked list to the double-linked list one step further and create a circular list by linking the last node to the first node (and the first node to the last one). If head references the first list node and tail references the last list node, the statements

```
head->prev = tail;
tail->next = head;
```

would accomplish this (Figure 4.25).

You could also create a circular list from a single-linked list by executing just the statement

```
tail->next = head;
```

This statement connects the last list element to the first list element. If you keep a pointer to only the last list element, tail, you can access the last element and the first element (tail->next) in O(1) time.

One advantage of a circular list is that you can continue to traverse in the forward (or reverse) direction even after you have passed the last (or first) list node. This enables you to visit all the list elements from any starting point. In a list that is not circular, you would have to start at the beginning or at the end if you wanted to visit all the list elements. A second advantage of a circular list is that you can never fall off the end of the list. There is a disadvantage: You must be careful not to set up an infinite loop.

FIGURE 4.25
Circular Linked List

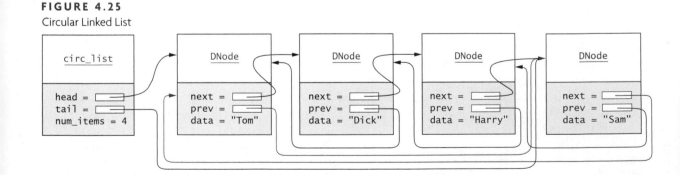

EXERCISES FOR SECTION 4.5

SELF-CHECK

1. Draw a single-linked list of **int** values containing the integers 5, 10, 7, and 30 and referenced by head. Complete the following fragment, which adds all **int** values in a list. Your fragment should walk down the list, adding any integers to sum and ignoring any objects in the list that are not **int** objects.

```
int sum = 0;
Node* node_ptr = _____;
while (node_ptr != NULL) {
  sum += _____;
}
node_ptr = _____;
}
```

2. Answer the following questions about lists.
   a. Each node in a single-linked list has a pointer to _____.
   b. In a double-linked list each node has a pointer to _____, and _____.
   c. To remove an item from a single-linked list you need a pointer to _____.
   d. To remove an item from a double-linked list you need a pointer to _____.

3. For the single-linked list in Figure 4.16, assume you have a pointer variable head (type Node*) that references the first node. Explain the effect of each statement in the following fragments.
   a. `head = new Node("Shakira", head->next);`
   b. `Node* node_ptr = head->next;`
   `node_ptr->next = node_ptr->next->next;`
   c. `Node* node_ptr = head;`
   `while (node_ptr->next != NULL)`
   `  node_ptr = node_ptr->next;`
   `  node_ptr->next = new Node("Tamika");`
   d. `Node* node_ptr = head;`
   `while (node_ptr != NULL && node_ptr->data != "Harry")`
   `  node_ptr = node_ptr->next;`
   `if (node_ptr != NULL) {`
   `  node_ptr->data = "Sally";`
   `  node_ptr->next = new Node("Harry", node_ptr->next->next);`
   `}`

4. For the double-linked list in Figure 4.20, explain the effect of each statement in the following fragments.
   a. `DNode* node_ptr = tail->prev;`
   `node_ptr->prev->next = tail;`
   `tail->prev = node_ptr->prev;`
   b. `DNode* node_ptr = head;`
   `head = new DNode("Tamika");`
   `head->next = node_ptr;`
   `node_ptr->prev = head;`
   c. `DNode* node_ptr = new DNode("Shakira");`
   `node_ptr->prev = head;`
   `node_ptr->next = head->next;`
   `head->next->prev = node_ptr;`
   `head->next = node_ptr;`

PROGRAMMING

1. Using the single-linked list shown in Figure 4.16, and assuming that head references the first Node and tail references the last Node, write statements to do each of the following.

   a. Insert "Bill" before "Tom".

   b. Remove "Sam".

   c. Insert "Bill" before "Tom".

   d. Remove "Sam".

2. Repeat Exercise 1 using the double-linked list shown in Figure 4.20.

4.6 The list Class and the Iterator

The list Class

The list class, part of the C++ standard library defined in header <list>, implements a double-linked list. A selected subset of the functions of this class are shown in Table 4.2. Because the list class, like the vector class, is a sequential container, it contains many of the functions found in the vector class as well as some additional functions.

Several functions use an iterator (or const_iterator) as an argument or return an iterator as a result. We discuss iterators next.

The Iterator

Let's say we want to process each element in a list. We *cannot* use the following loop to access the list elements in sequence, starting with the one at index 0.

```
// Access each list element and process it.
for (size_t index = 0; index < a_list.size(); index++) {
  // Do something with next_element, the element at
  // position index
  Item_Type next_element = a_list[index];  // Not valid
  ...
}
```

This is because the subscripting operator (operator[]) is not defined for the list as it is for the vector. Nor is the at function defined for a list, because the elements of a list are not indexed like an array or vector.

Instead, we can use the concept of an *iterator* to access the elements of a list in sequence. Think of an iterator as a moving place marker that keeps track of the current position in a particular linked list, and therefore, the next element to process (see Fig. 4.26). An iterator can be advanced forward (using operator++) or backward (using operator--).

TABLE 4.2
Selected Functions Defined by the Standard Library `list` Class

Function	Behavior
`iterator insert(iterator pos,` `    const Item_Type& item)`	Inserts a copy of `item` into the list at position `pos`. Returns an `iterator` that references the newly inserted item.
`iterator erase(iterator pos)`	Removes the item from the list at position `pos`. Returns an `iterator` that references the item following the one erased.
`void remove(const Item_Type& item)`	Removes all occurrences of `item` from the list.
`void push_front(const Item_Type& item)`	Inserts a copy of `item` as the first element of the list.
`void push_back(const Item_Type& item)`	Adds a copy of `item` to the end of the list.
`void pop_front()`	Removes the first item from the list.
`void pop_back()`	Removes the last item from the list.
`Item_Type& front();` `const Item_Type& front() const`	Gets the first element in the list. Both constant and modifiable versions are provided.
`Item_Type& back();` `const Item_Type& back() const`	Gets the last element in the list. Both constant and modifiable versions are provided.
`iterator begin()`	Returns an `iterator` that references the first item of the list.
`const_iterator() begin const`	Returns a `const_iterator` that references the first item of the list.
`iterator end()`	Returns an `iterator` that references the end of the list (one past the last item).
`const_iterator end() const`	Returns a `const_iterator` that references the end of the list (one past the last item).
`void swap(list<Item_Type> other)`	Exchanges the contents of this list with the `other` list.
`bool empty() const`	Returns **true** if the list is empty.
`size_t size() const`	Returns the number of items in the list.

You use an `iterator` like a pointer. The pointer dereferencing operator (`operator*`) returns a reference to the field `data` in the `DNode` object at the current `iterator` position. Earlier, in Section 4.5, we showed program fragments where the variable `node_ptr` was used to point to the nodes in a linked list. The `iterator` provides us with the same capabilities but does so while preserving information hiding. The internal structure of the `DNode` is not visible to the clients. Clients can access or modify the data and can move from one `DNode` in the list to another, but they cannot modify the structure of the linked list, since they have no direct access to the `prev` or `next` data fields.

Table 4.2 shows four functions that manipulate `iterator`s. Function `insert` (`erase`) adds (removes) a list element at the position indicated by an `iterator`. The `insert`

FIGURE 4.26
Double-Linked List with KW::list<Item_Type>::iterator

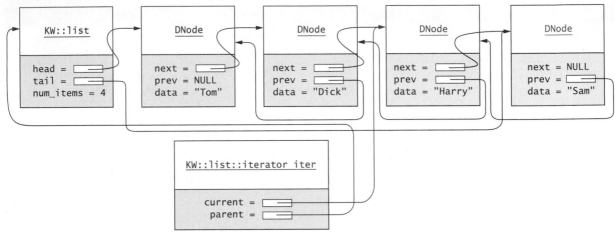

function returns an `iterator` to the newly inserted item, and the `erase` function returns an `iterator` to the item that follows the one erased. Function `begin` returns an `iterator` positioned at the first element of the list, and function `end` returns an `iterator` positioned just past the last list element.

EXAMPLE 4.5   Assume `iter` is declared as an `iterator` object for `list a_list`. We can use the following fragment to process each element in `a_list` instead of the one shown at the beginning of this section.

```
// Access each list element and process it.
for (list<Item_Type>::iterator iter = a_list.begin();
     iter != a_list.end(); ++iter) {

  // Do something with the next element (*iter)
  Item_Type next_element = *iter;
  ...
}
```

In this **for** statement, we use `iter` much as we would use an index to access the elements of a vector. The initialization parameter

```
list<Item_Type>::iterator iter = a_list.begin()
```

declares and initializes an `iterator` object of type `list<Item_Type>::iterator`. Initially this `iterator` is set to point to the first list element, which is returned by `a_list.begin()`. The test parameter

```
iter != a_list.end()
```

causes loop exit when the `iterator` has passed the last list element. The update parameter

```
++iter
```

advances the `iterator` to its next position in the list.

PROGRAM STYLE

Testing Whether There Are More List Nodes to Process

When testing whether there are more elements of an array or vector to process, we evaluate an expression of the form *index < array_size*, which will be **true** or **false**. However, we test whether there are more nodes of a list to process by comparing the current iterator position (iter) with a_list.end(), the iterator position just past the end of the list. We do this by evaluating the expression iter != a_list.end() instead of iter < a_list.end(). The reason we use != instead of < is that iterators effectively are pointers to the individual nodes and the physical ordering of the nodes within memory is not relevant. In fact, the last node in a linked list may have an address that is smaller than that of the first node in the list. Thus, using iter < a_list.end() would be incorrect because the operator < compares the actual memory locations (addresses) of the list nodes, not their relative positions in the list.

The other thing that is different is that we use prefix increment (++iter) instead of postfix increment with iterators. This results in more efficient code.

We stated that using an iterator to access elements in a list is similar to using a pointer to access elements in an array. In fact, an iterator is a generalization of a pointer. The following **for** statement accesses each element in the array declared as int an_array[SIZE].

```
for (int* next = an_array; next != an_array + SIZE; ++next) {
  // Do something with the next element (*next)
  int next_element = *next;
  ...
}
```

The **for** statements just discussed have a different form than what we are used to. These differences are discussed in the Program Style display above.

Common Requirements for Iterators

Each container in the STL is required to provide both an iterator and a const_iterator type. The only difference between the iterator and the const_iterator is the return type of the pointer dereferencing operator (operator*). The iterator returns a reference, and the const_iterator returns a **const** reference.

Table 4.3 lists the operators that iterator classes may provide. The iterator classes do not have to provide all of the operations listed. There is a hierarchical organization of iterator classes shown in Figure 4.27. For example, the figure shows a bidirectional_iterator as a derived class of a forward_iterator. This is to show that a bidirectional_iterator provides all of the operations of a forward_iterator plus the additional ones defined for the bidirectional_iterator. For example, you can use the decrement operator with a bidirectional_iterator to move the iterator back one item. The random_access_iterator (at the bottom of the diagram)

FIGURE 4.27
Iterator Hierarchy

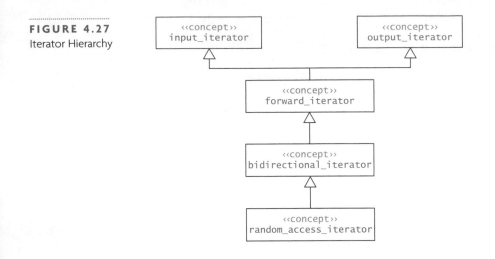

must provide all the operators in Table 4.3. A random_access_iterator can be moved forward or backward and can be moved past several items.

There are two forms shown in Table 4.3 for the increment and decrement operators. The prefix operator has no parameter. The postfix operator has an implicit type **int** parameter of 1.

Alhough we draw Figure 4.27 as a UML diagram, this is slightly misleading. Each of the iterator types represents what is called a *concept*. A concept represents a common interface that a generic class must meet. Thus a class that meets the requirements of a random_access_iterator is not necessarily derived from a class that meets the requirements of a bidirectional_iterator.

TABLE 4.3
The iterator Operators

Function	Behavior	Required for Iterator Type
const Item_Type& operator*	Returns a reference to the object referenced by the current iterator position that can be used on the right-hand side of an assignment. Required for all iterators except output_iterators.	All except output_iterator
Item_Type& operator*	Returns a reference to the object referenced by the current iterator position that can be used on the left-hand side of an assignment. Required for all iterators except input_iterators.	All except input_iterator
iterator& operator++()	Prefix increment operator. Required for all iterators.	All iterators
iterator operator++(int)	Postfix increment operator. Required for all iterators.	All iterators

TABLE 4.3 (cont.)

Function	Behavior	Required for Iterator Type
`iterator& operator--()`	Prefix decrement operator. Required for all bidirectional and random-access iterators.	`bidirectional_iterator` and `random_access_iterator`
`iterator operator--(int)`	Postfix decrement operator. Required for all bidirectional and random-access iterators.	`bidirectional_iterator` and `random_access_iterator`
`iterator& operator+=(int)`	Addition-assignment operator. Required for all random-access iterators.	`random_access_iterator`
`iterator operator+(int)`	Addition operator. Required for all random-access iterators.	`random_access_iterator`
`iterator operator-=(int)`	Subtraction-assignment operator. Required for all random-access iterators.	`random_access_iterator`
`iterator operator-(int)`	Subtraction operator. Required for all random-access iterators.	`random_access_iterator`

Removing Elements from a List

You can use an `iterator` to remove an element from a list as you access it. You use the `iterator` that refers to the item you want to remove as an argument to the `list<Item_Type>.erase` function. The erase function will return an `iterator` that refers to the item after the one removed. You use this returned value to continue traversing the list. You should not attempt to increment the `iterator` that was used in the call to `erase`, since it no longer refers to a valid list `DNode`.

EXAMPLE 4.6   Assume that we have a `list` of **int** values. We wish to remove all elements that are divisible by a particular value. The following function will accomplish this:

```
/** Remove items divisible by a given value.
    pre: a_list contains int values.
    post: Elements divisible by div have been removed.
*/
void remove_divisible_by(list<int>& a_list, int div) {
  list<int>::iterator iter = a_list.begin();
  while (iter != a_list.end()) {
    if (*iter % div == 0) {
      iter = a_list.erase(iter);
    } else {
      ++iter;
    }
  }
}
```

The expression `*iter` has the value of the current **int** value referenced by the iterator. The function call in the statement

```
iter = a_list.erase(iter);
```

removes the element referenced by iter and then returns an iterator that references the next element; thus, we do not want to increment iter if we call erase, but instead set iter to the value returned from the erase function. If we want to keep the value referenced by iter (the else clause), we need to increment the iterator iter so that we can advance past the current value. Note that we use the prefix increment operator because we do not need a copy of the iterator prior to incrementing it.

⊘ PITFALL

Attempting to Reference the Value of end()

The iterator returned by the end function represents a position that is just *past* the last item in the list. It does not reference an object. If you attempt to dereference an iterator that is equal to this value, the results are undefined. This means that your program may appear to work, but in reality there is a hidden defect. Some C++ library implementations test for the validity of an iterator, but such verification is not required by the C++ standard. When we show how to implement the list iterator, we will show an implementation that performs this validation.

EXAMPLE 4.7 Assume that we have a list of string values. We wish to locate the first occurrence of a string target and replace it with the string new_value. The following function will accomplish this:

```
/** Replace the first occurrence of target with new_value.
    pre: a_list contains string values.
    post: The first occurrence of target is replaced by new_value.
*/
void find_and_replace(list<string>& a_list,
                      const string& target,
                      const string& new_value) {
  list<string>::iterator iter = a_list.begin();
  while (iter != a_list.end()) {
    if (*iter == target) {
      *iter = new_value;
      break;  // Exit the loop.
    }
    else {
      ++iter;
    }
  }
}
```

EXERCISES FOR SECTION 4.6

SELF-CHECK

1. The function find, one of the STL algorithms, returns an iterator that references the first occurrence of the target (the third argument) in the sequence specified by the first two arguments. What does the following code fragment do?

   ```
   list<string>::iterator to_sam = find(my_list.begin(),
                                         my_list.end(), "Sam");
   --to_sam;
   my_list.erase(to_sam);
   ```

   where my_list is shown in the following figure:

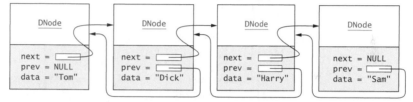

2. In Question 1, what if we change the statement

   ```
   --to_sam;
   ```

   to

   ```
   ++to_sam;
   ```

3. In Question 1, what if we omit the statement

   ```
   --to_sam;
   ```

PROGRAMMING

1. Write the function find_first by adapting the code shown in Example 4.7 to return an iterator that references the first occurrence of an object.
2. Write the function find_last by adapting the code shown in Example 4.7 to return an iterator that references the last occurrence of an object.
3. Write a function find_min that returns an iterator that references the minimum item in a list<Item_Type>, assuming that Item_Type implements the less-than operator.

4.7 Implementation of a Double-Linked List Class

We will implement a simplified version of the list class, which we will encapsulate in the namespace KW; thus our list will be called KW::list to distinguish it from the standard list, std::list. We will not provide a complete implementation, because we expect you to use the standard list class provided by the C++ standard library (in header <list>). The data fields for the KW::list class are shown in Table 4.4.

TABLE 4.4
Data Fields for the KW::list Class

Data Field	Attribute
DNode* head	A pointer to the first item in the list.
DNode* tail	A pointer to the last item in the list.
int num_items	A count of the number of items in the list.

Implementing the KW::list Functions

We need to implement the functions shown earlier in Table 4.2 for the list class.

```
namespace KW {

  template<typename Item_Type>
    class list {
      private:
        // Insert definition of nested class DNode here.
        #include "DNode.h"

      public:
        // Insert definition of nested class iterator here.
        #include "list_iterator.h"
        // Give iterator access to private members of list.
        friend class iterator;
        // Insert definition of nested class const_iterator here.
        #include "list_const_iterator.h"
        // Give const_iterator access to private members of list.
        friend class const_iterator;

      private:
        // Data fields
        /** A reference to the head of the list */
        DNode* head;
        /** A reference to the end of the list */
        DNode* tail;
        /** The size of the list */
        int num_items;
```

Note that the DNode is private, but that the iterator is public. We showed the DNode in Listing 4.3 and will describe the iterator later. Since the iterator and const_iterator need to access and modify the private members of the list class, we declare the iterator and const_iterator to be friends of the list class:

```
friend class iterator;
friend class const_iterator;
```

Members of friend classes, like stand-alone friend functions, have access to the private and protected members of the class that declares them to be friends.

The Default Constructor

The default constructor initializes the values of head, tail, and num_items. Initially the list is empty and both head and tail are NULL.

```
/** Construct an empty list. */
list() {
  head = NULL;
  tail = NULL;
  num_items = 0;
}
```

The Copy Constructor

Like the vector, the list class will dynamically allocate memory. Therefore we need to provide the copy constructor, destructor, and assignment operator. To make a copy we initialize the list to be an empty list and then insert the items from the other list one at a time.

```
/** Construct a copy of a list. */
list(const list<Item_Type>& other) {
  head = NULL;
  tail = NULL;
  num_items = 0;
  for (const_iterator itr = other.begin(); itr != other.end();
       ++itr) {
    push_back(*itr);
  }
}
```

The Destructor

The destructor walks through the list and deletes each DNode.

```
/** Destroy a list. */
~list() {
  while (head != NULL) {
    DNode* current = head;
    head = head->next;
    delete current;
  }
  tail = NULL;
  num_items = 0;
}
```

The Assignment Operator

The assignment operator is coded the same as we did for the vector. We declare a local variable that is initialized to the source of the assignment. This invokes the copy constructor. We then call the swap function, which exchanges the internal content of the target with the copy. The target is now a copy of the source, and the local variable is the original value of the destination. When the operator returns, the destructor is called on the local variable, deleting its contents.

```
/** Assign the contents of one list to another. */
list<Item_Type>& operator=(const list<Item_Type>& other) {
  // Make a copy of the other list.
  list<Item_Type> temp_copy(other);
  // Swap contents of self with the copy.
  swap(temp_copy);
  // Return -- upon return the copy will be destroyed.
  return *this;
}
```

The **push_front** Function

Function push_front inserts a new node at the head (front) of the list (see Figure 4.28). It allocates a new DNode that is initialized to contain a copy of the item being inserted. This DNode's prev data field is initialized to **NULL**, and its next data field is initialized to the current value of head. We then set head to point to this newly allocated DNode. Figure 4.28 shows the list object (data fields head, tail, and num_items) as well as the individual nodes.

```
void push_front(const Item_Type& item) {
  head = new DNode(item, NULL, head); // Step 1
  if (head->next != NULL)
    head->next->prev = head;   // Step 2
  if (tail == NULL)    // List was empty.
    tail = head;
  num_items++;
}
```

It is possible that the list was initially empty. This is indicated by tail being **NULL**. If the list was empty, then we set tail to also point to the newly allocated DNode.

The **push_back** Function

Fuction push_back appends a new element to the end of the list. If the list is not empty, we allocate a new DNode that is initialized to contain a copy of the item being inserted. This DNode's prev data field is initialized to the current value of tail, and its next data field is initialized to **NULL**. The value of tail->next is then set to point to this newly allocated node, and then tail is set to point to it as well. This is illustrated in Figure 4.29.

```
void push_back(const Item_Type& item) {
  if (tail != NULL) {
    tail->next = new DNode(item, tail, NULL); // Step 1
    tail = tail->next; // Step 2
    num_items++;
  } else {           // List was empty.
    push_front(item);
  }
}
```

If the list was empty, we call push_front.

The **insert** Function

Function insert has an iterator parameter pos that specifies where the new node will be inserted. The insert function tests for the special cases of inserting at either the front or the back. For these cases the push_front and push_back functions are called, respectively. We test for these cases by accessing the current data field of iterator pos. This data field references the node currently pointed to by the iterator. (We show the iterator class and its members shortly.)

```
iterator insert(iterator pos, const Item_Type& item) {
  // Check for special cases
  if (pos.current == head) {
    push_front(item);
    return begin();
  } else if (pos.current == NULL) {  // Past the last node.
    push_back(item);
    return iterator(this, tail);
  }
```

FIGURE 4.28
Adding to the Head of the List

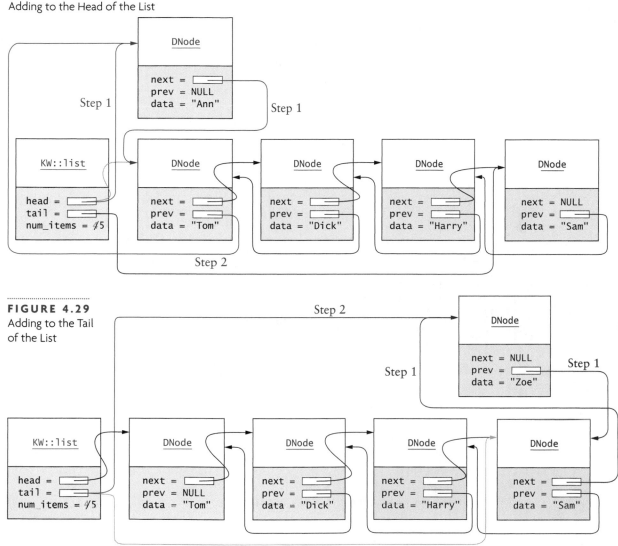

FIGURE 4.29
Adding to the Tail
of the List

If neither condition is true, we are inserting a new item in the middle of the list. First we allocate a new DNode, which is initialized to contain a copy of the item being inserted. This DNode's prev data field is initialized to point to the node before the position where we are inserting, and its next data field is initialized to point to the node at the position (pos.current) where we are inserting. This is illustrated in Figure 4.30.

```
// Create a new node linked before node referenced by pos.
DNode* new_node = new DNode(item,
                            pos.current->prev,
                            pos.current); // Step 1
```

FIGURE 4.30
Adding to the Middle
of the List

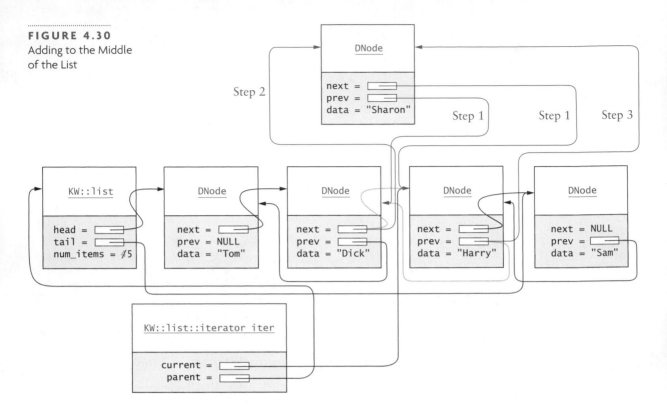

Then the links in the neighboring nodes are updated to point to the new node.

```
// Update links
pos.current->prev->next = new_node;      // Step 2
pos.current->prev = new_node;            // Step 3
```

Finally, num_items is incremented, and an iterator that refers to the newly inserted node is returned.

```
    num_items++;
    return iterator(this, new_node);
}
```

The **pop_front** Function

The pop_front function removes the first element from the list. It begins by verifying that there is at least one element (head != NULL). It saves a pointer to the first node, and then sets head to point to the node following the first node. The old first node is then deleted. If the list is not empty, the prev field in the first node is set to **NULL**, otherwise tail is set to **NULL**.

```
    void pop_front() {
      if (head == NULL)
        throw std::invalid_argument
          ("Attempt to call pop_front() on an empty list");
      DNode* removed_node = head;
      head = head->next;
```

```
      delete removed_node;
      if (head != NULL)
        head->prev = NULL;
      else
        tail = NULL;
      num_items--;
    }
```

The **pop_back** Function

The pop_back function removes the last element from the list. The logic is very similar to that of the pop_front function except that the node pointed to by tail is removed.

```
    void pop_back() {
      if (tail == NULL)
        throw std::invalid_argument
          ("Attempt to call pop_back() on an empty list");
      DNode* removed_node = tail;
      tail = tail->prev;
      delete removed_node;
      if (tail != NULL)
        tail->next = NULL;
      else
        head = NULL;
      num_items--;
    }
```

The **erase** Function

The erase function removes the item selected by its iterator parameter pos. It begins by verifying that the list is not empty and that pos is valid. It then computes the iterator that references the node following the one to be removed. This iterator is the return value of the function. Next the special cases of removing the first or last node are delegated to the pop_front and pop_back functions. If it is not one of these special cases, then the node to be removed is unlinked from its neighbors.

```
    iterator erase(iterator pos) {
      if (empty())
        throw std::invalid_argument
          ("Attempt to call erase on an empty list");
      if (pos == end())
        throw std::invalid_argument
          ("Attempt to call erase of end()");
      /* Create an iterator that references the position
         following pos. */
      iterator return_value = pos;
      ++return_value;
      // Check for special cases.
      if (pos.current == head) {
        pop_front();
        return return_value;
      } else if (pos.current == tail) {
        pop_back();
        return return_value;
```

```
        } else {  // Remove a node in the interior of the list.
          // Unlink current node.
          DNode* removed_node = pos.current;
          removed_node->prev->next = removed_node->next;
          removed_node->next->prev = removed_node->prev;
          delete removed_node;
          return return_value;
        }
      }
```

Implementing the `iterator`

Table 4.5 describes the data members of class `iterator`. An `iterator` object must store a pointer to the current item and a pointer to the `KW::list` object for which it is an iterator.

Figure 4.31 shows an example of a `KW::list` object and a `KW::list::iterator` object `iter`. The `iterator` currently references the node that contains `"Harry"`. Thus, the expression `*iter` gives us a reference to the string `"Harry"`. We can use this on either side of an assignment operator. Therefore we can change `"Harry"` to `"Henry"` by the statement

```
    *iter = "Henry";
```

The expression `*--iter` (equivalent to `*(--iter)`) would move the `iterator` backward so that it references the node containing `"Dick"` and then return a reference to that string.

TABLE 4.5
Data Fields of the `KW::list<Item_Type>::iterator` Class

Data Field	Attribute
`DNode* current`	A pointer to the current item.
`list<Item_Type>* parent`	A pointer to the list of which this `iterator` is a member.

FIGURE 4.31
Double-Linked List with `KW::list<Item_Type>::iterator`

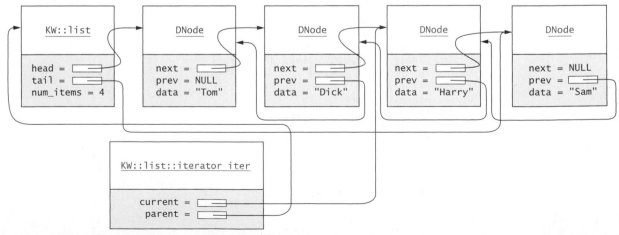

Declaring the Class `iterator`

We show the definition of the `iterator` class in Listing 4.4. In the following declaration

```
typename list<Item_Type>::DNode* current;
```

the keyword **typename** indicates that `DNode` is the name of a class that is nested within class `list<Item_Type>`. The keyword **typename** is required when the parent class is a template class. The identifier `current` is declared to be a pointer to a `DNode` object. We describe the `iterator` functions in the sections following the listing.

LISTING 4.4
The Nested Class `iterator`

```cpp
#ifndef LIST_ITERATOR_H_
#define LIST_ITERATOR_H_

// Nested class iterator.
class iterator {
  // Give the parent class access to this class.
  friend class list<Item_Type>;
  private:
    // Data fields
    /** A reference to the parent list */
    list<Item_Type>* parent;
    /** A pointer to the current DNode */
    typename list<Item_Type>::DNode* current;
    // Member functions
    /** Constructs an iterator that references a specific DNode.
        Note: this constructor is private. Only the list class
        can create one from scratch.
        @param my_parent A reference to the list
        @param position A pointer to the current DNode
    */
    iterator(list<Item_Type>* my_parent, DNode* position) :
      parent(my_parent), current(position) {}

  public:
    /** Returns a reference to the currently referenced item.
        @return A reference to the currently referenced item
        @throws std::invalid_argument if this iterator is at end
    */
    Item_Type& operator*() const {
      if (current == NULL)
        throw std::invalid_argument("Attempt to dereference end()");
      return current->data;
    }

    /** Returns a pointer to the currently referenced item.
        Item_Type must be a class or struct. This restriction
        is enforced by the compiler.
        @return A pointer to the currently referenced item
        @throws std::invalid_argument If this iterator is at end
    */
    Item_Type* operator->() const {
      if (current == NULL)
        throw std::invalid_argument("Attempt to dereference end()");
      return &(current->data);
    }
```

```
/** Advances the iterator forward.
    @return A modified version of this iterator that now
            references the next forward position
    @throws std::invalid_argument If this iterator is at end
*/
iterator& operator++() {
  if (current == NULL)
    throw std::invalid_argument("Attempt to advance past end()");
  current = current->next;
  return *this;
}


/** Moves the iterator backward.
    @return A modified version of this iterator that
            now references the previous position
    @throws std::invalid_argument If this iterator is at begin
*/
iterator& operator--() {
  if (current == parent->head)
    throw std::invalid_argument("Attempt to move before begin()");
  if (current == NULL)    // Past last element.
    current = parent->tail;
  else
    current = current->prev;
  return *this;
}


/** Postfix increment operator.
    @return A copy of this iterator before being advanced
*/
iterator operator++(int) {
  // Make a copy of the current value.
  iterator return_value = *this;
  // Advance self forward.
  ++(*this);
  // Return old value.
  return return_value;   /* Return the value prior to
                            increment */
}


/** Postfix decrement operator.
    @return A copy of this iterator before moving backward
*/
iterator operator--(int) {
  // Make a copy of the current value.
  iterator return_value = *this;
  // Move self backward.
  --(*this);
  // Return old value.
  return return_value;   /* Return the value prior to
                            decrement */
}


// Compare for equality.
bool operator==(const iterator& other) {
  return current == other.current;
}
```

```
      // Not equal
      bool operator!=(const iterator& other) {
        return !operator==(other);
      }
}; // End iterator

#endif
```

SYNTAX Accessing a Type Defined Inside a Template Class from Within a Template Class

FORM:

typename *template-class*::*the-type-name*

EXAMPLE:

typename std::list<Item_Type>::const_iterator

MEANING:

The identifier *the-type-name* is the name of a type and not the name of a data field or member function. Under some circumstances within a template class or function, the compiler cannot tell whether a reference to another template class identifier is a type name or an identifier that names a data field or function. Placing the keyword **typename** in front of such references resolves the ambiguity. Even where there is no ambiguity, the standard requires you to use the keyword **typename**. On the other hand, outside of template classes and functions there is no potential ambiguity, so the use of **typename** is illegal.

PITFALL

Misusing typename

If you fail to use the keyword **typename** where it is required, you may get a warning or error message. The g++ compiler, for example, gives the message:

```
warning: 'typename KW::list<Item_Type>::const_iterator is implicitly a
typename
warning: implicit typename is deprecated, please see the documentation
for details
```

Different compilers will have different error messages and may not issue a message under the same circumstances.

On the other hand, if you use the keyword **typename** outside of a template class or function, you will get an error message.

The Constructor

The KW::list::iterator constructor takes as a parameter a pointer to the DNode at which the iteration is to begin. This constructor is defined in the private part so that clients cannot create arbitrary iterators. Instead, the KW::list class will create and return iterator objects as needed. We can do this in the KW::list class because we declare it to be a friend of the KW::list::iterator class.

```
iterator(list<Item_Type>* my_parent, DNode* position) :
  parent(my_parent), current(position) {}
```

The Dereferencing Operator

The dereferencing operator (operator*) simply verifies that the current pointer is valid and then returns a reference to the data field in the DNode that it points to.

```
Item_Type& operator*() const {
  if (current == NULL)
    throw std::invalid_argument("Attempt to dereference end()");
  return current->data;
}
```

Member Access Operator

Since iterators can be used like pointers, the member access operator (operator->) is also defined. It also verifies that the current pointer is valid and then returns a pointer to (address of) the data field in the DNode that it points to.

```
Item_Type* operator->() const {
  if (current == NULL)
    throw std::invalid_argument("Attempt to dereference end()");
  return &(current->data);
}
```

The Prefix Increment and Decrement Operators

After validating the current pointer, the prefix increment operator sets current to current->next, and the prefix decrement operator sets current to current->prev. The modified object is then returned to the caller by dereferencing the this pointer. If the node referenced by current is the last list node, then the prefix increment operator sets current to **NULL**.

```
iterator& operator++() {
  if (current == NULL)
    throw std::invalid_argument("Attempt to advance past end()");
  current = current->next;
  return *this;
}

iterator& operator--() {
  if (current == parent->head)
    throw std::invalid_argument("Attempt to move before begin()");
  if (current == NULL)    // Past last element.
    current = parent->tail;
  else
    current = current->prev;
  return *this;
}
```

The Postfix Increment and Decrement Operators

The postfix increment and decrement operators first make a copy of the current iterator value. Then the corresponding prefix operator is applied and the copy is returned. If the node referenced by current is the last list node, then the postfix increment operator sets current to **NULL.**

```
iterator operator++(int) {
  // Make a copy of the current value.
  iterator return_value = *this;
  // Advance self forward.
  ++(*this);
  // Return old value.
  return return_value;    /* Return the value prior to
                             increment */
}

iterator operator--(int) {
  // Make a copy of the current value.
  iterator return_value = *this;
  // Move self backward.
  --(*this);
  // Return old value.
  return return_value;    /* Return the value prior to
                             decrement */
}
```

The `const_iterator`

The const_iterator is identical to the iterator, with two exceptions. The dereferencing operator returns a **const** reference, and the member access operator returns a **const** pointer. Even though the operators are defined in the same way as their corresponding operators in class iterator, the **const** in the operator heading means that the item referenced cannot be changed. The compiler will ensure that any attempt to do so will result in an error. The complete code for class const_iterator is available on the website. The member functions and data members are identical to those for class iterator (Listing 4.4) except for the two functions shown below.

```
/** Return a reference to the currently referenced item.
    @return A reference to the currently referenced item
    @throws std::invalid_argument If this const_iterator
                                    is at end
*/
const Item_Type& operator*() const {
  if (current == NULL)
    throw std::invalid_argument
      ("Attempt to dereference end()");
  return current->data;
}

/** Return a pointer to the currently referenced item.
    Item_Type must be a class or struct. This restriction
    is enforced by the compiler.
    @return A pointer to the currently referenced item
    @throws std::invalid_argument If this const_iterator
                                    is at end
```

```
  */
  const Item_Type* operator->() const {
    if (current == NULL)
      throw std::invalid_argument
        ("Attempt to dereference end()");
    return &(current->data);
  }
```

You need to use the `const_iterator` when a list is passed as a **const**. For example, the following function prints the contents of a list of **int**s.

```
void print_list(const list<int>& a_list) {
  list<int>::const_iterator iter = a_list.begin();
  while (iter != a_list.end()) {
    cout << *iter;
    ++iter;
    if (iter != a_list.end())
      cout << "  ==>  ";
  }
  cout << '\n';
}
```

⊘ PITFALL

Failure to Use const_iterator to Reference a const List

If we declared `iter` to be an iterator instead of a `const_iterator`, the function `print_list` would fail to compile, with an error message equivalent to:

```
test_list.cpp: In function 'void print_list(const KW::list<int>&)':
test_list.cpp:122: conversion from 'KW::list<int>::const_iterator' to
  non-scalar type 'KW::list<int>::iterator' requested
```

This is the error message produced by the g++ compiler. Other C++ compilers will produce similar error messages. If we were allowed to use an `iterator` (instead of a `const_iterator`), we could then use it to change the contents of the list that was passed as a parameter to the function `print_list`.

EXERCISES FOR SECTION 4.7

SELF-CHECK

1. Explain why we need both an `iterator` and a `const_iterator`.
2. Indicate whether you should use an `iterator` or a `const_iterator` as a parameter in new functions for the `list` class that would perform each of these operations. Also, provide a heading for each function.

   a. Insert a new element at the current iterator position.

   b. Replace the data stored in the currently selected item.

c. Retrieve the data stored in the currently selected item.

d. Insert a new element before the currently selected item.

3. Assume the list object in Figure 4.31 is named a_list and the iterator is named pos_a. Describe the effect of each statement in the following fragment on object a_list and the data field current of pos_a. Assume that the statements are executed in sequence.

```
++pos_a;
a_list.insert(pos_a, "Jane");
++pos_a;
++pos_a;
a_list.insert(pos_a, "Kim");
a_list.erase(pos_a);
```

PROGRAMMING

1. Implement the front function.

2. Implement the pop_back function.

3. Implement the begin function.

4. Implement the erase function.

4.8 Application of the list Class

In this section we introduce a case study that uses the C++ list class to solve a common problem: maintaining an ordered list.

CASE STUDY   Maintaining an Ordered List

Problem   As discussed in Section 4.5, we can use a linked list to maintain a list of students who are registered for a course. We want to maintain this list so that it will be in alphabetical order even after students have added and dropped the course.

Analysis   Instead of solving this problem just for a list of students, we will develop a general Ordered_List class that can be used to store any group of objects that can be compared using the less-than operator.

We can either extend the C++ list class to create a new class Ordered_List or create an Ordered_List class that uses a list to store the items. If we implement our Ordered_List class as an extension of list, a client will be able to use functions in the list class that can insert new elements or modify existing elements in such a way that the items are no longer in order. Therefore, we will use a list as a component of the Ordered_List.

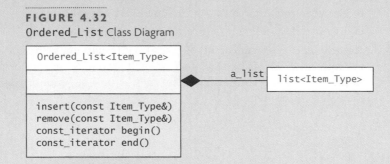

FIGURE 4.32
Ordered_List Class Diagram

Design   The class diagram in Figure 4.32 shows the relationships between the Ordered_List class and the list class. The filled diamond indicates that the list is a component of the Ordered_List.

Because we want to be able to make insertions and deletions in the ordered list, we must implement insert and remove functions. We also provide a const_iterator class and the functions begin and end to provide the user with the ability to access all of the elements in sequence efficiently. Note that we do not want to provide an iterator class, because it could be used to change the values in the list in such a way that order is no longer preserved. Because the list's erase function takes an iterator parameter and not a const_iterator, and because there is no efficient way to convert from a const_iterator to an iterator, we will not implement the erase function for the Ordered_List, even though erasing an element does not violate the ordering of the other elements. However, the remove function can be used to delete items from an ordered list. Table 4.6 shows the functions in class Ordered_List.

TABLE 4.6
Class Ordered_List

Data Field	Attribute
std::list<Item_Type> a_list	A linked list to contain the data.
Function	**Behavior**
void insert(const Item_Type& item)	Inserts item into the list preserving the list's order.
const_iterator begin() const	Returns a const_iterator to the beginning of the list.
const_iterator end() const	Returns a const_iterator to a position just past the end of the list.
public size_t size() const	Returns the size of the list.
public void remove(const Item_Type& item)	Removes item from the list.

Implementation

Defining the **const_iterator** Type

Because our functions return values of type const_iterator, we must define this type. We want the const_iterator to be the same as the const_iterator defined by the list class. This is done with the declaration:

```
typedef typename std::list<Item_Type>::const_iterator
    const_iterator;
```

The **typedef** keyword is used to declare the Ordered_List::const_iterator to be an *alias* for the list::const_iterator.

The **insert** Function

Let's say we have an ordered list that contains the data "Alice", "Andrew", "Caryn", and "Sharon", and we want to insert "Bill" (see Figure 4.33). If we start at the beginning of the list and access "Alice", we know that "Bill" must follow "Alice", but we can't insert "Bill" yet. If we access "Andrew", we know that "Bill" must follow "Andrew", but we can't insert "Bill" yet. However, when we access "Caryn", we know we must insert "Bill" before "Caryn". Therefore, to insert an element in an ordered list, we need to access the first element whose data value is larger than the value of the data in the element to be inserted. Once we have accessed the successor of our new node, we can insert a new node just before it.

Algorithm for Insertion

The algorithm for insertion is

1. Find the first item in the list that is greater than or equal to the item to be inserted.
2. Insert the new item before this one.

We can refine this algorithm as follows:

1.1 Create an iterator that starts at the beginning of the list.
1.2 **while** the iterator is not at the end and the item at the iterator position is less than the item to be inserted
1.3   Advance the iterator.
2. Insert the new item before the current iterator position.

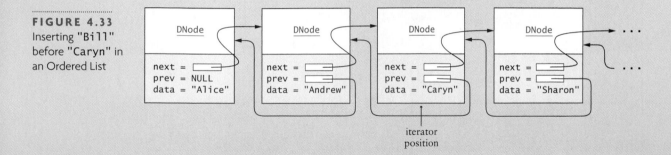

FIGURE 4.33
Inserting "Bill" before "Caryn" in an Ordered List

A straightforward coding of the insertion algorithm would be the following:

```
void insert(const Item_Type& an_item) {
  typename std::list<Item_Type>::iterator itr = a_list.begin();
  while (itr != a_list.end() && *itr < an_item)
    ++itr;
  // itr points to the first item >= an_item or the end.
  a_list.insert(itr, an_item);
}
```

Using Delegation for the Other Functions

The remaining functions in Table 4.6 are implemented via *delegation* to the list class. They merely call the corresponding function in the list. For example, the remove function is coded as follows.

```
void remove(const Item_Type& item)  {
  a_list.remove(item);
}
```

We can define the begin function as follows:

```
const_iterator begin() const {
  return a_list.begin();
}
```

The complete implementation is shown in Listing 4.5.

☑ PROGRAM STYLE

Delegation Pattern

Delegation is a programming technique or OOD pattern that is used frequently. Through delegation, you can easily implement a new class that has an existing class as a component. If the new class and old class have similar functions, then you can implement the new class functions by delegation to the functions in the existing class.

LISTING 4.5
Ordered_List.h

```
#ifndef ORDERED_LIST_H_
#define ORDERED_LIST_H_
#include <list>

/** The ordered list maintains a list of objects ordered by
    their less-than operator.
*/
template<typename Item_Type>
  class Ordered_List {

  private:
    /** A list to contain the ordered list */
    std::list<Item_Type> a_list;
```

```
public:
  // Typedefs
  typedef typename std::list<Item_Type>::const_iterator
    const_iterator;
  // Functions
  /** Insert a new item into the ordered list, maintaining order.
      @param an_item The item to be inserted
  */
  void insert(const Item_Type& an_item) {
    typename std::list<Item_Type>::iterator itr = a_list.begin();
    while (itr != a_list.end() && *itr < an_item)
      ++itr;  // itr points to the first item >= an_item
              // or the end
    a_list.insert(itr, an_item);
  }

  /** Remove an item from the ordered list.
      @param item The value to be removed
  */
  void remove(const Item_Type& item)  {
    a_list.remove(item);
  }

  /** Return an iterator to the beginning. */
  const_iterator begin() const {
    return a_list.begin();
  }

  /** Return an iterator to the end. */
  const_iterator end() const {
    return a_list.end();
  }
};

#endif
```

SYNTAX **Defining an Alias for a Type**

FORM:

typedef *original-type-name new-type-name*;

EXAMPLE:

```
typedef typename std::list<Item_Type>::const_iterator
  const_iterator;
typedef Item_Type item_type;
```

MEANING:

The identifier *new-type-name* may be used as a type name, and it will have the same meaning as *original-type-name*. In many compilers this is done by a straightforward text substitution. Thus error messages that make reference to *new-type-name* will be shown using *original-type-name*.

Testing   You can test the Ordered_List class by storing a collection of randomly generated positive integers in an Ordered_List. You can then insert a negative integer and an integer larger than any integer in the list. This tests the two special cases of inserting at the beginning and at the end of the list. You can then create an iterator and use it to traverse the list, displaying an error message if the current integer is smaller than the previous integer. You can also display the list during the traversal so that you can inspect it to verify that it is in order. Finally, you can remove the first element and the last element. Listing 4.6 shows a program that performs this test.

Function traverse_and_show traverses an ordered list passed as an argument using iterator iter to access the list elements. The **if** statement displays an error message if the previous value is greater than the current value (prev_item > this_item is **true**).

The main function calls traverse_and_show after all elements are inserted and after the three elements are removed. In function main, the loop

```
for (int i = 0; i < START_SIZE; i++) {
    int an_integer = rand() % MAX_INT;
    test_list.insert(an_integer);
}
```

fills the ordered list with randomly generated values between 0 and MAX_INT - 1. The function rand (defined in the header <cstdlib>) generates a random integer between 0 and the maximum value RAND_MAX. However, if it is not initialized, rand will generate exactly the same sequence of random numbers every time. The function srand is used to initialize the random number generator. A common practice to get different results each time a program is run is to initialize the random number generator to the current time of day in milliseconds since January 1, 1970. This is the value returned by the call to time(0). The function time is defined in the header <ctime>.

....
LISTING 4.6
Program test_ordered_list.cpp

```
#include "Ordered_List.h"
#include <cstdlib>
#include <ctime>
#include <iostream>
#include <ostream>
using std::cout;
using std::rand;
using std::srand;
using std::time;

/** Traverses the ordered list and displays each element.
    Displays an error message if an element is out of order.
    pre: The list elements are all positive and the list is
         not empty.
    @param test_list An ordered list
```

```
*/
void traverse_and_show(const Ordered_List<int>& test_list) {
  Ordered_List<int>::const_iterator iter = test_list.begin();
  int prev_item = *iter;
  // Traverse ordered list and display any value that
  // is out of order.
  ++iter;
  while (iter != test_list.end()) {
    int this_item = *iter++;
    cout << prev_item << '\n';
    if (prev_item > this_item) {
      cout << "*** FAILED, value is "
           << this_item << '\n';
    }
    prev_item = this_item;
  }
  cout << prev_item << '\n';
}

int main() {
  Ordered_List<int> test_list;
  const int MAX_INT = 500;
  const int START_SIZE = 100;
  // Initialize random number generator
  srand(time(0));
  // Create a random number generator.
  for (int i = 0; i < START_SIZE; i++) {
    int an_integer = rand() % MAX_INT;
    test_list.insert(an_integer);
  }

  // Add to beginning and end of list.
  test_list.insert(-1);
  test_list.insert(MAX_INT + 1);
  cout << "Original list\n";
  traverse_and_show(test_list);  // Traverse and display.

  // Remove first, last, and middle elements.
  int first = *(test_list.begin());
  test_list.remove(first);
  cout << "After removing first item\n";
  traverse_and_show(test_list);  // Traverse and display.
  int last = *(--test_list.end());
  test_list.remove(last);
  cout << "After removing last item\n";
  traverse_and_show(test_list);
  return 0;
}
```

EXERCISES FOR SECTION 4.8

SELF-CHECK

1. Why don't we implement the Ordered_List by extending list?
2. What other functions in the list class could we include in the Ordered_List class?

1. Write the code for the other functions of the `Ordered_List` class that are shown in Table 4.6.
2. Rewrite the `Ordered_List.insert` function to start at the end of the list and iterate using the `const_iterator` decrement operator (`operator--()`).

4.9 Standard Library Containers

The `vector` and the `list` are examples of what the C++ standard calls a *sequential container*. You may have observed that the interfaces (i.e., the sets of public members) are similar. As you will see when we revisit the `vector` in this section, they are more similar than we have presented them.

The C++ standard uses the term *container* to represent a class that can contain objects. It defines a common interface for all containers. It then splits the set of containers into sequential containers and *associative containers*. Common requirements unique to these subsets are also defined. Finally, the individual containers have their own additional requirements. This hierarchy is shown in Figure 4.34. Note that, like the iterator hierarchy discussed previously, this is not an inheritance hierarchy. Again, the term *concept* is used to represent the set of common requirements for the `container`, `sequence`, or `associative_container`. Although a `list` and a `vector` may have several member functions in common, they may not be used polymorphically. However, as we will discuss in the next section, both vectors and lists, as well as other sequences, can be used interchangeably by generic algorithms.

The basic difference between a sequence and an associative container is that items in a sequence (for example, a `vector` or a `list`) follow some linear arrangement. At any given time each element has a particular position relative to the other items in the container. In an associative container, on the other hand, there is no particular position for each item in the container. Items are accessed by value, rather than their position.

FIGURE 4.34
Container Class
Hierarchy

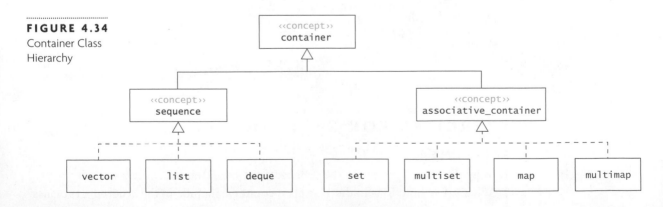

Common Features of Containers

The C++ standard lists several requirements that are common to all containers. There are a few features that can be considered fundamental:

- Containers grow as needed.
- Containers hold objects.

Table 4.7 shows selected **typedef**s and functions that are required for all containers. We have already seen and discussed some of these in the discussions of the vector and list. The iterator provides a common way to access all of the elements in a container.

TABLE 4.7

Common Requirements for Containers

typedefs	Meaning
value_type	The type of the objects stored in the container. Can be used by a template function that takes a container as a parameter without knowing the actual type of the objects in the container.
iterator	An iterator appropriate for the container.
const_iterator	A const_iterator appropriate for the container.
Constructors	**Purpose**
X()	Default constructor where X is the container type.
X(a)	Copy constructor where X is the container type and a is an object of this type.
Functions	**Behavior**
void ~X()	Destructor.
X& operator=(const X& a)	Assignment operator.
bool operator==(const X& a)	Equality operator. Containers must be of the same size and all corresponding objects must be equal.
bool operator!=(const X& a)	Negation of equal.
bool operator<(const X& a)	Less-than operator. Lexicographical comparison of each item in this container to the other container. Objects in the container must implement the less-than operator.
bool operator>(const X& a); bool operator<=(const X& a); bool operator>=(const X& a)	The other comparison operators are defined similarly to the less-than operator.
void swap(X& a)	Exchanges the contents of this container with another container of the same type. Note that this operation must be done in constant time.
iterator begin(); const_iterator begin() const	Returns an iterator or const_iterator to the first item in the container.

TABLE 4.7 (cont.)

Functions	Behavior
`iterator end();` `const_iterator end() const`	Returns an `iterator` or `const_iterator` that is just past the last item in the container.
`size_t size() const`	Returns the number of objects in the container.
`bool empty() const`	Returns **true** if the container is empty.

Sequences

The objects in a sequence are organized in a linear arrangement. Other than the first and last objects, each object has a predecessor and a successor. The ordering of the objects is determined by the user of the container. Table 4.8 shows some of the additional requirements common to sequences.

Optional Requirements for Sequences

The C++ standard defines three sequential containers: `vector`, `list`, and `deque`. We have seen the first two and will discuss the `deque` in Chapter 6. Implementors may define additional sequences. Table 4.9 shows some requirements that are common to some, but not all, sequences. The last column shows which sequences must define each function.

TABLE 4.8
Common Requirements for Sequences

Constructors	Purpose
`X(int num, const Item_Type& initial)`	Constructs the container of type X containing `num` copies of `initial`.
`X(const_iterator start,` `   const_iterator stop)`	Constructs the container of type X containing a copy of the items starting with the object referenced by the iterator `start` up to, but not including the iterator `stop`.

Functions	Behavior
`iterator insert(iterator pos,` `   const Item_Type& item)`	Insert a copy of `item` into the container before the position referenced by the iterator `pos`. Return an iterator that references the newly inserted item. For some containers other iterators may no longer be valid.
`iterator erase(iterator pos)`	Remove the item from the container referenced by the iterator `pos`. Return an iterator that references the object (or position) following `pos`. For some containers other iterators may no longer be valid.

TABLE 4.9
Requirements Applicable to Some, but Not All, Sequences

Function	Purpose	Required by
`Item_Type& front();` `const Item_Type& front() const`	Returns a reference to the first item in the container.	`vector, list, deque`
`Item_Type& back();` `const Item_Type& back() const`	Returns a reference to the last item in the container.	`vector, list, deque`
`void push_front(const Item_Type& item)`	Inserts a new item as the first item in the container.	`list, deque`
`void push_back(const Item_Type& item)`	Inserts a new item as the last item in the container.	`vector, list, deque`
`void pop_front()`	Removes the first item from the container.	`list, deque`
`void pop_back()`	Removes the last item from the container.	`vector, list, deque`

`Item_Type& operator[](int index);`
`const Item_Type& operator[](int index)`
`  const`
	Randomly accesses an item in the container via an index.	`vector, deque`

`Item_Type& at(int index);` `const Item_Type at(int index) const`	Randomly accesses an item in the container via an index. The value of the index is validated.	`vector, deque`

You may wonder why the standard does not require all of these functions for all sequences. The authors of the standard chose to require only those functions that could be implemented in constant time, or at least amortized constant time. Thus push_back is required for all sequences, but push_front is not required for the vector, where it would be O(*n*) because all elements currently in the vector would have to be shifted. Likewise, the subscripting operator is not required for the list because it would need to traverse the list starting at the beginning.

Associative Containers

The associative containers are designed for fast retrieval of data based on a unique value stored in each item, called its *key*. There are four associative containers: set, multiset, map, and multimap. The set and multiset store only keys, while the map and multimap associate a key with a value. We will discuss these containers in more detail in Chapter 9.

Vector Implementation Revisited

The KW::vector class we described in Section 4.3 does not exactly meet the requirements for a sequential container. Specifically, the insert and erase functions were defined in terms of an index rather than an iterator. (That was because iterators had not yet been introduced.) We also did not implement the functions begin and end. It is relatively easy to modify our KW::vector class so that it meets the requirements.

The `vector::iterator`

The simplest approach to defining the `iterator` and `const_iterator` for the vector is to define them to be equivalent to pointers. This is done as follows:

```
typedef Item_Type* iterator;
typedef const Item_Type* const_iterator;
```

The vector functions `begin` and `end` are then implemented as follows:

```
iterator begin() { return the_data; }
iterator end() { return the_data + num_items; }
```

Recall that the vector contents are stored in array `the_data`, so `the_data` is the address of the first element of this array and `the_data + num_items` is the address just past the last element.

This is the approach taken in many implementations of the standard, and is perfectly legal. A better approach, however, would be to define an `iterator` class that held both a pointer to an item and a pointer to the parent vector. The operators `*` and `->` could then validate the pointers before dereferencing them. Since this is a random-access `iterator`, the addition and subtraction operations must also be defined.

EXAMPLE 4.8   Earlier we implemented the `insert` function using an index rather than an iterator. The following uses the iterator (parameter `pos`) rather than the index.

```
iterator insert(iterator pos, const Item_Type& the_value) {
  // Validate pos
  if ((pos - begin()) < 0 || (end() - pos) < 0) {
    throw std::out_of_range
      ("position to insert is out of range");
  }
  // Ensure that there is space for the new item.
  if (num_items == current_capacity) {
    reserve(2 * current_capacity);
  }
  // Move data from pos to end() - 1 down.
  for (iterator p = end(); p > pos; p--) {
    *p = *(p - 1);
  }
  // Insert the new item.
  *pos = the_value;
  num_items++;
}
```

This code is equivalent to the version given previously if you substitute `begin()` + index for `pos` and `end()` - `begin()` for `num_items`.

EXERCISES FOR SECTION 4.9

SELF-CHECK

1. What kind of a container is an object of type `vector`? `set`? `map`? `list`?

2. Which container type requires more functions, vector or list? What are the additional functions required by that container type?

PROGRAMMING

1. Implement the erase function for KW::vector to take an iterator instead of an index to indicate the item to be removed.

2. Implement an iterator class for KW::vector that validates the pointer before dereferencing it.

4.10 Standard Library Algorithms and Function Objects

The find Function

In an earlier exercise we asked you to write a function to find a value in a vector. Let us assume that we want to find a value in a list instead. We could write the following:

```
list<int>::iterator find(list<int>& a_list, int target) {
  for (list<int>::iterator itr = a_list.begin();
       itr != a_list.end(); ++itr) {
    if (*itr == target)
      return itr;
  }
  return a_list.end();
}
```

But what if we wanted to find a string instead? We could replace **int** with string and rewrite this function. Rather than writing different copies of a function to work with different types, however, C++ allows us to define *template functions*. Template functions are like template classes in that we can define template parameters (generally types) that are then replaced with actual parameters at compile time.

Using templates we might try the following:

```
template<typename Item_Type>
  std::list<Item_Type>::iterator
    find(std::list<Item_Type>& a_list,
         const Item_Type& target) {
  typedef typename std::list<Item_Type>::iterator iterator;
  for (iterator itr = a_list.begin();
       itr != a_list.end(); ++itr) {
    if (*itr == target)
      return itr;
  }
  return a_list.end();
}
```

Unfortunately, this is not completely general. What if we want to search a vector instead of a list? Because the search loop is controlled by an iterator, the inventors of the STL chose to add an iterator to the container to be searched as a template parameter as well as the element data type. The STL template function find is effectively defined as follows:

```
template<typename Iterator, typename Item_Type>
  Iterator find(Iterator first, Iterator last,
                const Item_Type& target) {
    while (first != last) {
      if (*first == target)
        return first;
      ++first;
    }
    return first;
}
```

This function find has two iterator parameters (first and last). The parameter first points to the first element in the container; the parameter last points just past the last element in the container. The actual types of the iterators and the target are determined at compile time. If list_1 and vec_1 are a list<int> and a vector<string>, we can search these containers using the following function calls:

```
if (find(list_1.begin(), list_1.end(), 10) != list_1.end())
  cout << "list 1 contains 10\n";
else
  cout << "list 1 does not contain 10\n";
if (find(vec_1.begin(), vec_1.end(), "abc") != vec_1.end())
  cout << "vec_1 contains \"abc\"\n";
else
  cout << "vec_1 does not contain \"abc\"\n";
```

SYNTAX   Defining a Template Function

FORM:

template<typename T_1, ... , typename T_n>
  return-type function-name(T_i, ... , T_j)

EXAMPLES:

```
template<typename Item_Type>
  list<Item_Type>::iterator find(list<Item_Type>& a_list,
                                 const Item_Type& target)

template<typename iterator, typename Item_Type>
  iterator find(iterator first, iterator last,
                const Item_Type& target)
```

MEANING:

The function *function-name* takes parameters of the template types T_1 through T_n. The template parameter types are listed following the keyword **template** and must also be included in the function signature. The order of the parameters in the function signature does not need to be the same as they are following the keyword **template**, but each parameter type must be used at least once.

SYNTAX **Calling a Template Function**

FORM:
function-name(actual-parameter-list)

EXAMPLE:
find(list_1.begin(), list_1.end(), 10)

MEANING:

The types of the actual parameters are matched to the template type parameters. The template function is then instantiated with the parameter matching specified in the call. In our example the type of the actual argument list_1.begin() is a list<int>::iterator, as is the type of the second argument list_1.end(). The third parameter has the type **int**. Therefore, the template parameter Iterator is bound to list<int>::iterator, and the template parameter Item_Type is bound to **int**. The matching of the parameter types to template parameters is done at compile time. This is a very powerful feature of C++ that is used by the STL to do some fairly amazing things.

The actual types of the arguments to find do not have to be iterators defined by a container. Recall that an iterator is a generalization of a pointer. Therefore pointers can be used as well. For example, we can call find by passing pointers to the beginning and end of an array. In the following **if** statement, the pointer list_data points to the first element of the array and list_data + 7 points to the element just past the end of the array.

```
int list_data = {1, 4, 3, 5, 10, 8, 9};
...
if (find(list_data, list_data + 7, 10) != list_data + 7) ...
```

The Algorithm Library

The standard library contains several template functions defined in the header <algorithm>. Like find, many of them work on a pair of iterators that defines the sequence of input values. Some of them also take function objects (described later in this section) as parameters. Table 4.10 lists some of these functions. In all cases the range first..last represents values obtained by dereferencing an iterator starting at first and proceeding up to, but not including, last.

The template functions, or *algorithms*, perform fairly standard operations on containers, such as applying the same function to each element (for_each), copying values from one container to another (copy), seaching a container for a target value (find, find_if), or sorting a container (sort). Most of these algorithms are fairly simple loops, such as the find that was just discussed. You may then ask yourself; "Why not just code the loop when I need it?" There are two reasons: The first is to avoid "reinventing the wheel"—the library contains validated versions of these algorithms, whereas if you recode them yourself, you may have errors that you will have to fix rather than avoiding them in the first place. Secondly, the compiler can be designed to generate more efficient code when instantiating the library version of the algorithm than if you were to hand-code the equivalent C++ code.

TABLE 4.10
Selected Template Functions from the Standard Template Library

Function	Behavior
`template<typename II, typename F>` `  F for_each(II first, II last, F fun)`	Applies the function `fun` to each object in the sequence. The function `fun` is not supposed to modify its argument. The `iterator` argument II is required to be an input iterator. This means that the sequence is traversed only once.
`template<typename II, typename T>` `  II find(II first, II last, T target)`	Finds the first occurrence of `target` in the sequence. If not found, `last` is returned.
`template<typename II, typename P>` `  II find_if(II first, II last, P pred)`	Finds the first occurrence of an item in the sequence for which function `pred` returns true. If not found, `last` is returned.

`template<typename FI>`
`  FI min_element(FI first, FI last);`
`template<typename FI>`
`  FI max_element(FI first, FI last)`
	Finds the min/max element in the sequence `first..last`. FI is a forward iterator.

`template<typename II, typename OI>` `  OI copy(II first, II last, OI result)`	Copies the sequence `first..last` into `result..(result + (last - first))`. II is an input iterator, and OI is an output iterator.

`template<typename II, typename OI,`
`typename OP>`
`  OI transform(II first, II last,`
`  OI result, OP op)`
	Applies `op` to each element of the sequence `first..last` and places the result in `result..(result + (last - first))`.

`template<typename II1, typename II2,`
`typename OI, typename BOP>`
`  OI transform(II1 first1, II1 last1,`
`  II2 first2, OI result, BOP bin_op)`
	Applies `bin_op` to each pair of elements of the sequences `first1..last1` and `first2..(first2 + (last1 - first1))` and places the result in `result..(result + (last1 - first1))`

`template<typename T>` `  void swap(T& a, T& b)`	Exchanges the contents of a and b.
`template<typename FI1, typename FI2>` `  void iter_swap(FI1 a, FI1 b)`	Exchanges the values referenced by iterators a and b.
`template<typename BI>` `  void reverse(BI first, BI last)`	Reverses the sequence `first..last`. BI is a bidirectional iterator.
`template<typename RI>` `  void random_shuffle(RI first, RI last)`	Randomly rearranges the contents of `first..last`. RI is a random-access iterator.
`template<typename RI>` `  void sort(RI first, RI last)`	Sorts the contents of `first..last` based on the less-than operator applied to pairs of elements.
`template<typename RI, typename COMP>` `  void sort(RI first, RI last, COMP comp)`	Sorts the contents of `first..last` based on the binary operator COMP (a function operator). COMP is a function class that takes two arguments and returns a **bool**.

TABLE 4.10 (cont.)

Function	Behavior
template<typename II, typename T> T accumulate(II first, II last, T init)	Computes init plus the sum of the elements in first..last. Note that this function is defined in the header <numeric>.

template<typename II1, typename II2>
  bool equal(II1 first1, II1 last1,
  II2 first2);
template<typename II1, typename II2,
typename BP>
  bool equal(II1 first1, II1 last2,
  II2 first2, BP pred)
	Compares each element in the sequence first1..last1 to the corresponding elements in the sequence first2..first2 + (last1 - first1). If they are all equal, then this returns **true**. The second form uses the function object pred to perform the comparison.

EXAMPLE 4.9 The following will copy the contents of a_list into a_vector.

```
a_vector.resize(a_list.size());
copy(a_list.begin(), a_list.end(), a_vector.begin());
```

The first statement sets the size of a_vector to the same as a_list. It then calls template function copy to copy the elements from a_list to a_vector.

EXAMPLE 4.10 The following fragment will first sort the elements in vector<int> a_vector. Next it accumulates and displays the sum of the elements. The argument 0 to the accumulate function provides the initial value for the sum and specifies the type—**int** in this case. The first **if** statement displays an error message if the first element is not the smallest after the sort. Function min_element returns an iterator to the smallest element, which is compared to the first element in the sorted vector. Then it initializes iterator iter to point to the last element of the vector. Finally, the second **if** statement compares the last element with the largest element.

```
sort(a_vector.begin(), a_vector.end());    // Sort the vector.
// Accumulate the sum.
int sum = accumulate(a_vector.begin(), a_vector.end(), 0);
cout << "Sum is " << sum << endl;

// Check first element.
if (*a_vector.begin() !=
    *min_element(a_vector.begin(), a_vector.end()))
  cerr << "Error in sort\n";

// Check last element.
vector<int>::iterator iter(a_vector.end() - 1);
if (*iter != *max_element(a_vector.begin(), a_vector.end()))
  cerr << "Error in sort\n";
```

The swap Function

The swap function is defined as follows:

```
template<typename T>
  void swap(T& x, T& y) {
    T temp(x);      // temp is a copy of x.
    x = y;          // Assign y to x.
    y = temp;       // Assign the copy of x to y.
  }
```

In this definition, the template parameter T is a placeholder for the type of the data items being swapped. If we have two **int** variables i and j, we can call this function using the statement:

```
swap(i, j);
```

and if we have two pointer variables p and q, we can call this function using the statement.

```
swap(p, q);
```

In the first case the template parameter T is bound to the actual type, **int**, and in the second it is bound to the pointer type.

We used template function swap in Section 4.3 to exchange the contents of two variables:

```
std::swap(num_items, other.num_items);
std::swap(current_capacity, other.current_capacity);
std::swap(the_data, other.the_data);
```

The first two calls exchange a pair of **int** values; the last call exchanges the pointers to the two arrays.

Specializing the **swap** Function

But what if we have two vector variables v1 and v2 and execute the statement

```
swap(v1, v2);
```

In this case the copy constructor will be invoked to make a copy of v1 into temp. Then the assignment operator will be called to assign v2 to v1. Next, temp is assigned to v1 using the assignment operator again, and finally the destructor is called to destroy temp.

Since the standard swap uses the assignment operator, which in turn uses the copy constructor and swap member functions, we are making unnecessary copies. We can avoid this by providing what is known as a *specialization* of the swap function as follows:

```
template<typename Item_Type>
  inline void swap(vector<Item_Type>& x, vector<Item_Type>& y) {
    x.swap(y); }
```

By providing this function definition, the compiler will instantiate the vector::swap member function rather than the standard function swap when it is called with arguments of type vector. This function definition is placed in the vector.h file after the class definition.

SYNTAX   **Declaring inline Functions**

FORM:

inline *function-declaration* *{body}*

EXAMPLE:

```
inline void swap(vector<Item_Type>& x, vector<Item_Type>& y) {
  x.swap(y);
}
```

MEANING:

The compiler replaces a call to that function with the code contained in the function body. Such code executes faster. Since the compiler must be aware of the code to be generated, inline function definitions must be placed in header files.

PROGRAM STYLE

Specializing the swap Function

Any class that dynamically allocates memory, or contains objects with dynamically allocated memory—a vector, for example—should provide a swap member function and a specialization for the swap function. The swap member function should be written as follows:

```
void swap(class_name& other) {
  // Use the std::swap function to swap each data field.
  // . . .
}
```

The specialization should be defined in the declaration file (the .h file) and should be written as follows:

```
inline void swap(class-name& x, class-name& y) {
  x.swap(y);
}
```

Function Objects

One of the operators that can be overloaded by a class is the function call operator (operator()). A class that overloads this operator is called a *function class*, and an object of such a class is called a *function object*. As an example, we may want to find a value divisible by another value. We can create a function class Divisible_By whose constructor takes the divisor as an argument. Such a class is defined as follows:

```
class Divisible_By {
  private:
    int divisor;
  public:
    Divisible_By(int d) : divisor(d) {}
    bool operator()(int x) {
      return x % divisor == 0;
    }
};
```

Data field divisor stores the number we want to divide by. The definition of operator() specifies that the function result will be determined by testing the remainder resulting from the division of the function agument (int x) by the value of divisor. The expression Divisible_By(3) creates a function object that returns **true** if the argument passed to it is divisible by 3. Similarly the expression Divisible_By(5) creates a function object that tests for integers divisible by 5.

Table 4.11 describes the template function find_if as follows. Template parameter II is a placeholder for an input iterator; template parameter P is a placeholder for a function class with an operator() that returns a **bool** value.

The following code fragment uses function find_if and function class Divisible_By.

```
// Find first number divisible by 3 in list_1.
list<int>::iterator = iter;
iter = find_if(list_1.begin(), list_1.end(), Divisible_By(3));
if (iter != list_1.end())
  cout << "The first number divisible by 3 is " << *iter
      << endl;
else
  cout << "There are no numbers divisible by 3\n";

// Find first number divisible by 5 in list_1.
iter = find_if(list_1.begin(), list_1.end(), Divisible_By(5));
if (iter != list_1.end())
  cout << "The first number divisible by 5 is " << *iter
      << endl;
else
  cout << "There are no numbers divisible by 5\n";
```

The template function find_if is instantiated with an iterator bound to list<int>::iterator and with P bound to Divisible_By. This instantiation is called with two different function objects, but these function objects have the same type.

TABLE 4.11
Template Function find_if

Function	Behavior
template<typename II, typename P> II find_if(II first, II last, P pred)	Find the first occurrence of an item in the sequence for which function pred returns **true**. If not found, last is returned.

EXAMPLE 4.11   The function class `Square_Diff` saves its argument in data field `mean`. The function call operator `operator()` subtracts the value saved in `mean` from the input value and then returns the square of this difference.

```
/** Function class to compute the square of
    the difference of a value from the mean.
*/
class Square_Diff {
  private:
    /** The mean to be subtracted from each value. */
    double mean;

  public:
    /** Construct a Square_Diff object remembering
        the value of the mean.
        @param m The mean to be remembered
    */
    Square_Diff(double m) : mean (m) {}

    /** Subtract the mean from the input value and
        return the square of the difference.
        @param x The input value
        @return (x - mean) squared
    */
    double operator()(double x) {
      double diff = x - mean;
      return diff * diff;
    }
};
```

We can use function object `Square_Diff` to compute the standard deviation of a collection of real numbers using the formula below for standard deviation s, where m is the mean and x_i is the ith data item.

$$s = \sqrt{\frac{\sum_{i=0}^{n-1}(x_i - m)^2}{n-1}}$$

To get the mean, we first compute the sum of the data stored in container `input_data` (using function `accumulate`) and then divide by the number of values.

```
// Compute the sum of the input.
double sum =
    accumulate(input_data.begin(), input_data.end(), 0.0);
// Compute the mean.
double mean = sum / input_data.size();
```

We can use the `transform` algorithm (Table 4.12) with function class `Square_Diff` to transform the values in `input_data` into a sequence of squared deviations.

The following statement applies the function call operator in function class `Square_Diff` to each element of `input_data`. Because the third parameter is an iterator that points to the first element in `input_data`, the result of each call is saved back in `input_data`.

```
// Load the square deviation values.
transform(input_data.begin(), input_data.end(),
        input_data.begin(), Square_Diff(mean));
```

Finally we use accumulate to compute the sum of the squared deviations, and then the standard deviation is computed.

```
// Compute the sum of the squared deviations.
double sum_sq_dev =
  accumulate(input_data.begin(), input_data.end(), 0.0);
// Compute the standard deviation.
double stdev = sqrt(sum_sq_dev / (input_data.size() - 1.0));
```

TABLE 4.12
transform Algorithm

Function	Operator

template<typename II, typename OI, typename OP>
  OI transform(II first, II last,
  OI result, OP op)
	Applies op to each element of the sequence first..last and places the result in result..(result + (last - first))

EXERCISES FOR SECTION 4.10

SELF-CHECK

1. Explain the effect of each statement in the following fragment.
```
vector<int> a_list;
vector<int>::iterator iter;
iter = min_element(a_list.begin(), a_list.end());
cout << *iter << "\n";
iter = find(a_list.begin(), a_list.end(), 95);
if (iter != a_list.end())
  cout << *iter << "\n";
copy(a_list.begin(), a_list.end(), a_vector.begin());
sort(a_list.begin(), a_list.end());
reverse(a_list.begin(), a_list.end());
```

PROGRAMMING

1. Write the body of function swap.
2. Write the body of function accumulate.

Chapter Review

◆ The vector is a generalization of the array. As in the array, elements of a vector are accessed by means of an index. Unlike the array, the vector can grow or shrink. Items may be inserted or removed from any position. The C++ standard library provides the vector class, which uses an array as the underlying structure. This can be implemented by allocating an array that is larger than the number of items in the vector. As items are inserted into the vector, the items with higher indices are moved up to make room for the inserted item, and as items are removed, the items with higher indices are moved down to fill in the emptied space. When the array capacity is reached, a new array is allocated that is twice the size, and the old array is copied to the new one. By doubling the capacity, the cost of the copy is spread over each insertion, so that the copies can be considered to have a constant-time contribution to the cost of each insertion.

◆ A linked-list data structure consists of a set of nodes, each of which contains its data and a reference to the next node in the list. In a double-linked list, each node contains a reference to both the next and the previous node in the list. Insertion into and removal from a linked list is a constant-time operation.

◆ To access an item at a position indicated by an index in a linked list requires walking along the list from the beginning until the item at the specified index is reached. Thus, traversing a linked list using an index would be an $O(n^2)$ operation because we need to repeat the walk each time the index changes. The iterator provides a general way to traverse a list so that traversing a linked list using an iterator is an $O(n)$ operation. The C++ standard library provides the list class, which uses a double-linked list. We show an example of how this might be implemented.

◆ The vector and list are examples of the C++ standard library containers. The C++ standard requires that all containers provide a common interface (set of member functions and constructors). The containers are further organized into sequential containers and associative containers.

◆ An iterator provides us with the ability to access the items in a container sequentially. All containers must provide an iterator type and functions that return interators that reference the begining and end of the container.

◆ Iterators are organized in a hierarchy. The most restrictive iterators are the input and output iterators that allow traversal of a sequence only once, and the most general iterators allow for random access of the contents of a container.

◆ The C++ standard library provides a collection of algorithms that operate on sequences defined by iterators. These algorithms can be applied to the contents any of the containers using the iterators defined by that container.

Quick-Check Exercises

1. Elements of a vector are accessed by means of _____.
2. A vector can _____ or _____ as items are added or removed.
3. When we allocate a new array for an vector because the current capacity is exceeded, we make the new array at least _____. This allows us to _____.

4. In a single-linked list, if we want to remove a list element, which list element do we need to access? If `node_ptr` references this element, what statement removes the desired element?

5. Suppose a single-linked list contains three `DNodes` with data "him", "her", and "it" and `head` references the first element. What is the effect of the following fragment?

```
DNode* node_ptr = head->next;
node_ptr->data = "she";
```

6. Answer Question 5 for the following fragment.

```
DNode* node_ptr = head->next;
head.next = node_ptr->next;
```

7. Answer Question 5 for the following fragment.

```
head = new DNode("his", head);
```

8. An `iterator` allows us to access items of a `list` _____.

9. The C++ `list` class uses a _____.

Answers to Quick-Check Exercises

1. *an index*
2. *grow, shrink*
3. *twice the size; spread out the cost of the reallocation so that it is effectively a constant-time operation*
4. The predecessor of this node.

   ```
   node_ptr->next = node_ptr->next->next;
   ```
5. Replaces "her" with "she".
6. Deletes the second list element ("she").
7. Inserts a new first element containing "his".
8. *sequentially*
9. *double-linked list*

Review Questions

1. What is the difference between the size and the capacity of a `vector`? Why do we have a constructor that lets us set the initial capacity?
2. When we insert an item into an `vector`, why do we start copying from the end?
3. What is the advantage of a double-linked list over a single-linked list? What is the disadvantage?
4. Why is it more efficient to use an iterator to traverse a linked list?
5. What is the difference between a `forward_iterator` and a `bidirectional_iterator`?
6. What is the "rule of three"? Why is it important to follow this rule?

Programming Projects

1. Build a `Single_Linked_List` class. Your class should have the data members: `head`, `tail`, and `num_items`. Write the following member functions, which perform the same operations as the corresponding functions in the standard `list` class: `push_front`, `push_back`, `pop_front`, `pop_back`, `front`, `back`, `empty`, `size`. Also write the following member functions:
   - `void insert(size_t index, const Item_Type& item)`: Insert `item` at position `index` (starting at 0). Insert at the end if `index` is beyond the end of the list.

- `bool remove(size_t index)`: Remove the item at position `index`. Return **true** if successful; return **false** if `index` is beyond the end of the list.
- `size_t find(const Item_Type& item)`: Return the position of the first occurrence of `item` if it is found. Return the size of the list if it is not found.

2. Write an `iterator` class for class `Single_Linked_List`. Replace the **size_t** parameter or result in functions `insert`, `remove`, `find` with an `iterator`.

3. Develop a program to maintain a list of homework assignments. When an assignment is assigned, add it to the list, and when it is completed, remove it. You should keep track of the due date. Your program should provide the following services:
   - Add a new assignment.
   - Remove an assignment.
   - Provide a list of the assignments in the order they were assigned.
   - Find the assignment(s) with the earliest due date.

4. We can represent a polynomial as an ordered list of terms, where the terms are ordered by their exponents. To add two polynomials, you traverse both lists and examine the two terms at the current iterator position. If the exponent of one is smaller than the exponent of the other, then insert this one into the result and advance that list's iterator. If the exponents are equal, then create a new term with that exponent and the sum of the coefficients, and advance both iterators. For example:

   $3x^4 + 2x^2 + 3x + 7$ added to $2x^3 + 4x + 5$ is $3x^4 + 2x^3 + 2x^2 + 7x + 12$

   Write a program to read and add polynomials. You should define a class `Term` that contains the exponent and coefficient. This class should implement `operator<` by comparing the values of the exponents.

5. Write a program to manage a list of students waiting to register for a course as described in Section 4.5. Operations should include adding a new student at the end of the list, adding a new student at the beginning of the list, removing the student from the beginning of the list, and removing a student by name.

6. A circular linked list has no need of a head or tail. Instead you only need to reference an arbitrary item. Implement a circular linked-list class. Note that the `begin()` and `end()` functions will return iterators that reference the same node. You will, however, need to distinguish between them so that you can use the standard library algorithms.

7. The Josephus problem is named after the historian Flavius Josephus, who lived between the years 37 and 100 CE. Josephus was a reluctant leader of the Jewish revolt against the Roman Empire. When it appeared that Josephus and his band were to be captured, they resolved to kill themselves. Josephus persuaded the group by saying, "Let us commit our mutual deaths to determination by lot. He to whom the first lot falls, let him be killed by him that hath the second lot, and thus fortune shall make its progress through us all; nor shall any of us perish by his own right hand, for it would be unfair if, when the rest are gone, somebody should repent and save himself" (Flavius Josephus, *The Wars of the Jews*, Book III, Chapter 8, Verse 7, tr. William Whiston, 1737). Yet that is exactly what happened; Josephus was left for last, and he and the person he was to kill surrendered to the Romans. Although Josephus does not describe how the lots were assigned, the following approach is generally believed to be the way it was done. People form a circle and count around the circle some predetermined number. When this number is reached, that person receives a lot and leaves the circle. The count starts over with the next person. Using the circular linked list developed in Exercise 6, simulate this problem. Your program should take two parameters: n, the number of people that start, and m, the number of counts. For example, try n = 20 and m = 12. Where does Josephus need to be in the original list so that he is the last one chosen?

8. To mimic the procedure used by Josephus and his band strictly, the person eliminated remains in the circle until the next one is chosen. Modify your program to take this into account. Does this change affect the outcome?

9. The correlation coefficient of two input sequences is given by

$$r = \frac{n \sum x_i y_i - \sum x_i \sum y_i}{\sqrt{\left[n \sum x_i^2 - \left(\sum x_i \right)^2 \right] \left[n \sum y_i^2 - \left(\sum y_i \right)^2 \right]}}$$

Adapt Example 4.11 to compute the correlation coefficient from a sequence of pairs of input values from an input file. *Hint:* You will need to define function classes to compute the square of each input value and to compute the product of two input values. You can then use `transform` and `accumulate` to compute each of the individual terms in the formula.

10. A two-dimensional shape can be defined by its boundary polygon, which is simply a list of all coordinates ordered by a traversal of its outline. See the following figure for an example:

The left picture shows the original shape; the middle picture, the outline of the shape. The rightmost picture shows an abstracted boundary, using only the "most important" vertices. We can assign an importance measure to a vertex *P* by considering its neighbors *L* and *R*. We compute the distances *LP*, *PR*, and *LR*. Call these distances *l*1, *l*2, and *l*3. Define the importance as *l*1 + *l*2 − *l*3.

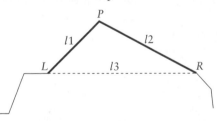

Use the following algorithm to find the n most important points.

1. **while** the number of points is greater than n
2.   Compute the importance of each point.
3.   Remove the least significant one.

Write a program to read a set of coordinates that form an outline and reduce the list to the n most significant ones, where n is an input value.

5

Stacks

In this chapter we illustrate how to use and implement an abstract data type known as a *stack*. A stack differs from a list in the following way. A client of a list can access any element and can insert elements at any location. However, a client of a stack can access only the element that was most recently inserted in the stack. This may seem like a serious restriction that would make stacks not very useful, but it turns out that stacks are actually one of the most commonly used data structures in computer science. For example, during program execution a stack is used to store information about the parameters and return addresses for all the functions that are currently executing (you will see how this is done in Chapter 7, "Recursion"). Compilers also use stacks to store information while evaluating expressions. Part of the reason for the widespread use of stacks is that a stack is relatively easy to implement. This was an important consideration for programming in languages that did not provide the capability for implementing ADTs as classes.

After describing the stack ADT and providing a header file for this ADT, we will discuss two simple applications of stacks: checking for palindromes and testing for balanced parentheses. We will then show how to implement stacks in two ways: using a standard container and a linked list. Finally, we will study how to use stacks to evaluate arithmetic expressions.

5.1 The Stack Abstract Data Type

In a cafeteria you can see stacks of dishes placed in spring-loaded containers. Usually several dishes are visible above the top of the container, and the rest are inside the container. You can access only the dish that is on top of the stack. If you want to place more dishes on the stack, you can place the dishes on top of those that are already there. The spring inside the stack container compresses under the weight of the additional dishes, adjusting the height of the stack so that only the top few dishes are always visible.

FIGURE 5.1
A Pez® Dispenser

Another physical example of stacklike behavior is a Pez® dispenser (see Figure 5.1). A Pez dispenser is a toy that contains candies. There is also a spring inside the dispenser. The top of the dispenser is a character's head. When you tilt the head back, a single piece of candy pops out. You can only extract one piece at a time. If you want to eat more than one piece, you have to open the dispenser multiple times. However, the behavior is not exactly like a stack because you can load the dispenser by putting in many candies at once.

In programming, a stack is a data structure with the property that only the top element of the stack is accessible. In a stack, the top element is the data value that was most recently stored in the stack. Sometimes this storage policy is known as Last-In, First-Out, or LIFO.

Next, we specify some of the operations that we might wish to perform on a stack.

Specification of the Stack Abstract Data Type

Because only the top element of a stack is visible, the operations performed by a stack are few in number. We need to be able to retrieve the top element (function top), remove the top element (function pop), push a new element onto the stack (function push), and test for an empty stack (function empty). Table 5.1 shows a specification for the Stack ADT, which specifies the stack operators. These are all defined in the header file for the STL container stack, <stack>.

TABLE 5.1
Specification of Stack ADT

Functions	Behavior
`bool empty() const`	Returns **true** if the stack is empty; otherwise, returns **false**.
`Item_Type& top();` `const Item_Type& top() const`	Returns the object at the top of the stack without removing it.
`void pop()`	Removes the object at the top of the stack.
`void push(const Item_Type& item)`	Pushes an item onto the top of the stack.
`size_t size() const`	Returns the number of items in the stack.

Listing 5.1 shows the class definition for the class `KW::stack`. This class definition implements the interface defined by Table 5.1 and is very similar to that defined by the C++ standard library. In the private part, the declaration

```
std::vector<Item_Type> container;
```

shows that we will use the STL vector for storage of the stack data. We discuss other approaches in Section 5.3. The line

```
#include "Stack.tc"
```

at the end of file `stack.h` inserts a file that implements the `KW::stack` member functions. We also discuss this file in Section 5.3.

LISTING 5.1
`KW::stack.h`

```
#ifndef STACK_H_
#define STACK_H_

/** Definition file for class KW::stack */
// Include directives needed by the implementation
#include <vector>

namespace KW {
  /** A stack is a data structure that provides last-in first-out
      access to the items that are stored in it. Only the most recently
      inserted item is accessible.
  */
  template<typename Item_Type>
    class stack {

    public:
      // Constructor and member functions

      /** Constructs an initially empty stack. */
      stack();

      /** Pushes an item onto the top of the stack.
          @param item The item to be inserted
      */
      void push(const Item_Type& item);
```

```
        /** Returns a reference to the object at the top of the stack
            without removing it.
            @return A reference to the object at the top of the stack
        */
        Item_Type& top();

        /** Returns a const reference to the object at the at the
            top of the stack without removing it.
            @return A const reference to the object at the top of the stack
        */
        const Item_Type& top() const;

        /** Removes the top item from the stack. */
        void pop();

        /** Determines whether the stack is empty. */
        bool empty() const;

        /** Returns the number of items in the stack. */
        size_t size() const;

    private:
        // Data fields
        /** A sequential container to contain the stack items */
        std::vector<Item_Type> container;

    }; // End class stack

    // Insert implementation of member functions here
    #include "Stack.tc"

} // End namespace KW
#endif
```

EXAMPLE 5.1   A stack names (type stack<string>) contains five strings as shown in Figure 5.2(a). The name "Rich" was placed on the stack before the other four names; "Jonathan" was the last element placed on the stack.

We create this stack using the following statements.

```
stack<string> names;
names.push("Rich");
names.push("Debbie");
names.push("Robin");
names.push("Dustin");
names.push("Jonathan");
```

For stack names in Figure 5.2(a), the value of names.empty() is false. The statement

```
string last = names.top();
```

stores "Jonathan" in last without changing names. The statement

```
names.pop();
```

removes "Jonathan" from names. The stack names now contains four elements and is shown in Figure 5.2(b). The statement

```
names.push("Philip");
```

pushes "Philip" onto the stack; the stack names now contains five elements and is shown in Figure 5.2(c).

FIGURE 5.2
Stack names

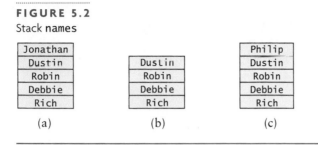

(a)   (b)   (c)

EXERCISES FOR SECTION 5.1

SELF-CHECK

1. Assume that the stack names is defined as in Figure 5.2(c) and perform the following sequence of operations. Indicate the result of each operation and show the new stack if it is changed.

```
names.push("Jane");
names.push("Joseph");
names.pop();
string next_top = names.top();
```

5.2 Stack Applications

In this section we will study two client programs that use stacks: a palindrome finder and a program that verifies that the parentheses in an expression are nested properly.

CASE STUDY   Finding Palindromes

Problem   A palindrome is a string that reads the same in either direction: left to right or right to left. For example, "kayak" is a palindrome, as is "I saw I was I." A well-known palindrome regarding Napoleon Bonaparte is "Able was I ere I saw Elba" (the island where he was sent in exile). We would like a program that reads a string and determines whether it is a palindrome.

Analysis This problem can be solved in many different ways. For example, you could set up a loop in which you compare the characters at each end of a string as you work towards the middle. If any pair of characters is different, the string can't be a palindrome. Another approach would be to scan a string backward (from right to left) and append each character to the end of a new string, which would become the reverse of the original string. Then you could see whether the strings were equal. The approach we will study here uses a stack to assist in forming the reverse of a string. It is not the most efficient way to solve the problem, but it makes good use of a stack.

w
a
s
I

If we scan the input string from left to right and push each character in the input string onto a stack of characters, we can form the reverse of the string by popping the characters and joining them together in the order that they come off the stack. For example, the stack at left contains the characters in the string "I saw".

If we pop them off and join them together, we will get "w" + "a" + "s" + " " + "I", or the string "was I". When the stack is empty, we can compare the string we formed with the original. If they are the same, the original string is a palindrome.

Data Requirements

PROBLEM INPUTS

An input string to be tested

PROBLEM OUTPUTS

A message indicating whether the string is a palindrome

Design We can define a class called Palindrome_Finder (Table 5.2) with data fields for storing the input string and the stack (stack<char> char_stack). The class needs functions to push all characters from the input string onto the stack (fill_stack), to build a string by popping the characters off the stack and joining them (build_reverse), and to compare the strings to see whether they are palindromes (is_palindrome).

Implementation Listing 5.2 shows the class definition and Listing 5.3 shows the implementation. The constructor calls function fill_stack to build the stack when a new Palindrome_Finder object is created. The loop

```
for (size_t i = 0; i < input_string.size(); i++) {
    char_stack.push(input_string[i]);
}
```

pushes each character in input_string onto the stack.

In function build_reverse, the loop

```
while (!char_stack.empty()) {
    // Remove top item from stack and append it to result.
    result += char_stack.top();
    char_stack.pop();
}
```

appends the top character on the stack to result, and then pops it off the stack.

TABLE 5.2
Class Palindrome_Finder

Data Fields	Attributes
`string input_string`	The input string.
`stack<char> char_stack`	The stack where characters are stored.
Functions	**Behavior**
`Palindrome_Finder(const string& str)`	Initializes a new `Palindrome_Finder` object, storing a copy of the parameter `str` in `input_string` and pushing each character onto the stack.
`void fill_stack()`	Fills the stack with the characters in `input_string`.
`string build_reverse()`	Returns the string formed by popping each character from the stack and joining the characters. Empties the stack.
`bool is_palindrome()`	Returns **true** if `input_string` and the string built by `build_reverse` have the same contents, except for case. Otherwise, returns **false**.

Function `is_palindrome` uses the equal algorithm to compare the `input_string` with the reverse string using a function object (see Section 4.10) that compares characters in a case-insensitive manner. The iterators for `input_string` and `reverse` select the next pair of characters to compare, starting with the first character in each string.

```
return equal(input_string.begin(), input_string.end(),
             reverse.begin(), Ci_Equal());
```

The class `Ci_Equal` is defined as follows:

```
/** Function class to perform case-insensitive comparison
    of characters. */
class Ci_Equal {
  public:
    bool operator()(char c1, char c2) {
      return toupper(c1) == toupper(c2);
    }
};
```

The equal algorithm uses the `operator()` defined in class `Ci_Equal` to compare corresponding elements in strings `input_string` and `reverse`; it returns **true** only if all characters being compared are equal, ignoring case.

LISTING 5.2
Palindrome_Finder.h

```
#ifndef PALINDROME_FINDER_H_
#define PALINDROME_FINDER_H

#include <string>
#include <stack>
```

```cpp
/** Class with functions to check whether a string is a palindrome. */
class Palindrome_Finder {

  public:
    /** Store the argument string in a stack of characters.
        @param str String of characters to store in the stack
    */
    Palindrome_Finder(const std::string& str): input_string(str) {
      fill_stack();
    }

    /** Function to determine whether input string is a palidrome. */
    bool is_palindrome();

  private:
    /** Function to fill a stack of characters from an input string. */
    void fill_stack();

    /** Function to build a string containing the characters in a stack.
        post: The stack is empty.
        @return The string containing the words in the stack
    */
    std::string build_reverse();

    /** String to store in stack. */
    std::string input_string;

    /** Stack to hold characters. */
    std::stack<char> char_stack;

};

#endif
```

....
LISTING 5.3
Palindrome_Finder.cpp

```cpp
/** Class with functions to check whether a string is a palindrome. */

#include "Palindrome_Finder.h"
#include <cctype>
#include <algorithm>
using namespace std;

/** Function to fill a stack of characters from an input string. */
void Palindrome_Finder::fill_stack() {
  for (size_t i = 0; i < input_string.size(); i++) {
    char_stack.push(input_string[i]);
  }
}

/** Function to build a string containing the characters in a stack.
    post: The stack is empty.
    @return The string containing the words in the stack
*/
```

```
string Palindrome_Finder::build_reverse() {
  string result;
  while (!char_stack.empty()) {
    // Remove top item from stack and append it to result.
    result += char_stack.top();
    char_stack.pop();
  }
  return result;
}

/** Function class to perform case-insensitive comparison
    of characters. */
class Ci_Equal {
  public:
    bool operator()(char c1, char c2) {
      return toupper(c1) == toupper(c2);
    }
};

bool Palindrome_Finder::is_palindrome() {
  string reverse = build_reverse();
  return equal(input_string.begin(), input_string.end(),
               reverse.begin(), Ci_Equal());
}
```

Testing   To test this class you should run it with several different strings, including both palindromes and nonpalindromes, as follows:

- A single character (always a palindrome)
- Multiple characters in one word
- Multiple words
- Different cases
- Even-length strings
- Odd-length strings
- An empty string (considered a palindrome)

☑ PROGRAM STYLE

Using an Iterator as a Loop Control Variable

The string class provides two ways to access individual characters: using an iterator or using an index. Therefore, you could write the loop in function fill_stack as follows:

```
for (string::const_iterator itr = input_string.begin();
     itr != input_string.end(); ++itr) {
  char_stack.push(*itr);
}
```

This is because the string class provides all of the functions required for a sequential container. Using an iterator instead of an index is more general and would allow you to replace the string input parameter with a list parameter.

An application of class `Palindrome_Finder` should have the following main function:

```
int main() {
  string line;
  cout << "Enter a string followed by a new line\n"
       << "To quit, enter an empty line: ";
  while (getline(cin, line) && (line != "")) {
    cout << line;
    if (Palindrome_Finder(line).is_palindrome())
      cout << " is a palindrome\n\n";
    else
      cout << " is not a palindrome\n\n";
    cout << "Enter a new string to test: ";
  }
}
```

CASE STUDY   Testing Expressions for Balanced Parentheses

Problem   When analyzing arithmetic expressions, it is important to determine whether an expression is balanced with respect to parentheses. For example, the expression

```
(w * (x + y) / z - (p / (r - q)))
```

is balanced. This problem is easy if all parentheses are the same kind—all we need to do is increment a counter each time we scan an opening parenthesis, and decrement the counter when we scan a closing parenthesis. If the counter is always greater than or equal to zero, and the final counter value is zero, the expression is balanced. However, if we can have different kinds of opening and closing parentheses, the problem becomes more difficult. For example,

```
(w * [x + y] / z - [p / {r - q}])
```

is balanced, but the expression

```
(w * [x + y) / z - [p / {r - q}])
```

is not, because the subexpression [x + y) is incorrect. In this expression, the set of opening parentheses includes the symbols {, [, (, and the set of closing parentheses includes the matching symbols },],).

Analysis   An expression is balanced if each subexpression that starts with the symbol { ends with the symbol }, and the same statement is true for the other symbol pairs. Another way of saying this is that an opening parenthesis at position k in the sequence {[(must be paired with the closing parenthesis at position k in the sequence }]). We can use a stack to determine whether the parentheses are balanced (or nested properly). We will scan the expression from left to right, ignoring all characters except for parentheses. We will push each open parenthesis onto a stack of characters. When we reach a closing parenthesis, we will see whether it matches the open parenthesis symbol on the top of the stack. If so, we will pop it off and continue the scan. If the characters don't match or the stack is empty, there is an error in the expression. If there are any characters left on the stack when we are finished, that also indicates an error.

Data Requirements

PROBLEM INPUTS

An expression string

PROBLEM OUTPUTS

A message indicating whether the expression has balanced parentheses

Design   We will write the function is_balanced to check for balanced parentheses. This function returns a **bool** value indicating whether the expression is balanced. We also need functions is_open and is_close to determine whether a character is an opening or closing parenthesis. Function is_balanced implements the following algorithm.

Algorithm for Function is_balanced

1.   Create an empty stack of characters.
2.   Assume that the expression is balanced (balanced is **true**).
3.   Set index to 0.
4.   **while** balanced is **true** and index < the expression's length
5.   Get the next character in the data string.
6.   **if** the next character is an opening parenthesis
7.   Push it onto the stack.
8.   **else if** the next character is a closing parenthesis
9.   Pop the top of the stack.
10.   **if** stack was empty or its top does not match the closing parenthesis
11.   Set balanced to **false**.
12.   Increment index.
13. Return **true** if balanced is **true** and the stack is empty.

The **if** statement at Step 6 tests each character in the expression, ignoring all characters except for opening and closing parentheses. If the next character is an opening parenthesis, it is pushed onto the stack. If the next character is a closing parenthesis, the nearest unmatched opening parenthesis is retrieved (by popping the stack) and compared to the closing parenthesis.

Implementation   Listing 5.4 shows the Paren_Checker program. The **while** loop in function is_balanced (Step 4 of the algorithm) begins by storing the next character in next_ch, starting with the character at the beginning of expression.

```
string::const_iterator iter = expression.begin();
while (balanced && (iter != expression.end())) {
  char next_ch = *iter;
```

Function is_open returns **true** if its type-char argument is in the string of opening parentheses, string OPEN; function is_close tests for closing parentheses (string CLOSE). If next_ch stores an opening parenthesis, the statement

```
s.push(next_ch);
```

pushes next_ch onto the stack s (a local stack<char>).

For each closing parenthesis, the top function retrieves the nearest unmatched opening parenthesis from the stack:

```
char top_ch = s.top();
```

Next, we see whether top_ch is a corresponding opening parenthesis to the next_ch closing parenthesis. This is done by comparing their positions in the list of opening and closing parentheses using the expression

```
OPEN.find(top_ch) == CLOSE.find(next_ch);
```

The function string::find returns the position of the character argument in the string. Thus we must be careful when defining the list of opening (OPEN) and closing (CLOSE) parentheses that the corresponding parentheses are in the same positions.

After the **while** loop finishes execution, the function result is returned. The result is **true** only when the expression is balanced and the stack is empty:

```
return balanced && s.empty();
```

LISTING 5.4
Paren_Checker.cpp

```
/** Program to check an expression for balanced parentheses. */

#include <stack>
#include <string>
#include <iostream>
using namespace std;

// The set of opening parentheses.
const string OPEN = "([{";
// The corresponding set of closing parentheses.
const string CLOSE = ")]}";

/** Function to determine whether a character is one of the opening
    parentheses (defined in constant OPEN).
    @param ch Character to be tested
    @return true If the character is an opening parenthesis
*/
bool is_open(char ch) {
  return OPEN.find(ch) != string::npos;
}

/** Function to determine whether a character is one of the closing
    parentheses (defined in constant CLOSE).
    @param ch Character to be tested
    @return true If the character is a closing parenthesis
```

```
*/
bool is_close(char ch) {
  return CLOSE.find(ch) != string::npos;
}

/** Test the input string to see that it contains balanced
    parentheses. This function tests an input string to
    see that each type of parenthesis is balanced. '(' is
    matched with ')', '[' is matched with ']', and '{' is
    matched with '}'.
    @param expression A string containing the expression to be examined
    @return true if all parentheses match
*/
bool is_balanced(const string& expression) {
  // A stack for the open parentheses that haven't been matched
  stack<char> s;
  bool balanced = true;
  string::const_iterator iter = expression.begin();
  while (balanced && (iter != expression.end())) {
    char next_ch = *iter;
    if (is_open(next_ch)) {
      s.push(next_ch);
    } else if (is_close(next_ch)) {
      if (s.empty()) {
        balanced = false;
      } else {
        char top_ch = s.top();
        s.pop();
        balanced =
          OPEN.find(top_ch) == CLOSE.find(next_ch);
      }
    }
    ++iter;
  }
  return balanced && s.empty();
}

/** Main function to test is_balanced. */
int main() {
  cout << "Enter an expression\n";
  string expression;
  while (getline(cin, expression) && (expression != "")) {
    cout << expression;
    if (is_balanced(expression)) {
      cout << " is balanced\n";
    } else {
      cout << " is not balanced\n";
    }
    cout << "Enter another expression: ";
  }
  return 0;
}
```

⊘ PITFALL

Attempting to Pop an Empty Stack

If you attempt to reference the top of or to pop an empty stack, your program will probably halt and report a run-time error. The nature of the error message will depend on the compiler and operating system. Under Linux you will probably get the message segmentation fault, and under Windows you will get an error dialog box reporting an illegal attempt to access memory. It is also possible that no error is reported at all. You can guard against this error by testing for a nonempty stack before calling top or pop.

☑ PROGRAM STYLE

Declaring Constants

We declared OPEN and CLOSE as global constants instead of declaring them locally in the functions where they are used (is_open and is_close). There are two reasons for this. First, it is a more efficient use of memory to declare them as constants instead of having to allocate storage for these constants each time the function is called. Also, if a new kind of parenthesis is introduced, it is easier to locate and update the class constants instead of having to find their declarations inside a function. However, relying on global constants makes functions less portable (less easy to drop in elsewhere), so this dependence should be mentioned in the function's comment header.

Testing   A simple test driver is included in Listing 5.4. Test this program by providing a variety of input expressions and displaying the result (**true** or **false**). You should try expressions that have several levels of nested parentheses. Also, try expressions that would be properly nested if the parentheses were all of one type, but are not properly nested because a closing parenthesis does not match a particular opening parenthesis (for example, {x + y] is not balanced because] is not the correct closing parenthesis for {). Also check expressions that have too many opening or closing parentheses. Finally, test for some strange strings such as "{[}]", which should fail. The string "{[a * + b]}", which is not a valid expression, should pass because its parentheses are balanced.

EXERCISES FOR SECTION 5.2

SELF-CHECK

1. The result returned by the palindrome finder depends on *all* characters in a string, including spaces and punctuation. Discuss how you would modify the palindrome finder so that only the *letters* in the input string were used to determine whether the input string was a palindrome. You should ignore any other characters.
2. Trace the execution of function `is_balanced` for each of the following expressions. Your trace should show the stack after each `push` or `pop` operation. Also show the values of `balanced`, `is_open`, and `is_close` after each closing parenthesis is processed.

   ```
   (a + b * {c / [d - e]}) + (d / e)
   (a + b * {c / [d - e}}) + (d / e)
   ```

PROGRAMMING

1. Write a function that reads a line and reverses the words in the line (not the characters) using a stack. For example, given the following input:

   ```
   The quick brown fox jumps over the lazy dog.
   ```

   you should get the following output:

   ```
   dog. lazy the over jumps fox brown quick The
   ```

2. Three different approaches to finding palindromes are discussed in the Analysis section of that case study. Code the first approach. You can use the `string` function `rbegin` to obtain a `reverse_iterator` that can be passed as an argument to the `equals` function.
3. Code the second approach to finding palindromes.

5.3 Implementing a Stack

Now that you have seen how to use a stack, we will discuss how to implement the Stack ADT. We will discuss more advanced applications afterwards. Readers who are interested primarily in stack applications can skip ahead to Section 5.5.

You may have recognized that a stack is very similar to a `vector`. In fact, the standard library defines the stack as a template class that takes any of the sequential containers as a template parameter. Thus, within the standard library a stack can be implemented using a `vector`, `list`, or `deque` as a component to hold the contents of the stack. We will describe the `deque` container in Chapter 6 when we discuss the Queue ADT. We show two implementations in this section: one that uses a standard template container and another that uses a special-purpose single-linked list.

FIGURE 5.3
Stack of **char** objects in a vector

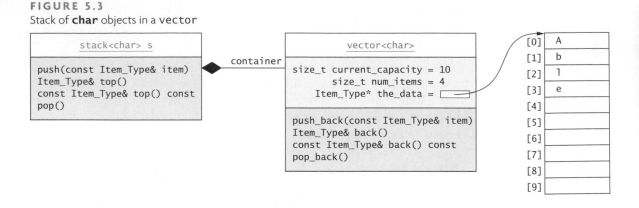

Figure 5.3 shows the characters of the string "Able" stored in stack<char> s. The vector<char> container is used to store the contents, where container[3] contains the character at the top of the stack.

Listing 5.5 (file Stack.tc) shows an implementation of the stack that is very similar to that given by the C++ standard library. Since all of the sequential containers provide the functions empty, size, back (equivalent to stack::top), push_back (equivalent to stack::push), and pop_back (equivalent to stack::pop), we could use any of these containers. The data member container represents the particular container object being used to store the stack elements. We discuss why we used the extension .tc after the listing.

Adapter Classes and the Delegation Pattern

The stack class uses the delegation pattern mentioned in Chapter 4 by making the functions in the underlying container class do its work for it. It is also said to be an *adapter class* because it adapts the functions available in another class to the interface its clients expect by giving different names to essentially the same operations. For example, if a vector is used as the container object, stack::push corresponds to vector::push_back, stack::top corresponds to vector::back, and so on.

LISTING 5.5
Stack.tc

```
#ifndef STACK_TC_
#define STACK_TC_

/** Construct an initially empty stack. */
template<typename Item_Type>
  stack<Item_Type>::stack() { }

/** Pushes an item onto the top of the stack.
    @param item The item to be inserted
*/
template<typename Item_Type>
  void stack<Item_Type>::push(const Item_Type& item) {
    container.push_back(item);
}
```

```
/** Returns a reference to the object at the top of the stack
    without removing it.
    @return A reference to the object at the top of the stack
*/
template<typename Item_Type>
  Item_Type& stack<Item_Type>::top() {
    return container.back();
}

/** Returns a const reference to the object at the
    top of the stack without removing it.
    @return A const reference to the object at the top of the stack
*/
template<typename Item_Type>
  const Item_Type& stack<Item_Type>::top() const {
    return container.back();
}

/** Removes the top item from the stack.
*/
template<typename Item_Type>
  void stack<Item_Type>::pop() {
    container.pop_back();
}

/** Determines whether the stack is empty. */
template<typename Item_Type>
  bool stack<Item_Type>::empty() const {
    return container.empty();
}

/** Returns the number of items in the stack. */
template<typename Item_Type>
  size_t stack<Item_Type>::size() const {
    return container.size();
}
#endif
```

Revisiting the Definition File `stack.h`

If you want to implement the stack using a vector object as a container, you must change the definition of the data member `container` in the private part of the class definition (Listing 5.1):

```
// Data fields
/** A sequential container to contain the stack items */
std::vector<Item_Type> container;
```

If you prefer to use a deque for a container, substitute deque<Item_Type> for vector<Item_Type> in the declaration of container.

The member function implementations shown in Listing 5.5 should be included after the class definition but before the end of the namespace. Template member function implementations must be included with the class definitions. In Listing 5.1, we used an include directive to insert the code for the member function definitions at the end of the stack.h file:

✓ PROGRAM STYLE

Reason for Including File Stack.tc in File stack.h

In earlier programming, we were able to write the definition file (extension .h) for a class and its implementation file (extension .cpp) as separate files, and we would include the .h file at the beginning of the .cpp file. C++ does not permit this for template classes, however, because for each instantiation of a template class in a client program the compiler needs to see the template to create an instantiation for those member functions that are used in the current instantiation. Therefore, we have placed the implementation in a separate file and given it the extension .tc to specify template implementation files. The .tc file, while not a typical header file, is still an included file, so it should not contain **using** directives or **using** statements.

An alternate approach would be to replace each function declaration in file stack.h with its actual definition (see Listing 5.6). This is simpler for the case where we only have a single implementation of an ADT; however, it does not provide a separate interface file and therefore makes it a bit more difficult to provide different implementations of the ADT.

```
// Insert implementation of member functions here
#include Stack.tc

} // End namespace KW
#endif
```

The include directive completes the definition of the file stack.h and allows us to compile file Stack.tc. The Program Style display above discusses why the definition file and implementation files were organized in this way. Listing 5.6 shows another way.

LISTING 5.6
stack.h with push Member Function Inserted

```
#ifndef STACK_H_
#define STACK_H_
#include <vector>

namespace KW {
  /** A stack is a data structure that provides last-in first-out
      access to the items that are stored in it. Only the most recently
      inserted item is accessible.
  */
  template<typename Item_Type>
    class stack {

    public:
      // Member functions
```

```
    /** Pushes an item onto the top of the stack.
        @param item The item to be inserted
    */
    void push(const Item_Type item) {
      container.push_back(item);
    }

  ...
  private:
    // Data fields
    /** A sequential container to contain the stack items */
    std::vector<Item_Type> container;

  };
}
#endif
```

Implementing a Stack as a Linked Data Structure

We can also implement a stack using a single-linked list of nodes. We show the stack containing the characters in "Able" in Figure 5.4, with the last character in the string stored in the node at the top of the stack. File Linked_Stack.tc defines a stack class that contains a collection of Node objects (see Section 4.5). Recall that inner class Node has data fields data (type Item_Type) and next (type Node*).

To use this implementation we need to replace the statements at the end of file stack.h (Listing 5.1) with the following:

```
    private:
      // Insert definition of class Node here
      #include "Node.h"

      /** A pointer to the top of the stack. */
      Node* top_of_stack;
  }; // End class stack

  // Insert implementation of member functions here
  #include "Linked_Stack.tc"
} // End namespace KW
#endif
```

Pointer variable top_of_stack (type Node*) points to the last element placed on the stack (see Section 4.5). Because it is easier to insert and remove from the head of a linked list, we will have top_of_stack point to the node at the head of the list.

Function push inserts a node at the head of the list. The statement

```
    top_of_stack = new Node(item, top_of_stack);
```

sets top_of_stack to point to the new node; top_of_stack->next references the old top of the stack. When the stack is empty, top_of_stack is **NULL**, so the attribute next for the first object pushed onto the stack (the item at the bottom) will be **NULL**.

Function top will return top_of_stack->data. Function empty tests for a value of top_of_stack equal to **NULL**. Function pop simply resets top_of_stack to the value stored in the next field of the list head and then deletes the old top of the stack (pointed to by old_top). Listing 5.7 shows the implementation file (Linked_Stack.tc).

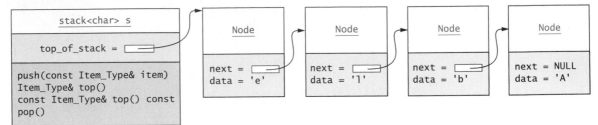

FIGURE 5.4
Stack of Character Objects in a Linked List

LISTING 5.7
Linked_Stack.tc

```
#ifndef LINKED_STACK_TC_
#define LINKED_STACK_TC_

/** Constructs an empty stack. */
template<typename Item_Type>
  stack<Item_Type>::stack() : top_of_stack(NULL) {}

/** Pushes an item onto the top of the stack.
    @param item The item to be inserted
*/
template<typename Item_Type>
  void stack<Item_Type>::push(const Item_Type& item) {
    top_of_stack = new Node(item, top_of_stack);
}

/** Returns a reference to the object at the top of the stack
    without removing it.
    @return A reference to the object at the top of the stack
*/
template<typename Item_Type>
  Item_Type& stack<Item_Type>::top() {
    return top_of_stack->data;
}

/** Returns a const reference to the object at the
    top of the stack without removing it.
    @return A const reference to the object at the top of the stack
*/
template<typename Item_Type>
  const Item_Type& stack<Item_Type>::top() const {
    return top_of_stack->data;
}

/** Removes the top item from the stack. */
template<typename Item_Type>
  void stack<Item_Type>::pop() {
    Node* old_top = top_of_stack;
    top_of_stack = top_of_stack->next;
    delete old_top;
}
```

```
/** Determines whether the stack is empty. */
template<typename Item_Type>
  bool stack<Item_Type>::empty() const {
    return top_of_stack == NULL;
}

/** Determines the size of the stack. */
template<typename Item_Type>
  size_t stack<Item_Type>::size() const {
  // Exercise
}

#endif
```

Comparison of Stack Implementations

The implementation shown in Listing 5.6 is very similar to the implementation provided by the C++ standard library. By delegating the operations to an underlying sequential container, we avoid having to implement these operations ourselves. By using the functions push_back, pop_back, and back, we are assured of constant time (O(1)) performance, since the C++ standard requires that implementations of the sequential containers provide these operations in (amortized) constant time.

Use of the standard containers has a space penalty, however. To achieve the amortized constant performance for push_back, and so forth, the vector and deque allocate additional space. As we showed in Section 4.3, the vector will allocate an array twice the current size whenever it needs to allocate additional space. As we will see in Chapter 6, the deque also allocates additional space. The standard list class is a double-linked list; thus each Node contains pointers to both a next and a previous entry. This flexibility is not needed for the stack.

We also showed how you could use your own linked data structure. This has the advantage of using exactly as much storage as is needed for the stack. However, you would also need to allocate storage for the links. Because all insertions and deletions are at one end, the flexibility provided by a linked data structure is not utilized. All stack operations using a linked data structure would be O(1).

EXERCISES FOR SECTION 5.3

SELF-CHECK

1. For the implementation of stack s using a linked list as the underlying data structure (see Figure 5.4), show how the underlying data structure changes after each statement below executes. What is the value of top_of_stack? Assume the characters in "C++" are stored on the stack (C pushed on first).

```
s.push('i');
s.push('s');
char ch1 = s.pop();
s.pop();
s.push(' ');
char ch2 = s.top();
```

PROGRAMMING

1. Write a function `size` for the linked stack implementation that returns the number of elements currently on the stack.

5.4 Additional Stack Applications

In this section we consider two case studies that are a bit more complicated than the earlier ones. They both relate to evaluating arithmetic expressions. The first problem is slightly easier, and it involves evaluating expressions that are in postfix form. The second problem discusses how to convert from *infix notation* (common mathematics notation) to postfix form.

Normally we write expressions using infix notation, in which binary operators (*, +, and so forth) are inserted between their operands. Infix expressions present no special problem to humans, because we can easily scan left and right to find the operands of a particular operator. A calculator (or computer), on the other hand, normally scans an expression string in the order that it is input (left to right). Therefore, it is easier to evaluate an expression if the user types the operands for each operator in before typing the operator (*postfix notation*). Table 5.3 shows some examples of expressions in postfix and infix form. The braces under each postfix expression will help you visualize the operands for each operator.

The advantage of the postfix form is that there is no need to group subexpressions in parentheses or even to consider operator precedence. (We talk more about postfix form in the second case study in this section.) The braces in Table 5.3 are for our convenience and are not required. The next case study develops a program that evaluates a postfix expression.

TABLE 5.3
Postfix Expressions

Postfix Expression	Infix Expression	Value
4 7 *	4 * 7	28
4 7 2 + *	4 * (7 + 2)	36
4 7 * 20 -	(4 * 7) - 20	8
3 4 7 * 2 / +	3 + ((4 * 7) / 2)	17

CASE STUDY   Evaluating Postfix Expressions

Problem   Write a class that evaluates a postfix expression. The postfix expression will be a string containing digit characters and operator characters from the set +, -, *, /. The space character will be used as a delimiter between tokens (integers and operators).

Analysis   In a postfix expression the operands precede the operators. A stack is the perfect place to save the operands until the operator is scanned. When the operator is scanned, its operands can be popped off the stack (the last operand scanned, the right operand, will be popped first). Therefore, our program will push each integer operand onto the stack. When an operator is read, the top two operands are popped, the operation is performed on its operands, and the result is pushed back onto the stack. We always pop two operators because we are assuming all operators are binary operators. Also, negative operands (indicated by unary minus) are not allowed. The final result should be the only value remaining on the stack when the end of the expression is reached.

Design   We will write class `Postfix_Evaluator` to evaluate postfix expressions. The class should define a function `eval`, which scans a postfix expression and processes each of its tokens, where a token is either an operand (an integer) or an operator. We also need a function `eval_op`, which evaluates each operator when it is scanned, and a function `is_operator`, which determines whether a character is an operator. Table 5.4 describes the class.

The algorithm for `eval` follows. The stack operators perform algorithm steps 1, 5, 7, 8, 10, and 11.

Table 5.5 shows the evaluation of the third expression in Table 5.3 using this algorithm. The arrow under the expression points to the character being processed; the stack diagram shows the stack after this character is processed.

TABLE 5.4
Class `Postfix_Evaluator`

Data Field	Attribute
`stack<int> operand_stack`	The stack of operands (**int** objects).
Public Functions	**Behavior**
`int eval(string expression)`	Returns the value of `expression`.
Private Functions	**Behavior**
`int eval_op(char op)`	Pops two operands and applies operator `op` to its operands, returning the result.
`bool is_operator(char ch) const`	Returns **true** if `ch` is an operator symbol.

TABLE 5.5
Evaluating a Postfix Expression

Expression	Action	Stack
4 7 * 20 – ↑	Push 4.	4
4 7 * 20 – ↑	Push 7.	7 4
4 7 * 20 – ↑	Pop 7 and 4. Evaluate 4 * 7. Push 28.	28
4 7 * 20 – ↑	Push 20.	20 28
4 7 * 20 – ↑	Pop 20 and 28. Evaluate 28 – 20. Push 8.	8
4 7 * 20 – ↑	Pop 8. Stack is empty. Result is 8.	

Algorithm for Function eval

1.   Empty the operand stack.
2.   **while** there are more tokens
3.   Get the next token.
4.   **if** the first character of the token is a digit
5.   Push the integer onto the stack.
6.   **else if** the token is an operator
7.   Pop the right operand off the stack.
8.   Pop the left operand off the stack.
9.   Evaluate the operation.
10.   Push the result onto the stack.
11. Pop the stack and return the result.

Implementation   Listing 5.8 shows the class definition file Postfix_Evaluator.h. The data fields include the string OPERATORS (defined in the implementation file to be "+-*/") and the operand stack (std::stack<int> operand_stack). The include file Syntax_Error.h, shown in Listing 5.9, defines the exception class Syntax_Error as a derived class of the exception class std::invalid_argument.

LISTING 5.8
Postfix_Evaluator.h

```
#ifndef POSTFIX_EVALUATOR_H_
#define POSTFIX_EVALUATOR_H_
```

```
#include <stack>
#include <string>
#include "Syntax_Error.h"

class Postfix_Evaluator {
  // Public member functions
  public:
    /** Evaluates a postfix expression.
        @param expression The expression to be evaluated
        @return The value of the expression
        @throws Syntax_Error if a syntax error is detected
    */
    int eval(const std::string& expression);

  // Private member functions
  private:
    /** Evaluates the current operator.
        This function pops the two operands off the operand
        stack and applies the operator.
        @param op A character representing the operator
        @throws Syntax_Error if top is attempted on an empty stack
    */
    int eval_op(char op);

    /** Determines whether a character is an operator.
        @param ch The character to be tested
        @return true if the character is an operator
    */
    bool is_operator(char ch) const {
      return OPERATORS.find(ch) != std::string::npos;
    }

    // Data fields
    static const std::string OPERATORS;
    std::stack<int> operand_stack;
};

#endif
```

....

LISTING 5.9
Syntax_Error.h

```
#ifndef SYNTAX_ERROR_H_
#define SYNTAX_ERROR_H_
#include <stdexcept>

class Syntax_Error : public std::invalid_argument {
  public:
    Syntax_Error(std::string msg) : std::invalid_argument(msg) {}
};
#endif
```

Listing 5.10 shows the implementation of the eval and eval_op functions. Function eval implements the algorithm shown in the design section. It begins by emptying the operand stack. We assume that there are spaces between operands and operators, so eval uses the istringstream (see *The C++ Primer*) to extract the individual tokens (character sequences delimited by spaces) in string expression.

```
// Process each token
istringstream tokens(expression);
char next_char;
while (tokens >> next_char) {
```

The expression

```
tokens >> next_char
```

will read the next nonblank character into next_char. If the character in next_char is a digit, this indicates that the next token is an integer. We put the first digit of this integer back into the istringstream using the statement

```
tokens.putback(next_char);
```

The putback function (member of the istream class) allows us to "unread" a single character. Now we read all the characters of the next integer into the **int** variable value using the statement

```
tokens >> value;
```

If the character in next_char is not a digit, then we check to be sure it is an operator. If it is an operator, then we call the eval_op fuction. Otherwise we indicate a syntax error by throwing the Syntax_Error exception.

Private function is_operator determines whether a character is an operator. When an operator is encountered, private function eval_op is called to evaluate it. This function pops the top two operands from the stack. The first item popped is the right-hand operand, and the second is the left-hand operand.

```
if (operand_stack.empty())
  throw Syntax_Error("Stack is empty");
int rhs = operand_stack.top();
operand_stack.pop();
if (operand_stack.empty())
  throw Syntax_Error("Stack is empty");
int lhs = operand_stack.top();
operand_stack.pop();
```

Notice that before we call the top function, we test to be sure that the operand_stack is not empty. If it is empty, we throw the Syntax_Error exception. If we omitted this test and attempted to pop an empty stack, we would probably get a run-time error.

A **switch** statement is then used to select the appropriate expression to evaluate for the given operator. For example, the following case processes the addition operator and saves the sum of lhs and rhs in result.

```
case '+' : result = lhs + rhs;
           break;
```

LISTING 5.10
Postfix_Evaluator.cpp

```cpp
/** Implementation of the postfix_evaluator. */

#include "Postfix_Evaluator.h"
#include <sstream>
#include <cctype>
using std::stack;
using std::string;
using std::istringstream;
using std::isdigit;

const std::string Postfix_Evaluator::OPERATORS = "+-*/";

/** Evaluates a postfix expression.
    @param expression The expression to be evaluated
    @return The value of the expression
    @throws Syntax_Error if a syntax error is detected
*/
int Postfix_Evaluator::eval(const std::string& expression) {
  // Be sure the stack is empty
  while (!operand_stack.empty())
    operand_stack.pop();

  // Process each token
  istringstream tokens(expression);
  char next_char;
  while (tokens >> next_char) {
    if (isdigit(next_char)) {
      tokens.putback(next_char);
      int value;
      tokens >> value;
      operand_stack.push(value);
    } else if (is_operator(next_char)) {
      int result = eval_op(next_char);
      operand_stack.push(result);
    } else {
      throw Syntax_Error("Invalid character encountered");
    }
  }
  if (!operand_stack.empty()) {
    int answer = operand_stack.top();
    operand_stack.pop();
    if (operand_stack.empty()) {
      return answer;
    } else {
      throw Syntax_Error("Stack should be empty");
    }
  } else {
    throw Syntax_Error("Stack is empty");
  }
}
```

```
/** Evaluates the current operator.
    This function pops the two operands off the operand
    stack and applies the operator.
    @param op A character representing the operator
    @throws Syntax_Error if top is attempted on an empty stack
*/
int Postfix_Evaluator::eval_op(char op) {
  if (operand_stack.empty())
    throw Syntax_Error("Stack is empty");
  int rhs = operand_stack.top();
  operand_stack.pop();
  if (operand_stack.empty())
    throw Syntax_Error("Stack is empty");
  int lhs = operand_stack.top();
  operand_stack.pop();
  int result = 0;
  switch(op) {
  case '+' : result = lhs + rhs;
             break;
  case '-' : result = lhs - rhs;
             break;
  case '*' : result = lhs * rhs;
             break;
  case '/' : result = lhs / rhs;
             break;
  }
  return result;
}
```

Testing   You will need to write a driver for the Postfix_Evaluator class. This driver should create a Postfix_Evaluator object, read one or more expressions, and report the result. It will also have to catch the Syntax_Error exception. A white-box approach to testing would lead you to consider the following test cases. First, you want to exercise each path in the eval_op function by entering a simple expression that uses each operator. Then you need to exercise the paths through eval by trying different orderings and multiple occurrences of the operators. These tests exercise the normal cases, so you next need to test for possible syntax errors. Consider the following cases: an operator without any operands, a single operand, an extra operand, an extra operator, a variable name, and finally an empty string.

☑ PROGRAM STYLE

Creating Your Own Exception Class

The program would work just the same if we did not bother to declare the Syntax_Error class and just threw a std::exception object each time an error occurred. However, we feel that this approach gives the user a more meaningful description of the cause of an error. Also, if other errors are possible in a client of this class, any Syntax_Error exception can be caught and handled in a separate **catch** clause.

CASE STUDY   Converting from Infix to Postfix

We normally write expressions in infix notation. Therefore, one approach to evaluating expressions in infix notation is first to convert it to postfix and then to apply the evaluation technique just discussed. We will show in this case study how to accomplish this conversion using a stack. An infix expression can also be evaluated directly using two stacks. This is left as a programming project.

Problem

To complete the design of an expression evaluator, we need a set of functions that convert infix expressions to postfix form. We will assume that the expression will consist only of spaces, operands, and operators, where the space is a delimiter character between tokens. All operands that are identifiers begin with a letter; all operands that are numbers begin with a digit. (Although we are allowing for identifiers, our postfix evaluator can't really handle them.)

Analysis

Table 5.3 showed the infix and postfix forms of four expressions. For each expression pair, the operands are in the same sequence; however, the placement of the operators changes in going from infix to postfix. For example, in converting

```
w - 5.1 / sum * 2
```

to its postfix form

```
w 5.1 sum / 2 * -
```

we see that the four operands (the tokens w, 5.1, sum, 2) retain their relative ordering from the infix expression, but the order of the operators is changed. The first operator in the infix expression, -, is the last operator in the postfix expression. Therefore, we can insert the operands in the output expression (postfix) as soon as they are scanned in the input expression (infix), but each operator should be inserted in the postfix string after its operands and in the order in which they should be evaluated, not the order in which they were scanned. For expressions without parentheses, there are two criteria that determine the order of operator evaluation:

- Operators are evaluated according to their precedence or rank. Higher-precedence operators are evaluated before lower-precedence operators. For example, *, /, and % (the multiplicative operators) are evaluated before +, -.
- Operators with the same precedence are evaluated in left-to-right order (left-associative rule).

If we temporarily store the operators on a stack, we can pop them whenever we need to and insert them in the postfix string in an order that indicates when they should be evaluated, rather than when they were scanned. For example, if we have the first two operators from the string "w - 5.1 / sum * 2" stored on a stack as follows,

operand_stack

```
 /
 -
```

the operator / (scanned second) must come off the stack and be placed in the postfix string before the operator - (scanned first). If we have the stack as just shown and the next operator is *, we need to pop the / off the stack and insert it in the postfix string before *, because the multiplicative operator scanned earlier (/) should be evaluated before the multiplicative operator (*) scanned later (the left-associative rule).

Design   Class `Infix_To_Postfix` contains functions needed for the conversion. The class should have a data field `operator_stack`, which stores the operators. It should also have a function `convert`, which does the initial processing of all tokens (operands and operators). Function `convert` needs to get each token (using an `istringstream` object) and process it. Each token that is an operand should be appended to the postfix string. Function `process_operator` will process each operator token. Function `is_operator` determines whether a token is an operator, and function `precedence` returns the precedence of an operator. Table 5.6 describes class `Infix_To_Postfix`.

The algorithm for function `convert` follows. The **while** loop extracts and processes each token, calling `process_operator` to process each operator token. After all tokens are extracted from the infix string and processed, any operators remaining on the stack should be popped and appended to the postfix string. They are appended to the end because they have lower precedence than those operators inserted earlier.

Algorithm for Function `convert`

1. Initialize `postfix` to an empty `string`.
2. Initialize the operator stack to an empty stack.
3. **while** there are more tokens in the infix string
4.   Get the next token.
5.   **if** the next token is an operand
6.   Append it to `postfix`.
7.   **else if** the next token is an operator
8.   Call `process_operator` to process the operator.
9.   **else**
10.   Indicate a syntax error.
11. Pop remaining operators off the operator stack and append them to `postfix`.

Function `process_operator`

The real decision making happens in function `process_operator`. By pushing operators onto the stack or popping them off the stack (and into the postfix string), this function controls the order in which the operators will be evaluated.

Each operator will eventually be pushed onto the stack. However, before doing this, `process_operator` compares the operator's precedence with that of the stacked operators, starting with the operator at the top of the stack. If the current operator has higher precedence than the operator at the top of the stack, it is pushed onto the stack immediately. This will ensure that none of the stacked operators can be inserted into the postfix string before it.

TABLE 5.6
Class `Infix_To_Postfix`

Data Field	Attribute
`stack<char> operator_stack`	Stack of operators.
`string postfix`	The postfix string being formed.
Public Functions	**Behavior**
`string convert(string infix)`	Extracts and processes each token in `infix` and returns the equivalent postfix string.
Private Functions	**Behavior**
`void process_operator(char op)`	Processes operator `op` by updating `operator_stack`.
`int precedence(char op) const`	Returns the precedence of operator `op`.
`bool is_operator(char ch) const`	Returns **true** if `ch` is an operator symbol.

However, if the operator at the top of the stack has higher precedence than the current operator, it is popped off the stack and inserted in the postfix string, because it should be performed before the current operator according to the precedence rule. Also, if the operator at the top of the stack has the same precedence as the current operator, it is popped off the stack and inserted into the postfix string, because it should be performed before the current operator according to the left-associative rule. After an operator is popped off the stack, we repeat the process of comparing the precedence of the operator currently at the top of the stack with the precedence of the current operator until the current operator is pushed onto the stack.

A special case is an empty operator stack. In this case, there are no stacked operators to compare with the new one, so we will simply push the current operator onto the stack. We use function top to access the operator at the top of the stack without removing it. Sometimes this is called *peeking the stack*.

Algorithm for Function `process_operator`

1.   **if** the operator stack is empty
2.   Push the current operator onto the stack.
     else
3.   **if** the precedence of the current operator is greater than the precedence of `stack.top()`
4.   Push the current operator onto the stack.
     else
5.   **while** the stack is not empty
             and the precedence of the current operator is
             less than or equal to the precedence of `stack.top()`
6.   Append `stack.top()` to `postfix` and pop the stack.
7.   Push the current operator onto the stack.

....
TABLE 5.7
Conversion of `w - 5.1 / sum * 2`

Next Token	Action	Effect on operator_stack	Effect on postfix
w	Append w to postfix.	⎵	w
-	The stack is empty Push - onto the stack.	-	w
5.1	Append 5.1 to postfix.	-	w 5.1
/	precedence(/) > precedence(-), Push / onto the stack.	/ -	w 5.1
sum	Append sum to postfix.	/ -	w 5.1 sum
*	precedence(*) equals precedence(/) Pop / off the stack and append to postfix.	-	w 5.1 sum /
*	precedence(*) > precedence(-), Push * onto the stack.	* -	w 5.1 sum /
2	Append 2 to postfix.	* -	w 5.1 sum / 2
End of input	Stack is not empty, Pop * off the stack and append to postfix.	-	w 5.1 sum / 2 *
End of input	Stack is not empty, Pop - off the stack and append to postfix.	⎵	w 5.1 sum / 2 * -

Table 5.7 traces the conversion of the infix expression `w - 5.1 / sum * 2` to the postfix expression `w 5.1 sum / 2 * -`. The final value of postfix shows that / is performed first (operands 5.1 and sum), * is performed next (operands 5.1 / sum and 2), and - is performed last.

Although the algorithm will correctly convert a well-formed expression and will detect some expressions with invalid syntax, it doesn't do all the syntax checking required. For example, an expression with extra operands would not be detected. We discuss this further in the testing section.

☑ PROGRAM STYLE

Using #ifdef, #else to Select a Stack Implementation

We select the stack implementation and define data field operator_stack using the #ifdef, #else compiler directive. This allows us to select either the stack implementation in the user namespace KW or the stack implementation in the standard namespace depending on the switch USEKW. If the switch USEKW is defined, the preprocessor inserts the following code:

```
#include "stack.h"
...
KW::stack<char> operator_stack;
```

If the switch USEKW is not defined, the preprocessor inserts the following code instead:

```
#include <stack>
...
std::stack<char> operator_stack;
```

We can define this switch when we compile the program using the -D compiler directive. For example, to use the KW implementation using the gcc compiler, we would compile using the following command:

```
g++ -DUSEKW -o Infix_To_Postfix Infix_To_Postfix.cpp
  Test_Infix_To_Postfix.cpp
```

The -DUSEKW defines the macro symbol USEKW. The -o specifies the name given to the executable file (Infix_To_Postfix). If this is omitted the executable file is given the strange name a.out. Without the -DUSEKW, the switch USEKW would not be defined, and the standard stack would be used. The various integrated development environments also provide a way to set this compiler directive.

Implementation   Listing 5.11 shows the definition for the Infix_To_Postfix class, and Listing 5.12 shows the implementation of the convert and process_operator functions. The convert function begins by initializing postfix and creating an istringsteam object infix_tokens. The tokens are extracted and processed within a **while** loop. The condition isalnum(next_token[0]) tests the first character of the next token to see whether the next token is an operand (identifier or number). Function isalnum (defined in <cctype>) returns **true** if next_token begins with a letter or digit. If this condition is true, the token is appended to postfix followed by a space character. The next condition,

```
    (is_operator(next_token[0]))
```

is true if next_token is an operator. If so, function process_operator is called. If the next token is not an operand or an operator, the Syntax_Error exception is thrown.

Once the end of the expression is reached, the remaining operators are popped off the stack and appended to postfix. Finally, postfix is converted to a string and returned.

Function process_operator uses private function precedence to determine the precedence of an operator (2 for *, /; 1 for +, −.). If the stack is empty or the condition

```
(precedence(op) > precedence(operator_stack.top()))
```

is true, the current operator, op, is pushed onto the stack. Otherwise, the **while** loop executes, popping all operators off the stack that have the same or greater precedence than op and appending them to the postfix string.

```
while (!operator_stack.empty()
        && (precedence(op) <= precedence(operator_stack.top()))) {
  postfix += operator_stack.top();
  postfix += " ";
  operator_stack.pop();
}
```

After loop exit, the statement

```
operator_stack.push(op);
```

pushes the current operator onto the stack.

In function precedence, the statement

```
return PRECEDENCE[OPERATORS.find(op)];
```

returns the element of int array PRECEDENCE selected by the function call OPERATORS.find(op). The precedence value returned will be 1 or 2.

LISTING 5.11
Infix_To_Postfix.h

```
#ifndef INFIX_TO_POSTFIX_H_
#define INFIX_TO_POSTFIX_H_

#include "Syntax_Error.h"
#include <string>
#ifdef USEKW
#include "stack.h"   // For KW::stack
#else
#include <stack>     // For standard stack
#endif

/** Class to convert infix expressions to postfix expressions. */
class Infix_To_Postfix {
  public:
    /** Extracts and processes each token in infix and returns the
        equivalent postfix string.
        @param expression The infix expression
        @return The equivalent postfix expression
        @throws Syntax_Error
    */
    std::string convert(const std::string& expression);

  private:
    /** Function to process operators.
        @param op The operator
        @throws Syntax_Error
    */
    void process_operator(char op);
```

```
        /** Determines whether a character is an operator.
            @param ch The character to be tested
            @return true if the character is an operator
        */
        bool is_operator(char ch) const {
          return OPERATORS.find(ch) != std::string::npos;
        }

        /** Determines the precedence of an operator.
            @param op The operator
            @return The precedence
        */
        int precedence(char op) const {
          return PRECEDENCE[OPERATORS.find(op)];
        }

        // Data fields
        static const std::string OPERATORS;
        static const int PRECEDENCE[];
        #ifdef USEKW
        KW::stack<char> operator_stack;
        #else
        std::stack<char> operator_stack;
        #endif
        std::string postfix;
};

#endif
```

....
LISTING 5.12
Infix_To_Postfix.cpp

```
/** Implementation of Infix_To_Postfix. */

#include "Infix_To_Postfix.h"
#include <sstream>
#include <cctype>
using std::string;
using std::istringstream;

const string Infix_To_Postfix::OPERATORS = "+-*/";
const int Infix_To_Postfix::PRECEDENCE[] = { 1, 1, 2, 2 };

/** Extracts and processes each token in infix and returns the
    equivalent postfix string.
    @param expression The infix expression
    @return The equivalent postfix expression
    @throws Syntax_Error
*/
string Infix_To_Postfix::convert(const string& expression) {
  postfix = "";
  while (!operator_stack.empty())
    operator_stack.pop();
  istringstream infix_tokens(expression);
  string next_token;
```

```
            while(infix_tokens >> next_token) {
              if (isalnum(next_token[0])) {
                postfix += next_token;
                postfix += " ";
              } else if (is_operator(next_token[0])) {
                process_operator(next_token[0]);
              } else {
                throw Syntax_Error("Unexpected Character Encountered");
              }
            } // End while
            // Pop any remaining operators and append them to postfix
            while (!operator_stack.empty()) {
              char op = operator_stack.top();
              operator_stack.pop();
              postfix += op;
              postfix += " ";
            }
            return postfix;
          }

          /** Function to process operators.
              @param op The operator
              @throws Syntax_Error
          */
          void Infix_To_Postfix::process_operator(char op) {
            if (operator_stack.empty()) {
              operator_stack.push(op);
            } else {
              if (precedence(op) > precedence(operator_stack.top())) {
                operator_stack.push(op);
              } else {
                // Pop all stacked operators with equal
                // or higher precedence than op.
                while (!operator_stack.empty()
                       && (precedence(op) <= precedence(operator_stack.top()))) {
                  postfix += operator_stack.top();
                  postfix += " ";
                  operator_stack.pop();
                }
                // assert: Operator stack is empty or current
                //         operator precedence > top of stack operator
                //         precedence;
                operator_stack.push(op);
              }
            }
          }
```

Testing   Listing 5.13 shows a main function that tests the `Infix_To_Postfix` class. When entering a test expression, be careful to type a space character between operands and operators.

Use enough test expressions to satisfy yourself that the conversion is correct for properly formed input expressions. For example, try different orderings and multiple occurrences of the operators. You should also try infix expressions where all operators have the same precedence (for example, all multiplicative).

If convert detects a syntax error, it will throw the exception `Syntax_Error`. The driver will catch this exception and display an error message. If an exception is not thrown, the driver will display the result. Unfortunately, not all possible errors are detected. For example, an adjacent pair of operators or operands is not detected. To detect this error, we would need to add a Boolean flag whose value indicates whether the last token was an operand. If the flag is **true**, the next token must be an operator; if the flag is **false**, the next token must be an operand. This modification is left as an exercise.

LISTING 5.13
Main Function to Test `Infix_To_Postfix`

```
/** Program to test the infix to postfix converter. */

#include "Infix_To_Postfix.h"
#include <iostream>
#include <string>
using namespace std;

int main() {
  Infix_To_Postfix infix_to_postfix;
  cout <<
    "Enter expressions to be converted, or press Return when done\n";
  string expression;
  while (getline(cin, expression)) {
    if (expression == "") break;
    try {
      string result = infix_to_postfix.convert(expression);
      cout << "== " << result << endl;
    } catch (Syntax_Error& ex) {
      cout << "Syntax Error: " << ex.what() << endl;
    }
    cout << "Enter next expression: ";
  }
}
```

CASE STUDY   Part 2: Converting Expressions with Parentheses

Problem   The ability to convert expressions with parentheses is an important (and necessary) addition. Parentheses are used to separate an expression into subexpressions.

Analysis   We can think of an opening parenthesis on an operator stack as a boundary or fence between operators. Whenever we encounter an opening parenthesis, we want to push it onto the stack. A closing parenthesis is the terminator symbol for a subexpression. Whenever we encounter a closing parenthesis, we want to pop off all operators on the stack until we pop the matching opening parenthesis. Neither opening nor closing parentheses should appear in the postfix expression. Because operators scanned after the opening parenthesis should be evaluated before the opening parenthesis, the precedence of the opening parenthesis must be smaller than any other operator. We also give a closing parenthesis the lowest precedence. This ensures that a "(" can only be popped by a ")".

Design   We should modify function `process_operator` to push each opening parenthesis onto the stack as soon as it is scanned. Therefore, the function should begin with the following new condition:

```
if (operator_stack.empty() || (op == '(')) {
  if (op == ')')
    throw Syntax_Error("Unmatched close parenthesis");
  operator_stack.push(op);
```

Note, if the stack is empty and the operator is a close parenthesis, we indicate a syntax error by throwing the `Syntax_Error` exception.

When a closing parenthesis is scanned, we want to pop all operators up to and including the matching opening parenthesis, inserting all operators popped (except for the opening parenthesis) in the postfix string. This will happen automatically in the following **while** statement if the precedence of the closing parenthesis is smaller than that of any other operator except for the opening parenthesis.

```
while (!operator_stack.empty()
       && (operator_stack.top() != '(')
       && (precedence(op) <= precedence(operator_stack.top()))) {
  postfix += operator_stack.top();
  postfix += " ";
  operator_stack.pop();
}
```

A closing parenthesis is considered processed when the corresponding opening parenthesis is popped from the stack, and the closing parenthesis is not placed on the stack. The following **if** statement executes after the **while** loop exit:

```
if (op == ')') {
  if (!operator_stack.empty()
    && (operator_stack.top() == '(')) {
    operator_stack.pop();
  } else {
    throw Syntax_Error("Unmatched close parentheses");
  }
}
```

Implementation   Listing 5.14 shows file `Infix_To_Postfix_Parens.cpp`, that contains modified versions of the `convert` and `process_operator` functions. The changes are shown in color. We have omitted parts that do not change.

········

LISTING 5.14
`Infix_To_Postfix_Parens.cpp`

```
/** Implementation of Infix_To_Postfix that processes parentheses.*/

#include "Infix_To_Postfix.h"
#include <sstream>
#include <cctype>
using std::string;
using std::istringstream;
```

```cpp
const string Infix_To_Postfix::OPERATORS = "+-*/()";
const int Infix_To_Postfix::PRECEDENCE[] = { 1, 1, 2, 2, -1, -1 };

/** Extract and process each token in infix and return the
    equivalent postfix string.
    @param expression The infix expression
    @return The equivalent postfix expression
    @throws Syntax_Error
*/
string Infix_To_Postfix::convert(const string& expression) {
  postfix = "";
  while (!operator_stack.empty())
    operator_stack.pop();
  istringstream infix_tokens(expression);
  string next_token;
  while(infix_tokens >> next_token) {
    if (isalnum(next_token[0])) {
      postfix += next_token;
      postfix += " ";
    } else if (is_operator(next_token[0])) {
      process_operator(next_token[0]);
    } else {
      throw Syntax_Error("Unexpected Character Encountered");
    }
  } // End while
  // Pop any remaining operators and append them to postfix
  while (!operator_stack.empty()) {
    char op = operator_stack.top();
    operator_stack.pop();
    if (op == '(') {
      throw Syntax_Error("Unmatched open parenthesis");
    }
    postfix += op;
    postfix += " ";
  }
  return postfix;
}

/** Function to process operators.
    @param op The operator
    @throws Syntax_Error
*/
void Infix_To_Postfix::process_operator(char op) {
  if (operator_stack.empty() || (op == '(')) {
    if (op == ')')
      throw Syntax_Error("Unmatched close parenthesis");
    operator_stack.push(op);
  } else {
    if (precedence(op) > precedence(operator_stack.top())) {
      operator_stack.push(op);
    } else {
      // Pop all stacked operators with equal
      // or higher precedence than op.
      while (!operator_stack.empty()
             && (operator_stack.top() != '(')
             && (precedence(op) <= precedence(operator_stack.top()))) {
        postfix += operator_stack.top();
        postfix += " ";
        operator_stack.pop();
      }
```

```
        // assert: Operator stack is empty or
        //         top of stack is '(' or current
        //         operator precedence > top of stack operator
        //         precedence;
        if (op == ')') {
          if (!operator_stack.empty()
              && (operator_stack.top() == '(')) {
            operator_stack.pop();
          } else {
            throw Syntax_Error("Unmatched close parentheses");
          }
        }
        else {
          operator_stack.push(op);
        }
      }
    }
  }
}
```

Testing   You can use the classes developed for the prior case studies to evaluate infix expressions with integer operands and nested parentheses. Your driver program will need to create instances of both classes and apply function convert to the Infix_To_Postfix_Parens object. The argument for convert will be the infix expression. The result will be its postfix form. Next, the driver will apply function eval of the Postfix_Evaluator object. The argument for eval will be the postfix expression returned by convert. Make sure there is a space before and after each parenthesis.

EXERCISES FOR SECTION 5.4

SELF-CHECK

1. Trace the evaluation of the following expression using class Postfix_Evaluator. Show the operand stack each time it is modified.

    10 2 * 5 / 6 2 5 * + -

2. Trace the conversion of the following expressions to postfix using class Infix_To_Postfix or Infix_To_Postfix_Parens. Show the operator stack each time it is modified.

    y - 7 * 35 + 4 / 6 - 10
    (x + 15) * (3 * (4 - (5 + 7 / 2)))

PROGRAMMING

1. Modify class Infix_To_Postfix to handle the exponentiation operator, indicated by the symbol ∧. The first operand is raised to the power indicated by the second operand. Assume that a sequence of ∧ operators will not occur and that precedence('∧') is greater than precedence('*').

2. Discuss how you would modify the infix-to-postfix convert function to detect a sequence of two operators or two operands.

C h a p t e r   R e v i e w

◆ A stack is a last-in, first-out data structure (LIFO). This means that the last item added to a stack is the first one removed.

◆ A stack is a simple but powerful data structure. It has only four operators: `empty`, `top`, `pop`, and `push`.

◆ Stacks are useful when we want to process information in the reverse of the order that it is encountered. For this reason, a stack was used to implement the balanced parenthesis checker and the palindrome finder.

◆ `std::stack` is implemented as an adapter of any sequential container class. The `stack` object contains a `container` object. The functions `push` and `pop` are delegated to the `push_back` and `pop_back` functions of the container, and the function `top` is delegated to the `back` function. We showed a `vector` as the default container, but the C++ standard library uses the `deque`. The deque is a data structure that combines the features of both a stack and a queue. We discuss the deque and its possible implementations in the next chapter.

◆ We showed an alternative stack implementation using a linked list as a container.

◆ Stacks can be applied in algorithms for evaluating arithmetic expressions. We showed how to evaluate postfix expressions and how to translate infix expressions with and without parentheses to postfix.

Quick-Check Exercises

1. A stack is a _____-in, _____-out data structure.
2. Draw this stack s using the implementation in file `Stack.tc`. How would you reference the character at the top of the stack?

   ```
   $
   *
   &
   ```

3. What is the value of `s.empty()` for the stack shown in Question 2?
4. What is returned by `s.pop()` for the stack shown in Question 2?
5. Draw the stack s for Question 2 using the implementation in file `Linked_Stack.tc`. How would you reference the character at the top of the stack?
6. What would be the postfix form of the following expression?
   ```
   x + y - 24  *  zone - ace /  25 + c1
   ```
   Show the contents of the operator stack just before each operator is processed and just after all tokens are scanned using function `Infix_To_Postfix::convert`.
7. Answer Question 7 for the following expression
   ```
   ( x + y - 24 ) * ( zone - ace / ( 25 + c1 ) )
   ```
8. The value of the expression 20 35 - 5 / 10 7 * + is _____. Show the contents of the operand stack just before each operator is processed and just after all tokens are scanned.

Answers to Quick-Check Exercises

1. A stack is a *last*-in, *first*-out data structure.

2. Each character in the following array is type **char**. Use the_data* to reference the character $ at the top of the stack.

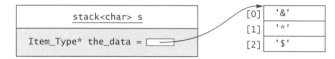

3. Function empty returns **false**.

4. pop returns a reference to the **char** object '$'.

5. Use top_of_stack–>data to reference the character $ at the top of the stack.

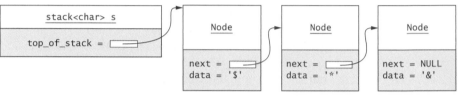

6. Infix: x + y - 24 * zone - ace / 25 + c1
   Postfix: x y + 24 zone * - ace 25 / - c1 +
   Operator stack before first + : | Empty stack (vertical bar is bottom of stack)
   Operator stack before first - : | +
   Operator stack before first * : | –
   Operator stack before second - : | –, *
   Operator stack before first / : | –
   Operator stack before second + : | –, /
   Operator stack after all tokens scanned: | +

7. Infix: (x + y - 24) * (zone – ace / (25 + c1))
   Postfix: x y + 24 - zone ace   25   c1 + / - *
   Operator stack before first (: | Empty stack (vertical bar is bottom of stack)
   Operator stack before first + : | (
   Operator stack before first - : | (, +
   Operator stack before first) : | (, –
   Operator stack before first * : | Empty stack
   Operator stack before second (: | *
   Operator stack before second - : | *, (
   Operator stack before second / : | *, (, –
   Operator stack before third (: | *, (, –, /
   Operator stack before second + : | *, (, –, /, (
   Operator stack before second) : | *, (, –, /, (, +
   Operator stack before third) : | *, (, –, /
   Operator stack after all tokens   scanned: | *

8. 20 35 – 5 / 10 7 * +   is 67 (–3 + 70)
   Operand stack just before - : | 20, 35
   Operand stack just before / : | –15, 5
   Operand stack just before * : | –3, 10, 7
   Operand stack just before + : | –3, 70
   Operand stack after all tokens : | 67

Review Questions

1. Show the effect of each of the following operations on stack s. Assume that y (type **char**) contains the character '&'. What are the final values of x and success and the contents of the stack s?

```
stack<char> s;
char x;
s.push('+');
if (!s.empty()) {
  x = s.top();
  s.pop();
  success = true;
} else {
  success = false;
}
if (!s.empty()) {
  x = s.top();
  s.pop();
  success = true;
} else {
  success = false;
}
s.push('(');
s.push(y);
if (!s.empty()) {
  x = s.top();
  s.pop();
  success = true;
} else {
  success = false;
}
```

2. Write a copy constructor and assignment operator for file Stack.tc.

3. Write a to_string function for file Linked_Stack.tc.

4. Write a copy constructor and assignment operator for file Linked_Stack.tc.

5. Write an infix expression that would convert to the postfix expression in Quick-Check Question 8.

6. Write a constructor for file Linked_Stack.tc that loads the stack from an iterator range. The last element in the range should be at the top of the stack.

7. Write a client that removes all negative numbers from a stack of **int** objects. If the original stack contained the integers 30, –15, 20, –25 (top of stack), the new stack should contain the integers 30, 20.

8. Write a function next_to_top that allows you to retrieve the element just below the one at the top of the stack without removing it. Write this function for both stack implementations. It should throw a std::out_of_range exception if the stack is empty or has only one element.

Programming Projects

1. Add a function is_palindrome_letters_only to the Palindrome_Finder class that bases its findings only on the letters in a string (ignoring spaces and other characters that are not letters).

2. We showed how to implement a stack using a vector, which has an array as its underlying data structure. Assume that the STL container classes are not available and write a file `Array_Stack.tc` that implements a stack using an array for storage.

3. Develop an Expression Manager that can do the following operations:

Balanced Symbols Check

- Read a mathematical expression from the user.
- Check and report whether the expression is balanced or not.
- {, }, (,), [,] are the only symbols considered for the check. All other characters can be ignored.

Infix to Postfix Conversion

- Read an infix expression from the user.
- Perform the Balanced Parentheses Check on the expression read.
- If the expression fails the Balanced Parentheses Check, report a message to the user that the expression is invalid.
- If the expression passes the Balanced Parentheses Check, convert the infix expression into a postfix expression and display it to the user.
- Operators to be considered are +, −, *, /, %.

Postfix to Infix Conversion

- Read a postfix expression from the user.
- Convert the postfix expression into an infix expression and display it to the user.
- Display an appropriate message if the postfix expression is not valid.
- Operators to be considered are +, −, *, /, %.

Evaluating a Postfix Expression

- Read the postfix expression from the user.
- Evaluate the postfix expression and display the result.
- Display an appropriate message if the postfix expression is not valid.
- Operators to be considered are +, −, *, /, %.
- Operands should be only integers.

Implementation

- Design a menu that requests user input to select from all the aforementioned operations.

4. Write a client program that uses the Stack abstract data type to simulate a session with a bank teller. Unlike most banks, this one has decided that the last customer to arrive will always be the first to be served. Create classes that represent information about a bank customer and a transaction. For each customer you need to store a name, current balance, and a reference to the transaction. For each transaction, you need to store the transaction type (deposit or withdrawal) and the amount of the transaction. After every five customers are processed, display the size of the stack and the name of the customer who will be served next.

5. Write a program to handle the flow of widgets into and out of a warehouse. The warehouse will have numerous deliveries of new widgets and orders for widgets. The widgets in a filled order are billed at a profit of 50 percent over their cost. Each delivery of new widgets may have a different cost associated with it. The accountants for the firm have instituted a last-in, first-out system for filling orders. This means that the newest widgets are the first ones sent out to fill an order. Also, the most recent orders are filled first. This function of inventory can be represented using two stacks: orders-to-be-filled and widgets-on-hand. When a delivery of new widgets is received, any unfilled orders (on the orders-to-be-filled stack) are processed and filled. After all orders are filled, if there are

widgets remaining in the new delivery, a new element is pushed onto the widgets-on-hand stack. When an order for new widgets is received, one or more objects are popped from the widgets-on-hand stack until the order has been filled. If the order is completely filled and there are widgets left over in the last object popped, a modified object with the quantity updated is pushed onto the widgets-on-hand stack. If the order is not completely filled, the order is pushed onto the orders-to-be-filled stack with an updated quantity of widgets to be sent out later. If an order is completely filled, it is not pushed onto the stack.

Write a class with functions to process the shipments received and to process orders. After an order is filled, display the quantity sent out and the total cost for all widgets in the order. Also indicate whether there are any widgets remaining to be sent out at a later time. After a delivery is processed, display information about each order that was filled with this delivery and indicate how many widgets, if any, were stored in the object pushed onto the widgets-on-hand stack.

6. You can combine the algorithms for converting between infix to postfix and for evaluating postfix to evaluate an infix expression directly. To do so you need two stacks: one to contain operators and the other to contain operands. When an operand is encountered, it is pushed onto the operand stack. When an operator is encountered, it is processed as described in the infix-to-postfix algorithm. When an operator is popped off the operator stack, it is processed as described in the postfix evaluation algorithm: The top two operands are popped off the operand stack, the operation is performed, and the result is pushed back onto the operand stack. Write a program to evaluate infix expressions directly using this combined algorithm.

7. Write a client program that uses the Stack abstract data type to compile a simple arithmetic expression without parentheses. For example, the expression

a + b * c - d

should be compiled according to the following table

Operator	Operand1	Operand2	Result
*	b	c	z
+	a	z	y
–	y	d	x

The table shows the order in which the operations are performed (*, +, –) and operands for each operator. The result column gives the name of an identifier (working backward from z) chosen to hold each result. Assume that the operands are the letters a through m and the operators are (+, –, *, /). Your program should read each character and process it as follows: If the character is blank, ignore it. If the character is neither blank nor an operand nor an operator, display an error message and terminate the program. If it is an operand, push it onto the operand stack. If it is an operator, compare its precedence to that of the operator on top of the operator stack. If the current operator has higher precedence than the one currently on top of the stack (or if the stack is empty), it should be pushed onto the operator stack. If the current operator has the same or lower precedence, the operator on top of the operator stack must be evaluated next. This is done by popping that operator off the operator stack along with a pair of operands from the operand stack and writing a new line in the output table. The character selected to hold the result should then be pushed onto the operand stack. Next, the current operator should be compared to the new top of the operator stack. Continue to generate output lines until the top of the operator stack has lower precedence than the current operator or until it is empty. At this point, push the current operator onto the top of the stack and examine the next character in the data string. When the end of the string is reached, pop any remaining operator along with its operand pair just described. Remember to push the result character onto the operand stack after each table line is generated.

6

Queues and Deques

Chapter Objectives

- ◆ To learn how to represent a waiting line (queue) and how to use the functions in the Queue ADT for insertion (push), for removal (pop), and for accessing the element at the front (front)
- ◆ To understand how to implement the Queue ADT using a single-linked list, a circular array, and a double-linked list
- ◆ To understand how to simulate the operation of a physical system that has one or more waiting lines using queues and random number generators
- ◆ To introduce the standard library deque class

In this chapter we study an abstract data type, the queue, that is widely used, like the stack, but differs from it in one important way. A stack is a LIFO (last-in, first-out) list, because the last element pushed onto a stack will be the first element popped off. A queue, on the other hand, is a FIFO (first-in, first-out) list, because the first element inserted in the queue will be the first element removed.

You will learn how to use a queue to store items (for example, customers) that will be accessed on a first-come, first-served basis. We will also show you how to implement queues. You will also learn how to use simulation to estimate the amount of time customers will spend waiting in a queue.

You will also learn about an abstract data type, the deque, that combines the features of a stack and a queue. We will also show you how to implement a deque.

FIGURE 6.1
Customers Waiting
in a Line or Queue

6.1 The Queue Abstract Data Type

The easiest way to visualize a queue is to think of a line of customers waiting for service, as shown in Figure 6.1. Usually, the next person to be served is the one who has been waiting the longest, and latecomers are added to the end of the line. The Queue ADT gets its name from the fact that such a waiting line is called a queue in English-speaking countries other than the United States.

A Queue of Customers

FIGURE 6.2
A Queue of Customers

Ticket agent

| Thome |
| Abreu |
| Jones |

A queue of three customers waiting to buy concert tickets is shown in Figure 6.2. The name of the customer who has been waiting the longest is Thome; the name of the most recent arrival is Jones. Customer Thome will be the first customer removed from the queue (and able to buy tickets) when a ticket agent becomes available, and customer Abreu will then become the first one in the queue. Any new customers will be inserted in the queue after customer Jones. We will revisit this queue in the next section.

A Print Queue

In computer science, queues are used in operating systems to keep track of tasks waiting for a scarce resource and to ensure that the tasks are carried out in the order in which they were generated. One example is a print queue. While surfing the Web, you may select several pages to be printed in a few seconds. Because a printer is a relatively slow device (several seconds per page), you will often select new pages to print faster than they can be printed. Rather than require you to wait until the current page is finished before you can select a new one, the operating system stores documents to be printed in a print queue (see Figure 6.3). Because they are stored in a queue, the pages will be printed in the same order as they were selected (first-in, first-out). The document first inserted in the queue will be the first one printed.

The Unsuitability of a "Print Stack"

Suppose your operating system used a stack (last-in, first-out) instead of a queue to store documents waiting to print. Then the most recently selected Web page would be the next page to print. This may not matter if only one person is using the printer. However, if the printer is connected to a computer network, this would be a big problem. Unless the print queue was empty when you selected a page to print (and the page printed immediately), that page would not print until all pages selected after it (by yourself or any other person on the network) were printed. If you were waiting by the printer for your page to print before going to your next class, you would have no way of knowing how long your wait might be. You would also be very unhappy if people who started after you had their documents printed before yours. So a print queue is a much more sensible alternative than a print stack.

Specification of the Queue ADT

Because only the front element of a queue is visible, the operations performed by a queue are few in number. We need to be able to retrieve the front element (function `front`), remove the front element (function `pop`), push a new element onto the queue (function `push`), and test for an empty stack (function `empty`). Table 6.1 shows a specification for the Queue ADT that specifies the queue operators. These are all defined in the header file for the STL container `queue`, `<queue>`.

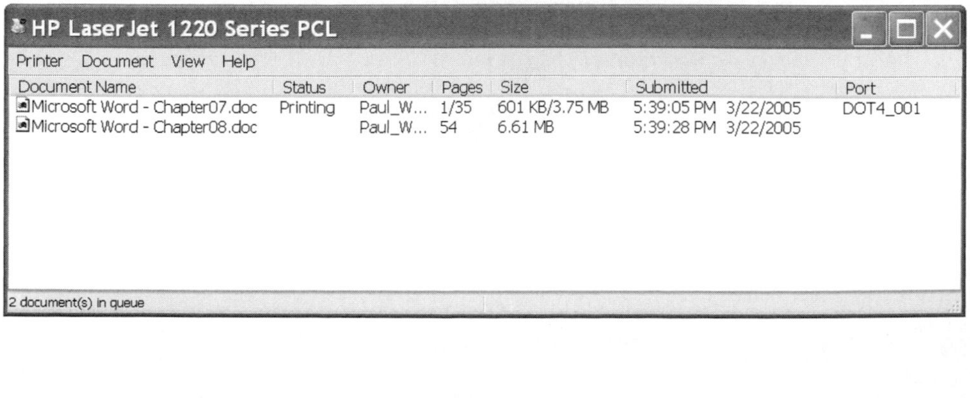

FIGURE 6.3
A Print Queue in the Windows Operating System

Document Name	Status	Owner	Pages	Size	Submitted		Port
Microsoft Word - Chapter07.doc	Printing	Paul_W...	1/35	601 KB/3.75 MB	5:39:05 PM	3/22/2005	DOT4_001
Microsoft Word - Chapter08.doc		Paul_W...	54	6.61 MB	5:39:28 PM	3/22/2005	

HP LaserJet 1220 Series PCL — Printer Document View Help

2 document(s) in queue

TABLE 6.1
Specification of Queue ADT

Function	Behavior
bool empty() const	Returns **true** if the queue is empty; otherwise returns **false**.
Item_Type& front(); const Item_Type& front() const	Returns the object at the front of the queue without removing it.
void pop()	Removes the object at the front of the queue.
void push(const Item_Type&)	Pushes an item onto the rear of the queue.
size_t size() const	Returns the number of items in the queue.

Listing 6.1 shows the class definition for the class KW::queue. This class definition implements the interface defined by Table 6.1 and is very similar to that defined by the C++ standard library. The colored lines show an implementation that uses the standard list class as a container. We will discuss this implementation and other possible implementations in Section 6.3.

LISTING 6.1
queue.h

```
#ifndef QUEUE_H_
#define QUEUE_H_

// Insert necessary include directives here.
#include <list>

namespace KW {

  /** A queue is a data structure that provides first-in first-out
      access to the items that are stored in it. Only the least recently
      inserted item is accessible.
  */
  template<typename Item_Type>
    class queue {

    public:

    // Constructor and member functions
    /** Constructs an empty queue. */
    queue();

    /** Pushes an item onto the back of the queue.
        @param item The item to be inserted
    */
    void push(const Item_Type& item);

    /** Returns a reference to the object at the front of the queue
        without removing it.
        @return A reference to the object at the front of the queue
    */
    Item_Type& front();
```

```
/** Returns a const reference to the object at the
    front of the queue without removing it.
    @return A const reference to the object at the front of the queue
*/
const Item_Type& front() const;

/** Removes the front item from the queue. */
void pop();

/** Determines whether the queue is empty. */
bool empty() const;

/** Returns the number of items in the queue */
size_t size() const;

private:
// Insert implementation-specific data fields
std::list<Item_Type> container;
}; // End class queue

// Insert member function implementation here
#include "List_Queue.tc"
} // End namespace KW
#endif
```

EXAMPLE 6.1   The queue names contains five strings as shown in Figure 6.4(a). The name "Jonathan" was placed in the queue before the other four names; "Rich" was the last element placed in the queue.

For queue names in Figure 6.4(a), the value of names.empty() is **false**. The statement

```
string first = names.front();
```

stores "Jonathan" in first without changing names. The statement

```
names.pop();
```

removes "Jonathan" from names. The queue names now contains four elements and is shown in Figure 6.4(b). The statement

```
names.push("Eliana");
```

adds "Eliana" to the end of the queue; the queue names now contains five elements and is shown in Figure 6.4(c).

FIGURE 6.4

Queue names

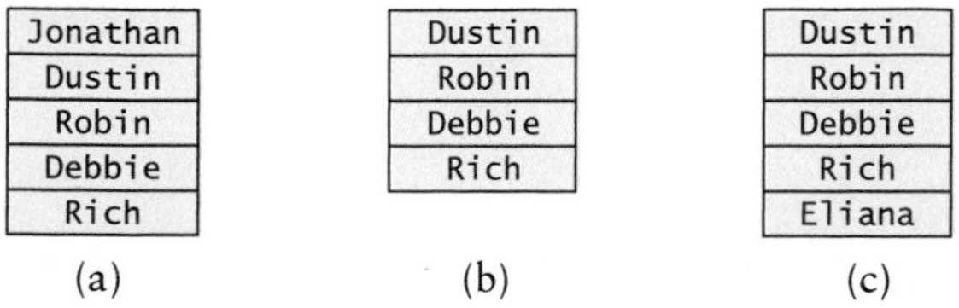

| Jonathan |
| Dustin |
| Robin |
| Debbie |
| Rich |

(a)

| Dustin |
| Robin |
| Debbie |
| Rich |

(b)

| Dustin |
| Robin |
| Debbie |
| Rich |
| Eliana |

(c)

EXERCISES FOR SECTION 6.1

SELF-CHECK

1. Draw the queue in Figure 6.2 as it will appear after the insertion of customer Harris and the removal of one customer from the queue. Which customer is removed? How many customers are left?

2. Assume that my_queue is an instance of a class that implements queue<string> and my_queue is an empty queue. Explain the effect of each of the following operations.
   ```
   my_queue.push("Hello");
   my_queue.push("Bye");
   cout << my_queue.front();
   my_queue.pop();
   my_queue.push("Welcome");
   if (!my_queue.empty()) {
     cout << my_queue.front();
     my_queue.pop();
     cout << ", new size is " << my_queue.size() << endl;
     cout << "Item in front is " << my_queue.front() << endl;
   }
   ```

6.2 Maintaining a Queue of Customers

In this section we present an application that maintains a queue of strings representing the names of customers waiting for service. Our goal is just to maintain the list of names and ensure that customers are inserted and removed properly.

CASE STUDY   Maintaining a Queue

Problem   Write a menu-driven program that maintains a list of customers waiting for service. This should be a first-in, first out list. The program user should be able to insert a new customer in the line, display the customer who is next in line, remove the customer who is next in line, and display the length of the line.

Analysis   As discussed earlier, a queue is a good data structure for storing a list of customers waiting for service, because they would expect to be served in the order in which they arrived. We can display the menu and then perform the requested operation by calling the appropriate queue function to update the customer list. We will input and output via cin and cout to display the menu, enter new customer names, and display results.

Problem Inputs

The operation to be performed

The name of a customer

Problem Outputs

The effect of each operation

Design   We will write a program `Maintain_Queue` to store the queue and control its processing. Program `Maintain_Queue` has a `queue<string>` variable `customers`. The `main` function displays a menu of choices and processes the user selection. The algorithm for function `main` follows.

Algorithm for `main`

1. **while** the user is not finished
2.   Display the menu and get the operation selected.
3.   Perform the operation selected.

We will be able to perform each selected operation by delegating to one of the functions in class `queue`.

Implementation   Listing 6.2 shows the program.

....
LISTING 6.2
Maintain_Queue.cpp

```cpp
/** Program to maintain a list of customers. */

#include <queue>
#include <string>
#include <iostream>
using namespace std;

/** Performs the operations selected on queue customers.
    pre:  customers has been created.
    post: customers is modified based on user selections.
*/
int main()
{
  queue<string> customers;
  string name;
  int choice_num = 0;
  string choices[] = {
    "push", "front", "pop", "size", "quit"};
  const int NUM_CHOICES = 5;

  // Perform all operations selected by user.
  while (choice_num < NUM_CHOICES - 1) {
    // Select the next operation.
    cout << "Select an operation on customer queue\n";
    for (int i = 0; i < NUM_CHOICES; i++) {
      cout << i << ": " << choices[i] << endl;
    }
```

```
        cin >> choice_num;
        switch (choice_num) {
        case 0:
          cout << "Enter new customer name\n";
          cin >> name;
          customers.push(name);
          break;
        case 1:
          cout << "Customer " << customers.front()
               << " is next in line\n";
          break;
        case 2:
          cout << "Customer " << customers.front()
               << " removed from line\n";
          customers.pop();
          break;
        case 3:
          cout << "Size of line is " << customers.size() << endl;
          break;
        case 4:
          cout << "Leaving customer queue.\n"
               << "Number of customers in queue is " << customers.size()
               << endl;
          break;
        default:
          cout << "Invalid selection\n";
          break;
        }
    } // End while.
    return 0;
}
```

In function main (Listing 6.2), the statements

```
    cout << "Select an operation on customer queue\n";
    for (int i = 0; i < NUM_CHOICES; i++) {
      cout << i << ": " << choices[i] << endl;
    }
```

display a menu of choices. The choice number is read into the variable choice_num.

After the selection is read into choice_num, the **switch** statement calls a queue function to perform the selected operation. For example, if the user clicks the push button, the statements

```
    cout << "Enter new customer name\n";
    cin >> name;
    customers.push(name);
```

read the customer name and insert it into the queue. The implementation of each case in the **switch** statement is rather straightforward.

Testing You can use program Maintain_Queue to test each of the different queue implementations discussed in the next section. You should verify that all customers are stored and retrieved in first-in, first-out order. Thoroughly test the queue by selecting different sequences of queue operations.

EXERCISES FOR SECTION 6.2

SELF-CHECK

1. Write an algorithm to display all the elements in a queue using just the queue operations. How would your algorithm change the queue?
2. Trace the following fragment for a stack<string> s and an empty queue<string> q.

```
string item;
while (!s.empty()) {
  item = s.top();
  s.pop()
  q.push(item);
}
while (!q.empty()) {
  item = q.front();
  q.pop();
  s.push(item);
}
```

   a. What is stored in stack s after the first loop executes? What is stored in queue q after the first loop executes?
   b. What is stored in stack s after the second loop executes? What is stored in queue q after the second loop executes?

PROGRAMMING

1. Add an option to Maintain_Queue to display all of the entries in the queue.

6.3 Implementing the Queue ADT

This section discusses how to implement the Queue ADT. You may have recognized that a queue is similar to a list in that you can insert an item at one end (list::push_back) and remove it from the other (list::pop_front). In fact, the standard library defines the queue as a template class that takes any of the sequential containers as a template parameter. However, the only sequential container that we have studied so far that provides both a push_back and pop_front function is the list. The standard library also defines an additional sequential container, called the deque, which does provide both push_back and pop_front functions. We will discuss the deque later in this chapter. In this section we discuss three approaches to implementing a queue: using a double-linked list (i.e., the standard list class), a single-linked list, and an array. We begin with the standard list class.

Using std::list as a Container for a Queue

Listing 6.3 (file List_Queue.tc) shows an implementation of class queue (Listing 6.1) that is very similar to that given by the C++ standard library. In this implementation, the data member container is type std::list<Item_Type>. As discussed earlier, file `List_Queue.tc` would be included after the definition of class `queue`, at the end of Listing 6.1.

Like the `stack` class (see Chapter 5), the queue is said to be an adapter class because it adapts the functions available in another class to the interface its clients expect by giving different names to essentially the same operations For example, if a `list` is used as the container object, `queue::push` would correspond to `list::push_back`. Similarly, `queue::front` would correspond to `list::front`, and so on. This is another example of delegation.

....

LISTING 6.3
List_Queue.tc

```
#ifndef LIST_QUEUE_TC_
#define LIST_QUEUE_TC_

/** Constructs an empty queue. */
template<typename Item_Type>
  queue<Item_Type>::queue() {}

/** Pushes an item onto the back of the queue.
    @param item The item to be inserted
*/
template<typename Item_Type>
  void queue<Item_Type>::push(const Item_Type& item) {
    container.push_back(item);
}

/** Returns a reference to the object at the front of the queue
    without removing it.
    @return A reference to the object at the front of the queue
*/
template<typename Item_Type>
  Item_Type& queue<Item_Type>::front() {
    return container.front();
}

/** Returns a const reference to the object at the
    front of the queue without removing it.
    @return A const reference to the object at the front of the queue
*/
template<typename Item_Type>
  const Item_Type& queue<Item_Type>::front() const {
    return container.front();
}

/** Removes the front item from the queue. */
template<typename Item_Type>
  void queue<Item_Type>::pop() {
    container.pop_front();
}

/** Determines whether the queue is empty. */
template<typename Item_Type>
  bool queue<Item_Type>::empty() const {
    return container.empty();
}
```

```
/** Returns the number of items in the queue. */
template<typename Item_Type>
  size_t queue<Item_Type>::size() const {
    return container.size();
}
#endif
```

Using a Single-Linked List to Implement the Queue ADT

We can implement a queue using our own single-linked list like the one shown in Figure 6.5. File Linked_Queue.tc defines a queue class that contains a collection of Node objects (see Figure 4.15). Recall that inner class Node has data fields data (type Item_Type) and next (type Node*).

To use this implementation we must include the file Node.h containing the definition of a node (see Chapter 4) in the definition file (queue.h) for class queue shown in Listing 6.1. We must also include the header file <cstddef> which defines **NULL**. We will place the include directive for <cstddef> at the beginning of file queue.h; we will place the include directive for "Node.h" in the private part of class KW::queue, just before the data field declarations.

```
// Insert necessary include directives here
#include <cstddef>
```

We must also replace the statements at the end of file queue.h with the following:

```
private:
  // Insert definition of Node here
  #include "Node.h"

  // Data Fields
  Node* front_of_queue;
  Node* back_of_queue;
}; // End class queue

// Insert implementation of member functions here
#include "Linked_Queue.tc"
} // End namespace KW
#endif
```

Insertions are at the rear of a queue, and removals are from the front. We need a reference to the last list node so that insertions can be performed in O(1) time; otherwise, we would have to start at the list head and traverse all the way down the list

FIGURE 6.5

A Queue as a Single-Linked List

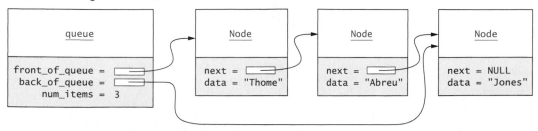

to do an insertion. There is a reference variable `front_of_queue` to the first list node (the list head) and a reference variable `back_of_queue` to the last list node. There is also a data field `num_items`.

The number of elements in the queue is changed by functions `push` and `pop`, so `num_items` must be incremented by one in `push` and decremented by one in `pop`. The value of `num_items` is tested in `empty` to determine the status of the queue. The function `size` simply returns the value of data field `num_items`.

Listing 6.4 shows file `Linked_Queue.tc`, which implements the operators for the Queue ADT (`queue.h`) shown in Listing 6.1. Function `push` treats insertion into an empty queue as a special case, because both `front_of_queue` and `back_of_queue` should both reference the new node after the insertion.

```
back_of_queue = new Node(item, NULL);
front_of_queue = back_of_queue;
```

If we insert into a queue that is not empty, the new node must be linked to the old `back_of_queue`, but `front_of_queue` is unchanged.

```
back_of_queue->next = new Node(item, NULL);
back_of_queue = back_of_queue->next;
```

If the queue is empty, function `front` will get a run-time error when it attempts to dereference the **NULL** pointer. Otherwise, it returns the element at the front of the queue:

```
return front_of_queue->data;
```

Function `pop` disconnects the node at the front of a nonempty queue and decrements `num_items`. Note that we also return the removed `Node` to the free storage pool using the **delete** statement.

```
Node* old_front = front_of_queue;
front_of_queue = front_of_queue->next;
if (front_of_queue == NULL) {
  back_of_queue = NULL;
}
delete old_front;
num_items--;
```

LISTING 6.4
Linked_Queue.tc

```
#ifndef LINKED_QUEUE_TC_
#define LINKED_QUEUE_TC_

/** Constructs an empty queue. */
template<typename Item_Type>
  queue<Item_Type>::queue() : front_of_queue(NULL), back_of_queue(NULL),
    num_items(0) {}

/** Pushes an item onto the back of the queue.
    @param item The item to be inserted
```

```cpp
*/
template<typename Item_Type>
  void queue<Item_Type>::push(const Item_Type& item) {
    if (front_of_queue == NULL) {
      back_of_queue = new Node(item, NULL);
      front_of_queue = back_of_queue;
    } else {
      back_of_queue->next = new Node(item, NULL);
      back_of_queue = back_of_queue->next;
    }
    num_items++;
}

/** Returns a reference to the object at the front of the queue
    without removing it.
    @return A reference to the object at the front of the queue
*/
template<typename Item_Type>
  Item_Type& queue<Item_Type>::front() {
    return front_of_queue->data;
}

/** Returns a const reference to the object at the
    front of the queue without removing it.
    @return A const reference to the object at the front of the queue
*/
template<typename Item_Type>
  const Item_Type& queue<Item_Type>::front() const {
    return front_of_queue->data;
}

/** Removes the front item from the queue. */
template<typename Item_Type>
  void queue<Item_Type>::pop() {
    Node* old_front = front_of_queue;
    front_of_queue = front_of_queue->next;
    if (front_of_queue == NULL) {
      back_of_queue = NULL;
    }
    delete old_front;
    num_items--;
}

/** Determines whether the queue is empty. */
template<typename Item_Type>
  bool queue<Item_Type>::empty() const {
    return front_of_queue == NULL;
}

/** Determines the size of the queue. */
template<typename Item_Type>
  size_t queue<Item_Type>::size() const {
    return num_items;
}

#endif
```

A complete definition and implementation of the queue class would include a copy constructor, assignment operator, swap function, and destructor as required by the "rule of three." However, our goal is to illustrate how to code the basic queue operators in Table 6.1, not to reinvent the wheel and provide an industrial-strength implementation, because one already exists (std::queue). Programming Project 1 asks you to provide the operators required by the "rule of three." Note that for the List_Queue.tc implementation, the default implementation of these functions is sufficient, because they are implemented by the std::list class; however, for the Linked_Queue.tc and Array_Queue.tc (discussed next), they are necessary because these implementations dynamically allocate storage.

Using a Circular Array for Storage in a Queue

Although the time efficiency of using a single- or double-linked list to implement the Queue ADT is acceptable, there is some space inefficiency. Each node of a single-linked list contains a pointer to its successor, and each node of a double-linked list contains pointers to its predecessor and successor. These additional pointers will increase the storage space required.

An alternative is to use an array. If we use an array, we can do an insertion at the rear of the array in $O(1)$ time. However, a removal from the front will be an $O(n)$ process if we shift all the elements that follow the first one over to fill the space vacated. We next discuss how to avoid this inefficiency.

Overview of the Design

File Array_Queue.tc (see Listing 6.5) defines a queue class that uses an object with four size_t data members (capacity, num_items, front_index, rear_index), and a pointer data member, the_data, which will point to a dynamically allocated array that provides storage for the queue elements. To use this implementation we must include the header file <algorithm>, which defines the swap template function, at the beginning of file queue.h; we then include the following in the data declarations.

```
// Data fields
/** The initial size of the data array */
static const size_t DEFAULT_CAPACITY = 10;
/** The current capacity of the data array */
size_t capacity;
/** The number of items in the queue */
size_t num_items;
/** The index of the front of the queue */
size_t front_index;
/** The index of the rear of the queue */
size_t rear_index;
/** Pointer to the array containing the data */
Item_Type* the_data;
```

The size_t fields front_index and rear_index are indices to the queue elements at the front and rear of the queue, respectively. The size_t field num_items keeps track of the actual number of items in the queue and allows us to determine easily whether the queue is empty (num_items is 0) or full (num_items is capacity).

It makes sense to store the first queue item in element 0, the second queue item in element 1, and so on. So we should set front_index to 0 and rear_index to –1 when we create an initially empty queue. Each time we do an insertion, we should increment num_items and rear_index by 1 so that front_index and rear_index will both be 0 if a queue has one element. Figure 6.6 shows an instance of a queue that is filled to its capacity (size == capacity). The queue contains the characters &, *, +, /, -, inserted in that order.

Because the queue in Figure 6.6 is filled to capacity, we cannot insert a new character without allocating more storage. However, we can remove a queue element by decrementing size and incrementing front to 1, thereby removing the_data[0] (the character &) from the queue. Figure 6.7 shows the queue after removal of the first element (it is still in the array, but not part of the queue). The queue contains the characters *, +, /, -, in that order.

Although the queue in Figure 6.7 is no longer filled, we cannot insert a new character, because rear_index is at its maximum value. One way to solve this problem is to shift the elements in array the_data so that the empty cells come after rear_index and then adjust front_index and rear_index accordingly. This array shifting must be done very carefully to avoid losing track of active array elements. It is also an $O(n)$ operation.

A better way to solve this problem is to represent the array field the_data as a circular array. In a circular array, the elements wrap around so that the first element actually follows the last. This is like counting modulo num_items; the array subscripts take on the values 0, 1, . . . , num_items – 1, 0, 1, and so on. This allows us to "increment" rear_index to 0 and store a new character in the_data[0]. Figure 6.8 shows the queue after inserting a new element (the character A). After the insertion, front_index is still 1 but rear_index becomes 0. The contents of the_data[0] changes from & to A. The queue now contains the symbols *, +, /, -, A, in that order.

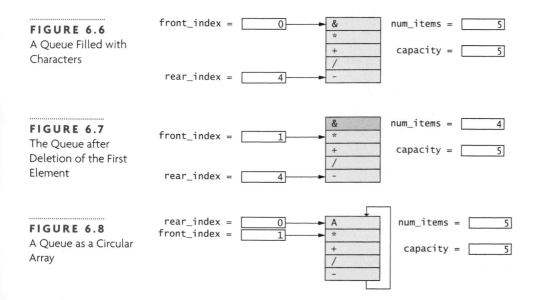

FIGURE 6.6
A Queue Filled with Characters

FIGURE 6.7
The Queue after Deletion of the First Element

FIGURE 6.8
A Queue as a Circular Array

EXAMPLE 6.2 The upper half of Figure 6.9 shows the effect of removing two elements from the queue just described. There are currently three characters in this queue (stored in the_data[3], the_data[4], and the_data[0]). The queue now contains the symbols /, -, A, in that order.

The lower half of Figure 6.9 shows the queue after insertion of a new character (B). The value of rear_index is incremented to 1 and the next element is inserted in the_data[1]. This queue element follows the character A in the_data[0]. The value of front_index is still 3 because the character / at the_data[3] has been in the queue the longest. the_data[2] is now the only queue element that is unused. The queue now contains the symbols /, -, A, B in that order.

FIGURE 6.9
The Effect of Two Deletions and One Insertion

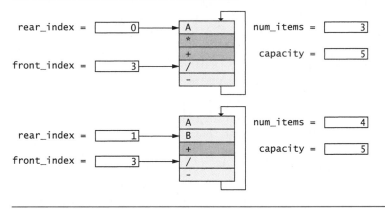

Implementing a Queue as a Circular Array

Listing 6.5 shows the file Array_Queue.tc, which implements the queue as a circular array.

The constructor sets num_items to 0 and front_index to 0 because array element the_data[0] is considered the front of the empty queue, and rear_index is initialized to capacity − 1 (instead of −1) because the queue is circular.

In function push, the statement

```
rear_index = (rear_index + 1) % capacity;
```

is used to increment the value of rear_index modulo capacity. When rear_index is less than capacity, this statement simply increments its value by one. But when rear_index becomes equal to capacity − 1, the next value of rear_index will be 0 (capacity mod capacity is 0), thereby wrapping the last element of the queue around to the first element. Because the constructor initializes rear_index to capacity − 1, the first queue element will be placed in the_data[0] as desired.

In function pop, front_index is incremented modulo capacity. In function front, the element at the_data[front_index] is returned, but front_index is not changed.

When the capacity is reached, we double the capacity and copy the array into the new one, as was done for the vector. However, we cannot simply use the reallocate function we developed for the vector, because of the circular nature of the array. We cannot copy over elements from the original array to the first half of the expanded array. Instead, we must first copy the elements from position front_index through the end of the original array to the beginning of the expanded array; then copy the elements from the beginning of the original array through rear to follow those in the expanded array (see Figure 6.10).

We begin by creating an array new_data, whose capacity is double that of the_data. The loop

```
size_t j = front_index;
for (size_t i = 0; i < num_items; i++) {
  new_data[i] = the_data[j];
  j = (j + 1) % capacity;
}
```

copies num_items elements over from the_data to the first half of new_data. In the copy operation

```
new_data[i] = the_data[j]
```

subscript i for new_data goes from 0 to num_items − 1 (the first half of new_data). Subscript j for the_data starts at front_index. The statement

```
j = (j + 1) % capacity;
```

increments the subscript for array the_data. Therefore, subscript j goes from front_index to capacity − 1 (in increments of 1) and then back to 0. So the elements are copied from the_data in the sequence the_data[front_index], ... , the_data[capacity - 1], the_data[0], ... , the_data[rear_index], where the_data[front_index] is stored in new_data[0] and the_data[rear_index] is stored in new_data[num_items - 1]. After exit from the copy loop, front_index is reset to 0 and rear_index is reset to num_items - 1 (see Figure 6.10).

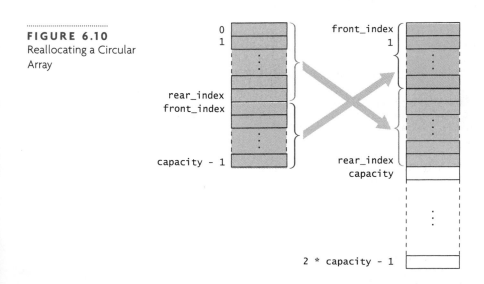

FIGURE 6.10
Reallocating a Circular
Array

By choosing a new capacity that is twice the current capacity, the cost of the reallocation is amortized across each insert, just as for a vector. Thus, insertion is still considered an O(1) operation.

....

LISTING 6.5
Array_Queue.tc

```
#ifndef ARRAY_QUEUE_TC_
#define ARRAY_QUEUE_TC_

/** Constructs an empty queue. */
template<typename Item_Type>
  queue<Item_Type>::queue() : capacity(DEFAULT_CAPACITY), num_items(0),
      front_index(0), rear_index(DEFAULT_CAPACITY - 1),
      the_data(new Item_Type[DEFAULT_CAPACITY]) {}

/** Pushes an item onto the rear of the queue.
    @param item The item to be inserted
*/
template<typename Item_Type>
  void queue<Item_Type>::push(const Item_Type& item) {
    if (num_items == capacity) {
      reallocate();
    }
    num_items++;
    rear_index = (rear_index + 1) % capacity;
    the_data[rear_index] = item;
}

/** Returns a reference to the object at the front of the queue
    without removing it.
    @return A reference to the object at the front of the queue
*/
template<typename Item_Type>
  Item_Type& queue<Item_Type>::front() {
    return the_data[front_index];
}

/** Returns a const reference to the object at the
    front of the queue without removing it.
    @return A const reference to the object at the front of the queue
*/
template <typename Item_Type>
  const Item_Type& queue<Item_Type>::front() const {
    return the_data[front_index];
}

/** Removes the front item from the queue. */
template<typename Item_Type>
  void queue<Item_Type>::pop() {
    front_index = (front_index + 1) % capacity;
    num_items--;
}
```

```
/** Determines whether the queue is empty */
template<typename Item_Type>
  bool queue<Item_Type>::empty() const {
    return num_items == 0;
}

/** Determines the size of the queue. */
template<typename Item_Type>
  size_t queue<Item_Type>::size() const {
    // Exercise
}

/** Doubles the capacity and reallocates the data.
    pre:  The array is filled to capacity.
    post: The capacity is doubled and the first half
          of the expanded array is filled with data.
*/
template<typename Item_Type>
  void queue<Item_Type>::reallocate() {
    size_t new_capacity = 2 * capacity;
    Item_Type* new_data = new Item_Type[new_capacity];
    size_t j = front_index;
    for (size_t i = 0; i < num_items; i++) {
      new_data[i] = the_data[j];
      j = (j + 1) % capacity;
    }
    front_index = 0;
    rear_index = num_items - 1;
    capacity = new_capacity;
    std::swap(the_data, new_data);

    delete[] new_data;
}

#endif
```

Comparing the Three Implementations

As mentioned earlier, all three implementations of the Queue ADT are comparable in terms of computation time. All operations are O(1) regardless of the implementation. Although reallocating an array is an O(n) operation, it is amortized over n items, so the cost per item is O(1).

In terms of storage requirements, both linked-list implementations require more storage because of the extra space required for links. To perform an analysis of the storage requirements, you need to know that C++ stores a copy of the data for a queue element in each node in addition to the links. Therefore, a node in a single-linked list would store a total of one pointer, a node in a double-linked list would store a total of two pointers, and a node in a circular array would store just the data. A circular array that is filled to capacity would require half the storage of a single-linked list to store the same number of elements (assuming that the data type requires the same amount of storage as a pointer). However, if the array were just reallocated, half the array would be empty, so it would require the same storage as a single-linked list.

EXERCISES FOR SECTION 6.3

SELF-CHECK

1. Show the new array for the queue in Figure 6.8 after the array size is doubled.
2. Redraw the queue in Figure 6.5 so that front_of_queue points to the list tail and back_of_queue points to the list head. Show the queue after an element is inserted and an element is removed. Explain why the approach used in the book is better.

PROGRAMMING

1. Write the size function for the Array_Queue.
2. Write a to_string() function for the List_Queue that return a string with all the elements that are in the queue. Enclose the queue elements in brackets and insert a comma between individual elements.
3. Do Programming Exercise 2 for the Array_Queue.

6.4 The Deque

A *deque* (pronounced "deck" or "DEE-queue") is an abstract data type that combines the features of a stack and a queue. The word "deque" is an abbreviation for "double-ended queue," and it means that you can insert, access, and remove items at either end. The C++ standard library takes this concept further and defines the class std::deque to be a sequence that, like the vector, supports random-access iterators (not supported by either the stack or the queue) in addition to constant-time insertion and removal from either end.

Specification of the Deque

Table 6.2 shows some of the member functions defined by the std::deque class. The deque represents a combination of a vector and a list in that it provides the constant-time insertion/removal from either end that is provided by the list and the constant-time random access provided by the vector. The deque is used by the C++ standard library as the default container for both the stack and the queue.

We now describe two approaches to implementing the deque. One is to adapt the circular array we used to implement the queue, and the other is the approach taken by the original Standard Template Library (the basis for the C++ standard library) and used by most C++ implementations.

Implementing the Deque Using a Circular Array

Earlier we showed how to use a circular array to implement a queue and showed how to implement the functions queue::push (equivalent to deque::push_back) and queue::pop (equivalent to deque::pop_front). Implementing functions push_front and pop_back is similar and is left as an exercise.

TABLE 6.2
Member Functions of Class **deque**

Member Function	Behavior
`const Item_Type&` `operator[](size_t index) const`	Returns a reference to the element at position `index` that can be used on the right-hand side of an assignment.
`Item_Type& operator[](size_t index)`	Returns a reference to the element at position `index` that can be used as the target of an assignment.
`Item_Type& at(size_t index);` `const Item_Type& at(size_t index) const`	The same as `operator[]` except that the index is validated. If the index is not valid, the `out_of_range` exception is thrown.
`iterator insert(iterator pos,` `const Item_Type& item)`	Inserts a copy of `item` into the deque at position `pos`. Returns an iterator that references the newly inserted item.
`iterator erase(iterator pos)`	Removes the item from the deque at position `pos`. Returns an iterator that references the item following the one erased.
`void remove(const Item_Type& item)`	Removes all occurrences of `item` from the deque.
`void push_front(const Item_Type& item)`	Inserts a copy of `item` as the first element of the deque.
`void push_back(const Item_Type& item)`	Adds a copy of `item` to the end of the deque.
`void pop_front()`	Removes the first item from the deque.
`void pop_back()`	Removes the last item from the deque.
`Item_Type& front();` `const Item_Type& front() const`	Gets the first element in the deque. Both constant and modifiable versions are provided.
`Item_Type& back();` `const Item_Type& back() const`	Gets the last element in the deque. Both constant and modifiable versions are provided.
`iterator begin()`	Returns an `iterator` that references the first item of the deque.
`const_iterator() begin const`	Returns a `const_iterator` that references the first item of the deque.
`iterator end()`	Returns an `iterator` that references the end of the deque (one past the last item).
`const_iterator end() const`	Returns a `const_iterator` that references the end of the deque (one past the last item).
`void swap(deque<Item_Type> other)`	Exchanges the contents of this deque with the `other` deque.
`bool empty() const`	Returns **true** if the deque is empty.
`size_t size() const`	Returns the number of items in the deque.
`void resize(size_t new_size)`	Changes the size of the deque to `new_size`. If `new_size` is smaller than the current size, then items are removed from the end. If `new_size` is larger than the current size, then default valued items are added to the end. The default valued item is the value returned by the default (no argument) constructor. For built-in types the default value is zero.

To obtain random access, consider that the ith element is at position front_index + i, assuming that i starts at 0 and this sum is not larger than capacity. If it is larger than capacity, we need to wrap around the end of the array using modulo arithmetic. The implementation of the index operator is as follows:

```
/** Returns a reference to an item in the deque based on an index. */
Item_Type& operator[](size_t i) {
  return the_data[(i + front_index) % capacity];
}
```

Implementation of the rest of the deque functions is left as a programming project. As we will discuss below, a randomly accessible circular array is part of the standard deque implementation. Thus, we will refer to this implementation of the deque as the class CArray. The C++ STL implementation of class deque is discussed next

The Standard Library Implementation of the Deque

The standard library implementation also uses a circular array, but the circular array contains pointers to fixed-size, dynamically allocated arrays that contain the data. This is illustrated in Figure 6.11. The first data item is located at index offset in the first data block, and the last item is located at index (offset + num_items - 1) % BLOCK_SIZE in the last data block. The value of offset is initially BLOCK_SIZE / 2 and is incremented by 1 each time an element is removed from the front of the deque.

You may wonder why the original designers chose this rather elaborate implementation rather than simply using a circular array. The reason has to do with the cost of the reallocation. Even though we amortize the cost of the reallocation so that each push_front or push_back is a constant-time operation, the reallocation can take a significant amount of time. This is because we make a copy of each object using the object's assignment operator. By storing only pointers in the circular array, the cost of reallocation is significantly reduced, because copying a pointer is a simple operation. Next you may wonder, why not just store pointers to single objects in the circular array? This would work, but dynamically allocating small objects has a significant space overhead. Thus, by allocating an array of objects, we minimize this space overhead and minimize the cost of the reallocation. For large collections of large objects, the deque can be used instead of the vector to minimize space overhead and the cost of reallocation.

FIGURE 6.11
Internal Structure of
Standard Implementation of **deque**

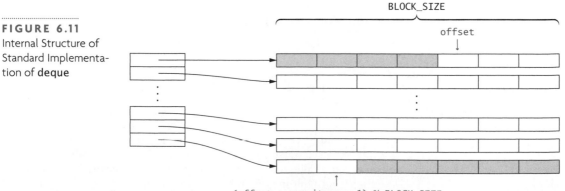

TABLE 6.3
deque Data Fields

Data Field	Attribute
`static const size_t BLOCK_SIZE`	The number of items in each data block array
`size_t offset`	The index of the first item in the first data block
`size_t num_items`	The number of items in the deque
`CArray<Item_Type*> the_data`	A circular array of pointers to the data blocks

We will leave the full implementation of the deque as a programming project, but we will discuss the data fields and the implementation of three functions: the index operator, push_back, and pop_front.

The Data Fields for the Deque

Table 6.3 shows the data fields for the deque class. The class CArray is the circular array implementation of the deque discussed at the beginning of this section. We assume that it has the operations operator[], push_front, push_back, pop_front, pop_back, front, back, and size.

The Index Operator

You can think of the data blocks as forming a two-dimensional array, where each row is a data block. The current capacity of the deque is defined by the size of the circular array times the size of a data block. The 0th item is at index offset in the 0th data block. Thus, to find the appropriate row you divide (i + offset) by BLOCK_SIZE. To find the column you compute (i + offset) % BLOCK_SIZE. The complete implementation of operator[] is as follows.

```
/** Returns a reference to an item referenced by an index.
    @param i the index
    @return A reference to deque[i]
*/
template<typename Item_Type>
  Item_Type& deque<Item_Type>::operator[](size_t i) {
    if (i >= num_items)
      throw std::out_of_range("Invalid index to deque::operator[]");
    size_t block_index = (offset + i) / BLOCK_SIZE;
    size_t data_index = (offset + i) % BLOCK_SIZE;
    return the_data[block_index][data_index];
  }
```

The **push_back** Function

The current capacity of the deque is the circular array's size times the BLOCK_SIZE. If the num_items plus offset is equal to the capacity, we need to increase the capacity by adding a new block. This is done by the statement:

```
the_data.push_back(new Item_Type[BLOCK_SIZE]);
```

Once the capacity is ensured, we can insert a new item by incrementing `num_items` and then storing the new item at position `num_items - 1`. The complete implementation of push_back follows.

```
/** Pushes an item onto the back of the deque.
    @param item The item to be inserted
*/
template<typename Item_Type>
  void deque<Item_Type>::push_back(const Item_Type& item) {
    size_t capacity = the_data.size() * BLOCK_SIZE;
    if ((num_items + offset) == capacity) {
      the_data.push_back(new Item_Type[BLOCK_SIZE]);
    }
    num_items++;
    (*this)[num_items - 1] = item;
}
```

The **pop_front** Function

To remove the front element, we merely need to decrement `offset`. If `offset` is now equal to `BLOCK_SIZE`, then the front block also needs to be removed and `offset` reset to zero. The code for pop_front is as follows:

```
/** Removes the front item from the deque. */
template<typename Item_Type>
  void deque<Item_Type>::pop_front() {
    offset++;
    if (offset == BLOCK_SIZE) {
      delete[] the_data.front();
      the_data.pop_front();
      offset = 0;
    }
    num_items--;
}
```

EXERCISES FOR SECTION 6.4

PROGRAMMING

1. Code the `push_front` and `pop_back` functions for the circular array class `CArray`.
2. Code the `push_front` and `pop_back` functions for the STL class `deque`.

6.5 Simulating Waiting Lines Using Queues

Simulation is a technique used to study the performance of a physical system by using a physical, mathematical, or computer model of the system. Through simulation, the designers of a new system can estimate the expected performance of the system before they actually build it. The use of simulation can lead to changes in the design that will improve the expected performance of the new system. Simulation is especially useful when the actual system would be too expensive to build or too dangerous to experiment with after its construction.

System designers often use computer models to simulate physical systems. In this section we will implement and test a computer model of an airline check-in counter in order to compare various strategies for improving service and reducing the waiting time for each passenger. We will use a queue to simulate the passenger waiting line. A special branch of mathematics called *queuing theory* has been developed to study these kinds of problems using mathematical models (systems of equations) instead of computer models.

CASE STUDY   Simulate a Strategy for Serving Airline Passengers

Problem   Blue Skies Airlines (BSA) is considering redesigning its ticket counters for airline passengers. The company would like to have two separate waiting lines: one for regular customers and one for frequent flyers. Assuming there is only one ticket agent available to serve all passengers, the company would like to determine the average waiting time for both types of passengers using various strategies for taking passengers from the waiting lines (see Figure 6.12).

A "democratic" strategy for serving passengers would be to take turns serving passengers from both lines (that is, one frequent flyer, one regular passenger, one frequent flyer, and so on). Another "democratic" strategy would be to serve the passenger who has been waiting in line the longest, but this would be the same as having a single queue. (Why?) An "elitist" strategy would be to serve any frequent flyer waiting in line before serving the regular passengers.

FIGURE 6.12
Passengers Waiting
in Lines

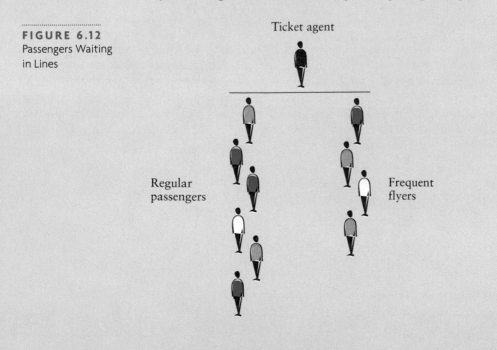

Ticket agent

Regular
passengers

Frequent
flyers

Analysis   Running a computer simulation is a good way to investigate the effect of different serving strategies. To run a computer simulation, we must keep track of the current time by maintaining a clock that is set to an initial time of zero. This clock will increase by one time unit until the simulation is finished. During each time interval, one or more of the following events may occur.

1. A new frequent flyer passenger arrives in line.
2. A new regular passenger arrives in line.
3. The ticket agent finishes serving a passenger and begins to serve a passenger from the frequent flyer line.
4. The ticket agent finishes serving a passenger and begins to serve a passenger from the regular passenger line.
5. The ticket agent is idle because there are no passengers in either line to serve.

The purpose of running the simulation is to determine statistics about the waiting times for frequent flyers and for regular passengers. In addition to the priority given to frequent flyers, the waiting times depend on the arrival rate of each type of passenger (number of passengers arriving per minute) and the time required to serve a passenger. There are different arrival rates for each kind of passenger. In addition to statistics on waiting times, we can display a minute-by-minute trace of events occurring during each minute of the simulation.

We can simulate different serving strategies by introducing a simulation variable frequent_flyer_max, which must be a positive integer. This will represent the number of consecutive frequent flyer passengers served between regular passengers. When frequent_flyer_max is 1, every other passenger served will be a regular passenger (the "democratic" strategy). When frequent_flyer_max is 2, every third passenger served will be a regular passenger. When frequent_flyer_max is a very large number, any frequent flyer passenger will be served before a regular passenger (the "elitist" strategy).

Design   To begin an object-oriented design, we look at the problem description and identify the classes. We can use the nouns in the problem statement as a starting point. Doing this we see that we have an agent, passengers, and two passenger queues. These are part of the simulation. This leads to the initial UML class diagram shown in Figure 6.13. The diagram shows that Passenger_Queue has a queue component and is itself a component of Airline_Checkin_Sim—the class that runs the simulation. Also, the queue stores objects of type Passenger.

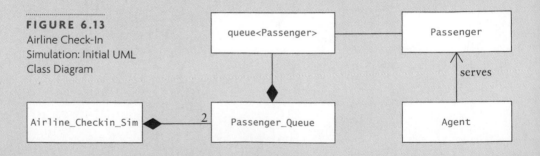

FIGURE 6.13
Airline Check-In
Simulation: Initial UML
Class Diagram

Next we develop a sequence diagram to see how the data flows between the objects and to identify the messages passed between them. In object-oriented design, when one object sends a message to another, this implies that the receiving object's class must have a function to respond to the message. The objects involved in the simulation are the `Airline_Checkin_Sim` instance, the two passenger queues, and `Passenger` objects.

Figure 6.14 shows the sequence diagram that is based on the events described in the analysis phase. The comments in the colored boxes show conditions that must be

FIGURE 6.14
Airline Check-In Simulation: Sequence Diagram

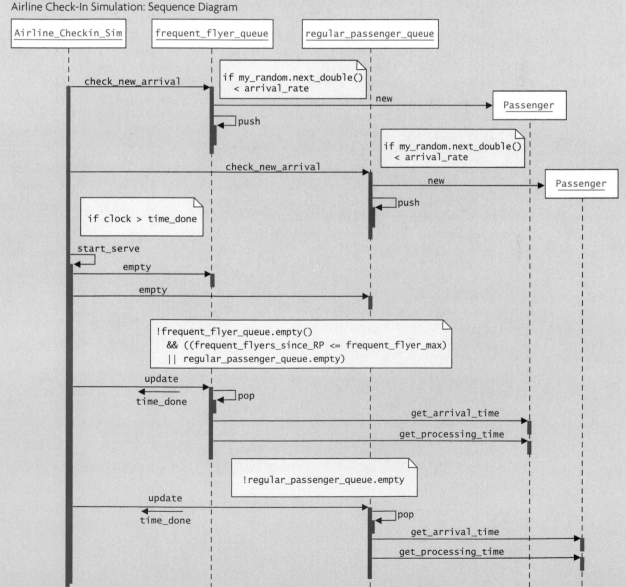

true before a message is sent. We will explain these conditions shortly. First the
`Airline_Checkin_Sim` object checks to see whether a new frequent flyer passenger has
arrived, by sending the `check_new_arrival` message to the `frequent_flyer_queue`. If
a new passenger has arrived (`my_random.next_double() < arrival_rate` is true), the
`frequent_flyer_queue` then creates a `Passenger` object (sending the `new` message) and
inserts it into the queue (by sending its queue component a `push` message, which is
shown as a message to self). Then the `Airline_Checkin_Sim` object checks to see
whether a regular passenger has arrived, and the same process is performed with the
`regular_passenger_queue`.

Then, if the agent is free (`clock > time_done`), the `Airline_Checkin_Sim` instance
determines the next passenger to be served by the agent. To see whether either or
both of the passenger queues have passengers waiting, the `Airline_Checkin_Sim`
instance sends the `empty` message to the queues. If there is a frequent flyer waiting
and the number of frequent flyers between regular passengers has not been
exceeded, or if there are no regular passengers waiting, then we simulate the agent
serving the next frequent flyer by sending the `update` message to the frequent flyer
queue. Otherwise, if there is a regular passenger waiting, we simulate the agent serving the next regular passenger in the queue by sending the `update` message to the
regular passenger queue. The response to this message (the return value from the
function) is the time at which the agent will next be free.

Notice that the agent does not actually appear as an actor at the top of the sequence
diagram. Therefore we can infer that the agent does not participate in the simulation. For the purposes of the simulation, the agent is either busy or idle and can thus
be represented by a Boolean expression. Also, the sequence diagram has identified
the functions that we need in each class. This leads to the revised UML class diagram shown in Figure 6.15.

FIGURE 6.15
Airline Check-In
Simulation: Updated
Class Diagram

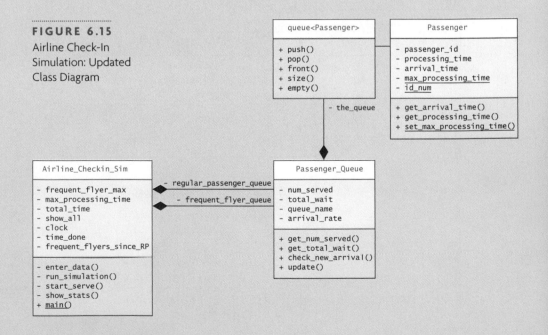

Class `Airline_Checkin_Sim`

The sequence diagram shown in Figure 6.14 represents the run_simulation function shown in Figure 6.15 for class Airline_Checkin_Sim. Table 6.4 shows its data fields and functions. Functions main, enter_data, and show_stats will be discussed briefly in the implementation. As an aid to testing our implementation, we want to have the option of printing a minute-by-minute state of the simulation and to track individual passengers. Thus, we add a show_all attribute to the Airline_Checkin_Sim class. If the value of show_all is true, we will essentially trace each action taken by the program through output to cout.

Class `Passenger_Queue`

The Passenger_Queue class stores the passenger queue and summary data about the queue (see Table 6.5). By encapsulating the queue within this class and having its functions manipulate both the queue and the summary data, we ensure that the summary data is always maintained. Specifically, when the function check_new_arrival determines that a new passenger has arrived, it inserts the passenger into the queue. When the update function removes a passenger, it updates the number of passengers served and the total wait time.

TABLE 6.4
Class Airline_Checkin_Sim

Data Field	Attribute
Passenger_Queue frequent_flyer_queue	The queue of frequent flyers
Passenger_Queue regular_passenger_queue	The queue of regular passengers
int frequent_flyer_max	The maximum number of frequent flyers to serve between regular passengers
int max_processing_time	The maximum time to serve a passenger
int total_time	The total time to run the simulation
bool show_all	A flag indicating whether to trace the simulation
int clock	The current clock time (initially zero)
int time_done	The time that the current passenger will be finished
int frequent_flyers_since_RP	The number of frequent flyers served since the last regular passenger
Function	**Behavior**
void run_simulation()	Controls the simulation. Executes the steps shown in Figure 6.14.
void enter_data()	Reads in the data for the simulation.
void start_serve()	Initiates service for a passenger.
void show_stats()	Displays the summary statistics.

TABLE 6.5
Class `Passenger_Queue`

Data Field	Attribute
`queue<Passenger> the_queue`	The queue of passengers
`int num_served`	The number from this queue that were served
`int total_wait`	The total time spent waiting by passengers that were in this queue
`string queue_name`	The name of this queue
`double arrival_rate`	The arrival rate for this queue
Function	**Behavior**
`Passenger_Queue(string queue_name)`	Constructs a new queue with the specified name.
`void check_new_arrival(int clock, bool show_all)`	Checks whether there was a new arrival for this queue and, if so, inserts the passenger into the queue.
`int update(int clock, bool show_all)`	Updates the total waiting time and number of passengers served when a passenger from this queue is served.
`int get_total_wait() const`	Returns the total waiting time for passengers in this queue.
`int get_num_served() const`	Returns the number of passengers served from this queue.

The **Passenger** Class

The `Passenger` class stores the following information about a passenger:

- A unique ID number
- The time the passenger arrived
- The actual processing time
- The maximum processing time

The ID number is used to identify passengers when the simulation is traced. It starts at 0 and is incremented by 1 each time a new `Passenger` object is created. Table 6.6 shows the class functions.

TABLE 6.6
Functions of the **Passenger** Class

Function	Behavior
`Passenger(int arrival_time)`	Constructs a new passenger, assigns it a unique ID and the specified arrival time. Computes a random processing time in the range 1 to `max_processing_time`.
`int get_arrival_time() const`	Returns the value of `arrival_time`.
`int get_processing_time() const`	Returns the value of `processing_time`.
`static void set_max_processing_time(int max_process_time)`	Sets the `max_processing_time` used to generate the random processing time.

Implementation   Coding the `Airline_Checkin_Sim` Class

The class and data field declarations for the `Airline_Checkin_Sim` class follow:

```cpp
#ifndef AIRLINE_CHECKIN_SIM_H_
#define ARRLINE_CHECKIN_SIM_H_

#include "Passenger_Queue.h"

/** Simulates the check-in process of an airline. */
class Airline_Checkin_Sim {

  public:

  Airline_Checkin_Sim () : frequent_flyer_queue("Frequent Flyer Queue"),
    regular_passenger_queue("Regular Passenger Queue"), clock(0),
    time_done(0) {}

  /** Run the simulation. */
  void run_simulation();

  /** Function to show the statistics. */
  void show_stats();

  /** Function to read the simulation parameters. */
  void enter_data();

  private:

  /** Function to start serving a passenger. */
  void start_serve();

  // Data Fields
  /** Queue of frequent flyers. */
  Passenger_Queue frequent_flyer_queue;

  /** Queue of regular passengers. */
  Passenger_Queue regular_passenger_queue;

  /** Maximum number of frequent flyers to be served
      before a regular passenger gets served. */
  int frequent_flyer_max;

  /** Maximum time to serve a passenger. */
  int max_processing_time;

  /** Total simulated time. */
  int total_time;

  /** If set true, print additional output. */
  bool show_all;

  /** Simulated clock. */
  int clock;

  /** Time that the agent will be done with the current passenger. */
  int time_done;
```

```
/** Number of frequent flyers served since the
    last regular passenger was served. */
int frequent_flyers_since_RP;

};

#endif
```

The `main` Function

The `main` function constructs an `Airline_Checkin_Sim` object, calls `enter_data` to read the input data, and then calls `run_simulation` to perform the simulation. After the simulation is complete, the `show_stats` function displays the summary results.

```
int main() {
  Airline_Checkin_Sim simulation;
  simulation.enter_data();
  simulation.run_simulation();
  simulation.show_stats();
}
```

The `enter_data` Function

The `enter_data` function (not shown) gets the input values shown in Table 6.7.

The `run_simulation` Function

The `run_simulation` function executes a loop once for each minute of simulated time. During each iteration, it calls function `check_new_arrival` on both the `frequent_flyer_queue` and the `regular_passenger_queue` to see whether any new passengers have arrived. Variable `show_all` is passed in both function calls. If the clock

TABLE 6.7
Airline Simulation Input Parameters

Internal Variable	Attribute	Conversion
`double frequent_flyer_queue.arrival_rate`	Expected number of frequent flyer arrivals per hour.	Divide input by 60 to obtain arrivals per minute.
`double regular_passenger_queue.arrival_rate`	Expected number of regular passenger arrivals per hour.	Divide input by 60 to obtain arrivals per minute.
`int max_processing_time`	Maximum service time in minutes.	None.
`int total_time`	Total simulation time in minutes.	None.
`bool show_all`	Flag. If **true**, display minute-by-minute trace of simulation.	Input beginning with 'Y' or 'y' will set this to **true**; other inputs will set it to **false**.

has advanced past the value of time_done, then the current passenger is finished with the ticket agent, so function start_serve is called to start the next passenger. Data field time_done is reset to the time the current passenger will be finished, which is the current clock time plus the service time.

```
void Airline_Checkin_Sim::run_simulation() {
  for (clock = 0; clock < total_time; clock++) {
    frequent_flyer_queue.check_new_arrival(clock, show_all);
    regular_passenger_queue.check_new_arrival(clock, show_all);
    if (clock >= time_done) {
      start_serve();
    }
  }
}
```

The start_serve Function

The start_serve function selects a queue and then calls that queue's update function to remove the next passenger and update the simulation variables.

If the frequent flyer queue is not empty, it is selected if either of the two following conditions is true:

- The number of frequent flyers who have been served since the last regular passenger is less than or equal to frequent_flyer_max.
- The regular passenger queue is empty.

Otherwise, start_serve selects the regular passenger queue. If both queues are empty, and show_all is true, start_serve prints a message that the agent is idle.

After selecting a queue, start_serve increments frequent_flyers_since_RP or sets it to zero, depending upon the passenger type being served.

```
void Airline_Checkin_Sim::start_serve() {
  if (!frequent_flyer_queue.empty ()
      && ( (frequent_flyers_since_RP <= frequent_flyer_max)
          || regular_passenger_queue.empty())) {
    // Serve the next frequent flyer.
    frequent_flyers_since_RP++;
    time_done = frequent_flyer_queue.update(clock, show_all);
  }
  else if (!regular_passenger_queue.empty()) {
    // Serve the next regular passenger.
    frequent_flyers_since_RP = 0;
    time_done = regular_passenger_queue.update(clock, show_all);
  }
  else if (show_all) {
    cout << "Time is " << clock
        << ": Server is idle\n";
  }
}
```

The show_stats Function

The show_stats function displays the total number of each kind of passenger and their average waiting time. It also displays the number of passengers left in each queue at the end of the simulation.

```
                   /** Function to show the statistics. */
                   void Airline_Checkin_Sim::show_stats() {
                     cout << "\nThe number of regular passengers served was "
                          << regular_passenger_queue.get_num_served() << endl;
                     double average_waiting_time =
                       double(regular_passenger_queue.get_total_wait())
                       / double(regular_passenger_queue.get_num_served());
                     cout << " with an average waiting time of "
                          << average_waiting_time << endl;
                     cout << "The number of frequent flyers served was "
                          << frequent_flyer_queue.get_num_served() << endl;
                     average_waiting_time =
                       double(frequent_flyer_queue.get_total_wait())
                       / double(frequent_flyer_queue.get_num_served());
                     cout << " with an average waiting time of "
                          << average_waiting_time << endl;
                     cout << "Passengers in frequent flyer queue: "
                          << frequent_flyer_queue.size() << endl;
                     cout << "Passengers in regular passenger queue: "
                          << regular_passenger_queue.size() << endl;
                   }
```

Coding Class **Passenger_Queue**

The class definition for Passenger_Queue follows. The constructor saves the name of
the queue so that it can be displayed when the show_all flag is set to show the
minute-by-minute trace of the simulation.

```
#ifndef PASSENGER_QUEUE_H
#define PASSENGER_QUEUE_H

#include <string>
#include <queue>
#include "Passenger.h"

/** Class to simulate a queue of passengers. */
class Passenger_Queue {

  public:

  // Constructor
  /** Constructs a Passenger_Queue with the given name.
      @param my_name The name of this queue
  */
   Passenger_Queue(std::string my_name) : num_served(0), total_wait(0),
     queue_name(my_name) {}

  /** Returns the number of passengers served.
      @return The number of passengers served
  */
  int get_num_served() const {
    return num_served;
  }
```

```
/** Returns the total wait time.
    @return The total wait time
 */
int get_total_wait() const {
  return total_wait;
}


/** Returns the queue name.
    @return The queue name
 */
std::string get_queue_name() const {
  return queue_name;
}


/** Sets the arrival rate.
    @param new_arrival_rate The value to set
 */
void set_arrival_rate(double new_arrival_rate) {
  arrival_rate = new_arrival_rate;
}


/** Determines whether the passenger queue is empty.
    @return true if the passenger queue is empty
 */
bool empty() const {
  return the_queue.empty();
}


/** Determines the size of the passenger queue.
    @return the size of the passenger queue
 */
size_t size() const {
  return the_queue.size();
}


/** Checks whether a new arrival has occurred.
    @param clock The current simulated time
    @param show_all Flag to indicate that detailed
                    data should be output
 */
void check_new_arrival(int clock, bool show_all);

/** Updates statistics.
    pre: The queue is not empty.
    @param clock The current simulated time
    @param show_all Flag to indicate whether to show detail
    @return Time passenger is done being served
 */
int update(int clock, bool show_all);

private:

// Data Fields
/**  The queue of passengers. */
std::queue<Passenger> the_queue;
```

```
/** The number of passengers served. */
int num_served;

/** The total time passengers were waiting. */
int total_wait;

/** The name of this queue. */
std::string queue_name;

/** The average arrival rate. */
double arrival_rate;
};

#endif
```

The function `check_new_arrival` is the most interesting part of the simulation program. Its purpose is to determine whether a new arrival occurs during a given time unit and, if so, to insert it in the appropriate passenger queue. During each time unit, `check_new_arrival` is applied to each passenger queue.

```
/** Checks whether a new arrival has occurred.
    @param clock The current simulated time
    @param show_all Flag to indicate that detailed
                    data should be output
*/
void Passenger_Queue::check_new_arrival(int clock, bool show_all) {
  if (my_random.next_double() < arrival_rate) {
    the_queue.push(Passenger(clock));
    if (show_all) {
      cout << "Time is "
           << clock <<  ": "
           << queue_name
           << " arrival, new queue size is "
           << the_queue.size() << endl;
    }
  }
}
```

The arrival of passengers is considered a "random event" because we cannot predict with certainty the time at which passengers arrive. The arrival rate tells us the average rate at which passengers will arrive. For example, an arrival rate of 0.25 means that on average 0.25 passengers will arrive every minute or, stated another way, one passenger will arrive every four minutes. However, this does not mean that passengers will arrive precisely at clock times 0, 4, 8, 12, and so on. A group of passengers may arrive in consecutive time units, and then we may not see another arrival for several more minutes. All we know is that if the simulation runs long enough, the number of passenger arrivals should be pretty close to the total simulation length times 0.25. In statistical terms, an arrival rate of 0.25 means that the probability of a passenger arrival in any given minute is 0.25, or 25 percent. To obtain the arrival rate, we divide the number of passengers expected per hour (a data item) by 60 because our clock increments every minute. If we expect more than 60 passengers per hour, we need to run the simulation with a smaller clock increment so that the arrival rate used by `check_new_arrival` is less than one.

We can use a pseudorandom number generator to determine whether a passenger has arrived in a given minute of the simulation. The C++ standard library includes the function `rand` that generates a random integer between 0 and `RAND_MAX`. As discussed in a subsequent section, we have encapsulated the function in the class `Random` and provided a function that returns a double value between 0 and 1. A global instance of the `Random` class (variable `my_random`) was defined in the file `Airline_Checkin_Sim.cpp`. The condition

```
my_random.next_double() < arrival_rate
```

compares the pseudorandom number generated to the value of `arrival_rate`. Because the values being compared are in the range 0.0–1.0, the probability that this condition will be true is proportional to the value of `arrival_rate`, as desired. If `arrival_rate` is 0.25, this condition should be true 25 percent of the time.

The `update` function removes a passenger from the queue, computes that passenger's waiting time (clock time – arrival time), and adds it to the total wait time. Next, `update` increments the count of passengers from this queue who have been served since the simulation began. Function `update` also computes the time that the agent will be finished with this passenger and returns the time to the caller.

```
/** Update statistics.
    pre: The queue is not empty.
    @param clock The current simulated time
    @param show_all Flag to indicate whether to show detail
    @return Time passenger is done being served
*/
int Passenger_Queue::update(int clock, bool show_all) {
  Passenger next_passenger = the_queue.front();
  the_queue.pop();
  int time_stamp = next_passenger.get_arrival_time();
  int wait = clock - time_stamp;
  total_wait += wait;
  num_served++;
  if (show_all) {
    cout << "Time is " << clock
         << ": Serving "
         << queue_name
         << " with time stamp "
         << time_stamp << endl;
  }
  return clock + next_passenger.get_processing_time();
}
```

Coding the **Passenger** Class

Data field `id_num` is the sequence number associated with a passenger. It is *static* because the same variable is used for all passengers and we don't want it reset to zero when a new passenger is created. Since the `max_processing_time` applies to all instances of `Passenger`, this is a static attribute, and the function `set_max_processing_time` is also static.

We will assume that the processing time is uniformly distributed between 1 and the `max_processing_time`. We call function `next_int` (member of the class `Random`) to generate a random **int** value between 0 and `max_processing_time - 1`. We compute the processing_time in the constructor. Listing 6.6 shows the `Passenger` class definition, and Listing 6.7 shows the implementation file `Passenger.cpp`. The implementation file contains the implementation of the constructor and definitions of the static members.

....

LISTING 6.6
Passenger.h

```cpp
#ifndef PASSENGER_H_
#define PASSENGER_H_

/** A class to represent a passenger. */
class Passenger {
  public:

  /** Creates a new passenger.
      @param arrive_time The time this passenger arrives */
  Passenger(int arrive_time);

  /** Gets the arrival time.
      @return The arrival time */
  int get_arrival_time() {
    return arrival_time;
  }

  /** Gets the processing time.
      @return The processing time */
  int get_processing_time() {
    return processing_time;
  }

  /** Gets the passenger ID.
      @return The passenger ID */
  int get_id() {
    return passenger_id;
  }

  /** Sets the maximum processing time.
      @param max_process_time The new value */
  static void set_max_processing_time(int max_process_time) {
    max_processing_time = max_process_time;
  }

  private:

  // Data Fields
  /** The ID number for this passenger. */
  int passenger_id;

  /** The time needed to process this passenger. */
  int processing_time;

  /** The time this passenger arrives. */
  int arrival_time;
```

```
/** The maximum time to process a passenger. */
static int max_processing_time;

/** The sequence number for passengers. */
static int id_num;

};

#endif
```

....
LISTING 6.7
Passenger.cpp

```
/** Implementation of the Passenger class. */

#include "Passenger.h"
#include "Random.h"
extern Random my_random;    // Declared in Airline_Checkin_Sim.cpp

/** Creates a new passenger.
   @param arrive_time The time this passenger arrives */
Passenger::Passenger(int arrive_time) {
  arrival_time = arrive_time;
  processing_time = 1 + my_random.next_int(max_processing_time);
  passenger_id = id_num++;
}

// Definition of static members.
/** The maximum time to process a passenger. */
int Passenger::max_processing_time;

/** The sequence number for passengers. */
int Passenger::id_num = 0;
```

Generating Pseudorandom Numbers

When you need a random number, as when playing a game, you can perform some procedure, such as spinning a wheel, in which imperceptibly small variations in the physical circumstances (hand position and force, condition of the bearings) all have large enough effects on the result to make it unpredictable.

When a computer needs a random number, it uses a mathematical process that is analogous to spinning a wheel, but because the computer is a machine designed to produce consistent results regardless of variations in its physical circumstances, the "wheel" is spun a controlled number of clicks each time, so the results are not truly random. However, if the size of the "wheel" and the algorithms for determining the number of clicks are chosen properly, the results can be made to appear to be random. We say that they appear to be random because they pass statistical tests. Such numbers are *pseudorandom numbers*, though they are often called "random."

The C++ standard library contains the function rand (declared in header <cstdlib>) that it inherits from the C standard library. This function returns a pseudorandom **int** value between 0 and RAND_MAX. There is also the function srand that is used to set the *seed* (starting value for first random number computation) of the random number generator. You should call this function once in any program that uses the random number generator so that the sequence generated is different each time the program is run. A common practice is to use the current date and time (expressed as milliseconds since January 1, 1970) as the seed to the random number generator.

Listing 6.8 shows the class Random, which encapsulates the C++ standard random number generator. The constructor calls the srand function to initialize the generator. The function next_double converts the value returned by rand into a **double** value between 0 and 1, and the function next_int returns an **int** in the range 0 through n, where n is the parameter.

....
LISTING 6.8
The Class Random

```
#ifndef RANDOM_H_
#define RANDOM_H_

#include <cstdlib>
#include <ctime>

/** Class to encapsulate the standard random number generator. */
class Random {

  public:

  /** Initializes the random number generator using the time
      as the seed.
  */
  Random() {
    std::srand(std::time(0));
  }

  /** Initializes the randon mumber generator using a
      supplied seed.
  */
  Random(int seed) {
    std::srand(seed);
  }

  /** Returns a random integer in the range 0 - n. */
  int next_int(int n) {
    return int(next_double() * n);
  }

  /** Return a random double in the range 0 - 1. */
  double next_double() {
    return double(std::rand()) / RAND_MAX;
  }

};

#endif
```

Testing   Figure 6.16 shows a sample run of the simulation program with the trace turned on. To test the simulation program, you should run it a number of times with the trace turned on and verify that passengers in the frequent flyer queue have the specified priority over regular passengers. Function `enter_data` should display the data values so that you can interpret the simulation results in a meaningful way. Also, make sure that the "server is idle" message is displayed only when both queues are empty. If both arrival rates are the same, check that the waiting times reflect the priority given to frequent flyers. Also see what happens when both kinds of passengers are treated equally (`frequent_flyer_since_RP` is 1).

When running the program, make sure that you use integer values for the total simulation time and for the service time. It is also a good idea to choose values for arrival rates and service time that keep the system from becoming saturated. The system will become saturated if the arrival rates are too large and passengers arrive more quickly than they can be served. This will result in very long queues and large waiting times. The system will become saturated if the total number of arrivals per minute (frequent flyer arrival rate + regular passenger arrival rate) is greater than the number of passengers being served in a minute: [1 / (`max_processing_time` / 2)].

After you are certain that the program runs correctly, you should turn off the trace and focus on the summary statistics. It is interesting to see how these values change for a particular set of arrival rates and service times. Remember, passenger arrivals are a random event, so the results should vary from one run to the next even if all input data stay the same.

....

FIGURE 6.16
Sample Run of Airline Check-In Simulation

```
C:\C++Book\programs\CH06>Airline_Checkin_Sim
Expected number of frequent flyer arrivals per hour: 15
Expected number of regular passenger arrivals per hour: 30
Enter the maximum number of frequent flyers
served between regular passengers 5
Enter the maximim service time in minutes 4
Enter the total simulation time in minutes 10
Display minute-by-minute trace of simulation (Y or N) y
Time is 0: Frequent Flyer Queue arrival, new queue size is 1
Time is 0: Serving Frequent Flyer Queue with time stamp 0
Time is 3: Server is idle
Time is 4: Frequent Flyer Queue arrival, new queue size is 1
Time is 4: Regular Passenger Queue arrival, new queue size is 1
Time is 4: Serving Regular Passenger Queue with time stamp 4
Time is 5: Regular Passenger Queue arrival, new queue size is 1
Time is 6: Regular Passenger Queue arrival, new queue size is 2
Time is 7: Frequent Flyer Queue arrival, new queue size is 2
Time is 7: Serving Frequent Flyer Queue with time stamp 4
Time is 8: Regular Passenger Queue arrival, new queue size is 3
Time is 9: Regular Passenger Queue arrival, new queue size is 4

The number of regular passengers served was 1
 with an average waiting time of 0
The number of frequent flyers served was 2
 with an average waiting time of 1.5
Passengers in frequent flyer queue: 1
Passengers in regular passenger queue: 4
```

EXERCISES FOR SECTION 6.5

SELF-CHECK

1. Show the output that would be generated by running the simulation program for 20 minutes with the following passenger arrivals when show_all is true and frequent_flyer_max is 1.

   A frequent flyer passenger arrives at clock = 0 and service time is 2
   A regular passenger arrives at clock = 0 and service time is 1
   A frequent flyer passenger arrives at clock = 1 and service time is 1
   A regular passenger arrives at clock = 1 and service time is 1
   A regular passenger arrives at clock = 2 and service time is 1
   A frequent flyer passenger arrives at clock = 3 and service time is 3
   A regular passenger arrives at clock = 3 and service time is 1
   A regular passenger arrives at clock = 4 and service time is 2
   A frequent flyer passenger arrives at clock = 5 and service time is 2

2. Answer Self-Check Exercise 1 when frequent_flyer_max is 2.

3. Function run_simulation begins with the statements

   ```
   frequent_flyer_queue.check_new_arrival(clock, show_all);
   regular_passenger_queue.check_new_arrival(clock, show_all);
   ```

   Would exchanging the order of these statements change the result? Explain your answer.

PROGRAMMING

1. Run the Airline_Checkin_Sim program with a variety of inputs to determine the maximum passenger arrival rate for a given average processing time and the effect of the frequent flyer service policy.

2. Modify the Airline_Checkin_Sim program to simulate every second of simulated time. Does this affect the results?

3. Write function enter_data.

Chapter Review

- ◆ The queue is an abstract data type with a first-in, first-out, or FIFO, structure. This means that the item that has been in the queue the longest will be the first one removed. Queues can be used to represent reservation lists and waiting lines (from which the data structure gets its name "queue").

- ◆ The C++ standard queue declares functions push to insert an item at the back, pop to remove an item from the front, and front to access the item at the front.

- ◆ We discussed three ways to implement the Queue ADT: as a double-linked list, a single-linked list, and a circular array. All three implementations support insertion and removal in $O(1)$ time; however, there will be a need for reallocation in the circular array implementation (amortized $O(1)$ time).

◆ To avoid the cost of building a physical system or running an actual experiment, computer simulation can be used to evaluate the expected performance of a system or operational strategy. We showed how to do this using a pair of queues to simulate passengers waiting for service at an airline ticket counter. We used pseudorandom numbers to determine whether a particular event occurs.

◆ The C++ standard `deque` combines the features of a stack, queue, vector, and linked list. It provides for constant-time insertion and removal from ether end, and random access. The STL implementation is designed to reduce the cost of reallocation and the space overhead that is encountered with large vectors of large objects. The C++ standard library uses the deque as the default container to implement both the stack and the queue.

Quick-Check Exercises

1. A queue is a _____-in, _____-out data structure.
2. Would a compiler use a stack or a queue in a program that converts infix expressions to postfix?
3. Would an operating system use a stack or a queue to determine which print job should be handled next?
4. Assume that a queue `q` of capacity 6 (circular array for storage) contains the five characters +, *, –, &, and #, where + is the first character inserted. Assume that + is stored in the first position in the array. What is the value of `q.front_index`? What is the value of `q.rear_index`?
5. Remove the first element from the queue in Exercise 4 and insert the characters \ and then %. Draw the new queue. What is the value of `q.front_index`? What is the value of `q.rear_index`?
6. If a single-linked list were used to implement the queue in Question 5, the character _____ would be at the head of the list and the character _____ would be at the tail of the list.
7. For a nonempty queue implemented as a single-linked list, the statement _____ would be used inside function `push` to store a new node whose data field is referenced by `item` in the queue; the statement _____ would be used to disconnect a node after its data was retrieved from the queue.
8. Pick the queue implementation (circular array, single-linked list, double-linked list, deque) that is most appropriate for each of the following conditions.
   a. Storage must be reallocated when the queue is full.
   b. This implementation is normally most efficient in use of storage.
   c. This is an existing class in the C++ STL.
9. Write an `if` statement that uses a pseudorandom number to assign `"heads"` or `"tails"` to a variable `coin_flip`. The probability of each should be 0.5. Assume the declaration `Random my_random;`.
10. Write a statement that uses a pseudorandom number to assign a value of 1 through 6 to a variable `die`, where each number is equally likely. Assume the declaration `Random my_random;`.

Answers to Quick-Check Exercises

1. *first, first*
2. stack
3. queue
4. `q.front_index` is 0; `q.rear_index` is 4.

5. q.rear_index
   q.front_index

%
*
–
&
#
\

q.front_index is 1; q.rear_index is 0.

6. '*', '%'

7. For insertion: back_of_queue->next = new Node(item, NULL);
   To disconnect the node to be removed: front_of_queue = front_of_queue->next;

8. a. Circular array
   b. Single-linked list
   c. Deque

9. if (my_random.next_double() < 0.5)
      coin_flip = "heads";
   else
      coin_flip = "tails";

10. die = 1 + 6 * my_random.next_int();

Review Questions

1. Show the effect of each of the following operations on queue q. Assume that y (type **char**) contains the character '&'. What are the final values of x and success (type **bool**) and the contents of queue q?

   ```
   queue<char> q;
   bool success = true;
   char x;
   q.push('+');
   x = q.pop();
   x = q.pop();
   success = true;
   q.push('(');
   q.push(y);
   x = q.pop();
   success = true;
   ```

2. Write a new queue function called move_to_rear that moves the element currently at the front of the queue to the rear of the queue. The element that was second in line will be the new front element. Do this using functions push, front, and pop.

3. Answer Question 2 without using functions push or pop for a single-linked list implementation of queue. You will need to manipulate the queue internal data fields directly.

4. Answer Question 2 without using functions push or pop for a circular array implementation of queue. You will need to manipulate the queue internal data fields directly.

5. Write a new queue function called move_to_front that moves the element at the rear of the queue to the front of the queue, while the other queue elements maintain their relative positions behind the old front element. Do this using functions push, front, and pop.

6. Answer Question 5 without using push and pop for a single-linked list implementation of the queue.

7. Answer Question 5 without using functions push or pop for a circular array implementation of the queue.

Programming Projects

1. Complete the definition file for class KW::queue by providing declarations for the copy constructor, assignment operator, destructor, and swap member function. Also define a specialization for the swap function following the class definition. Implement these operators as needed in files Linked_Queue.tc and Array_Queue.tc. Test your industrial-strength queue by adding extra operations to Maintain_Queue such as calls to destroy the queue and copy the queue.

2. Redo Project 6 from Chapter 5, assuming that widgets are shipped using a first-in, first-out inventory system.

3. Complete the implementation of the CArray class and the deque class.

4. Write a program that simulates the operation of a busy airport that has only two runways to handle all takeoffs and landings. You may assume that each takeoff or landing takes 15 minutes to complete. One runway request is made during each five-minute time interval, and the likelihood of a landing request is the same as for a takeoff request. Priority is given to planes requesting a landing. If a request cannot be honored, it is added to a takeoff or landing queue.

    Your program should simulate 120 minutes of activity at the airport. Each request for runway clearance should be time-stamped and added to the appropriate queue. The output from your program should include the final queue contents, the number of takeoffs completed, the number of landings completed, and the average number of minutes spent in each queue.

5. An operating system assigns jobs to print queues based on the number of pages to be printed (less than 10 pages, less than 20 pages, or more than 20 pages but less than 50 pages). You may assume that the system printers are able to print 10 pages per minute. Smaller print jobs are printed before larger print jobs, and print jobs of the same priority are queued up in the order in which they are received. The system administrators would like to compare the time required to process a set of print jobs using 1, 2, or 3 system printers.

    Write a program that simulates processing 100 print jobs of varying lengths using 1, 2, or 3 printers. Assume that a print request is made every minute and that the number of pages to print varies from 1 to 50 pages.

    The output from your program should indicate the order in which the jobs were received, the order in which they were printed, and the time required to process the set of print jobs. If more than one printer is being used, indicate which printer each job was printed on.

6. Write a menu-driven program that uses an array of queues to keep track of a group of executives as they are transferred from one department to another, get paid, or become unemployed. Executives within a department are paid based on their seniority, with the person who has been in the department the longest receiving the most money. Each person in the department receives $1000 in salary for each person in her department having less seniority than she has. Persons who are unemployed receive no compensation.

    Your program should be able to process the following set of commands:

Join *<person> <department>*	*<person>* is added to *<department>*.
Quit *<person>*	*<person>* is removed from his or her department.
Change *<person> <department>*	*<person>* is moved from old department to *<department>*.
Payroll	Each executive's salary is computed and displayed by department in decreasing order of seniority.

Hint: You might want to include a table that contains each executive's name and information and the location of the queue that contains his or her name, to make searching more efficient.

7. Simulate the operation of a bank. Customers enter the bank, and there are one or more tellers. If a teller is free, that teller serves the customer. Otherwise the customer enters the queue and waits until a teller is free. Your program should accept the following inputs:

   - The arrival rate for the customers
   - The average processing time
   - The number of tellers

   Use your program to determine how many tellers are required for a given arrival rate and average processing time.

8. Simulate a checkout area of a supermarket consisting of one super-express counter, two express counters, and num_std_lines standard counters. All customers with num_super or fewer items proceed to a super-express counter with the fewest customers, unless there is a free express or regular line, and those with between num_super and num_exp proceed to the express counter with the shortest line unless there is a free standard line. Customers with more than num_exp go to the standard counter with the shortest standard line.

   The number of items bought will be a random number in the range 1 to max_items. The time to process a customer is 5 seconds per item.

   Calculate the following statistics:

   - Average waiting time for each of the lines
   - Overall average waiting time
   - Maximum length of each line
   - Number of customers per hour for each line and overall
   - Number of items processed per hour for each line and overall
   - Average free time of each counter
   - Overall free time

   Note: The average waiting time for a line is the total of the customer waiting times divided by the number of customers. A customer's waiting time is the time from when he (or she) enters the queue for a given checkout line until the checkout processing begins. If the customer can find a free line, then the wait time is zero.

   Your program should read the following data:

num_super	The number of items allowed in the super-express line.
num_exp	The number of items allowed in the express line.
num_std_lines	The number of standard lines.
arrival_rate	The arrival rate of customers per hour.
max_items	The maximum number of items.
max_sim_time	The simulation time.

It may be that some lines do not get any business. In that case you must be sure, in calculating the average, not to divide by zero.

Recursion

Chapter Objectives

- ◆ To understand how to think recursively
- ◆ To learn how to trace a recursive function
- ◆ To learn how to write recursive algorithms and functions for searching arrays
- ◆ To understand how to use recursion to solve the Towers of Hanoi problem
- ◆ To understand how to use recursion to process two-dimensional images
- ◆ To learn how to apply backtracking to solve search problems such as finding a path through a maze

This chapter introduces a programming technique called *recursion* and shows you how to think recursively. You can use recursion to solve many kinds of programming problems that would be very difficult to conceptualize and solve without recursion. Computer scientists in the field of artificial intelligence (AI) often use recursion to write programs that exhibit intelligent behavior: playing games such as chess, proving mathematical theorems, recognizing patterns, and so on.

In the beginning of the chapter you will be introduced to recursive thinking and how to design a recursive algorithm and prove that it is correct. You will also learn how to trace a recursive function and use activation frames for this purpose.

Recursive algorithms and functions can be used to perform common mathematical operations such as computing a factorial or a greatest common divisor. Recursion can be used to process familiar data structures such as strings, arrays, and linked lists and to design a very efficient array search technique called binary search.

Recursion can be used to solve a variety of other problems. The case studies in this chapter use recursion to solve a game, to search for "blobs" in a two-dimensional image, and to find a path through a maze.

7.1 Recursive Thinking

Recursion is a problem-solving approach that can be used to generate simple solutions to certain kinds of problems that would be difficult to solve in other ways. In a recursive algorithm the original problem is split into one or more simpler versions of itself. For example, if the solution to the original problem involved n items, recursive thinking might split it into two problems: one involving $n - 1$ items and one involving just a single item. Then the problem with $n - 1$ items could be split again into one involving $n - 2$ items and one involving just a single item, and so on. If the solution to all the one-item problems is "trivial," we can build up the solution to the original problem from the solutions to the simpler problems.

As an example of how this might work, consider a collection of nested wooden figures as shown in Figure 7.1. If you wanted to write an algorithm to "process" this collection in some way (such as counting the figures or painting a face on each figure), you would have difficulty doing it, because you don't know how many objects are in the nest. But you could use recursion to solve the problem in the following way:

Recursive Algorithm to Process Nested Figures

1. **if** there is one figure in the nest
2.   Do whatever is required to the figure.
    else
3.   Do whatever is required to the outer figure in the nest.
4.   Process the nest of figures inside the outer figure in the same way.

In this recursive algorithm, the solution is trivial if there is only one figure: Perform Step 2. If there is more than one figure, perform Step 3 to process the outer figure. Step 4 is the recursive operation—recursively process the nest of figures inside the outer figure. This nest will, of course, have one less figure than before, so it is a simpler version of the original problem.

As another example, let's consider searching for a target value in an array. Assume that the array elements are sorted and are in increasing order. A recursive approach, which we will study in detail in Section 7.3, involves replacing the problem of searching an array of n elements with one of searching an array of $n/2$ elements. How do we do that? We compare the target value to the value of the element in the middle of the sorted array. If there is a match, we have found the target. If not, based on the result of the comparison, we search either the elements that come before the middle one or the elements that come after the middle one. So we have replaced the problem of searching an array with n elements to one that involves searching a smaller array with only $n/2$ elements. The recursive algorithm follows.

Recursive Algorithm to Search an Array

1.   **if** the array is empty
2.   Return −1 as the search result.
     else if the middle element matches the target
3.   Return the subscript of the middle element as the result.
     else if the target is less than the middle element
4.   Recursively search the array elements before the middle element and return the result.
     else
5.   Recursively search the array elements after the middle element and return the result.

The condition in Step 1 is true when there are no elements left to search. Step 2 returns −1 to indicate that the search failed. Step 3 executes when the middle element matches the target. Otherwise, we recursively apply the search algorithm (Steps 4 and 5), thereby searching a smaller array (approximately half the size), and return the result. For each recursive search, the region of the array being searched will be different, so the middle element will also be different.

The two recursive algorithms we showed so far follow this general approach:

General Recursive Algorithm

1.   **if** the problem can be solved directly for the current value of n
2.   Solve it.
     else
3.   Recursively apply the algorithm to one or more problems involving smaller values of n.
4.   Combine the solutions to the smaller problems to get the solution to the original.

Step 1 involves a test for what is called the *base case*: the value of *n* for which the problem can be solved easily. Step 3 is the *recursive case*, because there we recursively apply the algorithm. Because the value of *n* for each recursive case is smaller than the original value of *n*, each recursive case makes progress towards the base case. Whenever a split occurs, we revisit Step 1 for each new problem to see whether it is a base case or a recursive case.

Steps to Design a Recursive Algorithm

From what we have seen so far, we can summarize the characteristics of a recursive solution:

- There must be at least one case (the base case), for a small value of *n*, that can be solved directly.
- A problem of a given size (say, *n*) can be split into one or more smaller versions of the same problem (the recursive case).

Therefore, to design a recursive algorithm, we must

- Recognize the base case and provide a solution to it.
- Devise a strategy to split the problem into smaller versions of itself. Each recursive case must make progress toward the base case.
- Combine the solutions to the smaller problems in such a way that each larger problem is solved correctly.

Next we look at a recursive algorithm for a common programming problem. We will also provide a C++ function that solves this problem. All of the functions in this section and in the next will be found in file `Recursive_Functions.cpp` on this textbook's Web site.

EXAMPLE 7.1 Let's see how we could write our own recursive function for finding string length. How would you go about doing this? If there is a special character that marks the end of a string, then you can count all the characters that precede this special character. But if there is no special character, you might try a recursive approach. The base case is an empty string—its length is 0. For the recursive case, consider that each string has two parts: the first character and the "rest of the string." If you can find the length of the "rest of the string," you can then add 1 (for the first character) to get the length of the larger string. For example, the length of `"abcde"` is 1 + the length of `"bcde"`.

Recursive Algorithm for Finding the Length of a String

1. **if** the string is empty (has no characters)
2.   The length is 0.
    else
3.   The length is 1 plus the length of the string that excludes the first character.

We can implement this algorithm as a function with a `string` argument. The test for the base case is a string that contains no characters (`""`). In that case, the length is 0. In the recursive case,

```
return 1 + size(str.substr(1));
```

the function call `str.substr(1)` returns a string containing all characters in string `str` except for the character at position 0. Then we call function `size` again with this substring as its argument. The function result is one more than the value returned from the next call to `size`. Each time we reenter function `size`, the **if** statement executes with `str` referencing a string containing all but the first character in the previous call. Function `size` is called a *recursive function* because it calls itself.

```
/** Recursive function size (in Recursive_Functions.cpp).
    @param str The string
    @return The length of the string
*/
int size(string str) {
  if (str == "")
    return 0;
  else
    return 1 + size(str.substr(1));
}
```

EXAMPLE 7.2   Function `print_chars` is a recursive function that displays each character in its string argument on a separate line. In the base case (an empty string), the function return occurs immediately and nothing is displayed. In the recursive case, `print_chars` displays the first character of its string argument and then calls itself to display the characters in the rest of the string. If the initial call is `print_chars("hat")`, the function will display the lines

```
h
a
t
```

Unlike function `size` in Example 7.1, `print_chars` is a **void** function. However, both functions follow the format for the general recursive algorithm shown earlier.

```
/** Recursive function print_chars (in Recursive_Functions.cpp).
    post: The argument string is displayed, one character per line.
    @param str The string
*/
void print_chars(string str) {
  if (str == "") {
    return;
  } else {
    cout << str.at(0) << endl;
    print_chars(str.substr(1));
  }
}
```

You get an interesting result if you reverse the two statements in the recursive case.

```
/** Recursive function print_chars_reverse (in Recursive_Functions.cpp).
    post: The argument string is displayed in reverse,
          one character per line.
    @param str The string
*/
void print_chars_reverse(string str) {
  if (str == "") {
    return;
  } else {
    print_chars_reverse(str.substr(1));
    cout << str.at(0) << endl;
  }
}
```

Function `print_chars_reverse` calls itself to display the rest of the string before displaying the first character in the current string argument. The effect will be to delay displaying the first character in the current string until all characters in the rest of the string are displayed. Consequently, the characters in the string will be displayed in reverse order. If the initial call is `print_chars_reverse("hat")`, the function will display the lines

```
t
a
h
```

Proving That a Recursive Function Is Correct

To prove that a recursive function is correct, you must verify that you have performed correctly the design steps listed earlier. You can use a technique that mathematicians use to prove that a theorem is true for all values of n. A *proof by induction* works the following way:

- Prove the theorem is true for the base case of (usually) $n = 0$ or $n = 1$.
- Show that if the theorem is assumed true for n, then it must be true for $n + 1$.

We can extend the notion of an inductive proof and use it as the basis for proving that a recursive algorithm is correct. To do this:

- Verify that the base case is recognized and solved correctly.
- Verify that each recursive case makes progress toward the base case; that is, any new problems generated are smaller versions of the original problem.
- Verify that if all smaller problems are solved correctly, then the original problem is also solved correctly.

If you can show that your algorithm satisfies these three requirements, then your algorithm will be correct.

EXAMPLE 7.3   To prove that the `size` function is correct, we know that the base case is an empty string, and its length is correctly set at 0. The recursive case involves a call to `size` with a smaller string, so it is making progress toward the base case. Finally, if we know the length of the rest of the string, adding 1 gives us the length of the longer string consisting of the first character and the rest of the string.

Tracing a Recursive Function

Figure 7.2 traces the execution of the function call size("ace"). The diagram shows a sequence of recursive calls to function size. After returning from each call to size, we complete execution of the statement return 1 + size(...); by adding 1 to the result so far and then returning from the current call. The final result, 3, would be returned from the original call. The arrow alongside each word **return** shows which call to size is associated with that result. For example, 0 is the result of the function call size(""). After adding 1, we return 1, which is the result of the call size("e"), and so on. This process of returning from the recursive calls and computing the partial results is called *unwinding the recursion*.

The Stack and Activation Frames

You can also trace a recursive function by showing what C++ does when one function calls another. C++ maintains a stack, on which it saves new information in the form of an *activation frame*. The activation frame contains storage for the function arguments and any local variables as well as the return address of the instruction that called the function. Whenever a function is called, C++ pushes a new activation frame onto the stack and saves this information on the stack. This is done whether the function is recursive or not.

The left side of Figure 7.3 shows the activation frames on the stack after the last recursive call (corresponding to size("")) resulting from an initial call to size("ace"). At any given time, only the frame at the top of the stack is accessible, so its argument values will be used when the function instructions execute. When the **return** statement executes, control will be passed to the instruction at the specified return address, and this frame will be popped from the stack (Figure 7.3, right). The activation frame corresponding to the next-to-last call (size("e")) is now accessible.

FIGURE 7.2
Trace of size("ace")

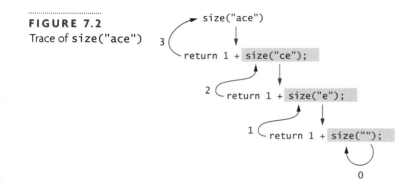

FIGURE 7.3
Stack Before and After Removal of Frame for `size("")`

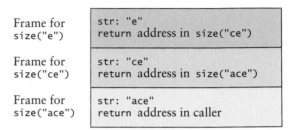

Frame for size("")	str: "" return address in size("e")
Frame for size("e")	str: "e" return address in size("ce")
Frame for size("ce")	str: "ce" return address in size("ace")
Frame for size("ace")	str: "ace" return address in caller

Run-time stack after all calls

Frame for size("e")	str: "e" return address in size("ce")
Frame for size("ce")	str: "ce" return address in size("ace")
Frame for size("ace")	str: "ace" return address in caller

Run-time stack after return from last call

You can think of the stack for a sequence of calls to a recursive function as an office tower in which an employee on each floor has the same list of instructions. The employee in the bottom office carries out part of the instructions on the list, calls the employee in the office above, and is put on hold. The employee in the office above starts to carry out the list of instructions, calls the employee in the next higher office, is put on hold, and so on. When the employee on the top floor is called, that

FIGURE 7.4
Trace of `size("ace")`
Using Activation Frames

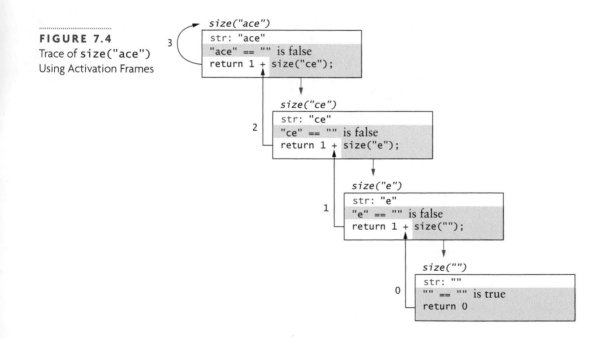

employee carries out the list of instructions to completion and then returns an answer to the employee below. The employee below then resumes carrying out the list of instructions and returns an answer to the employee on the next lower floor, and so on, until an answer is returned to the employee in the bottom office, who then resumes carrying out the list of instructions.

To make the flow of control easier to visualize, we will draw the activation frames from the top of the page down (see Figure 7.4). For example, the activation frame at the top, which would actually be at the bottom of the stack, represents the first call to the recursive function. The downward-pointing arrows connect each statement that calls a function with the frame for that particular execution of the function. The upward-pointing arrows show the return point from each lower-level call with the value returned alongside the arrow. For each frame, the return point is to the addition operator in the statement return 1 + size(...); For each frame, the code in the color screen is executed prior to the creation of the next activation frame; the rest of the code shown is executed after the return.

EXERCISES FOR SECTION 7.1

SELF-CHECK

1. Trace the execution of the call mystery(4) for the following recursive function using the technique shown in Figure 7.2. What does this function do?
```
int mystery(int n) {
  if (n == 0)
    return 0;
  else
    return n * n + mystery(n - 1);
}
```
2. Answer Exercise 1 using activation frames.
3. Trace the execution of print_chars("tic") (Example 7.2) using activation frames.
4. Trace the execution of print_chars_reverse("toc") using activation frames.
5. Prove that the print_chars function is correct.

PROGRAMMING

1. Write a recursive function to_number that forms the integer sum of all digit characters in a string. For example, the result of to_number("3ac4") would be 7. *Hint:* If next is a digit character ('0' through '9'), function is_digit(next) in header <cctype> will return true.
2. Write a recursive function repeater that returns a string with each character in its argument repeated. For example, if the string passed to repeater is "hello", repeater will return the string "hheelllloo".

7.2 Recursive Definitions of Mathematical Formulas

Mathematicians often use recursive definitions of formulas. These definitions lead very naturally to recursive algorithms.

EXAMPLE 7.4   The factorial of *n*, or *n*!, is defined as follows:

$$0! = 1$$

$$n! = n \times (n - 1)!$$

The first formula identifies the base case: *n* equal to 0. The second formula is a recursive definition. It leads to the following algorithm for computing *n*!.

Recursive Algorithm for Computing *n*!

1.   **if** *n* equals 0
2.   *n*! is 1.

      else
3. $n! = n \times (n - 1)!$

To verify the correctness of this algorithm, we see that the base case is solved correctly (0! is 1). The recursive case makes progress toward the base case, because it involves the calculation of a smaller factorial. Also, if we can calculate $(n - 1)!$, the recursive case gives us the correct formula for calculating *n*!.

The recursive function follows. The statement

```
return n * factorial(n - 1);
```

implements the recursive case. Each time `factorial` calls itself, the function body executes again with a different argument value. An initial function call such as `factorial(4)` will generate four recursive calls, as shown in Figure 7.5.

```
/** Recursive factorial function (in Recursive_Functions.cpp).
    pre: n >= 0
    @param n The integer whose factorial is being computed
    @return n!
*/
int factorial(int n) {
  if (n == 0)
    return 1;
  else
    return n * factorial(n - 1);
}
```

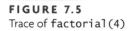

FIGURE 7.5
Trace of `factorial(4)`

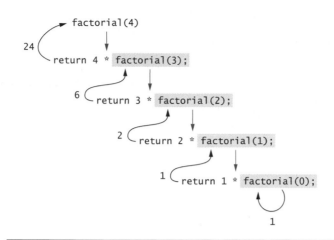

 PITFALL

Infinite Recursion and Stack Overflow

If you call function `factorial` with a negative argument, you will see that the recursion does not terminate. It will continue forever, because the stopping case, n equals 0, can never be reached, as n gets more negative with each call. For example, if the original value of n is –4, you will make function calls `factorial(-5)`, `factorial(-6)`, `factorial(-7)`, and so on. You should make sure that your recursive functions are constructed so that a stopping case is always reached. One way to prevent the infinite recursion in this case would be to change the terminating condition to n <= 0. However, this would incorrectly return a value of 1 for n! if n is negative. A better solution would be to throw an `invalid_argument` exception if n is negative.

If your program does not terminate properly, you may see an extremely long display on the console (if the console is being used to display its results). However, if the recursive call occurs before any output is displayed, you will see no output. Eventually you will get a run-time error because there is no more memory available for your program to execute any more function calls.

EXAMPLE 7.5   Let's develop a recursive function that raises a number x to a power n. You can raise a number to a power that is greater than 0 by repeatedly multiplying that number by itself. So if we know x^k, we can get x^{k+1} by multiplying x^k by x. The recursive definition is

$$x^n = x \times x^{n-1}$$

This gives us the first recursive case. You should know that any number raised to the power 0 is 1, so the base case is

$$x^0 = 1$$

What happens if n is negative? In this case, the answer can be determined by calling the recursive function with $-n$ (a positive integer) as the argument and dividing 1.0 by this result. So there are two recursive cases, as follows.

$$x^n = 1.0 / x^{-n}, \text{ for } n < 0$$

Recursive Algorithm for Calculating x^n

1. **if** n is 0
2.   The result is 1.
    else if n is greater than 0
3.   The result is $x \times x^{n-1}$.
    else if n is less than 0
4.   The result is $1.0 / x^{-n}$.

We show the function next.

```cpp
/** Recursive power function (in Recursive_Functions.cpp).
    @param x The number being raised to a power
    @param n The exponent
    @return x raised to the power n
*/
double power(double x, int n) {
  if (n == 0)
    return 1;
  else if (n > 0)
    return x * power(x, n - 1);
  else
    return 1.0 / power(x, -n);
}
```

EXAMPLE 7.6   The greatest common divisor (gcd) of two numbers is the largest integer that divides both numbers. For example, the gcd of 20, 15 is 5; the gcd of 36, 24 is 12; the gcd of 36, 18 is 18. The mathematician Euclid devised an algorithm for finding the greatest common divisor of two integers, m and n, based on the following definition:

Definition of gcd(m, n) for $m > n$

gcd(m, n) = n if n is a divisor of m

gcd(m, n) = gcd(n, m % n) if n isn't a divisor of m

This definition states that gcd(m, n) is n if n divides m. This is correct, because no number larger than n can divide n. Otherwise, the definition states that gcd(m, n) is the same as gcd(n, m % n), where m % n is the integer remainder of m divided by n. Therefore, gcd(20, 15) is the same as gcd(15, 5), or 5, because 5 divides 15. This recursive definition leads naturally to a recursive algorithm.

Recursive Algorithm for Calculating gcd(*m, n*) for *m* > *n*

1.   **if** n is a divisor of m
2.   The result is n.

      else
3.   The result is gcd($n, m \% n$).

To verify that this is correct, we need to make sure that there is a base case and that it is solved correctly. The base case is "n is a divisor of m." If so, the solution is n (n is the greatest common divisor), which is correct. Does the recursive case make progress toward the base case? It must, because both arguments in each recursive call are smaller than in the previous call, and the new second argument is always smaller than the new first argument ($m \% n$ must be less than n). Eventually a divisor will be found or the second argument will become 1. Since 1 is a base case (1 divides every integer), we have verified that the recursive case makes progress toward the base case.

Next, we show function gcd. Notice that the function introduces a new recursive case that transposes m and n if the initial value of n happens to be larger than m:

```
else if (m < n)
  return gcd(n, m);
```

This clause allows us to handle arguments that initially are not in the correct sequence.

```
/** Recursive gcd function (in Recursive_Functions.cpp).
    pre: m > 0 and n > 0
    @param m The larger number
    @param n The smaller number
    @return Greatest common divisor of m and n
*/
int gcd(int m, int n) {
  if (m % n == 0)
    return n;
  else if (m < n)
    return gcd(n, m);   // Transpose arguments.
  else
    return gcd(n, m % n);
}
```

Recursion Versus Iteration

You may have noticed that there are some similarities between recursion and iteration. Both techniques enable us to repeat a compound statement. In iteration, a loop repetition condition in the loop header determines whether we repeat the loop body or exit from the loop. We repeat the loop body while the repetition condition is true. In recursion, the condition usually tests for a base case. We stop the recursion when the base case is reached (the condition is true), and we execute the function body again when the condition is false. We can always write an iterative solution to a problem that is solvable by recursion. However, the recursive algorithm may be easier to conceptualize and may, therefore, lead to a function that is easier to write, read, and debug—all of which are very desirable attributes of code.

Tail Recursion or Last-Line Recursion

Most of the recursive algorithms and functions you have seen so far are examples of *tail recursion* or *last-line recursion*. In these algorithms, there is a single recursive call and it is the last line of the function. An example is the `factorial` function in Example 7.4.

```
int factorial(int n) {
  if (n == 0)
    return 1;
  else
    return n * factorial(n - 1);
}
```

It is a straightforward process to turn such a function into an iterative one, replacing the **if** statement with a loop, as we show next.

EXAMPLE 7.7   An iterative version of the `factorial` function follows.

```
/** Iterative factorial function.
    pre: n >= 0
    @param n The integer whose factorial is being computed
    @return n!
*/
int factorial_iter(int n) {
  int result = 1;
  for (int k = 1; k <= n; k++)
    result = result * k;
  return result;
}
```

Efficiency of Recursion

The iterative function `factorial_iter` multiplies all integers between 1 and n to compute n!. It may be slightly less readable than the recursive function `factorial`, but not much. In terms of efficiency, both algorithms are $O(n)$, because the number of loop repetitions or recursive calls increases linearly with n. However, the iterative version is probably faster, because the overhead for a function call and return would be greater than the overhead for loop repetition (testing and incrementing the loop control variable). The difference, though, would not be significant. Generally, if it is easier to conceptualize an algorithm using recursion, then you should code it as a recursive function, because the reduction in efficiency does not outweigh the advantage of readable code that is easy to debug.

A second factor to consider when discussing efficiency is memory usage. A recursive version can require significantly more memory that an iterative version because of the need to save local variables and parameters on a stack. The next example illustrates a simple recursive solution that is very inefficient in terms of time and memory utilization.

EXAMPLE 7.8   The Fibonacci numbers fib_n are a sequence of numbers that were invented to model the growth of a rabbit colony. Therefore, we would expect this sequence to grow very quickly, and it does. For example, fib_{10} is 55, fib_{15} is 610, fib_{20} is 6,765, and fib_{25} is 75,025 (that's a lot of rabbits!). The definition of this sequence follows:

$$fib_1 = 1$$
$$fib_2 = 1$$
$$fib_n = fib_{n-1} + fib_{n-2}$$

Next, we show a function that calculates the nth Fibonacci number. The last line codes the recursive case.

```
/** Recursive function to calculate Fibonacci numbers
    (in Recursive_Functions.cpp).
    pre: n >= 1.
    @param n The position of the Fibonacci number being calculated
    @return The Fibonacci number
*/
int fibonacci(int n) {
  if (n <= 2)
    return 1;
  else
    return fibonacci(n - 1) + fibonacci(n - 2);
}
```

Unfortunately, this solution is very inefficient because of multiple calls to `fibonacci` with the same argument. For example, calculating `fibonacci(5)` results in calls to `fibonacci(4)` and `fibonacci(3)`. Calculating `fibonacci(4)` results in calls to `fibonacci(3)` (second call) and also `fibonacci(2)`. Calculating `fibonacci(3)` twice results in two more calls to `fibonacci(2)` (three calls total), and so on (see Figure 7.6).

Because of the redundant function calls, the time required to calculate `fibonacci(n)` increases exponentially with n. For example, if n is 100, there are approximately 2^{100} activation frames. This number is approximately 10^{30}. If you could process one million activation frames per second, it would still take 10^{24} seconds, which is approximately 3×10^{16} years. However, it is possible to write recursive functions for computing Fibonacci numbers that have $O(n)$ performance. We show one such function next.

```
/** Recursive O(n) function to calculate Fibonacci numbers
    (in Recursive_Functions.cpp).
    pre: n >= 1
    @param fib_current The current Fibonacci number
    @param fib_previous The previous Fibonacci number
    @param n The count of Fibonacci numbers left to calculate
    @return The value of the Fibonacci number calculated so far
*/
int fibo(int fib_current, int fib_previous, int n) {
  if (n == 1)
    return fib_current;
  else
    return fibo(fib_current + fib_previous, fib_current, n - 1);
}
```

FIGURE 7.6
Function Calls Resulting
from fibonacci(5)

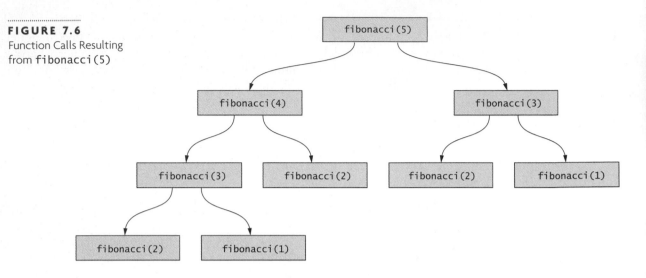

Unlike function fibonacci, function fibo does not follow naturally from the recursive definition of the Fibonacci sequence. In function fibo the first argument is always the current Fibonacci number, and the second argument is the previous one. We update these values for each new call. When n is 1 (the base case), we have calculated the required Fibonacci number, so we return its value (fib_current). The recursive case,

```
return fibo(fib_current + fib_previous, fib_current, n - 1);
```

passes the sum of the current Fibonacci number and the previous Fibonacci number to the first parameter (the new value of fib_current); it passes the current Fibonacci number to the second parameter (the new value of fib_previous); and it decrements n, making progress toward the base case.

To start this function executing, we need the following *wrapper function*, which is not recursive. This function is called a wrapper function because its only purpose it to call the recursive function and return its result. Its parameter, n, specifies the position in the Fibonacci sequence of the number we want to calculate. It calls the recursive function fibo, passing the first Fibonacci number as its first argument and n as its third.

```
/** Wrapper function for calculating Fibonacci numbers
    (in Recursive_Functions.cpp).
    pre: n >= 1
    @param n The position of the desired Fibonacci number
    @return The value of the nth Fibonacci number
*/
int fibonacci_start(int n) {
  return fibo(1, 0, n);
}
```

Figure 7.7 traces the execution of the function call fibonacci_start(5). Notice that the first arguments for the function calls to fibo form the sequence 1, 1, 2, 3, 5, which is the Fibonacci sequence. Also notice that the result of the first return (5) is simply passed on by each successive return. That is because the recursive case does not specify any operations other than returning the result of the next call.

FIGURE 7.7
Trace of
`fibonacci_start(5)`

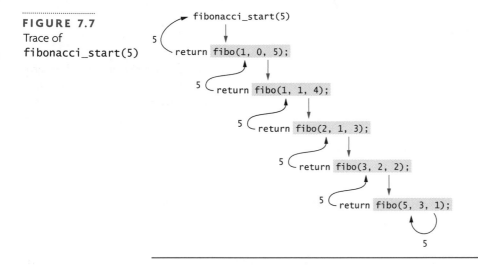

EXERCISES FOR SECTION 7.2

SELF-CHECK

1. Does the recursive algorithm for raising x to the power n work for negative values of n? Does it work for negative values of x? Indicate what happens if it is called for each of these cases.

2. Trace the execution of `fibonacci_start(5)` using activation frames.

3. For each of the following function calls, show the argument values in the activation frames that would be pushed onto the stack.

   a. `gcd(6, 21)`
   b. `factorial(5)`
   c. `gcd(31, 7)`
   d. `fibonacci(6)`
   e. `fibonacci_start(7)`

4. See for what value of n function `fibonacci` begins to take a long time to run on your computer (over 1 minute). Compare the performance of `fibonacci_start` and `fibo` for this same value.

PROGRAMMING

1. Write a recursive function for raising x to the power n that works for negative n as well as positive n.

2. Modify the `factorial` function to throw an `invalid_argument` exception if n is negative.

3. Write a program that has an iterative function for calculating Fibonacci numbers. Use an array that saves each Fibonacci number as it is calculated. Your function should take advantage of the existence of this array so that subsequent calls to the function simply retrieve the desired Fibonacci number if it has been calculated. If not, start with the largest Fibonacci number in the array rather than repeating all calculations.

7.3 Recursive Search

Searching a vector is an activity that can be accomplished using recursion. The simplest way to search a vector is a *linear search*. In a linear search, we examine one vector element at a time, starting with the first element or the last element, to see whether it matches the target. The vector element we are seeking may be anywhere in the vector, so on average we will examine $n/2$ items to find the target if it is in the vector. If it is not in the vector, we will have to examine all n elements (the worst case). This means linear search is an $O(n)$ algorithm.

Design of a Recursive Linear Search Algorithm

Let's consider how we might write a recursive algorithm that returns the subscript of a target item.

The base case would be an empty vector. If the vector is empty, the target cannot be there, so the result should be –1. If the vector is not empty, we will assume that we can examine just the first element of the vector, so another base case would be when the first vector element matches the target. If so, the result should be the subscript of the first vector element.

The recursive step would be to search the rest of the vector, excluding the first element. So our recursive step should search for the target starting with the current second vector element, which will become the first element in the next execution of the recursive step. The algorithm follows.

Algorithm for Recursive Linear Search

1.   **if** the vector is empty
2.   The result is –1.
    else if the first element matches the target
3.   The result is the subscript of the first element.
    else
4.   Search the vector excluding the first element and return the result.

Implementation of Linear Search

The following function, `linear_search`, shows the linear search algorithm for a vector of type `Item_Type`.

```
/** Recursive linear search function (in linear_search.h).
    @param items The vector being searched
    @param target The item being searched for
    @param pos_first The position of the current first element
    @return The subscript of target if found; otherwise -1
*/
template<typename Item_Type>
  int linear_search(const std::vector<Item_Type>& items,
                    const Item_Type& target, size_t pos_first) {
```

```
      if (pos_first == items.size())
        return -1;
      else if (target == items[pos_first])
        return pos_first;
      else
        return linear_search(items, target, pos_first + 1);
    }
```

The function parameter `pos_first` represents the subscript of the current first element. The first condition tests whether the vector left to search is empty. The condition (`pos_first == items.size()`) is true when the subscript of the current first element is beyond the bounds of the vector. If so, function `linear_search` returns -1. The statement

```
    return linear_search(items, target, pos_first + 1);
```

implements the recursive step; it increments `pos_first` to exclude the current first element from the next search.

To search a `vector<int>` `x` for `target`, you could use the function call

```
    linear_search(x, target, 0)
```

However, since the third argument would always be 0, we can define a nonrecursive wrapper function (also called `linear_search`) that has just two parameters: `items`, and `target`.

```
    /** Wrapper for recursive linear search function (in linear_search.h).
        @param items The vector being searched
        @param target The object being searched for
        @return The subscript of target if found; otherwise -1
    */
    template<typename Item_Type>
      int linear_search(const std::vector<Item_Type>& items,
                        const Item_Type& target) {
      return linear_search(items, target, 0);
    }
```

The sole purpose of this function is to call the recursive function, passing on its arguments with 0 as a third argument, and return its result. This function definition overloads the previous one.

Figure 7.8 traces the execution of the call to `linear_search` in the statement,

```
    int pos_hello = linear_search(greetings, string("Hello"));
```

Where the `vector<string>` greetings contains {"Hi", "Hello", "Shalom"}. The value returned to `pos_hello` will be 1.

Design of a Binary Search Algorithm

A second approach to searching is called *binary search*. Binary search can be performed only on a vector (or array) that has been sorted. In binary search, the stopping cases are the same as for linear search:

- When the vector is empty
- When the vector element being examined matches the target

FIGURE 7.8
Trace of `linear_search(greetings, "Hello")`

However, rather than examining the last vector element, binary search compares the "middle" element to the target. If there is a match, it returns the position of the middle element. Otherwise, because the vector has been sorted, we know with certainty which half of the vector must be searched to find the target. We then can exclude the other half of the vector (not just one element as with linear search). The binary search algorithm (first introduced in Section 7.1) follows.

Binary Search Algorithm

1.   **if** the vector is empty
2.   Return −1 as the search result.
     else if the middle element matches the target
3.   Return the subscript of the middle element as the result.
     else if the target is less than the middle element
4.   Recursively search the vector elements before the middle element and return the result.
     else
5.   Recursively search the vector elements after the middle element and return the result.

Figure 7.9 illustrates binary search for a vector with seven elements. The shaded elements are the ones that are being searched each time. The vector element in color is the one that is being compared to the target. In the first call, we compare "Dustin" to "Elliot". Because "Dustin" is smaller, we need to search only the part of the vector before "Elliot" (consisting of just 3 candidates). In the second call, we compare "Dustin" to "Debbie". Because "Dustin" is larger, we need to search only the shaded part of the vector after "Debbie" (consisting of just 1 candidate). In the third call, we compare "Dustin" to "Dustin", and the subscript of "Dustin" (2) is our result. If there were no match at this point (for example, the vector contained "Duncan" instead of "Dustin"), the vector of candidates to search would become an empty array.

Efficiency of Binary Search

Because we eliminate at least half of the elements from consideration with each recursive call, binary search is an $O(\log n)$ algorithm. To verify this, an unsuccessful search of a vector of size 16 could result in our searching vectors of size 16, 8, 4, 2, and 1 to determine that the target was not present. Thus a vector of size 16 requires a total of 5 probes in the worst case (16 is 2^4, so 5 is $\log_2 16 + 1$). If we double the size, we would need to make only 6 probes for a vector of size 32 in the worst case (32 is 2^5, so 6 is $\log_2 32 + 1$). The advantages of binary search become even more apparent for larger vectors. For a vector with 32,768 elements, the maximum num-

FIGURE 7.9
Binary Search for "Dustin"

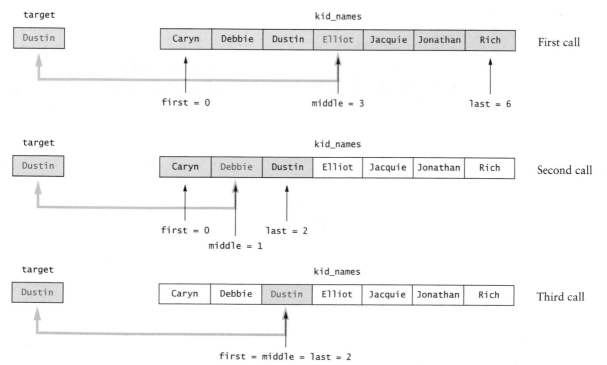

ber of probes required would be 16 ($\log_2$ 32,768 is 15), and if we expand the vector to 65,536 elements, we would increase the number of probes required only to 17.

Implementation of Binary Search

Listing 7.1 shows a recursive implementation of the binary search algorithm and its nonrecursive wrapper function. The parameters `first` and `last` are the subscripts of the first element and last element in the vector being searched. For the initial call to the recursive function from the wrapper function, `first` is 0 and `last` is `size - 1`.

The condition (`first > last`) becomes true when the list of candidates is empty, and -1 is returned. Otherwise, the statement

```
int middle = (first + last) / 2;
```

computes the subscript of the "middle" element in the current vector (midway between `first` and `last`).

Next the condition (`target == items[middle]`) compares the target to the middle element of the vector. If they match, the subscript `middle` is returned. Otherwise, if the condition (`target < items[middle]`) is true, the recursive step

```
return binary_search(items, first, middle - 1, target);
```

returns the result of searching the part of the current vector before the middle item (with subscripts `first` through `middle - 1`). If no conditions are true, the recursive step

```
return binary_search(items, middle + 1, last, target);
```

returns the result of searching the part of the current vector after the middle item (with subscripts `middle + 1` through `last`).

....

LISTING 7.1
Functions `binary_search`

```
/** Recursive binary search function (in binary_search.h).
    @param items The vector being searched
    @param first The subscript of the first element
    @param last The subscript of the last element
    @param target The item being searched for
    @return The subscript of target if found; otherwise -1
*/
template<typename Item_Type>
  int binary_search(const std::vector<Item_Type>& items,
                    int first, int last,
                    const Item_Type& target) {
  if (first > last)
    return -1;      // Base case for unsuccessful search.
  else {
    int middle = (first + last) / 2;  // Next probe index.
    if (target == items[middle])
      return middle;   // Base case for successful search.
    else if (target < items[middle])
      return binary_search(items, first, middle - 1, target);
    else
      return binary_search(items, middle + 1, last, target);
  }
}
```

```
/** Wrapper for recursive binary search function (in binary_search.h).
    @param items The vector being searched
    @param target The item being searched for
    @return The subscript of target if found; otherwise -1
*/
template<typename Item_Type>
  int binary_search(const std::vector<Item_Type>& items,
                    const Item_Type& target) {
    return binary_search(items, 0, items.size() - 1, target);
}
```

Figure 7.10 traces the execution of binary_search for the vector shown in Figure 7.9. The parameter items always references the same vector; however, the pool of candidates changes with each call.

FIGURE 7.10
Trace of binary_search(kid_names, "Dustin")

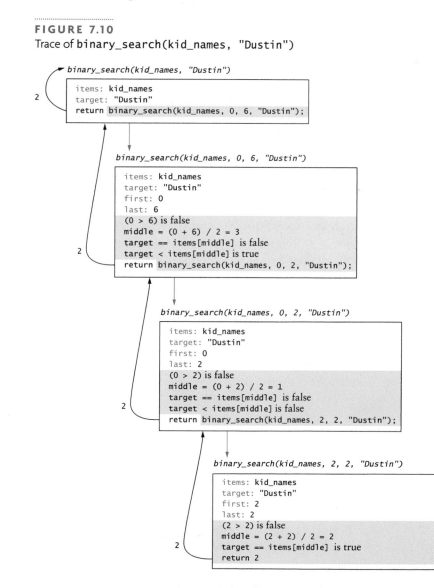

Testing Binary Search

To test the binary search algorithm, you must test vectors with an even number of elements and vectors with an odd number of elements. You must also test vectors that have duplicate items. Each vector must be tested for the following cases:

- The target is the element at each position of the vector, starting with the first position and ending with the last position. The purpose of this test is to ensure that all elements that are in the vector can be found.
- The target is less than the smallest vector element. The purpose of this test is to ensure that the function does not fall off the left end of the vector.
- The target is greater than the largest vector element. The purpose of this test is to ensure that the function does not fall off the right end of the vector.
- The target is a value between each pair of items in the vector. The purpose of this test is to ensure that the recursion terminates properly for target values that are between all element pairs in the vector.

EXERCISES FOR SECTION 7.3

SELF-CHECK

1. For the vector shown in Figure 7.9, show the values of first, last, and middle in successive frames when searching for a target of "Rich"; when searching for a target of "Alice"; when searching for a target of "Daryn".
2. How many elements will be compared to target for an unsuccessful binary search in a vector of 1000 items? What is the answer for 2000 items?
3. If there are multiple occurrences of the target item in a vector, what can you say about the subscript value that will be returned by linear_search? Answer the same question for binary_search.

PROGRAMMING

1. Write a recursive algorithm to find the sum of all values stored in a vector of integers.
2. Write a recursive linear search function with a recursive step that finds the last occurrence of a target in a vector, not the first. You will need to modify the linear search function so that the last element of the vector is always tested, not the first.

7.4 Problem Solving with Recursion

In this section we discuss recursive solutions to two problems. Our recursive solutions will break each problem up into multiple smaller versions of the original problem. Both problems are easier to solve using recursion because recursive thinking enables us to split each problem into more manageable subproblems. They would both be much more difficult to solve without recursion.

CASE STUDY   Towers of Hanoi

Problem   You may be familiar with a version of this problem that is sold as a child's puzzle. There is a board with three pegs and three disks of different sizes (see Figure 7.11). The goal of the game is to move the three disks from the peg where they have been placed (largest disk on the bottom, smallest disk on the top) to one of the empty pegs, subject to the following constraints:

- Only the top disk on a peg can be moved to another peg.
- A larger disk cannot be placed on top of a smaller disk.

FIGURE 7.11
Three-Disk Version of Towers of Hanoi

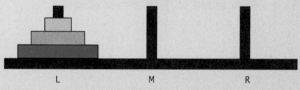

Analysis   We can solve this problem by displaying a list of moves to be made. The problem inputs will be the number of disks to move, the starting peg, the destination peg, and the temporary peg. We will write a program `Towers_Of_Hanoi` that contains a function `show_moves` that builds a string with all the moves.

TABLE 7.1
Inputs and Outputs for Towers of Hanoi Problem

Problem Inputs
Number of disks (an integer)
Letter of starting peg: L (left), M (middle), or R (right)
Letter of destination peg: (L, M, or R), but different from starting peg
Letter of temporary peg: (L, M, or R), but different from starting peg and destination peg
Problem Outputs
A list of moves

Design   We still need to determine a strategy for making a move. If we examine the situation in Figure 7.11 (all three disks on the L peg) we can derive a strategy to solve it. If we can figure out how to move the top two disks to the M peg (a two-disk version of the original problem), we can then place the bottom disk on the R peg (see Figure 7.12). Now all we need to do is move the two disks on the M peg to the R peg. If we can solve both of these two-disk problems, then the three-disk problem is also solved.

Solution to 3-Disk Problem: Move 3 Disks from Peg L to Peg R

1. Move the top two disks from peg L to peg M.
2. Move the bottom disk from peg L to peg R.
3. Move the top two disks from peg M to peg R.

FIGURE 7.12
Towers of Hanoi After the First Two Steps in Solution of the Three-Disk Problem

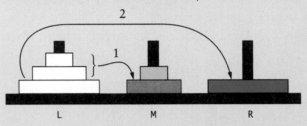

We can split the solution to each two-disk problem into three problems involving single disks. We solve the second two-disk problem next; the solution to the first one (move the top two disks from peg L to peg M) is quite similar.

Solution to 2-Disk Problem: Move Top 2 Disks from Peg M to Peg R

1. Move the top disk from peg M to peg L.
2. Move the bottom disk from peg M to peg R.
3. Move the top disk from peg L to peg R.

In Figure 7.13 we show the pegs after steps 1 and 2. When step 3 is completed, the three pegs will be on peg R.

FIGURE 7.13
Towers of Hanoi After First Two Steps in Solution of Two-Disk Problem

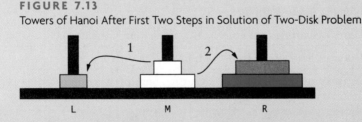

In a similar way, we can split a four-disk problem into two three-disk problems. Figure 7.14 shows the pegs after the top three disks have been moved from peg L to peg M. Because we know how to solve three-disk problems, we can also solve four-disk problems.

Solution to 4-Disk Problem: Move 4 Disks from Peg L to Peg R

1. Move the top three disks from peg L to peg M.
2. Move the bottom disk from peg L to peg R.
3. Move the top three disks from peg M to peg R.

FIGURE 7.14
Towers of Hanoi After the First Two Steps in Solution of the Four-Disk Problem

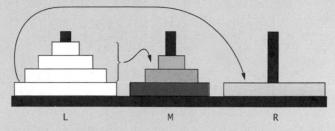

Next, we show a general recursive algorithm for moving *n* disks from one of the three pegs to a different peg.

Recursive Algorithm for *n*-Disk Problem: Move *n* Disks from the Starting Peg to the Destination Peg

1. **if** *n* is 1
2.   Move disk 1 (the smallest disk) from the starting peg to the destination peg.
3. **else**
4.   Move the top *n* − 1 disks from the starting peg to the temporary peg (neither starting nor destination peg).
5.   Move disk *n* (the disk at the bottom) from the starting peg to the destination peg.
6.   Move the top *n* − 1 disks from the temporary peg to the destination peg.

The stopping case is the one-disk problem. The recursive step enables us to split the *n*-disk problem into two (*n* − 1)-disk problems and a single-disk problem. Each problem has a different starting peg and destination peg.

Our recursive function, `show_moves`, will display the solution as a list of disk moves. For each move, we show the number of the disk being moved and its starting and destination pegs. For example, for the two-disk problem shown earlier (move two disks from the middle peg, M, to the right peg, R), the list of moves would be

```
Move disk 1 from peg M to peg L
Move disk 2 from peg M to peg R
Move disk 1 from peg L to peg R
```

The function `show_moves` must have the number of disks, the starting peg, the destination peg, and the temporary peg as its parameters. If there are n disks, the bottom disk has number n (the top disk has number 1). Table 7.2 describes the function required for program `Towers_Of_Hanoi`.

TABLE 7.2
Program `Towers_Of_Hanoi`

Function	Behavior
`void show_moves(int n, char start_peg,` `  char dest_peg, char temp_peg)`	Builds a string containing all moves for a game with n disks on `start_peg` that will be moved to `dest_peg`, using `temp_peg` for temporary storage of disks being moved.

Implementation   Listing 7.2 shows the program `Towers_Of_Hanoi`. In function `show_moves`, the stopping case is a single disk, which is "moved" from the start peg to the destination peg. The recursive step

```
show_moves(n - 1, start_peg, temp_peg, dest_peg);
cout << "Move disk " << n << " from peg " << start_peg
    << " to peg " << dest_peg << "\n";
show_moves(n - 1, temp_peg, dest_peg, start_peg);
```

calls `show_moves` to display the list of moves for the first (n – 1)-disk problem, displays the move required for the bottom disk (disk n), and then calls `show_moves` again to display the list of moves for the second (n – 1)-disk problem.

LISTING 7.2
`Towers_Of_Hanoi.cpp`

```
/** Recursive function for "moving" disks.
    pre: start_peg, dest_peg, temp_peg are different, n >= 1.
    post: displays a list of moves that solve the problem
          of moving n disks from start_peg to dest_peg.
    @param n is the number of disks
    @param start_peg is the starting peg
    @param dest_peg is the destination peg
    @param temp_peg is the temporary peg
    @return A string with all the required disk moves
*/
void show_moves(int n, char start_peg,
                char dest_peg, char temp_peg) {
  if (n == 1)
  {
    cout << "Move disk 1 from peg " << start_peg
        << " to peg " << dest_peg << "\n";
  }
  else
  { // Recursive step
    show_moves(n - 1, start_peg, temp_peg, dest_peg);
    cout << "Move disk " << n << " from peg " << start_peg
        << " to peg " << dest_peg << "\n";
    show_moves(n - 1, temp_peg, dest_peg, start_peg);
  }
}
```

Testing   Figure 7.15 shows the result of executing the following `main` function for the data 3, L, R ("move 3 disks from peg L to peg R"). The first three lines are the solution to the problem "move 2 disks from peg L to peg M," and the last three lines are the solution to the problem "move 2 disks from peg M to peg R."

```
int main() {
  int n_disks;
  char start_peg;
  char dest_peg;
  char temp_peg;
  cout << "Enter number of disks: ";
  cin >> n_disks;
  cout << "Enter start peg: ";
  cin >> start_peg;
```

```
        cout << "Enter destination peg: ";
        cin >> dest_peg;
        cout << "Enter temporary peg: ";
        cin >> temp_peg;
        show_moves(n_disks, start_peg, dest_peg, temp_peg);
    }
```

```
Command Prompt                                                    - □ ×
Move disk 1 from peg L to peg R
Move disk 2 from peg L to peg M
Move disk 1 from peg R to peg M
Move disk 3 from peg L to peg R
Move disk 1 from peg M to peg L
Move disk 2 from peg M to peg R
Move disk 1 from peg L to peg R
```

CASE STUDY   Counting Cells in a Blob

In the next case study we consider how we might process an image that is presented as a two-dimensional array of color values. The information in the two-dimensional array might come from a variety of sources. For example, it could be an image of part of a person's body that comes from an X-ray or an MRI, or it could be a picture of part of the earth's surface taken by a satellite. Our goal in this case study is to determine the size of any area in the image that is considered abnormal because of its color values.

Problem   You have a two-dimensional grid of cells, and each cell contains either a normal background color or a second color, which indicates the presence of an abnormality. The user wants to know the size of a blob: a collection of contiguous abnormal cells. The user will enter the position of a cell in the blob, and the count of all cells in that blob will be determined. As an example, Figure 7.16 shows a two-dimensional array with some abnormal cells in color. The size of the blob containing the cell at row 2, column 3 (rows and columns start at 0) is 4; the size of the blob containing the cell at row 3, column 1 is 2.

FIGURE 7.16
A Grid of Cells with
Abnormal Cells in Color

Analysis   Data Requirements

PROBLEM INPUTS
- The two-dimensional grid of cells
- The position of a cell in a blob

PROBLEM OUTPUTS
- The count of cells in the blob

Design Function `count_cells` in file `Blob.cpp` is a recursive function that is applied to a two-dimensional array. Its parameters are the array and the position (row and column) of a cell. The algorithm follows.

Algorithm for Function `count_cells`

1. **if** the cell `grid[r][c]` is outside the grid dimensions
2.   The result is 0.

   else if the color of the cell `grid[r][c]` is not the abnormal color

3.   The result is 0.

   else

4.   Set the color of cell `grid[r][c]` to a temporary color.
5.   The result is 1 plus the number of cells in each blob that includes a nearest neighbor.

The two stopping cases are reached if the coordinates of the cell are out of bounds or if the cell does not have the abnormal color and, therefore, can't be part of a blob. The recursive step involves counting 1 for a cell that has the abnormal color and adding the counts for the blobs that include each immediate neighbor cell. Each cell has eight immediate neighbors: two in the horizontal direction, two in the vertical direction, and four in the diagonal directions.

If no neighbor has the abnormal color, then the result will be just 1. If any neighbor cell has the abnormal color, then it will be counted along with all its neighbor cells that have the abnormal color, and so on until no neighboring cells with abnormal color are encountered (or the edge of the grid is reached). The reason for setting the color of cell `grid[r][c]` to the temporary color is to prevent it from being counted again when its neighbors' blobs are counted.

Implementation Listing 7.3 shows file `Blob.cpp`. The *enumeration* type `color` defines three enumerator values: `BACKGROUND`, `ABNORMAL`, and `TEMPORARY`. The first terminating condition

```
(r < 0 || r >= ROW_SIZE || c < 0 || c >= COL_SIZE)
```

is true if the cell position is outside the dimensions of the two-dimensional grid. The second terminating condition,

```
(grid[r][c] != ABNORMAL)
```

is true if the cell `grid[r][c]` has either the background color or the temporary color.

The recursive step is implemented by the statement

```
return 1
    + count_cells(grid, r - 1, c - 1) + count_cells(grid, r - 1, c)
    + count_cells(grid, r - 1, c + 1) + count_cells(grid, r, c + 1)
    + count_cells(grid, r + 1, c + 1) + count_cells(grid, r + 1, c)
    + count_cells(grid, r + 1, c - 1) + count_cells(grid, r, c - 1);
```

Each recursive call to `count_cells` has as its arguments the coordinates of a neighbor of the cell `grid[r][c]`. The value returned by each call will be the number of cells in the blob it belongs to, excluding the cell `grid[r][c]` and any other cells that may have been counted already.

····················

LISTING 7.3
`Blob.cpp`

```cpp
/** Program that solves problem of counting abnormal cells. */

enum color {BACKGROUND, ABNORMAL, TEMPORARY};
const int ROW_SIZE = 5;
const int COL_SIZE = 5;

// Insert main function here
...

/** Finds the number of cells in the blob that contains grid[r][c].
    pre:  Abnormal cells are in ABNORMAL color;
          Other cells are in BACKGROUND color.
    post: All cells in the blob are in the TEMPORARY color.
    @param r The row of a blob cell
    @param c The column of a blob cell
    @return The number of cells in the blob that contains grid[r][c]
*/
int count_cells(color grid[ROW_SIZE][COL_SIZE], int r, int c) {

  if (r < 0 || r >= ROW_SIZE || c < 0 || c >= COL_SIZE) {
    return 0;
  }
  else if (grid[r][c] != ABNORMAL) {
    return 0;
  }
  else  {
    grid[r][c] = TEMPORARY;
    return 1
      + count_cells(grid, r - 1, c - 1) + count_cells(grid, r - 1, c)
      + count_cells(grid, r - 1, c + 1) + count_cells(grid, r, c + 1)
      + count_cells(grid, r + 1, c + 1) + count_cells(grid, r + 1, c)
      + count_cells(grid, r + 1, c - 1) + count_cells(grid, r, c - 1);
  }
}
```

Testing   To test function `count_cells`, we will need to write a `main` function that declares and initializes the two-dimensional array `grid`. We can do this either by using an initializer list or by reading the cell values from a data file (see Programming Exercise 3 at the end of this section). A `main` function with an initializer list follows.

```cpp
#include <iostream>
int count_cells(color[ROW_SIZE][COL_SIZE], int, int);
int main() {
  color grid[ROW_SIZE][COL_SIZE] =
      {{BACKGROUND, ABNORMAL, BACKGROUND, ABNORMAL, ABNORMAL},
       {BACKGROUND, ABNORMAL, BACKGROUND, BACKGROUND, ABNORMAL},
       {BACKGROUND, BACKGROUND, BACKGROUND, ABNORMAL, BACKGROUND},
       {BACKGROUND, ABNORMAL, BACKGROUND, BACKGROUND, BACKGROUND},
       {BACKGROUND, ABNORMAL, BACKGROUND, ABNORMAL, BACKGROUND}};
```

```
        // Enter row and column of a cell in the blob.
        int row;
        std::cout << "Enter row: ";  std::cin >> row;
        int col;
        std::cout << "Enter column: ";  std::cin >> col;

        // Display results.
        std::cout << count_cells(grid, row, col) << "\n";
    }
```

When you test this program, make sure you verify that it works for the following cases:

- A starting cell that is on the edge of the grid
- A starting cell that has no neighboring abnormal cells
- A starting cell whose only abnormal neighbor cells are diagonally connected to it
- A "bull's-eye": a starting cell whose neighbors are all normal but their neighbors are abnormal
- A starting cell that is normal
- A grid that contains all abnormal cells
- A grid that contains all normal cells

EXERCISES FOR SECTION 7.4

SELF-CHECK

1. What is the big-O for the Towers of Hanoi as a function of n, where n represents the number of disks? Compare it to the function 2^n.
2. How many moves would be required to solve the five-disk problem?
3. Provide a "trace" of the solution to a four-disk problem by showing all the calls to show_moves that would be generated.
4. Explain why the first condition of function count_cells must precede the second condition.

PROGRAMMING

1. Modify function count_cells, assuming that cells must have a common side in order to be counted in the same blob. This means that they must be connected horizontally or vertically but not diagonally. Under this condition, the value of the function call count_cells(grid, 2, 3) would be 1, instead of 4, for the array in Figure 7.16.

2. Write a function `restore` that restores the grid back to its original state. You will need to reset the color of each cell that is in the temporary color back to its original color.
3. Write a function `fill_cells` that fills the two-dimensional array `grid` by reading each row's values from a data line consisting of 0s and 1s. The first data line in the input file will contain the number of rows and columns; the second data line will contain the values for row 0, and so on.

7.5 Backtracking

In this section we consider the problem-solving technique called *backtracking*. Backtracking is an approach to implementing systematic trial and error in a search for a solution. An application of backtracking is finding a path through a maze.

If you are attempting to walk through a maze, you will probably follow the general approach of walking down a path as far as you can go. Eventually either you will reach your destination and exit the maze, or you won't be able to go any further. If you exit the maze, you are done. Otherwise, you need to retrace your steps (backtrack) until you reach a fork in the path. At each fork, if there is a branch you did not follow, you will follow that branch hoping to reach your destination. If not, you will retrace your steps again, and so on.

What makes backtracking different from random trial and error is that backtracking provides a systematic approach to trying alternative paths and eliminating them if they don't work out. You will never try the exact same path more than once, and you will eventually find a solution path if one exists.

Problems that are solved by backtracking can be described as a set of choices made by some function. If at some point, it turns out that a solution is not possible with the current set of choices, the most recent choice is identified and removed. If there is an untried alternative choice, it is added to the set of choices, and search continues. If there is no untried alternative choice, then the next most recent choice is removed, and an alternative is sought for it. This process continues until either we reach a choice with an untried alternative and can continue our search for a solution, or we determine that there are no more alternative choices to try. Recursion allows us to implement backtracking in a relatively straightforward manner, because we can use each activation frame to remember the choice that was made at that particular decision point.

We will show how to use backtracking to find a path through a maze, but it can be applied to many other kinds of problems that involve a search for a solution. For example, a program that plays chess may use a kind of backtracking. If a sequence of moves it is considering does not lead to a favorable position, it will backtrack and try another sequence.

CASE STUDY   Finding a Path Through a Maze

Problem   Use backtracking to find and display the path through a maze. From each point in a maze, you can move to the next cell in the horizontal or vertical direction, if that cell is not blocked. So there are at most four possible moves from each point.

Analysis   Our maze will consist of a grid of cells like the grid used in the previous case study. The starting point is the cell at the top left corner (grid[0][0]), and the exit point is the cell at the bottom right corner (grid[ROW_SIZE - 1][COL_SIZE - 1]). All cells that can be part of a path will be in the BACKGROUND color. All cells that represent barriers and cannot be part of a path will be in the ABNORMAL color. To keep track of a cell that we have visited, we will set it to the TEMPORARY color. If we find a path, all cells on the path will be reset to the PATH color. So there are a total of four possible colors for a cell.

The cells in gray in Figure 7.17 right are on the path that would be found through the maze. The initial maze is shown at the left of Figure 7.17.

FIGURE 7.17
Finding a Path
through a Maze

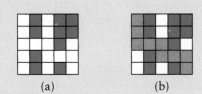

(a)   (b)

Design   The following recursive algorithm returns **true** if a path is found. It changes the color of all cells that are visited, but found not to be on the path, to the temporary color. In the recursive algorithm, each cell grid[r][c] being tested is reachable from the starting point. We can use recursion to simplify the problem of finding a path from cell grid[r][c] to the exit. We know that we can reach any unblocked neighbor cell that is in the horizontal or vertical direction from cell grid[r][c]. So a path exists from cell grid[r][c] to the maze exit if there is a path from a neighbor cell of grid[r][c] to the maze exit. If there is no path from any neighbor cell, we must backtrack and replace grid[r][c] with an alternative that has not yet been tried. That is done automatically through recursion. If there is a path, it will eventually be found and find_maze_path will return **true**.

Recursive Algorithm for find_maze_path(x, y)

1.   **if** the current cell is outside the maze
2.   Return **false** (you are out of bounds).
     else if the current cell is part of the barrier or has already been visited
3.   Return **false** (you are off the path or in a cycle).
     else if the current cell is the maze exit
4.   Recolor it to the path color and return **true** (you have successfully completed the maze).
     else // *Try to find a path from the current path to the exit:*

5.   Mark the current cell as on the path by recoloring it to the path color.

6.   **for** each neighbor of the current cell

7.   **if** a path exists from the neighbor to the maze exit

8.   Return **true**.

        // No neighbor of the current cell is on the path.

9.   Recolor the current cell to the temporary color (visited) and return **false**.

If no stopping case is reached (Steps 2, 3, or 4), the recursive case (the **else** clause) marks the current cell as being on the path and then tests whether there is a path from any neighbor of the current cell to the exit. If a path is found, we return **true** and begin unwinding from the recursion. During the process of unwinding from the recursion, the function will continue to return **true**. However, if all neighbors of the current cell are tested without finding a path, this means that the current cell cannot be on the path, so we recolor it to the temporary color and return **false** (Step 9). Next, we backtrack to a previous call and try to find a path through a cell that is an alternative to the cell just tested. The cell just tested will have been marked as visited (the temporary color), so we won't try using it again.

Notice that there is no attempt to find the *shortest* path through the maze. We just show the *first* path that is found.

Implementation

Listing 7.4 shows Maze.cpp. There is a wrapper function that calls recursive function find_maze_path with its argument values set to the coordinates of the starting point (grid[0][0]). The wrapper function returns the result of this call (**true** or **false**).

The recursive version of find_maze_path begins with three stopping cases: two unsuccessful and one successful (grid[r][c] is the exit point). The recursive case contains an **if** condition with four recursive calls. Because of short-circuit evaluation, if any call returns **true**, the rest are not executed. The arguments for each call are the coordinates of a neighbor cell. If a path exists from a neighbor to the maze exit, then the neighbor is part of the solution path, so we return **true**. If a neighbor cell is not on the solution path, we try the next neighbor until all four neighbors have been tested. If there is no path from any neighbor, we recolor the current cell to the temporary color and return **false**.

LISTING 7.4
Maze.cpp

```
/** Program that solves maze problems with backtracking. */
enum color {BACKGROUND, ABNORMAL, TEMPORARY, PATH};
const int ROW_SIZE = 5;
const int COL_SIZE = 5;

// Insert main function here
...

/** Wrapper function. */
bool find_maze_path(color grid[ROW_SIZE][COL_SIZE]) {
  return find_maze_path(grid, 0, 0);   // (0, 0) is the start point.
}
```

```
/** Attempts to find a path through cell grid[r][c].
    pre:  Possible path cells are in BACKGROUND color;
          barrier cells are in ABNORMAL color.
    post: If a path is found, all cells on it are set to the
          PATH color; all cells that were visited but are
          not on the path are in the TEMPORARY color.
    @param r The row of current point
    @param c The column of current point
    @return If a path through grid[r][c] is found, true;
            Otherwise, false
*/
bool find_maze_path(color grid[ROW_SIZE][COL_SIZE], int r, int c) {
  if (r < 0 || c < 0 || r >= ROW_SIZE || c >= COL_SIZE)
    return false;       // Cell is out of bounds.
  else if (grid[r][c] != BACKGROUND)
    return false;       // Cell is on barrier or dead end.
  else if (r == ROW_SIZE - 1 && c == COL_SIZE - 1) {
    grid[r][c] = PATH;          // Cell is on path
    return true;                // and is maze exit.
  }
  else {
    // Recursive case.
    // Attempt to find a path from each neighbor.
    // Tentatively mark cell as on path.
    grid[r][c] = PATH;
    if (find_maze_path(grid, r - 1, c)
        || find_maze_path(grid, r + 1, c)
        || find_maze_path(grid, r, c - 1)
        || find_maze_path(grid, r, c + 1 ) ) {
      return true;
    }
    else {
      grid[r][c] = TEMPORARY;  // Dead end.
      return false;
    }
  }
}
```

The Effect of Marking a Cell as Visited

If a path can't be found from a neighbor of the current cell to the maze exit, the current cell is considered a "dead end" and is recolored to the temporary color. You may be wondering whether the program would still work if we just recolored it to the background color. The answer is "Yes". In this case, cells that turned out to be dead ends or cells that were not visited would be in the background color after the program terminated. This would not affect the ability of the algorithm to find a path or to determine that none exists; however, it would affect the algorithm's efficiency. After backtracking, the function could try to place on the path a cell that had been found to be a dead end. The cell would be classified once again as a dead end. Marking it as a dead end (color TEMPORARY) the first time prevents this from happening.

To demonstrate the efficiency of this approach, we tested the program on a maze with 4 rows and 6 columns that had a single barrier cell at the maze exit. When we recolored each dead end cell in the TEMPORARY color, it took 93 recursive calls to find_maze_path to determine that a path did not exist. When we recolored each tested cell in the BACKGROUND color, it took 177,313 recursive calls to determine that a path did not exist.

Testing   To test function find_maze_path, we will need to write a main function that declares and initializes the two-dimensional array grid. A main function with an initializer list follows.

```cpp
#include <iostream>

bool find_maze_path(color[ROW_SIZE][COL_SIZE]);
bool find_maze_path(color[ROW_SIZE][COL_SIZE], int, int);

int main() {
  color grid[ROW_SIZE][COL_SIZE] =
      {{BACKGROUND, ABNORMAL, BACKGROUND, ABNORMAL, ABNORMAL},
       {BACKGROUND, ABNORMAL, BACKGROUND, ABNORMAL, ABNORMAL},
       {BACKGROUND, BACKGROUND, BACKGROUND, ABNORMAL, BACKGROUND},
       {BACKGROUND, ABNORMAL, BACKGROUND, BACKGROUND, BACKGROUND},
       {BACKGROUND, ABNORMAL, BACKGROUND, ABNORMAL, BACKGROUND}};

  // Display results.
  std::cout << std::boolalpha << find_maze_path(grid) << "\n";
}
```

You should test this with a variety of mazes, some that can be solved and some that can't (no path exists). You should also try a maze that has no barrier cells and one that has a single barrier cell at the exit point. In the latter case, no path exists.

EXERCISES FOR SECTION 7.5

SELF-CHECK

1. The terminating conditions in find_maze_path must be performed in the order specified. What could happen if the second or third condition were evaluated before the first? If the third condition were evaluated before the second condition?
2. Does it matter in which order the neighbor cells are tested in find_maze_path? How could this order affect the path that is found?

PROGRAMMING

1. Modify find_maze_path to push the coordinates of the cells that are on the path onto a stack (type std::stack<std::pair<int, int> >). The coordinates to be pushed are the arguments (r, c) whenever find_maze_path returns **true**.
2. Write a display_path function that takes the stack as an argument and pops its contents to display the actual path.

Chapter Review

◆ A recursive function has the following form, where Step 2 is the base case, and Steps 3 and 4 are the recursive case:

1.   **if** the problem can be solved for the current value of n
2.   Solve it.
   else
3.   Recursively apply the function to one or more problems involving smaller values of n.
4.   Combine the solutions to the smaller problems to get the solution to the original.

◆ To prove that a recursive algorithm is correct, you must

—Verify that the base case is recognized and solved correctly.

—Verify that each recursive case makes progress toward the base case.

—Verify that if all smaller problems are solved correctly, then the original problem must also be solved correctly.

◆ The operating system uses activation frames, stored on a stack, to keep track of argument values and return points during recursive function calls. Activation frames can be used to trace the execution of a sequence of recursive function calls.

◆ Mathematical sequences and formulas that are defined recursively can be implemented naturally as recursive functions.

◆ Two problems that can be solved using recursion were investigated: the Towers of Hanoi problem and counting cells in a blob.

◆ Backtracking is a technique that enables you to write programs that can be used to explore different alternative paths in a search for a solution.

Quick-Check Exercises

1. A recursive function has two cases: _____ and _____.
2. Each recursive call of a recursive function must lead to a situation that is _____ to the _____ case.
3. The control statement used in a recursive function is the _____ statement.
4. What three things are stored in an activation frame? Where are the activation frames stored?
5. You can sometimes substitute _____ for recursion.
6. Explain how a recursive function might cause a stack overflow exception.
7. If you have a recursive and an iterative function that calculate the same result, which do you think would be more efficient? Explain your answer.
8. Binary search is an O(___) algorithm, and linear search is an O(___) algorithm.
9. Towers of Hanoi is an O(___) algorithm. Explain your answer.
10. Why did you need to provide a wrapper function for recursive functions `linear_search` and `binary_search`?

Answers to Quick-Check Exercises

1. A recursive function has two cases: *base case* and *recursive case*.
2. Each recursive call of a recursive function must lead to a situation that is *closer* to the *base* case.
3. The control statement used in a recursive function is the ***if*** statement.
4. An activation frame stores the following information on the stack: the function argument values, the function local variable values, and the address of the return point in the caller of the function.
5. You can sometimes substitute *iteration* for recursion.
6. A recursive function that doesn't stop would continue to call itself, eventually pushing so many activation frames onto the stack that a stack overflow exception would occur.
7. An iterative function would generally be more efficient, because there is more overhead associated with multiple function calls.
8. Binary search is an $O(\log_2 n)$ algorithm, and linear search is an $O(n)$ algorithm.
9. Towers of Hanoi is an $O(2^n)$ algorithm, because each problem splits into two problems at the next lower level.
10. Both search functions should be called with the vector name and target as arguments. However, the recursive linear search function needs the subscript of the element to be compared to the target. The binary search function needs the search boundaries.

Review Questions

1. Explain the use of the stack and activation frames in processing recursive function calls.
2. What is a recursive data structure? Give an example of one.
3. For Towers of Hanoi, show the output lines generated by the function call `show_moves(3, 'R', 'M', 'L')`. Also, show the sequence of function calls.
4. For the counting cells in a blob problem, show the activation frames in the recursive calls to `count_cells` following `count_cells(grid, 4, 1)`.

Programming Projects

1. Test function `count_cells` using a data file made up of lines consisting of 0s and 1s with no spaces between them.
2. Test function `find_maze_path` using a data file made up of lines consisting of 0s and 1s with no spaces between them.
3. Show how you could use the following `TwoDArray` class in programs `Blob` and `Maze` to enable you to declare and use arrays of variable dimensions. The first line of a data file that is used to initialize the array should consist of the number of rows and number of columns in the array. The operator `[]` returns a pointer to the row. Since this is a pointer, we can then treat it as a one-dimensional array and apply the operator `[]` again to get a particular element (that is, if `x` is type `TwoDArray`, `x[i][j]` is the element of `x` at row `i`, column `j`.) Declaring the copy constructor and the assignment operator private has the effect of prohibiting these operations, as they are for one-dimensional arrays in C++.

```
#ifndef TWODARRAY_H_
#define TWODARRAY_H_

#include <cstddef>
```

```
/** Class to define a two dimensional array whose dimensions
      can be declared at run time.
*/
template<typename Item_Type>
  class TwoDArray {

  public:

    /** Construct a TwoDArray with n rows and m columns. */
    TwoDArray(size_t n, size_t m) :
      num_rows(n), num_cols(m), data(new Item_Type[n * m]) {}

    /** Destructor. */
    ~TwoDArray() { delete data; }

    /** Access a row. */
    Item_Type* operator[](size_t i) {
      return data + num_cols * i;
    }

    const Item_Type* operator[](size_t i) const {
      return data + num_cols * i;
    }

    /** Get the number of rows. */
    size_t get_num_rows() const {return num_rows;}

    /** Get the number of columns. */
    size_t get_num_cols() const {return num_cols;}

  private:

    /** Number of rows */
    size_t num_rows;
    /** Number of columns */
    size_t num_cols;
    /** The data array */
    Item_Type* data;

    // Prohibit copy and assignment
    TwoDArray(const TwoDArray&);
    TwoDArray& operator=(const TwoDArray&);

};

#endif
```

4. Write a recursive function that converts a decimal integer to a binary string. Write a recursive function that converts a binary string to a decimal integer.

5. As discussed in Chapter 5, a palindrome is a word that reads the same left to right as right to left. Write a recursive function that determines whether its argument string is a palindrome.

6. Write a program that will read a list of numbers and a desired sum, then determine the subset of numbers in the list that yield that sum if such a subset exists.

7. Write a recursive function that will dispense change for a given amount of money. The function will display all combinations of quarters, dimes, nickels, and pennies that equal the desired amount.

8. Write a recursive function for placing eight queens on a chessboard. The eight queens should be placed so that no queen can capture another. Recall that a queen can move in the horizontal, vertical, or diagonal direction.

   Hint: Obviously each queen must be in a different row and column. Let's assume that the `i`th queen (`i` runs from 0 to 7) is in column `i` and in `row[i]`. If for some `i` and `j`, `row[i] == row[j]`, then this is not a valid solution. To check the diagonals if `row[i] - row[j] == i - j` or `row[i] - row[j] == j - i`, then the two queens are on the same diagonal, and this not a valid solution.

   Use `i` as the parameter to the recursive function. The base case is `i == 8` when all queens have been assigned a row. The recursive case should try each possible row for queen `i`, and then see whether the `(i + 1)`th queen can find a safe position. If none of the rows for the `i`th queen is safe, then return **false**.

   There are 92 possible solutions. The following is one of them:

Chapter 8

Trees

Chapter Objectives

- To learn how to use a tree to represent a hierarchical organization of information
- To learn how to use recursion to process trees
- To understand the different ways of traversing a tree
- To understand the difference between binary trees, binary search trees, and heaps
- To learn how to implement binary trees, binary search trees, and heaps using linked data structures and arrays
- To learn how to use a binary search tree to store information so that it can be retrieved in an efficient manner
- To learn how to use a Huffman tree to encode characters using fewer bits than ASCII or Unicode, resulting in smaller files and reduced storage requirements

The data organizations you studied so far are linear, in that each element has only one predecessor or successor. Accessing all the elements in sequence is an O(*n*) process. In this chapter we begin our discussion of a data organization that is nonlinear or hierarchical: the *tree*. Instead of having just one successor, a node in a tree can have multiple successors; but it has just one predecessor. A tree in computer science is like a natural tree, which has a single trunk that may split off into two or more main branches. The predecessor of each main branch is the trunk. Each main branch may spawn several secondary branches (successors of the main branches). The predecessor of each secondary branch is a main branch. In computer science, we draw a tree from the top down, so the *root* of the tree is at the top of the diagram instead of the bottom.

Because trees have a hierarchical structure, we use them to represent hierarchical organizations of information, such as a class hierarchy, a disk directory and its

445

FIGURE 8.1
Part of the Programs Directory

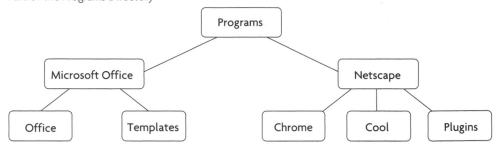

subdirectories (see Figure 8.1), or a family tree. You will see that trees are recursive data structures, because they can be defined recursively. For this reason, many of the functions used to process trees are written as recursive functions.

This chapter will focus on a restricted tree structure, a *binary tree*, in which each element has, at most, two successors. You will learn how to use linked data structures and arrays to represent binary trees. You will also learn how to use a special kind of binary tree called a *binary search tree* to store information (for example, the words in a dictionary) in an ordered way. Because each element of a binary tree can have two successors, you will see that searching for an item stored in a binary search tree is much more efficient than searching for an item in a linear data structure: (possibly $O(\log n)$ for a binary tree versus $O(n)$ for a list).

You also will learn about other kinds of binary trees. Expression trees are used to represent arithmetic expressions. The heap is an ordered tree structure that is used as the basis for a very efficient sorting algorithm and for a special kind of queue called the priority queue. The Huffman tree is used for encoding information and compressing files.

Trees

8.1 Tree Terminology and Applications

Tree Terminology

We use the same terminology to describe trees in computer science as we do trees in nature. In computer science, a tree consists of a collection of elements or nodes, with each node linked to its successors. The node at the top of a tree is called its root because computer science trees grow from the top down. The links from a node to its successors are called branches. The successors of a node are called its *children*. The predecessor of a node is called its *parent*. Each node in a tree has exactly one parent except for the root node, which has no parent. Nodes that have the same parent are *siblings*. A node that has no children is a *leaf node*. Leaf nodes are also known as *external nodes*, and nonleaf nodes are known as *internal nodes*.

A generalization of the parent-child relationship is the *ancestor-descendant relationship*. If node A is the parent of node B, which is the parent of node C, which in turn is the parent of node D, node A is an *ancestor* of nodes B, C, and D, and node D is a *descendant* of nodes A, B, and C. Sometimes we say that node A and node C are a grandparent and grandchild, respectively. The root node is an ancestor of every other node in a tree, and every other node in a tree is a descendant of the root node.

Figure 8.2 illustrates these features in a tree that stores a collection of words. The branches are the lines connecting a parent to its children. In discussing this tree, we will refer to a node by the string that it stores. For example, we will refer to the node that stores the string "dog" as node *dog*.

A *subtree* of a node is a tree whose root is a child of that node. For example, the nodes *cat* and *canine* and the branch connecting them are a subtree of node *dog*. The other subtree of node *dog* is the tree consisting of the single node *wolf*. The subtree consisting of the single node *canine* is a subtree of node *cat*.

FIGURE 8.2
A Tree of Words

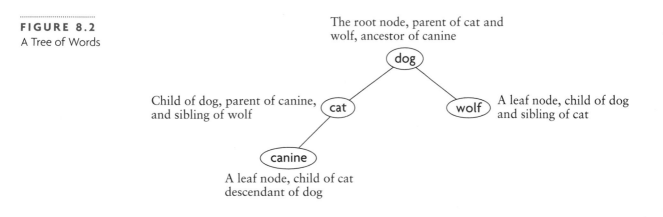

The root node, parent of cat and wolf, ancestor of canine

Child of dog, parent of canine, and sibling of wolf

A leaf node, child of dog and sibling of cat

A leaf node, child of cat descendant of dog

The *depth* of a node is a measure of its distance from the root. It is defined recursively as follows:

- If node *n* is the root of tree *T*, its depth is 0.
- If node *n* is not the root of tree *T*, its depth is 1 + the depth of its parent.

For the tree in Figure 8.2, node *dog* is at depth 0, nodes *cat* and *wolf* are at depth 1, and node *canine* is at depth 2. We will sometimes use the term *level* to refer to a node's depth in a tree.

The *height of a node* is the number of nodes in the longest path from that node to a leaf node. The height of nodes *canine* and *wolf* is 1, the height of node *cat* is 2, and the height of node *dog* is 3 (the longest path goes through the nodes *dog*, *cat*, and *canine*). An alternate definition of the height of a node is the number of branches in the longest path from the node to a leaf node plus one.

The *height of a tree* is the same as the height of its root node. The height of the tree in Figure 8.2 is 3.

Binary Trees

The tree in Figure 8.2 is a binary tree. Informally, this is a binary tree because each node has at most two branches to subtrees. A more formal definition for a binary tree follows:

A set of nodes *T* is a binary tree if either of the following is true:

- *T* is empty.
- If *T* is not empty, it has a root node *r* with 0, 1, or 2 binary subtrees whose roots are connected to *r* by a branch.

We refer to the left subtree as T_L and to the right subtree as T_R. Note that T_L, T_R, or both can be empty trees. For the tree in Figure 8.2, the right subtree of node *cat* is empty. The leaf nodes (*wolf* and *canine*) have empty left and right subtrees. This is illustrated in Figure 8.3, where the empty subtrees are indicated by the squares. Generally the empty subtrees are represented by NULL pointers, but another value may be chosen. From now on, we will consistently use a NULL pointer, and we will not draw the squares for the empty subtrees.

FIGURE 8.3

A Tree of Words with Empty Subtrees Indicated

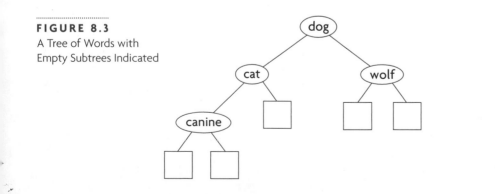

FIGURE 8.4
Expression Tree

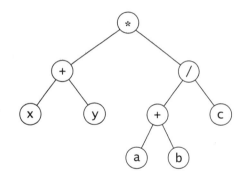

Some Types of Binary Trees

Next we discuss three different types of binary trees that are common in computer science.

An Expression Tree

Figure 8.4 shows a binary tree that stores an expression. Each node contains an operator (+, –, *, /, %) or an operand. The expression in Figure 8.4 corresponds to (x + y) * ((a + b) / c). Operands are stored in leaf nodes. Parentheses are not stored in the tree, because the tree structure dictates the order of operator evaluation. Operators in nodes higher up in the tree are evaluated after operators in nodes that are lower, so the operator * in the root node is evaluated last. If a node contains a binary operator, its left subtree represents the operator's left operand and its right subtree represents the operator's right operand. The left subtree of the root represents the expression x + y, and the right subtree of the root represents the expression (a + b) / c.

A Huffman Tree

Another use of a binary tree is to represent *Huffman codes* for characters that might appear in a text file. Unlike ASCII or Unicode encoding, which use the same number of bits to encode each character, a Huffman code uses different numbers of bits to encode the letters. It uses fewer bits for the more common letters (for example, space, *e*, *a*, and *t*) and more bits for the less common letters (for example, *q*, *x*, and *z*). On average, using Huffman codes to encode text files should give you files with fewer bits than you would get using other codes. Many programs that compress files use Huffman encoding to generate smaller files in order to save disk space or to reduce the time spent sending the files over the Internet.

Figure 8.5 shows the Huffman encoding tree for an alphabet consisting of the lowercase letters and the space character. All the characters are at leaf nodes. The data stored at internal nodes is not shown. To determine the code for a letter, you form a binary string by tracing the path from the root node to that letter. Each time you go left, append a 0, and each time you go right, append a 1. To reach the space character, you go right three times, so the code is 111. The code for the letter *d* is 10110 (right, left, right, right, left).

FIGURE 8.5
Huffman Code Tree

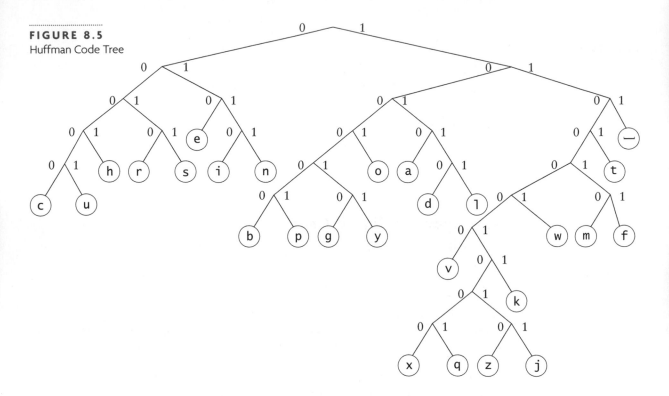

The two characters with a depth of 3 (space, *e*) are the most common and, therefore, have the shortest codes (111, 010). The next most common characters (*a*, *o*, *i*, and so forth) have a depth of 4.

You can store the code for each letter in an array. For example, the code for the space ' ' would be at position 0, the letter 'a' would be at position 1, and the code for letter 'z' would be at position 26. You can encode each letter in a file by looking up its code in the array.

However, to decode a file of letters and spaces, you walk down the Huffman tree, starting at the root, until you reach a letter. Once you have reached a letter, append that letter to the output text and go back to the root. Here is an example. The substrings that represent the individual letters are shown in alternate colors to help you follow the process. The underscore in the second line represents a space character (code is 111).

```
100010100111101010101000010101110100011
   g    o   _  e   a    g    l   e  s
```

Huffman trees are discussed further in Section 8.6.

Binary Search Trees

The tree in Figure 8.2 is a binary search tree because, for each node, all words in its left subtree precede the word in that node, and all words in its right subtree follow the word in that node. For example, for the root node *dog*, all words in its left subtree (*cat*, *canine*) precede *dog* in the dictionary, and all words in its right subtree (*wolf*) follow *dog*. Similarly, for the node *cat*, the word in its left subtree (*canine*) precedes it. There are no duplicate entries in a binary search tree.

More formally, we define a binary search tree as follows:

A set of nodes T is a binary search tree if either of the following is true:

- T is empty.
- If T is not empty, its root node has two subtrees, T_L and T_R, such that T_L and T_R are binary search trees and the value in the root node of T is greater than all values in T_L and is less than all values in T_R.

The order relations in a binary search tree expedite searching the tree. A recursive algorithm for searching a binary search tree follows:

1.   **if** the tree is empty
2.   Return NULL (target is not found).
       else if the target matches the root node's data
3.   Return the data stored at the root node.
       else if the target is less than the root node's data
4.   Return the result of searching the left subtree of the root.
       else
5.   Return the result of searching the right subtree of the root.

The first two cases are base cases and self-explanatory. In the first recursive case, if the target is less than the root node's data, we search only the left subtree (T_L) because all data items in T_R are larger than the root node's data and, therefore, larger than the target. Likewise we execute the second recursive step (search the right subtree) if the target is greater than the root node's data.

Just as with a binary search of an array (or vector), each probe into the binary search tree has the potential of eliminating half the elements in the tree. If the binary search tree is relatively balanced (that is, the depths of the leaves are approximately the same), searching a binary search tree is an $O(\log n)$ process, just like a binary search of an ordered array.

What is the advantage of using a binary search tree instead of just storing elements in a vector and then sorting it? A binary search tree never has to be sorted, because its elements always satisfy the required order relations. When new elements are inserted (or removed), the binary search tree property can be maintained. In contrast, a vector must be expanded whenever new elements are added, and it must be compacted whenever elements are removed. Both expanding and contracting involve shifting items and are thus $O(n)$ operations.

Fullness and Completeness

Trees grow from the top down, and each new value is inserted in a new leaf node. Trees have different shapes depending on how the values are inserted. The tree on the left in Figure 8.6 is called a *full binary tree* because all internal nodes have exactly two children. Note that the number of leaf nodes is one more than the number of internal nodes. This will be the case for a full binary tree of any height.

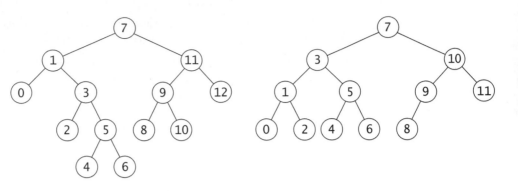

A *complete binary tree* of height h is filled up to depth $h - 1$ and, at depth h, any unfilled nodes are on the right (see Figure 8.6, right). A node is filled if it has a value stored in it. More formally, a binary tree of height h is complete if:

- All nodes at depth $h - 2$ and above have two children.
- When a node at depth $h - 1$ has children, all nodes to the left of it have two children.
- If a node at depth $h - 1$ has one child, it is a left child.

General Trees

A general tree is a tree that does not have the restriction that each node of a tree has at most two subtrees. So nodes in a general tree can have any number of subtrees. Figure 8.7 shows a general tree that represents a family tree showing the descendants of King William I (the Conqueror) of England.

We will not discuss general trees in detail. However, it is worth mentioning that a general tree can be represented using a binary tree. Figure 8.8 shows a binary tree representation of the family tree in Figure 8.7. We obtained it by connecting the left branch from a node to the oldest child (if any). Each right branch from a node is

FIGURE 8.7
Family Tree for the
Descendants of
William I of England

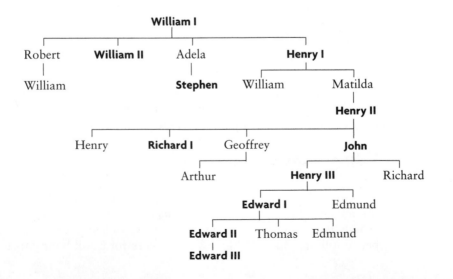

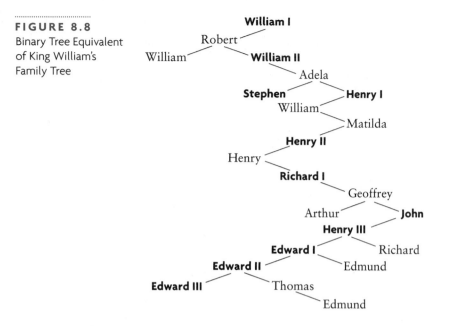

FIGURE 8.8
Binary Tree Equivalent
of King William's
Family Tree

connected to the next younger sibling (if any). For example in Figure 8.8, the left branch from William I is connected to his oldest child, Robert. The left branch from Robert is connected to his only son, William. The right branch from Robert is connected to his oldest sibling, William II, and so on.

Historical Note: The names of the men who became kings are in boldface type. You would expect the eldest son to succeed his father as king; however, this would not be the case if the eldest male died before his father. For example, Robert died before William I, so William II became king instead. Starting with King John (near the bottom of the tree), the eldest son of each king did become King of England.

EXERCISES FOR SECTION 8.1

SELF-CHECK

1. Draw binary expression trees for the following infix expressions. Your trees should enforce the C++ rules for operator evaluation (higher-precedence operators before lower-precedence operators and left associativity).

   a. x / y + a – b * c

   b. (x * a) – y / b * (c + d)

2. Using the Huffman tree in Figure 8.5,

   a. Write the binary string for the message "scissors cuts paper".

   b. Decode the following binary string:

   11000100010100010010111011000111111110001101010111101101001

3. For each of the following trees, answer these questions. What is its height? Is it a full tree? Is it a complete tree? Is it a binary search tree? If not, make it a binary search tree.

4. Represent the general tree in Figure 8.1 as a binary tree.

8.2 Tree Traversals

Often we want to determine the nodes of a tree and their relationship. We can do this by walking through the tree in a prescribed order and *visiting* the nodes (processing the information in the nodes) as they are encountered. This process is known as *tree traversal*. We will discuss three kinds of traversal in this section: *inorder*, *preorder*, and *postorder*. These three functions are distinguished by when they visit a node in relation to the nodes in its subtrees (T_L and T_R).

- Preorder: Visit root node, traverse T_L, traverse T_R.
- Inorder: Traverse T_L, visit root node, traverse T_R.
- Postorder: Traverse T_L, traverse T_R, visit root node.

Because trees are recursive data structures, we can write similar recursive algorithms for all three techniques. The difference in the algorithms is whether the root is visited before the children are traversed (pre), in between traversing the left and right children (in), or after the children are traversed (post).

Algorithm for Preorder Traversal

1. **if** the tree is empty
2.   Return.
    else
3.   Visit the root.
4.   Preorder traverse the left subtree.
5.   Preorder traverse the right subtree.

Algorithm for Inorder Traversal

1. **if** the tree is empty
2.   Return.
    else
3.   Inorder traverse the left subtree.
4.   Visit the root.
5.   Inorder traverse the right subtree.

Algorithm for Postorder Traversal

1. **if** the tree is empty
2.   Return.
    else
3.   Postorder traverse the left subtree.
4.   Postorder traverse the right subtree.
5.   Visit the root.

FIGURE 8.9
Traversal of a Binary
Tree

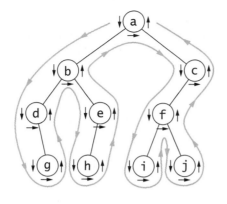

Visualizing Tree Traversals

You can visualize a tree traversal by imagining a mouse that walks along the edge of the tree. If the mouse always keeps the tree to the left (from the mouse's point of view), it will trace the route shown in color around the tree shown in Figure 8.9. This is known as an *Euler tour*.

If we record each node as the mouse first encounters it (indicated by the arrows pointing down in Figure 8.9), we get the following sequence:

```
a b d g e h c f i j
```

This is a preorder traversal, because the mouse visits each node before traversing its subtrees. The mouse also walks down the left branch (if it exists) of each node before going down the right branch, so the mouse visits a node, traverses its left subtree, and traverses its right subtree.

If we record each node as the mouse returns from traversing its left subtree (indicated by the arrows pointing to the right in Figure 8.9), we get the following sequence:

```
d g b h e a i f j c
```

This is an inorder traversal. The mouse traverses the left subtree, visits the root, and then traverses the right subtree. Node d is visited first because it has no left subtree.

If we record each node as the mouse last encounters it (indicated by the arrows pointing up in Figure 8.9), we get the following sequence:

```
g d h e b i j f c a
```

This is a postorder traversal, because we visit the node after traversing both its subtrees. The mouse traverses the left subtree, traverses the right subtree, and then visits the node.

Traversals of Binary Search Trees and Expression Trees

An inorder traversal of a binary search tree results in the nodes being visited in sequence by increasing data value. For example, for the binary search tree shown earlier in Figure 8.2, the inorder traversal would visit the nodes in the sequence:

canine, cat, dog, wolf

Traversals of expression trees give interesting results. If we perform an inorder traversal of the expression tree first shown in Figure 8.4 and repeated here, we visit the nodes in the sequence x + y * a + b / c. If we insert parentheses where they belong, we get the infix expression

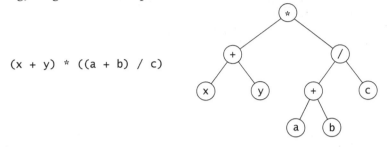

(x + y) * ((a + b) / c)

The postorder traversal of this tree would visit the nodes in the sequence

x y + a b + c / *

which is the postfix form of the expression. To illustrate this, we show the operand-operand-operator groupings under the expression.

The preorder traversal visits the nodes in the sequence

* + x y / + a b c

which is the prefix form of the expression. To illustrate this, we show the operator-operand-operand groupings under the expression.

EXERCISES FOR SECTION 8.2

SELF-CHECK

1. For the following trees:

   If visiting a node displays the integer value stored, show the inorder, preorder, and postorder traversal of each tree.

2. Draw an expression tree corresponding to each of the following:
   a. Inorder traversal is x / y + 3 * b / c (Your tree should represent the C++ meaning of the expression.)
   b. Postorder traversal is x y z + a b – c * / –
   c. Preorder traversal is * + a – x y / c d

3. Explain why the statement "Your tree should represent the C++ meaning of the expression" was not needed for parts b and c of Exercise 2.

8.3 Implementing a Binary_Tree Class

In this section we show how to use linked data structures to represent binary trees and binary tree nodes. We begin by focusing on the structure of a binary tree node.

The BTNode Class

Like a linked list, a node consists of a data part and links (references) to successor nodes. So that we can store any kind of data in a tree node, we will make the data part an object of type Item_Type. Instead of having a single link (pointer) to a successor node as in a list, a binary tree node must have links (pointers) to both its left and right subtrees. Figure 8.10 shows the structure of a binary tree node; Listing 8.1 shows its implementation.

Class BTNode is a stand-alone class. Since this class is merely a grouping of data, we use the **struct** keyword to declare it rather than the **class** keyword. (Recall that **struct** and **class** are synonymous except that, by default, members are public in a **struct**.) Even though the BTNode is only used within the Binary_Tree class, we do not define it as a nested class. Later, we will use the Binary_Tree and BTNode classes as base classes. Keeping the BTNode and Binary_Tree as distinct classes makes it easier to use them as base classes.

The constructor for class BTNode creates a leaf node (both left and right are NULL). The to_string function for the class just displays the data part of the node. Note that this function is declared virtual so that derived classes can override it. As was explained in Chapter 3, the virtual destructor is declared because some compilers issue a warning message if a class contains a virtual function but does not contain a virtual destructor. As shown, this destructor does nothing.

FIGURE 8.10
Linked Structure to Represent a Node

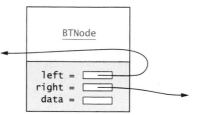

LISTING 8.1
BTNode.h

```cpp
#ifndef BTNODE_H_
#define BTNODE_H_
#include <sstream>

/** A node for a Binary Tree. */
template<typename Item_Type>
  struct BTNode
{
  // Data Fields
  Item_Type data;
  BTNode<Item_Type>* left;
  BTNode<Item_Type>* right;

  // Constructor
  BTNode(const Item_Type& the_data,
         BTNode<Item_Type>* left_val = NULL,
         BTNode<Item_Type>* right_val = NULL) :
    data(the_data), left(left_val),  right(right_val) {}

  // Destructor (to avoid warning message)
  virtual ~BTNode() {}

  // to_string
  virtual std::string to_string() const {
    std::ostringstream os;
    os << data;
    return os.str();
  }
}; // End BTNode

// Overloading the ostream insertion operator
template<typename Item_Type>
  std::ostream& operator<<(std::ostream& out,
                           const BTNode<Item_Type>& node) {
  return out << node.to_string();
}

#endif
```

The Binary_Tree Class

Table 8.1 shows the design of the Binary_Tree class. The single data field root points to the root node of a Binary_Tree object. It has protected visibility because we will need to access it in subclass Binary_Search_Tree, discussed later in this chapter. In Figure 8.11, we draw the expression tree for ((x + y) * (a / b)) using our BTNode representation.

EXAMPLE 8.1   Assume the tree drawn in Figure 8.11 is referenced by variable bT (type Binary_Tree).

- bT.root->data contains the char object '*'
- bT.root->left points to the left subtree of the root (the root node of tree x + y).
- bT.root->right points to the right subtree of the root (the root node of tree a / b).
- bT.root->right->data contains the char object '/'.

FIGURE 8.11
Linked Representation of the Expression Tree ((x + y) * (a / b))

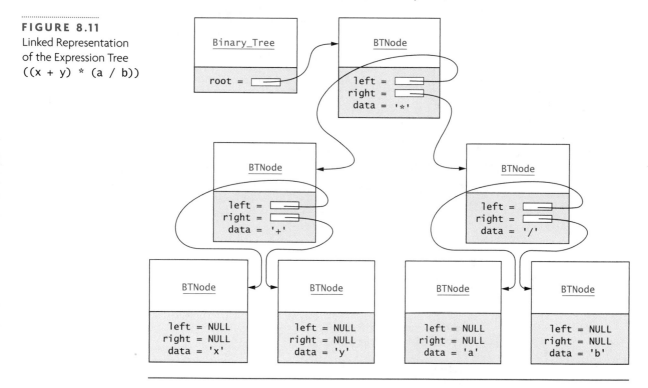

TABLE 8.1
Design of the Binary_Tree Class

Data Field	Attribute
BTNode<Item_Type>* root	Pointer to the root of the tree.
Constructor	**Behavior**
Binary_Tree()	Constructs an empty binary tree.
Binary_Tree(BTNode<Item_Type>* new_root)	Constructs a binary tree with the given node as the root.
Binary_Tree(Item_Type the_data, const Binary_Tree<Item_Type>& left_child, const Binary_Tree<Item_Type>& right_child)	Constructs a binary tree with the given data at the root and the two given subtrees.

....

TABLE 8.1 (cont.)

Function	Behavior
`Binary_Tree<Item_Type> get_left_subtree() const`	Returns the left subtree.
`Binary_Tree<Item_Type> get_right_subtree() const`	Returns the right subtree.
`const Item_Type& get_data() const`	Returns the data in the root.
`bool is_leaf() const`	Returns **true** if this tree is a leaf, **false** otherwise.
`bool is_null() const`	Returns **true** if this is an empty tree, **false** otherwise.
`string to_string() const`	Returns a string representation of the tree.
`static Binary_Tree<Item_Type> read_binary_tree(std::istream& in)`	Constructs a binary tree by reading its data from input stream in.

The class definition file follows.

```
#ifndef BINARY_TREE_H
#define BINARY_TREE_H

/** Class for a binary tree. */

#include <cstddef>
#include <sstream>
#include <stdexcept>
#include <string>
#include "BTNode.h"

template<typename Item_Type>
  class Binary_Tree
{
  public:

  // Constructors and Functions
  /** Construct an empty Binary_Tree. */
  Binary_Tree() : root(NULL) {}

  /** Construct a Binary_Tree with two subtrees.
      @param the_data The data at the root
      @param left_child The left subtree
      @param right_child The right subtree
  */
  Binary_Tree(const Item_Type& the_data,
              const Binary_Tree<Item_Type>& left_child
                = Binary_Tree(),
              const Binary_Tree<Item_Type>& right_child
                = Binary_Tree()) :
      root(new BTNode<Item_Type>(the_data, left_child.root,
                                 right_child.root)) {}

  /** Virtual destructor to avoid warnings. */
  virtual ~Binary_Tree() {}  // Do nothing.
```

```cpp
/** Return the left subtree. */
Binary_Tree<Item_Type> get_left_subtree() const;

/** Return the right subtree. */
Binary_Tree<Item_Type> get_right_subtree() const;

/** Return the data field of the root.
    @throws std::invalid_argument if empty tree
*/
const Item_Type& get_data() const;

/** Indicate that this is the empty tree. */
bool is_null() const;

/** Indicate that this tree is a leaf. */
bool is_leaf() const;

/** Return a string representation of this tree. */
virtual std::string to_string() const;

/** Read a Binary_Tree. */
static Binary_Tree<Item_Type> read_binary_tree(std::istream& in);

protected:

// Protected Constructor
/** Construct a Binary_Tree with a given node as the root */
Binary_Tree(BTNode<Item_Type>* new_root) : root(new_root) {}

// Data Field
BTNode<Item_Type>* root;

};   // End Binary_Tree

// Overloading the ostream insertion operator
template<typename Item_Type>
  std::ostream& operator<<(std::ostream& out,
                           const Binary_Tree<Item_Type>& tree) {
  return out << tree.to_string();
}

// Overloading the istream extraction operator
template<typename Item_Type>
  std::istream& operator>>(std::istream& in,
                           Binary_Tree<Item_Type>& tree) {
  tree = Binary_Tree<Item_Type>::read_binary_tree(in);
  return in;
}

// Implementation of member functions
...
#endif
```

The Constructors

There are three constructors: a no-parameter constructor, a constructor that creates a tree with a given node as its root, and a constructor that builds a tree from a data value and two trees.

The no-parameter constructor merely sets the data field root to NULL

```
Binary_Tree() : root(NULL) {}
```

The constructor that takes a BTNode as a parameter is a protected constructor. This is because client classes do not know about the BTNode class. This constructor can be used only by functions internal to the Binary_Tree class and its subclasses.

```
Binary_Tree(BTNode<Item_Type>* new_root) : root(new_root) {}
```

The third constructor takes three parameters: data to be referenced by the root node, and two Binary_Trees that will become its left and right subtrees.

```
Binary_Tree(const Item_Type& the_data,
            const Binary_Tree<Item_Type>& left_child
              = Binary_Tree(),
            const Binary_Tree<Item_Type>& right_child
              = Binary_Tree()):
    root(new BTNode<Item_Type>(the_data, left_child.root,
                               right_child.root)) {}
```

After its execution, the root node of the tree referenced by left_child (left_child.root) is pointed to by root->left, making left_child the left subtree of the new root node. If lT and rT are type Binary_Tree<char> and lT.root points to the root node of binary tree x + y and rT.root points to the root node of binary tree a / b, the statement

```
Binary_Tree<char> bT('*', lT, rT);
```

would cause bT to contain the tree shown in Figure 8.12.

Default values are provided for the second and third parameters. The default value is an empty tree (root value is NULL) created by the no-parameter constructor.

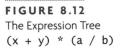

FIGURE 8.12
The Expression Tree
(x + y) * (a / b)

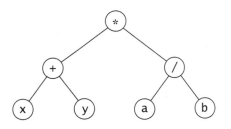

The **get_left_subtree** and **get_right_subtree** Functions

The get_left_subtree function returns a binary tree whose root is the left subtree of the object on which the function is called. It uses the protected constructor just discussed to construct a new Binary_Tree object whose root references the left subtree of this tree. The get_right_subtree function is symmetric.

```
/** Return the left-subtree. */
template<typename Item_Type>
  Binary_Tree<Item_Type>
    Binary_Tree<Item_Type>::get_left_subtree() const {
  if (root == NULL) {
    throw std::invalid_argument("get_left_subtree on empty tree");
  }
  return Binary_Tree<Item_Type>(root->left);
}
```

The `is_leaf` Function

The `is_leaf` function tests to see whether this tree has any subtrees. If there are no subtrees, then **true** is returned.

```
/** Indicate that this tree is a leaf. */
template<typename Item_Type>
  bool Binary_Tree<Item_Type>::is_leaf() const {
  if (root != NULL) {
    return root->left == NULL && root->right == NULL;
  } else
    return true;
}
```

The `to_string` Function

The `to_string` function generates a string representation of the `Binary_Tree` for output purposes. The string representation is a preorder traversal in which each local root is on a separate line. If a subtree is empty, the string `"NULL"` is displayed. The tree in Figure 8.12 would be displayed as follows:

```
*
+
x
NULL
NULL
y
NULL
NULL
/
a
NULL
NULL
b
NULL
NULL
```

The `to_string` function creates an `ostringstream` object. If the tree is empty, then it writes the string `"NULL\n"` to the `ostringstream`. Otherwise it writes the contents of the root using the `ostream` insertion operator followed by a newline character. Then it recursively applies the `to_string` function to the left and right subtrees.

```
/** Return a string representation of this tree. */
template<typename Item_Type>
  std::string Binary_Tree<Item_Type>::to_string() const {
  std::ostringstream os;
  if (is_null())
    os << "NULL\n";
  else {
    os << *root << '\n';
    os << get_left_subtree().to_string();
    os << get_right_subtree().to_string();
  }
  return os.str();
}
```

Reading a Binary Tree

If we use an istream to read the individual lines created by the to_string function previously discussed, we can reconstruct the binary tree using the algorithm:

1.   Read a line that represents information at the root.
2.   **if** it is "NULL"
3.   Return an empty tree.

    else

4.   Convert the input line to a data value.
5.   Recursively read the left child.
6.   Recursively read the right child.
7.   Return a tree consisting of the root and the two children.

The tree that is constructed will be type Binary_Tree<Item_Type>. The code for a function that implements this algorithm is shown in Listing 8.2.

....

LISTING 8.2
Function to Read a Binary Tree

```
template<typename Item_Type>
  Binary_Tree<Item_Type> Binary_Tree<Item_Type>::
    read_binary_tree(std::istream& in) {
  std::string next_line;
  getline(in, next_line);
  if (next_line == "NULL") {
    return Binary_Tree<Item_Type>();
  } else {
    Item_Type the_data;
    std::istringstream ins(next_line);
    ins >> the_data;
    Binary_Tree<Item_Type> left = read_binary_tree(in);
    Binary_Tree<Item_Type> right = read_binary_tree(in);
    return Binary_Tree<Item_Type>(the_data, left, right);
  }
}
```

Using **istream** and **ostream**

We can overload the istream extraction operator for the Binary_Tree class to call the read_binary_tree function and we can overload the ostream insertion operator to call the to_string function. By doing this, we can read and write Binary_Tree objects in the same manner as we read and write other objects.

```
// Overloading the ostream insertion operator.
template<typename Item_Type>
  std::ostream& operator<<(std::ostream& out,
                           const Binary_Tree<Item_Type>& tree) {
  return out << tree.to_string();
}
```

```
// Overloading the istream extraction operator.
template<typename Item_Type>
  std::istream& operator>>(std::istream& in,
                           Binary_Tree<Item_Type>& tree) {
  tree = Binary_Tree<Item_Type>::read_binary_tree(in);
  return in;
}
```

Copy Constructor, Assignment, and Destructor

We have not provided copy constructors, assignment operators, or functioning destructors for the Binary_Tree and BTNode classes. This is intentional. The purpose of these classes is to illustrate the binary tree ADT and not to provide a robust implementation. The constructor

```
Binary_Tree(const Item_Type& the_data,
            const Binary_Tree<Item_Type>& left_child,
            const Binary_Tree<Item_Type>& right_child)
```

and the functions get_left_subtree and get_right_subtree can result in multiple Binary_Tree objects containing pointers either directly or indirectly to a given BTNode object. One solution would be for this constructor and these functions to make a copy of the subtree arguments. Then the Binary_Tree destructor could call the root's BTNode destructor, which would then recursively call the destructors for all of the nodes in the tree. There are many cases where this would be very inefficient. Thus, we have decided to live with potential memory leaks for these classes.

An alternative would be to use what is known as a *smart pointer* for the pointers in the BTNode and Binary_Tree classes. A smart pointer is a class that acts like a pointer, but automatically deletes the object pointed to when the pointed-to object has no owners. We describe smart pointers in more detail in Appendix A.

EXERCISES FOR SECTION 8.3

SELF-CHECK

1. Draw the linked representation of the two trees below. See Figure 8.11 for an example.

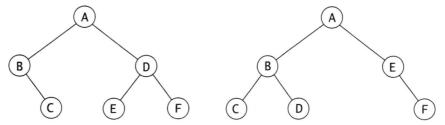

2. Show the tree that would be built by the following data lines:

```
30
15
4
NULL
NULL
20
18
NULL
19
NULL
NULL
NULL
35
32
NULL
NULL
38
NULL
NULL
```

3. What can you say about this tree?

4. Write the strings that would be displayed for the two binary trees in Figure 8.6.

PROGRAMMING

1. Write a function for the `Binary_Tree` class that returns the preorder traversal of a binary tree as a sequence of strings each separated by a space.

2. Write a function to display the postorder traversal of a binary tree in the same form as Programming Exercise 1.

3. Write a recursive member function to find the height of a `Binary_Tree`.

4. Write a recursive member function to find the number of nodes in a `Binary_Tree`.

5. Write a function to display the inorder traversal of a binary tree in the same form as Programming Exercise 1, except place a left parenthesis before each subtree and a right parenthesis after each subtree. Don't display anything for an empty subtree. For example, the expression tree shown in Figure 8.12 would be represented as (((x) + (y)) * ((a) / (b))).

8.4 Binary Search Trees

Overview of a Binary Search Tree

In Section 8.1 we provided the following recursive definition of a binary search tree:

A set of nodes T is a binary search tree if either of the following is true:

- T is empty
- If T is not empty, its root node has 0, 1, or 2 nonempty subtrees. Its left subtree, T_L, is a binary search tree that contains all values less than the value in

the root of T; its right subtree, T_R, is a binary search tree that contains all values greater than the value in the root of T.

We will assume that all entries saved in a binary search tree are unique (no duplicates). Figure 8.13 shows a binary search tree that contains the words in lowercase from the nursery rhyme "The House That Jack Built." We can use the following algorithm to find an object in a binary search tree.

Recursive Algorithm for Searching a Binary Search Tree

1.   **if** the root is NULL
2.   The item is not in the tree; return NULL.
3.   Compare the value of target, the item being sought, with root->data.
4.   **if** they are equal
5.   The target has been found, return the data at the root.
      else if target is less than root->data
6.   Return the result of searching the left subtree.
      else
7.   Return the result of searching the right subtree.

FIGURE 8.13
Binary Search Tree Containing All of the Words from "The House That Jack Built"

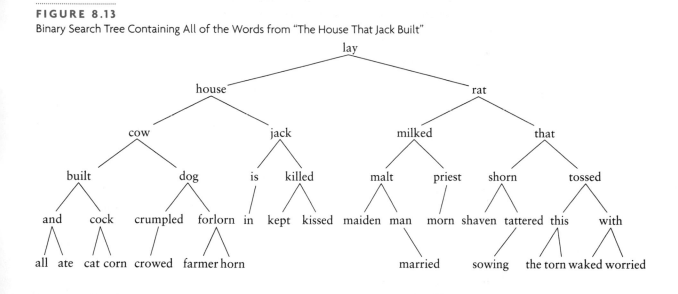

EXAMPLE 8.2   Suppose we wish to find *jill* in Figure 8.13. We first compare *jill* with *lay*. Because *jill* is less than *lay*, we continue the search with the left subtree and compare *jill* with *house*. Because *jill* is greater than *house*, we continue with the right subtree and compare *jill* with *jack*. Because *jill* is greater than *jack*, we continue with *killed* followed by *kept*. Now *kept* has no left child, and *jill* is less than *kept*, so we conclude that *jill* is not in this binary search tree. (She's in a different nursery rhyme.) Follow the entire path marked in color in Figure 8.14.

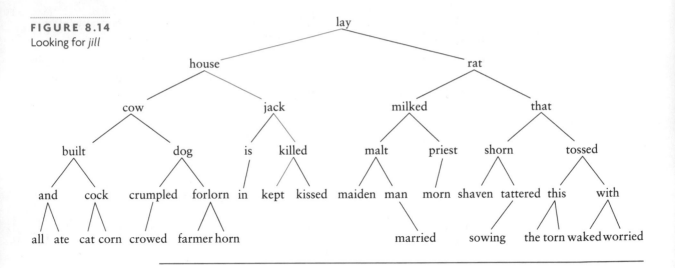

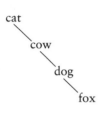

Performance

Searching the tree in Figure 8.13 is O(log *n*). However, if a tree is not very full, performance will be worse. The tree in the figure at left has only right subtrees, so searching it is O(*n*). In general, the performance is O(*h*), where *h* is the height of the tree.

The `Binary_Search_Tree` Class

Next we implement class `Binary_Search_Tree`. The type parameter specified when we create a new `Binary_Search_Tree` must implement the less-than operator (<).

Table 8.3 shows the design of this class. The class definition follows. Notice that class `Binary_Search_Tree` extends class `Binary_Tree` (see Figure 8.15). Class `Binary_Search_Tree` inherits the data field root from class `Binary_Tree` (declared as protected). Listing 8.3 shows the class definition. Functions insert and erase are declared `virtual` because we will extend `Binary_Search_Tree` in Chapter 11. The private member functions are used in the implementation of the public functions and are discussed subsequently.

TABLE 8.3
Design of the Class `Binary_Search_Tree`

Function	Behavior
`bool insert(const Item_Type& item)`	Inserts an item into the tree. Returns **true** if the item was inserted, **false** if the item was already in the tree.
`bool erase(const Item_Type& item)`	Remove an item from the tree. Returns **true** if the item was removed, **false** if the item was not in the tree.
`const Item_Type* find(const Item_Type& target) const`	Return a pointer to an item in the tree, or NULL if the item is not in the tree.

FIGURE 8.15
UML Diagram of
Binary_Search_Tree

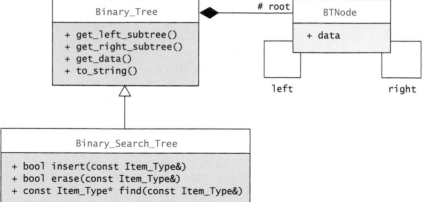

LISTING 8.3
Binary_Search_Tree.h

```
#ifndef BINARY_SEARCH_TREE_H
#define BINARY_SEARCH_TREE_H

#include "Binary_Tree.h"

/** Definition of the Binary Search Tree class.
    @param Item_Type The type of item to be stored in the tree
    Note: Item_Type must define the less-than operator as a
    total ordering.
*/
template<typename Item_Type>
  class Binary_Search_Tree : public Binary_Tree<Item_Type>
{
  public:
  // Constructor
  /** Construct an empty Binary_Search_Tree */
  Binary_Search_Tree() : Binary_Tree<Item_Type>() {}

  // Public Member Functions
  /** Insert an item into the tree.
      post: The item is in the tree.
      @param item The item to be inserted
      @return true if the item was not already
              in the tree, false otherwise
  */
  virtual bool insert(const Item_Type& item);

  /** Remove an item from the tree.
      post: The item is no longer in the tree.
      @param item The item to be removed
      @return true if the item was in the tree,
              false otherwise
  */
  virtual bool erase(const Item_Type& item);
```

```
        /** Determine whether an item is in the tree.
            @param item The item sought
            @return A const pointer to the item if in the
                    tree, or NULL if not
        */
        const Item_Type* find(const Item_Type& target) const;

    private:

        // Private Member Functions
        /** Insert an item into the tree.
            post: The item is in the tree.
            @param local_root A reference to the current root
            @param item The item to be inserted
            @return true if the item was not already in the
                    tree, false otherwise
        */
        virtual bool insert(BTNode<Item_Type>*& local_root,
                            const Item_Type& item);

        /** Remove an item from the tree.
            post: The item is no longer in the tree.
            @param local_root A reference to the current root
            @param item The item to be removed
            @return true if the item was in the tree,
                    false otherwise
        */
        virtual bool erase(BTNode<Item_Type>*& local_root,
                           const Item_Type& item);

        /** Determine whether an item is in the tree.
            @param local_root A reference to the current root
            @param target The item sought
            @return A const pointer to the item in the tree
        */
        const Item_Type* find(BTNode<Item_Type>* local_root,
                             const Item_Type& target) const;

        /** Find a replacement for a node that is being deleted.
            This function finds the rightmost local root that
            does not have a right child. The data in this local_root
            replaces the data in old_root. The pointer to local_root
            is then saved in old_root and local_root is replaced
            by its left child.
            @param old_root Reference to the pointer to old parent
            @param local_root Reference to the pointer to local root
        */
        virtual void replace_parent(BTNode<Item_Type>*& old_root,
                                    BTNode<Item_Type>*& local_root);

}; // End binary search tree

// Implementation of member functions
...

#endif
```

Implementing the **find** Functions

Earlier we showed a recursive algorithm for searching a binary search tree. Next we show how to implement this algorithm and a non-recursive starter function for the algorithm. Our function find will return a pointer to the data within the node that contains the information we are seeking.

Listing 8.4 shows the code for function find. In the starter function, the statement

```
return find(this->root, target);
```

calls the recursive find function with the tree root as its first parameter. When a template class (Binary_Tree in this case) is used as a base class of another template class (Binary_Search_Tree), the names of members of the base class are not found by the compiler unless they are qualified with the prefix this->. If bST is a Binary_Search_Tree, the function call bST.find(target) invokes the starter function.

The recursive function first tests the local root for NULL. If it is NULL, the object is not in the tree, so NULL is returned.

If the local root is not NULL, we see whether the target is less than the data at the local_root. If it is, we recursively call the function find, passing the left subtree of the local_root as the parameter.

```
return find(local_root->left, target);
```

If it is not, we see whether the data at the local_root is less than the target. (Recall that Item_Type is only required to implement the less-than operator.) If it is, we call find to search the right subtree.

```
return find(local_root->right, target);
```

If the target is not less than the data at the local_root, and if the data at the local_root is not less than the target, then we conclude that the target is equal to the data at the local_root. We then return a pointer to this data.

```
return &(local_root->data);
```

LISTING 8.4
Binary_Search_Tree find Function

```
template<typename Item_Type>
  const Item_Type* Binary_Search_Tree<Item_Type>::find(
    const Item_Type& target) const {
  return find(this->root, target);
}

template<typename Item_Type>
  const Item_Type* Binary_Search_Tree<Item_Type>::find(
    BTNode<Item_Type>* local_root,
    const Item_Type& target) const {
  if (local_root == NULL)
    return NULL;
  if (target < local_root->data)
    return find(local_root->left, target);
  else if (local_root->data < target)
    return find(local_root->right, target);
  else
    return &(local_root->data);
}
```

> ⊘ **PITFALL**
>
> ### Failure to Qualify a Template Base Class Member Name
>
> If you fail to qualify a template base class member name within a template derived class, you may get an error message. However, if this name happens to be defined outside the class, you will not get an error, but your program will not execute as expected. This is because the other name will be used. For example, if there was a global variable root, and we omitted this-> from the call to find, then find would start the search using the contents of this global variable.

Insertion into a Binary Search Tree

Inserting an item into a binary search tree follows a similar algorithm as searching for the item, because we are trying to find where in the tree the item would be, if it were there. In searching, a result of NULL is an indicator of failure; in inserting, we replace this NULL with a new leaf that contains the new item. If we reach a node that contains the object we are trying to insert, then we can't insert it (duplicates are not allowed), so we return **false** to indicate that we were unable to perform the insertion. The insertion algorithm follows.

Recursive Algorithm for Insertion in a Binary Search Tree

1. **if** the root is NULL
2.   Replace empty tree with a new tree with the item at the root and return **true**.
3. **else if** the item is equal to root->data
4.   The item is already in the tree; return **false**.
5. **else if** the item is less than root->data
6.   Recursively insert the item in the left subtree.
7. **else**
8.   Recursively insert the item in the right subtree.

The algorithm returns **true** when the new object is inserted and **false** if it is a duplicate (the second stopping case). The first stopping case tests for an empty tree. If so, a new Binary_Search_Tree is created, and the new item is stored in its root node (Step 2).

EXAMPLE 8.3   To insert *jill* into Figure 8.13, we would follow the steps shown in Example 8.2 except that when we reached *kept*, we would insert *jill* as the left child of the node that contains *kept* (see Figure 8.16).

FIGURE 8.16
Inserting *jill*

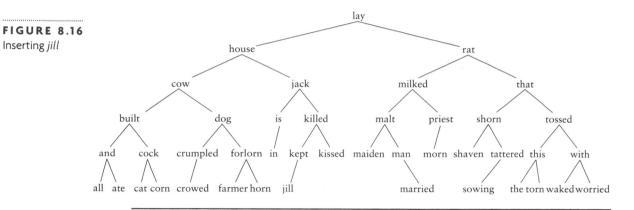

Implementing the **insert** Functions

Listing 8.5 shows the code for the starter and recursive insert functions. The recursive insert follows the algorithm presented earlier, except that the order of the tests needs to be changed similar to that used for find. This is because we only can perform a less-than comparison on Item_Type values.

In method insert, we define the parameter local_root as type BTNode<Item_Type>*& where there is both a * and a & following the type BTNode<Item_Type>. The * indicates that local_root is a pointer and the & indicates that local_root is a reference. When there is a * followed by a &, this indicates that local_root is a reference to a pointer to a BTNode<Item_Type>. Recall that when you pass an argument to a function by reference, any changes make to the corresponding parameter by the function are made to the argument.

The starter function calls the recursive function with the tree root as its argument. If the root was initially NULL, the statement

```
local_root =
   new BTNode<Item_Type>(item);
```

sets root to point to a newly created BTNode.

If the local_root is not NULL, then we follow the same pattern as in the find function and test to see whether the item to be inserted is less than local_root->data. If it is, we recursively call insert with local_root->left as the first argument.

```
return insert(local_root->left, item);
```

If item is not less than local_root->data, we then test to see whether local_root->data is less than item. If it is, we recursively call insert with local_root->right as the first argument.

```
return insert(local_root->right, item);
```

If both tests fail, then the item is already in the tree, and we return **false**.

If the item is not in the tree, the sequence of recursive calls will eventually lead to local_root being NULL. The statement

```
local_root =
   new BTNode<Item_Type>(item);
```

will set the caller's local_root->left or the caller's local_root->right to point to the newly created BTNode.

LISTING 8.5
Binary_Search_Tree insert Functions

```
template<typename Item_Type>
  bool Binary_Search_Tree<Item_Type>::insert(
    const Item_Type& item) {
  return insert(this->root, item);
}

template<typename Item_Type>
  bool Binary_Search_Tree<Item_Type>::insert(
    BTNode<Item_Type>*& local_root,
    const Item_Type& item) {
  if (local_root == NULL) {
    local_root =
      new BTNode<Item_Type>(item);
    return true;
  } else {
    if (item < local_root->data)
      return insert(local_root->left, item);
    else if (local_root->data < item)
      return insert(local_root->right, item);
    else {
      return false;
    }
  }
}
```

Removal from a Binary Search Tree

Removal also follows the search algorithm, except that when the item is found, it is removed. If the item is a leaf node, then its parent's reference to it is set to NULL, thereby removing the leaf node. If the item has only a left or right child, then the grandparent references the remaining child instead of the child's parent (the node we want to remove).

EXAMPLE 8.4   If we remove the node *is* from Figure 8.13, we can replace it with *in*. This is accomplished by changing the left child reference in *jack* (the grandparent) to reference *in* (see Figure 8.17).

FIGURE 8.17
Removing *is*

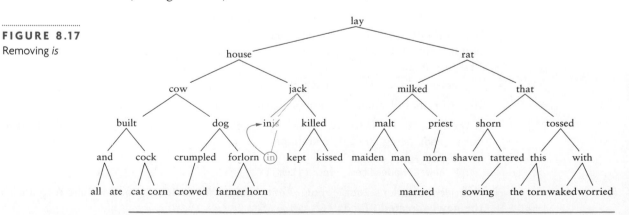

A complication arises when the item we wish to remove has two children. In this case we need to find a replacement parent for the children. Remember that the parent must be larger than all of the data fields in the left subtree and smaller than all of the data fields in the right subtree. If we take the largest item in the left subtree and promote it to be the parent, then all of the remaining items in the left subtree will be smaller. This item is also less than the items in the right subtree. This item is also known as the *inorder predecessor* of the item being removed. (We could use the inorder successor instead; this is discussed in the exercises.)

EXAMPLE 8.5   If we remove *house* from Figure 8.13, we look in the left subtree (root contains *cow*) for the largest item, *horn*. We then replace "house" with "horn" and remove the node *horn* (see Figure 8.18).

FIGURE 8.18
Removing *house*

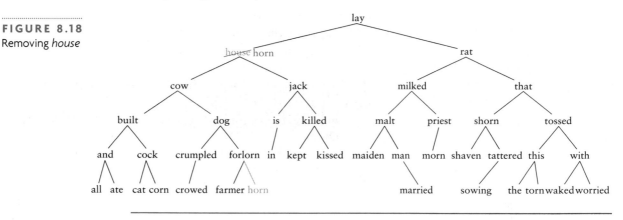

EXAMPLE 8.6   If we want to remove *rat* from the tree in Figure 8.13, we would start the search for the inorder successor at *milked* and see that it has a right child, *priest*. If we now look at *priest*, we see that it does not have a right child, but it does have a left child. We would then replace "rat" with "priest" and replace the reference to *priest* in *milked* with a reference to *morn* (the left subtree of the node *priest*). See Figure 8.19.

FIGURE 8.19
Removing *rat*

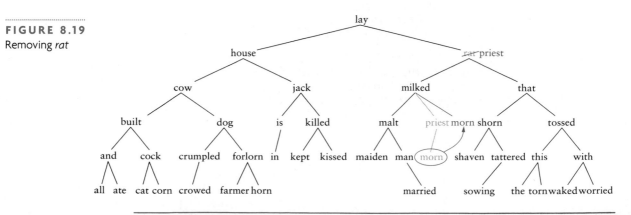

Recursive Algorithm for Removal from a Binary Search Tree

1.   **if** the root is NULL
2.   The item is not in tree – return NULL.
3.   Compare the item to the data at the local root.
4.   **if** the item is less than the data at the local root
5.   Return the result of deleting from the left subtree.
6.   **else if** the item is greater than the local root
7.   Return the result of deleting from the right subtree.
8.   **else**   // *The item is in the local root*
9.   **if** the local root has no children
10.   Set the parent of the local root to reference NULL.
11.   **else if** the local root has one child
12.   Set the parent of the local root to reference that child.
13.   **else**   // *Find the inorder predecessor*
14.   **if** the left child has no right child,
                    it is the inorder predecessor
15.   Set the parent of the local root to reference the left child.
16.   **else**
17.   Find the rightmost node in the right subtree of the left child.
18.   Copy its data into the local root's data and remove it by setting its parent to reference its left child.

Implementing the **erase** Functions

Listing 8.6 shows both the starter and the recursive erase functions. As with the insert function, the recursive erase function returns a **bool** value to indicate whether the item was removed or was not in the tree.

LISTING 8.6
Binary_Search_Tree erase Functions

```
template<typename Item_Type>
  bool Binary_Search_Tree<Item_Type>::erase(
    const Item_Type& item) {
  return erase(this->root, item);
}

template<typename Item_Type>
  bool Binary_Search_Tree<Item_Type>::erase(
    BTNode<Item_Type>*& local_root,
    const Item_Type& item) {
  if (local_root == NULL) {
    return false;
  } else {
    if (item < local_root->data)
      return erase(local_root->left, item);
```

```
        else if (local_root->data < item)
          return erase(local_root->right, item);
        else { // Found item
          BTNode<Item_Type>* old_root = local_root;
          if (local_root->left == NULL) {
            local_root = local_root->right;
          } else if (local_root->right == NULL) {
            local_root = local_root->left;
          } else {
            replace_parent(old_root, old_root->left);
          }
          delete old_root;
          return true;
        }
    }
  }
}
```

For the recursive function the two stopping cases are an empty tree and a tree whose root contains the item being removed. We first test to see whether the tree is empty (local root is NULL). If so, then the item sought is not in the tree, and **false** is returned. Next, local_root->data is compared to the item to be deleted. If the item to be deleted is less than local_root->data, it must be in the left subtree if it is in the tree at all, so we recursively call erase with local_root->left as the new local_root parameter.

```
        return erase(local_root->left, item);
```

Any change made to the local_root parameter by the recursive call will be made to the caller's local_root->left, thus changing the caller's left subtree.

If the local_root->data is less than the item to be deleted, the statement

```
        return erase(local_root->right, item);
```

affects the right subtree of local_root in a similar way.

If local_root->data is the item to be deleted, we have reached the second stopping case, beginning with the line

```
        else { // Found item
```

A pointer to the node containing the item is saved in old_root. If the node to be deleted has one child (or zero children), we set the local_root (parent of the deleted node) to point to its only grandchild (or NULL). Thus the node containing the item to be deleted (pointed to by old_root) has been unlinked from the tree.

If the node to be deleted (such as *jack*) has two children, we need to find the replacement for this node. This is done by the function replace_parent. Upon return from replace_parent the value in local_root->data will be the data value of the inorder predecessor of the item deleted. The pointer old_root will now point to the node that contained this value, and this node will have been unlinked from the tree. We describe how replace_parent does this next.

Whether the node to be deleted has zero, one, or two children, old_root points to a node that has been unlinked from the tree. We return this node to the free storage pool, and then return **true** to indicate that an item has been removed from the tree.

The `replace_parent` Function

The function `replace_parent` (see Listing 8.7) takes two reference parameters. The parameter `old_root` is a reference to a pointer to the node that contains the item to be removed. The parameter `local_root` is a reference to a pointer to a node that might contain the replacement value.

The function is initially called with `old_root` bound to the caller's `old_root` and with `local_root` bound to the caller's `old_root->left`. If this left child has no right sub-tree (as in deleting *jack*), the left child (node *is*) is the inorder predecessor. The first of the following statements,

```
old_root->data = local_root->data;
old_root = local_root;
local_root = local_root->left;
```

copies the left child's data into the `old_root`'s data (`"is"` to *jack*); the second statement now changes `old_root` to point to the left child; and the third statement resets the local node's left branch to reference its left child's left subtree (*in*).

If the left child of the node to be deleted has a right subtree, we recursively call `replace_parent`, leaving `old_root` referencing the node containing the item to be removed, and `local_root` referencing the current `local_root`'s right child.

```
replace_parent(old_root, local_root->right);
```

The recursion will terminate when `local_root` references a pointer to the rightmost child (a node with no right child) of the original parameter. This is illustrated in Figure 8.19. When the recursion reaches its stopping case, `old_root` will point to the node containing the value to be removed (*rat*). The left child (*milked*) of the node to be deleted (*rat*) has a right child (*priest*), which is its largest child. The parameter `local_root` will reference the node *priest*. Therefore, `old_root->data` will now contain `"priest"` (replacing `"rat"`). Then `old_root` is changed so that it points to the node *priest* and the node *morn* (the left child of *priest*) becomes the new right child of *milked*.

....
LISTING 8.7
Function `replace_parent`

```
template<typename Item_Type>
  void Binary_Search_Tree<Item_Type>::replace_parent(
    BTNode<Item_Type>*& old_root,
    BTNode<Item_Type>*& local_root) {
  if (local_root->right != NULL) {
    replace_parent(old_root, local_root->right);
```

```
    } else {
      old_root->data = local_root->data;
      old_root = local_root;
      local_root = local_root->left;
    }
  }
}
```

Testing a Binary Search Tree

To test a binary search tree, you need to verify that an inorder traversal will display the tree contents in ascending order after a series of insertions (to build the tree) and deletions are performed. You can base the main function of your testing code on that shown in Listing 4.3 (which validates these operations for an Ordered_List). You need to write a function that returns a vector of strings built from an inorder traversal. These strings should be in alphabetical order (see Programming Exercise 3).

CASE STUDY   Writing an Index for a Term Paper

Problem   You would like to write an index for a term paper. The index should show each word in the paper followed by the line number in which it occurred. The words should be displayed in alphabetical order. If a word occurs on multiple lines, the line numbers should be listed in ascending order. For example, the three lines

```
a, 3
a, 13
are, 3
```

show that the word "a" occurred on lines 3 and 13 and the word "are" occurred on line 3.

Analysis   A binary search tree is an ideal data structure to use for storing the index entries. We can store each word and its line number as a string in a tree node. For example, the two occurrences of the word "C++" on lines 5 and 10 could be stored as the strings "c++,   5" and "c++,   10". Each word will be stored in lowercase to ensure that it appears in its proper position in the index. The line number is right-justified so that the string "c++,   5" is considered less than the string "c++,   10". If the leading spaces were removed, this would not be the case ("c++, 5" is greater than "c++, 10"). After all the strings are stored in the search tree, we can display them in ascending order by performing an inorder traversal. Storing each word in a search tree is an $O(\log n)$ process, where n is the number of words currently in the tree. Storing each word in an ordered list would be an $O(n)$ process.

Design   We will use the Binary_Search_Tree just discussed to store the index. Function build_index will read each word from a data file and store it in the search tree. Function print_index will display the index.

Implementation   Listing 8.8 shows the program Index_Generator. In function build_index, the outer **while** loop reads each data line into next_line. After incrementing line_num, a new String_Tokenizer object (discussed after the listing) is created for the current data line. The inner **while** loop processes each token. The statements

```
string word = tokenizer.next_token();
to_lower(word);
```

extracts the next word from next_line and converts it to lower case. We then use an ostringstream to construct a string that consists of this word, followed by a comma, and followed by the value of line_num. The statements

```
os << right;
os << setw(3) << line_num;
```

formats line_num with leading spaces so that it occupies a total of 3 columns. Use of the manipulators right and setw are described in the *C++ Primer*.

Function print_index performs an inorder traversal of a Binary_Tree (recall that Binary_Tree is a base class of Binary_Search_Tree). This function is left as an exercise.

LISTING 8.8
Index_Generator.cpp

```cpp
/** Program to generate a simple index. */

#include <fstream>
#include <sstream>
#include <iostream>
#include <cctype>
#include <iomanip>
#include "String_Tokenizer.h"
#include "Binary_Search_Tree.h"

using namespace std;

/** Function to convert a string to lowercase.
    post: All characters in the string are converted
          to their lowercase equivalents.
    @param a_string The string to be converted
*/
void to_lower(string& a_string) {
  for (size_t i = 0; i < a_string.length(); i++)
    a_string[i] = tolower(a_string[i]);
}

/** Function to build the index.
    post: index contains the index of all words
          in the input file.
    @param index The Binary_Search_Tree that will
           contain the index
    @param in The istream that contains the file
```

```
*/
void build_index(Binary_Search_Tree<string>& index,
                 istream& in) {
  string next_line;
  int line_num = 0;
  while (getline(in, next_line)) {
    line_num++;
    String_Tokenizer tokenizer(next_line, " ,.:-!?/%\'\"");
    while (tokenizer.has_more_tokens()) {
      string word = tokenizer.next_token();
      to_lower(word);
      ostringstream os;
      os << word;
      os << ", ";
      os << right;
      os << setw(3) << line_num;
      index.insert(os.str());
    }
  }
}

/** Function to print the index in alphabetic order.
    Performs an inorder traversal of the index.
    @param index The Binary_Tree containing the index
           subtree being traversed.
*/
void print_index(const Binary_Tree<string>& index) {
  // Exercise
}

int main(int argc, char* argv[]) {
  // Exercise
}
```

The String_Tokenizer

Example P.16 in the C++ *Primer* showed how to use the string functions find_first_of and find_first_not_of to find individual tokens (substrings) in a longer string. A token is a substring that is delimited by a pair of delimiter characters (examples of delimiter characters are spaces and punctuation symbols).

We can use the code in that example to define a class String_Tokenizer (Listing 8.9). The constructor takes two string parameters: the line to be split and a string consisting of the delimiting characters. It initializes data members start and end to 0, but then calls function find_next to advance start to the first character that is not a delimiter and end to the first delimiter character after the character at start. The function has_more_tokens returns **true** if there are more substrings available. Function next_token returns the next substring (the characters between start and end). Before returning a token, it calls find_next to advance start and end to delimit the token following this one. Listing 8.9 shows the definition for the String_Tokenizer class, and Listing 8.10 shows the implementation.

....

LISTING 8.9
String_Tokenizer.h

```cpp
#ifndef STRING_TOKENIZER_H
#define STRING_TOKENIZER_H

#include <string>

/** The String_Tokenizer class splits a string into a sequence of
    subtrings, called tokens, separated by delimiters.
*/
class String_Tokenizer
{
  public:

  /** Construct a String_Tokenizer.
      @param source The string to be split into tokens
      @param delim The string containing the delimiters. If
                   this parameter is omitted, a space character is
                   assumed
  */
  String_Tokenizer(std::string source, std::string delim = " ") :
    the_source(source), the_delim(delim), start(0), end(0) {
    find_next();
  }

  /** Determine if there are more tokens.
      @return true if there are more tokens
  */
  bool has_more_tokens();

  /** Retrieve the next token.
      @return The next token. If there are no more tokens, an empty
              string is returned
  */
  std::string next_token();

  private:

  /** Position start and end so that start is the index of the start
      of the next token and end is the end.
  */
  void find_next();

  /** The string to be split into tokens */
  std::string the_source;

  /** The string of delimiters */
  std::string the_delim;

  /** The index of the start of the next token */
  size_t start;
```

```
    /** The index of the end of the next token */
    size_t end;
};

#endif
```

....

LISTING 8.10
String_Tokenizer.cpp

```
#include "String_Tokenizer.h"
using std::string;

/** Position start and end so that start is the index of the start
    of the next token and end is the end.
*/
void String_Tokenizer::find_next() {
  // Find the first character that is not a delimiter.
  start = the_source.find_first_not_of(the_delim, end);
  // Find the next delimiter.
  end = the_source.find_first_of(the_delim, start);
}

/** Determine if there are more tokens.
    @return true if there are more tokens
*/
bool String_Tokenizer::has_more_tokens() {
  return start != string::npos;
}

/** Retrieve the next token.
    @return The next token. If there are no more
            tokens, an empty string is returned
*/
string String_Tokenizer::next_token() {
  // Make sure there is a next token
  if (!has_more_tokens())
    return "";
  // Save the next token.
  string token = the_source.substr(start, end - start);
  // Find the following token.
  find_next();
  // Return the next token.
  return token;
}
```

Testing   To test program Index_Generator, write a main function that declares new ifstream and Binary_Tree<string> objects. The ifstream can reference any text file stored on your hard drive. Make sure that duplicate words are handled properly (including duplicates on the same line), that words at the end of each line are stored in the index, that empty lines are processed correctly, and that the last line of the document is also part of the index.

EXERCISES FOR SECTION 8.4

SELF-CHECK

1. Show the tree that would be formed for the following data items. Exchange the first and last items in each list, and rebuild the tree that would be formed if the items were inserted in the new order.

    a. happy, depressed, manic, sad, ecstatic

    b. 45, 30, 15, 50, 60, 20, 25, 90

2. Explain how the tree shown in Figure 8.13 would be changed if you inserted "mother". How would it be changed if you inserted "jane"? Does either of these insertions change the height of the tree?

3. Show or explain the effect of removing "kept" and "cow" from the tree in Figure 8.13.

4. In Exercise 3, a replacement must be chosen for the node *cow* because it has two children. What is the relationship between the replacement word and the word "cow"? What other word in the tree could also be used as a replacement for "cow"? What is the relationship between that word and the word "cow"?

5. The algorithm for deleting a node does not explicitly test for the situation where the node being deleted has no children. Explain why this is not necessary.

6. In Step 18 of the algorithm for deleting a node, when we replace the pointer to a node that we are removing with a pointer to its left child, why is it not a concern that we might lose the right subtree of the node that we are removing?

PROGRAMMING

1. Self-Check Exercise 4 indicates that there are two items that can be used to replace a data item in a binary search tree. Rewrite function erase so that it retrieves the leftmost element in the right subtree instead. You will also need to provide a function find_smallest_child.

2. Write a function that returns the tree contents in ascending order (using an inorder traversal) with newline characters separating the tree elements.

3. Write a main function to test a binary search tree based on Listing 4.3.

8.5 Heaps and Priority Queues

In this section, we discuss a binary tree that is ordered but in a different way than a binary search tree. In a *heap*, the value in each node is greater than all values in the node's subtrees. Figure 8.20 shows an example of a heap. Observe that 89 is the largest value. Observe that each parent is larger than its children, and that each parent has two children, with the exception of node 39 at the next-to-lowest level and the leaves. All nodes to the right of 39 (node 66) are leaf nodes. Furthermore, with the exception of 66, all leaves are at the lowest level.

FIGURE 8.20
Example of a Heap

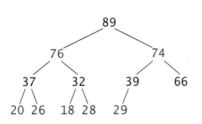

The heap shown in Figure 8.20 is called a *max heap* because the root node stores the largest value. It is also possible to build and use a *min heap*, in which each node's value is smaller than the values of its children, and the root node stores the smallest value.

A heap is a complete binary tree with the following properties:

- The value in the root is greater than or equal to all items in the tree.
- Every subtree is a heap

Inserting an Item into a Heap

We use the following algorithm for inserting an item into a heap. Our approach is to place each item initially in the bottom row of the heap and then move it up until it reaches the position where it belongs.

Algorithm for Inserting in a Heap

1. Insert the new item in the next position at the bottom of the heap.
2. `while` new item is not at the root and new item is larger than its parent
3.   Swap the new item with its parent, moving the new item up the heap.

New items are added to the last row of a heap. If a new item is smaller than or equal to its parent, nothing more need be done. If we insert 6 in the heap in Figure 8.20, 6 becomes the right child of 39, and we are done. However, if the new item is larger than its parent, the new item and its parent are swapped. This is repeated up the tree until the new item is in a position where it is no longer larger than its parent. For example, let's add 80 to the heap shown in Figure 8.21. Since 80 is larger than 66, these values are swapped as shown in Figure 8.22. Also, 80 is larger than 74, so these values are swapped resulting in the updated heap shown in Figure 8.23. But 80 is smaller than 89, so we are done.

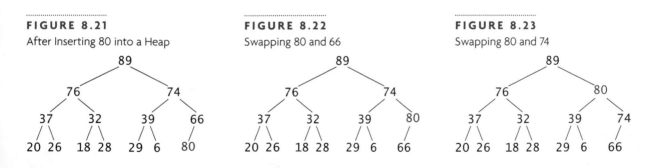

FIGURE 8.21
After Inserting 80 into a Heap

FIGURE 8.22
Swapping 80 and 66

FIGURE 8.23
Swapping 80 and 74

Removing an Item from a Heap

Removal from a heap is always from the top. The top item is first replaced with the last item in the heap (at the lower right-hand position), so that the heap remains a complete tree. If we used any other value, there would be a "hole" in the tree where that value used to be. Then the new item at the top is moved down the heap until it is in its proper position.

Algorithm for Removal from a Heap

1.   Remove the item in the root node by replacing it with the last item in the heap (LIH).
2.   `while` item LIH has children and item LIH is smaller than either of its children
3.   Swap item LIH with its larger child, moving LIH down the heap.

As an example, if we remove 89 from the heap shown in Figure 8.23, 66 replaces it as shown in Figure 8.24. Since 66 is smaller than both of its children, it is swapped with the larger of the two, 80, as shown in Figure 8.25. The result is still not a heap, because 66 is smaller than one of its children. Swapping 66 with its larger child, 74, restores the heap as shown in Figure 8.26.

Implementing a Heap

Because a heap is a complete binary tree, we can implement it efficiently using an array (or `vector`) instead of a linked data structure. We can use the first element (subscript 0) for storing the root data. We can use the next two elements (subscripts 1 and 2) for storing the two children of the root. We can use elements with subscripts 3, 4, 5, and 6 for storing the four children of these two nodes, and so on. Therefore, we can view a heap as a sequence of rows; each row is twice as long as the previous row. The first row (the root) has one item, the second row two, the third four, and so on. All of the rows are full except for the last one (see Figure 8.27).

Observe that the root, 89, is at position 0. The root's two children, 76 and 74, are at positions 1 and 2. For a node at position p, the left child is at $2p + 1$ and the right child is at $2p + 2$. A node at position c can find its parent at $(c - 1)/2$. Thus, as shown in Figure 8.27, the children of 32 (at position 4) are at positions 9 and 10.

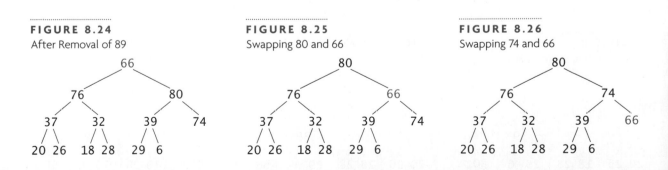

FIGURE 8.24
After Removal of 89

FIGURE 8.25
Swapping 80 and 66

FIGURE 8.26
Swapping 74 and 66

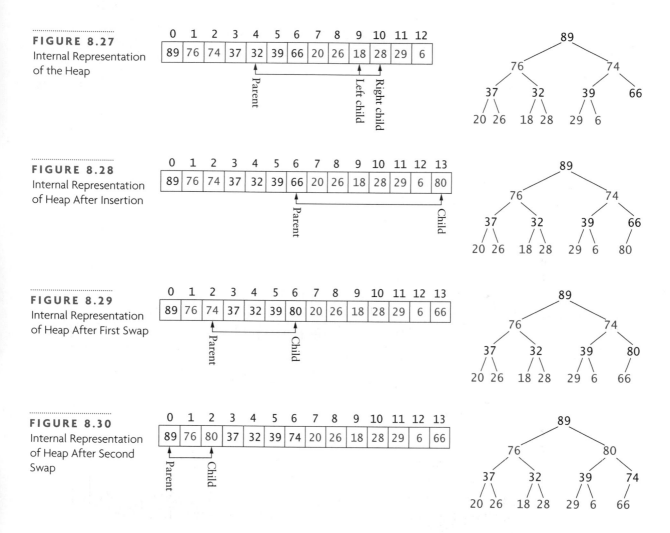

FIGURE 8.27
Internal Representation of the Heap

FIGURE 8.28
Internal Representation of Heap After Insertion

FIGURE 8.29
Internal Representation of Heap After First Swap

FIGURE 8.30
Internal Representation of Heap After Second Swap

Insertion into a Heap Implemented as a **vector**

We will use a vector for storing our heap because it is easier to expand and contract than an array. Figure 8.28 shows the heap after inserting 80 into position 13. This corresponds to inserting the new value into the lower right position as shown in the figure, right. Now we need to move 80 up the heap, by comparing it to the values stored in its ancestor nodes. The parent (66) is in position 6 (13 minus 1 is 12, divided by 2 is 6). Since 66 is smaller than 80, we need to swap as shown in Figure 8.29.

Now the child is at position 6 and the parent is at position 2 (6 minus 1 is 5, divided by 2 is 2). Since the parent, 74, is smaller than the child, 80, we must swap again as shown in Figure 8.30.

The child is now at position 2 and the parent at position 0. Since the parent is larger than the child, the heap property is restored. In the heap insertion and removal algorithms that follow, we will use table to reference the vector that stores the heap.

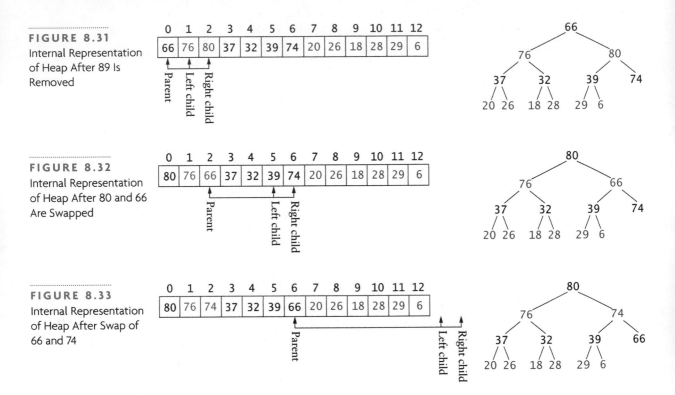

FIGURE 8.31
Internal Representation of Heap After 89 Is Removed

FIGURE 8.32
Internal Representation of Heap After 80 and 66 Are Swapped

FIGURE 8.33
Internal Representation of Heap After Swap of 66 and 74

Insertion of an Element into a Heap Implemented as a `vector`

1.   Insert the new element at the end of the `vector` and set `child` to `table.size() - 1`.
2.   Set `parent` to `(child - 1)/2`.
3.   **while** (`parent >= 0` and `table[parent] < table[child]`)
4.   Swap `table[parent]` and `table[child]`.
5.   Set `child` equal to `parent`.
6.   Set `parent` equal to `(child - 1)/2`.

Removal from a Heap Implemented as a **vector**

In removing elements from a heap, we must always remove the element at the top of the heap, which is the smallest element. We start with a `vector` that has been organized to form a heap. To remove the first item (89), we begin by replacing the first item with the last item, and then removing the last item. This is illustrated in Figure 8.31. The new value of the root (position 0) is smaller than both of its children (76 in position 1, and 80 in position 2). The larger of the two children (80 in position 2) is swapped with the parent as shown in Figure 8.32. Next, 66 is swapped with the larger of its two new children (74) and the heap is restored (Figure 8.33).

The algorithm for removal from a heap implemented as a **vector** follows:

Removing an Element from a Heap Implemented as a `vector`

1. Remove the last element (that is, the one at `size()` - 1) and set the item at 0 to this value.
2. Set parent to 0.
3. **while (true)**
4.   Set `left_child` to (2 * parent) + 1 and `right_child` to `left_child + 1`.
5.   **if** `left_child >= table.size()`
6.   Break out of loop.
7.   Assume `max_child` (the larger child) is `left_child`.
8.   **if** `right_child < table.size()` and `table[left_child] < table[right_child]`
9.   Set `max_child` to `right_child`.
10.   **if** `table[parent] < table[max_child]`
11.   Swap `table[parent]` and `table[max_child]`.
12.   Set parent to `max_child`.
    else
13.   Break out of loop.

The loop (Step 3) is terminated under one of two circumstances: Either the item has moved down the tree so that it has no children (line 5 is true), or it is larger than both its children (line 10 is false). In these cases, the loop terminates (line 6 or 13). This is shown in Figure 8.33. At this point the heap property is restored, and the next smallest item can be removed from the heap.

Performance of the Heap

The remove algorithm traces a path from the root to a leaf, and the insert algorithm traces a path from a leaf to the root. This requires at most h steps, where h is the height of the tree. The largest heap of height h is a full tree of height h. This tree has $2^h - 1$ nodes. The smallest heap of height h is a complete tree of height h, consisting of a full tree of height $h - 1$, with a single node as the left child of the leftmost child at height $h - 1$. Thus, this tree has $2^{(h-1)}$ nodes. Therefore, both `insert` and `remove` are $O(\log n)$, where n is the number of items in the heap.

Priority Queues

In computer science, a heap is used as the basis of a very efficient algorithm for sorting arrays, called heapsort, which you will study in Chapter 10. The heap is also used to implement a special kind of queue called a *priority queue*.

Sometimes a FIFO (First-In-First-Out) queue may not be the best way to implement a waiting line. In a print queue you might want to print a short document before some longer documents that were ahead of the short document in the queue. For example, if you were waiting by the printer for a single page to print, it would be very frustrating to have to wait until several documents of 50 pages or more were printed just because they entered the queue before yours did. Therefore, a better way to implement a print queue would be to use a priority queue. A priority queue is a data structure in which only the highest-priority item is accessible. During insertion, the position of an item in the queue is based on its priority relative to the priorities of other items in the queue. If a new item has higher priority than all items currently in the queue, it will be placed at the front of the queue and, therefore, will be removed before any of the other items inserted in the queue at an earlier time. This violates the FIFO property of an ordinary queue.

EXAMPLE 8.7　Figure 8.34 sketches a print queue that at first (top of diagram) contains two documents. We will assume that each document's priority is inversely proportional to its page count (priority is 1/page_count). The middle queue shows the effect of inserting a document 3 pages long. The bottom queue shows the effect of inserting a second one-page document: It follows the earlier document with that page length.

FIGURE 8.34
Insertion into a Priority Queue

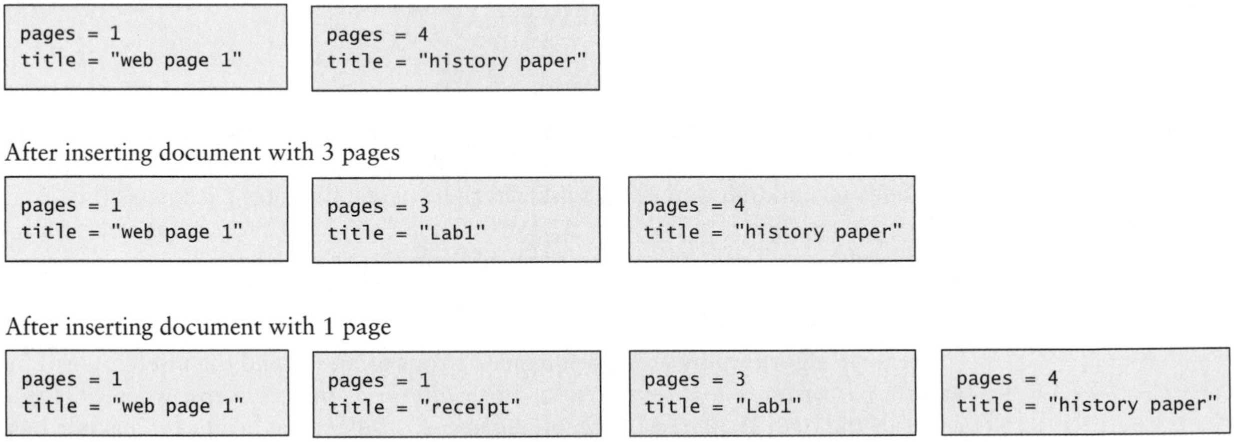

```
pages = 1                 pages = 4
title = "web page 1"      title = "history paper"
```

After inserting document with 3 pages

```
pages = 1                 pages = 3            pages = 4
title = "web page 1"      title = "Lab1"       title = "history paper"
```

After inserting document with 1 page

```
pages = 1                 pages = 1            pages = 3            pages = 4
title = "web page 1"      title = "receipt"    title = "Lab1"       title = "history paper"
```

The `priority_queue` Class

C++ provides a `priority_queue` class that uses the same interface as the queue given in Chapter 6. The differences are in the specification for the `top` and `pop` functions. These are defined to return the largest item in the queue rather than the oldest item in the queue. Table 8.5 summarizes the functions of the `priority_queue` class.

Using a Heap as the Basis of a Priority Queue

The largest item is always removed first from a priority queue (the largest item has the highest priority), just as it is for a heap. Because insertion into and removal from a heap is O(log *n*), a heap can be the basis for an efficient implementation of a priority queue. We will call our class KW::priority_queue to differentiate it from class std::priority_queue in the C++ standard library, which also uses a heap as the basis of its implementation. The interfaces for our class and the standard class are identical, but the implementations are slightly different.

TABLE 8.5
Functions of the `priority_queue` Class

Function	Behavior
`void push(const Item_Type& item)`	Inserts an item into the queue.
`void pop()`	Removes the largest entry if the queue is not empty. If the queue is empty, a run-time error may occur.
`const Item_Type& top() const`	Returns the largest entry without removing it. If the queue is empty, a run-time error may occur.
`size_t size() const`	Returns the number of items in the priority queue.
`bool empty() const`	Returns **true** if the queue is empty, **false** otherwise.

To remove an item from the priority queue, we take the first item from the vector; this is the largest item. We then remove the last item from the vector and put it into the first position of the vector, overwriting the value currently there. Then following the algorithm described earlier, we move this item down until it is larger than its children or it has no children.

Design of the `KW::priority_queue` Class

The design of the `KW::priority_queue` class is shown in Table 8.6. The data field `the_data` is used to store the heap. We discuss the purpose of data field `comp` shortly. By default, it acts like the less-than operator. The class definition follows.

```cpp
#ifndef PRIORITY_QUEUE_H
#define PRIORITY_QUEUE_H

#include <vector>
#include <functional>

namespace KW {

  /** Priority queue based on a heap stored in a vector. */
  template<typename Item_Type,
           typename Container = std::vector<Item_Type>,
           typename Compare = std::less<Item_Type> >
    class priority_queue {

    public:

      /** Construct an empty priority queue. */
      priority_queue() {}

      /** Insert an item into the priority queue. */
      void push(const Item_Type& item);

      /** Remove the largest item. */
      void pop();
```

```
                    /** Return true if the priority queue is empty. */
                    bool empty() const {return the_data.empty();}

                    /** Return the number of items in the priority queue. */
                    size_t size() const {return the_data.size();}

                    /** Return a reference to the smallest item */
                    const Item_Type& top() const {return the_data.front();}

                private:

                    /** The vector to hold the data */
                    Container the_data;

                    /** The comparator function object */
                    Compare comp;

                };

                // Implementation of Member Functions
                ...
            } // End namespace KW

            #endif
```

Specifying Defaults for a Template Class

The template class heading

```
template<typename Item_Type,
         typename Container = std::vector<Item_Type>,
         typename Compare = std::less<Item_Type> >
  class priority_queue {
```

prescribes defaults for data types `Container` (default is a `vector`) and `Compare` (default is operator `less`). In an application, the declaration

```
priority_queue<string> pQa;
```

creates a priority queue `pQa` that uses a `vector` (the default) for storage of string data and operator `less` (the default) for comparisons. The declaration

```
priority_queue<string, deque<string> > pQb;
```

creates a priority queue `pQb` that uses a `deque` for storage of string data and operator `less` (the default) for comparisons. We show how to specify a different comparison operator shortly.

TABLE 8.6
Design of `KW::priority_queue` Class

Data Field	Attribute
Container the_data	A sequential container to hold the data. A `std::vector` is used by default, but a deque may also be used.
Compare comp	The function object that performs comparison. By default, this function is equivalent to operator<(const Item_Type&, const Item_Type&).

The **push** Function

The push function appends the new item to the the_data, using its push_back function. It then moves this item up the heap until the container is restored to a heap.

```
template<typename Item_Type, typename Container, typename Compare>
  void priority_queue<Item_Type, Container, Compare>::push(
    const Item_Type& item) {
  the_data.push_back(item);
  int child = size() - 1;
  int parent = (child - 1) / 2;
  // Reheap
  while (parent >= 0
        && comp(the_data[parent], the_data[child])) {
    std::swap(the_data[child], the_data[parent]);
    child = parent;
    parent = (child - 1) / 2;
  }
}
```

The **while** loop condition,

```
while (parent >= 0
      && comp(the_data[parent], the_data[child])) {
```

first tests to see whether the index parent is greater than or equal to zero. If it is, it then tests to see whether the_data[parent] is less than the_data[child]. If it is, then we need to move the child up by calling on the standard swap function to exchange the values in the_data[parent] and the_data[child]. Otherwise the heap property has been restored, so the loop exits.

The **pop** Function

If there is a single item in the heap, the pop function removes it. Otherwise, the pop function removes the last item from the heap and places it at the top. Then it moves the item at the top down the heap until the heap property is restored. It then returns the original top of the heap.

```
template<typename Item_Type, typename Container, typename Compare>
  void priority_queue<Item_Type, Container, Compare>::pop() {
  if (size() == 1) {
    the_data.pop_back();
    return;
  }
  std::swap(the_data[0], the_data[size() - 1]);
  the_data.pop_back();
  int parent = 0;
  while (true) {
    int left_child = 2 * parent + 1;
    if (left_child >= size())
      break; // out of heap
    int right_child = left_child + 1;
    int max_child = left_child;
    if (right_child < size()
        && comp(the_data[left_child], the_data[right_child]))
      max_child = right_child;
```

```
                        // assert: max_child is the index of the larger child
                        if (comp(the_data[parent], the_data[max_child])) {
                          std::swap(the_data[max_child], the_data[parent]);
                          parent = max_child;
                        }
                        else
                          break;
                      }
                    }
```

Using a Compare Function Class

How do we compare elements in a priority queue? In many cases, we will insert objects that implement operator< and use their natural ordering. However, we may need to insert objects that do not implement operator<, or we may want to specify a different ordering from that defined by the object's operator<. For example, files to be printed may be ordered by their name using the operator< function, but we may want to assign priority based on their length.

To indicate that we want to use an ordering that is different than the natural ordering for the objects in our heap, we will provide a template argument that is a function class. This function class's operator() will perform the comparison.

EXAMPLE 8.8   The class Print_Document is used to define documents to be printed on a printer. This class implements the operator<, but its operator< function performs a lexical comparison of document names which has no bearing on their print order—we want the print order to be a function of the file size and time submitted. The class has a get_size function that gives the number of bytes to be transmitted to the printer, and a get_time_stamp function that gets the time that the print job was submitted. If we were to use either time or size alone, small documents could be delayed while big ones are printed, or the big documents would never be printed. By using a priority value that is a combination, we achieve a balanced usage of the printer.

We define a Compare function class for our Print_Document class as shown in Listing 8.11. The function order_value computes the weighted sum of the size and time_stamp using the weighting factors P1 and P2. Since we want the Print_Document whose order_value is the smallest to be printed first, the **return** statement actually applies the > operator to the two order_values. By making our compare function class implement a greater-than comparison, we invert the order of the items in the heap, effectively building a min heap instead of a max heap, so that the item at the top of the heap has the smallest order_value.

In a client program, we can use the statement

```
priority_queue<Print_Document,
    std::vector<Print_Document>, Compare_Print_Documents>
    print_queue;
```

to create a print queue.

....

LISTING 8.11
Compare_Print_Documents.h

```
#ifndef COMPARE_PRINT_DOCUMENTS_H
#define COMPARE_PRINT_DOCUMENTS_H

#include "Print_Document.h"

class Compare_Print_Documents
{
  public:

  bool operator()(const Print_Document& left,
                  const Print_Document& right) {
    return order_value(left) > order_value(right);
  }

  private:

  static const double P1 = 1.0;
  static const double P2 = 0.001;

  double order_value(const Print_Document& pd) {
    return P1 * pd.get_size() + P2 * pd.get_time_stamp();
  }

};

#endif
```

The `std::less` Function Class

If a Compare function class is not provided when the priority_queue is declared, the std::less class is used. This template class is defined in the header <functional> and it has a definition that is equivalent to the following:

```
template<typename value_type>
  struct less {
    bool operator()(const value_type& left,
                    const value_type& right) {
      return left < right;
    }
  };
```

EXERCISES FOR SECTION 8.5

SELF-CHECK

1. Show the heap that would be used to store the words *this, is, the, house, that, jack, built*, assuming they are inserted in that sequence. Exchange the order of arrival of the first and last words and build the new heap.

2. Draw the heaps for Exercise 1 as arrays.

3. Show the result of removing the number 76 from the heap in Figure 8.26. Show the new heap and its array representation.

4. The largest object should be removed first from a priority queue. Explain why operator `less` is used as the default to compare objects being placed in a priority queue instead of operator `greater`.

PROGRAMMING

1. Write a `Compare` function class that inserts `Person` objects in a priority queue based on the number of dependents a person has. The `Person` object with the largest number of dependents should be removed first.

8.6 Huffman Trees

In Section 8.1 we showed the Huffman coding tree and how it can be used to decode a message. We will now implement some of the functions needed to build a tree and decode a message. We will do this using a binary tree and a `priority_queue` (which also uses a binary tree).

A straight binary coding of an alphabet assigns a unique binary number k to each symbol in the alphabet a_k. An example of such a coding is ASCII, which is used by C++ for the **char** data type. There are 256 possible characters, and they are assigned a number between 0 and 255, which is a string of 8 binary digit ones. Therefore, the length of a message would be $8 \times n$, where n is the total number of characters in the message. For example, the message "go eagles" contains 9 characters and would require 9×8 or 72 bits. As shown in the example in Section 8.1, a Huffman coding of this message requires just 38 bits.

Table 8.8, based on data published in Donald Knuth, *The Art of Computer Programming, Vol 3: Sorting and Searching* (Addison-Wesley, 1973), p. 441, represents the relative frequencies of the letters in English text and is the basis of the tree shown in Figure 8.35. The letter *e* occurs an average of 103 times every 1,000 letters, or 10.3% of the letters are *e*'s. (This is a useful table to know if you are a fan of *Wheel of Fortune*.) We can use this Huffman tree to encode and decode a file of English text. However, files may contain other symbols or may contain these symbols in different frequencies than what is found in normal English. For this reason, you may want to build a custom Huffman tree based on the contents of the file you are encoding. You would then attach this tree to the encoded file so that it can be used to decode the file. We discuss how to build a Huffman tree in the next case study.

TABLE 8.8
Frequency of Letters in English Text

Symbol	Frequency	Symbol	Frequency	Symbol	Frequency
⎵	186	h	47	g	15
e	103	d	32	p	15
t	80	l	32	b	13
a	64	u	23	v	8
o	63	c	22	k	5
i	57	f	21	j	1
n	57	m	20	q	1
s	51	w	18	x	1
r	48	y	16	z	1

FIGURE 8.35
Huffman Tree Based on Frequency of Letters in English Text

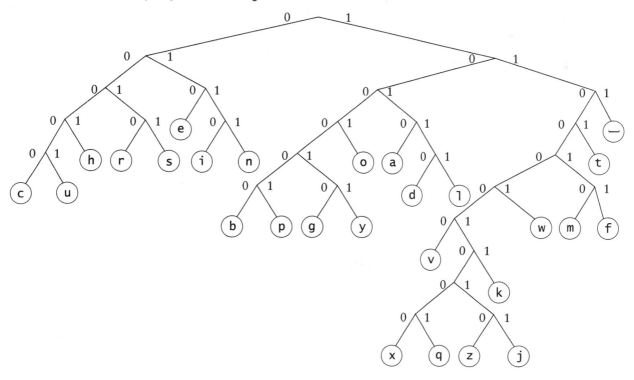

CASE STUDY   Building a Custom Huffman Tree

Problem   You want to build a custom Huffman tree for a particular file. Your input will consist of a vector of objects such that each object contains a symbol occurring in that file and the frequency of occurrence (weight) for the symbol in that file.

Analysis   Each node of a Huffman tree has storage for two data items: the weight of the node and the symbol associated with that node. All symbols will be stored at leaf nodes. The symbol part has no meaning for internal nodes. The weight of a leaf node will be the frequency of the symbol stored at that node. The weight of an internal node will be the sum of frequencies of all nodes in the subtree rooted at the internal node. For example, the internal node with leaf nodes c and u (on the left of Figure 8.35), would have a weight of 45 (22 + 23).

We will use a priority queue as the key data structure in constructing the Huffman tree. We will store individual symbols and subtrees of multiple symbols in order by their priority (frequency of occurrence). We want to remove symbols that occur less frequently first, because they should be lower down in the Huffman tree we are constructing. We discuss how this is done next.

FIGURE 8.36
Priority Queue with
the Symbols a, b, c, d,
and e

13	22	32	64	103
b	c	d	a	e

To build a Huffman tree, we start by inserting trees with just leaf nodes in a priority queue. Each leaf node will store a symbol and its weight. The queue elements will be ordered so that the leaf node with smallest weight (lowest frequency) is removed first. Figure 8.36 shows a priority queue, containing just the symbols a, b, c, d, e, that uses the weights shown in Table 8.8. The item at the front of the queue stores a reference to a tree with a root node that is a leaf node containing the symbol b with a weight (frequency) of 13. To represent the tree referenced by a queue element, we list the root node information for that tree. The queue elements are shown in priority order.

Now we start to build the Huffman tree. We build it from the bottom up. The first step is to remove the first two trees from the priority queue and combine them to form a new tree. The weight of the root node for this tree will be the sum of the weights of its left and right subtrees. We insert the new tree back into the priority queue. The priority queue now contains references to four binary trees instead of five. The tree referenced by the second element of the queue has a combined weight of 35 (13 + 22) as shown below.

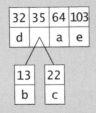

Again we remove the first two tree references and combine them. The new binary tree will have a weight of 67 in its root node. We put this tree back in the queue, and it will be the second element of the queue.

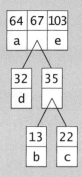

We repeat this process again. The new queue follows:

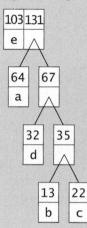

Finally we combine the last two elements into a new tree and put it into the priority queue. Now there is only one tree in the queue, so we have finished building the Huffman tree (see Figure 8.37). Table 8.9 shows the codes for this tree.

Design   The class Huff_Data will represent the data to be stored in each node of the Huffman binary tree. For a leaf, a Huff_Data object will contain the symbol and the weight.

Our class Huffman_Tree will have the functions and attributes listed in Table 8.10.

FIGURE 8.37
Huffman Tree of a, b, c, d, e

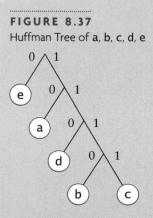

TABLE 8.9
Huffman Code of a, b, c, d, e

Symbol	Code
a	10
b	1110
c	1111
d	110
e	0

TABLE 8.10
Data Fields and Functions of Class `Huffman_Tree`

Data Field	Attribute
`Binary_Tree<Huff_Data> huff_tree`	The Huffman tree.

Function	Behavior
`void build_tree(const` `  vector<Huff_Data>& symbols)`	Builds the Huffman tree using the given alphabet and weights.
`string decode(const string&` `  coded_message) const`	Decodes a message using the generated Huffman tree.
`void print_code(ostream& out) const`	Outputs the resulting code.

Algorithm for Building a Huffman Tree

1. Construct a set of trees with root nodes that contain each of the individual symbols and their weights.
2. Place the set of trees into a priority queue.
3. `while` the priority queue has more than one item
4.   Remove the two trees with the smallest weights.
5.   Combine them into a new binary tree in which the weight of the tree root is the sum of the weights of its children.
6.   Insert the newly created tree back into the priority queue.

Each time through the `while` loop, two nodes are removed from the priority queue and one is inserted. Thus, effectively, one tree is removed, and the queue gets smaller with each pass through the loop.

Implementation   Listing 8.12 shows the class definition for class `Huffman_Tree`. The `Compare_Huffman_Tree` class and the functions are discussed in following subsections.

LISTING 8.12
Huffman_Tree.h

```
#ifndef HUFFMAN_TREE_H
#define HUFFMAN_TREE_H

#include <vector>
#include <string>
#include <ostream>
#include "Binary_Tree.h"

/** A datum in the Huffman_Tree */
struct Huff_Data
{
  // Data Fields
  /** The weight or probability assigned to this Huff_Data */
  double weight;
  /** The alphabet symbol if this is a leaf */
  char symbol;
```

```cpp
  // Constructor
  Huff_Data(double w, char c) : weight(w), symbol(c) {}
};

// ostream operator for Huff_Data
std::ostream& operator<<(std::ostream&, const Huff_Data&);

/** The comparator for Huff_Data. */
struct Compare_Huffman_Trees
{
  bool operator()(const Binary_Tree<Huff_Data>& left_tree,
                  const Binary_Tree<Huff_Data>& right_tree) {
    double wLeft = left_tree.get_data().weight;
    double wRight = right_tree.get_data().weight;
    return wLeft > wRight;
  }
};

/** Class to represent and build a Huffman tree. */
class Huffman_Tree
{
  public:

  /** Builds the Huffman tree using the given alphabet
      and weights.
      post: huff_tree contains the Huffman tree.
  */
  void build_tree(const std::vector<Huff_Data>& symbols);

  /** Output the resulting code.
      @param out An ostream to write the output
  */
  void print_code(std::ostream& out) const {
    print_code(out, "", huff_tree);
  }

  /** Function to decode a message that is input as a string of
      '1' and '0' characters.
      @param coded_message The input message as a string of
                            zeros and ones
      @return The decoded message as a string
  */
  std::string decode(const std::string& coded_message) const;

  private:

  /** Outputs the resulting code.
      @param ostream An ostream to write the output
      @param code The code up to this node
      @param tree The current node in the tree
  */
  void print_code(std::ostream& out, std::string code,
                  const Binary_Tree<Huff_Data>& tree) const;
  // Data fields
  Binary_Tree<Huff_Data> huff_tree;

};

#endif
```

The Comparator

Because the `Binary_Tree` class does not implement `operator<`, we need to define a comparator for use with our `priority_queue`. It will compare the weights in the `Huff_Data` objects stored in the root node of each Huffman tree, and, since we want the tree with the smallest weight to be removed first from the priority queue, we use the result of the greater than operator on the weights.

The **build_tree** Function

Function `build_tree` (see Listing 8.13) takes a vector of `Huff_Data` objects as its parameter. The statement

```
priority_queue<Binary_Tree<Huff_Data>,
   std::vector<Binary_Tree<Huff_Data> >,
   Compare_Huffman_Trees> the_queue;
```

creates a new priority queue for storing `Binary_Tree<Huff_Data>` objects using the `priority_queue`. (We could use either the standard priority queue or the KW priority queue.) This priority queue will use a `Compare_Huffman_Trees` comparator.

The **for** loop loads the priority queue with trees consisting of just leaf nodes. Each leaf node contains a `Huff_Data` object with the weight and alphabet symbol.

The **while** loop builds the tree. Each time through this loop, the trees with the smallest weights are removed and referenced by left and right. The statements

```
Huff_Data sum(wl + wr, 0);
Binary_Tree<Huff_Data> new_tree(sum, left, right);
the_queue.push(new_tree);
```

combine them to form a new `Binary_Tree` with a root node whose weight is the sum of the weights of its children and whose symbol is 0. This new tree is then inserted into the priority queue. The number of trees in the queue decreases by 1 each time we do this. Eventually there will only be one tree in the queue, and that will be the final Huffman tree. The last statement sets the variable `huff_tree` to contain this tree.

LISTING 8.13
The `build_tree` Function (Huffman_Tree.cpp)

```
void Huffman_Tree::build_tree(
  const std::vector<Huff_Data>& symbols) {
    priority_queue<Binary_Tree<Huff_Data>,
      std::vector<Binary_Tree<Huff_Data> >,
      Compare_Huffman_Trees> the_queue;
  for (size_t i = 0; i < symbols.size(); i++) {
    the_queue.push(Binary_Tree<Huff_Data>(symbols[i]));
  }
  // Build the tree.
  while (the_queue.size() > 1) {
    Binary_Tree<Huff_Data> left = the_queue.top();
    the_queue.pop();
    Binary_Tree<Huff_Data> right = the_queue.top();
    the_queue.pop();
    double wl = left.get_data().weight;
    double wr = right.get_data().weight;
    Huff_Data sum(wl + wr, 0);
```

```
        Binary_Tree<Huff_Data> new_tree(sum, left, right);
        the_queue.push(new_tree);
    }
    huff_tree = the_queue.top();
    the_queue.pop();
}
```

Testing Functions `print_code` and `decode` can be used to test the custom Huffman tree. Function `print_code` displays the tree, so you can examine it and verify that the Huffman tree that was built is correct based on the input data.

Function `decode` will decode a message that has been encoded using the code stored in the Huffman tree and displayed by `print_code`. So you can pass it a message string that consists of binary digits only and see whether it can be transformed back to the original symbols.

We will discuss testing the Huffman tree further in the next chapter when we continue the case study.

The `print_code` Function

To display the code for each alphabet symbol, we perform a preorder traversal of the final tree. The code so far is passed as a parameter, along with the current node. If the current node is a leaf, as indicated by the symbol not being 0, then the code is output. Otherwise the left and right subtrees are traversed. When we traverse the left subtree, we append a 0 to the code, and when we traverse the right subtree, we append a 1 to the code. Recall that at each level in the recursion there is a new copy of the parameters and local variables.

```
void Huffman_Tree::print_code(ostream& out, string code,
    const Binary_Tree<Huff_Data>& tree) const {
  Huff_Data the_data = tree.get_data();
  if (the_data.symbol != 0) {
    if (the_data.symbol == ' ') {
      out << "space: " << code << '\n';
    } else {
      out << the_data.symbol << ": " << code << '\n';
    }
  } else {
    print_code(out, code + "0", tree.get_left_subtree());
    print_code(out, code + "1", tree.get_right_subtree());
  }
}
```

The `decode` Function

To illustrate the decode process we will show a function that takes a `string` that contains a sequence of the digit characters `'0'` and `'1'` and decodes it into a message that is also a `string`. Function decode starts by setting `current_tree` to the Huffman tree. It then loops through the coded message one character at a time. If the character is a `'1'`, then `current_tree` is set to the right subtree; otherwise it is set to the left subtree. If the `current_tree` is now a leaf, the symbol is appended to the result, and `current_tree` is reset to the Huffman tree (see Listing 8.14). Note that this function is for testing purposes only. In actual usage, a message would be coded as a string of bits (not digit characters) and would be decoded one bit at a time.

···········

LISTING 8.14
The decode Function (Huffman_Tree.cpp)

```cpp
string Huffman_Tree::decode(const string& coded_message) const {
  string result;
  Binary_Tree<Huff_Data> current_tree = huff_tree;
  for (size_t i = 0; i < coded_message.length(); i++) {
    if (coded_message[i] == '1') {
      current_tree = current_tree.get_right_subtree();
    } else {
      current_tree = current_tree.get_left_subtree();
    }
    if (current_tree.is_leaf()) {
      Huff_Data the_data = current_tree.get_data();
      result += the_data.symbol;
      current_tree = huff_tree;
    }
  }
  return result;
}
```

☑ **PROGRAM STYLE**

A Generic Huffman_Tree Class

We chose to implement a nongeneric Huffman_Tree class to simplify the coding.
However, it may be desirable to build a Huffman tree for storing strings (for example, to
encode words in a document instead of the individual letters) or for storing groups of
pixels in an image file. We can do this by making the Huffman_Tree, Huff_Data and
Compare_Huffman_Tree classes template classes. The template parameter would represent the type of the symbols. The implementation of the member functions would need
to be included in the .h file that contains the class definitions.

EXERCISES FOR SECTION 8.6

SELF-CHECK

1. What is the Huffman code for the letters a, j, k, l, s, t, v using Figure 8.35?
2. Create the Huffman code tree for the following frequency table:

Symbol	Frequency
*	50
+	30
–	25
/	10
%	5

3. What would the Huffman code look like if all symbols in the alphabet had equal frequency?

PROGRAMMING

1. Write a function encode for the Huffman_Tree class that encodes a string of letters that is passed as its first argument. Assume that a second parameter, codes (type const vector<string>&), contains the code strings (binary digits) for the symbols (space at position 0, *a* at position 1, *b* at position 2, and so on).

Chapter Review

◆ A tree is a recursive, nonlinear data structure that is used to represent data that is organized as a hierarchy.

◆ A binary tree is a collection of nodes with three components: a reference to a data object, a reference to a left subtree, and a reference to a right subtree. A binary tree object has a single data field, which references the root node of the tree.

◆ In a binary tree used to represent arithmetic expressions, the root node should store the operator that is evaluated last. All internal nodes store operators, and the leaf nodes store operands. An inorder traversal (traverse left subtree, visit root, traverse right subtree) of an expression tree yields an infix expression, a preorder traversal (visit root, traverse left subtree, traverse right subtree) yields a prefix expression, and a postorder traversal (traverse left subtree, traverse right subtree, visit root) yields a postfix expression.

◆ A binary search tree is a tree in which the data stored in the left subtree of every node is less than the data stored in the root node, and the data stored in the right subtree of every node is greater than the data stored in the root node. The performance is proportional to the height of the tree and can range from $O(n)$ (for trees that resemble linked lists) to $O(\log n)$ (if the tree is full). An inorder traversal visits the nodes in increasing order.

◆ A heap is a complete binary tree in which the data in each node is greater (less) than the data in both its subtrees. A heap can be implemented very effectively as an array or vector. The children of the node at subscript p are at subscripts $2p + 1$ and $2p + 2$. The parent of child c is at $(c - 1)/2$. The item at the top of a max (min) heap is the largest (smallest) item.

◆ Insertion and removal in a heap are both $O(\log n)$. For this reason, a heap can be used to implement a priority queue efficiently. A priority queue is a data structure in which the item with the highest priority is removed next. The item with the highest priority is at the top of a heap and is always removed next.

◆ A Huffman tree is a binary tree used to store a code that facilitates file compression. The length of the bit string corresponding to a symbol in the file is inversely proportional to its frequency, so the symbol with the highest frequency of occurrence has the shortest length. In building a Huffman tree, a priority queue is used to store the symbols and trees formed so far. Each step in building the Huffman tree consists of removing two items and forming a new tree with these two items as the left and right subtrees of the new tree's root node. A reference to each new tree is inserted in the priority queue.

Quick-Check Exercises

1. For the following expression tree

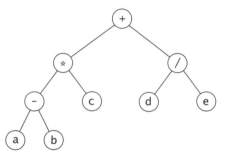

   a. Is the tree full? _____ Is the tree complete? _____
   b. List the order in which the nodes would be visited in a preorder traversal.
   c. List the order in which the nodes would be visited in an inorder traversal.
   d. List the order in which the nodes would be visited in a postorder traversal.
2. Searching a full binary search tree is O(____).
3. A heap is a binary tree that is a (full / complete) tree.
4. Show the binary search tree that would result from inserting the items 35, 20, 30, 50, 45, 60, 18, 25 in this sequence.
5. Show the binary search tree in Exercise 4 after 35 is removed.
6. Show the max heap that would result from inserting the items from Exercise 4 in the order given.
7. Draw the max heap from Exercise 6 as an array.
8. Show the max heap in Exercise 7 after 60 is removed.
9. In a Huffman tree, the item with the highest frequency of occurrence will have the _____ code.
10. List the code for each symbol shown in the following Huffman tree.

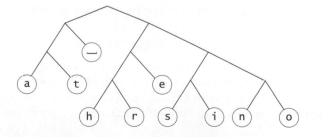

Answers to Quick-Check Exercises

1. **a.** Not full, complete
   b. + * − a b c / d e
   c. a − b * c + d / e
   d. a b − c * d e / +
2. $O(\log n)$.
3. A heap is a binary tree that is a *complete* tree.
4.

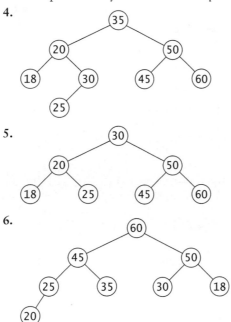

5.

6.

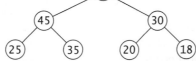

7. 60, 45, 50, 25, 35, 30, 18, 20, where 60 is at position 0 and 20 is at position 7.
8.

9. In a Huffman tree, the item with the highest frequency of occurrence will have the *shortest* code.

10.

Symbol	Code	Symbol	Code
Space	01	n	1110
a	000	o	1111
e	101	r	1001
h	1000	s	1100
i	1101	t	001

Review Questions

1. Draw the tree that would be formed by inserting the words in this question into a binary search tree. Use lowercase letters.
2. Show all three traversals of this tree.
3. Show the tree from Question 1 after removing *draw*, *by*, and *letters* in that order.
4. Answer Question 1, but store the words in a heap instead of a binary search tree.
5. Given the following frequency table, construct a Huffman code tree. Show the initial priority queue and all changes in its state as the tree is constructed.

Symbol	Frequency
x	34
y	28
w	20
a	10
b	8
c	5

Programming Projects

1. Assume that a class `Expression_Tree` has a data field that is a `Binary_Tree`. Write an instance function to evaluate an expression stored in a binary tree whose nodes contain either integer values (stored in `string` objects) or operators (stored in `string` objects). Your function should implement the following algorithm:

   Algorithm to Evaluate an Expression Tree

   1.   **if** the root node is an integer
   2.   Return the integer value.
   3.   **else if** the root node is an operator symbol
   4.   Let `left_val` be the value obtained by recursively applying this algorithm to the left subtree.
   5.   Let `right_val` be the value obtained by recursively applying this algorithm to the right subtree.
   6.   Return the value obtained by applying the operator in the root node to `left_val` and `right_val`.

   Use function `read_binary_tree` to read the expression tree in.

2. Write an application to test the `Huffman_Tree` class. Your application will need to read a text file and build a frequency table for the characters occurring in that file. Once that table is built, create a Huffman code tree and then a string consisting of `'0'` and `'1'` digit characters that represents the code string for that file. Read that string back in and recreate the contents of the original file.

3. Solve Programming Project 4 in Chapter 6, "Queues and Deques", using the class `priority_queue`.

4. Build a generic `Huffman_Tree<T>` class such that the symbol type T is specified when the tree is created. Test this class by using it to encode the words in your favorite nursery rhyme.

5. In a breadth-first traversal of a binary tree, the nodes are visited in an order prescribed by their depth. First visit the node at depth 0, the root node. Then visit the nodes at depth 1, in left-to-right order, and so on. You can use a queue to implement a breadth-first traversal of a binary tree:

Algorithm for Breadth-First Traversal of a Binary Tree

1. Insert the root node in the queue.
2. **while** the queue is not empty
3.   Remove a node from the queue and visit it.
4.   Place references to its left and right subtrees in the queue.

Code this algorithm and test it on several binary trees.

6. Define an `Index_Tree` class such that each node has data fields to store a word, the count of occurrences of that word in a document file, and the line number for each occurrence. Use a `list` to store the line numbers. Use an `Index_Tree` object to store an index of words appearing in a text file and then display the index by performing an inorder traversal of this tree.

7. Morse code (see Table 8.11) is a common code that is used to encode messages consisting of letters and digits. Each letter consists of a series of dots and dashes; for example, the code for the letter *a* is •— and the code for the letter *b* is —•••. Store each letter of the alphabet in a node of a binary tree of depth 4. The root node is at depth 0 and stores no letter. The left node at depth 1 stores the letter *e* (code is •) and the right node stores the letter *t* (code is —). The four nodes at depth 2 store the letters with codes (••, •—, —•, ——). To build the tree (see Figure 8.38), read a file in which each line consists of a letter followed by its code. The letters should be ordered by tree depth. To find the position for a letter in the tree, scan the code and branch left for a dot and branch right for a dash. Encode a message by replacing each letter by its code symbol. Then decode the message using the Morse code tree. Make sure you use a delimiter symbol between coded letters.

TABLE 8.11
Morse Code for Letters

a	•—	b	—•••	c	—•—•
d	—••	e	•	f	••—•
g	——•	h	••••	i	••
j	•———	k	—•—	l	•—••
m	——	n	—•	o	———
p	•——•	q	——•—	r	•—•
s	•••	t	—	u	••—
v	•••—	w	•——	x	—••—
y	—•——	z	——••		

Morse Code Tree

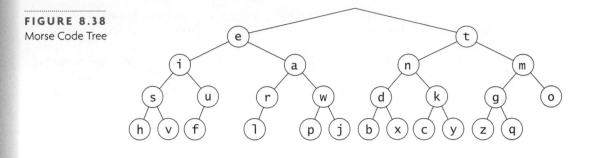

Chapter 9

Sets and Maps

Chapter Objectives

- ◆ To understand the C++ map and set containers and how to use them
- ◆ To learn about hash coding and its use to facilitate efficient search and retrieval
- ◆ To study two forms of hash tables—open addressing and chaining—and to understand their relative benefits and performance tradeoffs
- ◆ To learn how to implement both hash table forms
- ◆ To be introduced to the implementation of maps and sets
- ◆ To see how two earlier applications can be more easily implemented using map objects for data storage

I n Chapter 4 we introduced the C++ containers, focusing on the sequential containers vector and list. We also described the third sequential container, the deque, in Chapter 6. Searching for a particular value in a sequential container is generally an O(n) process. The exception is a binary search of a sorted object, which is an O(log n) process.

In this chapter we consider the other part of the container framework: the associative containers. The main purpose of associative containers is to enable efficient search and retrieval of information. It is also possible to remove elements from these collections without moving other elements around. By contrast, if an element is removed from a vector object, the elements that follow it are normally shifted over to fill the vacated space.

Included in the associative containers are the set and the map. These classes provide efficient search and retrieval of entries. The set is an implementation of the Set abstract data type. The map provides efficient search and retrieval of entries that consist of pairs of objects. The first object in each pair is the key, and the second object is the information associated with that key. You retrieve an object from a map by specifying its key.

We also study the hash table data structure. The hash table is a very important data structure that has been used very effectively in compilers for storing tables of symbols (identifiers) and in building dictionaries. It can be used as the underlying data structure for a map or set implementation. It stores objects at arbitrary locations and offers an average constant time for insertion, removal, and searching.

We will see two ways to implement a hash table and how to use it as the basis for a class that implements the map or set. We will not show you the complete implementation of an object that implements map or set, because we expect that you will use the ones provided by the C++ standard library. However, we will certainly tell you what you need to know to implement them.

9.1 Associative Container Requirements

We introduced the container class hierarchy in Chapter 4. We covered the part of that hierarchy that focuses on the sequential containers and their implementors. In this section we explore the Set interface and its implementors.

Figure 9.1 shows the part of the C++ standard library container hierarchy that relates to sets. In includes the set, multiset, map, and multimap. They are implemented in C++ using a special kind of binary search tree called the Red-Black tree (discussed in Chapter 11).

The Set Abstraction

What mathematicians call a set can be thought of as a collection of objects. There is the additional requirement that the elements contained in the set be unique. For example, if we have the set of fruits {"apples", "oranges", and "pineapples"} and add "apples" to it, we still have the same set. Also, we usually want to know whether or not a particular object is a member of the set rather than where in the set it is located. Thus, if s is a set, we would be interested in the expression contains(s, "apples") which returns the value **true** if "apples" is in set s and **false** if it is not.

FIGURE 9.1
The Set Hierarchy

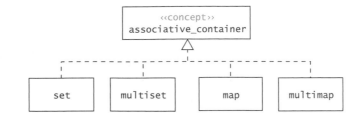

We assume that you are familiar with sets from a course in discrete mathematics. Just as a review, however, the operations that are performed on a mathematical set are testing for membership, adding elements, and removing elements. Other common operations on a mathematical set are *set union* (A ∪ B), *set intersection* (A ∩ B), and *set difference* (A − B). There is also a subset operator (A ⊂ B). These operations are defined as follows:

- The union of two sets A, B is a set whose elements belong either to A or B or to both A and B. Example: {1, 3, 5, 7} ∪ {2, 3, 4, 5} is {1, 2, 3, 4, 5, 7}
- The intersection of sets A, B is the set whose elements belong to both A and B. Example: {1, 3, 5, 7} ∩ {2, 3, 4, 5} is {3, 5}.
- The difference of sets A, B is the set whose elements belong to A but not to B. Examples: {1, 3, 5, 7} − {2, 3, 4, 5} is {1, 7}; {2, 3, 4, 5} − {1, 3, 5, 7} is {2, 4}
- Set A is a subset of set B if every element of set A is also an element of set B. Example: {1, 3, 5, 7} ⊂ {1, 2, 3, 4, 5, 7} is true.

The set Functions

A set has required functions for testing for set membership (find), testing for an empty set (empty), determining the set size (size), creating an iterator over the set (begin, end), adding an element (insert), and removing an element (erase). There are no set union, set intersection, or set difference member functions. However, these operators are defined in the algorithm header for all containers, not just sets.

Table 9.1 shows the commonly used functions of the set class. The set is a template class that takes the following template parameters:

- Key_Type: The type of the item contained in the set
- Compare: A function class that determines the ordering of the keys. By default this is the less-than operator.
- Allocator: The memory allocator for key objects. We will use the library-supplied default.

Although not a requirement of the Set abstraction, C++ stores items in a set as ordered by their Compare function. Thus, if you iterate through a set, you will get a sorted list of the contents.

Table 9.2 shows the set functions defined in the algorithm header that can be applied to any container. As shown in Table 9.2, the last function parameter is a comparison function (optional) that determines when one element is less than another. The default is the less-than operator. In Tables 9.1 and 9.2, type parameters II, II1, and II2 represent input iterators; type parameter OI represents an output iterator.

....

TABLE 9.1
Some **set** Member Functions

Function	Behavior
template<typename II> set(II first, II last)	Constructs a set from the sequence of objects represented by the iterator range first . . . last.
iterator begin(); const iterator begin() const	Returns an iterator to the first item in the set.
iterator end(); const_iterator end()	Returns an iterator to one past the last item in the set.
bool empty()	Returns **true** if there are no items in the set.
int size()	Returns the number of items in the set.
pair<iterator, bool> insert(const Key_Type& item)	Inserts an item into the set. If the item is not in the set, the returned **iterator** will reference the inserted item, and the **bool** parameter will be **true**. If the item is already in the set, the returned **iterator** (the **iterator** parameter) will reference the item that is currently in the set, and the **bool** parameter will be **false**.
template<typename II> void insert(II first, II last)	Inserts the items from the sequence of objects represented by the iterator range first . . . last. Duplicate values are not inserted. The iterator range must not reference elements in the target set.
void erase(const Key_Type& item)	Removes the item from the set.
iterator find(const Key_Type& item)	Returns an iterator that references the item in the set. If the item is not present, end() is returned.

....

TABLE 9.2
Set Functions from <algorithm>

Function	Behavior
template<typename II1, typename II2, typename OI, typename Compare> OI set_difference(II1 first1, II1 last1, II2 first2, II2 last2, OI result, Compare less)	Forms the set difference of the element in the sorted sequence first1 . . . last1 and the elements in the sorted sequence first2 . . . last2. The set difference is stored in result. An iterator to the end of result is returned.
template<typename II1, typename II2, typename OI, typename Compare> OI set_intersection(II1 first1, II1 last1, II2 first2, II2 last2, OI result, Compare less)	Forms the set intersection of the element in the sorted sequence first1 . . . last1 and the elements in the sorted sequence first2 . . . last2. The set difference is stored in result. An iterator to the end of result is returned.
template<typename II1, typename II2, typename OI, typename Compare> OI set_union(II1 first1, II1 last1, II2 first2, II2 last2, OI result, Compare less)	Forms the set union of the element in the sorted sequence first1 . . . last1 and the elements in the sorted sequence first2 . . . last2. The set union is stored in result. An iterator to the end of result is returned.

Function insert(const Key_Type& item) returns two results, a **bool** value and an
iterator to the set, as denoted by the result type pair<bool, iterator>. We discuss
class pair at the end of Section 9.1. We show how to use these functions next.

EXAMPLE 9.1   Listing 9.1 contains a main function that creates two sets: set1 and set2. It loads
these sets from two arrays and then forms their set union, difference, and intersection. The statement

```
set1.insert(data1, data1 + 3);
```

uses the insert operator with two iterator arguments to load the data from string
array data1 into set1. Notice that the second iterator, data1 + 3, is just past the
third (and last) element of array data1.

The statement

```
cout << "set1 is " << set1 << endl;
```

uses the overloaded insertion operator << (in file Set_Functions.h) to display the
elements of the first set including braces and commas. Notice that the elements are
displayed in alphabetical order. We discuss the insertion operator in the next section.

The statement

```
set_union(set1.begin(), set1.end(),
          set2.begin(), set2.end(),
          inserter(set_u, set_u.begin()));
```

uses function set_union to form the union of set1 and set2 in the initially empty
set<string> set_u. Instead of using an output iterator for the last argument, we use
the iterator adapter inserter, which inserts elements into a container rather than
overwriting existing elements in a container. The inserter takes two arguments: a
container and an iterator within the container. Each insertion appends the next element to the current end of the container.

Running the main function generates the following output lines. The last line shows
the result of comparing the result of set1.find(string("Apples")) to the result of
set1.end(). They are not equal if "Apples" is a set element.

```
set1 is {Apples, Oranges, Pineapples}
set2 is {Apples, Grapes, Peaches}
set1 + set2 is {Apples, Grapes, Oranges, Peaches, Pineapples}
set1 - set2 is {Oranges, Pineapples}
set1 * set2 is {Apples}
"Apples" is an element of set1 is true
```

········

LISTING 9.1
Illustrating the Use of Sets

```
#include <set>
#include <string>
#include <iostream>
#include <algorithm>
#include <iterator>
#include "Set_Functions.h"    // for operator<<

using namespace std;
```

```cpp
int main()
{
  set<string> set1;
  set<string> set2;
  set<string> set_u;
  set<string> set_d;
  set<string> set_i;

  string data1[] = {"Apples", "Oranges", "Pineapples"};
  string data2[] = {"Peaches", "Apples", "Grapes"};

  set1.insert(data1, data1+3);
  set2.insert(data2, data2+3);
  cout << "set1 is " << set1 << endl;
  cout << "set2 is " << set2 << endl;

  set_union(set1.begin(), set1.end(),
            set2.begin(), set2.end(),
            inserter(set_u, set_u.begin()));
  cout << "set1 + set2 is " << set_u << endl;

  set_difference(set1.begin(), set1.end(),
                 set2.begin(), set2.end(),
                 inserter(set_d, set_d. begin()));
  cout << "set1 - set2 is " << set_d << endl;

  set_intersection(set1.begin(), set1.end(),
                   set2.begin(), set2.end(),
                   inserter(set_i, set_i. begin()));
  cout << "set1 * set2 is " << set_i << endl;

  bool is_member = (set1.find(string("Apples")) != set1.end());
  cout << "\"Apples\" is an element of set1 is "
       << boolalpha << is_member << endl;

  return 0;
}
```

The **set** Operators +, –, *, and <<

We showed how to perform the set operators union (+), difference (–), and intersection (*) using the functions in the `algorithm` header. However, it would be instructive to implement these operators using the set member operators. The code for these operators and function contains is in file `Set_Functions.h`.

The union operation can be defined as:

```cpp
/** Construct the union of two sets. */
template<typename Key_Type, typename Compare>
  std::set<Key_Type, Compare> operator+(
      const std::set<Key_Type, Compare>& left,
      const std::set<Key_Type, Compare>& right) {
  typename std::set<Key_Type, Compare> result(left);
  result.insert(right.begin(), right.end());
  return result;
}
```

This function begins by loading set `result` with the elements in the `left` set. Then all elements in the `right` set are inserted.

Set difference is a bit more complicated. Again we load set `result` with the elements in the `left` set. Then we use a loop to erase each element in the `right` set from the `result` set.

```
/** Construct the difference of two sets. */
template<typename Key_Type, typename Compare>
  std::set<Key_Type, Compare> operator-(
      const std::set<Key_Type, Compare>& left,
      const std::set<Key_Type, Compare>& right) {
  typename std::set<Key_Type, Compare> result(left);
  for (typename std::set<Key_Type, Compare>::const_iterator
      itr = right.begin(); itr != right.end(); ++itr)
    result.erase(*itr);
  return result;
}
```

There is no function in class `set` that performs a test for set membership. However, we can implement a function `contains` using the result of the set search function `find`.

```
template<typename Key_Type, typename Compare>
  bool contains(const std::set<Key_Type, Compare>& s,
               const Key_Type& k) {
  return s.find(k) != s.end();
}
```

The `ostream` insertion operator `<<` inserts each set element in output stream `out`, preceding each element except for the first with a comma. The first element is preceded by an open brace, and the last element is followed by a close brace.

```
// Overloading the ostream insertion operator
template<typename Item_Type>
  std::ostream& operator<<(std::ostream& out,
                          const std::set<Item_Type>& a_set) {
  out << "{";
  bool first = true;
  for (typename std::set<Item_Type>::const_iterator
      itr = a_set.begin(); itr != a_set.end(); ++itr) {
    if (first)
      out << *itr;
    else
      out << ", " << *itr;
    first = false;
  }
  return out << "}";
}
```

Comparison of **vector**s and **set**s

The `vector` and `set` both implement the common requirements of the container classes. They also both have `insert` and `erase` functions, but these functions have different signatures and slightly different meanings. With the `vector` you must specify the location where the item is to be inserted, but with the `set` you do not. The `set` has an `insert` function (not shown in Table 9.1) that takes a position argument as a "hint" to speed up the insertion, but the exact position where the item goes is not under the caller's control. Also, in addition to the iterator referencing the inserted item, the set's insert function also returns a **bool** value indicating whether or not the item was inserted.

Unlike a vector, a set does not have an subscript operator function (operator[]). Therefore, elements cannot be accessed by index. So if seta is a set object, the expression seta[0] would cause the syntax error

```
no match for 'std::set<int, std::less<int>, std::allocator<int> >&
[int]' operator
```

Although you can't reference a specific element of a set, you can iterate through all its elements using an iterator object. The following loop accesses each element of set object seta, and the elements will be accessed in sorted order. We used such a loop in the functions shown earlier for overloading operator - and operator <<. Note that the iterator itr must be type const_iterator because you can't change a set's contents using an iterator.

```
// Create an iterator to seta.
for (set<string>::const_iterator itr = seta.begin();
     itr != seta.end(); ++itr) {
  string next_item = *itr;
  // Do something with next_item
  ...
}
```

The multiset

The multiset is the same as the set except that it does not impose the requirement that the items be unique. Thus the insert function always inserts a new item, and duplicate items will be retained. However, the erase function removes all occurrences of the specified item because there may be duplicates.

The functions lower_bound and upper_bound can be used to select the group of entries that match a desired value. If the item is present, function lower_bound returns an iterator to the first occurrence of the specified value. Function upper_bound returns an iterator to the smallest item that is larger than the specified value. The desired entries are between the iterators returned by these two functions. If the item is not present, function lower_bound returns an iterator to the smallest element that is larger than the specified entry, and function upper_bound returns the same value. The following function determines the number of occurrences of the string target in the multiset<string> words_set.

```
int count_occurrences(const multiset<string>& words_set,
                      const string& target) {
  multiset<string>::const_iterator first_itr =
    words_set.lower_bound(target);
  multiset<string>::const_iterator last_itr =
    words_set.upper_bound(target);
  int count = 0;
  for (multiset<string>::const_iterator itr = first_itr;
       itr != last_itr; ++itr)
    ++count;
  return count;
}
```

These functions are also defined for the set. They can be used to define a subset by setting a pair of iterators to two values within the set. For example, if the set fruits is {"Apples", "Grapes", "Oranges", "Peaches", "Pears", "Pineapples", "Tomatoes"}, then

```
lower_bound("Peaches")
```

would return an iterator to "Peaches", and

```
upper_bound("Pineapples")
```

would return an iterator to "Tomatoes". These two iterators would define the subset of fruits between "Peaches" and "Pineapples".

Standard Library Class pair

The C++ standard library defines the class pair in the header <utility>. This class is a simple grouping of two values of different types. The members are named first and second. Pairs are used as the return type from functions that need to return two values, such as the set::insert function, and as the element type for maps (described in Section 9.2).

Since all of its members are public, it is declared as a **struct**. Listing 9.2 shows an equivalent definition of class pair.

....
LISTING 9.2
Equivalent Definition of the struct pair (Part of the Standard Header <utility>)

```
template<typename Type1, typename Type2>
  struct pair {
  Type1 first;
  Type2 second;

  // Construct a pair from two values
  pair(const Type1& x, const Type2& y) : first(x), second(y) {}

  // Construct a pair using default values for the types
  pair() : first(Type1()), second(Type2()) {}

  // Construct a pair from two values that are assignable to the
  // target types
  template<typename Other_T1, typename Other_T2>
    pair(const pair<Other_T1, Other_T2>& other) {
      first = other.first;
      second = other.second;
  }
};
```

The template form of the constructor allows for initialization of a pair using values for which there is an assignment defined. For example, the declaration:

```
pair<string, double> my_pair("Hello", 5);
```

creates pair<string, double> my_pair and initializes its data fields to the arguments listed. The argument types are **const char** * and **int**, which can be assigned to a string and a **double**, respectively.

A template function is defined to create a pair object from two arguments.

```
template<typename Type1, typename Type2>
  make_pair(const Type1& first_value, const Type2& second_value) {
    return pair<Type1&, Type2&>(first_value, second_value);
}
```

Also, the less-than operator is defined for class pair. The results of this operator are based on the first values, if they are not equal, and on the second values if the first values are equal.

```
template<typename Type1, typename Type2>
  bool operator<(pair<Type1, Type2>& left, pair<Type1, Type2>& right) {
    return (left.first < right.first)
            || (!(right.first < left.first)
                && (left.second < right.second));
}
```

EXERCISES FOR SECTION 9.1

SELF-CHECK

1. Explain the effect of the following function calls.
```
set<string> s;
s.insert("hello");
s.insert("bye");
s.insert(s.begin(), s.end());
set<string> t;
t.insert("123");
cout << t << endl;
cout << (t - s) << endl;
cout << (s - t) << endl;
cout << contains(s, "ace") << endl;
cout << contains(s, "123") << endl;
s = s * t;
cout << s << endl;
t = t * s;
cout << t << endl;
```

2. Rewrite the preceding fragment above replacing the set operators with the functions from the algorithm header.

3. Redo Self-Check Exercise 1 for s and t declared as type multiset<string>.

4. Show the sets m and n after each of the following operations.
```
multiset<int> m;
set<int> n;
m.insert(25); m.insert(37); m.insert(27); m.insert(37);
n.insert(25); n.insert(37); n.insert(27); n.insert(37);
m.erase(25); m.erase(37);
n.erase(25); n.erase(37);
```

PROGRAMMING

1. Implement the set intersection operator * using set member functions.

2. Implement the set union operator + by delegating to function `set_union` from the algorithm header.

3. Implement the set difference operator - by delegating to function `set_difference`.

4. Implement the set intersection operator * by delegating to function `set_intersection`.

9.2 Maps and Multimaps

The `map` is related to the `set`. Mathematically a map is a set of ordered pairs whose elements are known as the key and the value. The key is required to be unique, as are the elements of a set, but the value is not necessarily unique. For example, the following would be a map:

{(**J**, Jane), (**B**, Bill), (**S**, Sam), (**B1**, Bob), (**B2**, Bill)}

The keys in this example are strings consisting of one or two characters, and each value is a person's name. The keys are unique but not the values (there are two Bills). The key is based on the first letter of the person's name. The keys **B1** and **B2** are the keys for the second and third person whose name begins with the letter B.

You can think of each key as "mapping" to a particular value (hence the name *map*). For example, the key **J** maps to the value Jane. The keys **B** and **B2** map to the value Bill. You can also think of the keys as forming a set (*keys*) and the values as forming a set (*values*). Each element of *keys* maps to a particular element of *values*, as shown in Figure 9.2. In mathematical set terminology, this is a *many-to-one mapping* (that is, more than one element of *keys* may map to a particular element of *values*). For example, both keys **B** and **B2** map to the value Bill. This is also an *onto mapping* in that all elements of *values* have a corresponding member in *keys*.

A `map` can be used to enable efficient storage and retrieval of information in a table. The key is a unique identification value associated with each item stored in a table. The "value" in the key/value pair might be an object, or even a pointer to an object, with objects in the class distinguished by some attribute associated with the key that is then mapped to the value.

FIGURE 9.2
Example of Mapping

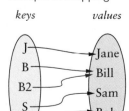

EXAMPLE 9.2 When information about an item is stored in a table, the information stored may consist of a unique ID (identification code, which may or may not be a number) as well as descriptive data. The unique ID would be the key, and the rest of the information would represent the value associated with that key. Some examples follow:

Type of Item	Key	Value
University student	Student ID number	Student name, address, major, grade-point average
Customer for on-line store	E-mail address	Customer name, address, credit card information, shopping cart
Inventory item	Part ID	Description, quantity, manufacturer, cost, price

In the preceding examples, the student ID number may be assigned by the university, or it may be the student's social security number. The e-mail address is a unique address for each customer, but it is not numeric. Similarly, a part ID could consist of a combination of letters and digits.

In comparing maps to indexed collections, you can think of the keys as selecting the elements of a map, just as indexes select elements in a vector object. The keys for a map, however, can have arbitrary values (not restricted to 0, 1, 2, and so on, as for indexes). As you will see later, the subscript operator is overloaded for the map class, so you can have statements of the form:

```
v = a_map[k];    // Assign to v the value for key k
a_map[k] = v1;   // Set the value for key k to v1
```

where k is of the key type, v and v1 are of the value type, and a_map is a map.

The map Functions

A map is effectively defined as a set whose items are pairs. The member functions defined for both are the same except for the type of the parameters. The map is a template class that takes the following template parameters:

- Key_Type: The type of the keys contained in the key set
- Value_Type: The type of the values in the value set
- Compare: A function class that determines the ordering of the keys. By default this is the less-than operator.
- Allocator: The memory allocator for key objects. We will use the library-supplied default.

Items are stored in a map as ordered by their Compare function. Thus, if you iterate through a map, you will get a sorted list of the contents. The Compare function is used to create the function class Key_Compare, which compares only the Key_Type part of the pair<const Key_Type, Value_Type> items (called Entry_Type) that are stored in a map. (Note that the key for an entry can't be changed, but the value can be.)

```
struct Key_Compare {
  bool operator()(const Entry_Type& left,
                  const Entry_Type& right) const {
    return left.first < right.first;
  }
};
```

If the set is defined, the map could be defined as shown in Listing 9.3. The map functions are all implemented by delegation to the corresponding set function. For example:

```
std::pair<iterator, bool> insert(const Entry_Type& item) {
  return the_set.insert(item);
}
```

In addition to the set functions, the map class overloads the subscript operator such that the key is used as an index (for example, a_map[k]). For this reason, a map is also known as an *associative array*.

The code that overloads the subscript operator is placed at the end of the public part of the class definition and begins as follows:

```
Value_Type& operator[](const Key_Type& key) {
  std::pair<iterator, bool> ret
    = the_set.insert(Entry_Type(key, Value_Type()));
```

This statement inserts into the_set a pair consisting of the key and a dummy value. The return value (assigned to ret) will be a pair<iterator, bool>. The iterator will reference the Entry_Type object that was inserted if the key was not already mapped. Thus, using the subscript operator to access a key in a map has the side effect of inserting that key with a default value if it is not already present. However, the iterator will reference the Entry_Type object that was already in the_set if the key is already mapped.

Because changing a value that is in a set could destroy the ordering of the items, the set::iterator's dereferencing operators always return a **const** reference to the object referenced. We need to return a non-**const** reference to the Value_Type part of the Entry_Type object. Thus we need to use a const_cast to remove the **const** qualification.

```
Entry_Type& entry(const_cast<Entry_Type&>(*(ret.first)));
```

SYNTAX   const_cast

FORM:

const_cast<*target_type*>(*value*)

EXAMPLE:

const_cast(Entry_Type&)(*(ret.first))

MEANING:

If the type of *value* was a **const** reference type (or **const** pointer type), it is converted to *target_type*, where *target_type* is the corresponding non-**const** reference (or pointer) type. You must be careful using this construct, because it allows you to violate the protection provided by the language. For example, a **const_cast** could be used to change the key of the item stored in either a set or a map. The set and map use binary search trees, so changing a value could make the tree cease to be a binary search tree. The insert, erase, and find operations would no longer work. In this case we knew that the Value_Type part of the Entry_Type could be changed without harming the structure of the_set.

LISTING 9.3
map.h

```
#ifndef MAP_H_
#define MAP_H_

#include <set>
#include <utility>

namespace KW
{
  /** Definition of the map class using the std::set. */
  template<typename Key_Type, typename Value_Type>
    class map {

      public:

      // Define the Entry_Type.
      typedef std::pair<const Key_Type, Value_Type> Entry_Type;

      // Compare only the keys.
      struct Key_Compare {
        bool operator()(const Entry_Type& left,
                        const Entry_Type& right) const {
          return left.first < right.first;
        }
      };

      // Define the iterator types
      typedef typename std::set<Entry_Type,
          Key_Compare>::iterator iterator;
      typedef typename std::set<Entry_Type,
          Key_Compare>::const_iterator const_iterator;

      // Delegate the functions.
      iterator begin() {
        return the_set.begin();
      }

      const_iterator begin() const {
        return the_set.begin();
      }
```

```
      iterator end() {
        return the_set.end();
      }

      const_iterator end() const {
        return the_set.end();
      }

      bool empty() {
        return the_set.empty();
      }

      int size() {
        return the_set.size();
      }

      std::pair<iterator, bool> insert(const Entry_Type& item) {
        return the_set.insert(item);
      }

      void erase(const Key_Type& key) {
        the_set.erase(Entry_Type(key, Value_Type()));
      }

      iterator find(const Key_Type& key) {
        return the_set.find(Entry_Type(key, Value_Type()));
      }

      // Overload the subscript operator
      Value_Type& operator[](const Key_Type& key) {
        std::pair<iterator, bool> ret
          = the_set.insert(Entry_Type(key, Value_Type()));
        Entry_Type& entry(const_cast<Entry_Type&>(*(ret.first)));
        return entry.second;
      }

      private:
      std::set<Entry_Type, Key_Compare> the_set;

  }; // End map

} // End namespace KW

#endif
```

The implementation of the map shown in Listing 9.3 is for illustration purposes only, and other than operator[] it is not fully functional. Specifically, the iterator cannot be defined as shown. Instead, an iterator class needs to be defined so that its dereferencing operators perform the const_cast. Then we wouldn't need to do the const_cast in operator[], and the iterator returned from insert and find would be useful.

EXAMPLE 9.3 The following statements build a map object that contains the mapping shown in Figure 9.2.

```
map<string, string> a_map;
a_map["J"] = "Jane";
a_map["B"] = "Bill";
a_map["S"] = "Sam";
a_map["B1"] = "Bob";
a_map["B2"] = "Bill";
```

The statement

```
cout << "B1 maps to " << a_map["B1"] << endl
```

would display B1 maps to Bob. The statement

```
cout << "Bill maps to " << a_map["Bill"] << endl;
```

would display "Bill maps to " because "Bill" is a value, not a key. However, a side effect of this statement is that "Bill" would now be a key in the map associated with the empty string. Recall that if a key is not in a map when the subscript operator is applied, the key is inserted and mapped to the default value for the value type. For string, the default value is an empty string.

EXAMPLE 9.4 In Section 8.4 we examined a case study that used a binary search tree to store an index of words occurring in a term paper. Each data element in the tree was a string consisting of a word followed by a 3-digit line number.

Although this is one approach to storing an index, it would be more useful to store each word and all the line numbers for that word as a single index entry. We could do this by storing the index in a map in which each word is a key and its associated value is a list of all the line numbers at which the word occurs. As we build the index, each time a word is encountered, its list of line numbers would be retrieved (using the word as a key), and the most recent line number would be appended to this list (a list<int>). For example, if the word *fire* has already occurred on lines 4 and 8 and we encounter it again on line 20, the list<int> associated with *fire* would reference the three **int**s 4, 8, and 20.

Listing 9.4 shows function build_index (adapted from build_index in Listing 8.8). Parameter index is a map with key type string and value type list<int>.

```
typedef std::map<std::string, std::list<int> > map_type;
```

If we wanted to use the map class shown in Listing 9.3, we would change this declaration to

```
typedef KW::map<std::string, std::list<int> > map_type;
```

The statement

```
index[word].push_back(line_num);
```

retrieves the value (a list<int>) associated with the next word. If there was no value associated with the next word, an empty list (the default for list<int>) is inserted into the map. The push_back function is then called on this list object to append the line_num. Recall that the String_Tokenizer class was also described in Section 8.4.

....
LISTING 9.4
Function `build_index`

```
/** Reads each word (a key) in the data file in and stores it
    in a map along with a list of line numbers (a value).
    pre:  index is an empty map.
    post: lowercase form of each word with all its
          line numbers is stored in index.
    @param in An istream attached to the data file
    @param index The index
*/
void build_index(istream& in, map_type& index) {
  string next_line;  // Each data line
  int line_num = 0;  // Line number
  // Keep reading lines until done
  while (getline(in, next_line)) {
    line_num++;
    // Create a String_Tokenizer for the current data line
    // using punctuation and white space as delimiters
    String_Tokenizer tokenizer(next_line, " ,.:-!?/%\'\"");
    // Insert each token in the index
    while (tokenizer.has_more_tokens()) {
      string word = tokenizer.next_token();
      to_lower(word);
      index[word].push_back(line_num);
    }
  }
}
```

⊘ **PITFALL**

Side Effect of Retrieving a Missing Key

In function `build_index`, the statement

`index[word].push_back(line_num);`

uses the expression `index[word]` to retrieve the value (a list) associated with string
word. If this is the first occurrence of word, a side effect of the retrieval is that an empty
list is inserted in index as the value associated with word, and the line number is
inserted into this list. This is just what we want to happen. However, there are other situations when we don't want to insert a new entry into the map if the key is missing. In
these cases, we should use `find` to perform the retrieval, as in the following fragment.

```
const_iterator itr_word = index.find(word);
if (itr_word != index.end())
  cout << "first occurrence is on line # " << itr_word->second.front()
       << endl;
else
  cout << word << " is not in the index\n"
```

The **if** statement displays either the line number of the first occurrence of word
(`itr_word->second.front()`) or a message that word is not present.

Defining the Compare Function

The default value for the Compare template parameter is the Key_Type's less-than operator. If Key_Type is a primitive type or the string class, the < operator is defined. However, let us assume that we wanted to use the class Person, with data fields family_name and given_name to be the key in a map. The family_name should determine the ordering of Person objects. However, if two Person objects have the same family_name, then we need to use the given_name. We would define the following function class to compare Person objects.

```
struct Compare_Person {
  bool operator()(const Person& p1, const Person& p2) {
    if (p1.family_name < p2.family_name)
      return true;
    else
      return (p1.family_name == p2.family_name)
             && (p1.given_name < p2.given_name);
  }
}
```

⊘ PITFALL

Not Defining the Compare Function as a Total Ordering Relationship

Suppose we defined Compare_Person as follows:

```
struct Compare_Person {
  bool operator()(const Person& p1, const Person& p2) {
    if (p1.family_name < p2.family_name)
      return true;
    else
      return p1.given_name < p2.given_name;
  }
}
```

Then "Jones, Tom" (family_name is "Jones", given_name is "Tom") would be less than "Smith, John" (family_name is "Smith", given_name is "John") as expected, but "Smith, John" would also be less than "Jones, Tom" (since "John" < "Tom"). A map with this as a Compare function will give very strange results.

The multimap

Like the multiset, the multimap removes the restriction that the keys are unique. The subscript operator is not defined for the multimap. Instead, lower_bound and upper_bound must be used to obtain a range of iterators that reference the values mapped to a given key.

EXAMPLE 9.5 Earlier we showed how to use a map<string, list<int> > to create an index. We could use a multimap<string, int> instead for this purpose. Each word would be inserted into the multimap along with the line number. There could be duplicate entries for the same word. The function to create the index is the same as shown in Listing 9.4 except that the statement

```
index.insert(pair<string, int>(word, line_num));
```

is used instead of

```
index[word].push_back(line_num);
```

Listing 9.5 shows the `print_index` function. It uses a **for** loop to iterate through the multimap index.

```
for (multimap<string, int>::const_iterator itr = index.begin();
     itr != index.end(); ) {
```

Notice that we do not increment the iterator; this will be done in the loop body. At the top of the loop the iterator `itr` is positioned at a new word, and references the `pair<string, int>` that contains this word and the first line number on which it occurs. The word and the first line number are output using the statement:

```
// Print the word
string word = itr->first;
cout << word << ": ";
// Print the first line number
cout << itr->second;
```

Now we use the `upper_bound` function to obtain an `iterator` that is at the next word (or the end).

```
multimap<string, int>::const_iterator next_word
    = index.upper_bound(word);
```

This `iterator` is used as the upper bound on the loop that prints the remaining line numbers.

```
while (itr != next_word) {
  cout << ", " << itr->second;
  ++itr;
}
```

LISTING 9.5

The `print_index` Function (Part of `multimap_index_generator.cpp`)

```
void print_index(const multimap<string, int>& index) {
  for (multimap<string, int>::const_iterator itr = index.begin();
       itr != index.end(); ) {
    // Print the word
    string word = itr->first;
    cout << word << ": ";
    // Print the first line number
    cout << itr->second;
    // Print the rest of the line numbers
    multimap<string, int>::const_iterator next_word
      = index.upper_bound(word);
    ++itr;
    while (itr != next_word) {
      cout << ", " << itr->second;
      ++itr;
    }
    cout << '\n';
  }
}
```

EXERCISES FOR SECTION 9.2

SELF-CHECK

1. If you were using a map to store the following lists of items, which data field would you select as the key and why?
    a. textbook title, author, ISBN (International Standard Book Number), year, publisher
    b. player's name, uniform number, team, position
    c. computer manufacturer, model number, processor, memory, disk size
    d. department, course title, course ID, section number, days, time, room
2. Show the map a_map created by the following statements. What would be displayed if you accessed the entries using an iterator and displayed the values of the first and second data fields of each entry on a line separated by a colon?

```
a_map.insert(1234, "sam");
a_map.insert(2456, "bill");
a_map[2222] = "hal";
a_map[1234] = "sally";
cout << a_map[1111];
```

3. Suppose the fragment in Self-Check Exercise 2 were modified to create a multimap, b_map, instead. Show that multimap. What would be displayed if you accessed the entries using an iterator and displayed the value of the first and second data fields of each entry on a line separated by a colon? All values for a given key should appear on the same line separated by commas.

PROGRAMMING

1. Write statements to create a map object that stores each word occurring in a term paper along with the number of times the word occurs.
2. Write statements to perform the display described in Self-Check Exercise 2.
3. Write statements to perform the display described in Self-Check Exercise 3.

9.3 Hash Tables

The C++ standard library uses a special type of binary search tree, called a *balanced binary search tree*, to implement the set and map classes. This provides access to items in O(log *n*) time. Sets and maps can also be implemented using a data structure known as a *hash table*, which has some advantages over balanced search trees. The goal behind the hash table is to be able to access an entry based on its key value, not its location. In other words, we want to be able to access an element directly through its key value (associative retrieval), rather than having to determine its location first by searching for the key value in an array or a tree. Using a hash table enables us to retrieve an item in constant time (expected O(1)). We say expected O(1) rather than just O(1), because there will be some cases where the performance will be much worse than O(1) and may even be O(n), but on the average we expect that it will be O(1).

Hash Codes and Index Calculation

The basis of hashing (and hash tables) is to transform the item's key value to an integer value (its *hash code*) which will then be transformed into a table index. Figure 9.3 illustrates this process for a table of size n. We discuss how this might be done in the next few examples.

EXAMPLE 9.6   Consider the Huffman code problem discussed in Section 8.6. To build the Huffman tree, you needed to know the number of occurrences of each character in the text being encoded. Let's assume that the text contained only the ASCII characters. We could use a table of size 128, one element for each possible character, and let the **char** value for each character be its location in the table. Using this approach, table element 65 would give us the number of occurrences of the letter A, table element 66 would give us the number of occurrences of the letter B, and so on. The hash code for each character is its **char** value (a number), which is also its index in the table. In this case, we could calculate the table index for character ascii_char using the following assignment statement, where ascii_char represents the character we are seeking in the table.

```
int index = ascii_char;
```

EXAMPLE 9.7   Let's consider a slightly harder problem: Assume that out text is not in English and instead uses the Unicode characters, and we want to know the number of occurrences of each character. There are over 65,000 Unicode characters, however. For any file, let's assume that at most 100 different characters actually appear. So, rather than use a table with 65,536 elements, it would make sense to try to store these items in a much smaller table (say 200 elements). If the hash code for each character is its Unicode value, we need to convert this value (between 0 and 65,536) to an array index between 0 and 199. We can calculate the array index for character uni_char (type **wchar_t**) as:

```
int index = uni_char % 200
```

Because the range of Unicode values (the key range) is much larger than the index range, it is likely that some characters in our text will have the same index value. Because we can store only one key-value pair in a given array element, a situation known as a *collision* results. We discuss how to deal with collisions shortly.

FIGURE 9.3
Index Calculation for a Key

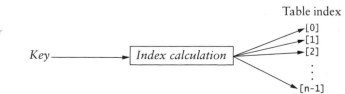

Functions for Generating Hash Codes

In most applications, the keys that we will want to store in a table will consist of strings of letters or digits rather than a single character (for example, a social security number, a person's name, or a part ID). We need a way to map each string to a particular table index. Again, we have a situation in which the number of possible key values is much larger than the table size. For example, if a string can store up to 10 letters or digits, the number of possible strings is 62^{10} (approximately 8.4×10^{17}), assuming the English alphabet with 52 letters (upper- and lower-case) and 10 digit characters.

Generating good hash codes for arbitrary strings or arbitrary objects is somewhat of an experimental process. Simple algorithms tend to generate a lot of collisions. For example, simply summing the **char** values for all characters in a string would generate the same hash code for words that contained the same letters, but in different orders, such as "sign" and "sing", which would have the same hash code using this algorithm ('s' + 'i' + 'n' + 'g'). One algorithm that has shown good results uses the following formula.

$$s_0 \times 31^{n-1} + s_1 \times 31^{n-2} + s_2 \times 31^{n-3} + \cdots + s_{n-1}$$

where s_i is the ith character of the string and n is the length of the string. (The number 31 is a prime number; the use of prime numbers in hash functions tends to reduce the number of collisions.)

This is the formula used by a hash function in the Java **String** class. Since C++ does not provide a standard hash function for the **string** class, we will borrow this one. Using it, the string "Cat" would have a hash code of 'C' $\times$ 31^2 + 'a' $\times$ 31 + 't'. This is the number 67,510. To get a table index, the hash function must take this result modulo the table size.

As previously discussed, the integer value returned by this function can't be unique, because there are too many possible strings. However, the probability of two strings having the same hash code value is relatively small, because this function distributes the hash code values fairly evenly throughout the range of **int** values.

Because the hash codes are distributed evenly throughout the range of **int** values, this function will appear to produce a random value that can be used as the table index for retrieval. If the object is not already present in the table, the probability that the table slot with this index will be empty is proportional to how full the table is.

Although the hash function result appears to be random and gives a random distribution of keys, keep in mind that the calculation is deterministic. This means that you will always get the same hash code for a particular key.

One additional criterion for a good hash function, besides providing a random distribution, is that it be relatively simple and efficient (fast) to compute. It doesn't make much sense to use a hash function whose computation is an $O(n)$ process to avoid doing an $O(n)$ search.

DESIGN CONCEPT

Proposed Standard Hash Function Class

Although hash tables were not included in the original C++ standard, there has long been a desire for their inclusion. Currently the C++ standard is undergoing revision, and hash tables are one of the proposed additions. One issue with including hash tables is how to designate the hash function. The proposed solution is to define a template function class hash. This class would be specialized for the primitive types and other library-defined types such as string. The type hash<*type*> would then designate the hash function class for the type *type*, and hash<*type*>() would designate the function object. The expression hash<*type*>() (*key*) would then evaluate the function for the value *key*.

Open Addressing

Next we consider two ways to organize hash tables: *open addressing* and chaining. In open addressing, each hash table element (type Entry_Type*) points to a single key-value pair. We can use the following simple approach (called *linear probing*) to access an item in a hash table. If the index calculated for an item's key is occupied by an item with that key, we have found the item. If that element contains an item with a different key, we increment the index by one. We keep incrementing the index (modulo the table size) until either we find the key we are seeking or we reach a NULL entry. A NULL entry indicates that the key is not in the table.

Algorithm for Accessing an Item in a Hash Table with Linear Probing

1. Compute the index by taking the key's hash function modulo the size of the table.
2. **if** table[index] is NULL
3.   The item is not in the table.
4. **else if** table[index]->first is equal to the key
5.   The item is in the table.
   else
6.   Continue to search the table by incrementing the index until either the item is found or a NULL entry is found.

Step 1 ensures that the index is within the table range (0 through table.size() − 1). If the condition in Step 2 is true, the table index does not reference an object, so the item is not in the table. The condition in Step 4 is true if the item being sought is at position index, in which case the item is located. Steps 1 through 5 can be done in O(1) expected time.

Step 6 is necessary for two reasons. The values returned by the hash function are not unique, so the item being sought can have the same hash code as another one in the table. Also, the remainder calculated in Step 1 can yield the same index for different hash code values. Both of these cases are examples of collisions.

Table Wraparound and Search Termination

Notice that as you increment the table index, your table should wrap around (as in a circular array), so that the element with subscript 0 "follows" the element with subscript `table.size()` - 1. This enables you to use the entire table, not just the part with subscripts larger than the hash code value, but it leads to the potential for an infinite loop in Step 6 of the algorithm. If the table is full and the objects examined so far do not match the one you are seeking, how do you know when to stop? One approach would be to stop when the index value for the next probe is the same as the initial hash code value computed for the key. This means that you have come full circle to the starting value for the index. A second approach would be to ensure that the table is never full by increasing its size after an insertion if its occupancy rate exceeds a specified threshold. This is the approach that we take in our implementation.

EXAMPLE 9.8

We illustrate the insertion of five names in a table of size 5 and in a table of size 11. Table 9.3 shows the names, the corresponding hash code (result of the hash function `hash_fcn`), the hash code modulo 5, and the hash code modulo 11. We picked prime numbers (5 and 11) because empirical tests have shown that hash tables with a size that is a prime number often give better results.

For a table of size 5 (an occupancy rate of 100 percent), "Tom", "Dick", and "Sam" have hash indexes of 4, and "Harry" and "Pete" have hash indexes of 3; whereas for a table length of 11 (an occupancy rate of 45 percent), "Dick" and "Sam" have hash indexes of 5, but the others have hash indexes that are unique. We see how the insertion process works next.

For a table of size 5, if "Tom" and "Dick" are the first two entries, "Tom" would be stored at the element with index 4, the last element in the table. Consequently, when "Dick" is to be added, element 4 is already occupied, so the hash index is incremented to 0 (the table wraps around to the beginning), and "Dick" is stored there.

TABLE 9.3
Names and `hash_fcn` Values for Table Sizes 5 and 11

Name	hash_fcn()	hash_fcn()%5	hash_fcn()%11
"Tom"	84274	4	3
"Dick"	2129869	4	5
"Harry"	69496448	3	10
"Sam"	82879	4	5
"Pete"	2484038	3	7

```
[0]  "Dick"
[1]  NULL
[2]  NULL
[3]  NULL
[4]  "Tom"
```

"Harry" is stored in position 3 (the hash index), and "Sam" is stored in position 1, because its hash index is 4 but the elements at 4 and 0 are already filled.

```
[0]  "Dick"
[1]  "Sam"
[2]  NULL
[3]  "Harry"
[4]  "Tom"
```

Finally, "Pete" is stored in position 2, because its hash index is 3 but the elements at positions 3, 4, 0, and 1 are filled.

```
[0]  "Dick"
[1]  "Sam"
[2]  "Pete"
[3]  "Harry"
[4]  "Tom"
```

For the table of size 11, the entries would be stored as shown in the following table, assuming that they were inserted in the order "Tom", "Dick", "Harry", "Sam", and finally "Pete". Insertions go more smoothly for the table of size 11. The first collision occurs when "Sam" is stored, so "Sam" is stored at position 6 instead of position 5.

```
[0]   NULL
[1]   NULL
[2]   NULL
[3]   "Tom"
[4]   NULL
[5]   "Dick"
[6]   "Sam"
[7]   "Pete"
[8]   NULL
[9]   NULL
[10]  "Harry"
```

For the table of size 5, retrieval of "Tom" can be done in one step. Retrieval of all of the others would require a linear search because of collisions that occurred when they were inserted. For the table of size 11, retrieval of all but "Sam" can be done in one step, and retrieval of "Sam" requires only two steps. This example illustrates that the best way to reduce the probability of a collision is to increase the table size.

Traversing a Hash Table

One thing that you cannot do is traverse a hash table in a meaningful way. If you visit the hash table elements in sequence and display the objects stored, you would display the strings "Dick", "Sam", "Pete", "Harry", "Tom" for the table of length 5 and the strings "Tom", "Dick", "Sam", "Pete", "Harry" for a table of length 11. In either case, the list of names is in arbitrary order.

Deleting an Item Using Open Addressing

When an item is deleted, we cannot just set its table entry to NULL. If we do, then when we search for an item that may have collided with the deleted item, we may incorrectly conclude that the item is not in the table. (Because the item that collided was inserted after the deleted item, we will have stopped our search prematurely.) By storing a dummy value when an item is deleted, we force the search algorithm to keep looking until either the desired item is found or a NULL value, representing a free cell, is located.

Although the use of a dummy value solves the problem, keep in mind that it can lead to search inefficiency, particularly when there are many deletions. Removing items from the table does not reduce the search time, because the dummy value is still in the table and is part of a search chain. In fact, you cannot even replace a deleted value with a new item, because you still need to go to the end of the search chain to ensure that the new item is not already present in the table. So deleted items waste storage space and reduce search efficiency. In the worst case, if the table is almost full and then most of the items are deleted, you will have O(n) performance when searching for the few items remaining in the table.

Reducing Collisions by Expanding the Table Size

Even with a good hashing function, there is still the problem of collisions resulting from taking the hash value modulo the table size. The first step in reducing these collisions is to use a prime number for the size of the table.

Additionally, the probability of a collision is proportional to how full the table is. Therefore, when the hash table becomes sufficiently full, a larger table should be allocated and the entries reinserted.

We previously saw examples of expanding the size of an array. Generally, what we did was to allocate a new array with twice the capacity of the original, copy the values in the original array to the new array, and then reference the new array instead of the original. This approach will not work with hash tables. If you use it, some search chains will be broken because the new table does not wrap around in the same way as the original table. The last element in the original table will be in the middle of the new table, and it does not wrap around to the first element of the new table. Therefore, you expand a hash table using the following *rehashing* algorithm:

Algorithm for Rehashing

1. Allocate a new hash table with twice the capacity of the original.
2. Reinsert each old table entry that has not been deleted into the new hash table.
3. Reference the new table instead of the original.

Step 2 reinserts each item from the old table into the new table instead of copying it over to the same location. Notice that deleted items are not reinserted into the new table, thereby saving space and reducing the length of some search chains. We illustrate this in the hash table implementation.

Reducing Collisions Using Quadratic Probing

The problem with linear probing is that it tends to form clusters of keys in the table, causing longer search chains. For example, if the table already has keys with hash codes of 5 and 6, a new item that collides with either of these keys will be placed at index 7. An item that collides with any of these three items will be placed at index 8, and so on. Figure 9.4 shows a hash table of size 11 after inserting elements with hash codes in the sequence 5, 6, 5, 6, 7. Each new collision expands the cluster by one element, thereby increasing the length of the search chain for each element in that cluster. For example, if another element is inserted with any hash code in the range 5 through 9, it will be placed at position 10, and the search chain for items with hash codes of 5 and 6 would include the elements at indexes 7, 8, 9, and 10.

One approach to reduce the effect of clustering is to use *quadratic probing* instead of linear probing. In quadratic probing, the increments form a quadratic series ($1 + 2^2 + 3^2 + \cdots$). Therefore, the next value of index is calculated using the steps:

```
probe_num++;
index = (start_index + probe_num * probe_num % table.size());
```

where start_index is the index calculated using the hash function and probe_num starts at 0. Ignoring wraparound, if an item has a hash code of 5, successive values of index will be 6 (5 + 1), 9 (5 + 4), 14 (5 + 9), . . . , instead of 6, 7, 8, ... Similarly, if the hash code is 6, successive values of index will be 7, 10, 15, and so on. Unlike linear probing, these two search chains have only one table element in common (at index 6).

Figure 9.5 illustrates the hash table after elements with hash codes in the same sequence as in the preceding table (5, 6, 5, 6, 7) have been inserted with quadratic probing. Although the cluster of elements looks similar, their search chains do not overlap as much as before. Now the search chain for an item with a hash code of 5 consists of the elements at 5, 6, and 9, and the search chain for an item with a hash code of 6 consists of the elements at positions 6 and 7.

FIGURE 9.4

Clustering with Linear Probing

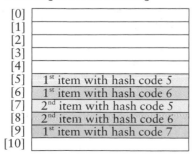

[0]	
[1]	
[2]	
[3]	
[4]	
[5]	1st item with hash code 5
[6]	1st item with hash code 6
[7]	2nd item with hash code 5
[8]	2nd item with hash code 6
[9]	1st item with hash code 7
[10]	

FIGURE 9.5

Insertion with Quadratic Probing

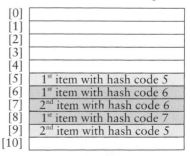

[0]	
[1]	
[2]	
[3]	
[4]	
[5]	1st item with hash code 5
[6]	1st item with hash code 6
[7]	2nd item with hash code 6
[8]	1st item with hash code 7
[9]	2nd item with hash code 5
[10]	

Problems with Quadratic Probing

One disadvantage of quadratic probing is that the next index calculation is a bit time consuming as it involves a multiplication, an addition, and a modulo division. A more efficient way to calculate the next index follows:

```
k += 2;
index = (index + k) % table.size();
```

which replaces the multiplication with an addition. If the initial value of k is −1, successive values of k will be 1, 3, 5, 7, ... If the hash code is 5, successive values of index will be 5, 6 (5 + 1), 9 (5 + 1 + 3), 14 (5 + 1 + 3 + 5), ... The proof of the equality of these two approaches to calculating index is based on the following mathematical series:

$$n^2 = 1 + 3 + 5 + \cdots + 2n - 1$$

A more serious problem with quadratic probing is that not all table elements are examined when looking for an insertion index, so it is possible that an item can't be inserted even when the table is not full. It is also possible that your program can get stuck in an infinite loop while searching for an empty slot. It can be proved that if the table size is a prime number and the table is never more than half-full, this can't happen. However, requiring that the table be half-empty at all times wastes quite a bit of memory. For these reasons, we will use linear probing in our implementation.

Chaining

An alternative to open addressing is a technique called *chaining*, in which each table element references a linked list that contains all the items that hash to the same table index. This linked list is often called a *bucket*, and this approach is sometimes called *bucket hashing*. Figure 9.6 shows the result of chaining for our earlier example with a table of size 5. Each new element with a particular hash index can be placed at the beginning or the end of the associated linked list. The algorithm for accessing such a table is the same as for open addressing, except for the step for resolving collisions. Instead of incrementing the table index to access the next item with a particular hash code value, you traverse the linked list referenced by the table element with index hash<Key_Type>()(key) % table.size(), where hash<type>() is the hash function for the Key_Type and key is the key.

One advantage of chaining is that only items that have the same value for hash<Key_Type>()(key) % table.size() will be examined when looking for an object. In open addressing, search chains can overlap, so a search chain may include items in the table that have different starting index values.

A second advantage is that you can store more elements in the table than the number of table slots (indexes), which is not the case for open addressing. If each table index already references a linked list, additional items can be inserted in an existing list without increasing the table size (number of indexes).

Once you have determined that an item is not present, you can insert it either at the beginning or at the end of the list. To delete an item, simply remove it from the list. In contrast to open addressing, removing an item actually deletes it, so it will not be part of future search chains.

FIGURE 9.6
Example of Chaining

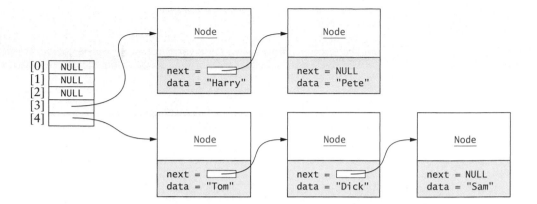

Performance of Hash Tables

The load factor for a hash table is the number of filled cells divided by table size. The load factor has the greatest effect on hash table performance. The lower the load factor, the better the performance, because there is less chance of a collision when a table is sparsely populated. If there are no collisions, the performance for search and retrieval is $O(1)$, regardless of the table size.

Performance of Open Addressing Versus Chaining

Donald Knuth (in *Searching and Sorting*, vol. 3 of *The Art of Computer Programming*, Addison-Wesley, 1973) derived the following formula for the expected number of comparisons, c, required for finding an item that is in a hash table using open addressing with linear probing and a load factor L:

$$c = \frac{1}{2}\left(1 + \frac{1}{1-L}\right)$$

Table 9.4 (second column) shows the value of c for different values of load factor (L). It shows that if L is 0.5 (half-full), the expected number of comparisons required is 1.5. If L increases to 0.75, the expected number of comparisons is 2.5, which is still very respectable. If L increases to 0.9 (90 percent full), the expected number of comparisons is 5.5. This is true regardless of the size of the table.

Using chaining, if an item is in the table, on average we have to examine the table element corresponding to the item's hash code and then half of the items in each list. The average number of items in a list is L, the number of items divided by the table size. Therefore, we get the formula

$$c = 1 + \frac{L}{2}$$

for a successful search. Table 9.4 (third column) shows the results for chaining. For values of L between 0.0 and 0.75, the results are similar to those of linear probing, but chaining gives better performance than linear probing for higher load factors. Quadratic probing (not shown) gives performance that is between those of linear probing and chaining.

TABLE 9.4
Number of Probes for Different Values of Load Factor (*L*)

L	Number of Probes with Linear Probing	Number of Probes with Chaining
0	1.00	1.00
0.25	1.17	1.13
0.5	1.50	1.25
0.75	2.50	1.38
0.85	3.83	1.43
0.9	5.50	1.45
0.95	10.50	1.48

Performance of Hash Tables Versus Sorted Arrays and Binary Search Trees

If we compare hash table performance with binary search of a sorted array, the number of comparisons required by binary search is $O(\log n)$, so the number of comparisons increases with table size. A sorted array of size 128 would require up to 7 probes (2^7 is 128), which is more than for a hash table of any size that is 90 percent full. A sorted array of size 1024 would require up to 10 probes (2^{10} is 1024). A binary search tree would yield the same results.

You can insert into or remove elements from a hash table in $O(1)$ expected time. Insertion or removal from a binary search tree is $O(\log n)$, but insertion or removal from a sorted array is $O(n)$ (you need to shift the larger elements over). Worst-case performance for a hash table or a binary search tree is $O(n)$.

Storage Requirements for Hash Tables, Sorted Arrays, and Trees

The performance of hashing is certainly preferable to that of binary search of an array (or a binary search tree), particularly if *L* is less than 0.75. However, the tradeoff is that the lower the load factor, the more unfilled storage cells there are in a hash table, whereas there are no empty cells in a sorted array. Because a binary search tree requires two pointers per node (the left subtree and the right subtree), more storage would be required for a binary search tree than for a hash table with a load factor of 0.75.

EXAMPLE 9.9   A hash table of size 100 with open addressing could store 75 items with a load factor of 0.75. This would require storage for 100 pointers. Storage would be required for 150 pointers to store the 75 items in a binary search tree.

Storage Requirements for Open Addressing and Chaining

Next, we consider the effect of chaining on storage requirements. For a table with a load factor of *L*, the number of table elements required is *n* (the size of the table). For open addressing, the number of pointers to an item (a key-value pair) is *n*. For chaining, the average number of nodes in a list is *L*. If we use the C++ `list` class, there will be two pointers in each node (the next list element and the previous element). However, we could use our own single-linked list and eliminate the previous-element pointer (at some time cost for deletions). Therefore, we will require storage for $n + L$ references.

EXAMPLE 9.10 If we have 60,000 items in our hash table and use open addressing, we would need a table size of 80,000 to have a load factor of 0.75 and an expected number of comparisons of 2.5. Next, we calculate the table size, n, needed to get similar performance using chaining:

$$2.5 = 1 + \frac{L}{2}$$
$$5.0 = 2 + L$$
$$3 = \frac{60,000}{n}$$
$$n = 20,000$$

A hash table of size 20,000 requires storage space for 20,000 lists. There will be 60,000 nodes in the table (one for each item). If we use single-linked lists of nodes, we will need storage for 60,000 pointers (1 pointer per node). This is the same as the storage needed for open addressing.

EXERCISES FOR SECTION 9.3

SELF-CHECK

1. For the hash table search algorithm shown in this section, why was it unnecessary to test whether all table entries had been examined as part of Step 5?
2. For the items in the 5-element table of Table 9.3, compute hash_fcn(key) % table.size() for table sizes of 7 and 13. What would be the position of each item in tables of these sizes using open addressing and linear probing? Answer the same question for chaining.
3. The following table stores **int** keys with the values shown. Show one sequence of insertions that would store the keys as shown. Which elements were placed in their current position because of collisions? Show the table that would be formed by chaining.

Index	Key
[0]	24
[1]	6
[2]	20
[3]	
[4]	14

4. For Table 9.3 and the table size of 5 shown in Example 9.8, discuss the effect of deleting the entry for "Dick" and replacing it with a NULL value. How would this affect the search for "Sam", "Pete", and "Harry"? Answer both questions if you replace the entry for "Dick" with the string "deleted" instead of NULL.

5. Explain what is wrong with the following strategy to reclaim space that is filled with deleted items in a hash table: When attempting to insert a new item in the table, if you encounter an item that has been deleted, replace the deleted item with the new item.

6. Compare the storage requirement for a hash table with open addressing, a table size of 500, and a load factor of 0.5 with a hash table that uses chaining and gives the same performance.

PROGRAMMING

1. Code the following algorithm for finding the location of an object as a function. Assume that table (a hash table vector), and a key (of type Key_Type) to be located in the table are passed as arguments, and hash_fcn(Key_Type) is a hash function defined for Key_Type. Return the object's position if it is found; table.size() if the object is not found.

    1.   Compute the index by taking the hash_fcn(key) % table.size().
    2.   **if** table[index] is NULL
    3.   The object is not in the table.
          else if table[index]->first is equal to the key
    4.   The object is in the table.
          else
    5.   Continue to search the table (by incrementing index) until either the object is found or a NULL entry is found.

9.4 Implementing the Hash Table

In this section, we discuss how to implement a hash table. We will show implementations for hash tables using open addressing and chaining.

The KW::hash_map ADT

We will show more than one way to implement a hash table. Both will be implementations of a class called hash_map (in namespace KW). The interface for these classes is shown in Table 9.5.

The Entry_Type

A hash table stores key-value pairs, therefore the hash_map will define the type Entry_Type as follows:

```
typedef std::pair<const Key_Type, Value_Type> Entry_Type;
```

TABLE 9.5
Interface for the hash_map Class

Function	Behavior
`iterator begin();` `const iterator begin() const`	Returns an iterator to the first entry in the map.
`iterator end();` `const_iterator end()`	Returns an iterator to one past the last entry in the map.
`bool empty()`	Returns **true** if there are no entries in the map.
`size_t size()`	Returns the number of entries in the map.
`pair<iterator, bool> insert(const` `  Entry_Type& entry)`	Inserts an entry into the map. If the key is not in the map, the returned iterator will reference the inserted entry, and the **bool** result will be **true**. If the key is already in the map, the returned iterator will reference the entry that is currently in the map with this key, and the **bool** result will be **false**.
`void erase(const Key_Type& key)`	Removes the item from the map.
`iterator find(const Key_Type& key)`	Returns an iterator that references the item in the map. If the item is not present, `end()` is returned.
`Value_Type& operator[](const` `  Key_Type& key)`	Returns a reference to the value associated with `key`. If `key` is not associated with a value, inserts a default value into the map and returns a reference to the inserted object.

TABLE 9.6
Data Fields for the Class hash_map as Implemented by Hash_Table_Open.h

Data Field	Attribute
`hash<Key_Type> hash_fcn`	The function object that will compute the hash function for the Key_Type.
`size_t num_keys`	The number of keys in the table, excluding keys that were deleted.
`std::vector<Entry_Type*> the_table`	The hash table vector.
`static const size_t INITIAL_CAPACITY`	The initial capacity.
`const double LOAD_THRESHOLD`	The maximum load factor.
`size_t num_deletes`	The number of deleted keys.
`const Entry_Type dummy`	A dummy entry to represent deleted keys.
`const Entry_Type* DELETED`	A pointer to the dummy entry.

Class hash_map as Implemented by Hash_Table_Open.h

Data Declarations and Constructor

In a hash table that uses open addressing, we represent the hash table as a vector of pointers to Entry_Type objects (initial size is INITIAL_CAPACITY). We describe the data fields in Table 9.6. The Entry_Type* object DELETED is used to indicate that the entry at a particular table element has been deleted; a NULL pointer indicates that a table element was never occupied.

We will use the proposed standard hash function class described earlier to represent the hash function. Thus the data field hash_fcn will contain an instance of this function class instantiated for the Key_Type. We will describe how to define this class for a given type in Section 9.5.

The data field declarations and constructor for KW::hash_map (as implemented by Hash_Table_Open.h) follow.

```
/** Definition of the hash_map class. This definition is similar
    to the unordered_map that has been proposed for the next
    version of the C++ standard.
    @param Key_Type The type of the keys
    @param Value_Type The type of the values
*/
template<typename Key_Type, typename Value_Type>
  class hash_map {

    public:

    // Typedefs
    typedef std::pair<const Key_Type, Value_Type> Entry_Type;

    // Forward declaration of iterator
    class iterator;
    class const_iterator;

    /** Construct an empty hash_map. */
    hash_map() :
      hash_fcn(hash<Key_Type>()), num_keys(0),
      the_table(INITIAL_CAPACITY, NULL),
      LOAD_THRESHOLD(0.75),
      num_deletes(0) {}
    ...

    private:

      /** The hash function object */
      hash<Key_Type> hash_fcn;

      /** The number of items currently in the map */
      size_t num_keys;

      /** The vector containing the hash_table */
      std::vector<Entry_Type*> the_table;

      /** The initial capacity */
      static const size_t INITIAL_CAPACITY = 100;
```

```
/** The maximum load factor */
const double LOAD_THRESHOLD;

/** The number of deleted keys */
size_t num_deletes;

/** A dummy entry and a pointer to it */
static Entry_Type dummy;
static Entry_Type* const DELETED;

}; // End hash_map

template<typename Key_Type, typename Value_Type>
  typename hash_map<Key_Type, Value_Type>::Entry_Type
    hash_map<Key_Type, Value_Type>::dummy =
      std::pair<const Key_Type, Value_Type>(
              Key_Type(), Value_Type());

template<typename Key_Type, typename Value_Type>
  typename hash_map<Key_Type, Value_Type>::Entry_Type* const
    hash_map<Key_Type, Value_Type>::DELETED =
      &hash_map<Key_Type, Value_Type>::dummy;
```

The **static** data member DELETED is used to indicate that an entry in the table has been deleted. It is initialized to point to a unique object (dummy). Static data members must be initialized outside of the class declaration. The syntax is similar to that used for member function implementations. For nontemplate classes, the initialization statements would appear in the .cpp file along with the member function implementations. However, for a template class they must appear in the include file (.h) and must be qualified by the class name, including template parameters.

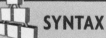

SYNTAX   Initializing Static Data Members of a Template Class

FORM:

template<*template parameter declarations*>
  type class_name<*template parameters*>::*member_name* = *value*;

EXAMPLE:

```
template<typename Key_Type, typename Value_Type>
  typename hash_map<Key_Type, Value_Type>::Entry_Type
    hash_map<Key_Type, Value_Type>::dummy =
      std::pair<const Key_Type, Value_Type>(Key_Type(), Value_Type());
```

MEANING:

Memory is allocated for the static object *class_name*::*member_name*, and it is initialized to the specified *value*. This can become quite complicated, especially where the type of the data member is also defined within the template class. In this example typename hash_map<Key_Type, Value_Type>::Entry_Type is the *type* of the data field, hash_map is the *class*, dummy is the *member name*, and std::pair<const Key_Type, Value_Type>(Key_Type(), Value_Type()) is the *value*.

We want DELETED to represent a unique value that will not point to a valid item. Furthermore, once initialized, we do not want the value of DELETED to change. Notice in the declaration for DELETED that the **const** qualification appears after the * and before the data member name. This declares DELETED to be a constant pointer (i.e., the value of the pointer does not change) as compared with a pointer to **const** (i.e., the value pointed to does not change).

SYNTAX   Constant Pointer Declaration

FORM:

type* const *name*;

EXAMPLE:

```
static Entry_Type* const DELETED;
```

MEANING:

By placing the **const** qualifier after the *, the identifier name is declared to be a constant pointer. That is the value of the pointer (the address of the location pointed to) remains constant. The value pointed to, however, is not declared to be a constant.

The locate Function

Several functions use a private function locate that searches the table (using linear probing) until it finds either the target key or an empty slot. By expanding the table when its load factor exceeds the LOAD_THRESHOLD, we ensure that there will always be an empty slot in the table. Table 9.7 summarizes these private functions.

The algorithm for function locate follows. Listing 9.6 shows the function.

Algorithm for hash_map::locate(const Key_Type& key)

1.   Set index to hash_fcn(key) % the_table.size(), where hash_fcn is the hash function.
2.   **while** the_table[index] is not empty and the key is not at the_table[index]
3.   Increment index modulo the_table.size().
4.   Return the index.

TABLE 9.7
Private Functions for Class hash_map as Implemented by Hash_Table_Open.h

Function	Behavior
size_t locate(const Key_Type& key)	Returns the index of the specified key if present in the table; otherwise, returns the index of the first available slot.
void rehash()	Doubles the capacity of the table and permanently removes deleted items.

LISTING 9.6

Function `hash_map::locate` (in `Hash_Table_Open.h`)

```
/** Locates the entry in the hash table that contains the target key
    or finds the next free entry.
    @param key The key being sought
    @return The position of the key or the first empty slot if
            the key is not in the table
*/
size_t locate(const Key_Type& key) {
  size_t index = hash_fcn(key) % the_table.size();
  while (the_table[index] != NULL
         && (the_table[index] == DELETED
         || the_table[index]->first != key))
    index = (index + 1) % the_table.size();
  return index;
}
```

Notice that the function call `hash_fcn(key)` calls the hash function object for the `Key_Type`. We will discuss how this is provided below. Loop exit occurs if `the_table[index]` is `NULL` (an empty entry is reached) or if the key is at `the_table[index]`. This will happen if the condition (`the_table[index] == DELETED || the_table[index]->first != key`) is false. The condition can be false only if the table item at `index` was not deleted and the key at `the_table[index]` is the key being sought. The order of these conditions is critical. Short-circuit evaluation ensures that the key at `the_table[index]` is checked only after it is determined that `the_table[index]` is not a deleted item.

The **insert** Function

Next we write the algorithm for function `insert`. After inserting a new entry, the function checks to see whether the load factor exceeds the `LOAD_THRESHOLD`. If so, it calls function `rehash` to expand the table and reinsert the entries. By checking the load factor before searching the table, we are assured that if the item is not in the table, we will find an empty slot quickly, and that is the slot where the item will be inserted. If we checked the load threshold after inserting a new item, the new item would get moved and we would have to look for it to create the return iterator value. Listing 9.7 shows the code for function `insert`.

☑ PROGRAM STYLE

Use of `size_t` versus `int` for Indexes

Notice that we declared `index` to be of type **`size_t`**. This is an unsigned type, which is the type returned by the `vector` `size()` function. The C++ compiler defines this type as an unsigned integer type that has sufficient range to represent all index values. (The specific type depends on the architecture of the computer on which the program is to be executed.) By using an unsigned value we are sure that the result of the modulo operator (`%`) is in the range 0 to `the_table.size()` - 1. If we defined `index` and `hash_fcn` to return **`int`** values, then the result of `hash_fcn` could be negative and the result of the modulo operator could also be negative.

Algorithm for hash_map::insert(const Entry_Type& entry)

1. Check for need to rehash.
2. Find the first table element that is empty or the table element that contains the key.
3. **if** an empty element was found
4.   Insert the new item and increment num_keys.
5.   Return make_pair(*iterator to the inserted item*, true)
6. **else** // *key was found*
7.   Return make_pair(*iterator to the found item*, false)

LISTING 9.7
Function hash_map::insert (in Hash_Table_Open.h)

```
/** Inserts an item into the map.
    post: The key is associated with the value in the map.
    @param entry The key, value pair to be inserted
    @return An iterator to the inserted item and true
            if the entry was inserted; an iterator to the existing
            item and false if the item is already present
*/
std::pair<iterator, bool> insert(const Entry_Type& entry) {
  double load_factor = double(num_keys + num_deletes) / the_table.size();
  if (load_factor > LOAD_THRESHOLD) {
    rehash(); // Double the size of the table.
  }
  // Find the position in the table.
  size_t index = locate(entry.first);
  // See whether it is empty.
  if (the_table[index] == NULL) {
    // Create a new entry.
    the_table[index] = new Entry_Type(entry);
    num_keys++;
    return std::make_pair(iterator(this, index), true);
  } else {
    // Item is already in the table.
    return std::make_pair(iterator(this, index), false);
  }
}
```

Ⓧ PITFALL

Integer Division for Calculating Load Factor

Before calling function rehash, function insert calculates the load factor by dividing the number of filled slots by the table size. This is a simple computation, but if you forget to convert the numerator or denominator to **double**, the load factor will be zero (because of integer division), and the table will not be expanded. This will slow down the performance of the table when it becomes nearly full, and it will cause an infinite loop (in function locate) when the table is completely filled.

The Subscript Operator (`operator[]`)

The code for the subscript operator is similar to what was shown before when we implemented the map using the set (see Section 9.2). The difference is that the insert function for hash_map returns an iterator that can be used directly. The algorithm follows, and the code is shown in Listing 9.8

Algorithm for the Subscript Operator (`operator[]`)

1. Call `insert` to insert a new entry consisting of the key and a default `Value_Type` object.
2. Use the iterator returned from the call to `insert` to return a reference to the value that corresponds to the key.

Remember that `insert` adds an item if the key is not found in the map. If the key is currently associated with a value in the map, then Step 1 will return an `iterator` that references that entry. Otherwise, Step 1 will return an `iterator` that references the inserted default value.

LISTING 9.8
Subscript Operator (in `Hash_Table_Open.h`)

```
/** Accesses a value in the map, using the key as an index.
    @param key The key of the item being sought
    @return A reference to the associated value. If the
            key was not in the map, a default value is inserted and
            a reference to this value is returned.
*/
Value_Type& operator[](const Key_Type& key) {
  // Try to insert a dummy item.
  std::pair<iterator, bool> ret = insert(Entry_Type(key, Value_Type()));
  // Return a reference to the value found or inserted.
  return ret.first->second;
}
```

The **erase** Function

Next, we write the algorithm for function erase. Note that we "remove" a table element by setting it to point to object DELETED. We leave the implementation as an exercise.

Algorithm for erase(const Key_Type& key)

1. Find the first table element that is empty or the table element that contains the key.
2. **if** an empty element is found
3.   Return.
4. **else**
5.   The key is found.
        Remove this table element by setting it to point to DELETED, increment num_deletes, and decrement num_keys.

The **rehash** Function

Finally, we write the algorithm for private function rehash. Listing 9.9 shows the function.

Algorithm for rehash

1.   Allocate a new hash table that is double the size.
2.   Reset the number of keys and number of deletions to 0.
3.   Reinsert each table entry that has not been deleted in the new hash table.

LISTING 9.9

Function `hash_map::rehash` (in `Hash_Table_Open.h`)

```
/** Expand the table size when load_factor exceeds LOAD_THRESHOLD.
    post: The size of the table is doubled.
          Each nondeleted entry from the original table is
          reinserted into the expanded table.
          The value of num_keys is reset to the number of items
          actually inserted; num_deletes is reset to 0.
*/
void rehash() {
  // Create a new table whose size is double the current table.
  std::vector<Entry_Type*> other_table(the_table.size() * 2, NULL);

  // Swap this table with the current table.
  the_table.swap(other_table);

  // Reinsert all items from old table to new.
  num_deletes = 0;
  for (size_t i = 0; i < other_table.size(); i++) {
    if ((other_table[i] != NULL) && (other_table[i] != DELETED)) {
      size_t index = locate(other_table[i]->first);
      the_table[index] = other_table[i];
    }
  }
}
```

The Copy Constructor, Assignment Operator, and Destructor

Because the `vector<Entry_Type*>` table contains pointers to dynamically allocated `Entry_Type` objects, we need to implement the copy constructor and assignment operators so that they make copies of the objects pointed to when a `hash_map` is copied. We also need to delete these dynamically allocated objects when a `hash_map` is destroyed.

The copy constructor initializes the data fields to the same values as the no-parameter constructor and then calls the `insert` function to insert each item from `hash_map` `other` into `the_table`.

```
/** Copy Constructor.
    @param other The other map to be copied
*/
hash_map(const hash_map<Key_Type, Value_Type>& other) :
    hash_fcn(hash<Key_Type>()), num_keys(0),
            the_table(other.the_table.size(), NULL),
    LOAD_THRESHOLD(0.75),
    num_deletes(0) {
  for (size_t i = 0; i < other.the_table.size(); i++) {
    if (other.the_table[i] != NULL && other.the_table[i] != DELETED)
      insert(Entry_Type(other.the_table[i]->first,
                        other.the_table[i]->second));
  }
}
```

The assignment operator and destructor are left as exercises.

TABLE 9.8
Data Fields for Class `hash_map` Implemented by `Hash_Table_Chain.h`

Data Field	Attribute
`hash<Key_Type> hash_fcn`	The hash function object.
`size_t num_keys`	The number of keys in the map.
`std::vector<std::list<Entry_Type> > the_buckets`	A vector of lists containing the items.
`static const size_t INITIAL_CAPACITY`	The initial size of the vector.
`static double LOAD_THRESHOLD`	The maximum load factor before rehashing.

Class hash_map as Implemented by `Hash_Table_Chain.h`

Next we turn our attention to `Hash_Table_Chain.h`, which implements `hash_map` using chaining. We will represent the hash table as a vector of linked lists as shown in Table 9.8. Even though a hash table that uses chaining can store any number of elements in the same slot, we will expand the table if the number of entries becomes three times the number of slots (`LOAD_THRESHOLD` is 3.0) to keep the performance at a reasonable level.

Listing 9.10 shows the data fields and the constructor for `Hash_Table_Chain.h`.

LISTING 9.10
Data Fields and Constructor for `hash_map` as Implemented by `Hash_Table_Chain.h`

```
/** Definition of the hash_map class. This definition is similar
    to the unordered_map that has been proposed for the next
    version of the C++ standard.
    @param Key_Type The type of the keys
    @param Value_Type The type of the values
*/
template<typename Key_Type, typename Value_Type>
  class hash_map {

    public:

    // Typedefs
    typedef std::pair<const Key_Type, Value_Type> Entry_Type;

    // Forward declaration of iterator
    class iterator;
    class const_iterator;

    /** Construct an empty hash_map. */
    hash_map() :
      hash_fcn(hash<Key_Type>()), num_keys(0),
              the_buckets(INITIAL_CAPACITY), LOAD_THRESHOLD(3.0)  {
    }
    ...

    private:
```

```
/** The hash function object */
hash<Key_Type> hash_fcn;

/** The number of items currently in the map */
size_t num_keys;

/** Vector of lists containing the buckets */
std::vector<std::list<Entry_Type> > the_buckets;

/** The initial capacity */
static const size_t INITIAL_CAPACITY = 100;

/** The maximum load factor */
const double LOAD_THRESHOLD;

}; // End hash_map
```

Next we discuss functions insert and erase. Instead of introducing a locate function to search a list for the key, we will include a search loop in each function.

We begin with the algorithm for insert. Listing 9.11 shows its code.

Algorithm for insert(const Entry_Type& entry)

1. Check for need to rehash.
2. Set index to hash_fcn(key) % the_buckets.size().
3. Search the list at the_buckets[index] to find the key.
4. **if** not found
5. Append a new entry to the end of this list.
6. Return make_pair(*iterator to the inserted item*, true)
7. **else**
8. Return make_pair(*iterator to the found item*, false)

LISTING 9.11
Function hash_map::insert(const Entry_Type& entry) (in Hash_Table_Chain.h)

```
/** Inserts an item into the map.
    post: The key is associated with the value in the map.
    @param entry The key, value pair to be inserted
    @return an iterator to the inserted item and true
            if the entry was inserted, an iterator to the existing
            item and false if the item is already present
*/
std::pair<iterator, bool>
  insert(const Entry_Type& entry) {

  // Check for the need to rehash.
  double load_factor = double(num_keys) / the_buckets.size();
  if (load_factor > LOAD_THRESHOLD) {
    rehash();
  }

  // Find the position in the table.
  size_t index = hash_fcn(entry.first) % the_buckets.size();
```

```
    // Search for the key.
    typename std::list<Entry_Type>::iterator pos
      = the_buckets[index].begin();
    while (pos != the_buckets[index].end()
          && pos->first != entry.first) ++pos;
    if (pos == the_buckets[index].end()) {  // Not in table
      the_buckets[index].push_back(Entry_Type(entry));
      num_keys++;
      return std::make_pair(iterator(this, index,
                                    --(the_buckets[index].end())),
                          true);
    } else { // Already there
      return std::make_pair(iterator(this, index, pos), false);
    }
}
```

Next, we write the algorithm for function erase. We leave the implementation of rehash and erase as an exercise.

Algorithm for hash_map::erase(const Key_Type& key)

1.   Set index to hash_fcn(key) % the_buckets.size().
2.   Search the list at table[index] to find the key.
3.   **if** the search is successful
4.   Erase the entry with this key and decrement num_keys.

Copy Constructor, Assignment, and Destructor

Because Hash_Table_Chain.h uses a std::vector<std::list<Entry_Type> > to hold the hash table, the default copy constructor and assignment operator will make a deep copy of the hash_map, and the default destructor will delete any dynamically allocated objects.

Testing the Hash Table Implementations

We discuss two approaches to testing the hash table implementations. One way is to create a file of key-value pairs and then read each key-value pair and insert it in the hash table, observing how the table is filled. To do this, you need to write a to_string function for the table that captures the index of each table element that is not NULL and then the contents of that table element. For open addressing, the contents would be the string representation of the key-value pair. For chaining, you could use an iterator to traverse the linked list at that table element and append each key-value pair to the result string (see the Programming Exercises for this section).

If you use a data file, you can carefully test different situations. The following are some of the cases you should examine:

- Does the array index wrap around as it should?
- Are collisions resolved correctly?
- Are duplicate keys handled appropriately? Is the new value retrieved instead of the original value?
- Are deleted keys retained in the table, but no longer accessible via operator[]?
- Does rehashing occur when the load factor reaches 0.75 (3.0 for chaining)?

By stepping through the `insert` function you can observe how the table is probed and the search chain that is followed to access or retrieve a key.

An alternative to creating a data file is to insert randomly generated integers in the hash table. This will allow you to create a very large table with little effort. The following loop generates SIZE key-value pairs. Each key is an integer between 0 and RAND_MAX. For each table entry, the value is the same as the key. The `hash<int>` function returns a "random" value based on the **int** value provided. We describe one possible implementation in the next section.

```
for (int i = 0; i < SIZE; i++) {
  int next_int = rand();
  hash_table[next_int] = next_int;
}
```

Because the keys are generated randomly, you can't investigate the effect of duplicate keys as you can with a data file. However, you can build arbitrarily large tables and observe how the elements are placed in the table. After the table is complete, you can interactively enter items to retrieve, delete, and insert and verify that they are handled properly.

If you are using open addressing, you can add statements to count the number of items probed each time an insertion is made. You can accumulate these totals and display the average search chain length. If you are using chaining, you can also count the number of probes made and display the average. After all items have been inserted, you can calculate the average length of each linked list and compare that with the number predicted by the formula provided in the discussion of performance in Section 9.3.

EXERCISES FOR SECTION 9.4

SELF-CHECK

1. The following table stores **int** keys and needs to be rehashed. Where would each key be placed in the new table resulting from rehashing the current table?

Index	Key
[0]	24
[1]	6
[2]	20
[3]	
[4]	14

PROGRAMMING

1. Write an erase function for `Hash_Table_Open.h`.
2. Write `rehash` and erase functions for class `Hash_Table_Chain.h`.
3. Write a `to_string` function for class `Hash_Table_Open.h`.

4. Write a to_string function for class Hash_Table_Chain.h.

5. Write a function size for both hash table implementations.

6. Modify function locate to count and display the number of probes made each time it is called. Accumulate these in a data field num_probes and count the number of times locate is called in another data field. Provide a function that returns the average number of probes per call to locate.

9.5 Implementation Considerations for the hash_map

Defining the Hash Function Class

The definition for the template hash function class is as follows

```
/** Hash Function Objects Template */
template<typename Key_Type>
  struct hash {
    size_t operator()(const Key_Type&);
};
```

Since this is a function class, it declares the function call operator (operator()). However, no implementation is provided. Instead, specializations are provided for the built-in types and library-defined types such as string.

Specialization for string

The specialization for the string class is shown below. It evaluates the polynomial:

$$s_0 \times 31^{n-1} + s_1 \times 31^{n-2} + s_2 \times 31^{n-3} + \cdots + s_{n-1}$$

which we discussed previously. Once the hash class becomes part of the C++ standard, standard library implementors will provide an appropriate function, but it may be different from what we have shown here.

```
// Specialization for string
#include <string>
template<>
  struct hash<std::string> {
    size_t operator()(const std::string& s) {
      size_t result = 0;
      for (size_t i = 0; i < s.length(); i++) {
        result = result * 31 + s[i];
      }
      return result;
    }
};
```

Specialization for int

One possible hash function for **int** values is the value itself. This, however, does not tend to distribute the keys through the hash table. A better approach is to multiply the **int** value by some large prime number and take the result modulo the word size.

This is the approach used by the random number generator and demonstrated in the following code. The number shown is a large prime number and the integer multiplication is performed modulo the word size. The `size_t` function casts the result to type `size_t`.

```
// Specialization for int
template<>
  struct hash<int> {
    size_t operator()(int i) {
      return size_t(4262999287U * i);
    }
};
```

Specialization for Your Own Classes

To use objects of your own classes as keys in a `hash_map`, you need to define the equality operator (`==`) and specialize the `hash` function class. The `hash` function will be used to start the search, and the equality operator will be used to finish it. For this to work, the `hash` function must obey the following contract:

If obj1 == obj2 is true, then hash<*type*>()(obj1) == hash<*type*>()(obj2)

where `obj1` and `obj2` are objects of type *type*.

Consequently, you should make sure that your function uses the same data field(s) as your equality operator. We provide an example next.

EXAMPLE 9.11   Class `Person` has data field `IDNumber`, which is used to determine whether two `Person` objects are equal. The equality operator returns **true** only if the objects' `IDNumber` fields have the same contents.

```
bool operator==(const Person& other) const {
  return IDNumber == other.IDNumber;
}
```

To satisfy its contract, function `hash<Person>` must also be specialized as follows. Now two objects that are considered equal will also have the same hash code.

```
template<>
  struct hash<Person> {
    size_t operator()(const Person& p) {
      return hash<string>()(p.IDNumber);
    }
};
```

The hash_map::iterator and hash_map::const_iterator

Our goal in this chapter was to show you how to implement the operators in our hash table, not to implement a `hash_map` that has the same functionality as the `std::map` class. To complete the limited implementation we have shown so far, we need to implement the `iterator` and `const_iterator` classes.

TABLE 9.9

Design of the hash_map::iterator for Hash_Table_Open.h

Data Field	Attribute
hash_map<Key_Type, Value_Type>* the_parent	A pointer to the hash_map that this iterator is iterating through.
size_t the_index	The index in the table for the current entry.
Public Member Functions	**Behavior**
Entry_Type& operator*()	Returns a reference to the Entry_Type that is referenced by this iterator.
Entry_Type* operator->()	Returns a pointer to the Entry_Type that is referenced by this iterator.
iterator& operator++()	Prefix increment operator. Advances this iterator to the next entry in the table that is occupied.
iterator operator++(int)	Postfix increment operator. Saves the current value of this iterator. Increments this iterator and then returns the saved value.
bool operator==(const iterator& other) const	Returns **true** if this iterator and the other iterator are the same.
Private Member Functions	**Behavior**
iterator(const hash_map<Key_Type>* parent, size_t index)	Constructs an iterator that starts at the specified index, or at the next occupied table entry following index.
void advance()	If the_index is not at an occupied position in the table, advances it to the next occupied position.

The const_iterator is the same except that the return type from operator*() is a const Entry_Type& and the return type from operator->() is a const Entry_Type*. Also the const_iterator must provide a public constructor that converts from an iterator to a const_iterator. The definition of this constructor is as follows:

```
const_iterator(const typename hash_map<Key_Type,
               Value_Type>::iterator& other)
    : the_parent(other.the_parent), the_index(other.the_index) {}
```

The other constructors for iterator and const_iterator are private because we do not want the client programs to create arbitrary iterators. The only valid iterator objects are ones created by the member functions of the hash_map that owns the iterator. Therefore, the iterator and const_iterator classes must declare the hash_map as a friend. The iterator must also declare the const_iterator as a friend for the conversion constructor just described.

The iterator for the Hash_Table_Chain.h implementation is similar to that for the Hash_Table_Open.h implementation. An additional data field of type std::list<Entry_Type>::iterator is needed to keep track of the position within the list in the_bucket[the_index].

Implementation of the iterators is left as a Programming Project (see Project 6).

EXERCISES FOR SECTION 9.5

PROGRAMMING

1. Write statements to display all key, value pairs in hash_map object m, one pair per line. You will need to create an iterator to access the map entries.
2. Assume a Person has data fields last_name and first_name. Write an equality operator that returns **true** if two Person objects have the same first and last names. Write a hash<Person> function class that satisfies the hash function contract. Make sure that your hash<Person>() function does not return the same value for Henry James and James Henry. Your equality operator should return a value of **false** for these two people.

9.6 Additional Applications of Maps

In this section we will consider two case studies that use a Map object. We take another look at the telephone directory case first presented in Chapter 1 and revisited in Chapter 4.

CASE STUDY   Implementing the Phone Directory Using a Map

Problem   In Section 1.4 we introduced the Phone_Directory ADT (see Table 1.5), which contained functions (load_data, lookup_entry, add_or_change_entry, remove_entry, save) for processing a phone directory consisting of name-number pairs.

Initially we implemented this ADT using an array (Section 1.7) and later a vector (Section 4.2) to store Directory_Entry objects. To look up a name or to change an existing name, we performed a linear search of the array, which is an $O(n)$ operation. By using a map we can obtain a more efficient implementation.

Analysis   The Phone_Directory is essentially a map. It relates names (which must be unique) to phone numbers. For the entries shown in the following table, the name is the key field and the phone number is the value field.

Index	Value
Jane Smith	215-555-1234
John Smith	215-555-1234
Bill Jones	508-555-6123

Phone_Directory API	map API
add_or_change_entry	operator[]
lookup_entry	find
remove_entry	erase
load_data	None
save	None

Thus, we can implement the Phone_Directory ADT by using a map<string, string> object for the phone directory. The map<string, string> object would contain the key-value pairs { ("Jane Smith", "215-555-1234"), ("John Smith", "215-555-1234"), ("Bill Jones", "508-555-6123") }.

Design We need to design the class Map_Based_PD, which implements the Phone_Directory ADT. Data field the_directory is type map<string, string>. Table 9.10 shows the functions required by the Phone_Directory ADT and the corresponding function or functions in the map interface. Three of these functions have direct correspondents.

Implementation In the following functions, data field the_directory is type map<string, string>. Function add_or_change_entry uses the subscript operator to change or add a new name-number pair to the directory.

```
string Phone_Directory::add_or_change_entry(
    const string& name, const string& number) {
  string old_number = the_directory[name];
  the_directory[name] = number;
  modified = true;
  return old_number;
}
```

The first statement retrieves the old number associated with the name. If there was none, a default value (empty string) is inserted. The second statement then changes the value to the desired number.

This is slightly inefficient since we do two searches of the map. We could adapt the code for operator[] (Listing 9.3) and use the insert function. If the returned pair<iterator, bool> indicates that the name was already in the map, we could then use the returned iterator to retrieve the old name and set the new one. The revised function is as follows.

```
string Phone_Directory::add_or_change_entry(
    const string& name, const string& number) {
  string old_number = "";
  pair<iterator, bool> ret =
    the_directory.insert(pair<string, string>(name, number));
  if (!ret.second) { // Name already in the directory
    old_number = ret.first->second;
    ret.first->second = number;
  }
  modified = true;
  return old_number;
}
```

The `lookup_entry` function uses the `find` function to locate the directory entry. The entry key field (`name`) is passed as an argument. If the returned `iterator` is not equal to `end()`, then the name is retrieved and returned. Otherwise, an empty string is returned.

```
/** Look up an entry.
    @param name The name of the person
    @return The number. If not in the directory, an empty string
*/
string Phone_Directory::lookup_entry(const string& name) const
{
  const_iterator itr = the_directory.find(name);
  if (itr != the_directory.end())
    return itr->second;
  else
    return "";
}
```

The `remove_entry` function uses the `erase(const Key_Type& key)` function to delete a directory entry. First we use the subscript operator to retrieve the old number. Thus we always are inserting a value and then removing it. We could avoid this by using the `find` function and then the `erase(iterator)` function, but there may not be any advantage to this. This is because for a binary search tree, the `erase` may require searching the tree, even though an `iterator` is provided. It depends on the implementation of the binary search tree and the `iterator` class.

```
string Phone_Directory::remove_entry(const string& name)
{
  string old_number = the_directory[name];
  the_directory.erase(name);
  modified = old_number != string();
  return old_number;
}
```

The `load_data` function reads the entries from a data file and stores them in a `map`. We will write the loop that does the read and store operations. It uses the subscript operator to add an entry with the given name and number.

```
while (getline(in, name)) {
  if (getline(in, number)) {
    the_directory[name] = number;
  }
}
```

To save the directory, we need to extract each name-number pair sequentially from the map and write them out. We can use a **for** loop and an iterator:

```
for (iterator itr = the_directory.begin();
     itr != the_directory.end(); ++ itr) {
  out << itr->first << "\n";
  out << itr->second << "\n";
}
```

Testing To test this code, you need to modify the `PD_Application.cpp` file to include `Map_Based_PD.h` and compile and link this modified source file with the `Map_Based_PD.cpp`.

The rest of the `main` function used to test the application would be the same.

CASE STUDY   Completing the Huffman Coding Problem

Problem   In Chapter 8 we showed how to compress a file by using a Huffman tree to encode the symbols occurring in the file so that the most frequently occurring characters had the shortest binary codes. The input to function `build_tree` of class `Huffman_Tree` was a `Huff_Data` vector consisting of (weight, symbol) pairs, where the weight in each pair was the frequency of occurrence of the corresponding symbol. We need a function to build this vector for any data file so that we can create the Huffman tree. Once the tree is built, we need to encode each symbol in the input file by writing the corresponding bit string for that symbol to the output file.

Analysis   A map is a very useful data structure for both these tasks: creating the vector of `Huff_Data` elements and replacing each input character by its bit string code in the output file. For either situation we need to look up a symbol in a table. Using a map ensures that the table lookup is an $O(\log n)$ process.

To build the frequency table, we need to read a file and count the number of occurrences of each symbol in the file. The symbol will be the key for each entry in a `map<char, int>` object, and the corresponding value will be the count of occurrences so far. As each symbol is read, we retrieve its map entry and increment the corresponding count. If the symbol is not yet in the frequency table, the map subscript operator will insert a zero the first time we reference it.

Once we have the frequency table, we can construct the Huffman tree using a priority queue as explained in Section 8.6. Then we need to build a code table that stores the bit string code associated with each symbol to facilitate encoding the data file. Storing the code table in a `map<char, Bit_String>` object makes the encoding process more efficient, because we can look up the symbol and retrieve its bit string code ($O(\log n)$ process). To build the code table, we do a preorder traversal of the Huffman tree.

Design   The algorithm for building the frequency table follows. After all characters are read, we iterate through the map and create the corresponding `Huff_Data` item, a (weight, symbol) pair.

Algorithm for `build_frequency_table`

1. **while** there are more characters in the input file
2.   Read a character.
3.   Increment the entry in the map associated with this character.
4. **for** each entry in the map
5.   Store its data as a weight-symbol pair in the `vector<Huff_Data>`.
6. Return the `vector<Huff_Data>`.

We can use a `map<char, Bit_String>` object that stores each symbol and its corresponding bit string code (a string of 0 and 1 bits) to encode the file. Class `Bit_String` may be downloaded from the Web site for this textbook.

Function `build_code` builds the code table by performing a preorder traversal of the Huffman tree. The code table should be declared as a data field:

```
map<char, Bit_String> code_map;
```

As we traverse the tree, we keep track of the bit string code so far. When we traverse left, we append a 0 to the bit string, and when we traverse right, we append a 1 to the bit string. If we encounter a symbol in a node, we insert that symbol along with a copy of the code so far (a new entry) in the code table. Because all symbols are stored in leaf nodes, we return immediately without going deeper in the tree.

Algorithm for Function `build_code`

1.   Get the data at the current root.
2.   **if** reached a leaf node
3.   Insert the symbol and bit string code so far as a new code table entry.
4.   **else**
5.   Append a 0 to the bit string code so far.
6.   Apply the function recursively to the left subtree.
7.   Append a 1 to the bit string code.
8.   Apply the function recursively to the right subtree.

Finally, to encode the file, we read each character, look up its bit string code in the code table map, and then write it to the output file.

Algorithm for Function `encode`

1.   **while** there are more characters in the input file
2.   Read a character and get its corresponding bit string code.
3.   Write its bit string to the output file.

Implementation   Listing 9.12 shows the code for function `build_frequency_table`. The **while** loop builds the frequency table (`map frequencies`). Once the table is built, we use a **for** loop to traverse the `map`, retrieving each entry from the map and using its data to create a new `Huff_Data` element for vector `result`. When we finish, we return `result` as the function result.

LISTING 9.12
Function `build_frequency_table`

```
vector<Huff_Data> Huffman_Tree::build_frequency_table(istream& in) {
  map<char, int> frequencies;
  char c;
  while (in.get(c)) {
    frequencies[c]++;
  }
  vector<Huff_Data> result;
  for (map<char, int>::iterator itr = frequencies.begin();
       itr != frequencies.end(); ++itr) {
    result.push_back(Huff_Data(itr->second, itr->first));
  }
  return result;
}
```

Next, we show function build_code. We provide a starter function that initializes code_map to an empty map and calls the recursive function that implements the algorithm discussed in the Design section.

```
/** Starter function to build the code table.
    post: The table is built.
*/
void build_code() {
  code_map.clear();
  build_code(huff_tree, Bit_String());
}
/** Recursive function to perform breadth-first traversal
    of the Huffman tree and build the code table.
    @param tree The current tree root
    @param code The code string so far
*/
void Huffman_Tree::build_code(const Binary_Tree<Huff_Data>& tree,
                              const Bit_String& code) {
  if (tree.is_leaf()) {
    Huff_Data datum = tree.get_data();
    code_map[datum.symbol] = code;
  } else {
    // Append 0 to code so far and traverse left
    Bit_String left_code(code);
    left_code.append(false);
    build_code(tree.get_left_subtree(), left_code);
    // Append 1 to code so far and traverse right
    Bit_String right_code(code);
    right_code.append(true);
    build_code(tree.get_right_subtree(), right_code);
  }
}
```

Function encode reads each character again, looks up its bit string code, and writes it to the output file. We assume that the code table is in map code_map (a data field).

```
/** The map to store the code table. */
map<char, Bit_String> code_map
```

Following is the encode function.

```
/** Encodes a data file by writing it in compressed bit string form.
    @param in The input stream
    @param out The output stream
*/
void Huffman_Tree::encode(std::istream& in, std::ostream& out) {
  Bit_String result;
  char next_char;
  while (in.get(next_char)) {
    result += code_map[next_char];
  }
  result.write(out);
}
```

Testing To test these functions completely, you need to download class Bit_String (see Project 1) and write a main function that calls them in the proper sequence. For interim testing, you can read a data file and display the frequency table that is constructed to verify that it is correct. You can also use the string class instead of class Bit_String in functions build_code and encode. The resulting code string would consist of a sequence of digit characters '0' and '1' instead of a sequence of 0 and 1 bits. But this would enable you to verify that the program works correctly.

EXERCISES FOR SECTION 9.6

PROGRAMMING

1. Complete function load_data for class Map_Based_PD.
2. Complete function save for class Map_Based_PD.

Chapter Review

- The standard library class set is a data type that supports the same operations as a mathematical set. We use set objects to store a collection of elements that are not ordered by position. Each element in the collection is unique. A set is a useful data structure when we only need to determine whether or not a particular element is in a collection, not its position or relative order.

- The standard library class map enables a user to access information (a value) corresponding to a specified key. Each key is unique and is mapped to a value that may or may not be unique. Maps are useful for retrieving or updating the value corresponding to a given key.

- A hash table uses hashing to transform an item's key into a table index so that insertions, retrievals, and deletions can be performed in expected $O(1)$ time. When the hash function is applied to a key, it should return an integer value that appears to be a random number. A good hash function should be easy to compute and should distribute its values evenly throughout the range of unsigned integer (size_t) values. We use modulo division to transform the hash code value to a table index.

- A collision occurs when two keys hash to the same table index. Collisions are expected, and hash tables utilize either open addressing or chaining to resolve collisions. In open addressing, each table element points to a key-value pair, or is NULL if it is empty. During insertion, a new entry is stored at the table element corresponding to its hash index if it is empty; otherwise, it is stored in the next empty location following the one selected by its hash index. In chaining, each table element is a linked list of key-value pairs with that hash index. During insertion, a new entry is stored in the linked list of key-value pairs for its hash index.

◆ In open addressing, linear probing is often used to resolve collisions. In linear probing, finding a target or an empty table location involves incrementing the table index by 1 after each probe. This approach may cause clusters of keys to occur in the table, leading to overlapping search chains and poor performance. To minimize the harmful effect of clustering, quadratic probing increments the index by the square of the probe number. Quadratic probing can, however, cause a table to appear to be full when there is still space available, and it can lead to an infinite loop.

◆ The best way to avoid collisions is to keep the table load factor relatively low by rehashing when the load factor reaches a value such as 0.75 (75 percent full). To rehash, you increase the table size and reinsert each table element.

◆ In open addressing, you can't remove an element from the table when you delete it, but you must mark it as deleted. In chaining, you can remove a table element when you delete it. In either case, traversal of a hash table visits its entries in an arbitrary order.

◆ Using a hash-table based implementation of the set and map gives search and retrieval operations that have expected constant ($O(1)$) time.

◆ The standard library implementation of the set and map use a Red-Black tree. Search and retrieval operations are $O(\log n)$). The tree implementation enables you to traverse the key-value pairs in a meaningful way and allows for subsets based on a range of key values.

Quick-Check Exercises

1. If s is a set that contains the characters 'a', 'b', 'c', write a statement to insert the character 'd'.

2. What is the effect of each of the following function calls, given the set in Exercise 1, and what does it return? (Function contains is defined in Set_Functions.h.)
   ```
   s.insert('a');
   s.insert('A');
   next = 'b';
   contains(s, next);
   ```
   For questions 3 through 7, a Map, m, contains the following entries: (1234, "Jane Doe"), (1999, "John Smith"), (1250, "Ace Ventura"), (2000, "Bill Smythe"), (2999, "Nomar Garciaparra").

3. What is the effect of the statement m[1234] = "Jane Smith";?

4. What is returned by m[1234]? What is returned by m[1500]?

5. If the entries for Map m are stored in a hash table of size 1000 with open addressing and linear probing, where would each of the items be stored? Assume that the hash function is the identity function.

6. Answer Question 5 for the case where the entries were stored using quadratic probing.

7. Answer Question 5 for the case where the entries were stored using chaining.

Answers to Quick-Check Exercises

1. `s.add('d');`
2. `s.add('a');`   `// add 'a', duplicate - returns false`
   `s.add('A');`   `// add 'A', returns true`
   `next = 'b';`
   `s.contains(next);` `// 'b' is in the set, returns true`
3. The value associated with key 1234 is changed to `"Jane Smith"`. The string `"Jane Doe"` is returned.
4. The string `"Jane Doe"`, and then the empty string.
5. 1234 at 234, 1999 at 999, 1250 at 250, 2000 at 000, 2999 at 001.
6. 1234 at 234, 1999 at 999, 1250 at 250, 2000 at 000, 2999 at 003.
7. 2000 in a linked list at 000, 1234 in a linked list at 234, 1250 in a linked list at 250, 1999 and 2999 in a linked list at 999.

Review Questions

1. Show where the following keys would be placed in a hash table of size 5 using open addressing: 1000, 1002, 1007, 1003. Where would these keys be after rehashing to a table of size 11?
2. Answer Question 1 for a hash table that uses chaining.
3. Write a `to_string` function for class `hash_map`. This function should display each table element that is not `NULL` and is not deleted.
4. Class `Hash_Table_Chain.h` uses the class `std::list`, which is implemented as a double-linked list. Write the `insert` function using a single-linked list to hold elements that hash to the same index.
5. Write the `operator[]` function for the class in Question 4.
6. Write the `erase` function for the class in Question 4.

Programming Projects

1. Complete all functions of class `Huffman_Tree` and test them out using a document file and a C++ source file on your computer. You can download class `Bit_String` from the Web site for this textbook.
2. Use a `map` to store the frequency counts for all the words in a large text document. When you are done, display the contents of this `map`. Next, store its contents in an array. Sort the array in decreasing order by frequency and display it.
3. Modify Project 2 to save the line numbers for every occurrence of a word as well as the count.
4. (Based on example in Brian W. Kernighan and Rob Pike, *The Practice of Programming*, Addison Wesley, 1999) We want to generate "random text" in the style of another author. Your first task is to collect a group of prefix strings of two words that occur in a text file and associate them with a list of suffix strings using a `map`. For example, the text for Charles Dickens' "A Christmas Carol" contains the four phrases:

   Marley was dead: to begin with.
   Marley was as dead as a door-nail.
   Marley was as dead as a door-nail.
   Marley was dead.

The prefix string "Marley was" would be associated with the vector containing the four suffix strings "dead:", "as", "as", "dead.". You must go through the text and examine each successive pair of two-word strings to see whether that pair is already in the map as a key. If so, add the next word to the vector that is the value for that prefix string. For example, in examining the first two sentences shown, you would first add to the entry ("Marley was", vector "dead:"). Next you would add the entry ("was dead", vector "as"). Next you would add the entry ("dead as", vector "a"), and so on. When you retrieve the prefix "Marley was" again, you would modify the vector that is its value, and the entry would become ("Marley was", vector "dead:", "as"). When you are all finished, add the entry "THE_END" to the suffix list for the last prefix placed in the map.

Once you have scanned the complete text, it is time to use the map to begin generating new text that is in the same style as the old text. Output the first prefix you placed in the map: "Marley was". Then retrieve the vector that is the value for this prefix. Randomly select one of the suffixes, and then output the suffix. For example, the output text so far might be "Marley was dead" if the suffix "dead" was selected from the vector of suffixes for "Marley was". Now continue with the two-word sequence consisting of the second word from the previous prefix and the suffix (that would be the string "was dead"). Look it up in the map, randomly select one of the suffixes, and output it. Continue this process until the suffix "THE_END" is selected.

5. Complete Hash_Table_Open.h so that it fully implements the map interface described in Table 9.5. As part of this, implement the iterator and const_iterator as described in Section 9.5.

6. Complete Hash_Table_Chain.h so that it fully implements the map interface, and test it out. Complete class iterator and const_iterator as described in Project 5.

7. Revise function insert for Hash_Table_Open to place a new item into an already deleted spot in the search chain. Don't forget to check the scenario where the key has already been inserted.

Sorting

Chapter Objectives

- ◆ To learn how to use the standard sorting functions in `algorithm.h`
- ◆ To learn how to implement the following sorting algorithms: selection sort, bubble sort, insertion sort, Shell sort, merge sort, heapsort, and quicksort
- ◆ To understand the difference in performance of these algorithms, and which to use for small arrays, which to use for medium arrays, and which to use for large arrays

Sorting is the process of rearranging the data in an array or container so that the data elements are in increasing (or decreasing) order. Because sorting is done so frequently, computer scientists have devoted much time and effort to developing efficient algorithms for sorting arrays. Even though many languages (including C++) provide sorting utilities, it is still very important to study these algorithms, because they illustrate several well-known ways to solve the sorting problem, each with its own merits. You should know how they are written so that you can duplicate them if you need to use them with languages that don't have sorting utilities.

Another reason for studying these algorithms is that they illustrate some very creative approaches to problem solving. For example, the insertion sort algorithm adapts an approach used by card players to arrange a hand of cards; the merge sort algorithm builds on a technique used to sort external data files. Several algorithms use divide-and-conquer to break a larger problem into more manageable subproblems. The Shell sort is a very efficient sort that works by sorting many small subarrays using insertion sort, which is a relatively inefficient sort when used by itself. The merge sort and quicksort algorithms are both recursive. The heapsort uses a heap as its underlying data structure. The final reason for studying sorting is to learn how computer scientists analyze and compare the performance of several different algorithms that do the same operation.

We will cover three quadratic ($O(n^2)$) sorting algorithms that are fairly simple and appropriate for sorting small arrays but are not recommended for large arrays. We will also discuss three sorting algorithms that give improved performance ($O(n \log n)$) on large arrays and one that gives performance that is much better than $O(n^2)$, but not as good as $O(n \log n)$.

Our goal is to provide a sufficient selection of quadratic sorts and faster sorts. A few other sorting algorithms are described in the programming projects.

10.1 Using C++ Sorting Functions

The Standard C++ Library (in `algorithm.h`) provides two sorting functions with the following prototypes:

```
template template<typename RI>
  void sort(RI first, RI last);

template<typename RI, typename Compare>
  void sort(RI first, RI last, Compare comp);
```

Each function uses a pair of random-access iterators (`typename RI`). Recall from Chapter 4 that a random-access iterator is an iterator that can move forward or backward and in increments greater than 1. The first iterator in the pair references the first element of the sequence to be sorted, and the second iterator in the pair references 1 past the last element in the sequence. The second version of the function has a type `Compare` parameter, through which the user can specify a comparison operator. If a `Compare` parameter is not specified, the operator `<` is used to compare adjacent elements of a sequence. Therefore, the elements of the sequence will be sorted in increasing order.

Because these functions require random-access iterators, they can be used only with vectors, deques, and ordinary C pointers (for sorting arrays). The `list` container supports only bidirectional iterators, so it provides its own `sort` member function.

There are also two functions named `stable_sort`, which are similar to the `sort` functions. The primary difference is that elements that are equal may not retain their relative ordering when `sort` is used, but they will retain their relative ordering when `stable_sort` is used. In other words, if there are two occurrences of an item, the one that is first in the unsorted array is only guaranteed to be first in the sorted array if `stable_sort` is used. The `sort` function is slightly faster than `stable_sort`, so it should be used whenever the relative ordering of equal elements is not of concern.

The actual type of random-access iterator passed to function `sort` will depend on whether we are sorting an array, vector, or deque. The compiler attempts to match the actual types of the arguments to the template parameters. If we use the second version of function `sort`, we must also pass an object that implements a comparison function.

EXAMPLE 10.1   If array `items` stores a collection of 16 integers, the statement

```
sort(items, items + 16);
```

sorts the array. The statement

```
sort(items, items + 8);
```

sorts only the first half of the array, leaving the rest untouched. The function call

```
sort(items, items + 16, greater<int>());
```

sorts the array in descending order using function `greater<int>`, which implements the comparison operator > for integers (defined in library `functional`).

EXAMPLE 10.2   The following statements sort the elements of vector `v` and deque `d`.

```
sort(v.begin(), v.end());
sort(d.begin(), d.end());
```

The following statement shows how to sort the elements in vector v in descending order by using the comparison function `greater<int>()`.

```
sort(v.begin(), v.end(), greater<int>());
```

EXAMPLE 10.3   In Section 9.2, we wrote the following `Compare_Person` function class:

```
struct Compare_Person {
  bool operator()(const Person& p1, const Person& p2) {
    return (p1.family_name < p2.family_name)
           || (p1.family_name == p2.family_name)
           && (p1.given_name < p2.given_name);
  }
```

If people_list is a vector of Person objects, the statement

```
sort(people_list.begin(), people_list.end(), Compare_Person());
```

sorts the elements in people_list in ascending order based on their names. The client program must include header file "People.h", which defines class Person and struct Compare_Person.

EXERCISES FOR SECTION 10.1

SELF-CHECK

1. Assume ar is an array of **int**, v is a vector of **double**, and people is a vector of Person objects. Describe the effect of executing each of the following function calls.

   a. sort(ar, ar + 10);
   b. sort(people.begin(), people.end(), Compare_Person());
   c. sort(v.begin(), v.end(), greater<double>());

PROGRAMMING

1. Write a function call to sort the last half of vector people using the ordering determined by class Compare_Person.
2. Write a function call to sort the first 20 elements of array ar in descending order.
3. Write a function call to sort people using the natural ordering.

10.2 Selection Sort

Selection sort is a relatively easy-to-understand algorithm that sorts an array (or sequence) by making several passes through the array, selecting the next smallest item in the array each time and placing it where it belongs in the array. We illustrate all the sorting algorithms using an array of integer values for simplicity.

We show the algorithm next, where n is the number of elements in an array with subscripts 0 through n − 1, and fill is the subscript of the element that will store the next smallest item in the array.

Selection Sort Algorithm

1.   **for** fill = 0 to n − 2 do
2.   Set pos_min to the subscript of the smallest item in the subarray starting at subscript fill.
3.   **if** the next smallest item is not at position fill
                  Exchange the item at pos_min with the one at fill.

Step 2 involves a search for the smallest item in each subarray. It requires a loop in which we compare each element in the subarray, starting with the one at position fill + 1, with the smallest value found so far. In the refinement of Step 2 shown in the following algorithm (Steps 2.1 through 2.4), we use pos_min to store the subscript of the smallest value found so far. We assume that its initial position is fill.

Refinement of Selection Sort Algorithm (Step 2)

2.1   Initialize pos_min to fill.

2.2   **for** next = fill + 1 to n - 1

2.3   **if** the item at next is less than the item at pos_min

2.4   Reset pos_min to next.

First the selection sort algorithm finds the smallest item in the array (smallest is 20) and moves it to position 0 by exchanging it with the element currently at position 0. At this point, the sorted part of the array (in color in the diagrams on the right) consists of the new element at position 0. The values to be exchanged are shaded dark in the diagrams on the left.

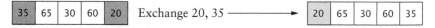

Next the algorithm finds the smallest item in the subarray starting at position 1 (next smallest is 30) and exchanges it with the element currently at position 1:

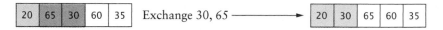

At this point, the sorted portion of the array consists of the elements at positions 0 and 1. Next the algorithm selects the smallest item in the subarray starting at position 2 (next smallest is 35) and exchanges it with the element currently at position 2:

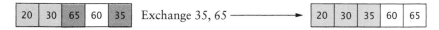

At this point, the sorted portion of the array consists of the elements at positions 0, 1, and 2. Next the algorithm selects the smallest item in the subarray starting at position 3 (next smallest is 60). Because 60 is already at position 3, there is no exchange:

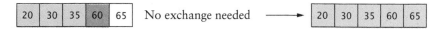

The element at position 4, the last position in the array, must store the largest value (largest is 65), so the array is sorted.

Analysis of Selection Sort

Steps 2 and 3 are performed n – 1 times. Step 3 performs an exchange of items if required; consequently, there are at most n – 1 exchanges (**O**(*n*)).

Step 2.3 involves a comparison of items and is performed (n – 1 – fill) times for each value of fill. Because fill takes on all values between 0 and n – 2, the following series computes the number of executions of Step 2.3:

$$(n - 1) + (n - 2) + \cdots + 3 + 2 + 1$$

This is a well-known series that can be written in closed form as

$$\frac{n \times (n - 1)}{2} = \frac{n^2}{2} - \frac{n}{2}$$

For very large n we can ignore all but the most significant term in this expression, so the number of comparisons is $O(n^2)$. Because the number of comparisons increases with the square of n, the selection sort is called a quadratic sort.

If the array happens to be sorted before selection sort begins, no exchanges will be required. The number of comparisons will still be $O(n^2)$, but the number of exchanges is $O(1)$.

Code for Selection Sort Using Iterators

Listing 10.1 shows the code for two sort functions that follow the algorithm just described. In writing the code for these functions and all the other functions in this chapter, we follow the approach taken by the C++ implementors of function std::sort. However, we give each sort function a distinct name, rather than calling them all sort. To use these functions, you must include file SelectionSort.h. You must also prefix the sort function with KW::.

```
#include "SelectionSort.h"
...

KW::selection_sort(x, x + 100);
```

Both sort functions in Listing 10.1 can sort arrays, vectors, or deques. The first one can sort a container that stores elements of any object type for which the operator < is defined. The second sort function has a template parameter Compare, which represents a comparison object. The first function uses the condition (*next < *pos_min) to compare the elements referenced by the two iterators; the second function uses the condition (comp(next, pos_min)), which calls the comparison operator to compare these elements.

LISTING 10.1
SelectionSort.h

```
#ifndef SELECTIONSORT_H_
#define SELECTIONSORT_H_

#include <algorithm>

namespace KW {
```

```
/** Sort data in the specified sequence using selection sort.
    @param RI An iterator that meets the
              random-access iterator requirements
    @param first An iterator that references the first element
                 of the sequence to be sorted
    @param last An iterator that references one past the
                end of the sequence to be sorted
*/
template<typename RI>
  void selection_sort(RI first, RI last) {
  for (RI fill = first; fill != last - 1; ++fill) {
    // Invariant: Elements at positions first through fill - 1 are sorted.
    RI pos_min = fill;
    for (RI next = fill + 1; next != last; ++next) {
      // Invariant: pos_min references the smallest item in
      //            positions fill through next - 1.
      if (*next < *pos_min) {
        pos_min = next;
      }
    }
    // Assert: pos_min references the smallest item in positions fill
    // through last - 1.
    // If the next smallest item is not at fill, exchange *fill and
    // *pos_min.
    if (fill != pos_min)
      std::iter_swap(pos_min, fill);
  }
}

/** Sort data in the specified range using selection sort.
    @param RI An iterator that meets the
              random-access iterator requirements
    @param first An iterator that references the beginning
                 of the sequence to be sorted
    @param last An iterator that references 1 past the
                end of the sequence to be sorted
    @param comp An object that implements a comparison function
*/
template<typename RI, typename Compare>
  void selection_sort(RI first, RI last,
                      Compare comp) {
  for (RI fill = first; fill != last - 1; ++fill) {
    // Invariant: Elements at positions first through fill - 1 are sorted.
    RI pos_min = fill;
    for (RI next = fill + 1; next != last; ++next) {
      // Invariant: pos_min references the smallest item in
      //            positions fill through next - 1.
      if (comp(*next, *pos_min)) {
        pos_min = next;
      }
    }
    // Assert: pos_min references the smallest item in positions fill
    // through last - 1.
```

```
      // If the next smallest item is not at fill, exchange *fill and
      // *pos_min.
      if (fill != pos_min)
        std::iter_swap(pos_min, fill);
    }
  }

} // End namespace KW

#endif
```

Code for an Array Sort

Many textbooks provide functions that sort a specific kind of array, usually type
int[], rather than a container. Although these functions are less general, they are
often a little easier to code. Listing 10.2 shows a selection sort function that sorts
an array of **int**s. As you might expect, it is very similar to the first selection_sort
function in Listing 10.1.

LISTING 10.2
SelectionSortArray.h

```
#ifndef SELECTIONSORTARRAY_H_
#define SELECTIONSORTARRAY_H_

#include <algorithm>

namespace KW {

/** Sort data in an int[] array using selection sort.
    @param the_array The array to be sorted
    @param size The number of elements in the_array
*/
void selection_sort_array(int the_array[], int size) {
  for (int fill = 0; fill != size - 1; ++fill) {
    // Invariant: Elements at positions first through fill - 1 are sorted.
    int pos_min = fill;
    for (int next = fill + 1; next != size; ++next) {
      // Invariant: pos_min references the smallest item in
      //            positions fill through next - 1.
      if (the_array[next] < the_array[pos_min]) {
        pos_min = next;
      }
    }
    // Assert: pos_min references the smallest item in positions fill
    // through last - 1.
    // If the next smallest item is not at fill, exchange *fill and
    // *pos_min.
    if (fill != pos_min)
      std::swap(the_array[pos_min], the_array[fill]);
  }
}

} // End namespace KW

#endif
```

EXERCISES FOR SECTION 10.2

SELF-CHECK

1. Show the progress of each pass of the selection sort for the following array. How many passes are needed? How many comparisons are performed? How many exchanges? Show the array after each pass.

   40 35 80 75 60 90 70 75

2. How would you modify the code for selection sort to arrange an array of values in decreasing sequence? How could you accomplish this without changing the function shown in Listing 10.1?

3. Modify the selection sort algorithm to exchange the elements at positions `fill` and `pos_min` even when they are equal. How does this affect big-**O** for exchanges? Discuss whether the time saved by eliminating unnecessary exchanges would exceed the cost of testing whether `pos_min` equals `fill`.

PROGRAMMING

1. Modify the first selection sort function to incorporate the change in Self-Check Exercise 3.

2. Add statements to trace the progress of the first selection sort. Display the container contents after each exchange.

10.3 Bubble Sort

The next quadratic sorting algorithm, *bubble sort*, compares adjacent array elements and exchanges their values if they are out of order. In this way the smaller values bubble up to the top of the array (toward the first element) while the larger values sink to the bottom of the array; hence the name.

Bubble Sort Algorithm

1.   **do**
2.   **for** each pair of adjacent array elements
3.   **if** the values in a pair are out of order
4.   Exchange the values
5.   **while** the array is not sorted.

As an example, we will trace through one execution of Step 2, or one pass through an array being sorted. By scanning the diagrams of Figure 10.1 from left to right, you can see the effect of each comparison. The pair of array elements being compared is shown in a darker color in each diagram. The first pair of values (`table[0]` is 60, `table[1]` is 42) is out of order, so the values are exchanged. The next pair of values (`table[1]` is now 60, `table[2]` is 75) is compared in the second array shown in Figure 10.1; this pair is in order, and so is the next pair (`table[2]` is 75, `table[3]`

FIGURE 10.1
One Pass of Bubble
Sort

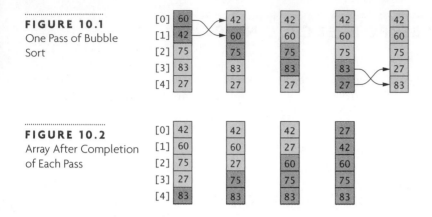

FIGURE 10.2
Array After Completion
of Each Pass

is 83). The last pair (`table[3]` is 83, `table[4]` is 27) is out of order, so the values are exchanged as shown is the last diagram, and 83 has sunk to the bottom of the array.

The last array shown in Figure 10.1 is closer to being sorted than is the original. The only value that is out of order is the number 27 in `table[3]`. Unfortunately, it will be necessary to complete three more passes through the array before this value bubbles up to the top of the array. In each of these passes only one pair of values will be out of order, so only one exchange will be made. The contents of array `table` after the completion of each pass is shown in Figure 10.2; the portion that is sorted is shown in color.

At the end of pass 1 only the last array element must be in its correct place, at the end of pass 2 the last two array elements must be in their correct places, and so on. There is no need to examine array elements that are already in place, so there is one less pair to test in the next pass. Only one pair will be tested during the last pass.

After the completion of four passes ($n - 1$ is 4), the array is now sorted. Sometimes an array will become sorted before $n - 1$ passes. This situation can be detected if a pass is made through the array without doing any exchanges. This is the reason for the **bool** flag exchanges in the following refined bubble sort algorithm: to keep track of whether any exchanges were made during the current pass (exchanges is set to **false** when the pass begins and is reset to **true** after an exchange).

Refinement of Bubble Sort Algorithm (Steps 2–4)

2.1   Initialize exchanges to **false**. // *No exchanges yet—array may be sorted*

2.2   **for** each pair of adjacent array elements

3.   **if** the values in a pair are out of order

4.1   Exchange the values.

4.2   Set exchanges to **true**. // *Made an exchange, array not sorted*

Analysis of Bubble Sort

Because the actual numbers of comparisons and exchanges performed depend on the array being sorted, the bubble sort algorithm provides excellent performance in some cases and very poor performance in other cases. It works best when an array is nearly sorted to begin with.

Because all adjacent pairs of elements in the unsorted region are compared in each pass and there may be $n - 1$ passes, the number of comparisons is represented by the series

$$(n - 1) + (n - 2) + \cdots + 3 + 2 + 1$$

However, if the array becomes sorted early, the later phases and comparisons are not performed. In the worst case the number of comparisons is $O(n^2)$. Unfortunately, each comparison can lead to an exchange if the array is badly out of order. The worst case occurs when the array is inverted (that is, the array elements are in descending order), and the number of exchanges is $O(n^2)$.

The best case occurs when the array is already sorted. Only one pass will be required, in which there are $n - 1$ comparisons ($O(n)$ comparisons). If the array is sorted, there will be no exchanges, so the number of exchanges is 0 ($O(1)$ exchanges).

In estimating the worst-case performance of a sorting algorithm on a large array whose initial element values are determined arbitrarily, the definition of big-O requires us to be pessimistic. For this reason, bubble sort is considered a quadratic sort, and its performance is usually worse than selection sort ($O(n)$) because the number of exchanges can be $O(n^2)$.

Code for Bubble Sort

Listing 10.3 shows the code for the bubble sort function in file BubbleSort.h. Notice that the outer **do** . . . **while** loop terminates when the condition (exchanges) is false. This indicates the array is sorted, because no exchanges occurred during the pass just completed. If the array does not become sorted until all n - 1 passes are completed, then an extra pass will be required. However, the inner loop will be exited immediately, because last - pass will be equal to first. The variable pass is the number of the current pass, starting at 1 for the first pass.

The inner loop control variable, first_of_pair, is the subscript of the first element of each pair. The initial value of first_of_pair is first. The final value must be 1 less than the last subscript in the unsorted region. If the last element in the array is referenced by last - 1, the final value of first_of_pair is last - pass. Coding the bubble sort function with a comparison function object as a parameter is left as an exercise.

....
LISTING 10.3
BubbleSort.h

```
#ifndef BUBBLESORT_H_
#define BUBBLESORT_H_

#include <algorithm>

namespace KW {
```

```
/** Sort data in the specified sequence using bubble sort.
    @param RI An iterator that meets the
              random-access iterator requirements
    @param first An iterator that references
              the first element in the sequence to be sorted
    @param last An iterator that references
              1 past the end of the sequence
*/
template<typename RI>
  void bubble_sort(RI first, RI last) {
  int pass = 1;
  bool exchanges;
  do {
    // Invariant: Elements after position last - pass
    // are in place.
    exchanges = false;  // No exchanges yet.
    // Compare each pair of adjacent elements.
    for (RI first_of_pair = first;
         first_of_pair != last - pass; ++first_of_pair) {
      RI second_of_pair = first_of_pair + 1;
      if (*second_of_pair < *first_of_pair) {
        // Exchange pair.
        std::iter_swap(first_of_pair, second_of_pair);
        exchanges = true;  // Set flag.
      }
    }
    pass++;
  } while (exchanges);
  // Assert: Array is sorted.
}

} // End namespace KW

#endif
```

EXERCISES FOR SECTION 10.3

SELF-CHECK

1. How many passes of bubble sort are needed to sort the following array of integers? How many comparisons are performed? How many exchanges? Show the array after each pass.

   40 35 80 75 60 90 70 75

2. How would you modify the bubble sort function to arrange an array of values in decreasing sequence?

PROGRAMMING

1. Add statements to trace the progress of bubble sort. Display the container contents after each pass is completed.

2. Code bubble sort with a Compare function template parameter.

3. Implement a bubble sort function that sorts an array of type **int**[] using subscripts instead of iterators.

10.4 Insertion Sort

Our next quadratic sorting algorithm, *insertion sort*, is based on the technique used by card players to arrange a hand of cards. The player keeps the cards that have been picked up so far in sorted order. When the player picks up a new card, the player makes room for the new card and then inserts it in its proper place.

The left diagram of Figure 10.3 shows a hand of cards (ignoring suits) after three cards have been picked up. If the next card is an 8, it should be inserted between the 6 and 10, maintaining the numerical order (middle diagram). If the next card is a 7, it should be inserted between the 6 and 8 as shown on the right in Figure 10.3.

To adapt this insertion algorithm to an array that has been filled with data, we start with a sorted subarray consisting of the first element only. For example, in the left-most array of Figure 10.4, the initial sorted subarray consists of only the first value, 30. The array element(s) that are in order after each pass are in color, and the elements waiting to be inserted are in gray. We first insert the second element (25). Because it is smaller than the element in the sorted subarray, we insert it before the old first element (30), and the sorted subarray has two elements (25, 30 in second diagram). Next, we insert the third element (15). It is also smaller than all the elements in the sorted subarray, so we insert it before the old first element (25), and the sorted subarray has three elements (15, 25, 30 in third diagram). Next, we insert the fourth element (20). It is smaller than the second and third elements in the sorted subarray so we insert it before the old second element (25), and the sorted subarray has four elements (15, 20, 25, 30 in the fourth diagram). Finally we insert the last element (28). It is smaller than the last element in the sorted subarray, so we insert it before the old last element (30) and the array is sorted. The algorithm follows.

FIGURE 10.3
Picking Up a Hand of Cards

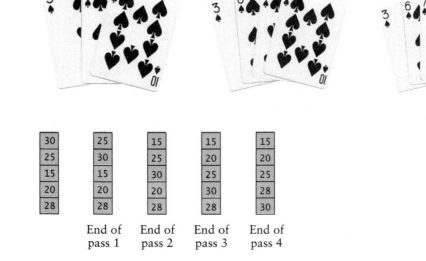

FIGURE 10.4
An Insertion Sort

Insertion Sort Algorithm

1.   **for** each array element from the second element to the last element
2.   Insert the selected element where it belongs in the array, increasing the length of the sorted subarray by 1 element.

To accomplish Step 2, the insertion step, we need to make room for the element to be inserted (saved in next_val) by shifting all values that are larger than it, starting with the last value in the sorted subarray.

Refinement of Insertion Sort Algorithm (Step 2)

2.1   next_pos is a pointer to the element to insert.
2.2   Save the value of the element to insert in next_val.
2.3   **while** next_pos > first and the element at next_pos – 1 > next_val
2.4   Shift the element at next_pos – 1 to position next_pos.
2.5   Decrement next_pos by 1.
2.6   Insert next_val at next_pos.

We illustrate these steps in Figure 10.5. For the array shown on the left, the first three elements are in the sorted subarray, and the next element to insert is 20, referenced by next_pos. First we save 20 in next_val. Then we shift the value just above it (30) down one position (see the second array in Figure 10.5), and then we shift the value just above the last one moved (25) down one position (see third array in Figure 10.5). After these shifts (third array), there will temporarily be two copies of the last value shifted (25). The first of these (shown in white background in Figure 10.5) is overwritten when the value in next_val is moved into its correct position. The four-element sorted subarray is shown in color on the right of Figure 10.5.

Analysis of Insertion Sort

The insertion step is performed $n - 1$ times. In the worst case, all elements in the sorted subarray are compared to next_val for each insertion, so the maximum number of comparisons is represented by the series

$$1 + 2 + 3 + \cdots + (n - 2) + (n - 1)$$

which is $O(n^2)$. In the best case (when the array is already sorted), only one comparison is required for each insertion, so the number of comparisons is $O(n)$. The number of shifts performed during an insertion is one less than the number of comparisons or, when the new value is the smallest so far, the same as the number of

FIGURE 10.5
Inserting the Fourth
Array Element

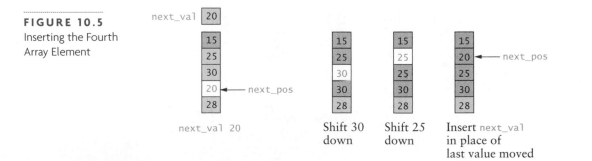

comparisons. However, a shift in an insertion sort requires the movement of only one item, whereas in a bubble sort or a selection sort an exchange involves a temporary item and requires the movement of three items. A C++ array of objects contains the actual objects, and it is these actual objects that are changed.

Code for Insertion Sort

Listing 10.4 shows header file `InsertionSort.h`. We use function `KW::insert` to perform the insertion step shown earlier. It would be more efficient to insert this code inside the **for** statement; however, using a function will make it easier later to implement the Shell sort algorithm.

Function `insert` is supposed to shift all elements in the range `first` through `next_pos - 1` that are greater than the next element to be inserted (`next_val`). We can't declare variable `next_val` without knowing the data type of the array elements, so we use the following **while** loop, which actually exchanges each element to be shifted with its successor (using function `std::iter_swap`).

```
while (next_pos != first && *next_pos < *(next_pos - 1)) {
  std::iter_swap(next_pos, next_pos - 1);  // Exchange.
  --next_pos;  // Check next smaller element.
}
```

Loop exit will occur if the first element has been shifted (`next_pos` equals `first`), or if the next element to shift (`*(next_pos - 1)`) is less than or equal to the element just shifted (`*next_pos`). Notice that you can't transpose the order of the two tests in the **while** condition, because `*(next_pos - 1)` would reference a storage location outside the array when `next_pos` equals `first`. Although this does more work than necessary (swapping a pair of elements instead of shifting an element), it does implement the insertion sort algorithm and the performance is still $O(n^2)$.

LISTING 10.4
InsertionSort.h

```
#ifndef INSERTIONSORT_H_
#define INSERTIONSORT_H_

#include <algorithm>

namespace KW {

/** Sort data in the specified range using insertion sort.
    @param RI An iterator that meets the
            random-access iterator requirements
    @param first An iterator that references
            the first element in the sequence to be sorted
    @param last An iterator iterator that references
            1 past the end of the sequence
*/
template<typename RI>
  void insertion_sort(RI first, RI last) {
  for (RI next_pos = first + 1; next_pos != last; ++next_pos) {
    // Invariant: elements at position first through
    //            next_pos - 1 are sorted.
```

```
      // Insert element at position next_pos in the sorted subarray.
      insert(first, next_pos);
  }
}

/** Insert the element at position next_pos in the sorted subarray
    using swap.
    pre:  elements at position 0 through next_pos - 1 are sorted.
    post: elements at position 0 through next_pos are sorted.
    @param RI An iterator that meets the
           random-access iterator requirements
    @param first An iterator that references
           the first element in the sequence to be sorted
    @param next_pos An iterator that references
           the element to insert
*/
template<typename RI>
  void insert(RI first, RI next_pos) {
  while (next_pos != first && *next_pos < *(next_pos - 1)) {
    std::iter_swap(next_pos, next_pos - 1); //  Exchange pair of values
    --next_pos;  // Check next smaller element
  }
}

} // End namespace KW

#endif
```

Using `iterator_traits` to Determine the Data Type of an Element

The following version of function `insert` follows the algorithm more closely. The statement

```
    typename std::iterator_traits<RI>::value_type next_val = *next_pos;
```

declares variable `next_val` and stores the element referenced by `next_pos` in it. The template class `iterator_traits` is defined in the header `<iterator>`, and `value_type` represents the data type of the element referenced by the iterator `next_pos`.

```
    template<typename RI>
      void insert(RI first, RI next_pos) {
      typename std::iterator_traits<RI>::value_type next_val
          = *next_pos;  // next_val is element to insert.
      while (next_pos != first
             && next_val < *(next_pos - 1)) {
        *next_pos = *(next_pos - 1);
        --next_pos;  // Check next smaller element.
      }
      *next_pos = next_val;  // Store next_val where it belongs.
    }
```

DESIGN CONCEPT

Iterator Traits

You may wonder how the `iterator_traits` determines the type of the object that the iterator references. Basically, the iterator provides this information. In Chapter 4 we described the `list` container and showed how to implement its iterator. To keep the explanation simple, we omitted several details, one of which we will now explain.

Each container class is required to provide certain **typedef**s, including one named `value_type`. Thus, our `list` class should have had the following declaration:

```
template<typename Item_Type>
  class list {
    public:
      typedef Item_Type value_type;
      ...
```

Likewise, the `iterator` class (defined within the `list` class) should have the declaration:

```
class iterator {
  typedef typename list<Item_Type>::value_type value_type;
```

The `iterator_traits` class is then defined as follows:

```
template<typename Iterator>
  struct iterator_traits {
  typedef typename Iterator::value_type value_type;
  ...
};
```

When the compiler sees the function call:

```
sort(v.begin(), v.end())
```

it determines that the type of the expressions `v.begin()` and `v.end()` is `vector<int>::iterator` and thus the template parameter `Iterator` is bound to this type. Therefore the expression

```
typename iterator_traits<Iterator>::value_type
```

becomes

```
typename iterator_traits<vector<int>::iterator>::value_type
```

Since ordinary pointers can be used as iterators, we need to add an additional specialization for `iterator_traits`.

```
template<typename T>
  struct iterator_traits<T*> {
    typedef T value_type;
    ...
};
```

Now in the function call

```
sort(a, a + 20)
```

where a is an array of **int**, the parameter type is int*, and the template parameter `Iterator` is bound to this type. Thus the expression

```
typename iterator_traits<Iterator>::value_type
```

becomes

```
typename iterator_traits<int*>::value_type
```

The compiler then associates T with **int**, so that the declaration

```
typedef T value_type;
```

becomes

```
typedef int value_type;
```

EXERCISES FOR SECTION 10.4

SELF-CHECK

1. Sort the following array using insertion sort. How many passes are needed? How many comparisons are performed? How many exchanges? Show the array after each pass.

   40   35   80   75   60   90   70   75

PROGRAMMING

1. Eliminate function `insert` in Listing 10.4 and write its code inside the **for** statement.
2. Add statements to trace the progress of insertion sort. Display the container contents after the insertion of each value.
3. Write the insertion sort with a `Compare` template parameter.
4. Implement an insertion sort function that sorts an array of type **int**[] using subscripts instead of iterators.

10.5 Comparison of Quadratic Sorts

Table 10.1 summarizes the performance of the three quadratic sorts for large values of n. Although these algorithms are $O(n^2)$ on average, the best-case performance for bubble sort and insertion sort is only $O(n)$. To give you some idea as to what these numbers mean, Table 10.2 shows some values of n and n^2. If n is not too large (say, 100 or less), it really doesn't matter which sorting algorithm you use. Of the three, insertion sort gives the best performance for most arrays, because it takes advantage of any partial sorting that is in the array and uses less costly shifts instead of exchanges to rearrange array elements. In the next section, we discuss a variation on insertion sort, known as Shell sort, that has $O(n^{3/2})$ or better performance.

The best-case performance occurs when an array is already sorted. In this case, there are no exchanges performed in bubble sort and only n comparisons because only one pass through the array is required. However, unless the array is nearly sorted, bubble sort's performance usually exhibits its worst-case behavior, $O(n^2)$. For this reason, bubble sort generally performs much worse than the others.

Since the time to sort an array of n elements is proportional to n^2, none of these algorithms is particularly good for large arrays (that is, $n > 100$). The best sorting algorithms provide $n \log n$ average-case behavior and are considerably faster for large arrays. In fact, one of the algorithms that we will discuss has $n \log n$ worst-case behavior. You can get a feel for the difference in behavior by comparing the last column of Table 10.2 with the middle column.

Recall from Chapter 2 that big-O analysis ignores any constants that might be involved or any overhead that might occur from function calls needed to perform an exchange or comparison. However, the tables give you an estimate of the relative performance of the different sorting algorithms.

We haven't talked about storage usage for these algorithms. All the quadratic sorts require storage for the array being sorted. However, there is only one copy of this array, so the array is sorted in place. There are also requirements for variables that store iterators to particular elements, loop control variables, and temporary variables. However, for large n, the size of the array dominates these other storage considerations.

TABLE 10.1
Comparison of Quadratic Sorts

	Number of Comparisons		Number of Exchanges	
	Best	Worst	Best	Worst
Selection sort	$O(n^2)$	$O(n^2)$	$O(n)$	$O(n)$
Bubble sort	$O(n)$	$O(n^2)$	$O(1)$	$O(n^2)$
Insertion sort	$O(n)$	$O(n^2)$	$O(n)$	$O(n^2)$

TABLE 10.2
Comparison of Rates of Growth

n	n^2	$n \log n$
8	64	24
16	256	64
32	1,024	160
64	4,096	384
128	16,384	896
256	65,536	2,048
512	262,144	4,608

Comparisons versus Exchanges

We have analyzed comparisons and exchanges separately, but you may be wondering whether one is more costly (in terms of computer time) than the other. In C++, an exchange requires your computer to swap two objects using a third object as an intermediary. A comparison requires your computer to evaluate the < operator, or call a comparison function. The cost of executing a comparison function depends on its complexity, but it will probably be more than that of an exchange because of the overhead to call and execute the function. An exchange requires physically moving the information in each object. The cost of an exchange is proportional to the size of the objects being exchanged and, therefore, may be more costly than a comparison for large objects.

EXERCISES FOR SECTION 10.5

SELF-CHECK

1. Complete Table 10.2 for $n = 1024$ and $n = 2048$.
2. What do the new rows of Table 10.2 tell us about the increase in time required to process an array of 1024 elements versus an array of 2048 elements for $O(n)$, $O(n^2)$, and $O(n \log n)$ algorithms?

10.6 Shell Sort: A Better Insertion Sort

Next we describe the *Shell sort*, which is a type of insertion sort, but with $O(n^{3/2})$ or better performance. Unlike the other algorithms, Shell sort is named after its discoverer, Donald Shell (D. L. Shell, "A High-Speed Sorting Procedure," *Communications of the ACM,* Vol. 2, No. 7 [1959], pp. 30–32). You can think of the Shell sort as a divide-and-conquer approach to insertion sort. Instead of sorting the entire array at the start, the idea behind Shell sort is to sort many smaller subarrays using insertion sort before sorting the entire array. The initial subarrays will contain two or three elements, so the insertion sorts will go very quickly. After each collection of subarrays is sorted, a new collection of subarrays with approximately twice as many elements as before will be sorted. The last step is to perform an insertion sort on the entire array, which has been presorted by the earlier sorts.

As an example, let's sort the following array using initial subarrays with only two and three elements. We determine the elements in each subarray by setting a gap value between the subscripts in each subarray. We will explain how we pick the gap values later. We will use an initial gap of 7.

[0]	[1]	[2]	[3]	[4]	[5]	[6]	[7]	[8]	[9]	[10]	[11]	[12]	[13]	[14]	[15]
40	35	80	75	60	90	70	75	55	90	85	34	45	62	57	65

A gap of 7 means the first subarray has subscripts 0, 7, 14 (element values 40, 75, 57, shown in light color); the second subarray has subscripts 1, 8, 15 (element values 35, 55, 65, shown in dark color); the third subarray has subscripts 2, 9 (element values 80, 90, shown in gray); and so on. There are seven subarrays. We start the process by inserting the value at position 7 (value of gap) into its subarray (elements at 0 and 7). Next, we insert the element at position 8 into its subarray (elements at 1 and 8). We continue until we have inserted the last element (at position 15) in its subarray (elements at 1, 8, and 15). The result of performing insertion sort on all seven subarrays with two or three elements follows.

[0]	[1]	[2]	[3]	[4]	[5]	[6]	[7]	[8]	[9]	[10]	[11]	[12]	[13]	[14]	[15]
40	35	80	75	34	45	62	57	55	90	85	60	90	70	75	65

Next we use a gap of 3. There are only three subarrays, and the longest one has six elements. The first subarray has subscripts 0, 3, 6, 9, 12, 15; the second subarray has subscripts 1, 4, 7, 10, 13; the third subarray has subscripts 2, 5, 8, 11, 14.

[0]	[1]	[2]	[3]	[4]	[5]	[6]	[7]	[8]	[9]	[10]	[11]	[12]	[13]	[14]	[15]
40	35	80	75	34	45	62	57	55	90	85	60	90	70	75	65

We start the process by inserting the element at position 3 (value of gap) into its subarray. Next, we insert the element at position 4, and so on. The result of all insertions is as follows.

[0]	[1]	[2]	[3]	[4]	[5]	[6]	[7]	[8]	[9]	[10]	[11]	[12]	[13]	[14]	[15]
40	34	45	60	35	55	62	57	60	65	70	75	75	85	80	90

Finally, we use a gap of 1, which performs an insertion sort on the entire array. Because of the presorting, it will require 1 comparison to insert 34, 1 comparison to insert 45 and 60, 3 comparisons to insert 35, 2 comparisons to insert 55, 1 comparison to insert 62, 2 comparisons to insert 57, 2 comparisons to insert 60, and only 1 comparison to insert each of the remaining values.

The algorithm for Shell sort follows. Steps 2 through 4 correspond to the insertion sort algorithm shown earlier. Because the elements with subscripts 0 through gap - 1 are the first elements in their subarrays, we begin Step 4 by inserting the element at position gap instead of at position 1 as we did for the insertion sort. Step 1 sets the initial gap between subscripts to n/2, where n is the number of array elements. To get the next gap value, Step 6 divides the current gap value by 2.2 (chosen by experimentation). We want the gap to be 1 during the last insertion sort so that the entire array will be sorted. Step 5 ensures this by resetting gap to 1 if it is 2.

Shell Sort Algorithm

1.   Set the initial value of gap to n/2.
2.   **while** gap > 0
3.   **for** each array element from position gap to the last element
4.   Insert this element where it belongs in its subarray.
5.   **if** gap is 2, set it to 1.
6.   **else** gap = gap/2.2.

Refinement of Step 4, the Insertion Step

4.1   next_pos is an iterator to the element to insert.

4.2   Save the value of the element to insert in next_val.

4.3   **while** next_pos > first + gap and the element at next_pos – gap > next_val

4.4   Shift the element at next_pos – gap to position next_pos.

4.5   Decrement next_pos by gap.

4.6   Insert next_val at next_pos.

Analysis of Shell Sort

You may wonder why Shell sort is an improvement over regular insertion sort, because it ends with an insertion sort of the entire array. Each later sort (including the last one) will be performed on an array whose elements have been presorted by the earlier sorts. Because the behavior of insertion sort is closer to $O(n)$ than to $O(n^2)$ when an array is nearly sorted, the presorting will make the later sorts, which involve larger subarrays, go more quickly. As a result of presorting, only 19 comparisons were required to perform an insertion sort on the last 15-element array shown in the previous section. This is critical, because it is precisely for larger arrays where $O(n^2)$ behavior would have the most negative impact. For the same reason, the improvement of Shell sort over insertion sort is much more significant for large arrays.

A general analysis of Shell sort is an open research problem in computer science. The performance depends on how the decreasing sequence of values for gap is chosen. It is known that Shell sort is $O(n^2)$ if successive powers of 2 are used for gap (that is, 32, 16, 8, 4, 2, 1). If successive values for gap are of the form $2^k - 1$ (that is, 31, 15, 7, 3, 1), however, it can be proven that the performance is $O(n^{3/2})$. This sequence is known as Hibbard's sequence. There are other sequences that give similar or better performance.

We have presented an algorithm that selects the initial value of gap as $n/2$ and then divides by 2.2 and truncates to the next lowest integer. Empirical studies of this approach show that the performance is $O(n^{5/4})$ or maybe even $O(n^{7/6})$, but there is no theoretical basis for this result (M. A. Weiss, *Data Structures and Problem Solving Using Java* [Addison Wesley, 1998], p. 230).

Code for Shell Sort

Listing 10.5 shows the code for Shell sort. Function insert has a third parameter, gap. The expression after &&,

```
while ((next_pos > first + gap - 1)  // First element not shifted.
        && (next_val < *(next_pos - gap))) {
```

compares elements that are separated by the value of gap instead of by 1. The expression before && is false if next_pos is an iterator to the first element in a subarray. The statements in the while loop shift the element at next_pos down by gap (one position in the subarray) and reset next_pos to refer to the element just moved.

LISTING 10.5
ShellSort.h

```cpp
#ifndef SHELLSORT_H_
#define SHELLSORT_H_

namespace KW {

/** Sort data in the specified range using Shell sort.
    @param RI An iterator that meets the
            random-access iterator requirements
    @param first An iterator that references
            the first element in the sequence to be sorted
    @param last An iterator that references
            1 past the end of the sequence
*/
template<typename RI>
  void shell_sort(RI first, RI last) {
  // Set initial gap between adjacent elements.
  int gap = (last - first) / 2;
  while (gap > 0) {
    for (RI next_pos = first + gap;
         next_pos != last; ++next_pos) {
      // Insert element at next_pos in its subarray.
      KW::insert(first, next_pos, gap);
    }  // End for.

    // Reset gap for next pass.
    if (gap == 2) {
      gap = 1;
    } else {
      gap = int(gap / 2.2);
    }
  }
}

/** Insert the element at position next_pos in the sorted subarray.
    pre:  elements at position 0 through next_pos - 1 are sorted.
    post: elements at position 0 through next_pos are sorted.
    @param RI An iterator that meets the
            random-access iterator requirements
    @param first An iterator that references
            the first element in the sequence to be sorted
    @param next_pos An iterator that references
            the element to insert
    @param gap The gap between elements in the sequence to be sorted
*/
template<typename RI>
  void insert(RI first, RI next_pos,
              int gap) {
  typename std::iterator_traits<RI>::value_type next_val = *next_pos;
  // Shift all values > next_val in subarray down by gap.
  while ((next_pos > first + gap - 1)  // First element not shifted.
         && (next_val < *(next_pos - gap))) {
    *next_pos = *(next_pos - gap);   // Shift down.
    next_pos -= gap;      // Check next position in subarray.
```

```
    }
    *next_pos = next_val;
}

} // End namespace KW

#endif
```

EXERCISES FOR SECTION 10.6

SELF-CHECK

1. Trace the execution of Shell sort on the following array. Show the array after all sorts when the gap is 3 and after the final sort when the gap is 1. List the number of comparisons and exchanges required when the gap is 3 and when the gap is 1. Compare this with the number of comparisons and exchanges that would be required for a regular insertion sort.

   40 35 80 75 60 90 70 65

2. For the example of Shell sort shown in this section, determine how many comparisons and exchanges are required to insert all the elements for each gap value. Compare this with the number of comparisons and exchanges that would be required for a regular insertion sort.

PROGRAMMING

1. Eliminate function `insert` in Listing 10.5 and write its code inside the **for** statement.
2. Add statements to trace the progress of Shell sort. Display each value of `gap` and display the container contents after all subarrays for that `gap` value have been sorted.
3. Implement a Shell sort function that sorts an array of type **int**[] using subscripts instead of iterators.

10.7 Merge Sort

The next algorithm that we will consider is called *merge sort*. A *merge* is a common data processing operation that is performed on two sequences of data (or data files) with the following characteristics:

- The objects in both sequences are ordered by the same comparison operator (that is, both sequences are sorted).

The result of the merge operation is to create a third sequence that contains all of the objects from the first two sorted sequences. For example, if the first sequence is 3, 5, 8, 15 and the second sequence is 4, 9, 12, 20, the final sequence will be 3, 4, 5, 8, 9, 12, 15, 20. The algorithm for merging the two sequences is as follows:

Merge Algorithm

1. Access the first item from both sequences.
2. `while` not finished with either sequence
3.   Compare the current items from the two sequences, copy the smaller current item to the output sequence, and access the next item from the input sequence whose item was copied.
4. Copy any remaining items from the first sequence to the output sequence.
5. Copy any remaining items from the second sequence to the output sequence.

The `while` loop (Step 2) merges items from both input sequences to the output sequence. The current item from each sequence is the one that has been most recently accessed but not yet copied to the output sequence. Step 3 compares the two current items and copies the smaller one to the output sequence. If input sequence A's current item is the smaller one, the next item is accessed from sequence A and becomes its current item. If input sequence B's current item is the smaller one, the next item is accessed from sequence B and becomes its current item. After the end of either sequence is reached, Step 4 or Step 5 copies the items from the other sequence to the output sequence. Note that either Step 4 or Step 5 is executed, but not both.

As an example, consider the sequences shown in Figure 10.6. Steps 2 and 3 will first copy the items from sequence A with the values 244 and 311 to the output sequence; then items from sequence B with values 324 and 415 will be copied; and then the item from sequence A with value 478 will be copied. At this point, we have copied all items in sequence A, so we exit the `while` loop and copy the remaining items from sequence B (499, 505) to the output (Steps 4 and 5).

Analysis of Merge

For two input sequences that contain a total of n elements, we need to move each element from its input sequence to its output sequence, so the time required for a merge is $O(n)$. How about the space requirements? We need to be able to store both initial sequences and the output sequence. So the array cannot be merged in place, and the additional space usage is $O(n)$.

Code for Merge

Listing 10.6 shows the code for the merge algorithm. Iterators `left` and `right` select the next element to be inserted in the output sequence from the left and right input

FIGURE 10.6
Merge Operation

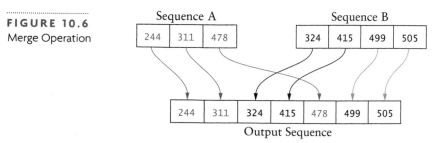

Output Sequence

sequences, respectively. Algorithm Steps 4 and 5 are implemented as **while** loops at the end of the function.

·······················

LISTING 10.6
Merge Function

```
/** Merge data in two sorted input sequences
    into a sorted output sequence.
    pre:  Both input sequences are sorted.
    post: The output sequence is sorted and contains all elements
          in both input sequences.
    @param RI An iterator that meets the
              random-access iterator requirements
    @param left An iterator that references
              the first element in the left sequence
    @param end_left An iterator that references
              1 past the end of the left sequence
    @param right An iterator that references
              the first element in the right sequence
    @param end_right An iterator that references
              1 past the end of the right sequence
    @param out An iterator that references
              the first element in the output sequence
*/
template<typename RI>
  void merge(RI left, RI end_left,
             RI right, RI end_right,
             RI out) {
  // While there is data in both input sequences
  while (left != end_left && right != end_right) {
    // Find the smaller and
    // insert it into the output sequence.
    if (*left < *right) {
      *out++ = *left++;
    } else {
      *out++ = *right++;
    }
  }

  // Assert: one of the sequences has more items to copy.
  // Copy remaining input from left sequence into the output.
  while (left != end_left) {
    *out++ = *left++;
  }

  // Copy remaining input from right sequence into output.
  while (right != end_right) {
    *out++ = *right++;
  }
}
```

PROGRAM STYLE

By using the postincrement operator on the iterators, you can copy the current item from one input sequence, append it to the end of the output sequence, and then increment the iterators to that input sequence and the output sequence in one statement. The statement:

```
*out++ = *left++;
```

is equivalent to the following three statements, executed in the order shown:

```
*out = *left;
++out;
++left;
```

Both the single statement and the group of three statements maintain the invariant that the iterator `left` references the next item to insert from the left input sequence.

Algorithm for Merge Sort

We can modify merging to serve as an approach to sorting a single, unsorted table as follows:

1.   Split the table into two halves.
2.   Sort the left half.
3.   Sort the right half.
4.   Merge the two.

What sort algorithm should we use to do Steps 2 and 3? We can use the merge sort algorithm we are developing! The base case will be a table of size 1, which is already sorted, so there is nothing to do for the base case. We write the algorithm next, showing its recursive step.

Algorithm for Merge Sort

1.   **if** the table has more than one element
2.   Store the first half of the table in `left_table`.
3.   Store the second half of the table in `right_table`.
4.   Recursively apply the merge sort algorithm to `left_table`.
5.   Recursively apply the merge sort algorithm to `right_table`.
6.   Call the merge function with `left_table` and `right_table` as the input sequences and the original table as the output sequence.

Trace of Merge Sort Algorithm

Each recursive call to function `merge_sort` with a table that has more than one element splits the array argument into a left array and a right array, where each new array is approximately half the size of the array argument. We then sort each of these arrays, beginning with the left half, by recursively calling function `merge_sort` with the left array and right array as arguments. After returning from the sort of the left array and right array at each level, we merge these two halves together back into the space occupied by the array that was split. Figure 10.7 illustrates this process. The left subarray in each recursive call (in gray) will be sorted before the processing of its corresponding right subarray (in color) begins. Lines 4 and 6 merge two one-element arrays to form a sorted two-element array. At line 7, the two sorted two-element arrays (50, 60 and 30, 45) are merged into a sorted four-element array. Next the right subarray in color on line 1 would be sorted in the same way. When done, the sorted subarray (15, 20, 80, 90) will be merged with the sorted subarray on line 7.

FIGURE 10.7
Trace of Merge Sort

| 50 | 60 | 45 | 30 | 90 | 20 | 80 | 15 |

1. *Split array into two 4-element arrays*

| 50 | 60 | 45 | 30 |

2. *Split left array into two 2-element arrays*

| 50 | 60 |

3. *Split left array (50, 60) into two 1-element arrays*

| 50 | 60 |

4. *Merge two 1-element arrays into a 2-element array*

| 45 | 30 |

5. *Split right array from Step 2 into two 1-element arrays*

| 30 | 45 |

6. *Merge two 1-element arrays into a 2-element array*

| 30 | 45 | 50 | 60 |

7. *Merge two 2-element arrays into a 4-element array*

Analysis of Merge Sort

In Figure 10.7, the size of the arrays being sorted decreases from 8 to 4 (line 1) to 2 (line 2) to 1 (line 3). After each pair of subarrays is sorted, the pair will be merged to form a larger sorted array. Rather than showing a time sequence of the splitting and merging operations, we summarize them as follows.

| 50 | 60 | 45 | 30 | 90 | 20 | 80 | 15 |

1. *Split the 8-element array*

| 50 | 60 | 45 | 30 | 90 | 20 | 80 | 15 |

2. *Split the 4-element arrays*

| 50 | 60 | 45 | 30 | 90 | 20 | 80 | 15 |

3. *Split the 2-element arrays*

| 50 | 60 | 30 | 45 | 20 | 90 | 15 | 80 |

4. *Merge the 1-element arrays into 2-element arrays*

| 30 | 45 | 50 | 60 | 15 | 20 | 80 | 90 |

5. *Merge the 2-element arrays into 4-element arrays*

| 15 | 20 | 30 | 45 | 50 | 60 | 80 | 90 |

6. *Merge the 4-element arrays into an 8-element array*

Lines 1 through 3 show the splitting operations, and lines 4 through 6 show the merge operations. Line 4 shows the two-element arrays formed by merging one-element arrays, line 5 shows the four-element arrays formed by merging 2-element arrays, and line 6 shows the sorted array. Because each of these lines involves a movement of n elements from smaller-size arrays to larger arrays, the effort to do each merge is $O(n)$. The number of lines that require merging (three in this case) is $\log n$ because each recursive step splits the array in half. So the total effort to reconstruct the sorted array through merging is $O(n \log n)$.

Recall from our discussion of recursion that whenever a recursive function is called, a copy of the local variables is saved on the run-time stack. Thus, as we go down the recursion chain, sorting the `left_tables`, a sequence of `right_tables` of size $n/2$, $n/4, \ldots, n/2^k$ is allocated. Since $n/2 + n/4 + \cdots + 2 + 1 = n - 1$, a total of n additional storage locations are required.

Code for Merge Sort

Listing 10.7 shows file `MergeSort.h` with code for the merge sort algorithm. The statement

```
typedef typename
    std::iterator_traits<RI>::value_type value_type;
```

uses class `iterator_traits` to define `value_type` as the data type of the elements being sorted. The statement

```
RI middle = first + (last - first) / 2;
```

positions iterator `middle` at the middle element in the sequence being sorted. The vectors `left_table` and `right_table` store the elements in the left and right sequences, respectively. After these vectors are sorted, their contents are merged into the original array, starting at the position selected by the current value of iterator `first`.

LISTING 10.7
MergeSort.h

```
#ifndef MERGESORT_H_
#define MERGESORT_H_

namespace KW {

/** Sort data in the specified range using merge sort.
    @param RI An iterator that meets the
           random-access iterator requirements
    @param first A random access iterator that references
           the first element in the sequence to be sorted
    @param last A random-access iterator that references
           1 past the end of the sequence
*/
```

```
template<typename RI>
  void merge_sort(RI first, RI last) {
  if (last - first > 1) {
    // Split table into two new half tables.
    typedef typename
      std::iterator_traits<RI>::value_type value_type;
    RI middle = first + (last - first) / 2;
    std::vector<value_type> left_table(first, middle);
    std::vector<value_type> right_table(middle, last);

    // Sort the halves.
    KW::merge_sort(left_table.begin(), left_table.end());
    KW::merge_sort(right_table.begin(), right_table.end());

    // Merge the halves back into the original table.
    merge(left_table.begin(), left_table.end(),
          right_table.begin(), right_table.end(),
          first);
  }
}
// See Listing 10.6 for merge function
...
} // End namespace KW

#endif
```

EXERCISES FOR SECTION 10.7

SELF-CHECK

1. Trace the execution of the merge sort on the following array, providing a figure similar to Figure 10.7.

   55 50 10 40 80 90 60 100 70 80 20

2. For the array in Question 1, show the vectors `left_table` and `right_table` for each recursive call to function `merge_sort` in Listing 10.7 and show the array elements after returning from each call to `merge`. How many times is `merge_sort` called, and how many times is `merge` called?

PROGRAMMING

1. Add statements that trace the progress of the `merge` function by displaying the container after each merge operation. Also display the vectors `left_table` and `right_table`.

2. Implement a merge sort function that sorts an array of type `int[]` using subscripts instead of iterators.

10.8 Heapsort

The merge sort algorithm has the virtue that its time is $O(n \log n)$, but it still requires, at least temporarily, n extra storage locations. This next algorithm can be implemented without requiring any additional storage. It uses a heap to store the array and so is called *heapsort*.

Heapsort Algorithm

We introduced the heap in Section 8.5. As stated there, a max heap is a data structure that maintains the largest value at the top. Figure 10.8 shows an example of such a heap.

Once we have a heap, we can remove one item at a time from the heap. The item removed is always the top element, and we will place it at the bottom of the heap. When we reheap, the larger of a node's two children is always moved up the heap, so the new heap will have the next largest item as its root. Figure 10.9 shows the heap after we have removed one item, and Figure 10.10 shows the heap after we have removed two items. In both figures, the items in color have been removed from the heap. As we continue to remove items from the heap, the heap size shrinks as the number of the removed items increases. Figure 10.11 shows the heap after we have emptied it.

If we implement the heap using an array, each element removed will be placed at the end of the array, but in front of the elements that were removed earlier. After we remove the last element, the array will be sorted. We illustrate this next.

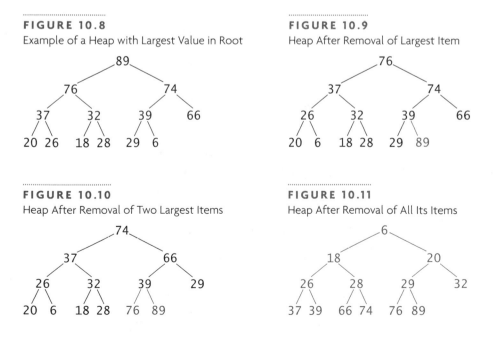

FIGURE 10.8
Example of a Heap with Largest Value in Root

FIGURE 10.9
Heap After Removal of Largest Item

FIGURE 10.10
Heap After Removal of Two Largest Items

FIGURE 10.11
Heap After Removal of All Its Items

FIGURE 10.12
Internal Representation of the Heap Shown in Figure 10.8

[0]	[1]	[2]	[3]	[4]	[5]	[6]	[7]	[8]	[9]	[10]	[11]	[12]
89	76	74	37	32	39	66	20	26	18	28	29	6

FIGURE 10.13
Internal Representation of the Heaps Shown in Figures 10.9 through 10.11

[0]	[1]	[2]	[3]	[4]	[5]	[6]	[7]	[8]	[9]	[10]	[11]	[12]
76	37	74	26	32	39	66	20	6	18	28	29	89

[0]	[1]	[2]	[3]	[4]	[5]	[6]	[7]	[8]	[9]	[10]	[11]	[12]
74	37	66	26	32	39	29	20	6	18	28	76	89

.
.
.

[0]	[1]	[2]	[3]	[4]	[5]	[6]	[7]	[8]	[9]	[10]	[11]	[12]
6	18	20	26	28	29	32	37	39	66	74	76	89

Figure 10.12 shows the array representation of the original heap. As before, the root, 89, is at position 0. The root's two children, 76 and 74, are at positions 1 and 2. For a node at position p, the left child is at $2p + 1$ and the right child is at $2p + 2$. A node at position c can find its parent at $(c - 1) / 2$.

Figure 10.13 shows the array representation of the heaps in Figures 10.9 through 10.11. The items in color have been removed from the heap and are sorted. Each time an item is removed, the heap part of the array decreases by one element and the sorted part of the array increases by one element. In the array at the bottom of Figure 10.13, all items have been removed from the heap and the array is sorted.

From our foregoing observations, we can sort the array that represents a heap in the following way.

Algorithm for In-Place Heapsort

1. Build a heap by rearranging the elements in an unsorted array.
2. `while` the heap is not empty
3.   Remove the first item from the heap by swapping it with the last item in the heap and restoring the heap property.

Each time through the loop (Steps 2 and 3), the largest item remaining in the heap is placed at the end of the heap, just before the previously removed items. Thus, when the loop terminates, the items in the array are sorted. In Section 8.5 we discussed how to remove an item from a heap and restore the heap property. We also implemented a pop function for a heap in a vector.

Algorithm to Build a Heap

Step 1 of the algorithm builds a heap. If we want to sort the sequence `table` bounded by the iterators `first` through `last`, we can consider the first item to be a heap of one item. We now consider the general case where the items in the sequence from `table[first]` through `table[first + n - 1]` form a heap; the items from `table[first + n]` through `table[last - 1]` are not in the heap. As each item is inserted, we must "reheap" to restore the heap property.

Refinement of Step 1 for In-Place Heapsort

1.1.   `while` n is less than the number of items in the sequence

1.2.   Increment n by 1. This inserts a new item into the heap.

1.3.   Restore the heap property.

Analysis of Heapsort Algorithm

From our knowledge of binary trees, we know that a heap of size n has log n levels. Building a heap requires finding the correct location for an item in a heap with log n levels. Because we have n items to insert and each insert (or remove) is O(log n), building a heap is O(n log n). Similarly, we have n items to remove from the heap, so that is also O(n log n). Because we are storing the heap in the original sequence, no extra storage is required.

Code for Heapsort

Listing 10.8 shows file `HeapSort.h`. The `heap_sort` function merely calls the `build_heap` function which codes Step 1 of the in-place heapsort algorithm. Next, it calls the `shrink_heap` function, which codes Steps 2 and 3 of the algorithm. Function `shrink_heap` is based on the `pop` function shown earlier in Section 8.5. Both functions use function `std::iter_swap` to swap the items in the sequence.

You have to be careful with pointer arithmetic in functions `build_heap` and `shrink_heap`. In `build_heap`, the statements

```
RI child = first + n - 1;
RI parent = first + (child - first - 1) / 2;  // Find parent.
```

set `child` to reference the next element to be inserted. The subscript of the parent would normally be obtained by subtracting one from the child subscript and dividing by 2. The second statement above accomplishes this. Similarly, in `shrink_heap`, you need to calculate the left child subscript by adding 1 to 2 times the parent subscript. This is accomplished by the statement

```
RI left_child = first + 2 * (parent - first) + 1;
```

⊘ PITFALL

Invalid Pointer Arithmetic

In the statement

```
RI parent = first + (child - first - 1) / 2;   // Find parent.
```

the expression part is algebraically equivalent to `(first + child - 1)/2`. However, using this expression would cause a syntax error indicating invalid pointer addition. You can't add pointers, because pointers represent addresses and the result of adding two addresses is not logically meaningful. However, you can subtract two pointers, or you can add or subtract a constant (an *offset*) to a pointer. An analogy would be comparing times. If you arrived at place A at 4 PM and at place B at 6 PM, you could subtract the two times to determine that it took you 2 hours to go from place A to place B. But adding the two times would not be meaningful.

LISTING 10.8
HeapSort.h

```
#ifndef HEAPSORT_H_
#define HEAPSORT_H_

#include <algorithm>

namespace KW {

/** Sort data in the specified range using heapsort.
    @param RI An iterator that meets the
            random-access iterator requirements
    @param first A random access iterator that references
            the first element in the sequence to be sorted
    @param last A random-access iterator that references
            1 past the end of the sequence
*/
template<typename RI>
  void heap_sort(RI first, RI last) {
    build_heap(first, last);
    shrink_heap(first, last);
}

/** build_heap transforms the sequence into a heap.
    @param RI An iterator that meets the
            random-access iterator requirements
    @param first A random-access iterator that references
            the first element in the sequence to be sorted
    @param last A random-access iterator that references
            1 past the end of the sequence
*/
template<typename RI>
  void build_heap(RI first, RI last) {
  int n = 1;
```

```cpp
    // Invariant: table[first] through table[first + n - 1] is a heap.
    while (n < (last - first)) {
      ++n;  // Add a new item to the heap and reheap.
      RI child = first + n - 1;
      RI parent = first + (child - first - 1) / 2;  // Find parent.
      while (parent >= first
              && *parent < *child) {
        std::iter_swap(parent, child); // Exchange elements.
        child = parent;
        parent = first + (child - first - 1) / 2;
      }
    }
  }

  /** shrink_heap transforms a heap into a sorted sequence.
      @param RI An iterator that meets the
              random-access iterator requirements
      @param first A random-access iterator that references
              the first element in the sequence to be sorted
      @param last A random-access iterator that references
              1 past the end of the sequence
  */
  template<typename RI>
    void shrink_heap(RI first, RI last) {
    RI n = last;
    /* Invariant: table[first] through table[first + n - 1] forms a heap.
       table[first + n] through table[last - 1] is sorted.
    */
    while (n != first) {
      --n;
      std::iter_swap(first, n);
      RI parent = first;
      while (true) {
        RI left_child = first + 2 * (parent - first) + 1;
        if (left_child >= n) {
          break;       // No more children.
        }
        RI right_child = left_child + 1;
        // Find the larger of the two children.
        RI max_child = left_child;
        if (right_child < n    // There is a right child.
            && *left_child < *right_child) {
          max_child = right_child;
        }
        // If the parent is smaller than the larger child,
        if (*parent < *max_child) {
          // Swap the parent and child.
          std::iter_swap(parent, max_child);
          // Continue at the child level.
          parent = max_child;
        } else {   // Heap property is restored.
          break;  // Exit the loop.
        }
      }
    }
  }

} // End namespace KW

#endif
```

EXERCISES FOR SECTION 10.8

SELF-CHECK

1. Build the heap from the numbers in the following list. How many exchanges were required? How many comparisons?

   55 50 10 40 80 90 60 100 70 80 20

2. Shrink the heap from Question 1 to create the array in sorted order. How many exchanges were required? How many comparisons?

3. Implement a heap sort function that sorts an array of type `int[]` only.

10.9 Quicksort

The next algorithm we will study is called *quicksort*. Developed by C. A. R. Hoare in 1962, it works in the following way: Given an array (or sequence) to sort, quicksort rearranges this array into two parts so that all the elements in the left subarray are less than or equal to a specified value (called the *pivot*) and all the elements in the right subarray are greater than the pivot. The pivot is placed between the two parts. Thus all of the elements on the left of the pivot value are smaller than all elements on the right of the pivot value, so the pivot value is in its correct position. By repeating this process on the two halves, the whole array becomes sorted.

As an example of this process, let's sort the following array.

44	75	23	43	55	12	64	77	33

We will assume that the first array element (44) is arbitrarily selected as the pivot value. A possible result of rearranging, or *partitioning*, the element values follows.

12	33	23	43	44	55	64	77	75

After the partitioning process, the pivot value, 44, is at its correct position. All values less than 44 are in the left subarray, and all values larger than 44 are in the right subarray, as desired. The next step would be to apply quicksort recursively to the two subarrays on either side of the pivot value, beginning with the left subarray (12, 33, 23, 43). Here is the result when 12 is the pivot value:

12	33	23	43

The pivot value is in the first position. Because the left subarray does not exist, the right subarray (33, 23, 43) is sorted next, resulting in the following situation.

12	23	33	43

The pivot value 33 is in its correct place, and the left subarray (23) and right sub-array (43) have single elements, so they are sorted. At this point, we are finished sorting the left part of the original subarray, and quicksort is applied to the right subarray (55, 64, 77, 75). In the following array, all the elements that have been placed in their proper position are in the darker color.

12	23	33	43	44	55	64	77	75

If we use 55 for the pivot, its left subarray will be empty after the partitioning process, and the right subarray 64, 77, 75 will be sorted next. If 64 is the pivot, the situation will be as follows, and we sort the right subarray (77, 75) next.

55	64	77	75

If 77 is the pivot and we move it where it belongs, we end up with the following array. Because the left subarray (75) has a single element, it is sorted, and we are done.

75	77

Algorithm for Quicksort

The algorithm for quicksort follows. We will describe how to do the partitioning later. We assume that the sequence is bounded by the iterators first and last and that pivot is a pointer to the pivot value after partitioning. There are two recursive calls, which execute if the sequence has more than one element. In the first call, the new sequence to be sorted is in the iterator range first through pivot; in the second call, the new sequence to be sorted is in the iterator range pivot + 1 through last. Note that the element pointed to by pivot is ignored, since it is in its proper position. If either new sequence contains just one element (or zero elements), an immediate return will occur.

Algorithm for Quicksort

1. if the sequence has more than one element
2.   Partition the elements in the sequence in the iterator range first through last so that the pivot value is in its correct place and is pointed to by pivot.
3.   Recursively apply quicksort to the sequence in the iterator range first through pivot.
4.   Recursively apply quicksort to the sequence in the iterator range pivot + 1 through last.

Analysis of Quicksort

If the pivot value is a random value selected from the current sequence, then statistically it is expected that half of the items in the sequence will be less than the pivot value and half will be greater than the pivot value. After partitioning, if the left and right sequences have the same number of elements (the best case), there will be log *n* levels of recursion. At each level, the partitioning process involves moving every element into its correct partition, so quicksort is $O(n \log n)$, just like merge sort.

But what if the split is not 50-50? Let us consider the case where each split is 90-10. Instead of a 100-element array being split into two 50-element arrays, there will be one array with 90 elements and one with just 10. The 90-element array may be split 50-50, or it may also be split 90-10. In the latter case, there would be one array with 81 elements and one with just 9 elements. Generally, for random input, the splits will not be exactly 50-50, but neither will they all be 90-10. An exact analysis is difficult and beyond the scope of this book, but the running time will be bound by a constant $\times$ *n* log *n*.

There is one situation, however, where quicksort gives very poor behavior. If, each time we partition the array, we end up with a subarray that is empty, the other subarray will have one less element than the one just split (only the pivot value will be removed). Therefore, we will have *n* levels of recursive calls (instead of log *n*), and the algorithm will be $O(n^2)$. Because of the overhead of recursive function calls (versus iteration), quicksort will take longer and require more extra storage on the runtime stack than any of the earlier quadratic algorithms for this particular case. We will discuss a way to handle this situation later.

Code for Quicksort

Listing 10.9 shows file `QuickSort.h` with function `quick_sort`. We discuss the partition function next.

LISTING 10.9
QuickSort.h

```
#ifndef QUICKSORT_H_
#define QUICKSORT_H_

#include <algorithm>

namespace KW {

/** Sort data in the specified range using quicksort.
    @param RI An iterator that meets the
           random-access iterator requirements
    @param first An iterator that references
           the first element in the sequence to be sorted
    @param last An iterator that references
           1 past the end of the sequence
*/
template<typename RI>
  void quick_sort(RI first, RI last) {
  if (last - first > 1) {  // There is data to be sorted.
    // Partition the table.
    RI pivot = partition(first, last);

    // Sort the left half.
    KW::quick_sort(first, pivot);
```

```
      // Sort the right half.
      KW::quick_sort(pivot + 1, last);
    }
}
// Insert partition function. See Listing 10.10
...

} // End namespace KW

#endif
```

Algorithm for Partitioning

The partition function selects the pivot and performs the partitioning operation. When we are selecting the pivot, it does not really matter which element is the pivot value (if the arrays are randomly ordered to begin with). For simplicity we chose the element at position first. We then begin searching for the first value at the left end of the subarray that is greater than the pivot value. When we find it, we search for the first value at the right end of the subarray that is less than or equal to the pivot value. These two values are exchanged, and we repeat the search and exchange operations. This is illustrated in Figure 10.14, where iterator up points to the first value greater than the pivot and iterator down points to the first value less than or equal to the pivot value. The elements less than the pivot are in light color and the elements greater than the pivot are in gray.

The value 75 is the first value at the left end of the array that is larger than 44, and 33 is the first value at the right end that is less than or equal to 44, so these two values are exchanged. The iterators up and down are advanced again, as shown in Figure 10.15.

The value 55 is the next value at the left end that is larger than 44, and 12 is the next value at the right end that is less than or equal to 44, so these two values are exchanged, and up and down are advanced again, as shown in Figure 10.16.

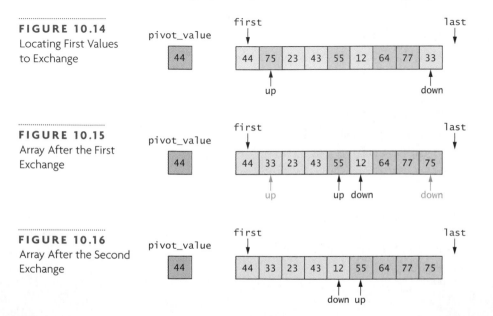

FIGURE 10.14 Locating First Values to Exchange

FIGURE 10.15 Array After the First Exchange

FIGURE 10.16 Array After the Second Exchange

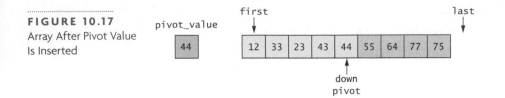

FIGURE 10.17
Array After Pivot Value
Is Inserted

After the second exchange, the first five array elements contain the pivot value and all values less than or equal to the pivot; the last four elements contain all values larger than the pivot. The value 55 is selected once again by up as the next element larger than the pivot; 12 is selected by down as the next element less than or equal to the pivot. Since up has now "passed" down, these values are not exchanged. Instead, the pivot value (subscript first) and the value at position down are exchanged. This puts the pivot value in its proper position (the new subscript is down) as shown in Figure 10.17.

The partition process is now complete, and the value of down is returned to the iterator pivot. Function quick_sort will be called recursively to sort the left sequence and the right sequence. The algorithm for partition follows.

Algorithm for partition Function

1. Define the pivot value as the contents of table[first].
2. Initialize up to first + 1 and down to last - 1.
3. **do**
4.   Increment up until up selects the first element greater than the pivot value or up has reached last - 1.
5.   Decrement down until down selects the first element less than or equal to the pivot value or down has reached first.
6.   **if** up < down then
7.   Exchange table[up] and table[down].
8. **while** up is to the left of down
9. Exchange table[first] and table[down].
10. Return the value of down to pivot.

Code for partition

The code for partition is shown in Listing 10.10. The **while** statement:

```
while ((up != last - 1) && !(*first < *up)) {
    ++up;
}
```

advances the iterator up until it is equal to last - 1 or until it references an item that is greater than the pivot value (pointed to by first). Note that the condition !(*first < *up) is equivalent to (*first >= *up); however, we can't use >= as the comparison operator. Similarly, the **while** statement:

```
while (*first < *down) {
    --down;
}
```

decrements the iterator down until it references an item in table that is less than or equal to the pivot value. The **do . . . while** condition

(up < down)

ensures that the partitioning process will continue while up is to the left of down.

What happens if there is a value in the array that is the same as the pivot value? The index down will stop at such a value. If up has stopped prior to reaching that value, *up and *down will be exchanged, and the value equal to the pivot will be in the left partition. If up has passed this value, and therefore passed down, *first will be exchanged with *down (same value as *first), and the value equal to the pivot will still be in the left partition.

What happens if the pivot value is the smallest value in the array? Since the pivot value is at *first, the loop will terminate with down equal to first. In this case, the left partition is empty. Figure 10.18 shows an array for which this is the case.

By similar reasoning we can show that up will stop at last - 1 if there is no element in the array larger than the pivot. In this case, down will also stay at last - 1, and the pivot value (*first) will be swapped with the last value in the array, so the right partition will be empty. Figure 10.19 shows an array for which this is the case.

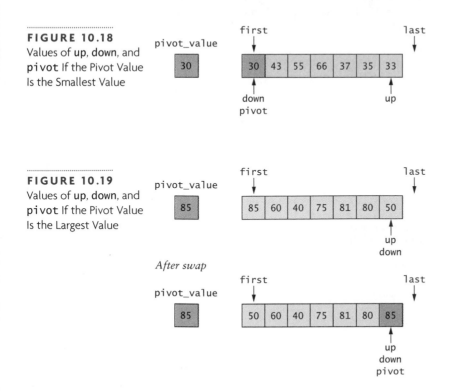

FIGURE 10.18
Values of **up**, **down**, and **pivot** If the Pivot Value Is the Smallest Value

FIGURE 10.19
Values of **up**, **down**, and **pivot** If the Pivot Value Is the Largest Value

---

LISTING 10.10

Quicksort `partition` Function (First Version)

```
/** Partition the table so that values in the iterator range
        first through pivot are less than or equal to the pivot value,
        and values in the iterator range pivot + 1 through last
        are greater than the pivot value.
        @param RI An iterator that meets the
                random-access iterator requirements
        @param first An iterator that references
                the first element in the sequence to be sorted
        @param last An iterator that references
                1 past the end of the sequence
        @return The position of the pivot value (originally at first)
*/
template<typename RI>
  RI partition(RI first, RI last) {
  // Start up and down at either end of the sequence.
  // The first table element is the pivot value.
  RI up = first + 1;
  RI down = last - 1;
  do {
    /* Invariant:
        All items in table[first] through table[up - 1] <= table[first]
        All items in table[down + 1] through table[last - 1] > table[first]
    */
    while ((up != last - 1) && !(*first < *up)) {
      ++up;
    }
    // Assert: up equals last-1 or table[up] > table[first].
    while (*first < *down) {
      --down;
    }
    // Assert: down equals first or table[down] <= table[first].
    if (up < down) {    // if up is to the left of down,
      // Exchange table[up] and table[down].
      std::iter_swap(up, down);
    }
  } while (up < down); // Repeat while up is left of down.

  // Exchange table[first] and table[down] thus putting the
  // pivot value where it belongs.
  // Return position of pivot.
  std::iter_swap(first, down);
  return down;
}
```

A Revised Partition Algorithm

We stated earlier that quicksort is $O(n^2)$ when each split yields one empty subarray. Unfortunately, that would be the case if the array was sorted. So the worst possible performance occurs for a sorted array, which is not very desirable.

A better solution is to pick the pivot value in a way that is less likely to lead to a bad split. One approach is to examine the first, middle, and last elements in the

FIGURE 10.20
Sorting First, Middle, and Last Elements in Array

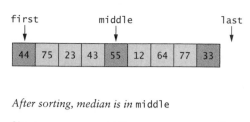

After sorting, median is in middle

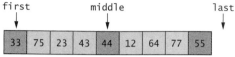

array and select the median of these three values as the pivot. We can do this by sorting the three-element subarray (in color in Figure 10.20). After sorting, the smallest of the three values is pointed to by first, the median is pointed to by middle, and the largest of the three is pointed to by last - 1.

At this point, we can exchange the first element with the middle element (the median) and use the partition algorithm shown earlier, which uses the first element (now the median) as the pivot value. When we exit the partitioning loop, *first and *down are exchanged, moving the pivot value where it belongs (back to the middle position). This revised partition algorithm follows.

Algorithm for Revised partition Function

1. Sort table[first], table[middle], and table[last - 1].
2. Move the median value to the first position (the pivot value) by exchanging table[first] and table[middle].
3. Initialize up to first + 1 and down to last - 1.
4. **do**
5.   Increment up until up selects the first element greater than the pivot value or up has reached last - 1.
6.   Decrement down until down selects the first element less than or equal to the pivot value or down has reached first.
7.   **if** up < down then
8.   Exchange table[up] and table[down]
9. **while** up is to the left of down.
10. Exchange table[first] and table[down].
11. Return the value of down to pivot.

You may be wondering whether you can avoid the double shift (Steps 2 and 10) and just leave the pivot value at table[middle], where it belongs. The answer is "Yes", but you would also need to modify the partition algorithm further if you did this. Programming Project 6 addresses this issue and the construction of an industrial-strength quicksort function.

Code for Revised partition Function

Listing 10.11 shows the revised version of function partition with function bubble_sort3, which applies the bubble sort algorithm to the three selected items in table so that

```
table[first] <= table[middle] <= table[last - 1]
```

Function partition begins with a call to function bubble_sort3 and then calls swap to make the median the pivot. The rest of the function is unchanged.

LISTING 10.11

Revised partition Function and bubble_sort3

```
/** Partition the table so that values in the iterator range
    first through pivot are less than or equal to the pivot value,
    and values in the iterator range pivot + 1 through last
    are greater than the pivot value. The pivot value is the
    median of the first, middle, and last elements.
    @param RI An iterator that meets the
            random-access iterator requirements
    @param first An iterator that references
            the first element in the sequence to be sorted
    @param last An iterator that references
            1 past the end of the sequence
    @return The position of the pivot value (originally at first)
*/
template<typename RI>
  RI partition(RI first, RI last) {
  /* Put the median of table[first], table[middle], table[last - 1]
     into table[first], and use this value as the pivot.
  */
  bubble_sort3(first, last);
  // Swap first element with middle element.
  std::iter_swap(first, first + (last - first) / 2);

  // Continue with rest of partition function in Listing 10.10.
  // Start up and down at either end of the sequence.
  // The first table element is the pivot value.
  RI up = first + 1;
  RI down = last - 1;
  do {
    /* Invariant:
       All items in table[first] through table[up - 1] <= table[first]
       All items in table[down + 1] through table[last - 1] > table[first]
    */
    while ((up != last - 1) && !(*first < *up)) {
      ++up;
    }
    // Assert: up equals last - 1 or table[up] > table[first].
    while (*first < *down) {
      --down;
    }
```

```
      // Assert: down equals first or table[down] <= table[first].
      if (up < down) {    // if up is to the left of down,
        // Exchange table[up] and table[down].
        std::iter_swap(up, down);
      }
  } while (up < down);  // Repeat while up is left of down.

  // Exchange table[first] and table[down] thus putting the
  // pivot value where it belongs.
  // Return position of pivot.
  std::iter_swap(first, down);
  return down;
}

/** Sort first, middle, and last elements of sequence.
    @param RI An iterator that meets the
            random-access iterator requirements
    @param first An iterator that references
            the first element in the sequence to be sorted
    @param last An iterator that references
            1 past the end of the sequence
*/
template<typename RI>
  void bubble_sort3(RI first, RI last) {
  RI middle = first + (last - first) / 2;
  /* Perform bubble sort on table[first], table[middle],
     table[last - 1].
  */
  if (*middle < *first) {
    std::iter_swap(first, middle);
  }
  // Assert: table[first] <= table[middle].
  if (*(last - 1) < *middle) {
    std::iter_swap(middle, last - 1);
  }
  // Assert: table[last] is the largest value of the three.
  if (*middle < *first) {
    std::iter_swap(first, middle);
  }
  // Assert: table[first] <= table[middle] <= table[last - 1].
}
```

PITFALL

Falling Off Either End of the Array

A common problem when incrementing up or down during the partition process is falling off either end of the array. We used the condition

`((up != last - 1) && !(*first < *up))`

to keep up from falling off the right end of the array. Self-Check Exercise 3 asks why we don't need to write similar code to avoid falling off the left end of the array.

EXERCISES FOR SECTION 10.9

SELF-CHECK

1. Trace the execution of quicksort on the following array, assuming that the first item in each subarray is the pivot value. Show the elements referenced by `first` and `last - 1` for each recursive call and the elements in the iterator range `first` through `last` after returning from each call. Also, show the pivot value during each call and the value returned to `pivot`. How many times is `quick_sort` called, and how many times is `partition` called?

    55 50 10 40 80 90 60 100 70 80 20

2. Redo Question 1 using the revised `partition` algorithm, which does a preliminary sort of three elements and selects their median as the pivot value.

3. Explain why the condition (`*first < *down`) in the loop that decrements `down` does not need to be written as ((`*first < *down`) && (`down != first`)). That is, why is the expression after && unnecessary?

PROGRAMMING

1. Insert statements to trace the quicksort algorithm. After each call to `partition`, display the elements selected by `first`, `pivot`, and `last - 1` and the sequence in the iterator range `first` through `last`.

2. Implement a quicksort function that sorts an array of type **int**[] using subscripts instead of iterators.

10.10 Testing the Sort Algorithms

To test the sorting algorithms, we need to exercise them with a variety of test cases. We want to make sure that they work, and we also want to get some idea of their relative performance when sorting the same container (array, vector, or deque). We should test the functions with small containers, large containers, containers whose elements are in random order, containers that are already sorted, and containers with duplicate copies of the same value.

Listing 10.12 shows a driver program that tests the standard `sort` function and the `KW::quick_sort` function on the same vector of random integer values. Function `next_int` of class `Random` (see Listing 6.8) generates random integer values.

Function `clock` (in library file `ctime`) returns a value that approximates the amount of time that a program has been running. We call it before and after a sort function and display the difference. This gives us a measure of the sorting time and allows us to compare its performance to that of the standard sort.

Function `verify` verifies that the vector elements are sorted by checking that each element in the vector is not less than its predecessor. Function `dump_table` (not shown) should display the first 10 elements and last 10 elements of the vector (or the entire contents if the vector has 20 or fewer elements).

Because we used distinct names for the sorting functions in this chapter, you can compare one to the other. Just replace the call to `std::sort` with the second sorting function.

....

LISTING 10.12
Driver to Test Sort Algorithms

```
/** Driver function to test sorts. */

#include <iostream>
#include <iterator>
#include <vector>
#include "Random.h"
#include "QuickSort.h"
#include <ctime>

using namespace std;

template<typename RI>
  bool verify(RI first, RI last);

template<typename RI>
  void dump_table(RI first, RI last);

int main() {
  vector<int> a_vec;
  int num_items;
  Random rand;

  // Fill vector a_vec with random numbers.
  cout << "Enter vector size: ";
  cin >> num_items;
  for (int i = 0; i < num_items; i++) {
    a_vec.push_back(rand.next_int(2 * num_items));
  }
  vector<int> copy_vec = a_vec;    // A copy of a_vec.

  // Sort and verify using standard sorting algorithm.
  long int start = clock();
  std::sort(a_vec.begin(), a_vec.end());
  cout << "time for standard sort: " << (clock() - start) << endl;
  if (verify(a_vec.begin(), a_vec.end()))
    cout << "standard sort successful\n";
  else
    cout << "standard sort failed\n";
  dump_table(a_vec.begin(), a_vec.end());
```

```
      // Sort and verify using KW sorting function.
      start = clock();
      KW::quick_sort(copy_vec.begin(), copy_vec.end());
      cout << "time for KW sort: " << (clock() - start) << endl;
      if (verify(copy_vec.begin(), copy_vec.end()))
        cout << "KW sort successful\n";
      else
        cout << "KW sort failed\n";
      dump_table(copy_vec.begin(), copy_vec.end());

      return 0;
}

template<typename RI>
  bool verify(RI first, RI last) {
  while (first != last - 2) {
    if (*(first + 1) < *first)
      return false;
    ++first;
  }
  return true;
}

template<typename RI>
  void dump_table(RI first, RI last) {
  // Exercise
}
```

EXERCISES FOR SECTION 10.10

SELF-CHECK

1. Explain why function verify will always determine whether an array is sorted. Does verify work if an array contains duplicate values?

PROGRAMMING

1. Write function dump_table.
2. Modify the driver function to fill the vector with a collection of integers read from a file.

10.11 The Dutch National Flag Problem (Optional Topic)

A variety of partitioning algorithms for quicksort have been published. Most are variations on the one presented in this text. There is another popular variation that uses a single left-to-right scan of the array (instead of scanning left and scanning right as we did). The following case study illustrates a partitioning algorithm that combines both scanning techniques to partition an array into three segments. The famous computer scientist Edsger W. Dijkstra described this problem in his book *A Discipline of Programming* (Prentice-Hall, 1976).

CASE STUDY   The Problem of the Dutch National Flag

Problem   The Dutch national flag consists of three stripes that are colored (from top to bottom) red, white, and blue as shown in Figure 10.21. Because we only have two colors in this book, we use gray for red. Unfortunately, when the flag arrived, it looked like Figure 10.22; threads of each of the colors were all scrambled together! Fortunately, we have a machine that can unscramble it, but it needs software.

Analysis   Our unscrambling machine has the following abilities:

- It can look at one thread in the flag and determine its color.
- It can swap the position of two threads in the flag.

Our machine can also execute **while** loops and **if** statements.

FIGURE 10.21
The Dutch National Flag

FIGURE 10.22
Scrambled Dutch National Flag

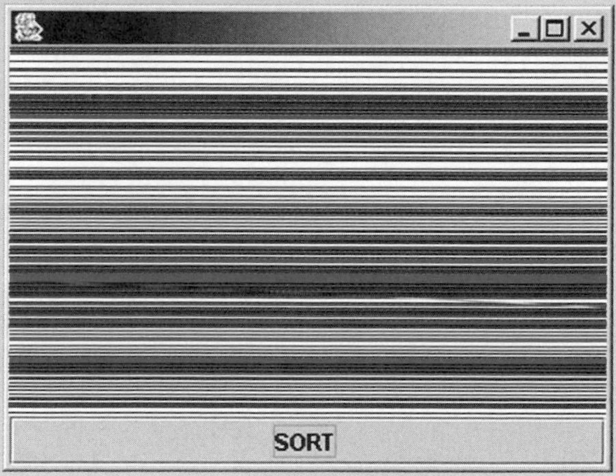

Design   Loop Invariant

When we partitioned the array in quicksort, we split the array into three regions. Values between first and up were less than or equal to the pivot; values between down and last were greater than the pivot, and values between up and down were unknown. We started with the unknown region containing the whole array (first == up, and down == last). The partitioning algorithm preserves this invariant while shrinking the unknown region. The loop terminates when the unknown region becomes empty (up > down).

Values < pivot	Unknown	Values > pivot

first   up   down   last

Because our goal is to have three regions when we are done, let us define four regions: the red region, the white region, the blue region, and the unknown region. Now initially the whole flag is unknown. When we get done, however, we would like the red region on top, the white region in the middle, and the blue region on the bottom. The unknown region must be empty.

Let us assume that the threads are stored in an array `threads` and that the total number of threads is `HEIGHT`. Let us define `red` to be the upper bound of the red region, `white` to be the lower bound of the white region, and `blue` to be the lower bound of the blue region. Then, if our flag is complete, we can say the following:

- If $0 \leq i <$ `red`, then `threads[i]` is red.
- If `white` $< i \leq$ `blue`, then `threads[i]` is white.
- If `blue` $< i <$ `HEIGHT`, then `threads[i]` is blue.

What about the case where `red` $\leq i \leq$ `white`? When the flag is all sorted, `red` should equal `white`, so this region should not exist. However, when we start, everything is in this region, so a thread in that region can have any color.

Thus we can define the following loop invariant:

- If $0 \leq i <$ `red`, then `threads[i]` is red.
- If `red` $\leq i \leq$ `white`, then the color is unknown.
- If `white` $< i \leq$ `blue`, then `threads[i]` is white.
- If `blue` $< i <$ `HEIGHT`, then `threads[i]` is blue.

This is illustrated in Figure 10.23. The red region is at the top.

FIGURE 10.23
Dutch National Flag
Loop Invariant

[0]

[red]

[white]

[blue]

[HEIGHT]

Algorithm   We can solve our problem by establishing the loop invariant and then executing a loop that both preserves the loop invariant and shrinks the unknown region.

1. Set `red` to 0, `white` to `HEIGHT - 1`, and `blue` to `HEIGHT - 1`. This establishes our loop invariant, with the unknown region the whole flag and the red, white, and blue regions empty.

2. **while** `red` < `white`

3.   Shrink the distance between `red` and `white` while preserving the loop invariant.

Preserving the Loop Invariant

Let us assume that we now know the color of threads[white] (the thread at position white). Our goal is to either leave threads[white] where it is (in the white region if it is white) or "move it" to the region where it belongs. There are three cases to consider:

Case 1: The color of threads[white] is white. In this case we merely decrement the value of white to restore the invariant. By doing so, we increase the size of the white region by one thread.

Case 2: The color of threads[white] is red. We know from our invariant that the color of threads[red] is unknown. Therefore, if we swap the thread at threads[red] with the one at threads[white], we can then increment the value of red and preserve the invariant. By doing this, we add the thread to the end of the red region and reduce the size of the unknown region by one thread.

Case 3: The color of threads[white] is blue. We know from our invariant that the color of threads[blue] is white. Thus, if we swap the thread at threads[white] with the thread at threads[blue] and then decrement both white and blue, we preserve the invariant. By doing this, we insert the thread at the beginning of the blue region and reduce the size of the unknown region by one thread.

Implementation   A graphical implementation of this program is beyond the scope of this text. We show the coding of the sort algorithm in Listing 10.13.

LISTING 10.13
Dutch National Flag Sort

```
void sort() {
  int red = 0;
  int white = height - 1;
  int blue = height - 1;
  /* Invariant:
     0 <= i < red        ==>threads[i].get_color() == RED
     red <= i <= white ==>threads[i].get_color() is unknown
     white < i < blue  ==>threads[i].get_color() == WHITE
     blue < i < height ==>threads[i].get_color() == BLUE
  */
  while (red <= white) {
    if (threads[white].get_color() == WHITE) {
      white--;
    } else if (threads[white].get_color() == RED) {
      swap(red, white);
      red++;
    } else {  // threads[white].get_color() == BLUE
      swap(white, blue);
      white--;
      blue--;
    }
  }
  // Assert: red == white so unknown region is now empty.
}
```

EXERCISES FOR SECTION 10.11

PROGRAMMING

1. Adapt the Dutch National Flag algorithm to do the quicksort partitioning. Consider the red region to be those values less than the pivot, the white region to be those values equal to the pivot, and the blue region to be those values greater than the pivot. You should initially sort the first, middle, and last items and use the middle value as the pivot value.

Chapter Review

- ◆ We analyzed several sorting algorithms; their performance is summarized in Table 10.3.
- ◆ The three quadratic algorithms, $O(n^2)$, are selection sort, bubble sort, and insertion sort. They give satisfactory performance for small arrays (up to 100 elements). Generally, insertion sort is considered to be the best of the quadratic sorts. Bubble sort is a good choice when the array is likely to be nearly sorted, but it should be avoided otherwise.
- ◆ Shell sort, $O(n^{5/4})$, gives satisfactory performance for arrays up to 5000 elements.
- ◆ Quicksort has average-case performance of $O(n \log n)$, but if the pivot is picked poorly, the worst-case performance is $O(n^2)$.
- ◆ Merge sort and heapsort have $O(n \log n)$ performance.
- ◆ The standard library header `<algorithm>` defines a `sort` and `stable_sort` algorithm. The `sort` algorithm is similar to the second version of quicksort that we presented, except that when the partition length becomes less than a threshold, insertion sort is used. The `stable_sort` algorithm is a merge sort.

TABLE 10.3
Comparison of Sort Algorithms

	Number of Comparisons		
	Best	**Average**	**Worst**
Selection sort	$O(n^2)$	$O(n^2)$	$O(n^2)$
Bubble sort	$O(n)$	$O(n^2)$	$O(n^2)$
Insertion sort	$O(n)$	$O(n^2)$	$O(n^2)$
Shell sort	$O(n^{7/6})$	$O(n^{5/4})$	$O(n^2)$
Merge sort	$O(n \log n)$	$O(n \log n)$	$O(n \log n)$
Heapsort	$O(n \log n)$	$O(n \log n)$	$O(n \log n)$
Quicksort	$O(n \log n)$	$O(n \log n)$	$O(n^2)$

Quick-Check Exercises

1. Name three quadratic sorts.
2. Name two sorts with $n \log n$ worst-case behavior.
3. Which algorithm is particularly good for an array that is already sorted? Which is particularly bad? Explain your answers.
4. What determines whether you should use a quadratic sort or a logarithmic sort?
5. Which quadratic sort's performance is least affected by the ordering of the array elements? Which is most affected?
6. What is a good all-purpose sorting algorithm for medium-sized arrays?

Answers to Quick-Check Exercises

1. Selection sort, insertion sort, bubble sort
2. Merge sort, heapsort
3. Bubble sort is good—it requires $n - 1$ comparisons with no exchanges. Quicksort can be bad if the first element is picked as the pivot value, because the partitioning process always creates one subarray with a single element.
4. Array size
5. Selection sort is least affected; bubble sort is most affected.
6. Shell sort or any $O(n \log n)$ sort

Review Questions

1. When does quicksort work best, and when does it work worst?
2. Write a recursive procedure to implement the insertion sort algorithm.
3. What is the purpose of the pivot value in quicksort? How did we first select it in the text, and what is wrong with that approach for choosing a pivot value?
4. For the following array

   30 40 20 15 60 80 75 4 20

   show the new array after each pass of insertion sort, bubble sort, and selection sort. How many comparisons and exchanges are performed by each?
5. For the array in Question 4, trace the execution of Shell sort.
6. For the array in Question 4, trace the execution of merge sort.
7. For the array in Question 4, trace the execution of quicksort.
8. For the array in Question 4, trace the execution of heapsort.
9. The shaker sort is an adaptation of the bubble sort that alternates the direction in which the array elements are scanned during each pass. The first pass starts its scan with the first element, moving the larger element in each pair down the array. The second pass starts its scan with the next-to-last element, moving the smaller element in each pair up the array, and so on. Indicate what the advantage of the shaker sort might be.

Programming Projects

1. Use the random number generator in class Random to store a list of 1000 pseudorandom integer values in an array. Apply each of the sort functions described in this chapter to the array and determine the number of comparisons and exchanges. Make sure the same array is passed to each sort function.

2. Investigate the effect of array size and initial element order on the number of comparisons and exchanges required by each of the sorting algorithms described in this chapter. Use arrays with 100 and 10,000 integers. Use three initial orderings of each array (randomly ordered, inversely ordered, and ordered). Be certain to sort the same six arrays with each sort function.

3. Implement the shaker sort algorithm described in Review Question 9.

4. A variation of the merge sort algorithm can be used to sort large sequential data files. The basic strategy is to take the initial data file, read in several (say 10) data records, sort these records using an efficient array-sorting algorithm, and then write these sorted groups of records (runs) alternately to one of two output files. After all records from the initial data file have been distributed to the two output files, the runs on these output files are merged one pair of runs at time and written to the original data file. After all runs from the output file have been merged, the records on the original data file are redistributed to the output files, and the merging process is repeated. Runs no longer need to be sorted after the first distribution to the temporary output files.

   Each time runs are distributed to the output files, they contain twice as many records as the time before. The process stops when the length of the runs exceeds the number of records in the data file. Write a program that implements merge sort for sequential data files. Test your program on a file with several thousand data values.

5. Write a function that sorts a linked list.

6. Write an industrial-strength quicksort function with the following enhancements:

   a. If an array segment contains 20 elements or fewer, sort it using insertion sort.

   b. After sorting the first, middle, and last elements, use the median as the pivot, instead of swapping the median with the first element. (Save this value in `pivot_val`). Because the first and last elements are in the correct partitions, it is not necessary to test them before advancing `up` and `down`. This is also the case after each exchange, so increment `up` and decrement `down` at the beginning of the **do ... while** loop. Also, it is not necessary to test whether `up` is less than `last` before incrementing `up`, because the condition `pivot_val < *up` is false when `up` equals `last - 1` (the median must be $\geq$ the last element in the array).

7. In the early days of data processing (before computers), data was stored on punched cards. A machine to sort these cards contained 12 bins (one for each digit value and + and –). A stack of cards was fed into the machine, and the cards were placed into the appropriate bin, depending on the value of the selected column. By restacking the cards so that all zeros were first, followed by the ones, followed by the twos, and so forth, and then sorting on the next column, the whole deck of cards could be sorted. This process, known as radix sort, requires $c \times n$ passes, where c is the number of columns and n is the number of cards.

   We can simulate the action of this machine using an array of queues. During the first pass, the least significant digit (the ones digit) of each number is examined and the number is added to the queue whose subscript matches that digit. After all numbers have been processed, the elements of each queue are added to an eleventh queue, starting with `queue[0]`, followed by `queue[1]`, and so forth. The process is then repeated for the next significant digit, taking the numbers out of the eleventh queue. After all the digits have been processed, the eleventh queue will contain the numbers in sorted order.

   Write a program that implements radix sort on an array of **int** values. You will need to make 10 passes, because an **int** can store numbers up to 2,147,483,648.

Chapter 11

Self-Balancing
Search Trees

Chapter Objectives

- ◆ To understand the impact that balance has on the performance of binary search trees
- ◆ To learn about the AVL tree for storing and maintaining a binary search tree in balance
- ◆ To learn about the Red-Black tree for storing and maintaining a binary search tree in balance
- ◆ To learn about 2-3 trees, 2-3-4 trees, and B-trees and how they achieve balance
- ◆ To understand the process of search and insertion in each of these trees and to be introduced to removal

In Chapter 8 we introduced the binary search tree. The performance (time required to find, insert, or remove an item) of a binary search tree is proportional to the total height of the tree, where we defined the height of a tree as the maximum number of nodes along a path from the root to a leaf. A full binary tree of height k can hold $2^k - 1$ items. Thus, if the binary search tree were full and contained n items, the expected performance would be $O(\log n)$.

Unfortunately, if we build the binary search tree as described in Chapter 8, the resulting tree is not necessarily complete or close to being complete. Thus the actual performance is worse than expected. In this chapter we explore two algorithms for building binary search trees so that they are as full as possible. We call these trees *self-balancing* because they attempt to achieve a balance so that the height of each left subtree and right subtree are equal or nearly equal.

Finally we look at the B-tree and its specializations, the 2-3 and 2-3-4 trees. These are not binary search trees, but they achieve and maintain balance.

In this chapter we focus on algorithms and functions for search and insertion. We also discuss removing an item, but we have left the details of removal to the programming projects.

11.1   Tree Balance and Rotation

Why Balance Is Important

Figure 11.1 shows an example of a valid, but extremely unbalanced, binary search tree. Searches or insertions into this tree would be $O(n)$, not $O(\log n)$. Figure 11.2 shows the binary search tree resulting from inserting the words of the sentence "The quick brown fox jumps over the lazy dog." It too is not well balanced, having a height of 7 but containing only nine words. (Note that the string "The" is the smallest, because it begins with an uppercase letter.)

FIGURE 11.1
Very Unbalanced Binary
Search Tree

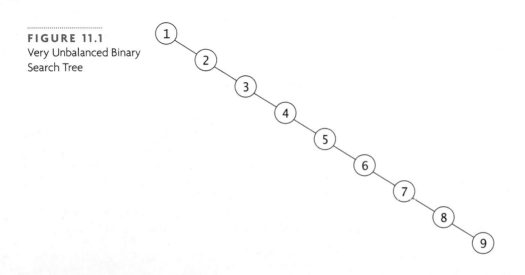

Rotation

FIGURE 11.2

Realistic Example of an Unbalanced Binary Search Tree

To achieve self-adjusting capability, we need an operation on a binary search tree that will change the relative heights of left and right subtrees but preserve the binary search tree property—that is, the items in each left subtree are less than the item at the root, and the items in each right subtree are greater than the item in the root. In Figure 11.3 we show an unbalanced binary search tree with a height of 4 right after the insertion of node 7. The height of the left subtree of the root (20) is 3, and the height of the right subtree is 1.

We can transform the tree in Figure 11.3 by doing a *right rotation* around node 20, making 10 the root and 20 the root of the right subtree of the new root (10). Because 20 is now the right subtree of 10, we need to move node 10's old right subtree (root is 15). We will make it the left subtree of 20, as shown in Figure 11.4.

After these changes the new binary search tree has a height of 3 (one less than before), and the left and right subtrees of the new root (10) have a height of 2, as shown in Figure 11.5. Note that the binary search tree property is maintained for all the nodes of the tree.

This result can be generalized. If node 15 had children, its children would have to be greater than 10 and less than 20 in the original tree. The left and right subtrees of node 15 would not change when node 15 was moved, so the binary search tree property would still be maintained for all children of node 15 in the new tree (> 10 and < 20). We can make a similar statement for any of the other leaf nodes in the original tree.

Algorithm for Rotation

Figure 11.6 illustrates the internal representation of the nodes of our original binary search tree whose branches (indicated by arrows in color) will be changed by rotation. Initially, root references node 20. Rotation right is achieved by the following algorithm.

Algorithm for Rotation Right

1. Remember the value of root->left (temp = root->left).
2. Set root->left to the value of temp->right.
3. Set temp->right to root.
4. Set root to temp.

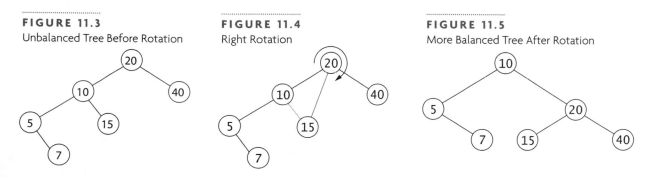

FIGURE 11.3
Unbalanced Tree Before Rotation

FIGURE 11.4
Right Rotation

FIGURE 11.5
More Balanced Tree After Rotation

Figure 11.7 shows the rotated tree. Step 1 sets `temp` to reference the left subtree (node 10) of the original root. Step 2 resets the original root's left subtree to reference node 15. Step 3 resets node `temp`'s right subtree to reference the original root. Then Step 4 sets `root` to reference node `temp`. The internal representation corresponds to the tree shown in Figure 11.5.

The algorithm for *left rotation* is symmetric to that for right rotation and is left as an exercise.

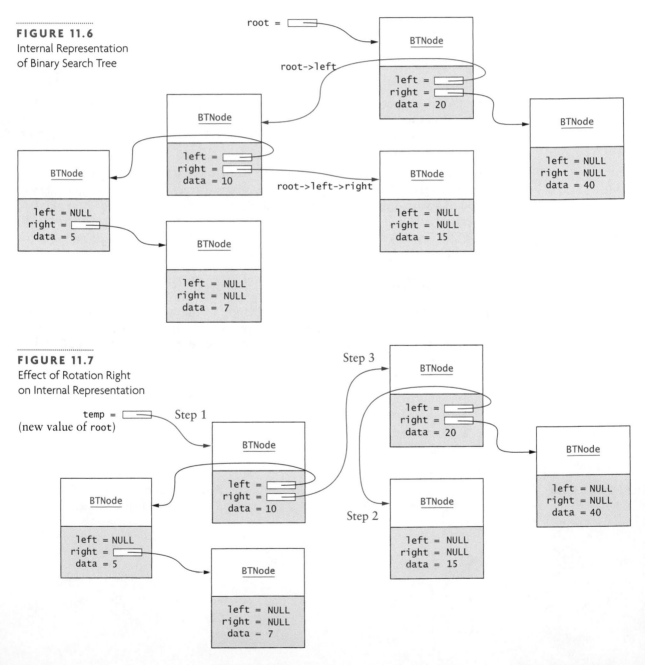

FIGURE 11.6
Internal Representation
of Binary Search Tree

FIGURE 11.7
Effect of Rotation Right
on Internal Representation

Implementing Rotation

Listing 11.1 shows class `BST_With_Rotate`. This class is an extension of the `Binary_Search_Tree` class described in Chapter 8, and it will be used as the base class for the other search trees discussed in this chapter. For this reason, it has visibility **protected**. It contains the functions rotate_left and rotate_right. These functions take a reference to a pointer to a `BTNode` that is the root of a subtree and modify it to the root of the rotated tree.

LISTING 11.1
BST_With_Rotate.h

```
#ifndef BST_WITH_ROTATE_H_
#define BST_WITH_ROTATE_H_
#include "Binary_Search_Tree.h"

/** This class extends the Binary_Search_Tree by adding the rotate
    operations. Rotate will change the balance of a search
    tree while preserving the search tree property.
    Used as a common base class for self-adjusting trees.
*/
template<typename Item_Type>
  class BST_With_Rotate : public Binary_Search_Tree<Item_Type> {

  protected:

  /** rotate_right
      pre:  local_root is the root of a binary search tree
      post: local_root->left is the root of a binary search tree
            local_root->left->left is raised one level
            local_root->left->right does not change levels
            local_root->right is lowered one level
            local_root is set to the new root
    @param local_root The root of the binary tree to be rotated
  */
  void rotate_right(BTNode<Item_Type>*& local_root) {
    BTNode<Item_Type>* temp = local_root->left;
    local_root->left = temp->right;
    temp->right = local_root;
    local_root = temp;
  }

  // Insert rotate_left here
  // Exercise
};

#endif
```

Figure 11.8 is a UML class diagram that shows the relationships between `BST_With_Rotate` and the other classes in the hierarchy. `BST_With_Rotate` is a subclass of `Binary_Tree` as well as `Binary_Search_Tree`. Class `Binary_Tree` has the data field root, which points to the `BTNode` that is the root of the tree. The figure shows that a `BTNode` contains a data field named data (of type `Item_Type`) and two pointers to a `BTNode`. The names of the pointers are left and right, as shown on the lines from the `BTNode` to itself.

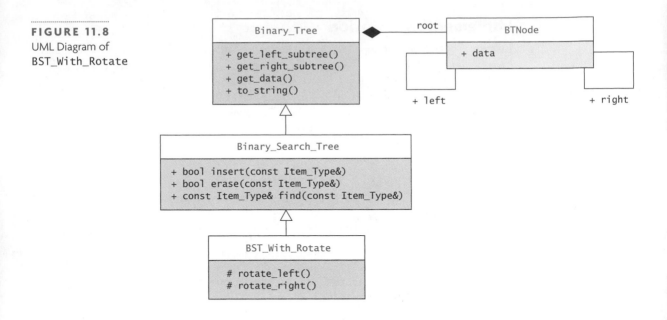

FIGURE 11.8
UML Diagram of
BST_With_Rotate

EXERCISES FOR SECTION 11.1

SELF-CHECK

1. Draw the binary search tree that results from inserting the words of the sentence "Now is the time for all good men to come to the aid of their party." What is its height? Compare this with 4, the smallest integer greater than $\log_2 13$, where 13 is the number of distinct words in this sentence.

2. Try to construct a binary search tree that contains the same words as in Question 1, but has a maximum height of 4.

3. Describe the algorithm for rotation left.

PROGRAMMING

1. Add the rotate_left function to the BST_With_Rotate class.

11.2 AVL Trees

Two Russian mathematicians, G. M. Adel'son-Vel'skiĭ and E. M. Landis, published a paper in 1962 that describes an algorithm for maintaining overall balance of a binary search tree. Their algorithm keeps track of the difference in height of each subtree. As items are added to (or removed from) the tree, the balance (that is, the difference in the heights of the subtrees) of each subtree from the insertion point up to the root is updated. If the balance ever gets out of the range −1 . . . +1, the subtree is rotated to bring it back into balance. Trees using this approach are known as *AVL trees* after the initials of the inventors. As before, we define the height of a tree as the number of nodes in the longest path from the root to a leaf node, including the root.

Balancing a Left-Left Tree

The following tree results from inserting 20 in a tree that already contains node 50 (the root) and node 40. Such a tree is called a Left-Left tree because its root and the left subtree of the root are both left-heavy. The balance of the root is −2, so this tree is unbalanced.

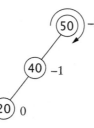

If we rotate the tree right around the root, we get the following balanced tree. This tree is also a binary search tree, but all nodes have a balance of 0.

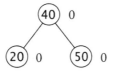

Figure 11.9 shows a general binary search tree with a balance of −2 caused by an insertion into its left-left subtree. Each white triangle with label a, b, or c represents a tree of height k; the shaded area at the bottom of the left-left triangle (tree a) indicates an insertion into this tree (its height is now $k + 1$). We use the formula

$$h_R - h_L$$

to calculate the balance for each node, where h_L and h_R are the heights of the left and right subtrees, respectively. The actual heights are not important; it is their relative difference that matters. The right subtree (b) of node 25 has a height of k; its left subtree (a) has a height of $k + 1$, so its balance is −1. The right subtree (of node 50) has a height of k; its left subtree has a height of $k + 2$, so its factor is −2. Such a tree is called a Left-Left tree because its root and the left subtree of the root are both left-heavy.

Figure 11.10 shows this same tree after a rotation right. The new tree root is node 25. Its right subtree (root 50) now has tree b as its left subtree. Notice that balance has now been achieved. Also, the overall height has not increased. Before the insertion, the tree height was $k + 2$; after the rotation, the tree height is still $k + 2$.

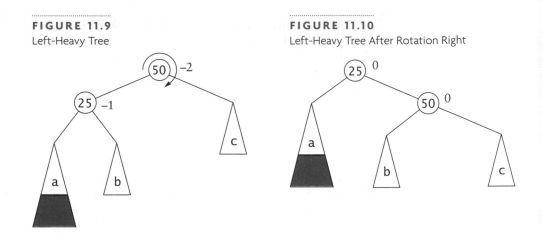

Balancing a Left-Right Tree

The following tree results from inserting 40 in the tree consisting of nodes 50 (the root) and node 20. This tree is called a Left-Right tree because its root (node 50) is left-heavy but the left subtree of the root (node 20) is right-heavy.

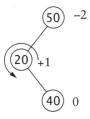

We cannot fix this with a simple rotation right as in the Left-Left case. (See Self-Check Exercise 2 at the end of this section.) However, we can fix this tree by first rotating left around node 20, giving the following tree.

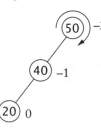

This tree is still unbalanced, so we next rotate right around node 50, giving the following balanced tree. All nodes have a balance of 0.

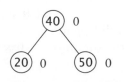

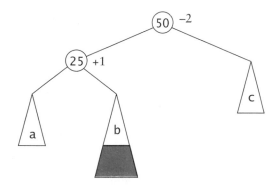

FIGURE 11.11
Left-Right Tree

Balance $50 = (k - (k + 2))$

Balance $25 = ((k + 1) - k)$

As you can see, in this case the resulting tree is balanced. This occurs when the left-right subtree (40) is balanced. In the general case, however, the left-right subtree will not be balanced.

Figure 11.11 shows a general Left-Right tree with subtrees a, b, and c all originally the same height. (They were all height 0 in the simple case just discussed.) After insertion into tree b, the tree is unbalanced and has the balances shown. We discuss the insertion and balancing process in more detail next.

Figure 11.12 shows the Left-Right tree in Figure 11.11 with tree b expanded. Node 40, the root of subtree b, has subtrees b_L and b_R. Figure 11.12 shows the effect of an insertion into b_L, making node 40 left-heavy. If the left subtree is rotated left, as shown in Figure 11.13, the overall tree is now a Left-Left tree, similar to the case of Figure 11.9. Now, if the modified tree is rotated right, overall balance is achieved, as shown in Figure 11.14. Figures 11.15 through 11.17 illustrate the effect of these double rotations after insertion into b_R.

In both cases, the new tree root is 40; its left subtree has node 25 as its root, and its right subtree has node 50 as its root. The balance of the root is 0. If the critically unbalanced situation was due to an insertion into subtree b_L, the balance of the root's left child is 0 and the balance of the root's right child is +1 (Figure 11.14). For insertion into subtree b_R, the balance of the root's left child is –1 and the balance of the root's right child is 0 (Figure 11.17).

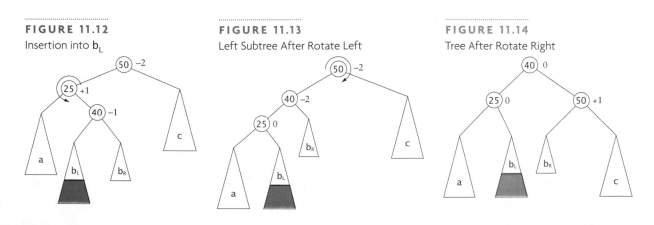

FIGURE 11.12
Insertion into b_L

FIGURE 11.13
Left Subtree After Rotate Left

FIGURE 11.14
Tree After Rotate Right

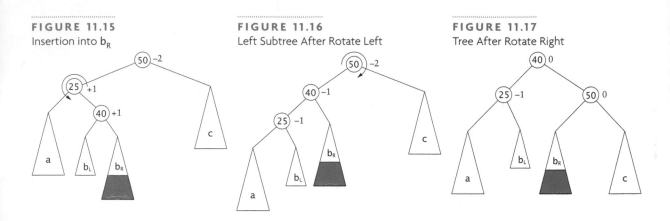

FIGURE 11.15
Insertion into b_R

FIGURE 11.16
Left Subtree After Rotate Left

FIGURE 11.17
Tree After Rotate Right

Four Kinds of Critically Unbalanced Trees

How do we recognize unbalanced trees and determine what to do to balance them? For the Left-Left tree shown in Figure 11.9 (parent and child nodes are both left-heavy, parent balance is –2, child balance is –1), the remedy is to rotate right around the parent.

For the Left-Right example shown in Figure 11.12 (parent is left-heavy with balance –2, child is right-heavy with balance +1), the remedy is to rotate left around the child and then rotate right around parent. We list the four cases that need rebalancing and their remedies next.

- Left-Left (parent balance is –2, left child balance is –1): Rotate right around parent.
- Left-Right (parent balance is –2, left child balance is +1): Rotate left around child, then rotate right around parent.
- Right-Right (parent balance is +2, right child balance is +1): Rotate left around parent.
- Right-Left (parent balance is +2, right child balance is –1): Rotate right around child, then rotate left around parent.

EXAMPLE 11.1

We will build an AVL tree from the words in the sentence "The quick brown fox jumps over the lazy dog."

After inserting the words *The*, *quick*, and *brown*, we get the following tree.

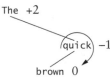

The subtree with the root *quick* is left-heavy by 1, but the overall tree with the root of *The* is right-heavy by 2 (Right-Left case). We must first rotate the subtree around *quick* to the right:

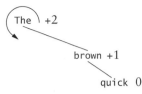

Then rotate left about *The*:

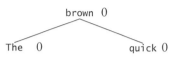

We now proceed to insert *fox* and *jumps*:

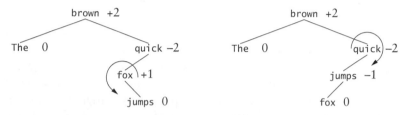

The subtree rooted about *quick* is now left-heavy by 2 (Left-Right case). Because this case is symmetric with the previous one, we rotate left about *fox* and then right about *quick*, giving the following result.

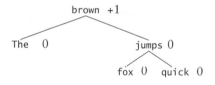

We now insert *over*.

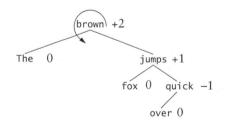

The subtrees at *quick* and *jumps* are unbalanced by 1. The subtree at *brown*, however, is right-heavy by 2 (Right-Right case), so a rotation left solves the problem.

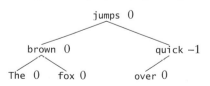

We can now insert *the*, *lazy*, and *dog* without any additional rotations being necessary.

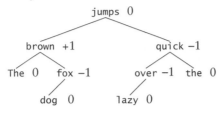

Implementing an AVL Tree

We begin by deriving the class AVL_Tree from BST_With_Rotate (see Listing 11.1). Figure 11.18 is a UML class diagram showing the relationship between AVL_Tree and BST_With_Rotate. The AVL_Tree class contains the **bool** data field increase, which indicates whether the current subtree height has increased as a result of the insertion. We override the functions insert and erase but inherit function find, because searching a balanced tree is no different from searching an unbalanced tree. Listing 11.2 shows the class definition for AVL_Tree. We also extend the class BTNode with AVLNode. Within this class we add the additional field balance.

FIGURE 11.18
UML Class Diagram of AVL_Tree

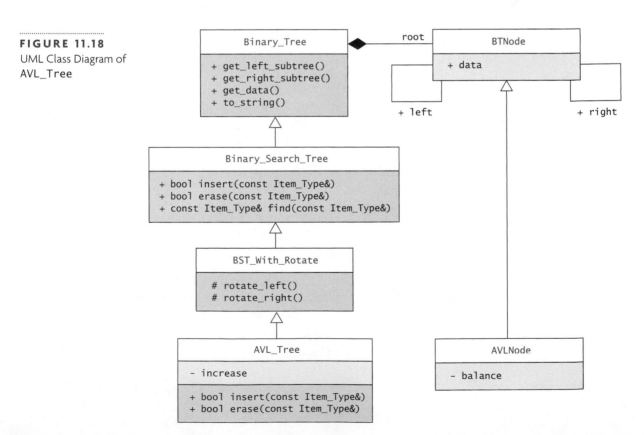

....
LISTING 11.2
AVL_Tree Class Definition (AVL_Tree.h)

```cpp
#ifndef AVL_TREE_H
#define AVL_TREE_H

#include "BST_With_Rotate.h"
#include "AVLNode.h"

/** Definition of the AVL Binary Search Tree class.
    @param Item_Type The type of item to be stored in the tree
    Note: Item_Type must define the less-than operator as a
    total ordering.
*/
template<typename Item_Type>
  class AVL_Tree : public BST_With_Rotate<Item_Type> {

  public:
  // Constructor
  /** Construct an empty AVL_Tree */
  AVL_Tree() : BST_With_Rotate<Item_Type>() {}

  // Public Member Functions
  /** Insert an item into the tree.
      post: The item is in the tree.
      @param item The item to be inserted
      @return true only if the item was not
              already in the tree
  */
  virtual bool insert(const Item_Type& item) {
    return insert(this->root, item); }

  /** Remove an item from the tree.
      post: The item is no longer in the tree.
      @param item The item to be removed
      @return true only if the item was in the tree
  */
  virtual bool erase(const Item_Type& item) {
    return erase(this->root, item); }

  private:
  // Private member functions declarations
  ...

  // Data Fields
  /** A flag to indicate that the height of the tree has increased */
  bool increase;

}; // End of AVL_Tree class definition

// Implementation of member functions
...
#endif
```

The **AVLNode** Class

The AVLNode class is shown in Listing 11.3. It is an extension of the BTNode class. It adds the data field balance, which has the enum type balance_type, which defines the values LEFT_HEAVY, BALANCED, and RIGHT_HEAVY.

....
LISTING 11.3
The AVLNode Class (AVLNode.h)

```
#ifndef AVLNODE_H_
#define AVLNODE_H_
#include <sstream>

/** A node for an AVL Tree. */
template<typename Item_Type>
  struct AVLNode : public BTNode<Item_Type> {

  enum  balance_type {LEFT_HEAVY = -1, BALANCED = 0, RIGHT_HEAVY = +1};
  // Additional data field
  balance_type balance;

  // Constructor
  AVLNode(const Item_Type& the_data, BTNode<Item_Type>* left_val = NULL,
          BTNode<Item_Type>* right_val = NULL) :
    BTNode<Item_Type>(the_data, left_val, right_val), balance(BALANCED) {}

  // Destructor (to avoid warning message)
  virtual ~AVLNode() {}

  // to_string
  virtual std::string to_string() const {
    std::ostringstream os;
    os << balance << ": " << this->data;
    return os.str();
  }
}; // End AVLNode

#endif
```

Inserting into an AVL Tree

The easiest way to keep a tree balanced is never to let it become unbalanced. If any node becomes critical and needs rebalancing, rebalance immediately. You can identify critical nodes by checking the balance at the root node of a subtree as you return to each parent node along the insertion path. If the insertion was in the left subtree and the left subtree height has increased, you must check to see whether the balance for the root node of the left subtree has become critical (−2 or +2). If so, we need to fix it by calling rebalance_left (rebalance a left-heavy tree when balance is −2) or rebalance_right (rebalance a right-heavy tree when balance is +2). A symmetric strategy should be followed after returning from an insertion into the right subtree. The **bool** variable increase is set before return from recursion to indicate to the next higher level that the height of the subtree has increased. This information is then used to adjust the balance of the next level in the tree. The following algorithm is based on the algorithm for inserting into a binary search tree, described in Chapter 8.

Algorithm for Insertion into an AVL Tree

1.   **if** the root is NULL
2.   Create a new tree with the item at the root and return **true**.
     else if the item is equal to root->data
3.   The item is already in the tree; return **false**.
     else if the item is less than root->data
4.   Recursively insert the item in the left subtree.
5.   **if** the height of the left subtree has increased (increase is **true**)
6.   Decrement balance.
7.   **if** balance is zero, reset increase to **false**.
8.   **if** balance is less than -1
9.   Reset increase to **false**.
10.   Perform a rebalance_left.
     else if the item is greater than root->data
11.   The processing is symmetric to Steps 4 through 10. Note that balance is incremented if increase is true.

After returning from the recursion (Step 4), examine the member data field increase to see whether the left subtree has increased in height. If it did, then decrement the balance. If the balance had been +1 (current subtree was right-heavy), it is now zero, so the overall height of the current subtree is not changed. Therefore, reset increase to **false** (Steps 5–7).

If the balance was -1 (current subtree was left-heavy), it is now -2, and a rebalance_left must be performed. The rebalance operation reduces the overall height of the tree by 1, so increase is reset to **false**. Therefore, no more rebalancing operations will occur, so we can fix the tree by either a single rotation (Left-Left case) or a double rotation (Left-Right case) (Steps 8–10).

Recursive **insert** Function

The recursive insert function is called by the insert starter function (see Listing 11.2); it begins as follows:

```
/** Insert an item into the tree.
    post: The item is in the tree.
    @param local_root A reference to the current root
    @param item The item to be inserted
    @return true only if the item was not already in the tree
*/
virtual bool insert(BTNode<Item_Type>*& local_root,
                    const Item_Type& item) {
```

We begin by seeing whether the local_root is NULL. If it is, then we set local_root to point to a new AVLNode that contains the item to be inserted. We then set increase to **true** and return **true**.

```
if (local_root == NULL) {
  local_root = new AVLNode<Item_Type>(item);
  increase = true;
  return true;
}
```

Next we compare the inserted item with the data field of the current node. (As with the Binary_Search_Tree, we need to change the order of the tests from that shown in the algorithm.)

If it is less than this value, we recursively call the insert function (Step 4 of the insertion algorithm), passing local_root->left as the parameter and saving the return value in the **bool** variable return_value.

```
if (item < local_root->data) {
  bool return_value = insert(local_root->left, item);
```

Upon return from the recursion, we examine the member data field increase. If increase is **true**, then the height of the left subtree has increased. Now we need to examine the current value of the local_root's balance. However, local_root is of type pointer to BTNode, and balance is a data field in the type AVLNode. The node that local_root points to is in fact an AVLNode. Thus we can create a pointer value that points to this node of the desired type using the dynamic cast.

```
if (increase) {
  AVLNode<Item_Type>* AVL_local_root =
    dynamic_cast<AVLNode<Item_Type>*>(local_root);
```

There are three cases to consider: AVL_local_root->balance is BALANCED, AVL_local_root->balance is RIGHT_HEAVY, and AVL_local_root->balance is LEFT_HEAVY. In the first case the local root is now LEFT_HEAVY. The overall height at local_root increases, so we leave increase set to **true**. (See Figure 11.19.)

```
switch (AVL_local_root->balance) {
  case AVLNode<Item_Type>::BALANCED :
  // local root is now left heavy
  AVL_local_root->balance = AVLNode<Item_Type>::LEFT_HEAVY;
  break;
```

In the second case, the local root is now balanced. In this case the overall height of the tree at local_root has not changed, so we set increase to **false**. (See Figure 11.20.)

```
case AVLNode<Item_Type>::RIGHT_HEAVY :
  // local root is now right heavy
  AVL_local_root->balance = AVLNode<Item_Type>::BALANCED;
  // Overall height of local root remains the same
  increase = false;
  break;
```

In the third case, the node at local_root was already LFFT_HEAVY, and now it is critically unbalanced. Thus we need to correct the balance. This is done by the function

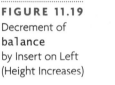

FIGURE 11.19
Decrement of
balance
by Insert on Left
(Height Increases)

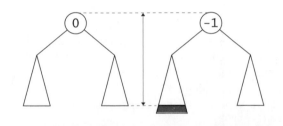

balance before insert is 0   balance is decreased due to insert;
Overall height increased

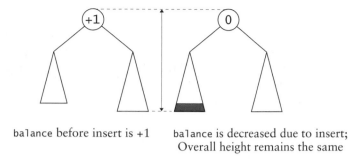

FIGURE 11.20
Decrement of
`balance`
by Insert on Left
(Height Does Not
Change)

balance before insert is +1   balance is decreased due to insert;
                                 Overall height remains the same

`rebalance_left`. The result of `rebalance_left` is that the overall height of the tree at `local_root` remains unchanged; thus we set `increase` to **false**.

```
case AVLNode<Item_Type>::LEFT_HEAVY :
  // local root is now critically unbalanced
  rebalance_left(local_root);
  increase = false;
  break;
```

After exiting the **switch** statement we return the saved `return_value`.

```
  } // End switch
} // End (if increase)
return return_value;
} // End (if item < local_root->data)
```

Next we test to see whether `local_root->data` is less than the `item`. The processing is symmetric with the case in which `item` is less than `local_root->data` and is left as an exercise.

If `item` is not less than `local_root->data` and `local_root->data` is not less than `item`, then they must be equal; we set `increase` to **false**, leave the `local_root` unchanged, and return **false** (algorithm Step 3).

```
else {
  increase = false;
  return false;
}
```

Initial Algorithm for `rebalance_left`

Function `rebalance_left` rebalances a left-heavy tree. Such a tree can be a Left-Left tree (fixed by a single right rotation) or a Left-Right tree (fixed by a left rotation followed by a right rotation). If its left subtree is right-heavy, we have a Left-Right case, so we first rotate left around the left subtree. Finally we rotate the tree right.

1.   **if** the left subtree has positive balance (Left-Right case)
2.   Rotate left around left subtree root.
3.   Rotate right.

The algorithm for `rebalance_right` is left as an exercise.

The Effect of Rotations on Balance

The rebalancing algorithm just presented is incomplete. So far we have focused on changes to the root reference and to the internal branches of the tree being balanced, but we have not adjusted the balances of the nodes. In the beginning of this section we showed that for a Left-Left tree, the balances of the new root node and of its right child are 0 after a right rotation; the balances of all other nodes are unchanged (see Figure 11.10).

The Left-Right case is more complicated. We made the following observation after studying the different cases.

The balance of the root is 0. If the critically unbalanced situation was due to an insertion into subtree b_L, the balance of the root's left child is 0 and the balance of the root's right child is +1 (Figure 11.14). For insertion into subtree b_R, the balance of the root's left child is −1, and the balance of the root's right child is 0 (Figure 11.17). So we need to change the balances of the new root node and both its left and right children; all other balances are unchanged. We will call insertion into subtree b_L the Left-Right-Left case and insertion into subtree b_R the Left-Right-Right case. There is a third case where the left-right subtree is balanced; this occurs when a left-right leaf is inserted into a subtree that has only a left child. In this case after the rotates are performed, the root, left child, and right child are all balanced.

Revised Algorithm for `rebalance_left`

Based on the foregoing discussion we can now develop the complete algorithm for `rebalance_left`, including the required balance changes. It is easier to store the new balance for each node before the rotation than after.

1. **if** the left subtree has a positive balance (Left-Right case)
2.   **if** the left-right subtree has a negative balance (Left-Right-Left case)
3.   Set the left subtree (new left subtree) balance to 0.
4.   Set the left-left subtree (new root) balance to 0.
5.   Set the local root (new right subtree) balance to +1.
        else if the left-right subtree has a positive balance (Left-Right-Right case)
6.   Set the left subtree (new left subtree) balance to −1.
7.   Set the left-left subtree (new root) balance to 0.
8.   Set the local root (new right subtree) balance to 0.
        else (Left-Right Balanced case)
9.   Set the left subtree (new left subtree) balance to 0.
10.   Set the left-left subtree (new root) balance to 0.
11.   Set the local root (new right subtree) balance to 0.
12.   Rotate the left subtree left.
    else (Left-Left case)
13.   Set the left subtree balance to 0.
14.   Set the local root balance to 0.
15. Rotate the local root right.

The algorithm for `rebalance_right` is left as an exercise.

Function **rebalance_left**

The code for rebalance_left is shown in Listing 11.4. First we test to see whether the left subtree is right-heavy (Left-Right case). If so, the Left-Right subtree is examined. Depending on its balance, the balances of the left subtree and local root are set as previously described in the algorithm. The rotations will reduce the overall height of the tree by 1. The left subtree is then rotated left, and then the tree is rotated right.

If the left child is LEFT_HEAVY, the rotation process will restore the balance to both the tree and its left subtree and reduce the overall height by 1; the balance for the left subtree and local root are both set to BALANCED. The tree is then rotated right to correct the imbalance.

....
LISTING 11.4
The rebalance_left Function

```
template<typename Item_Type>
  void AVL_Tree<Item_Type>::rebalance_left(BTNode<Item_Type>*& local_root)
{
  // Cast local_root to an AVLNode pointer
  AVLNode<Item_Type>* AVL_local_root =
    dynamic_cast<AVLNode<Item_Type>*>(local_root);
  // Obtain reference to the left child
  AVLNode<Item_Type>* left_child =
    dynamic_cast<AVLNode<Item_Type>*>(local_root->left);
  // See whether left-right-heavy
  if (left_child->balance == AVLNode<Item_Type>::RIGHT_HEAVY) {
    // Obtain a reference to the left-right child
    AVLNode<Item_Type>* left_right_child =
      dynamic_cast<AVLNode<Item_Type>*>(left_child->right);
    // Adjust the balances to be the new values after rotations are
    // performed
    if (left_right_child->balance == AVLNode<Item_Type>::LEFT_HEAVY) {
      left_child->balance = AVLNode<Item_Type>::BALANCED;
      left_right_child->balance = AVLNode<Item_Type>::BALANCED;
      AVL_local_root->balance = AVLNode<Item_Type>::RIGHT_HEAVY;
    } else if (left_right_child->balance
                == AVLNode<Item_Type>::BALANCED) {
      left_child->balance = AVLNode<Item_Type>::BALANCED;
      left_right_child->balance = AVLNode<Item_Type>::BALANCED;
      AVL_local_root->balance = AVLNode<Item_Type>::BALANCED;
    } else {
      left_child->balance = AVLNode<Item_Type>::LEFT_HEAVY;
      left_right_child->balance = AVLNode<Item_Type>::BALANCED;
      AVL_local_root->balance = AVLNode<Item_Type>::BALANCED;
    }
    // Perform left rotation
    rotate_left(local_root->left);
  } else { // Left-Left case
    /* In this case the left child (the new root) and the
       local root (new right child) will both be balanced
       after the rotation.
```

```
    */
    left_child->balance = AVLNode<Item_Type>::BALANCED;
    AVL_local_root->balance = AVLNode<Item_Type>::BALANCED;
  }
  // Finally rotate right
  rotate_right(local_root);
}
```

We also need a `rebalance_right` function that is symmetric with `rebalance_left` (that is, all `left`s are changed to `right`s and all `right`s are changed to `left`s). Coding of this function is left as an exercise.

Removal from an AVL Tree

When we remove an item from a left subtree, the balance of the local root is increased, and when we remove an item from the right subtree, the balance of the local root is decreased. We can adapt the algorithm for removal from a binary search tree to become an algorithm for removal from an AVL tree. We need to maintain a data field `decrease` that tells the previous level in the recursion that there was a decrease in the height of the subtree that was just returned from. (This data field is analogous to the data field `increase`, which is used in the insertion to indicate that the height of the subtree has increased.) We can then increment or decrement the local root balance. If the balance is outside the threshold, then the rebalance functions (`rebalance_left` or `rebalance_right`) are used to restore the balance.

We need to modify functions `rebalance_left` and `rebalance_right` so that they set the balance value correctly if the left (or right) subtree is balanced. This is also a left-left (right-right) case that is corrected by a single rotate. (See Figures 11.59 and 11.60 in the Programming Projects at the end of this chapter.) When a subtree changes from either left-heavy or right-heavy to balanced, then the height has decreased, and `decrease` should remain **true**; when the subtree changes from balanced to either left-heavy or right-heavy, then `decrease` should be reset to **false**. We also need to provide functions similar to the ones needed for removal in a binary search tree. Implementing removal is left as a programming project.

Also, observe that the effect of rotations is not only to restore balance but to decrease the height of the subtree being rotated. Thus, while only one call to `rebalance_left` or `rebalance_right` was required for insertion, during removal each recursive return could result in a further need to rebalance.

Performance of the AVL Tree

Because each subtree is kept as close to balanced as possible, one would expect that the AVL tree provides the expected $O(\log n)$ performance. Each subtree is allowed to be out of balance by ±1. Thus, the tree may contain some holes.

It can be shown that in the worst case the height of an AVL tree can be 1.44 times the height of a complete binary tree that contains the same number of items. However, this would still yield $O(\log n)$ performance, because we ignore constants.

The worst-case performance is very rare. Empirical tests (see, for example, Donald Knuth, *The Art of Computer Programming, Vol 3: Searching and Sorting* [Addison-

Wesley, 1973], p. 460) show that, on the average, $\log_2 n + 0.25$ comparisons are required to insert the *n*th item into an AVL tree. Thus the average performance is very close to that of the corresponding complete binary search tree.

EXERCISES FOR SECTION 11.2

SELF-CHECK

1. Show how the final AVL tree for the "The quick brown fox . . . dog" changes as you insert "apple", "cat", and "hat" in that order.
2. Show the effect of just rotating right on the tree in Figure 11.11. Why doesn't this fix the problem?
3. Build an AVL tree that inserts the integers 30, 40, 15, 25, 90, 80, 70, 85, 15, 72 in the given order.
4. Build the AVL tree from the sentence "Now is the time for all good men to come to the aid of their party."

PROGRAMMING

1. Program the `rebalance_right` function.
2. Program the code in the `insert` function for the case where `local_root->data < item`.

11.3 Red-Black Trees

We discuss another approach to keeping a tree balanced, called the *Red-Black tree*. Rudolf Bayer developed the Red-Black tree as a special case of his B-tree (the topic of Section 11.4); Leo Guibas and Robert Sedgewick refined the concept and introduced the color convention. A Red-Black tree maintains the following invariants:

1. A node is either red or black.
2. The root is always black.
3. A red node always has black children. (A NULL pointer is considered to refer to a black node.)
4. The number of black nodes in any path from the root to a leaf is the same.

Figure 11.21 shows an example of a Red-Black tree. Invariant 4 states that a Red-Black tree is always balanced because the root node's left and right subtrees must be the same black-height, where the black-height is determined by counting just black nodes. Notice that by the standards of the AVL tree this tree is out of balance and would be considered a Left-Right tree. However, by the standards of the Red-Black tree it is balanced, because there are two black nodes (counting the root) in any path from the root to a leaf. (We have one color in this textbook other than black, so we will use that color to indicate a red node.)

FIGURE 11.21
Red-Black Tree

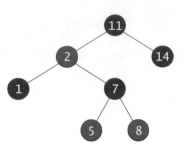

Insertion into a Red-Black Tree

The algorithm for insertion follows the same recursive search process used for all binary search trees to reach the insertion point. When a leaf is found, the new item is inserted, and it is initially given the color red, so invariant 4 will be maintained. If the parent is black, we are done.

However, if the parent is also red, then invariant 3 has been violated. Figure 11.22(a) shows the insertion of 35 as a red child of 30. If the parent's sibling is also red, then we can change the grandparent's color to red and change both the parent and parent's sibling to black. This restores invariant 3 but does not violate invariant 4. (See Figure 11.22(b).) If the root of the overall tree is now red, we can change it to black to restore invariant 2, and still maintain invariant 4 (the heights of all paths to a leaf are increased by 1). (See Figure 11.22(c).)

If we insert a value with a red parent, but that parent does not have a red sibling (see Figure 11.23(a)), then we change the color of the grandparent to red and the parent to black (see Figure 11.23(b)). Now we have violated invariant 4, as there are more black nodes on the side of the parent. We correct this by rotating about the grandparent so that the parent moves into the position where the grandparent was, thus restoring invariant 4 (see Figure 11.23(c)).

FIGURE 11.22
Insertion into a
Red-Black Tree, Case 1

FIGURE 11.23
Insertion into a
Red-Black Tree, Case 2

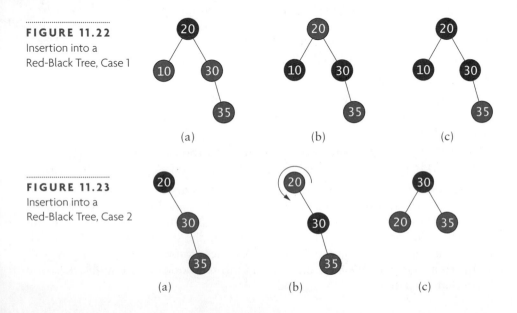

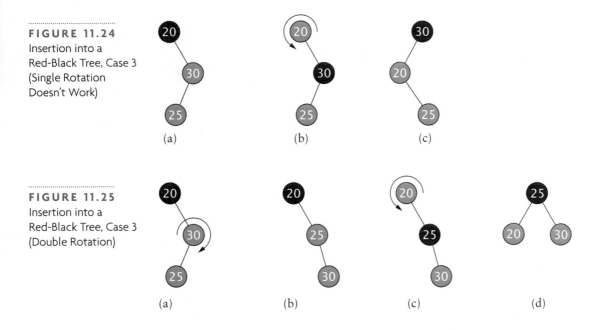

FIGURE 11.24
Insertion into a
Red-Black Tree, Case 3
(Single Rotation
Doesn't Work)

FIGURE 11.25
Insertion into a
Red-Black Tree, Case 3
(Double Rotation)

The preceding maneuver works only if the inserted value is on the same side of its parent as the parent is to the grandparent. Figure 11.24(a) shows 25 inserted as the left child of 30, which is the right child of 20. If we change the color of the grandparent (20) to red and the parent (30) to black (see Figure 11.24(b)) and then rotate (see Figure 11.24(c)), we are still left with a red parent–red child combination. Before changing the color and rotating about the grandparent level, we must first rotate about the parent so that the red child is on the same side of its parent as the parent is to the grandparent (see Figure 11.25(b)). We can then change the colors (see Figure 11.25(c)) and rotate (see Figure 11.25(d)).

More than one of these cases can occur. Figure 11.26 shows the insertion of the value 4 into the Red-Black tree of Figure 11.21. Upon return from the insertion to the parent (node 5), it may be discovered that a red node now has a red child, which is a violation of invariant 3. If this node's sibling (node 8) is also red (case 1), then they must have a black parent. If we make the parent red (node 7) and both of the parent's children black, invariant 4 is preserved, and the problem is shifted up, as shown in Figure 11.27.

Looking at Figure 11.27 we see that 7 is red and that its parent, 2, is also red. However, we can't simply change 2's color as we did before, because 2's sibling, 14, is black. This problem will require one or two rotations to correct.

Because the red child (7) is not on the same side of its parent (2) as the parent is to the grandparent (11), this is an example of Case 3. We rotate the tree left (around node 2) so that the red node 2 is on the same side of red node 7 as node 7 is to the grandparent (11) (see Figure 11.28). We now change node 7 to black and node 11 to red (Figure 11.29) and rotate right around node 11, restoring the balance of black nodes as shown in Figure 11.30.

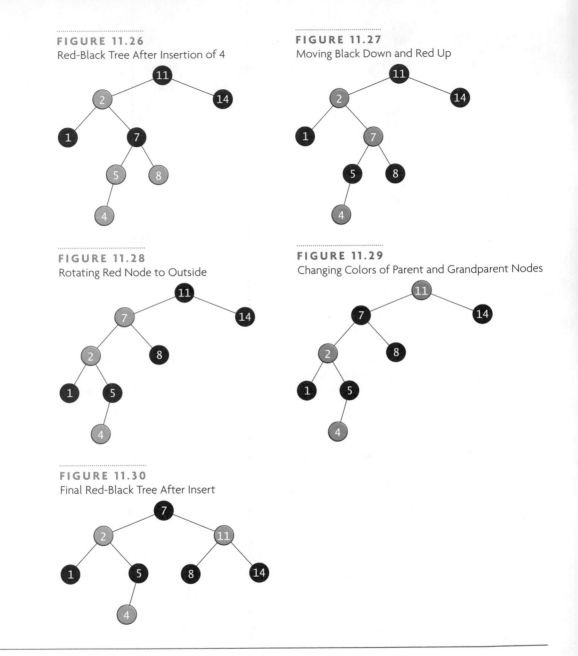

FIGURE 11.26
Red-Black Tree After Insertion of 4

FIGURE 11.27
Moving Black Down and Red Up

FIGURE 11.28
Rotating Red Node to Outside

FIGURE 11.29
Changing Colors of Parent and Grandparent Nodes

FIGURE 11.30
Final Red-Black Tree After Insert

EXAMPLE 11.2 We will now build the Red-Black tree for the sentence "The quick brown fox jumps over the lazy dog."

We start by inserting *The*, *quick*, and *brown*.

The parent of *brown* (*quick*) is red, but the sibling of *quick* is black (NULL nodes are considered black), so we have an example of Case 2 or Case 3. Because the child is not on the same side of the parent as the parent is to the grandparent, this is Case 3. We first rotate right about *quick* to get the child on the same side of the parent as the parent is to the grandparent.

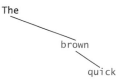

We then change the colors of *The* and *brown*.

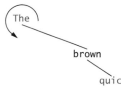

Then we rotate left about *The*.

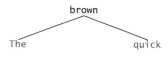

Next we insert *fox*.

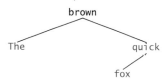

We see that *fox* has a red parent (*quick*) whose sibling is also red (*The*). This is a Case 1 insertion, so we can change the color of the parent and its sibling to black and the grandparent to red.

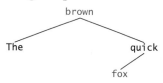

Since the root is red, we can change it to black without violating the rule of balanced black nodes.

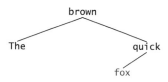

Now we add *jumps*, which gives us another Case 3 insertion.

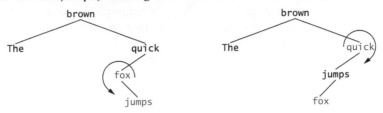

This triggers a double rotation. First rotate left about *fox* and change the color of its parent *jumps* to black and its grandparent *quick* to red. Next, rotate right about *quick*.

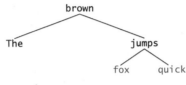

Next we insert *over*.

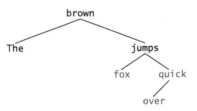

Because *quick* and *fox* are red, we have a Case 1 insertion, so we can move the black in *jumps* down, changing the color of *jumps* to red and *fox* and *quick* to black.

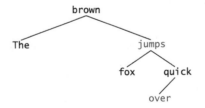

Next we add *the*. No changes are required, because its parent is black.

When compared to the corresponding AVL tree, this tree looks out of balance. But the black nodes are in balance (2 in each path).

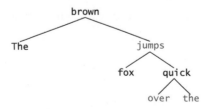

Now we insert *lazy*.

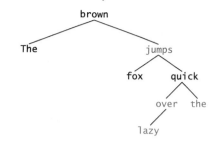

Because *over* and *the* are both red, we can move the black at *quick* down (Case 1).

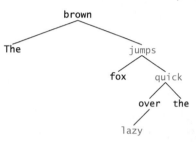

But now *quick* is a red node with a red parent (*jumps*), but whose sibling is black (*The*). Because *quick* and *jumps* are both right children, this is an example of Case 2. This triggers a rotate left around *brown*.

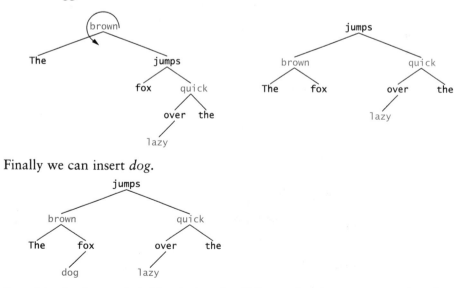

Finally we can insert *dog*.

Surprisingly, the result is identical to the AVL tree for the same input, but the intermediate steps were very different.

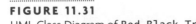

FIGURE 11.31
UML Class Diagram of Red_Black_Tree

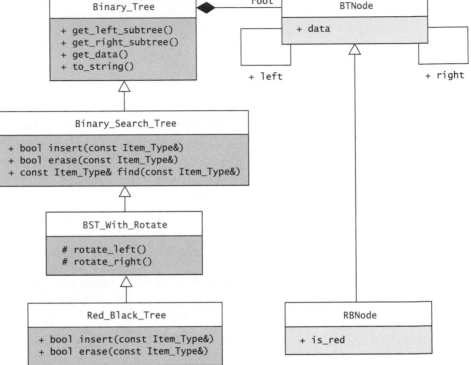

Implementation of Red-Black Tree Class

We begin by deriving the class Red_Black_Tree from BST_With_Rotate (see Listing 11.1). Figure 11.31 is a UML class diagram showing the relationship between Red_Black_Tree and BST_With_Rotate. The Red_Black_Tree class overrides the insert and erase functions. The class BTNode is extended with the RBNode class. This class has the additional data field is_red to indicate red nodes. Listing 11.5 shows the RBNode class.

LISTING 11.5
The RBNode Class

```
#ifndef RBNODE_H_
#define RBNODE_H_
#include <sstream>

/** A node for a Red-Black Tree. */
template<typename Item_Type>
  struct RBNode : public BTNode<Item_Type> {

  // Additional Data Field
  bool is_red;
```

```
// Constructor
RBNode(const Item_Type& the_data, BTNode<Item_Type>* left_val = NULL,
       BTNode<Item_Type>* right_val = NULL) :
  BTNode<Item_Type>(the_data, left_val, right_val), is_red(true) {}

// Destructor (to avoid warning message)
virtual ~RBNode() {}

// to_string
virtual std::string to_string() const {
  std::ostringstream os;
  if (is_red)
    os << "  red: " << this->data;
  else
    os << " black: " << this->data;
  return os.str();
}
}; // End RBNode

#endif
```

Algorithm for Red-Black Tree Insertion

Insert *over*

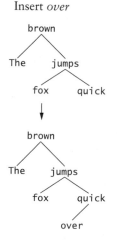

The foregoing outline of the Red-Black tree insertion algorithm is from the point of view of the node being inserted. It can be, and has been, implemented using a data structure that has a pointer to the parent of each node stored in it so that, given a pointer to a node, one can access the parent, grandparent, and the parent's sibling (the node's aunt or uncle).

We are going to present a recursive algorithm where the need for fixups is detected from the grandparent level. This algorithm has one additional difference from the algorithm as presented in the foregoing examples: Whenever a black node with two red children is detected on the way down the tree, it is changed to red and the children are changed to black (for example, *jumps* and its children in the figure at left). If this change causes a problem, it is fixed on the way back up. This modification simplifies the logic a bit and improves the performance of the algorithm. This algorithm is also based on the algorithm for inserting into a binary search tree that was described in Chapter 8.

Algorithm for Red-Black Tree Insertion

  1.   **if** the root is NULL
  2.   Insert a new Red-Black node and color it black.
  3.   Return **true.**
  4.   **else if** the item is equal to root->data
  5.   The item is already in the tree; return **false.**
  6.   **else if** the item is less than root->data
  7.   **if** the left subtree is NULL
  8.   Insert a new Red-Black node as the left subtree and color it red.
  9.   Return **true.**
10.   **else**

11.		**if** both the left child and the right child are red
12.		Change the color of the children to black and change local root to red.
13.		Recursively insert the item into the left subtree.
14.		**if** the left child is now red
15.		**if** the left grandchild is now red (grandchild is an "outside" node)
16.		Change the color of the left child to black and change the local root to red.
17.		Rotate the local root right.
18.		**else if** the right grandchild is now red (grandchild is an "inside" node)
19.		Rotate the left child left.
20.		Change the color of the left child to black and change the local root to red.
21.		Rotate the local root right.
22.	**else**	
23.		Item is greater than root->data; process is symmetric and is left as an exercise.
24.	**if** the local root is the root of the tree	
25.		Force its color to be black.

In C++ we can pass arguments to functions by reference. This means that a change made to the parameter's value by the function results in a change to the argument object that was passed to the function. We will pass the local root of a Red-Black tree by reference as an argument to the insert function. Thus, in Step 8, we replace the NULL pointer to the left subtree with the inserted node.

If the left subtree is not NULL (Steps 10 through 21), we recursively apply the algorithm (Step 13). But before we do so, we see whether both children are red. If they are, we change the local root to red and change the children to black (Steps 11 and 12). (If the local root's parent was red, this condition will be detected at that level during the return from the recursion.)

Upon return from the recursion (Step 14), we see whether the local root's left child is now red. If it is, we need to check its children (the local root's grandchildren). If one of them is red, then we have a red parent with a red child, and a rotation is necessary. If the left grandchild is red, a single rotation will solve the problem (Steps 15 through 17). If the right grandchild is red, a double rotation is necessary (Steps 18 through 21). Note that there may be only one grandchild or no grandchildren. However, if there are two grandchildren, they cannot both be red, because they would have been changed to black by Steps 11 and 12, as described in the previous paragraph.

The `insert` Starter Function

The `insert` starter function checks for a NULL root and inserts a single new node. Since the root of a Red-Black tree is always black, we set the newly inserted node to black.

```
template<typename Item_Type>
  bool Red_Black_Tree<Item_Type>::insert(const Item_Type& item) {
  if (this->root == NULL) {
    RBNode<Item_Type>* new_root = new RBNode<Item_Type>(item);
    new_root->is_red = false;
    this->root = new_root;
    return true;
  }
```

Otherwise the recursive `insert` function is called. This function takes two parameters: the node that is the local root of the subtree into which the item is to be inserted, and the item to be inserted. Upon return the value of the first parameter is modified to be the node that is the root of the subtree that now contains the inserted item.

The root is replaced by the recursive `insert` function, the color of the root is set to black, and the return value from the recursive `insert` function is returned to the caller.

```
  else {
    // Call the recursive insert function.
    bool return_value = insert(this->root, item);
    // Force the root to be black
    set_red(this->root, false);
    return return_value;
  }
}
```

The Recursive `insert` Function

The recursive `insert` function begins by comparing the item to be inserted with the data field of the local root. If it is less, then `local_root->left` is checked to see whether it is NULL. If so, then we insert a new node and return (Steps 7 through 9).

```
if (item < local_root->data) {
  if (local_root->left == NULL) {
    local_root->left = new RBNode<Item_Type>(item);
    return true;
  }
```

Otherwise, check to see whether both children are red. If so, we make them black and change the local root to red. This is done by the function `move_black_down`. Then we recursively call the `insert` function, using `root->left` as the new local root (Steps 11–13).

```
  else {
    // Check for two red children, swap colors if found
    move_black_down(local_root);
    // Recusively insert into the left subtree
    bool return_value = insert(local_root->left, item);
```

It is upon return from the recursive `insert` that things get interesting. Upon return from the recursive call, `local_root->left` refers to the parent of a Red-Black subtree that may be violating the rule against adjacent red nodes. Therefore we check the left child to see whether it is red (Step 14).

```
// See if the left-child is red
if (is_red(local_root->left)) {
```

If the left child is red, then we need to check its two children. First we check the left grandchild (Step 15).

```
if (is_red(local_root->left->left)) {
    // Child and left-left grandchild are both red
```

If the left-left grandchild is red, we have detected a violation of invariant 3 (no consecutive red children), and we have a left-left case. Thus we change colors and perform a single rotation, returning the resulting local root to the caller (Steps 16–17).

```
// Need to change colors and rotate
set_red(local_root->left, false);
set_red(local_root, true);
rotate_right(local_root);
return return_value;
```

If the left grandchild is not red, we then check the right grandchild. If it is red, the process is symmetric to the preceding case, except that a double rotation will be required (Steps 18–21).

```
// Else check right grandchild
else if (is_red(local_root->left->right)) {
    // This will require a double rotation.
    set_red(local_root->left->right, false);
    set_red(local_root, true);
    rotate_left(local_root->left);
    rotate_right(local_root);
    return return_value;
}
```

If upon return from the recursive call the left child is black, the return is immediate, and all of this complicated logic is skipped. Similarly, if neither the left nor right grandchild is also red, nothing is done.

If the item is not less than `local_root->data`, we check to see whether `local_root->data` is less than the item. The process is symmetric and is left as an exercise (Step 23 and Programming Exercise 1).

If they are equal (both comparisons fail), then the item is already in the tree; **false** is returned (algorithm Step 5).

The Functions `is_red` and `set_red`

Because the pointers in the nodes are of type `BTNode<Item_Type>*`, but are in fact `RBNode<Item_Type>*`, we need to use the `dynamic_cast` operator to cast the pointers to the proper type to be able to access the `is_red` data field. To facilitate this we define two functions: one to determine whether a node is red and the other to set the value of the `is_red` field. These are shown below.

```
/** Determine whether a node is red.
    @param node A pointer to a BTNode<Item_Type>
    @return true if node points to a RBNode<Item_Type> that is red
*/
static bool is_red(BTNode<Item_Type>* node) {
  RBNode<Item_Type>* RB_node =
    dynamic_cast<RBNode<Item_Type>*>(node);
  if (RB_node != NULL) {
    return RB_node->is_red;
  } else {
    return false;
  }
}


/** Set the color of a node.
    @param node A pointer to a BTNode<Item_Type>
    @param red A bool value that is true if the
           node is to be set red, false if to be set black
*/
static void set_red(BTNode<Item_Type>* node, bool red) {
  RBNode<Item_Type>* RB_node =
    dynamic_cast<RBNode<Item_Type>*>(node);
  if (RB_node != NULL) {
    RB_node->is_red = red;
  }
}
```

Removal from a Red-Black Tree

Removal follows the algorithm for a binary search tree that was described in Chapter 8. Recall that we remove a node only if it is a leaf or if it has only one child. Otherwise, the node that contains the inorder predecessor of the value being removed is the one that is removed. If the node that is removed is red, there is nothing further that must be done, because red nodes do not affect a Red-Black tree's balance. If the node to be removed is black and has a red child, then the red child takes its place, and we color it black. However, if we remove a black leaf, then the black height is now out of balance. There are several cases that must be considered. We will describe them in Programming Project 6 at the end of this chapter.

Performance of a Red-Black Tree

It can be shown that the upper limit of the height for a Red-Black tree is $2 \log_2 n + 2$, which is still $O(\log n)$. As with the AVL tree, the average performance is significantly better than the worst-case performance. Empirical studies (see Robert Sedgewick, *Algorithms in C++*, 3rd edition [Addison-Wesley, 1998], p. 570) show that the average cost of a search in a Red-Black tree built from random values is $1.002 \log_2 n$. Thus, both the AVL and Red-Black trees give performance that is close to that of a complete binary search tree.

EXERCISES FOR SECTION 11.3

SELF-CHECK

1. Show how the Red-Black tree for the "The quick brown fox . . . dog" changes as you insert "apple", "cat", and "hat" in that order.
2. Insert the numbers 6, 3, and 0 in the Red-Black tree in Figure 11.21.
3. Build the Red-Black tree from the sentence "Now is the time for all good men to come to the aid of their party." Is it the same as the AVL tree?

PROGRAMMING

1. Program the insert function for the case where local_root->data is less than the item.

11.4 2-3 Trees

In this section we begin our discussion of three nonbinary trees. We begin with the *2-3 tree*, named for the number of possible children from each node (either two or three). A 2-3 tree is made up of nodes designated as *2-nodes* and *3-nodes*. A 2-node is the same as a binary search tree node: It consists of a data field and references to two children, one child containing values less than the data field and the other child containing values greater than the data field. A 3-node contains two data fields, ordered so that the first is less than the second, and references to three children: one child containing values less than the first data field, one child containing values between the two data fields, and one child containing values greater than the second data field.

Figure 11.32 shows the general forms of a 2-node (data item is x) and a 3-node (data items are x and y). The children are represented as subtrees. Figure 11.33 shows an example of a 2-3 tree. There are only two 3-nodes in this tree (the right and right-right nodes); the rest are 2-nodes.

A 2-3 tree has the additional property that all of the leaves are at the lowest level. This is how the 2-3 tree maintains balance. This will be further explained when we study the insertion and removal algorithms.

FIGURE 11.32
2-Node and 3-Node

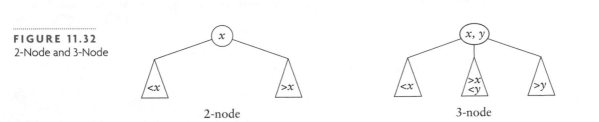

FIGURE 11.33
Example of a 2-3 Tree

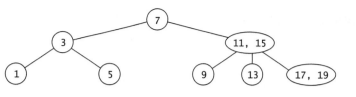

Searching a 2-3 Tree

Searching a 2-3 tree is very similar to searching a binary search tree.

1.   **if** the local root is NULL
2.   Return NULL; the item is not in the tree.
3.   **else if** this is a 2-node
4.   **if** the item is equal to the data1 field
5.   Return the data1 field.
6.   **else if** the item is less than the data1 field
7.   Recursively search the left subtree.
8.   **else**
9.   Recursively search the right subtree.
10.   **else** // *This is a 3-node*
11.   **if** the item is equal to the data1 field
12.   Return the data1 field.
13.   **else if** the item is equal to the data2 field
14.   Return the data2 field.
15.   **else if** the item is less than the data1 field
16.   Recursively search the left subtree.
17.   **else if** the item is less than the data2 field
18.   Recursively search the middle subtree.
19.   **else**
20.   Recursively search the right subtree.

EXAMPLE 11.3   To search for 13 in Figure 11.33, we would compare 13 with 7 and see that it is greater than 7, so we would search the node that contains 11 and 15. Because 13 is greater than 11 but less than 15, we would next search the middle child, which contains 13: success! The search path is shown in color in Figure 11.34.

FIGURE 11.34
Searching a 2-3 Tree

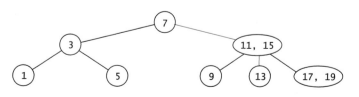

Inserting an Item into a 2-3 Tree

A 2-3 tree maintains balance by being built from the bottom up, not the top down. Instead of hanging a new node onto a leaf, we insert the new node into a leaf, as discussed in the following paragraphs. We search for the insertion node using the normal process for a 2-3 tree.

Inserting into a 2-Node Leaf

Figure 11.35, left, shows a 2-3 tree with three 2-nodes. We want to insert 15. Because the leaf we are inserting into is a 2-node, then we can insert 15 directly, creating a new 3-node (Figure 11.35 right).

Inserting into a 3-Node Leaf with a 2-Node Parent

If we want to insert a number larger than 7 (say 17), that number will be virtually inserted into the 3-node at the bottom right of the tree, giving the virtual node in gray in Figure 11.36. Because a node can't store three values, the middle value will propagate up to the 2-node parent, and the virtual node will be split into two new 2-nodes containing the smallest and largest values. Because the parent is a 2-node, it will be changed to a 3-node, and it will reference the three 2-nodes, as shown in Figure 11.37.

Let's now insert the numbers 5, 10, and 20. Each of these would go into one of the leaf nodes (all 2-nodes), changing them to 3-nodes, as shown in Figure 11.38.

Inserting into a 3-Node Leaf with a 3-Node Parent

In the tree in Figure 11.38 all the leaf nodes are full, so if we insert any other number, one of the leaf nodes will need to be virtually split, and its middle value will propagate to the parent. Because the parent is already a 3-node, it will also need to be split.

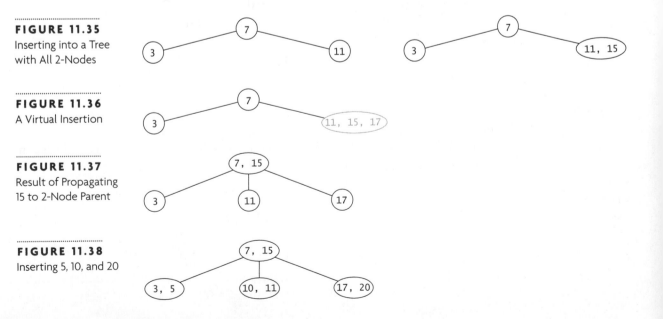

FIGURE 11.35
Inserting into a Tree with All 2-Nodes

FIGURE 11.36
A Virtual Insertion

FIGURE 11.37
Result of Propagating 15 to 2-Node Parent

FIGURE 11.38
Inserting 5, 10, and 20

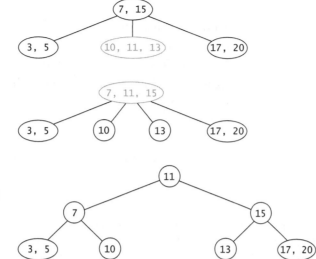

FIGURE 11.39
Virtually Inserting 13

FIGURE 11.40
Virtually Inserting 11

FIGURE 11.41
Result of Making 11 the
New Root

For example, if we were to insert 13, it would be virtually inserted into the leaf node with values 10 and 11 (see Figure 11.39). This would result in two new 2-nodes with values 10 and 13, and 11 would propagate up to be virtually inserted in the 3-node at the root (see Figure 11.40). Because the root is full, it would split into two new 2-nodes with values 7 and 15, and 11 would propagate up to be inserted in a new root node. The net effect is an increase in the overall height of the tree, as shown in Figure 11.41.

We summarize these observations in the following insertion algorithm.

Algorithm for Insertion into a 2-3 Tree

1.　　**if** the root is NULL
2.　　　　Create a new 2-node that contains the new item.
3.　　**else if** the item is in the local root
4.　　　　Return **false**.
5.　　**else if** the local root is a leaf
6.　　　　**if** the local root is a 2-node
7.　　　　　　Expand the 2-node to a 3-node and insert the item.
8.　　　　**else**
9.　　　　　　Split the 3-node (creating two 2-nodes) and pass the new parent and right child back up the recursion chain.
10.　　**else**
11.　　　　**if** the item is less than the smaller item in the local root
12.　　　　　　Recursively insert into the left child.
13.　　　　**else if** the local root is a 2-node
14.　　　　　　Recursively insert into the right child.
15.　　　　**else if** the item is less than the larger item in the local root
16.　　　　　　Recursively insert into the middle child.

17.   **else**
18.   Recursively insert into the right child.
19.   **if** a new parent was passed up from the previous level of recursion
20.   **if** the new parent will be the tree root
21.   Create a 2-node whose data item is the passed-up parent, left child is the old root, and right child is the passed-up child. This 2-node becomes the new root.
22.   **else**
23.   Recursively insert the new parent at the local root.
24.   Return **true**.

EXAMPLE 11.4   We will create a 2-3 tree using "The quick brown fox jumps over the lazy dog." The initial root contains *The*, *quick*. If we insert *brown*, we will split the root. Because *brown* is between *The* and *quick*, it gets passed up and will become the new root.

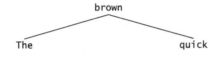

We now insert *fox* as the left neighbor of *quick*, creating a new 3-node.

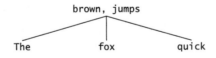

Next, *jumps* is inserted between *fox* and *quick*, thus splitting this 3-node, and *jumps* gets passed up and inserted next to *brown*.

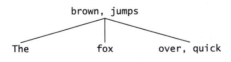

Then *over* is inserted next to *quick*.

Now we insert *the*. It will be inserted to the right of *over*, *quick*, splitting that node, and *quick* will be passed up. It will be inserted to the right of *brown*, *jumps*, splitting that node as well, causing *jumps* to be passed up to the new root.

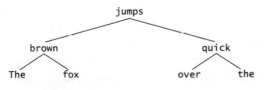

Finally, *lazy* and *dog* are inserted next to *over* and *fox*, respectively.

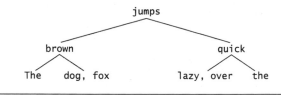

Analysis of 2-3 Trees and Comparison with Balanced Binary Trees

The 2-3 tree resulting from the preceding example is a balanced tree of height 3 that requires fewer complicated manipulations. There were no rotations, as were needed to build the AVL and Red-Black trees, which were both height 4. The number of items that a 2-3 tree of height h can hold is between $2^h - 1$ (all 2-nodes) and $3^h - 1$ (all 3-nodes). Therefore, the height of a 2-3 tree is between $\log_3 n$ and $\log_2 n$. Thus the search time is $O(\log n)$, since logarithms are all related by a constant factor, and constant factors are ignored in big-O notation.

Removal from a 2-3 Tree

Removing an item from a 2-3 tree is somewhat the reverse of the insertion process. To remove an item, we must first search for it. If the item to be removed is in a leaf with two items, we simply delete it. If the item to be removed is not in a leaf, we remove it by swapping it with its inorder predecessor in a leaf node and deleting it from the leaf node. If removing a node from a leaf causes the leaf to become empty, items from the sibling and parent can be redistributed into that leaf, or the leaf may be merged with its parent and sibling nodes. In the latter case, the height of the tree may decrease. We illustrate these cases next.

If we remove the item 13 from the tree shown in Figure 11.42, its node becomes empty, and item 15 in the parent node has no left child. We can merge 15 and its right child to form the virtual leaf node {15, 17, 19}. Item 17 moves up to the parent node; item 15 is the new left child of 17 (see Figure 11.43).

FIGURE 11.42
Removing 13 from a
2-3 Tree

FIGURE 11.43
2-3 Tree After Redistribution of Nodes
Resulting from Removal

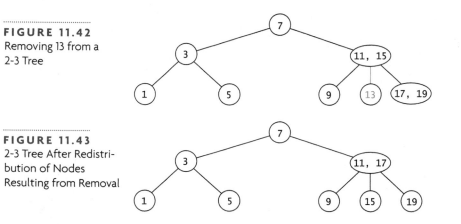

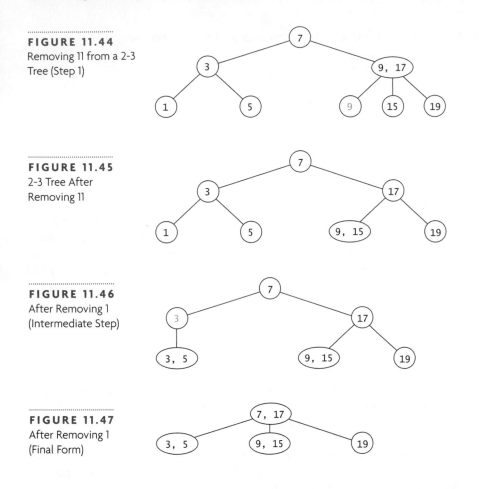

FIGURE 11.44
Removing 11 from a 2-3
Tree (Step 1)

FIGURE 11.45
2-3 Tree After
Removing 11

FIGURE 11.46
After Removing 1
(Intermediate Step)

FIGURE 11.47
After Removing 1
(Final Form)

We next remove 11 from the 2-3 tree. Because this is not a leaf, we replace it with its predecessor, 9, as shown in Figure 11.44. We now have the case where the left leaf node of 9 has become empty. So we merge 9 into its right leaf node as shown in Figure 11.45.

Finally, let's consider the case in which we remove the value 1 from Figure 11.45. First, 1's parent (3) and its right sibling (5) are merged to form a 3-node, as shown in Figure 11.46. This has the effect of deleting 3 from the next higher level. Therefore, the process repeats, and 3's parent (7) and 7's right child (17) are merged as shown in Figure 11.47. The merged node becomes the root.

The 2-3 tree served as an inspiration for the more general 2-3-4 tree and B-tree. Rather than show an implementation of the 2-3 tree, which has some rather messy complications, we will describe and implement the more general 2-3-4 tree in the next section.

EXERCISES FOR SECTION 11.4

SELF-CHECK

1. Show the following tree after inserting each of the following values one at a time: 1, 4, 9.

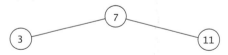

2. Show the following tree after inserting each of the following one at a time: 9, 13.

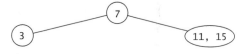

3. Show the 2-3 tree that would be built for the sentence "Now is the time for all good men to come to the aid of their party."

11.5 2-3-4 and B-Trees

The 2-3 tree was the inspiration for the more-general B-tree, which allows up to n children per node, where n may be a very large number. The B-tree was designed for building indexes to very large databases stored on a hard disk.

The 2-3-4 tree is a specialization of the B-tree. It is called a specialization because it is basically a B-tree with n equal to 4. The 2-3-4 tree is also interesting because the Red-Black tree can be considered a 2-3-4 tree in a binary-tree format.

2-3-4 Trees

2-3-4 trees expand on the idea of 2-3 trees by adding the *4-node* (see Figure 11.48). This is a node with three data items and four children. Figure 11.49 shows an example of a 2-3-4 tree.

FIGURE 11.48
2-, 3-, and 4-Nodes

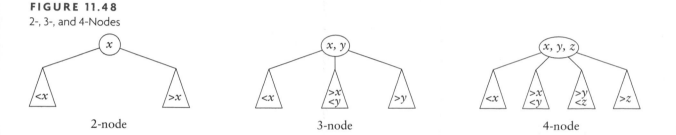

FIGURE 11.49
Example of a 2-3-4 Tree

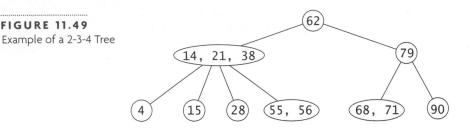

The addition of this third data item simplifies the insertion logic. We can search for the leaf in the same way as for a 2-3 tree. If a 4-node is encountered at any point, we will split it, as discussed subsequently. Therefore, when we reach a leaf, we are guaranteed that there will be room to insert the item.

For the 2-3-4 tree shown in Figure 11.49, a number larger than 62 would be inserted in a leaf node in the right subtree. A number between 63 and 78, inclusive, would be inserted in the 3-node (68, 71), making it a 4-node. A number larger than 79 would be inserted in the 2-node (90), making it a 3-node.

When inserting a number smaller than 62 (say, 25), we would encounter the 4-node (14, 21, 38). We would immediately split it into two 2-nodes and insert the middle value (21) into the parent (62) as shown in Figure 11.50. Doing this guarantees that there will be room to insert the new item. We perform the split from the parent level and immediately insert the middle item from the split child in the parent node. Because we are guaranteed that the parent is not a 4-node, we will always have room to do this. We do not need to propagate a child or its parent back up the recursion chain. Consequently the recursion becomes tail recursion.

In this example, splitting the 4-node was not necessary. We could have merely inserted 25 as the left neighbor of 28. However, if the leaf being inserted into was a 4-node, we would have had to split it and propagate the middle item back up the recursion chain, just as we did for the 2-3 tree. The choice always to split a 4-node when it is encountered while searching for an insertion spot results in prematurely splitting some nodes, but it simplifies the algorithm and has minimal impact on the overall performance.

Now we can insert 25 as the left neighbor of 28 as shown in Figure 11.51.

FIGURE 11.50
Result of Splitting a
4-Node

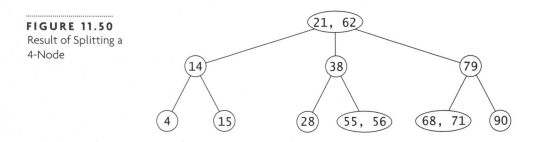

FIGURE 11.51
2-3-4 Tree After
Inserting 25

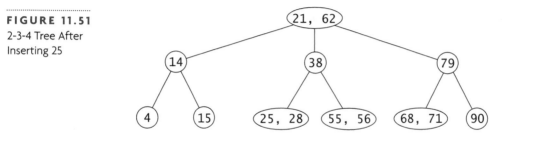

EXAMPLE 11.5 We will again use the sentence "The quick brown fox jumps over the lazy dog." After the first three words are inserted, the root contains *The*, *brown*, and *quick*.

```
The, brown, quick
```

This is a 4-node. Prior to inserting *fox*, this node is split.

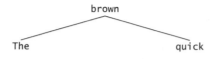

Because *fox* is larger than *brown*, we recursively apply the insert to *quick*. Because *fox* is smaller than *quick*, we obtain the following tree.

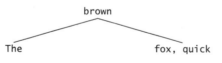

Because *jumps* is larger than *brown* and between *fox* and *quick*, we insert it as follows.

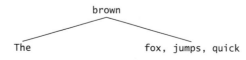

Next, we consider *over*. This is larger than *brown*. The right child of *brown*, however, is a 4-node, so we split it and insert its middle value, *jumps*, next to *brown*.

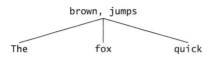

Because *over* is larger than *jumps*, we insert it next to *quick*.

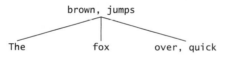

The next word, *the*, gets inserted to the right of *quick*.

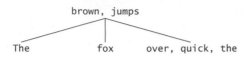

The next word, *lazy*, is larger than *jumps*, and we find that the right child of the node containing *jumps* is a 4-node, so it gets split.

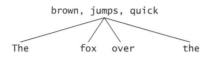

Now we need to insert *lazy*. However, before we insert *lazy*, we observe that the root is a 4-node. So we immediately split it.

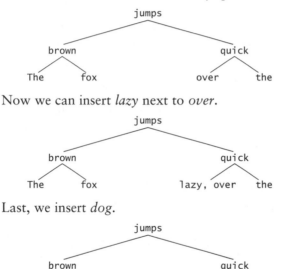

Now we can insert *lazy* next to *over*.

Last, we insert *dog*.

Implementation of the Two_Three_Four_Tree Class

Instead of defining specialized nodes for a 2-3-4 tree, we can define a general node that holds up to CAP - 1 data items and CAP children, where CAP is a template parameter. The information will be stored in the array data of size CAP - 1, and the pointers to the children will be stored in the array child of size CAP. The information values will be sorted so that data[0] < data[1] < data[2] < .... The data field size will indicate how many data values are in the node. The children will be associated with the data values such that child[0] points to the subtree with items smaller than data[0], child[size] points to the subtree with items larger than data[size - 1], and for 0 < i < size, child[i] points to items greater than data[i - 1] and smaller than data[i].

We show the class Node for a 2-3-4 tree next. Notice that the data field root is declared to be of type Node<4>*.

```
/** The reference to the root. */
Node<4>* root;
```

This is because for the 2-3-4 tree the node has a CAP of 4. In the next section we discuss how this can be generalized to any value. Note also that while the Node is generalized, the algorithm and code for the Two_Three_Four_Tree is not.

Listing 11.6 shows the data field root and inner class Node. The algorithm follows.

LISTING 11.6
The Data Fields and Constructor of Class Two_Three_Four_Tree and Class Node

```
template<typename Item_Type>
  class Two_Three_Four_Tree {

  // Inner Class
  /** A Node represents a node in a 2-3-4 tree. CAP represents
      the maxumum number of children. For a 2-3-4 tree CAP is 4.
      This class has no functions; it is merely a container of
      private data.
  */
  template<size_t CAP>
    struct Node {

      /** The number of data items in this node */
      size_t size;

      /** The information */
      Item_Type data[CAP - 1];

      /** The links to the children. child[i] refers to
          the subtree of children < data[i] for i < size
          and to the subtree of children > data[size - 1]
          for i == size. */
      Node* child[CAP];

      Node() {
        for (size_t i = 0; i < CAP; i++) {
          if (i < CAP - 1)
            data[i] = Item_Type();
          child[i] = NULL;
        }
      }
  };

  // Data Fields
  /** The reference to the root. */
  Node<4>* root;

  public:
  /** Create an empty Two_Three_Four_Tree */
  Two_Three_Four_Tree() : root(NULL) {}

  ...
```

Algorithm for Insertion into a 2-3-4 Tree

1. **if** the root is NULL
2.   Create a new 2-node with the item.
3.   Return **true**.
4. **if** the root is a 4-node
5.   Split it into two 2-nodes, making the middle value the new root.
6. Set index to 0.
7. **while** the item is less than data[index]
8.   Increment index.
9. **if** the item is equal to data[index]
10.   Return **false**.

    else

11.   **if** child[index] is NULL
12.   Insert the item into the local root at index, moving the existing data and child values to the right.

      else if child[index] does not reference a 4-node

13.   Recursively continue the search with child[index] as the local root.

      else

14.   Split the node referenced by child[index].
15.   Insert the parent into the local root at index.
16.   **if** the new parent is equal to the item, return **false**.
17.   **if** the item is less than the new parent
18.   Recursively continue the search with child[index] as the local root.

        else

19.   Recursively continue the search with child[index + 1] as the local root.

The **insert** Starter Function

If the root is NULL, then a new 2-node is created and becomes the root.

```
/** Insert an object into the tree.
    @param obj The object to be inserted
    @return true if the item was inserted
*/
bool insert(const Item_Type& item) {
  if (root == NULL) {
    root = new Node<4>;
    root->data[0] = item;
    root->size = 1;
    return true;
  }
```

Otherwise, we see whether the root is a 4-node. If it is, then it is split, and the new parent becomes the new root (Step 5).

```
    if (root->size == 3) {
      Item_Type new_parent;
      Node<4>* new_child;
      split_node(root, new_parent, new_child);
      Node<4>* new_root = new Node<4>;
      new_root->data[0] = new_parent;
      new_root->child[0] = root;
      new_root->child[1] = new_child;
      new_root->size = 1;
    }
```

Then we recursively insert starting at the root.

```
    return insert(root, item);
  }
```

Recursive **insert** Function

We begin by finding index such that the value to be inserted is less than or equal to data[index] or index is equal to the number of data items in the node (Steps 6–8) .

```
  /** Recursive function to insert an object into the tree.
      @param local_root The local root
      @param item The item to be inserted
      @return true if the item was inserted,
              false if the item is already in the tree
  */
  bool insert(Node<4>* local_root, const Item_Type& item) {
    size_t index = 0;
    while (index < local_root->size
           && local_root->data[index] < item) {
      index++;
    }
    // index == local_root->size or item <= local_root.data[index]
```

Next we see whether the item is equal to data[index]. If so, we return **false** (Steps 9, 10).

```
    if (index != local_root->size
        && !(item < local_root->data[index])) {
    // Item is already in the tree.
    return false;
  }
```

If child[index] is NULL, insert the item into the local root (Step 12).

```
    if (local_root->child[index] == NULL) {
      insert_into_node(local_root, index, item, NULL);
      return true;
    }
```

If child[index] does not reference a 4-node, then we recursively continue the insert at this child (Step 13).

```
    else if (local_root->child[index]->size < 3) {
      return insert(local_root->child[index], item);
    }
```

Otherwise we need to split the child and insert the middle value from this child into the current root at index (Steps 14–15).

```
      else {
        Item_Type new_parent;
        Node<4>* new_child;
        split_node(local_root->child[index], new_parent, new_child);
        insert_into_node(local_root, index,
                         new_parent, new_child);
```

The newly inserted parent could be equal to the item to be inserted. If it is, then we return **false**. Otherwise we continue to insert recursively either at child[index] or at child[index + 1], depending on whether the inserted item is less than or greater than the newly inserted parent (Steps 16–19).

```
      if (item < local_root->data[index]) {
        return insert(local_root->child[index], item);
      } else if (local_root->data[index] < item) {
        return insert(local_root->child[index + 1], item);
      } else {
        return false;
      }
    }
  }
```

The **split_node** Function

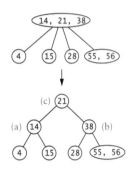

The split_node function takes a 4-node as its parameter. The function changes this node into a 2-node that contains the left data item and the left two children, creates a new 2-node with the right data item and the right two children, and sets new_parent to the middle item. The caller of split_node will either insert the middle item into the existing parent node, or it will insert the middle item into a new node if the root is being split (the case shown in the figure at left).

```
void split_node(Node<4>* node, Item_Type& new_parent,
                Node<4>*& new_child) {
  new_child = new Node<4>;
  new_parent = node->data[1];
  new_child->size = 1;
  new_child->data[0] = node->data[2];
  new_child->child[0] = node->child[2];
  new_child->child[1] = node->child[3];
  node->size = 1;
}
```

The **insert_into_node** Function

The insert_into_node function shifts the data and child values to the right and inserts the new value and child at the indicated index.

```
void insert_into_node(Node<4>* node, size_t index,
                      const Item_Type& item, Node<4>* child) {
  for (size_t i = node->size; i > index; i--) {
    node->data[i] = node->data[i - 1];
    node->child[i + 1] = node->child[i];
  }
  node->data[index] = item;
  node->child[index + 1] = child;
  node->size++;
}
```

We will not discuss deletion, but it is similar to deletion from a 2-3 tree.

Relating 2-3-4 Trees to Red-Black Trees

A Red-Black tree is a binary-tree equivalent of a 2-3-4 tree. A 2-node is a black node (see Figure 11.52). A 4-node is a black node with two red children (see Figure 11.53). A 3-node can be represented as either a black node with a left red child or a black node with a right red child (see Figure 11.54).

Suppose we want to insert a value z that is greater than y into the 3-node shown at the top of Figure 11.54 (tree with black root y). Node z would become the red right child of black node y, and the subtree with label $>y$ would be split into two parts, giving the 4-node shown in Figure 11.53.

Suppose, on the other hand, we want to insert a value z that is between x and y into the 3-node shown at the bottom of Figure 11.54 (tree with black root x). Node z would become the red left child of red node y (see the left diagram in Figure 11.55), and a double rotation would be required. First rotate right around y (the middle diagram) and then rotate left around x (the right diagram). This corresponds to the situation shown in Figure 11.56 (a 4-node with x, z, y).

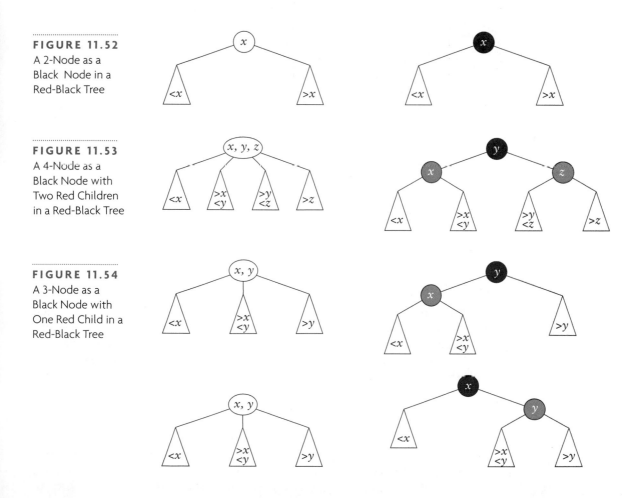

FIGURE 11.52
A 2-Node as a Black Node in a Red-Black Tree

FIGURE 11.53
A 4-Node as a Black Node with Two Red Children in a Red-Black Tree

FIGURE 11.54
A 3-Node as a Black Node with One Red Child in a Red-Black Tree

FIGURE 11.55
Inserting into the Middle of a 3-Node (Red-Black Tree Equivalent)

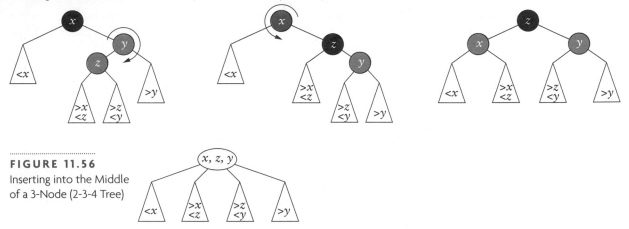

FIGURE 11.56
Inserting into the Middle
of a 3-Node (2-3-4 Tree)

B-Trees

A *B-tree* extends the idea behind the 2-3 and 2-3-4 trees by allowing a maximum of CAP - 1 data items in each node. Other than the root, each node contains between (CAP - 1)/2 and CAP - 1 data items. Figure 11.57 shows an example of a B-tree with CAP equal to 5. The *order of a B-tree* is defined as the maximum number of children for a node, so this is a B-tree of order 5. Except for the root, each node is a leaf node.

B-trees were developed to store indexes to databases stored on disk. Disk storage is broken into blocks, and the time to access a block is significant compared to the time required to manipulate data once it is in internal memory. The nodes of a B-tree are sized to fit in a block, so each disk access to the index retrieves exactly one B-tree node. The time to retrieve a block is large compared to the time required to process it in memory, so by making the tree nodes as large as possible, we reduce the number of disk accesses required to find an item in the index. Assuming that a block can store a node for a B-tree of order 200, each node would store at least 100 items. This would enable 100^4, or 100 million, items to be accessed in a B-tree of height 4.

The insertion process for a B-tree is similar to that for a 2-3 or 2-3-4 tree, and each insertion is into a leaf. For example, a number less than 10 would be inserted into the leftmost leaf; a number greater than 40 would be inserted into the rightmost leaf; and numbers between 11 and 39 would be inserted into one of the interior leaves. If the leaf being inserted into is full, it is split into two nodes, each containing approximately half the items, and the middle item is passed up to the split node's parent. If the parent is full, it is split and its middle item is passed up to its parent, and so on. If a node being split is the root of the B-tree, a new root node is created, thereby increasing the height of the B-tree. The children of the new root will be the two nodes that resulted from splitting the old root. Figure 11.58 shows the B-tree after inserting 17. The node {13, 15, 18, 20} was split, and 17 was passed up. Then the old root node was split, and 22 was passed up to the new root.

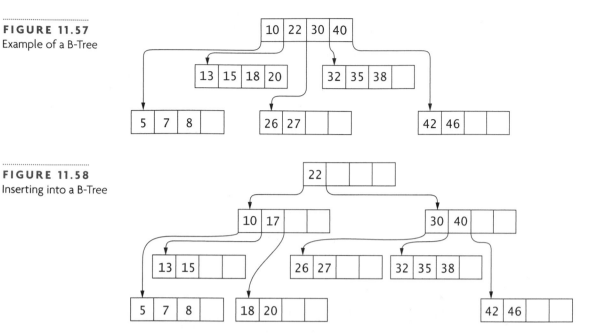

FIGURE 11.57
Example of a B-Tree

FIGURE 11.58
Inserting into a B-Tree

Implementing the B-Tree

In the 2-3-4 tree implementation, we made the Node class a template, giving it the parameter CAP that represented the maximum number of children. We can use this same Node class in the B_Tree, but now the template parameter applies to the whole class. Thus we begin the declaration of the B_Tree class as follows:

```
template<typename Item_Type, size_t CAP>
  class B_Tree {

  // Inner Class
  /** A Node represents a node in a B-tree. CAP represents
      the maxumum number of children. This class has no functions;
      it is merely a container of private data.
  */
  struct Node {
    ...
  };

  // Data Fields
  /** The reference to the root. */
  Node* root;
```

The definition of the Node class is the same as shown in Listing 11.6.

The insert function is very similar to that for the 2-3 and 2-3-4 trees. It searches the current Node for the item until it reaches a leaf, and then inserts the item into that leaf. If the leaf is full, it is split. In the 2-3 tree we described this process as a virtual insertion into the full leaf and then using the middle data value as the parent of the split-off node. This parent value was then inserted into the parent node during the return process of the recursion. In the 2-3-4 tree we avoided this complication by splitting a full node during the search process, thus the search process never terminated with a full node. If the maximum number of children is odd (and thus there are an even number of data values), splitting on the way up the recursion chain results in the split node and the split-off node having equal numbers of data values. If the split on the way down is applied to this case, the split node and split-off node can be misbalanced, with one node having one less than half the values and the other having one more. If the number of children is even (and thus there are an odd number of data values), splitting on the way down is simpler, since the center value is well defined, while after the virtual insertion there is a choice for the center value. However, the result has to be that either split node or the split-off node has one more data value than the other.

Therefore, we will use a generalization of the insertion algorithm described for the 2-3 tree.

Algorithm for Insertion into a B-Tree

1. **if** the root is NULL
2.   Create a new Node that contains the inserted item.
3. **else** search the local root for the item
4.   **if** the item is in the local root
5.   Return **false.**
6.   **else**
7.   **if** the local root is a leaf
8.   **if** the local root is not full
9.   Insert the new item.
10.   Return NULL as the new_child and **true** to indicate successful insertion.
11.   **else**
12.   Split the local root.
13.   Return the new_parent and a pointer to the new_child and **true** to indicate successful insertion.
14.   **else**
15.   Recursively call the insert function.
16.   **if** the returned new_child is not NULL
17.   **if** the local root is not full
18.   Insert the new_parent and new_child into the local root.
19.   Return **NULL** as the new_child and **true** to indicate successful insertion
20.   **else**
21.   Split the local root.
22.   Return the new_parent and a pointer to the new_child and **true** to indicate successful insertion.
23.   **else**
24.   Return the success/fail indicator for the insertion.

In this algorithm we described multiple return values. There is the **bool** return value that indicates success or failure of the insertion. There is the new_parent of the split-off node, and there is a pointer to the split-off node, which we call the new_child. We implement this by using the return value from the insert function as the success/fail indicator, and passing new_parent and new_child as reference parameters. If there is no new_child, NULL is returned, and the value in new_parent is not changed.

Code for the **insert** Function

The code for the insert function is shown in Listing 11.7. It is very similar to the code for the 2-3-4 tree. Instead of a linear search, we use a binary search to locate the item in the local root. The binary_search function returns a pointer to the item if it is present or a pointer to the position where the item should be inserted. We convert the returned pointer into an index using the statement

```
size_t index = pointer - local_root->data;
```

In the 2-3-4 tree, if the local root was a leaf and the item was not found, we could insert it. With the B-tree we need to test to see whether the local root is full. If it is full, we need to split the local root; otherwise we can insert. In either case we return **true**.

```
if (local_root->size < CAP - 1) {
  insert_into_node(local_root, index, item, NULL);
  new_child = NULL;
} else {
  split_node(local_root, index, item, NULL, new_parent, new_child);
}
return true;
```

If the local root is not a leaf, then we recursively call the insert function using local_root->child[index] as the local_root argument. However, in contrast to the 2-3-4 tree, we do not test this Node's size prior to the recursive call; rather, we test to see whether a new_child is returned. If one is, and the local_root is full, it is split; otherwise we insert the new_parent and new_child into the local_root.

```
bool result = insert(local_root->child[index],
                     item, new_parent, new_child);
if (new_child != NULL) {
  if (local_root->size < CAP - 1) {
    insert_into_node(local_root, index, new_parent, new_child);
    new_child = NULL;
  } else {
    split_node(local_root, index, new_parent, new_child,
               new_parent, new_child);
  }
}
return result;
```

The insert_into_node functions for the B-tree and 2-3-4 tree are the same. The split_node functions, however are different. We describe the split_node function next.

LISTING 11.7
The `insert` Function from `B_Tree.h`

```
/** Recursive function to insert an object into the tree.
    @param local_root The local root
    @param item The item to be inserted
    @param new_parent The parent of the split node
    @param new_child Pointer to the subtree containing items
                     greater than the new_parent
    @return true if the item was inserted,
            false if the item is already in the tree
*/
bool insert(Node* local_root, const Item_Type& item,
            Item_Type& new_parent, Node*& new_child) {
  Item_Type* pointer = binary_search(local_root->data,
                                     local_root->data + local_root->size,
                                     item);
  size_t index = pointer - local_root->data;
  // index == local_root->size or item <= local_root.data[index]

  if (index != local_root->size
      && !(item < local_root->data[index])) {
    // Item is already in the tree.
    return false;
  }
  // See if local_root is a leaf
  if (local_root->child[index] == NULL) {
    if (local_root->size < CAP - 1) {
      insert_into_node(local_root, index, item, NULL);
      new_child = NULL;
    } else {
      split_node(local_root, index, item, NULL, new_parent, new_child);
    }
    return true;
  } else {
    bool result = insert(local_root->child[index],
                         item, new_parent, new_child);
    if (new_child != NULL) {
      if (local_root->size < CAP - 1) {
        insert_into_node(local_root, index, new_parent, new_child);
        new_child = NULL;
      } else {
        split_node(local_root, index, new_parent, new_child,
                   new_parent, new_child);
      }
    }
    return result;
  }
}
```

The `split_node` Function

The `split_node` function will perform the virtual insertion of the new item (and its child) into the node and split it so that half of the items remain, and that half are moved to the split-off node. The middle value becomes the parent of the split-off node. This is illustrated in Figure 11.59.

FIGURE 11.59
Splitting the Node

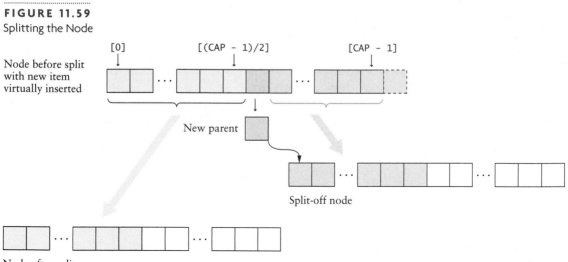

Node before split
with new item
virtually inserted

Node after split

The code for the split_node function is shown in Listing 11.8. Because we cannot insert the new item into the node before it is split, we need to do the split first in such a way that space is available in either the original node or the split-off node for the new item. After the split we want half of the items to remain in the original node and the other half moved to the split-off node. The number of items is CAP - 1; thus half of them is (CAP - 1)/2, and the other half is (CAP - 1) - (CAP - 1)/2. The reason that the other half is not simply (CAP - 1)/2 is that CAP - 1 may be an odd number. Thus we move (CAP - 1) - (CAP - 1)/2 items, unless the new item is to be inserted into the split-off node, in which case we move one fewer item. The number of items to be moved is computed using the following statements:

```
// Determine number of items to move
size_t num_to_move = (CAP - 1) - (CAP - 1)/2;
// If insert is to the right half, move one less item
if (index > (CAP - 1)/2)
  num_to_move--;
```

The standard copy algorithm is then used to move the data and the corresponding children.

```
std::copy(node->data + (CAP - 1) - num_to_move,
          node->data + (CAP - 1), new_child->data);
std::copy(node->child + CAP - num_to_move, node->child + CAP,
          new_child->child + 1);
node->size = (CAP - 1) - num_to_move;
new_child->size = num_to_move;
```

Now we are ready to insert the new item and set the new_child->child[0] pointer. There are three cases: the item is to be inserted as the middle item, the item is to be inserted into the original node, and the item is to be inserted into the new_child. If the item is to be inserted into the middle, then it becomes the new_parent, and its child becomes new_child->child[0].

```
if (index == (CAP - 1)/2) { // Insert into the middle
  new_parent = item;
  new_child->child[0] = child;
}
```

Otherwise we can use the insert_into_node function to insert the item into either the original node or the new_child.

```
if (index < (CAP - 1)/2) { // Insert into the left
  insert_into_node(node, index, item, child);
} else { // Insert into right
  insert_into_node(new_child, index - (CAP - 1)/2 - 1, item, child);
}
```

In either case, after the insert the last item in the original node becomes the new_parent, and its child becomes new_child->child[0]

```
// The rightmost item of the node becomes the new parent
new_parent = node->data[node->size-1];
// Its child is now the left child of the split-off node
new_child->child[0] = node->child[node->size];
node->size--;
```

....

LISTING 11.8
Function split_node from B_Tree.h

```
/** Function to virtually insert a new item into a full
    node and split the result into two nodes.
    pre:  node->data[index - 1] < item < node->data[index]
          and node->size = CAP-1.
    post: Node is split and the item is inserted in the left, right,
          or center. The center item becomes the parent of the right half.
    @param node The node to insert the value into
    @param index The index where the inserted item is to be placed
    @param item The value to be inserted
    @param child The right child of the value to be inserted
    @param new_parent The item that is the parent of the split-
                      off child
    @param new_child The split-off child
*/
void split_node(Node* node, size_t index,
                const Item_Type& item, Node* child,
                Item_Type& new_parent, Node*& new_child) {
  // Create new child
  new_child = new Node;
  // Determine number of items to move
  size_t num_to_move = (CAP - 1) - (CAP - 1)/2;
  // If insert is to the right half, move one less item
  if (index > (CAP - 1)/2)
    num_to_move--;

  // Move items
  std::copy(node->data + (CAP - 1) - num_to_move,
            node->data + (CAP - 1), new_child->data);
  std::copy(node->child + CAP - num_to_move, node->child + CAP,
            new_child->child + 1);
  node->size = (CAP - 1) - num_to_move;
  new_child->size = num_to_move;
```

```
// Insert new item
if (index == (CAP - 1)/2) { // Insert into the middle
  new_parent = item;
  new_child->child[0] = child;
} else {
  if (index < (CAP - 1)/2) { // Insert into the left
    insert_into_node(node, index, item, child);
  } else { // Insert into right
    insert_into_node(new_child, index - (CAP - 1)/2 - 1, item, child);
  }
  // The rightmost item of the node becomes the new parent
  new_parent = node->data[node->size-1];
  // Its child is now the left child of the split-off node
  new_child->child[0] = node->child[node->size];
  node->size--;
}
}
```

Removal from B-Tree

Removing an item from a B-tree is a generalization of removing an item from a 2-3 tree. If the item to be removed is in a leaf, it is removed; otherwise it is replaced by its inorder predecessor that is in a leaf. If the leaf is now less than half full, items from a sibling node and the parent are redistributed into that leaf. However, if the sibling is itself exactly half full, the leaf, its parent, and sibling are merged into a single node, deleting the leaf from the parent node. If the parent node is now half full, the process of node re-redistribution or merging is repeated during the recursive return process.

We illustrate this process by deleting the item 18 from Figure 11.58. The leaf node that contained 18 would have only one item, so we merge it with its parent and left sibling into a new node (13, 15, 17, 20), as shown in Figure 11.60.

The problem is that the parent of (13, 15, 17, 20) has only one item (10), so it is merged with its parent and right sibling to form a new root node (10, 22, 30, 40) as shown in Figure 11.61. Note that the height of the resulting B-tree has been reduced by 1.

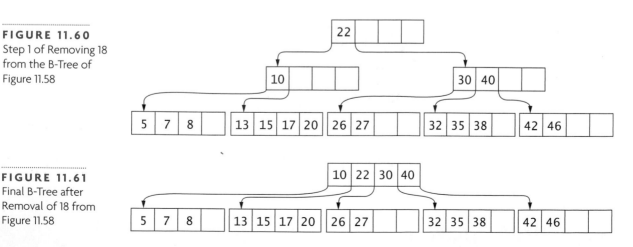

FIGURE 11.60
Step 1 of Removing 18 from the B-Tree of Figure 11.58

FIGURE 11.61
Final B-Tree after Removal of 18 from Figure 11.58

FIGURE 11.62
Example of a B+ Tree

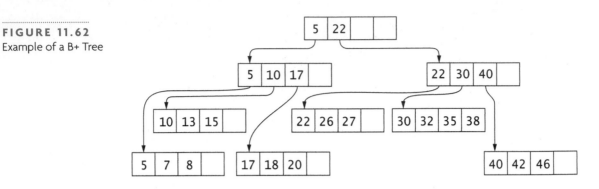

B+ Trees

We stated earlier that B-trees were developed and are still used to create indexes for databases. The `Node` is stored on a disk block, and the pointers are pointers to disk blocks instead of being memory addresses. The `Item_Type` is a key-value pair, where the value is also a pointer to a disk block. Because all of the child pointers in the leaf nodes are `NULL`, there is a significant amount of wasted space. A modification to the B-tree, known as the B+ tree, was developed to reduce this wasted space. In the B+ tree the leaves contain the keys and pointers to the corresponding values. The internal nodes contain only keys and pointers to children. In the B-tree there are `CAP` pointers to children and `CAP` - 1 values. In the B+ tree the parent's value is repeated as the first value; thus there are `CAP` pointers and `CAP` keys. An example of a B+ tree is shown in Figure 11.62.

EXERCISES FOR SECTION 11.5

SELF-CHECK

1. Show the following tree after inserting each of the following values one at a time: 1, 5, 9, and 13.

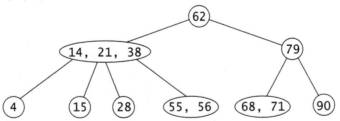

2. Build a 2-3-4 tree to store the words in the sentence "Now is the time for all good men to come to the aid of their party."
3. Draw the Red-Black tree equivalent of the 2-3-4 tree shown in Exercise 1.

4. Draw the 2-3-4 tree equivalent to the following Red-Black tree.

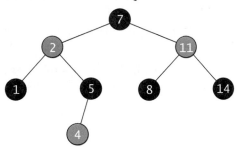

5. Draw a B-tree with CAP = 4 that stores the sequence of integers: 20, 30, 8, 10, 15, 18, 44, 26, 28, 23, 25, 43, 55, 36, 44, 39.

6. Remove items 30, 26, 15, and 17 from the B-tree in Figure 11.58.

7. Draw the B+ tree that would be formed by inserting the integers shown in Exercise 5.

PROGRAMMING

1. Code the find function for the 2-3-4 tree.

2. Code the binary_search function for the B-tree.

Chapter Review

◆ Tree balancing is necessary to ensure that a search tree has $O(\log n)$ behavior. Tree balancing is done as part of an insertion or removal.

◆ An AVL tree is a balanced binary tree in which each node has a balance value that is equal to the difference between the heights of its right and left subtrees ($h_R - h_L$). A node is balanced if it has a balance value of 0; a node is left-(right-)heavy if it has a balance of -1 ($+1$). Tree balancing is done when a node along the insertion (or removal) path becomes critically out of balance; that is, when the absolute value of the difference of the height of its two subtrees is 2. The rebalancing is done after returning from a recursive call in the insert or remove function.

◆ For an AVL tree, there are four kinds of imbalance and a different remedy for each.

—Left-Left (parent balance is -2, left child balance is -1): Rotate right around parent.

—Left-Right (parent balance is -2, left child balance is $+1$): Rotate left around child, then rotate right around parent.

—Right-Right (parent balance is +2, right child balance is +1): Rotate left around parent.

—Right-Left (parent balance is +2, right child balance is –1): Rotate right around child, then rotate left around parent.

◆ A Red-Black tree is a balanced tree with red and black nodes. After an insertion or removal, the following invariants must be maintained for a Red-Black tree.

—A node is either red or black.

—The root is always black.

—A red node always has black children. (A NULL reference is considered to refer to a black node.)

—The number of black nodes in any path from the root to a leaf is the same.

◆ To maintain tree balance in a Red-Black tree, it may be necessary to recolor a node and also to rotate around a node. The rebalancing is done inside the insert or remove function, right after returning from a recursive call.

◆ Trees whose nodes have more than two children are an alternative to balanced binary search trees. These include 2-3 and 2-3-4 trees. A 2-node has two children, a 3-node has three children, and a 4-node has four children. The advantage to these trees is that keeping the trees balanced is a simpler process. Also, the tree may be less deep because a 3-node can have three children and a 4-node can have four children, but they still have O(log n) behavior.

◆ A 2-3-4 tree can be balanced on the way down the insertion path by splitting a 4-node into two 2-nodes before inserting a new item. This is easier than splitting nodes and rebalancing after returning from an insertion.

◆ A B-tree is a tree whose nodes can store up to CAP items and is a generalization of a 2-3-4 tree. B-trees are used as indexes to large databases stored on disk. The value of CAP is chosen so that each node is as large as it can be and still fit in a disk block. The time to retrieve a block is large compared to the time required to process it in memory, so by making the tree nodes as large as possible, we reduce the number of disk accesses required to find an item in the index.

◆ A B+ tree is a variation on the B-tree that stores keys and pointers to data in the leaf nodes and keys and pointers to child nodes in the internal nodes. The parent of a child node is repeated as the first key of the child. Thus each node holds CAP keys and CAP pointers.

Quick-Check Exercises

1. Show the following AVL tree after inserting *mouse*. What kind of imbalance occurs, and what is the remedy?

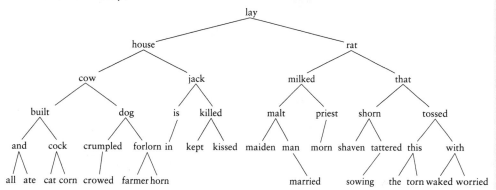

2. Show the following Red-Black tree after inserting 12 and then 13. What kind of rotation, if any, is performed?

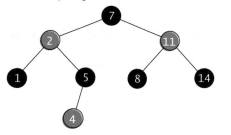

3. Show the following 2-3 tree after inserting 45 and then 20.

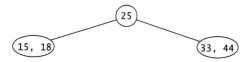

4. Show the following 2-3-4 tree after inserting 40 and then 50.

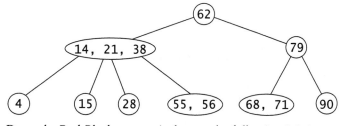

5. Draw the Red-Black tree equivalent to the following 2-3-4 tree.

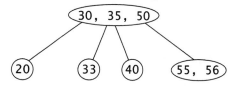

6. Draw the 2-3-4 tree equivalent to the following Red-Black tree.

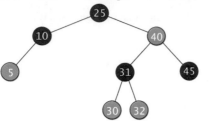

7. Show the following B-tree after inserting 45 and 21.

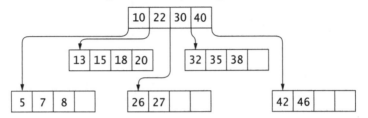

Answers to Quick-Check Exercises

1. When *mouse* is inserted (to the right of *morn*), node *morn* has a balance of +1, and node *priest* has a balance of –2. This is a case of Left-Right imbalance. Rotate left around *morn* and right around *priest*. Node *mouse* will have *morn* (*priest*) as its left (right) subtree.

2. When we insert 12 as a red node, it has a black parent, so we are done. When we insert 13, we have the situation shown in the first of the following figures. This is the mirror image of case 3 in Figure 11.25. We correct it by first rotating left around 12, giving the second of the following figures. Then we change 14 to red and 13 to black and rotate right around 13, giving the tree in the third figure.

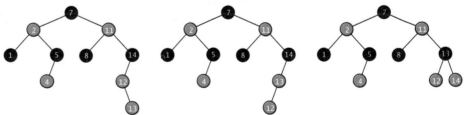

3. The 2-3 tree after inserting 45 is as follows.

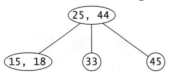

The 2-3 tree after inserting 20 is as follows.

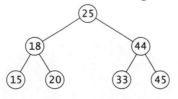

4. When 40 is inserted, the 4-node 14, 21, 38 is split and 21 is inserted into the root, 62. The node 14 has the children 4 and 15, and the node 38 has the children 28 and the 3-node 55, 56. We then insert 40 into the 3-node, making it a 4-node. The result follows.

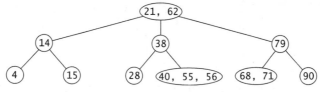

When we insert 50, the 4-node 40, 55, 56 is split and the 55 is inserted into the 2-node 38. Then 50 is inserted into the resulting 2-node, 40, making it a 3-node, as follows.

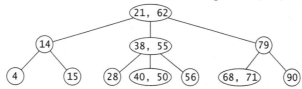

5. The equivalent Red-Black tree follows.

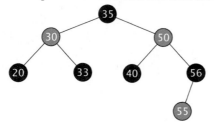

6. The equivalent 2-3-4 tree follows.

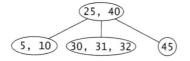

7. Insert 45 in a leaf.

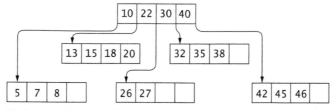

To insert 21, we need to split node {13, 15, 18, 20} and pass 18 up. Then we split the root and pass 22 up to the new root.

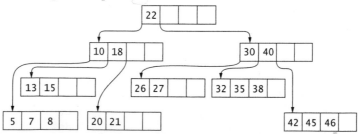

Review Questions

1. Draw the mirror images of the three cases for insertion into a Red-Black tree and explain how each situation is resolved.
2. Show the AVL tree that would be formed by inserting the month names (12 strings) in their normal calendar sequence.
3. Show the Red-Black tree that would be formed by inserting the month names in their normal calendar sequence.
4. Show the 2-3 tree that would be formed by inserting the month names in their normal calendar sequence.
5. Show the 2-3-4 tree that would be formed by inserting the month names in their normal calendar sequence.
6. Show a B-tree of capacity 5 that would be formed by inserting the month names in their normal calendar sequence.

Programming Projects

1. Code the missing functions for insertion in the AVL_Tree class. Use it to insert a collection of randomly generated numbers. Insert the same numbers in a binary search tree that is not balanced. Verify that each tree is correct by performing an inorder traversal. Also, display the format of each tree that was built and compare their heights.
2. Code the Red_Black_Tree class by coding the missing functions for insertion. Redo Project 1 using this class instead of the AVL_Tree class.
3. Code the Two_Three_Four_Tree class by coding the missing functions. Redo Project 1 using this class instead of the AVL_Tree class.
4. Code the Two_Three_Tree class. Redo Project 1 using this class instead of the AVL_Tree class.
5. Complete the AVL_Tree class by providing the missing functions for removal. Demonstrate that these functions work.

    Review the changes required for functions rebalance_left, and rebalance_right discussed at the end of Section 11.2. Also, modify rebalance_left (and rebalance_right) to consider the cases where the left (right) subtree is balanced. This case can result when there is a removal from the right (left) subtree that causes the critical imbalance to occur. This is still a Left-Left (Right-Right) case, but after the rotation the overall balances are not zero. This is illustrated in Figures 11.63 and 11.64, where an item is removed from subtree c.

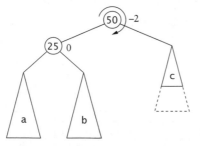

FIGURE 11.63
Left-Left Imbalance with Left Subtree Balanced

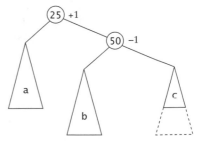

FIGURE 11.64
All Trees Unbalanced After Rotation

A remove can also result in a left-right (or right-left) case where the left-right (right-left) subtree is balanced. This is illustrated in Figures 11.65 through 11.67. The `rebalance_left` and `rebalance_right` functions already handle this case, because it also occurs when the inserted node causes unbalance in the left-right (or right-left) subtree.

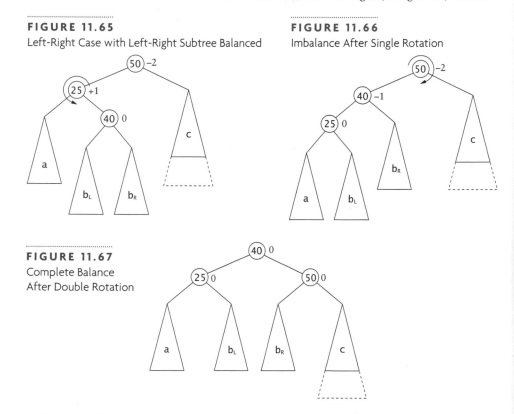

FIGURE 11.65
Left-Right Case with Left-Right Subtree Balanced

FIGURE 11.66
Imbalance After Single Rotation

FIGURE 11.67
Complete Balance
After Double Rotation

6. Complete the `Red_Black_Tree` class by coding the missing functions for removal. The functions `erase` and `find_largest_child` are adapted from the corresponding functions of the `Binary_Search_Tree` class. These adaptations are similar to those done for the AVL tree. A data field `fixup_required` performs a role analogous to the `decrease` data field in the AVL tree. It is set when a black node is removed. Upon return from a function that can remove a node, this variable is tested. If the removal is from the right, then a new function `fixup_right` is called. If the removal is from the left, then a new function `fixup_left` is called.

The `fixup_right` function must consider five cases, as follows:

- **Case 1:** Parent is red and sibling has a red right child. Figure 11.68(a) shows a red node P that is the root of a subtree that has lost a black node X from its right subtree. The root of the left subtree is S, and it must be a black node. If this subtree has a red right child, as shown in the figure, we can restore the black balance. First we rotate the left subtree left and change the color of the parent to black (see Figure 11.68(b)). Then we rotate right about the parent as shown in Figure 11.68(c). This restores the black balance. As shown in the figure, the node S may also have a left child. This does not affect the results.

FIGURE 11.68
Red-Black Removal Case 1

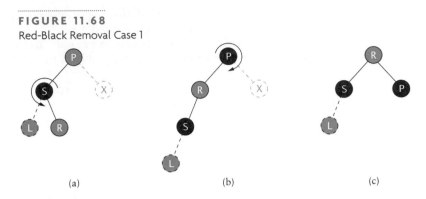

(a)   (b)   (c)

- **Case 2:** Parent is red, and sibling has only a left red child. Figure 11.69(a) shows the case where the red parent P has a left child S that has a red left child L. In this case we change the color of S to red and the color of P to black. Then we rotate right as shown in Figure 11.69(b).

FIGURE 11.69
Red-Black Removal Case 2

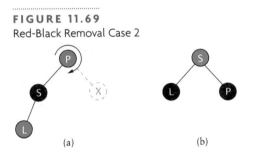

(a)   (b)

- **Case 3:** Parent is red, and the left child has no red children. Figure 11.70(a) shows the case where the red parent P has a left child S that has no children. As in the next two cases, this fixup process is started at the bottom of the tree but can move up the tree. In this case S may have black children, and X may represent the root of a subtree whose black height is one less than the black height of S. The correction is quite easy. We change P to black and S to red (see Figure 11.70(b)). Now the balance is restored, and the black height at P remains the same as it was before the black height at X was reduced.

FIGURE 11.70
Red-Black Removal Case 3

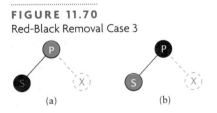

(a)   (b)

- **Case 4:** Parent is black and left child is red. Figure 11.71(a) shows the case where the parent P is black and the left child S is red. Since the black heights of S and X were equal before removing X, S must have two black children. We first change the color of the left child to black as shown in Figure 11.71(b). We rotate the child S left and change the color of P to red as shown in Figure 11.71(c). Then we rotate right twice, so that S is now where P was, thus restoring the black balance.

FIGURE 11.71
Red-Black Removal Case 4

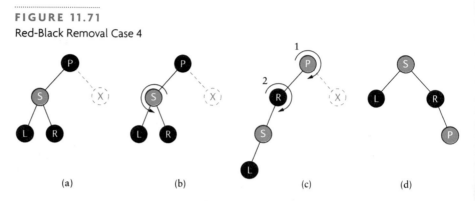

(a)   (b)   (c)   (d)

- **Case 5:** Parent is black and left child is black. Figure 11.72(a) shows the case where P is back and S is black. We then change the color of the parent to red and rotate. The black height of P has been reduced. Thus we repeat the process at the next level (P's parent).

FIGURE 11.72
Red-Black Removal Case 5

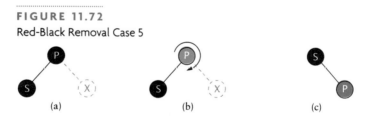

(a)   (b)   (c)

Chapter

Graphs

Chapter Objectives

- ◆ To become familiar with graph terminology and the different types of graphs
- ◆ To study a Graph ADT and different implementations of the Graph ADT
- ◆ To learn the breadth-first and depth-first search traversal algorithms
- ◆ To learn some algorithms involving weighted graphs
- ◆ To study some applications of graphs and graph algorithms

O ne of the limitations of trees is that they cannot represent information structures in which a data item has more than one parent. In this chapter we introduce a data structure known as a *graph* that will allow us to overcome this limitation.

Graphs and graph algorithms were being studied long before computers were invented. The advent of the computer made the application of graph algorithms to real-world problems possible. Graphs are especially useful in analyzing networks. Thus it is not surprising that much of modern graph theory and application was developed at Bell Laboratories, which needed to analyze the very large communications network that is the telephone system. Graph algorithms are also incorporated into the software that makes the Internet function. You can also use graphs to describe a road map, airline routes, or course prerequisites. Computer chip designers use graph algorithms to determine the optimal placement of components on a silicon chip.

You will learn how to represent a graph, find the shortest path through a graph, and find the minimum subset of a graph.

12.1 Graph Terminology

A graph is a data structure that consists of a set of *vertices* (or nodes) and a set of *edges* (relations) between the pairs of vertices. The edges represent paths or connections between the vertices. Both the set of vertices and the set of edges must be finite, and either set may be empty. If the set of vertices is empty, naturally the set of edges must also be empty. We restrict our discussion to simple graphs in which there is at most one edge from a given vertex to another vertex.

EXAMPLE 12.1 The following set of vertices, V, and set of edges, E, define a graph that has five vertices, with labels A through E, and four edges.

$V = \{A, B, C, D, E\}$

$E = \{\{A, B\}, \{A, D\}, \{C, E\}, \{D, E\}\}$

Each edge is set of two vertices. There is an edge between A and B (the edge {A, B}), between A and D, between C and E, and between D and E. If there is an edge between any pair of vertices x, y, this means there is a path from vertex x to vertex y and vice versa. We discuss the significance of this shortly.

Visual Representation of Graphs

Visually we represent vertices as points or labeled circles and the edges as lines joining the vertices. Figure 12.1 shows the graph from Example 12.1.

There are many ways to draw any given graph. The physical layout of the vertices, and even their labeling, are not relevant. Figure 12.2 shows two ways to draw the same graph.

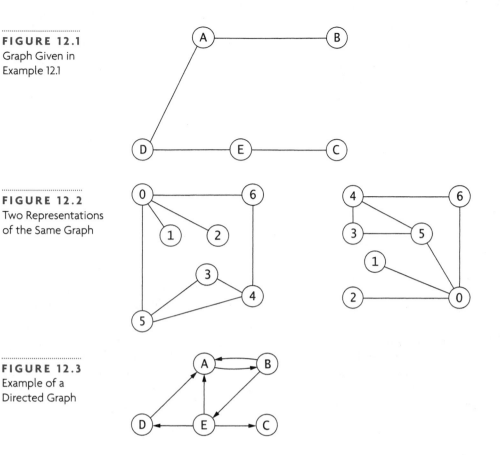

FIGURE 12.1
Graph Given in
Example 12.1

FIGURE 12.2
Two Representations
of the Same Graph

FIGURE 12.3
Example of a
Directed Graph

Directed and Undirected Graphs

The edges of a graph are *directed* if the existence of an edge from A to B does not necessarily guarantee that there is a path in both directions. A graph that contains directed edges is known as a *directed graph* or *digraph*, and a graph that contains undirected edges is known as an *undirected graph*, or simply a graph. A directed edge is like a one-way street; you can travel on it only in one direction. Directed edges are represented as lines with an arrow on one end, whereas undirected edges are represented as single lines. The graph in Figure 12.1 is undirected; Figure 12.3 shows a directed graph. The set of edges for the directed graph follows:

$$E = \{(A, B), (B, A), (B, E), (D, A), (E, A), (E, C), (E, D)\}$$

Notice the difference in the notation. Each edge in the edge list for the directed graph is an ordered pair of vertices, instead of a set as in an undirected graph. The edge (A, B) is an edge *from* A *to* B. Observe that there is both an edge from A to B and an edge from B to A, but these are the only two vertices in which there is an edge in both directions. Our convention will be that the ordered pair (u, v) means an edge to v (the *destination*) from u (the *source*). We denote an edge in an undirected graph as the set $\{u, v\}$, which means that the edge goes both from u to v and from v to u. Therefore, you can create a directed graph that is equivalent to an undirected graph

FIGURE 12.4
Example of a
Weighted Graph

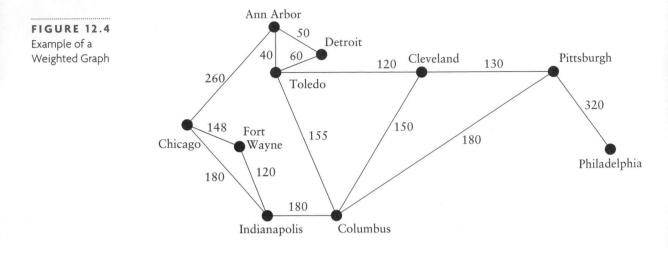

by substituting for each edge {*u*, *v*} the ordered pairs (*u*, *v*) and (*v*, *u*). In general, when we describe graph algorithms in this chapter, we will use the ordered-pair notation (*u*, *v*) for an edge.

The edges in a graph may have values associated with them, known as their *weights*. A graph with weighted edges is known as a *weighted graph*. In an illustration of a weighted graph the weights are shown next to the edges. Figure 12.4 shows an example of a weighted graph. Each weight is the distance between the two cities (vertices) connected by the edge. Generally the weights are nonnegative, but there are graph problems and graph algorithms that deal with negative-weighted edges.

Paths and Cycles

One reason we study graphs is to find pathways between vertices. We use the following definitions to describe pathways between vertices.

- A vertex is *adjacent* to another vertex if there is an edge *to* it *from* that other vertex. In Figure 12.4, Philadelphia is adjacent to Pittsburgh. In Figure 12.3 A is adjacent to D, but since this is a directed graph, D is *not* adjacent to A.

- A *path* is a sequence of vertices in which each successive vertex is adjacent to its predecessor. In Figure 12.5, the following sequence of vertices is a path: Philadelphia → Pittsburgh → Columbus → Indianapolis → Chicago.

- In a *simple path* the vertices and edges are distinct, except that the first and last vertex may be the same. In Figure 12.5 the path Philadelphia → Pittsburgh → Columbus → Indianapolis → Chicago is a simple path. The path Philadelphia → Pittsburgh → Columbus → Indianapolis → Chicago → Fort Wayne → Indianapolis is a path, but not a simple path. (See Figure 12.6.)

- A *cycle* is a simple path in which only the first and final vertices are the same. In Figure 12.7, the path Pittsburgh → Columbus → Toledo → Cleveland → Pittsburgh is a cycle. For an undirected graph, a cycle must contain at least three distinct vertices. Thus Pittsburgh → Columbus → Pittsburgh is not considered a cycle.

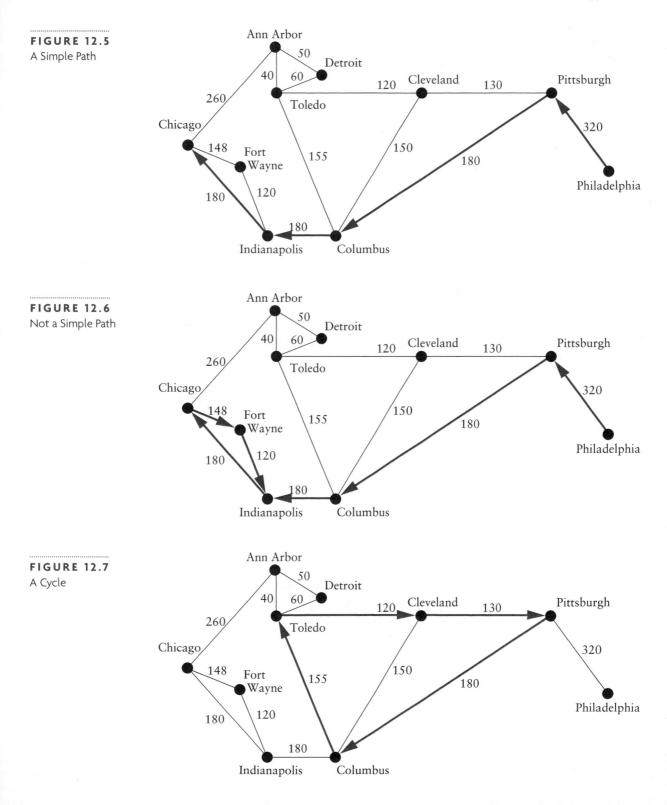

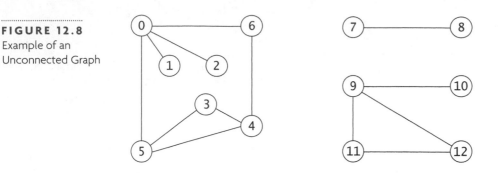

FIGURE 12.8
Example of an
Unconnected Graph

- An undirected graph is called a *connected graph* if there is a path from every vertex to every other vertex. Figure 12.7 is a connected graph, whereas Figure 12.8 is not.

- If a graph is not connected, it is considered unconnected, but it will still consist of *connected components*. A connected component is a subset of the vertices and the edges connected to those vertices in which there is a path between every pair of vertices in the component. A single vertex with no edges is also considered a connected component. Figure 12.8 consists of the connected components {0, 1, 2, 3, 4, 5, 6}, {7, 8}, and {9, 10, 11, 12}.

Relationship Between Graphs and Trees

The graph is the most general of the data structures we have studied. It allows for any conceivable relationship among the data elements (the vertices). A tree is actually a special case of a graph. Any graph that is connected and contains no cycles can be viewed as a tree by picking one of its vertices (nodes) as the root. For example, the graph shown in Figure 12.1 can be viewed as a tree if we consider the node labeled D to be the root. (See Figure 12.9.)

Graph Applications

We can use graphs to help in solving a number of different kinds of problems. For example, we might want to know whether there is a connection from one node in a network to all others. If we can show that the graph is connected, then a path must exist from one node to every other node.

In college you must take some courses before you take others. These are called prerequisites. Some courses have multiple prerequisites, and some prerequisites have

FIGURE 12.9
A Graph Viewed as
a Tree

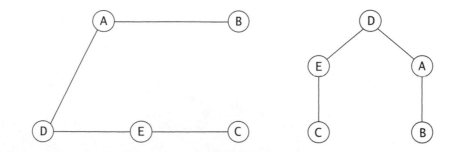

prerequisites of their own. It can be quite confusing. You may even feel that there is a loop in the maze of prerequisites and that it is impossible to schedule your classes to meet the prerequisites. We can represent the set of prerequisites by a directed graph. If the graph has no cycles, then we can find a solution. We can also find the cycles.

Another application would be finding the least-cost path or shortest path from each vertex to all other vertices in a weighted graph. For example, in Figure 12.4 we might want to find the shortest path from Philadelphia to Chicago. Or we might want to create a table showing the distance (miles in the shortest route) between each pair of cities.

EXERCISES FOR SECTION 12.1

SELF-CHECK

1. In the graph shown in Figure 12.1, what vertices are adjacent to D? In Figure 12.3?
2. In Figure 12.3, is it possible to get from A to all other vertices? How about from C?
3. In Figure 12.4, what is the shortest path from Philadelphia to Chicago?

12.2 The Graph ADT and Edge Class

A very extensive graph library has been developed for C++ by the organization known as Boost (see www.boost.org). Several of Boost's libraries have been proposed for incorporation into the next revision of the C++ standard. The Boost Graph Library is the subject of its own book (Jeremy Siek, Lie-Quan Lee, and Andrew Lumsdaine, *The Boost Graph Library: User Guide and Reference Manual* [Addison-Wesley, 2002]). This library is quite elaborate and provides much more than is needed for this text. Therefore, we will design our own library that is sufficient for the applications mentioned at the end of the previous section.

To write these programs, we need to be able to navigate through a graph, or *traverse* it (visit all its vertices). To accomplish this, we need to be able to advance from one vertex in a graph to all its adjacent vertices. Therefore, we need to be able to do the following:

1. Create a graph with the specified number of vertices.
2. Iterate through all of the vertices in the graph.
3. Iterate through the vertices that are adjacent to a specified vertex.
4. Determine whether an edge exists between two vertices.
5. Determine the weight of an edge between two vertices.
6. Insert an edge into the graph.

We will use an abstract class to specify these requirements. The declaration for this class is shown in Listing 12.1.

....

LISTING 12.1
Graph.h

```
#ifndef GRAPH_H_
#define GRAPH_H_

#include "Edge.h"
#include <iosfwd>

/** Abstract class to specify a Graph ADT. A graph is a set
    of vertices and a set of edges. Vertices are
    represented by integers from 0 to n - 1. Edges
    are ordered pairs of vertices.
*/
class Graph {

  public:

  // Forward declaration of iterator class
  class iterator;

  // Constructor
  /** Construct a graph.
      @param n The number of vertices
      @param d True if this is a directed graph
  */
  Graph(int n, bool d) : num_v(n), directed(d) {}

  // Virtual Destructor
  virtual ~Graph() {}

  // Accessors
  /** Return the number of vertices.
      @return The number of vertices
  */
  int get_num_v() const {return num_v;}

  /** Determine whether this is a directed graph.
      @return true if this is a directed graph
  */
  bool is_directed() const {return directed;}

  /** Insert a new edge into the graph.
      @param edge The new edge
  */
  virtual void insert(const Edge& edge) = 0;

  /** Determine whether an edge exists.
      @param source The source vertex
      @param dest The destination vertex
      @return true if there is an edge from source to dest
  */
  virtual bool is_edge(int source, int dest) const = 0;
```

```
/** Get the edge between two vertices.
    @param source The source vertex
    @param dest The destination vertex
    @return The Edge between these two vertices or an Edge
            with a weight of numeric_limits<double>::infinity()
            if there is no edge
*/
virtual Edge get_edge(int source, int dest) const = 0;

/** Return an iterator to the first edge adjacent
    to the specified vertex.
    @param source The source vertex
    @return An iterator to the edges
            adjacent to source
*/
virtual iterator begin(int source) const = 0;

/** Return an iterator one past the last edge adjacent
    to a specified vertex.
    @param source The source vertex
*/
virtual iterator end(int source) const = 0;

/** Load the edges of a graph from the data in an input file.
    The file should contain a series of lines, each line
    with two or three data values. The first is the source,
    the second is the destination, and the optional third
    is the weight.
    @param in The istream that is connected
              to the file that contains the data
*/
void load_edges_from_file(std::istream& in);

/** Factory function to create a graph and load the data from an input
    file. The first line of the input file should contain the number
    of vertices. The remaining lines should contain the edge data as
    described under load_edges_from_file.
    @param in The istream that is connected to the file that contains
              the data
    @param is_directed true if this is a directed graph, false otherwise
    @param type The string "Matrix" if an adjacency matrix is to be
                created, and the string "List" if an adjacency list
                is to be created.
    @throws std::invalid_argument if type is neither "Matrix" nor "List"
 */
static Graph* create_graph(std::istream& in, bool is_directed,
                           const std::string& type);

// Definition of nested classes iter_impl and iterator
...

protected:
```

```
// Data fields
/** The number of vertices */
int num_v;
/** Flag to indicate whether this is a directed graph */
bool directed;

}; // End class Graph

#endif
```

Representing Vertices and Edges

Before we can implement this abstract class, we must decide how to represent the vertices and edges of a graph. We can represent the vertices by integers from 0 up to, but not including, |V| (|V| means the cardinality of V, or the number of vertices in set V). For edges we will define the class Edge, which will contain the source vertex, the destination vertex, and the weight. For unweighted edges we will use the default weight of 1.0. Table 12.1 shows the Edge class. Observe that an Edge is directed. For undirected graphs we will always have two Edge objects: one in each direction for each pair of vertices that has an edge between them. A vertex is represented by a type **int** variable.

TABLE 12.1
The Edge Class

Data Field	Attribute
int dest	The destination vertex for an edge.
int source	The source vertex for an edge.
double weight	The weight.
Constructor	**Purpose**
Edge(int source, int dest, double w = 1.0)	Constructs an Edge from source to dest. Sets the weight to w. If w is not specified, then the weight is set to 1.0.
Edge()	Constructs a dummy edge with source and dest set to –1 and weight to infinity.
Edge(const Edge& other)	Constructs an Edge that is a copy of other.
Member Function	**Behavior**
bool operator==(const Edge& other)	Compares two edges for equality. Edges are equal if their source and destination vertices are the same. The weight is not considered.
int get_dest()	Returns the destination vertex.
int get_source()	Returns the source vertex.
double get_weight()	Returns the weight.
string to_string()	Returns a string representation of the edge.
ostream& operator<<(ostream&, const Edge&)	Overloaded ostream insertion operator.

EXERCISES FOR SECTION 12.2

SELF-CHECK

1. Use the constructors in Table 12.1 to create the Edge objects connecting vertices 9 through 12 for the graph in Figure 12.8.

PROGRAMMING

1. Implement the Edge class.

12.3 Implementing the Graph ADT

Because graph algorithms have been studied and implemented throughout the history of computer science, many of the original publications of graph algorithms and their implementations did not use an object-oriented approach and did not even use abstract data types. The implementation of the graph was done in terms of fundamental data structures that were used directly in the algorithm. Different algorithms would use different representations.

Two representations of graphs are most common:

- The edges in a graph are represented by an array of lists called the *adjacency lists*, where each list stores the vertices adjacent to a particular vertex.
- The edges are represented by a two-dimensional array, called an *adjacency matrix*, with |V| rows and |V| columns.

Adjacency List

An adjacency list representation of a graph uses an array of lists. There is one list for each vertex. Figure 12.10 shows an adjacency list representation of a directed graph. The list referenced by array element 0 shows the vertices (1 and 3) that are adjacent to vertex 0. The vertices are in no particular order. For simplicity, we are showing just the destination vertex as the value field in each node of the adjacency list, but in the actual implementation the entire Edge will be stored. Instead of storing value = 1 (the destination vertex) in the first vertex adjacent to 0, we will store a reference to the Edge (0, 1, 1.0) where 0 is the source, 1 is the destination, and 1.0 is the weight. The Edge must be stored (not just the destination) because weighted graphs can have different values for weights.

For an undirected graph (or simply a "graph"), symmetric entries are required. Thus, if {u, v} is an edge, then v will appear on the adjacency list for u and u will appear on the adjacency list for v. Figure 12.11 shows the adjacency list representation for an undirected graph. The actual lists will store references to Edges.

FIGURE 12.10
Adjacency List
Representation of a
Directed Graph

FIGURE 12.11
Adjacency List
Representation of an
Undirected Graph

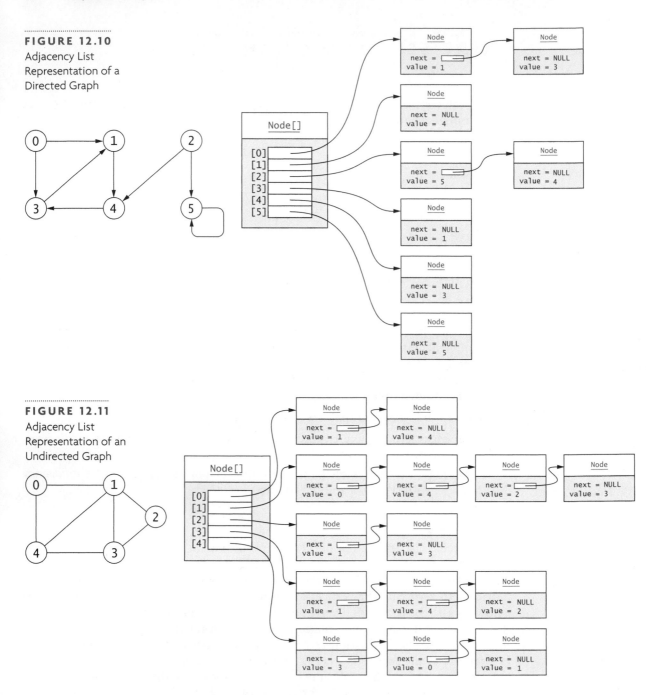

Adjacency Matrix

The adjacency matrix uses a two-dimensional array to represent the graph. For an unweighted graph the entries in this matrix can be **bool** values, where **true** represents the presence of an edge and **false** its absence. Another popular method is to use the value 1 for an edge and 0 for no edge. The integer coding has benefits over the **bool** approach for some graph algorithms that use matrix multiplication.

For a weighted graph the matrix would contain the weights. Since 0 is a valid weight (for example, if the edges represent electrical connections and the weights are the resistances), we will use numeric_limits<double>::infinity() (a special **double** value in C++ that approximates the mathematical behavior of infinity) to indicate the absence of an edge, and in an unweighted graph we will use a weight of 1.0 to indicate the presence of an edge.

Figure 12.12 shows a directed graph and the corresponding adjacency matrix. Instead of using Edge objects, an edge is indicated by the value 1.0, and the lack of an edge is indicated by a blank space.

If the graph is undirected, then the matrix is symmetric, and only the lower diagonal of the matrix need be saved (the colored squares in Figure 12.13).

Overview of the Hierarchy

We will describe C++ classes that use each representation. Each class will extend a common abstract base class, Graph, that was introduced in Section 12.2. The class Edge was also described in that section.

We will define the class Graph to represent a graph in general. The classes List_Graph and Matrix_Graph will provide concrete representations of graphs using an adjacency list and adjacency matrix, respectively (see Figure 12.14). The Graph class contains the inner classes iterator and iter_impl (as indicated by the ⊕ symbol). The iter_impl class is abstract. The Matrix_Graph class and List_Graph class will each contain an inner class iter_impl that implements the abstract functions of Graph::iter_impl.

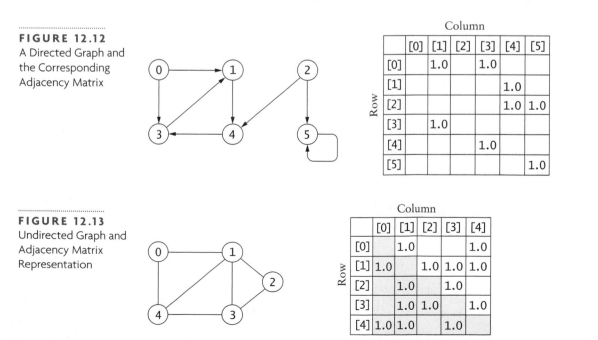

FIGURE 12.12
A Directed Graph and the Corresponding Adjacency Matrix

Column

	[0]	[1]	[2]	[3]	[4]	[5]
[0]		1.0		1.0		
[1]					1.0	
[2]					1.0	1.0
[3]		1.0				
[4]				1.0		
[5]						1.0

FIGURE 12.13
Undirected Graph and Adjacency Matrix Representation

Column

	[0]	[1]	[2]	[3]	[4]
[0]		1.0			1.0
[1]	1.0		1.0	1.0	1.0
[2]		1.0		1.0	
[3]		1.0	1.0		1.0
[4]	1.0	1.0		1.0	

FIGURE 12.14
UML Class Diagram of
Graph Class Hierarchy

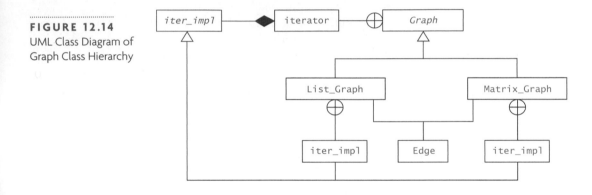

Class Graph

We will use an abstract class, Graph, as the common base class for graph implementations. This will enable us to implement some of the functions in the abstract base class and leave other functions that are implementation-specific to its derived classes. Graph algorithms will be designed to work on objects that meet the requirements defined by this abstract class. This class is summarized in Table 12.2. Note that the abstract member functions insert, is_edge, get_edge, begin, and end are not shown; they are discussed when the actual classes are implemented.

Implementation

The implementation is shown in Listing 12.2. Function load_edges_from_file reads edges from individual lines of a data file (see Programming Exercise 1).

TABLE 12.2
The Abstract Class **Graph**

Data Field	Attribute
bool directed	**true** if this is a directed graph.
int num_v	The number of vertices.
Constructor	**Purpose**
Graph(int n, bool d)	Constructs an empty graph with the specified number of vertices (n) and with the specified directed flag (d). If directed is **true**, this is a directed graph.
virtual ~Graph()	The destructor.
Function	**Behavior**
int get_num_v()	Gets the number of vertices.
bool is_directed()	Returns **true** if the graph is a directed graph.
void load_edges_from_file(istream& in)	Loads edges from a data file.
static Graph* create_graph (istream& in, bool is_directed, const string& type)	Factory function to create a graph and load the data from an input of the specified type.

....
LISTING 12.2
Graph.cpp

```cpp
#include "Graph.h"
#include "Matrix_Graph.h"
#include "List_Graph.h"
#include <string>
#include <istream>
#include <sstream>
#include <stdexcept>
#include <limits>
using std::string;
using std::istream;
using std::istringstream;
using std::numeric_limits;

/** Load the edges of a graph from the data in an input file.
    The file should contain a series of lines, each line
    with two or three data values. The first is the source,
    the second is the destination, and the optional third
    is the weight.
    @param in The istream that is connected
           to the file that contains the data
*/
void Graph::load_edges_from_file(istream& in) {
  // Programming exercise
}


/** Factory function to create a graph and load the data from an input
    file. The first line of the input file should contain the number
    of vertices. The remaining lines should contain the edge data as
    described under load_edges_from_file.
    @param in The istream that is connected to the file that contains
              the data
    @param is_directed true if this is a directed graph, false otherwise
    @param type The string "Matrix" if an adjacency matrix is to be
                created, and the string "List" if an adjacency list
                is to be created
    @throws std::invalid_argument if type is neither "Matrix" nor "List"
*/
Graph* Graph::create_graph(istream& in, bool is_directed,
                            const std::string& type) {
  int n;
  in >> n;
  in.ignore(numeric_limits<int>::max(), '\n'); // Skip rest of this line
  Graph* return_value = NULL;
  if (type == "Matrix")
    return_value = new Matrix_Graph(n, is_directed);
  else if (type == "List")
    return_value = new List_Graph(n, is_directed);
  else
    throw std::invalid_argument("Unrecognized Graph Type");
  return_value->load_edges_from_file(in);
  return return_value;
}
```

The `iterator` and `iter_impl` Classes

Listing 12.3 shows the definition of the `iterator` and `iter_impl` classes. The `iter_impl` class is an abstract class that declares the functions required to implement a forward iterator. The `iterator` class contains a data field that is a pointer to an `iter_impl` object. The member functions of the `iterator` class delegate to the `iter_impl`. The functions `begin` and `end` in the concrete graph implementation classes will construct an `iterator` object with a pointer to an `iter_impl` object that is of the appropriate class for that implementation. We will discuss this again when we discuss the implementations.

....
LISTING 12.3
Definition of the `iterator` and `iter_impl` Classes from `Graph.h`

```
/** An iterator provides sequential access to the edges
    adjacent to a given vertex.
*/
class iterator {

  public:
  Edge operator*() {
    return ptr_to_impl->operator*();
  }

  iterator& operator++() {
    ++(*ptr_to_impl);
    return *this;
  }

  iterator operator++(int) {
    iterator temp(*this);
    ++(*ptr_to_impl);
    return temp;
  }

  bool operator==(const iterator& other) const {
    return *ptr_to_impl == *other.ptr_to_impl;
  }

  bool operator!=(const iterator& other) const {
    return !((*this) == other);
  }

  ~iterator() {delete ptr_to_impl;}

  iterator(const iterator& other) :
    ptr_to_impl(other.ptr_to_impl->clone()) {}

  /** Constructor.
      @param p_graph Pointer to the graph being iterated over
      @param p_impl Pointer to iterator implementation
  */
  iterator(iter_impl* p_impl) : ptr_to_impl(p_impl) {}
```

```
    private:
    /** Pointer to the implementation */
    iter_impl* ptr_to_impl;
}; // End iterator

/** The iter_impl class defines abstract functions
      to implement the iterator operations.
*/
class iter_impl {
  public:
  virtual Edge operator*() = 0;
  virtual iter_impl& operator++() = 0;
  virtual bool operator==(const iter_impl&) const = 0;
  virtual iter_impl* clone() = 0;
  virtual ~iter_impl() {}
};
```

The List_Graph Class

The List_Graph class extends the Graph class by providing an internal representation using a vector of lists. Table 12.3 describes the List_Graph class. The class declaration is shown in Listing 12.4.

TABLE 12.3
The List_Graph Class

Data Field	Attribute
vector<list<Edge> > edges	A vector of lists to contain the edges that originate with each vertex.
Constructor	**Purpose**
List_Graph(int n, bool d)	Constructs a graph with the specified number of vertices and directionality.
Public Member Functions	**Behavior**
iterator begin(int source) const	Returns an iterator to the edges that originate from a given vertex.
iterator end(int source) const	Returns an iterator that is one past the edges that originate from a given vertex.
Edge get_edge(int source, int dest) const	Gets the edge between two vertices.
void insert(const Edge& e)	Inserts a new edge into the graph.
bool is_edge(int source, int dest) const	Determines whether an edge exists from vertex source to vertex dest.

....

LISTING 12.4
List_Graph.h

```
#ifndef LIST_GRAPH_H_
#define LIST_GRAPH_H_

#include "Graph.h"
#include <list>
#include <vector>
using std::list;
using std::vector;

/** A List_Graph is an implementation of the Graph
    abstract class that uses a vector of lists
    to contain the edges adjacent to a given vertex.
*/
class List_Graph : public Graph {

  public:

    // Constructors
    /** Constructs a graph with the specified number of
        vertices and directionality.
        @param n The number of vertices
        @param d The directionality flag
    */
    List_Graph(int n, bool d);

    // Declaration of abstract functions.
    /** Insert a new edge into the graph.
        @param edge The new edge
    */
    void insert(const Edge& edge);

    /** Determines whether an edge exists.
        @param source The source vertex
        @param dest The destination vertex
        @return true if there is an edge from source to dest
    */
    bool is_edge(int source, int dest) const;

    /** Get the edge between two vertices. If an
        edge does not exist, an Edge with a weight
        of numeric_limits<double>::infinity() is returned.
        @param source The source vertex
        @param dest The destination vertex
        @return The edge between these two vertices
     */
    Edge get_edge(int source, int dest) const;

    /** Return an iterator to the edges adjacent
        to a given vertex.
        @param source The source vertex
        @return An iterator positioned at the beginning
                of the vertices adjacent to source
    */
    iterator begin(int source) const;
```

```
    /** Return an iterator that is one past the
        edges adjacent to a given vertex.
        @param source The source vertex
        @return An iterator positioned one past the
                edges adjacent to source
    */
    iterator end(int source) const;

  private:

    // Data field
    /** The vector of lists of edges */
    std::vector<std::list<Edge> > edges;

  public:

    // iter_impl class
...

}; // end List_Graph

#endif
```

The Constructor

The constructor allocates a vector of lists, one for each vertex. This is done by calling the `resize` function for the vector to ensure that it has one entry for each vertex.

```
    /** Constructs a graph with the specified number of
        vertices and directionality.
        @param n The number of vertices
        @param d The directionality flag
    */
    List_Graph::List_Graph(int n, bool d) : Graph(n, d) {
      edges.resize(n);
    }
```

The **is_edge** Function

The function `is_edge` determines whether an edge exists by searching the list associated with the source vertex for an entry. This is done by calling the `find` function for the `list`.

```
    /** Determines whether an edge exists.
        @param source The source vertex
        @param dest The destination vertex
        @return true if there is an edge from source to dest
    */
    bool List_Graph::is_edge(int source, int dest) const {
      list<Edge>::const_iterator itr = find(edges[source].begin(),
                                            edges[source].end(),
                                            Edge(source, dest));
      return itr != edges[source].end();
    }
```

Observe that we had to create a dummy Edge object for the find function to search for. The Edge equality operator does not check the edge weights, so the weight parameter is not needed. The find function (defined in <algorithm>) will return an iterator to the item if it is in the list, or it will return an iterator to the end of the list. Thus, if the iterator returned from find is not end(), then the Edge is in the list.

The **get_edge** Function

Similar to is_edge, the get_edge function also requires a search using the find function. If the returned iterator is not end(), we return the Edge referenced by the returned iterator. If it is end(), we return an Edge with a weight of infinity.

```
/** Get the edge between two vertices. If an
    edge does not exist, an Edge with a weight
    of numeric_limits<double>::infinity() is returned.
    @param source The source vertex
    @param dest The destination vertex
    @return The edge between these two vertices
*/
Edge List_Graph::get_edge(int source, int dest) const {
  list<Edge>::const_iterator itr = find(edges[source].begin(),
                                        edges[source].end(),
                                        Edge(source, dest));
  if (itr != edges[source].end())
    return *itr;
  else
    return Edge(source, dest, numeric_limits<double>::infinity());
}
```

The **insert** Function

The insert function inserts a new edge (source, dest, weight) into the graph by adding that edge's data to the list of adjacent vertices for that edge's source. If the graph is not directed, it adds a new edge in the opposite direction (dest, source, weight) to the list of adjacent vertices for that edge's destination.

```
/** Insert a new edge into the graph.
    @param edge The new edge
*/
void List_Graph::insert(const Edge& edge) {
  edges[edge.get_source()].push_back(edge);
  if (!is_directed()) {
    edges[edge.get_dest()].push_back(Edge(edge.get_dest(),
                                          edge.get_source(),
                                          edge.get_weight()));
  }
}
```

The **begin** and **end** Functions

The begin and end functions dynamically allocate new List_Graph::iter_impl objects that in turn contain begin and end iterators to the list associated with the specified vertex. The pointer to this iter_impl object is then passed to the Graph::iterator constructor.

```
/** Return an iterator to the edges adjacent
    to a given vertex.
    @param source The source vertex
    @return An iterator positioned at the beginning
            of the vertices adjacent to source
*/
Graph::iterator List_Graph::begin(int source) const {
    return Graph::iterator(new iter_impl(edges[source].begin()));
}

/** Return an iterator that is one past the edges
    adjacent to a given vertex.
    @param source The source vertex
    @return An iterator positioned one past the
            edges adjacent to source
*/
Graph::iterator List_Graph::end(int source) const {
    return Graph::iterator(new iter_impl(edges[source].end()));
}
```

The `List_Graph::iter_impl` Class

The `List_Graph::iter_impl` class is a subclass of the `Graph::iter_impl` class. Recall that the `Graph::iter_impl` class is abstract, and that all of its member functions are abstract. The `List_Graph::iter_impl` class provides implementations of the minimum iterator functions that are defined for the `Graph::iterator`. We designed the `Graph::iterator` this way to provide a common interface for iterators defined for different `Graph` implementations. If we had only the `List_Graph`, we could use the `list<Edge>::iterator` directly as the `Graph::iterator`.

One major difference between the `Graph::iterator` and other iterator classes is the behavior of the dereferencing operator (`operator*()`). In other iterator classes we have shown, the dereferencing operator returns a reference to the object that the iterator refers to. Thus the iterator can be used to change the value of the object referred to. (It is for that reason that we define both an `iterator` and `const_iterator`.) The `Graph::iterator`, and thus the `iter_impl` classes, however, return a *copy* of the referenced `Edge` object. Thus changes made to an `Edge` via a `Graph::iterator` will not change the `Edge` within the graph.

Listing 12.5 shows the `List_Graph::iter_impl`. It extends the `Graph::iter_impl` class and defines implementations for the abstract functions `operator*`, `operator++`, `operator==`, and `clone`. The only one of these that is a bit tricky is the equality operator. The equality operator declaration begins with:

```
bool operator==(const Graph::iter_impl& other) const {
```

This declaration states that `other` is of type `Graph::iter_impl`, which is an abstract class. In principle it is possible that a `Graph::iterator` that was returned from a `List_Graph` class and a `Graph::iterator` from a `Matrix_Graph` (or other implementation) could be compared.

Thus the `List_Graph::iter_impl::operator==` function must determine whether the `other` parameter refers to an object of the same class or to an object of some other subclass. This is done using the `dynamic_cast` operator (see Section 3.3).

```
          const iter_impl* ptr_other =
            dynamic_cast<const iter_impl*>(&other);
```

If other refers to an object of a different class, then ptr_other will be **NULL**.

The List_Graph::iter_impl Class from List_Graph.h

```
/** Implementation class for an iterator to the edges.
*/
class iter_impl : public Graph::iter_impl {

  private:
  // Constructor
  /** Construct an iter_impl for a given vertex.
      @param start An iterator to the list of edges adjacent
                   to the desired vertex
  */
  iter_impl(std::list<Edge>::const_iterator start) : current(start) {}

  public:
  /** Return the current edge */
  Edge operator*() {
    return *current;
  }

  /** Advance to the next edge */
  Graph::iter_impl& operator++() {
    ++current;
    return *this;
  }

  /** Determine whether two iter_impl objects are equal */
  bool operator==(const Graph::iter_impl& other) const {
    const iter_impl* ptr_other =
      dynamic_cast<const iter_impl*>(&other);
    if (ptr_other == NULL) return false;
    return current == ptr_other->current;
  }

  /** Make a deep copy of this iter_impl */
  Graph::iter_impl* clone() {
    return new iter_impl(current);
  }

  private:
  // Data fields

  /** Iterator to the list of edges */
  std::list<Edge>::const_iterator current;
  friend class List_Graph;

}; // End iter_impl
```

The `Matrix_Graph` Class

The `Matrix_Graph` class extends the `Graph` class by providing an internal representation using a two-dimensional array for storing the edge weights. The rows represent the source of each edge, and the columns represent the destination. This array is implemented by dynamically allocating an array of dynamically allocated arrays. Since dynamically allocated arrays are implemented as pointers, the resulting type is a pointer to a pointer.

```
double** edges;
```

When a new `Matrix_Graph` object is created, the constructor sets the number of rows (vertices) in this array. For a directed graph, each row is then allocated to hold the same number of columns, one for each vertex. For an undirected graph, only the lower diagonal of the array is needed. Thus the first row has one column, the second two, and so on. The `is_edge` and `get_edge` functions when operating on an undirected graph must test to see whether the destination is greater than the source, if it is, they then must access the row indicated by the destination and the column indicated by the source.

The `iter_impl` class presents a challenge. An `iter_impl` object must keep track of the current source (row) and current destination (column). The dereferencing operator (`operator*`) must then create and return an `Edge` object. (This is why we designed the `Graph::iterator` to return an `Edge` value rather than an `Edge` reference.)

The other complication for the `iter_impl` class is the increment operator. When this operator is called, the iterator must be advanced to the next defined edge, skipping those columns whose weights are infinity.

The implementation of the `Matrix_Graph` is left as a project (Programming Project 1).

Comparing Implementations

Time Efficiency

The two implementations present a tradeoff. Which is best depends upon the algorithm and the density of the graph. The density of a graph is the ratio of $|E|$ to $|V|^2$. A *dense graph* is one in which $|E|$ is close to but less than $|V|^2$, and a *sparse graph* is one in which $|E|$ is much less than $|V|^2$. Therefore, for a dense graph we can assume that $|E|$ is $O(|V|^2)$, and for a sparse graph we can assume that $|E|$ is $O(|V|)$.

Many graph algorithms are of the form:

1.   **for** each vertex u in the graph
2.   **for** each vertex v adjacent to u
3.   Do something with edge (u, v).

For an adjacency list representation, Step 1 is $O(|V|)$ and Step 2 is $O(|E_u|)$, where $|E_u|$ is the number of edges that originate at vertex u. Thus the combination of Steps 1 and 2 will represent examining each edge in the graph, giving $O(|E|)$. On the other hand, for an adjacency matrix representation, Step 2 is also $O(|V|)$, and thus the overall algorithm is $O(|V|^2)$. Thus, for a sparse graph the adjacency list gives better performance for this type of algorithm, whereas for a dense graph the performance is the same for either representation.

Some graph algorithms are of the form

1.   **for** each vertex u in some subset of the vertices
2.   **for** each vertex v in some subset of the vertices
3.   **if** (u, v) is an edge
4.   Do something with edge (u, v).

For an adjacency matrix representation, Step 3 tests a matrix value and is $O(1)$, so the overall algorithm is $O(|V|^2)$. For an adjacency list representation, however, Step 3 searches a list and is $O(|E_u|)$, so the combination of Steps 2 and 3 is $O(|E|)$ and the overall algorithm is $O(|V||E|)$. For a dense graph the adjacency matrix gives the best performance for this type of algorithm, and for a sparse graph the performance is the same for both representations.

Thus, if a graph is dense, the adjacency matrix representation is best, and if a graph is sparse, the adjacency list representation is best. Intuitively, this makes sense, because a sparse graph will lead to a sparse matrix, or one in which most entries are infinity. These entries are not included in a list representation, so they will have no effect on processing time. They are included in a matrix representation, however, and will have an undesirable impact on processing time.

Storage Efficiency

Notice that storage is allocated for all vertex combinations (or at least half of them) in an adjacency matrix. So the storage required is proportional to $|V|^2$. If the graph is sparse (not many edges), there will be a lot of wasted space in the adjacency matrix. In an adjacency list, only the adjacent edges are stored.

On the other hand, in an adjacency list, each edge is represented by an `Edge` object containing data about the source, destination, and weight. There are also pointers to the next and previous edges in the list. In a matrix representation, only the weight associated with an edge is stored. So each element in an adjacency list requires approximately five times the storage of an element in an adjacency matrix. (If we used a single-linked list rather than the standard list, this would be reduced to four times the storage, since the pointer to the previous edge would be eliminated.)

Based on this we can conclude that the break-even point in terms of storage efficiency occurs when approximately 20 percent of the adjacency matrix is filled with meaningful data. That is, the adjacency list uses less (more) storage when less than (more than) 20 percent of the adjacency matrix would be filled.

EXERCISES FOR SECTION 12.3

SELF-CHECK

1. Represent the following graphs using adjacency lists.

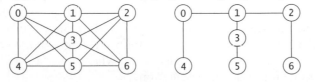

2. Represent the graphs in Exercise 1 using an adjacency matrix.

3. For each graph in Exercise 1, what are the |*V*|, the |*E*|, and the density? Which representation is best for each graph? Explain your answers.

PROGRAMMING

1. Implement the `load_edges_from_file` function for class `Graph`. If there are two values on a line, an edge with the default weight of 1.0 is inserted; if there are three values, the third value is the weight.

12.4 Traversals of Graphs

Most graph algorithms involve visiting each vertex in a systematic order. Just as with trees, there are different ways to do this. The two most common traversal algorithms are breadth first and depth first. Although these are graph traversals, they are more commonly called *breadth-first* and *depth-first search*.

Breadth-First Search

In a breadth-first search, we visit the start node first, then all nodes that are adjacent to it next, then all nodes that can be reached by a path from the start node containing two edges, three edges, and so on. The requirement for a breadth-first search is that we must visit all nodes for which the shortest path from the start node is length *k* before we visit any node for which the shortest path from the start node is length *k* + 1. You can visualize a breadth-first traversal by "picking up" the graph at the vertex that is the start node, so the start node will be the highest node and the rest of the nodes will be suspended underneath it, connected by their edges. In a breadth-first search, the nodes that are higher up in the picked-up graph are visited before nodes that are lower in the graph.

Breadth-first search starts at some vertex. Unlike the case of a tree, there is no special start vertex, so we will arbitrarily pick the vertex with label 0. We then visit it by identifying all vertices that are adjacent to the start vertex. Then we visit each of these vertices, identifying all of the vertices adjacent to them. This process continues until all vertices are visited. If the graph is not a connected graph, then the process is repeated with one of the unidentified vertices. In the discussion that follows, we use color to distinguish among three states for a node: identified (light color), visited (dark color), and not identified (white). Initially, all nodes are not identified. If a node is in the identified state, that node was encountered while visiting another, but it has not yet been visited.

FIGURE 12.15
Graph to Be Traversed
Breadth First

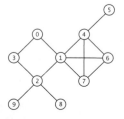

Example of Breadth-First Search

Consider the graph shown in Figure 12.15. We start at vertex 0 and color it light (see Figure 12.16(a)). We visit 0 and see that 1 and 3 are adjacent, so we color them light (to show that they have been identified). We are finished visiting 0 and now color it dark (see Figure 12.16(b)). So far we have visited node 0.

FIGURE 12.16
Example of a Breadth-First Search

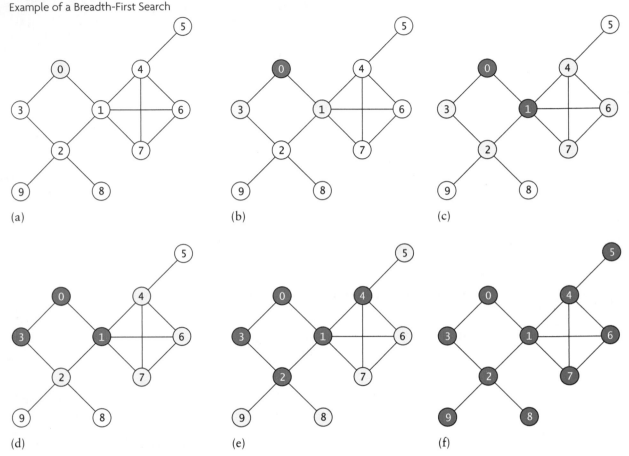

We always select the first node that was identified (light color) but not yet visited and visit it next. Therefore, we visit 1 and look at its adjacent vertices: 0, 2, 4, 6, and 7. We skip 0, because it is not colored white, and color the others light. Then we color 1 dark (see Figure 12.16(c)). Now we have visited nodes 0 and 1.

Then we look at 3 (the first of the light-colored vertices in Figure 12.16(c) to have been identified) and see that its adjacent vertex, 2, has already been identified and 0 has been visited, so we are finished with 3 (see Figure 12.16(d)). Now we have visited nodes 0, 1, and 3, which are the starting vertex and all vertices adjacent to it.

Now we visit 2 and see that 8 and 9 are adjacent. Then we visit 4 and see that 5 is the only adjacent vertex not identified or visited (Figure 12.16(e)). Finally, we visit 6 and 7 (the last vertices that are two edges away from the starting vertex), then 8, 9, and 5, and see that there are no unidentified vertices (Figure 12.16(f)). The vertices have been visited in the sequence 0, 1, 3, 2, 4, 6, 7, 8, 9, 5.

Algorithm for Breadth-First Search

To implement breadth-first search, we need to be able to determine the first identified vertex that has not been visited, so that we can visit it. To ensure that the identified vertices are visited in the correct sequence, we will store them in a queue (first-in, first-out). When we need a new node to visit, we remove it from the queue. We summarize the process in the following algorithm.

Algorithm for Breadth-First Search

1. Take an arbitrary start vertex, mark it identified (color it light), and place it in a queue.
2. **while** the queue is not empty
3.   Take a vertex, u, out of the queue and visit u.
4.   **for** all vertices, v, adjacent to this vertex, u
5.   **if** v has not been identified or visited
6.   Mark it identified (color it light).
7.   Insert vertex v into the queue.
8.   We are now finished visiting u (color it dark).

Table 12.4 traces this algorithm on the graph shown earlier in Figure 12.15. The initial queue contents is the start node, 0. The first line shows that after we finish visiting vertex 0, the queue contains nodes 1 and 3, which are adjacent to node 0 and are colored light in Figure 12.16(b). The second line shows that after removing 1 from the queue and visiting 1, we insert its neighbors that have not yet been identified or visited: nodes 2, 4, 6, and 7.

Table 12.4 shows that the nodes were visited in the sequence 0, 1, 3, 2, 4, 6, 7, 8, 9, 5. There are other sequences that would also be valid breadth-first traversals.

TABLE 12.4
Trace of Breadth-First Search of Graph in Figure 12.15

Vertex Being Visited	Queue Contents After Visit	Visit Sequence
0	1 3	0
1	3 2 4 6 7	0 1
3	2 4 6 7	0 1 3
2	4 6 7 8 9	0 1 3 2
4	6 7 8 9 5	0 1 3 2 4
6	7 8 9 5	0 1 3 2 4 6
7	8 9 5	0 1 3 2 4 6 7
8	9 5	0 1 3 2 4 6 7 8
9	5	0 1 3 2 4 6 7 8 9
5	empty	0 1 3 2 4 6 7 8 9 5

FIGURE 12.17
Breadth-First Search
Tree of Graph in
Figure 12.15

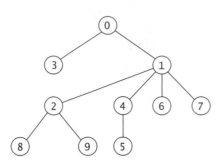

We can also build a tree that represents the order in which vertices would be visited in a breadth-first traversal, by attaching the vertices as they are identified to the vertex from which they are identified. Such a tree is shown in Figure 12.17. Observe that this tree contains all of the vertices and some of the edges of the original graph. A path starting at the root to any vertex in the tree is the shortest path in the original graph from the start vertex to that vertex, where we consider all edges to have the same weight. Therefore, the shortest path is the one that goes through the smallest number of vertices. We can save the information we need to represent this tree by storing the parent of each vertex when we identify it (Step 7 of the breadth-first algorithm).

Refinement of Step 7 of Breadth-First Search Algorithm

7.1   Insert vertex v into the queue.

7.2   Set the parent of v to u.

Performance Analysis of Breadth-First Search

The loop at Step 2 will be performed for each vertex. The inner loop at Step 4 is performed for $|E_v|$ (the number of edges that originate at that vertex). The total number of steps is the sum of the edges that originate at each vertex, which is the total number of edges. Thus the algorithm is $O(|E|)$.

Implementing Breadth-First Search

Listing 12.6 shows function breadth_first_search. Notice that nothing is done when we have finished visiting a vertex (algorithm Step 8).

This function declares three data structures: vector<int> parent, vector<bool> identified, and queue<int> the_queue. The vector identified is used to keep track of the nodes that have been previously encountered, and the_queue is used to store nodes that are waiting to be visited.

The function returns vector parent, which could be used to construct the breadth-first search tree. The element parent[v] contains the parent of vertex v in the tree. The statement

```
parent[neighbor] = current;
```

is used to "insert an edge into the breadth-first search tree". It does this by setting the parent of a newly identified node (neighbor) as the node being visited (current).

If we run the `breadth_first_search` function on the graph shown in Figure 12.15, then the vector parent will be defined as follows:

vector<int> parent	
[0]	-1
[1]	0
[2]	1
[3]	0
[4]	1
[5]	4
[6]	1
[7]	1
[8]	2
[9]	2

If you compare vector parent to Figure 12.17, you can see that parent[i] is the parent of vertex i. For example, the parent of vertex 4 is vertex 1. The entry parent[0] is −1 because node 0 is the start vertex.

Although vector parent could be used to construct the breadth-first search tree, we are generally not interested in the complete tree but rather in the path from the root to a given vertex. Using vector parent to trace the path from that vertex back to the root would give you the reverse of the desired path. For example, the path derived from parent for vertex 4 to the root would be 4 to 1 to 0. If you place these vertices in a stack and then pop the stack until it is empty, you will get the path from the root: 0 to 1 to 4.

LISTING 12.6
Breadth_First_Search.cpp

```cpp
#include <vector>
#include <queue>
#include "Graph.h"
using namespace std;

/** Perform a breadth-first search of a graph.
    The vector p will contain the predecessor of each
    vertex in the breadth-first search tree.
    @param graph The graph to be searched
    @param start The start vertex
    @return The vector of parents
*/
vector<int> breadth_first_search(const Graph& graph, int start) {
    int num_v = graph.get_num_v();
    queue<int> the_queue;
    vector<int> parent(num_v, -1);
    vector<bool> identified(num_v, false);
    identified[start] = true;
    the_queue.push(start);
```

```
/* While the queue is not empty */
while (!the_queue.empty()) {
  /* Take a vertex, current, out of the queue
     (Begin visiting current).*/
  int current = the_queue.front();
  the_queue.pop();
  /* For all vertices, neighbor, adjacent to current */
  Graph::iterator itr = graph.begin(current);
  while (itr != graph.end(current)) {
    Edge edge = *itr;
    int neighbor = edge.get_dest();
    /* If neighbor has not been identified */
    if (!identified[neighbor]) {
      /* Mark it identified */
      identified[neighbor] = true;
      /* Place it into the queue */
      the_queue.push(neighbor);
      /* Insert the edge (current, neighbor)
         into the tree */
      parent[neighbor] = current;
    }
    ++itr;
  }
  // Finished visiting current.
}
return parent;
}
```

Depth-First Search

Another way to traverse a graph is depth-first search. In depth-first search you start at a vertex, visit it, and choose one adjacent vertex to visit. Then choose a vertex adjacent to that vertex to visit, and so on until you go no further. Then back up and see whether a new vertex (one not previously visited) can be found. In the discussion that follows, we use color to distinguish among three states for a node: being visited (light color), finished visiting (dark color), and not yet visited (white). Initially, of course, all nodes are not yet visited. Note that the light color is used in depth-first search to indicate that a vertex is *in the process of being visited*, whereas it was used in our discussion of breadth-first search to indicate that the vertex was *identified*.

Example of Depth-First Search

Consider the graph shown in Figure 12.18. We can start at any vertex, but for simplicity we will start at 0. The vertices adjacent to 0 are 1, 2, 3, and 4. We mark 0 as being visited (color it light; see Figure 12.19(a)). Next we consider 1. We mark 1 as being visited (see Figure 12.19(b)). The vertices adjacent to 1 are 0, 3, and 4. But 0 is being visited, so we recursively apply the algorithm with 3 as the start vertex. We mark 3 as being visited (see Figure 12.19(c)). The vertices adjacent to 3 are 0, 1, and 4. Because 0 and 1 are already being visited, we recursively apply the algorithm with

FIGURE 12.18
Graph to Be Traversed
Depth First

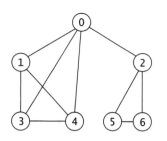

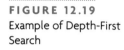

FIGURE 12.19
Example of Depth-First
Search

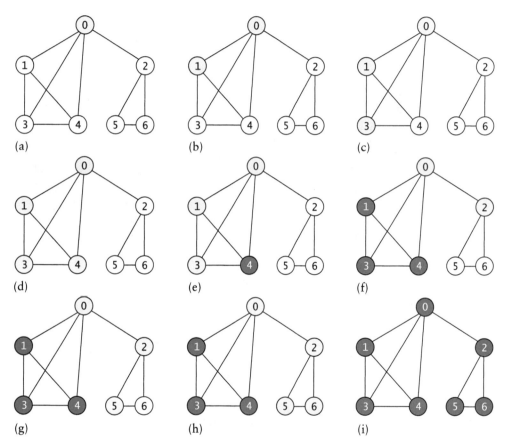

4 as the start vertex. We mark 4 as being visited (see Figure 12.19(d)). The vertices adjacent to 4 are 0, 1, and 3. All of these are being visited, so we mark 4 as finished (see Figure 12.19(e)) and return from the recursion. Now all of the vertices adjacent to 3 have been visited, so we mark 3 as finished and return from the recursion. Now all of the vertices adjacent to 1 have been visited, so we mark 1 as finished and return from the recursion to the original start vertex, 0. The order in which we started to visit vertices is 0, 1, 3, 4; the order in which vertices have become finished so far is 4, 3, 1.

We now consider vertex 2, which is adjacent to 0 but has not been visited. We mark 2 as being visited (see Figure 12.19(f)) and consider the vertices adjacent to it: 5 and 6. We mark 5 as being visited (see Figure 12.19(g)) and consider the vertices adjacent to it: 2 and 6. Because 2 is already being visited, we next visit 6. We mark 6 as being visited (see Figure 12.19(h)). The vertices adjacent to 6 (2 and 5) are already being visited. Thus we mark 6 as finished and recursively return. The vertices adjacent to 5 have all been visited, so we mark 5 as finished and return from the recursion. All of the vertices adjacent to 2 have been visited, so we mark 2 as finished and return from the recursion.

Finally, we come back to 0. Because all of the vertices adjacent to it have also been visited, we mark 0 as finished, and we are done (see Figure 12.19(i)). The order in which we started to visit all vertices is 0, 1, 3, 4, 2, 5, 6; the order in which we finished visiting all vertices is 4, 3, 1, 6, 5, 2, 0. The *discovery order* is the order in which the vertices are discovered. The *finish order* is the order in which the vertices are finished. We consider a vertex to be finished when we return to it after finishing all its successors.

Figure 12.20 shows the depth-first search tree for the graph in Figure 12.18. A preorder traversal of this tree yields the sequence in which the vertices were visited: 0, 1, 3, 4, 2, 5, 6. The dashed lines are the other edges in the graph that are not part of the depth-first search tree. These edges are called *back edges* because they connect a vertex with its ancestors in the depth-first search tree. Observe that vertex 4 has two ancestors in addition to its parent, 3: 1 and 0. Vertex 1 is a grandparent, and vertex 0 is a great-grandparent.

Algorithm for Depth-First Search

Depth-first search is used as the basis of other graph algorithms. However, rather than embedding the depth-first search algorithm into these other algorithms, we will implement the depth-first search algorithm to collect information about the vertices, which we can then use in these other algorithms. The information we will collect is the discovery order (or the visit order) and the finish order.

The depth-first search algorithm follows. Step 5 recursively applies this algorithm to each vertex as it is discovered.

FIGURE 12.20
Depth-First Search Tree
of Figure 12.18

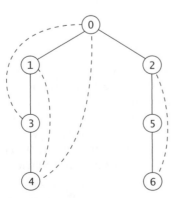

Algorithm for Depth-First Search

1. Mark the current vertex, u, visited (color it light), and enter it in the discovery order list.
2. **for** each vertex, v, adjacent to the current vertex, u
3.   **if** v has not been visited
4.   Set parent of v to u.
5.   Recursively apply this algorithm starting at v.
6. Mark u finished (color it dark) and enter u into the finish order list.

Observe that Step 6 is executed after the loop in Step 2 has examined all vertices adjacent to vertex u. Also, the loop at Step 2 does not select the vertices in any particular order.

Table 12.5 shows a trace of the algorithm as applied to the graph shown in Figure 12.19. We list each visit or finish step in column 1. Column 2 lists the vertices adjacent to each vertex when it begins to be visited. The discovery order (the order in which the vertices are visited) is 0, 1, 3, 4, 2, 5, 6. The finish order is 4, 3, 1, 6, 5, 2, and 0.

Performance Analysis of Depth-First Search

The loop at Step 2 is executed $|E_v|$ (the number of edges that originate at that vertex) times. The recursive call results in this loop being applied to each vertex. The total number of steps is the sum of the edges that originate at each vertex, which is the total number of edges $|E|$. Thus the algorithm is $\mathbf{O}(|E|)$.

....

TABLE 12.5
Trace of Depth-First Search of Figure 12.19

Operation	Adjacent Vertices	Discovery (Visit) Order	Finish Order
Visit 0	1, 2, 3, 4	0	
Visit 1	0, 3, 4	0, 1	
Visit 3	0, 1, 4	0, 1, 3	
Visit 4	0, 1, 3	0, 1, 3, 4	
Finish 4			4
Finish 3			4, 3
Finish 1			4, 3, 1
Visit 2	0, 5, 6	0, 1, 3, 4, 2	
Visit 5	2, 6	0, 1, 3, 4, 2, 5	
Visit 6	2, 5	0, 1, 3, 4, 2, 5, 6	
Finish 6			4, 3, 1, 6
Finish 5			4, 3, 1, 6, 5
Finish 2			4, 3, 1, 6, 5, 2
Finish 0			4, 3, 1, 6, 5, 2, 0

There is an implicit Step 0 to the algorithm that colors all of the vertices white. This is $O(|V|)$, thus the total running time of the algorithm is $O(|V|+|E|)$.

Implementing Depth-First Search

The function `depth_first_search` is designed to be used as a building block for other algorithms. When called, this function performs a depth-first search on a graph and records the start time, finish time, start order, and finish order. For an unconnected graph, or for a directed graph (whether connected or not), a depth-first search may not visit each vertex in the graph. Thus, once the recursive function returns, the vertices need to be examined to see whether they all have been visited; if not, the recursive process repeats, starting with the next unvisited vertex. Thus, the depth-first search can generate more than one tree. We will call this collection of trees a *forest*.

The starter function clears and resizes the vectors `parent`, `visited`, `discovery_order`, and `finish_order` and initializes all elements of `parent` to -1 (no parent). In the starter function in Listing 12.7, the **for** statement that begins with lines

```
for (int i = 0; i < num_v; i++) {
   if (!visited[i]) {
      depth_first_search(graph, i, parent,
```

calls the recursive depth-first search function. The recursive `depth_first_search` follows the algorithm shown earlier. If the graph is connected, all vertices will be visited after the return from the initial call to the recursive `depth_first_search`. If the graph is not connected, additional calls will be made using a start vertex that has not been visited.

....
LISTING 12.7
Depth_First_Search.cpp

```cpp
#include <vector>
#include "Graph.h"
using namespace std;

/** Perform a depth first search of a graph (recursive function).
    @param graph The graph to be searched
    @param current The current vertex being visited
    @param parent The parents in the depth-first search tree
    @param discovery_order The discovery order for each vertex
    @param finish_order The finish order for each vertex
    @param visited The vector that records whether a vertex has been
                   visited
    @param discovery_index The index into the discovery_order vector
    @param finish_index The index into the finish_order vector
*/
void depth_first_search(const Graph& graph, int current,
                        vector<int>& parent,
                        vector<int>& discovery_order,
                        vector<int>& finish_order,
                        vector<bool>& visited,
```

```
                              int& discovery_index,
                              int& finish_index) {
    visited[current] = true;
    discovery_order[discovery_index++] = current;
    /* For each vertex adjacent to the current vertex. */
    for (Graph::iterator itr = graph.begin(current);
         itr != graph.end(current); ++itr) {
      int neighbor = (*itr).get_dest();
      // if neighbor has not been visited
      if (!visited[neighbor]) {
        /* Insert (current, neighbor) into the depth-
           first search tree */
        parent[neighbor] = current;
        // Recursively apply the algorithm starting at neighbor.
        depth_first_search(graph, neighbor,
                           parent, discovery_order,
                           finish_order, visited,
                           discovery_index, finish_index);
      }
    }
    // Mark current finished
    finish_order[finish_index++] = current;
}

/** Perform a depth-first search of a graph (starter function).
    @param graph The graph to be searched
    @param start The start vertex
    @param parent The parents in the depth-first search tree
    @param discovery_order The discovery order for each vertex
    @param finish_order The finish order for each vertex
*/
void depth_first_search(const Graph& graph, int start,
                        vector<int>& parent,
                        vector<int>& discovery_order,
                        vector<int>& finish_order) {
  int num_v = graph.get_num_v();
  parent.clear();
  parent.resize(num_v, -1);
  discovery_order.clear();
  discovery_order.resize(num_v, -1);
  finish_order.clear();
  finish_order.resize(num_v, -1);
  vector<bool> visited(num_v, false);
  int discovery_index = 0;
  int finish_index = 0;
  for (int i = 0; i < num_v; i++) {
    if (!visited[i]) {
      depth_first_search(graph, i, parent,
                         discovery_order,
                         finish_order,
                         visited,
                         discovery_index,
                         finish_index);
    }
  }
}
```

Testing Function depth_first_search

Next, we show a main function that tests the class. It is a simple driver program that can be used to read a graph and then initiate a depth-first traversal. The function create_graph creates a Graph of the desired implementation, reads the source and destination vertices, and inserts the edge into the graph. After the traversal, the driver program displays the vectors that represent the search results.

```
/** Main function to demonstrate the algorithm.
    pre: argv[1] is the name of the input file.
    pre: argv[2] is the type of graph.
    @param argc The count of command line arguments
    @param argv The command line arguments
*/
int main(int argc, char* argv[]) {
  if (argc < 3) {
    cerr << "Usage Depth_First_Search <input> <graph type>\n";
    return 1;
  }
  ifstream in(argv[1]);
  if (!in) {
    cerr << "Unable to open " << argv[1] << " for input\n";
    return 1;
  }
  Graph* g = Graph::create_graph(in, false, "List");
  vector<int> parent;
  vector<int> discovery_order;
  vector<int> finish_order;
  depth_first_search(*g, 0, parent, discovery_order, finish_order);
  cout << setw(4) << "i";
  cout << setw(8) << "discovery_order";
  cout << setw(8) << "finish_order";
  cout << setw(8) << "parent";
  cout << endl;
  for (int i = 0; i < g->get_num_v(); i++) {
    cout << setw(4) << i;
    cout << setw(8) << discovery_order[i];
    cout << setw(8) << finish_order[i];
    cout << setw(8) << parent[i];
    cout << endl;
  }
}
```

EXERCISES FOR SECTION 12.4

SELF-CHECK

1. Show the breadth-first search trees for the following graphs.

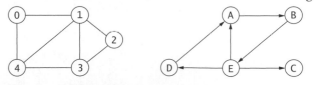

2. Show the depth-first search trees for the graphs in Exercise 1.

PROGRAMMING

1. Provide all accessor functions for class `Depth_First_Search` and the constructor that specifies the order of start vertices.
2. Implement function `depth_first_search` without using recursion. *Hint:* Use a stack to save the parent of the current vertex when you start to search one of its adjacent vertices.

12.5 Applications of Graph Traversals

CASE STUDY   Shortest Path Through a Maze

Problem   We want to design a program that will find the shortest path through a maze. In Chapter 7 we showed how to write a recursive program that found a solution to a maze. That program used a backtracking algorithm that visited alternate paths. When it found a dead end, it backed up and tried another path, and eventually it found a solution.

Figure 12.21 shows a maze solution generated by this recursive program. The light gray cells are barriers in the maze. The white squares show the solution path, the black squares show the squares that were visited but rejected, and the dark gray squares were not visited. As you can see, the program did not find an optimal solution. (This is a consequence of the program advancing the solution path to the South before attempting to advance it to the East.) We want to find the shortest path, defined as the one with the fewest decision points in it.

Analysis   We can represent the maze shown in Figure 12.21 by a graph, where we place a node at each decision point and at each dead end, as shown in Figure 12.22.

Now that we have the maze represented as a graph, we need to find the shortest path from the start point (vertex 0) to the end point (vertex 12). The breadth-first search function will return the shortest path from each vertex to its parent (the vector of parent vertices), and we can use this vector to find the shortest path to the end point. Recall that our shortest path will contain the smallest number of vertices, but not necessarily the smallest number of cells, in the path.

Design   Your program will need the following data structures:

- An external representation of the maze, consisting of the number of vertices and the edges
- An object of a class that implements the `Graph` interface
- A vector to hold the predecessors returned from the `breadth_first_search` function
- A stack to reverse the path

FIGURE 12.21
Recursive Solution to a Maze

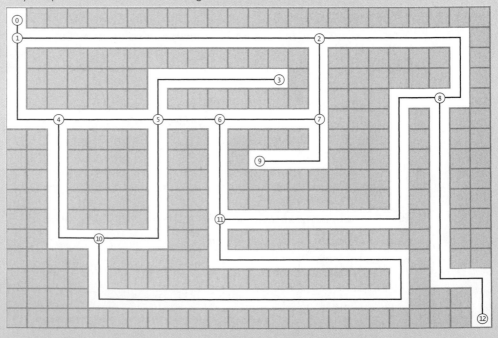

FIGURE 12.22
Graph Representation of the Maze in Figure 12.21

The algorithm is as follows:

1. Read in the number of vertices and create the graph object.
2. Read in the edges and insert the edges into the graph.
3. Call the `breadth_first_search` function with this graph and the starting vertex as its argument. The function returns the vector parent.
4. Start at v, the end vertex.
5. **while** v is not –1
6.   Push v onto the stack.
7.   Set v to parent[v].
8. **while** the stack is not empty
9.   Pop a vertex off the stack and output it.

Implementation

Listing 12.8 shows the program. We assume that the graph that represents the maze is stored in a text file. The first line of this file contains the number of vertices. The edges are on subsequent lines. The rest of the code follows the algorithm.

LISTING 12.8

Program to Solve a Maze Using a Breadth-First Search (`Maze.cpp`)

```cpp
#include <iostream>
#include <fstream>
#include <vector>
#include <stack>
#include "Graph.h"

using namespace std;

vector<int> breadth_first_search(const Graph&, int);

/** Program to solve a maze represented as a graph.
    This program performs a breadth-first search of the graph
    to find the "shortest" path from the start vertex to the
    end. It is assumed that the start vertex is 0, and the
    end vertex is num_v - 1.
    @param argc Count of command line arguments
    @param argv The command line arguments
    @pre argv[1] Contains the name of the input file
    @pre argv[2] Contains the type of graph
*/
int main(int argc, char* argv[]) {
  if (argc < 3) {
    cerr << "Usage Maze <input> <graph type>\n";
    return 1;
  }
  ifstream in(argv[1]);
  if (!in) {
    cerr << "Unable to open " << argv[1] << " for input\n";
    return 1;
  }
  Graph* the_maze = Graph::create_graph(in, false, "List");
```

```
        // Perform breadth-first search
    vector<int> parent = breadth_first_search(*the_maze, 0);
        // Construct the path
        stack<int> the_path;
        int v = the_maze->get_num_v() - 1;
        while (parent[v] != -1) {
            the_path.push(v);
            v = parent[v];
        }
        // Output the path
        cout << "The Shortest path is:\n";
        while (!the_path.empty()) {
            cout << the_path.top() << endl;
            the_path.pop();
        }
    }
```

Testing   Test this program with a variety of mazes. Use mazes for which the original program finds the shortest path and mazes for which it does not. For the graph shown in Figure 12.23, the shortest path from 0 to 12 is $0 \to 1 \to 2 \to 8 \to 12$.

FIGURE 12.23
Solution to Maze in Figure 12.21

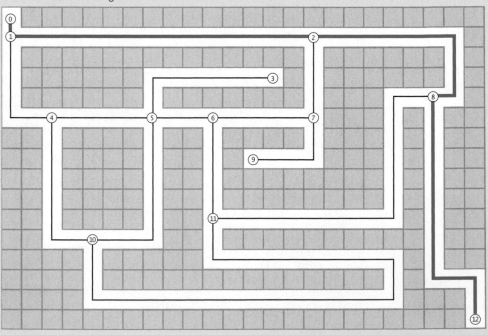

CASE STUDY   Topological Sort of a Graph

Problem   There are many problems in which one activity cannot be started before another one has been completed. One that you may have already encountered is determining the order in which you can take courses. Some courses have prerequisites. Some have more than one prerequisite. Furthermore, the prerequisites may have prerequisites. Figure 12.24 shows the courses and prerequisites of a computer science program at the authors' university.

Graphs such as the one shown in Figure 12.24 are known as *directed acyclic graphs* (DAGs). They are directed graphs that contain no cycles; that is, there are no loops, so once you pass through a vertex, there is no path back to that vertex. Figure 12.25 shows another example of a DAG.

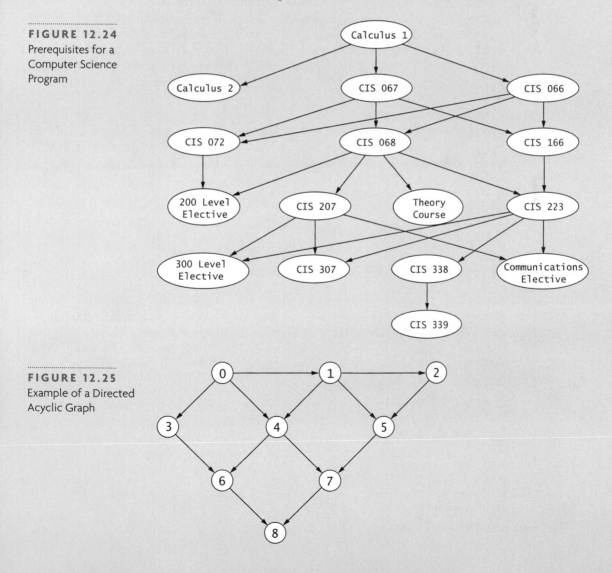

A *topological sort* of the vertices of a DAG is an ordering of the vertices such that if (u, v) is an edge, then u appears before v. This must be true for all edges. For example, 0, 1, 2, 3, 4, 5, 6, 7, 8 is a valid topological sort of the graph in Figure 12.25, but 0, 1, 5, 3, 4, 2, 6, 7, 8 is not, because $2 \rightarrow 5$ is an edge, but 5 appears before 2. There are many valid paths through the prerequisite graph and many valid topological sorts. Another valid topological sort is 0, 3, 1, 4, 6, 2, 5, 7, 8.

Analysis   If there is an edge from u to v in a DAG, then if we perform a depth-first search of this graph, the finish time of u must be after the finish time of v. When we return to u, either v has not been visited or it has finished. It is not possible that v would be visited but not finished, because if it were possible, we would discover u on a path that had passed through v. That would mean that there is a loop or cycle in the graph.

For example, in Figure 12.25 we could start the depth-first search at 0, then visit 4, followed by 6, followed by 8. Then, returning to 4, we would have to visit 7 before returning to 0. Then we would visit 1, and from 1 we would see that 4 has finished. Alternatively, we could start at 0 and then go to 1, and we would see that 4 has not been visited. What we cannot have happen is that we start at 0, then visit 4, and eventually get to 1 before finishing 4.

Design   If we perform a depth-first search of a graph and then order the vertices by the inverse of their finish order, we will have one topological sort of a directed acyclic graph. The topological sort produced by listing the vertices in the inverse of their finish order after a depth-first search of the graph in Figure 12.25 is 0, 3, 1, 4, 6, 2, 5, 7, 8.

Algorithm for Topological Sort

1. Read the graph from a data file.
2. Perform a depth-first search of the graph.
3. List the vertices in reverse of their finish order.

Implementation   We can use our depth_first_search function to implement this algorithm. Listing 12.9 shows a program that does this. It begins by reading the graph from an input file. It then calls the depth_first_search function, passing vectors parent, discovery_order, and finish_order by reference. Upon return, these vectors will be filled with the desired information. If we output the finish_order vector starting at get_num_v() - 1, we will obtain the topological sort of the graph.

LISTING 12.9
Topological_Sort.cpp

```
#include <iostream>
#include <fstream>
#include <vector>
#include "Graph.h"
using namespace std;
```

```
void depth_first_search(const Graph&, int,
                        vector<int>&, vector<int>&,
                        vector<int>&);

/** This program outputs the topological sort of a directed graph
    that contains no cycles.
    pre: argv[1] will contain the file name that contains the graph.
    pre: argv[2] will contain the type of graph representation.
    @param argc The count of command line arguments
    @param argv The command line arguments
*/
int main(int argc, char* argv[]) {
  if (argc < 3) {
    cerr << "Usage Topological_Sort <input> <graph type>\n";
    return 1;
  }
  ifstream in(argv[1]);
  if (!in) {
    cerr << "Unable to open " << argv[1] << " for input\n";
    return 1;
  }
  Graph* the_graph = Graph::create_graph(in, true, argv[2]);
  // Perform the depth-first search
  vector<int> parent;
  vector<int> discovery_order;
  vector<int> finish_order;
  depth_first_search(*the_graph, 0, parent, discovery_order,
                     finish_order);
  cout << "The Topological Sort is\n";
  for (int i = the_graph->get_num_v() - 1; i >= 0; i--)
    cout << finish_order[i] << endl;
  return 0;
}
```

Testing   Test this program using several different graphs. Use sparse graphs and dense graphs. Make sure that each graph that you try has no loops or cycles. If it does, the algorithm may display an invalid output.

EXERCISES FOR SECTION 12.5

SELF-CHECK

1. Draw the depth-first search tree of the graph in Figure 12.24 and then list the vertices in reverse finish order.
2. List some alternative topological sorts for the graph in Figure 12.24.

12.6 Algorithms Using Weighted Graphs

Finding the Shortest Path from a Vertex to All Other Vertices

The breadth-first search discussed in Section 12.4 found the shortest path from the start vertex to all other vertices, assuming that the length of each edge was the same. We now consider the problem of finding the shortest path where the length of each edge may be different—that is, in a weighted directed graph such as that shown in Figure 12.26. The computer scientist Edsger W. Dijkstra developed an algorithm, now called Dijkstra's algorithm (E. W. Dijkstra, "A Note on Two Problems in Connection with Graphs," *Numerische Mathematik*, Vol. 1 [1959], pp. 269–271), to solve this problem. This algorithm makes the assumption that all of the edge values are positive.

For Dijkstra's algorithm we need two sets, S and $V - S$, and two vectors, d and p. S will contain the vertices for which we have computed the shortest distance, and $V - S$ will contain the vertices that we still need to process. The entry $d[v]$ will contain the shortest distance from s to v, and $p[v]$ will contain the predecessor of v in the path from s to v.

We initialize S by placing the start vertex, s, into it. We initialize $V - S$ by placing the remaining vertices into it. For each v in $V - S$, we initialize d by setting $d[v]$ equal to the weight of the edge $w(s, v)$ for each vertex, v, adjacent to s and to ∞ for each vertex that is not adjacent to s. We initialize $p[v]$ to s for each v in $V - S$.

For example, given the graph shown in Figure 12.26, the set S would initially be {0}, $V - S$ would be {1, 2, 3, 4}. The vectors d and p would be defined as follows.

v	d[v]	p[v]
1	10	0
2	∞	0
3	30	0
4	100	0

FIGURE 12.26
Weighted Directed
Graph

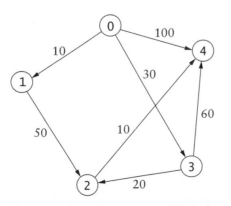

The first row shows that the distance from vertex 0 to vertex 1 is 10 and that vertex 0 is the predecessor of vertex 1. The second row shows that vertex 2 is not adjacent to vertex 0.

We now find the vertex u in $V - S$ that has the smallest value of $d[u]$. Using our example, this is 1. We now consider the vertices v that are adjacent to u. If the distance from s to u ($d[u]$) plus the distance from u to v (that is, $w(u, v)$) is smaller than the known distance from s to v, $d[v]$, then we update $d[v]$ to be $d[u] + w(u, v)$, and we set $p[v]$ to u. In our example the value of $d[1]$ is 10, and $w(1, 2)$ is 50. Since 10 + 50 = 60 is less than ∞, we set $d[2]$ to 60 and $p[2]$ to 1. We remove 1 from $V - S$ and place it into S. We repeat this until $V - S$ is empty.

After the first pass through this loop, S is {0, 1}, $V - S$ is {2, 3, 4} and d and p are as follows:

v	d[v]	p[v]
1	10	0
2	60	1
3	30	0
4	100	0

We again select u from $V - S$ with the smallest $d[u]$. This is now 3. The adjacent vertices to 3 are 2 and 4. The distance from 0 to 3, $d[3]$, is 30. The distance from 3 to 2 is 20. Because 30 + 20 = 50 is less than the current value of $d[2]$, 60, we update $d[2]$ to 50 and change $p[2]$ to 3. Also, because 30 + 60 = 90 is less than 100, we update $d[4]$ to 90 and set $p[4]$ to 3.

Now S is {0, 1, 3}, and $V - S$ is {2, 4}. The vectors d and p are as follows:

v	d[v]	p[v]
1	10	0
2	50	3
3	30	0
4	90	3

Next we select vertex 2 from $V - S$. The only vertex adjacent to 2 is 4. Since $d[2] + w(2, 4) = 50 + 10 = 60$ is less than $d[4]$, 90, we update $d[4]$ to 60 and $p[4]$ to 2. Now S is {0, 1, 2, 3}, $V - S$ is {4}, and d and p are as follows:

v	d[v]	p[v]
1	10	0
2	50	3
3	30	0
4	60	2

Finally we remove 4 from $V - S$ and find that it has no adjacent vertices. We are now done. The vector d shows the shortest distances from the start vertex to all other vertices, and the vector p can be used to determine the corresponding paths. For example, the path from vertex 0 to vertex 4 has a length of 60, and it is the reverse of 4, 2, 3, 0; therefore, the shortest path is $0 \rightarrow 3 \rightarrow 2 \rightarrow 4$.

Dijkstra's Algorithm

1. Initialize S with the start vertex, s, and $V - S$ with the remaining vertices.
2. **for** all v in $V - S$
3.   Set $p[v]$ to s.
4.   **if** there is an edge (s, v)
5.   Set $d[v]$ to $w(s, v)$.
    else
6.   Set $d[v]$ to ∞.
7. **while** $V - S$ is not empty
8.   **for** all u in $V - S$, find the smallest $d[u]$.
9.   Remove u from $V - S$ and add u to S.
10.   **for** all v adjacent to u in $V - S$
11.   **if** $d[u] + w(u, v)$ is less than d$[v]$.
12.   Set $d[v]$ to $d[u] + w(u, v)$.
13.   Set $p[v]$ to u.

Analysis of Dijkstra's Algorithm

Step 1 requires $|V|$ steps.

The loop at Step 2 will be executed $|V - 1|$ times.

The loop at Step 7 will also be executed $|V - 1|$ times.

Within the loop at Step 7 we have to consider Steps 8 and 9. For these steps we will have to search each value in $V - S$. This decreases each time through the loop at Step 7, so we will have $|V| - 1 + |V| - 2 + \cdots 1$. This is $O(|V|^2)$. Therefore, Dijkstra's algorithm as stated is $O|V|^2)$. We will look at possible improvements to this for sparse graphs when we discuss a similar algorithm in the next subsection.

Implementation

Listing 12.10 provides a straightforward implementation of Dijkstra's algorithm using set<int> v_minus_s to represent set $V - S$. The function takes as inputs the graph and starting point, and it outputs predecessor and distance vectors passed through parameters. We use iterators to traverse v_minus_s.

If we used an adjacency list representation for the graph (i.e., class List_Graph, described earlier), then we would code Step 10 (update the distances) to iterate through the edges adjacent to vertex u, and then update the distance if the destination vertex was in v_minus_s. The modified code follows:

```
    // Update the distances
    for (Graph::iterator itr = graph.begin(u);
         itr != graph.end(u); ++itr) {
      Edge edge = *itr;
      int v = edge.get_dest();
      if (contains(v_minus_s, v)) {
        double weight = edge.get_weight();
        if (dist[u] + weight < dist[v]) {
          dist[v] = dist[u] + weight;
          pred[v] = u;
        }
      }
    }
  }
```

LISTING 12.10

Dijkstra's Shortest-Path Algorithm (`Dijkstra.cpp`)

```
#include <iostream>
#include <fstream>
#include <vector>
#include <set>
#include "Graph.h"

using namespace std;

/** Dijkstra's Shortest-Path algorithm.
    @param graph The weighted graph to be searched
    @param start The start vertex
    @param pred Output vector to contain the predecessors
           in the shortest path
    @param dist Output vector to contain the distance
           in the shortest path
*/
void dijkstras_algorithm(const Graph& graph,
                         int start,
                         vector<int>& pred,
                         vector<double>& dist) {
  int num_v = graph.get_num_v();
  // Use a set to represent V - S
  set<int> v_minus_s;
  // Initialize V - S.
  for (int i = 0; i < num_v; i++) {
    if (i != start) {
      v_minus_s.insert(i);
    }
  }
  // Initialize pred and dist
  for (set<int>::iterator itr = v_minus_s.begin();
       itr != v_minus_s.end(); ++itr) {
    pred[*itr] = start;
    dist[*itr] = graph.get_edge(start, *itr).get_weight();
  }
```

```
    // Main loop
    while (!v_minus_s.empty()) {
      // Find the value u in V - S with the smallest dist[u].
      double min_dist = numeric_limits<double>::infinity();
      int u = -1;
      for (set<int>::iterator itr = v_minus_s.begin();
           itr != v_minus_s.end(); ++itr) {
        int v = *itr;
        if (dist[v] < min_dist) {
          min_dist = dist[v];
          u = v;
        }
      }
      // Remove u from v_minus_s
      v_minus_s.erase(u);
      // Update the distances
      for (set<int>::iterator itr = v_minus_s.begin();
           itr != v_minus_s.end(); ++itr) {
        int v = *itr;
        if (graph.is_edge(u, v)) {
          double weight = graph.get_edge(u, v).get_weight();
          if (dist[u] + weight < dist[v]) {
            dist[v] = dist[u] + weight;
            pred[v] = u;
          }
        }
      }
    }
  }
  ...
```

Minimum Spanning Trees

A *spanning tree* is a subset of the edges of a graph such that there is only one edge between any two vertices, and all of the vertices are connected. If we have a spanning tree for a graph, then we can access all the vertices of the graph from the start node. The *cost* of a spanning tree is the sum of the weights of the edges. We want to find the *minimum spanning tree*, or the spanning tree with the smallest cost. For example, if we want to start up our own long-distance phone company and need to connect the cities shown in Figure 12.4, finding the minimum spanning tree would allow us to build the cheapest network.

We will discuss the algorithm published by R. C. Prim (R. C. Prim, "Shortest Connection Networks and Some Generalizations," *Bell System Technical Journal*, Vol. 36 [1957], pp. 1389–1401) for finding the minimum spanning tree of a graph. It is very similar to Dijkstra's algorithm, but Prim published his algorithm in 1957, two years before Dijkstra's paper, which contains an algorithm for finding the minimum spanning tree that is essentially the same as Prim's as well as the previously discussed algorithm for finding the shortest paths.

Overview of Prim's Algorithm

The vertices are divided into two sets: S, the set of vertices in the spanning tree, and $V - S$, the remaining vertices. As in Dijkstra's algorithm, we maintain two vectors: $d[v]$ will contain the length of the shortest edge from a vertex in S to the vertex v

that is in $V - S$, and $p[v]$ will contain the source vertex for that edge. The only difference between the algorithm to find the shortest path and the algorithm to find the minimum spanning tree is the contents of $d[v]$. In the algorithm to find the shortest path, $d[v]$ contains the total length of the path from the starting vertex. In the algorithm to find the minimum spanning tree, $d[v]$ contains only the length of the final edge. We show the essentials of Prim's algorithm next.

Prim's Algorithm for Finding the Minimum Spanning Tree

1.   Initialize S with the start vertex, s, and $V - S$ with the remaining vertices.
2.   **for** all v in $V - S$
3.   Set $p[v]$ to s.
4.   **if** there is an edge (s, v)
5.   Set $d[v]$ to $w(s, v)$.
        else
6.   Set $d[v]$ to ∞.
7.   **while** $V - S$ is not empty
8.   **for** all u in $V - S$, find the smallest $d[u]$.
9.   Remove u from $V - S$ and add it to S.
10.   Insert the edge $(u, p[u])$ into the spanning tree.
11.   **for** all v in $V - S$
12.   **if** $w(u, v) < d[v]$
13.   Set $d[v]$ to $w(u, v)$.
14.   Set $p[v]$ to u.

In the vector d, $d[v]$ contains the length of the shortest known (previously examined) edge from a vertex in S to the vertex v, while v is a member of $V - S$. In the vector p, the value $p[v]$ is the source vertex of this shortest edge. When v is removed from $V - S$, we no longer update these entries in d and p.

EXAMPLE 12.2   Consider the graph shown in Figure 12.27. We initialize S to {0} and $V - S$ to {1, 2, 3, 4, 5}. The smallest edge from u to v, where u is in S and v is in $V - S$, is the edge (0, 2). We add this edge to the spanning tree, and add 2 to S (see Figure 12.28(a)).

FIGURE 12.27
Graph for Example 12.2

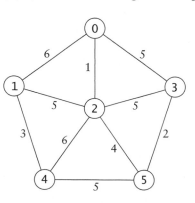

....

FIGURE 12.28

Building a Minimum Spanning Tree Using Prim's Algorithm

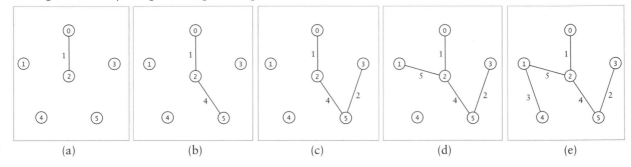

(a)   (b)   (c)   (d)   (e)

The set S is now $\{0, 2\}$ and $V - S$ is $\{1, 3, 4, 5\}$. We now have to consider all of the edges (u, v), where u is either 0 or 2, and v is 1, 3, 4, or 5 (there are eight possible edges). The smallest one is $(2, 5)$. We add this to the spanning tree, and S now is $\{0, 2, 5\}$ and $V - S$ is $\{1, 3, 4\}$ (see Figure 12.28(b)). The next smallest edge is $(5, 3)$. We insert that into the tree and add 3 to S (see Figure 12.28(c)). Now $V - S$ is $\{1, 4\}$. The smallest edge is $(2, 1)$. After adding this edge (see Figure 12.28(d)), we are left with $V - S$ being $\{4\}$. The smallest edge to 4 is $(1, 4)$. This is added to the tree, and the spanning tree is complete (see Figure 12.28(e)).

Analysis of Prim's Algorithm

Step 8 is $O(|V|)$. Because this is within the loop at Step 7, it will be executed $O(|V|)$ times for a total time of $O(|V|^2)$. Step 11 is $O(|E_u|)$, the number of edges that originate at u. Because Step 11 is inside the loop of Step 7, it will be executed for all vertices; thus, the total is $O(|E|)$. Because $|V|^2$ is greater than $|E|$, the overall cost of the algorithm is $O(|V|^2)$.

By using a priority queue to hold the edges from S to $V - S$, we can improve on this algorithm. Then Step 8 is $O(\log n)$, where n is the size of the priority queue. In the worst case, all of the edges are inserted into the priority queue, the overall cost of the algorithm is then $O(|E| \log |V|)$. We say that the algorithm is $O(|E| \log |V|)$ instead of saying that it is $O(|E| \log |E|)$, even though the maximum size of the priority queue is $|E|$, because $|E|$ is bounded by $|V|^2$ and $\log |V|^2$ is $2 \times \log |V|$.

For a dense graph, where $|E|$ is approximately $|V|^2$, this is not an improvement, but it is an improvement for a sparse graph, where $|E|$ is significantly less than $|V|^2$. Furthermore, computer science researchers have developed improved priority queue implementations that give $O(|E| + |V| \log |V|)$ or better performance.

Implementation

Listing 12.11 shows an implementation of Prim's algorithm using a priority queue to hold the edges from S to $V - S$. The vectors p and d given in the previous algorithm description are not needed, because the priority queue contains complete edges. For a given vertex d, if a shorter edge is discovered, we do not remove the entry containing the longer edge from the priority queue. We merely insert new edges as they are discovered. Therefore, when the next shortest edge is removed from the priority queue, it may have a destination that is no longer in $V - S$. In that case, we continue to remove edges from the priority queue until we find one with a destination that is still in $V - S$. This is done with the following loop:

```
do {
  edge = pQ.top();
  pQ.pop();
  dest = edge.get_dest();
} while(!contains(v_minus_s, dest));
```

LISTING 12.11
Prim's Minimum Spanning Tree Algorithm (`Prim.cpp`)

```cpp
#include <iostream>
#include <fstream>
#include <vector>
#include <set>
#include <queue>
#include "Graph.h"
#include "set_functions.h"

using namespace std;

/** Comparator function class to compare Edge weights. */
struct Compare_Edges {
  typedef Edge value_type;
  bool operator()(const Edge& left, const Edge& right) {
    return left.get_weight() < right.get_weight();
  }
};

/** Prim's Minimum Spanning Tree algorithm.
    @param graph The weighted graph to be searched
    @param start The start vertex
    @return A vector of edges that forms the MST
*/
vector<Edge> prims_algorithm(const Graph& graph,
                             int start) {
  vector<Edge> result;
  int num_v = graph.get_num_v();
  // Use a set to represent V - S
  set<int> v_minus_s;
  // Declare the priority queue
  priority_queue<Edge, vector<Edge>, Compare_Edges> pQ;
  // Initialize V - S.
  for (int i = 0; i < num_v; i++) {
    if (i != start) {
      v_minus_s.insert(i);
    }
  }
  int current = start;
```

```
// Main loop
while (!v_minus_s.empty()) {
  // Update priority queue
  Graph::iterator iter = graph.begin(current);
  while (iter != graph.end(current)) {
    Edge edge = *iter++;
    int dest = edge.get_dest();
    if (contains(v_minus_s, dest)) {
      pQ.push(edge);
    }
  }
  // Find the shortest edge whose source is in S and
  // destination is in V - S.
  int dest;
  Edge edge;
  do {
    edge = pQ.top();
    pQ.pop();
    dest = edge.get_dest();
  } while(!contains(v_minus_s, dest));
  // Take dest out of v_minus_s
  v_minus_s.erase(dest);
  // Add edge to result
  result.push_back(edge);
  // Make this the current vertex
  current = dest;
}
return result;
}
...
```

EXERCISES FOR SECTION 12.6

SELF-CHECK

1. Trace the execution of Dijkstra's algorithm to find the shortest path from Philadelphia to the other cities shown in the following graph.

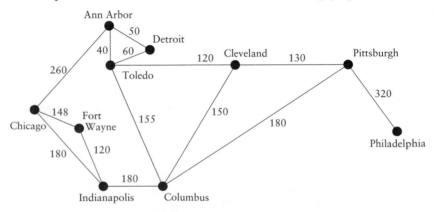

2. Trace the execution of Dijkstra's algorithm to find the shortest paths from vertex 0 to the other vertices in the following graph.

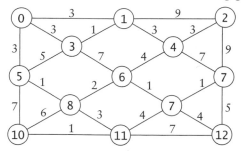

3. Trace the execution of Prim's algorithm to find the minimum spanning tree for the graph shown in Question 2.

4. Trace the execution of Prim's algorithm to find the minimum spanning tree for the graph shown in Question 1.

Chapter Review

♦ A graph consists of a set of vertices and a set of edges. An edge is a pair of vertices. Graphs may be either undirected or directed. Edges may have a value associated with them known as the weight.

♦ In an undirected graph, if $\{u, v\}$ is an edge, then there is a path from vertex u to vertex v, and vice versa.

♦ In a directed graph, if (u, v) is an edge, then (v, u) is not necessarily an edge.

♦ If there is an edge from one vertex to another, then the second vertex is adjacent to the first. A path is a sequence of adjacent vertices. A path is simple if the vertices in the path are distinct except, perhaps, for the first and last vertex, which may be the same. A cycle is a path in which the first and last vertexes are the same.

♦ A graph is considered connected if there is a path from each vertex to every other vertex.

♦ A tree is a special case of a graph. Specifically, a tree is a connected graph that contains no cycles.

♦ Graphs may be represented by an array of adjacency lists. There is one list for each vertex, and the list contains the edges that originate at this vertex.

♦ Graphs may be represented by a two-dimensional square array called an adjacency matrix. The entry $[u][v]$ will contain a value to indicate that an edge from u to v is present or absent.

◆ A breadth-first search of a graph finds all vertices reachable from a given vertex via the shortest path, where the length of the path is based on the number of vertices in the path.

◆ A depth-first search of a graph starts at a given vertex and then follows a path of unvisited vertices until it reaches a point where there are no unvisited vertices that are reachable. It then backtracks until it finds an unvisited vertex, and then continues along the path to that vertex.

◆ A topological sort determines an order for starting activities which are dependent on the completion of other activities (prerequisites). The finish order derived from a depth-first traversal represents a topological sort.

◆ Dijkstra's algorithm finds the shortest path from a start vertex to all other vertices, where the distance from one vertex to another is determined by the weight of the edge between them.

◆ Prim's algorithm finds the minimum spanning tree for a graph. This consists of the subset of the edges of a connected graph whose sum of weights is the minimum and the graph consisting of only the edges in the subset is still connected.

Quick-Check Exercises

1. For the following graph:
   a. List the vertices and edges.
   b. True or false: The path 0, 1, 4, 6, 3 is a simple path.
   c. True or false: The path 0, 3, 1, 4, 6, 3, 2 is a simple path.
   d. True or false: The path 3, 1, 2, 4, 7, 6, 3 is a cycle.

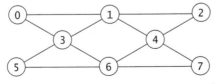

2. Identify the connected components in the following graph.

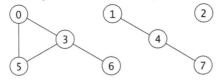

3. For the following graph
   a. List the vertices and edges.
   b. Does this graph contain any cycles?

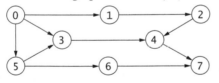

4. Show the adjacency matrices for the graphs shown in Questions 1, 2, and 3.
5. Show the adjacency lists for the graphs shown in Questions 1, 2, and 3.
6. Show the breadth-first search tree for the graph shown in Question 1, starting at vertex 0.
7. Show the depth-first search tree for the graph shown in Question 3, starting at vertex 0.
8. Show a topological sort of the vertices in the graph shown in Question 3.
9. In the following graph, find the shortest path from 0 to all other vertices.

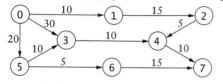

10. In the following graph, find the minimum spanning tree.

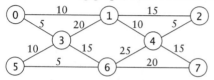

Answers to Quick-Check Exercises

1. **a.** Vertices: {0, 1, 2, 3, 4, 5, 6, 7}. Edges: {{0, 1}, {0, 3}, {1, 2}, {1, 3}, {1, 4}, {2, 4}, {3, 5}, {3, 6}, {4, 6}, {4, 7}, {5, 6}, {6, 7}}.
   b. True.
   c. False.
   d. True.
2. The connected components are {0, 3, 5, 6}, {1, 4, 7}, and {2}.
3. **a.** Vertices: {0, 1, 2, 3, 4, 5, 6, 7}. Edges: {(0, 1), (0, 3), (0, 5), (1, 2), (2, 4), (3, 4), (4, 7), (5, 3), (5, 6), (6, 7)}.
   b. The graph contains no cycles.
4. For the graph shown in Question 1:

Column

	[0]	[1]	[2]	[3]	[4]	[5]	[6]	[7]
[0]		1		1				
[1]	1		1	1	1			
[2]		1			1			
[3]	1	1				1	1	
[4]		1	1				1	1
[5]				1			1	
[6]				1	1	1		1
[7]					1		1	

Row

For Question 2:

Column

	[0]	[1]	[2]	[3]	[4]	[5]	[6]	[7]
[0]				1		1		
[1]					1			
[2]								
[3]	1					1	1	
[4]		1						1
[5]	1			1				
[6]				1				
[7]					1			

Row

For Question 3:

Column

	[0]	[1]	[2]	[3]	[4]	[5]	[6]	[7]
[0]		1		1		1		
[1]			1					
[2]					1			
[3]					1			
[4]								1
[5]				1			1	
[6]								1
[7]								

Row

5. For Question 1:

[0] → 1 → 3
[1] → 0 → 2 → 3 → 4
[2] → 1 → 4
[3] → 0 → 1 → 5 → 6
[4] → 1 → 2 → 6 → 7
[5] → 3 → 6
[6] → 3 → 4 → 5 → 7
[7] → 4 → 6

For Question 2:

[0] → 3 → 5
[1] → 4
[2] →
[3] → 0 → 5 → 6
[4] → 1 → 7
[5] → 0 → 3
[6] → 3
[7] → 4

For Question 3:

[0] → 1 → 3 → 5
[1] → 2
[2] → 4
[3] → 4
[4] → 7
[5] → 3 → 6
[6] → 7
[7] →

6.

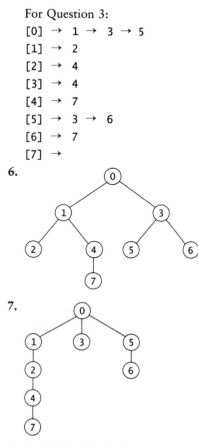

7.

8. 0, 5, 6, 3, 1, 2, 4, 7.

9.

Vertex	Distance	Path
1	10	0 → 1
2	25	0 → 1 → 2
3	30	0 → 3 (or 0 → 5 → 3)
4	30	0 → 1 → 2 → 4
5	20	0 → 5
6	25	0 → 5 → 6
7	40	0 → 5 → 6 → 7 (or 0 → 1 → 2 → 4 → 7)

10.

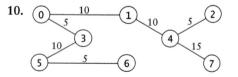

Review Questions

1. What are the different types of graphs?
2. What are the different types of paths?
3. What are two common functions for representing graphs? Can you think of other functions?
4. What is a breadth-first search? What can it be used for?
5. What is a depth-first search? What can it be used for?
6. Under what circumstances are the paths found by Dijkstra's algorithm not unique?
7. Under what circumstances is the minimum spanning tree unique?
8. What is a topological sort?

Programming Projects

1. Design and implement the `Matrix_Graph` class.
2. Rewrite function `dijkstras_algorithm` to use a priority queue as we did for function `prims_algorithm`. When inserting edges into the priority queue, the weight is replaced by the total distance from the source vertex to the destination vertex. The source vertex, however, remains unchanged, because it is the predecessor in the shortest path.
3. In both Prim's algorithm and Dijkstra's algorithm, edges are retained in the priority queue even though a shorter edge to a given destination vertex has been found. This can be avoided, and thus performance improved, by using a `Modifiable_Priority_Queue`. Extend the `priority_queue` class described in Chapter 8 as follows:

```
#ifndef MODIFIABLE_PRIORITY_QUEUE_H
#define MODIFIABLE_PRIORITY_QUEUE_H

#include <iostream>
#include <vector>
#include <functional>
#include <utility>

namespace KW {

    /** A modifiable priority queue based on a heap stored in a vector.
        Like the priority_queue, items are inserted in any order and
        removed in priority order, with the largest (as defined by the
        Compare function) removed first. The insert function will return
        a value known as a locator. The locator may be used to replace a
        value in the priority queue.
    */
    template<typename Item_Type, typename Compare = std::less<Item_Type> >
      class Modifiable_Priority_Queue {

        public:

        /** Construct an empty priority queue */
        Modifiable_Priority_Queue() {}

        /** Insert an item into the priority queue.
            @param item The item to be inserted
            @return A locator to the item
```

```
*/
int insert(const Item_Type& item);

/** Return a reference to the largest item */
const Item_Type& top() const {return the_data.front();}

/** Remove the largest item */
void pop();

/** Replace the item at the specified location.
    @param loc The locator value of the current item
    @param new_value The new value
*/
void replace_item(int loc, const Item_Type& new_value);

/** Return true if the priority queue is empty */
bool empty() const {return the_data.empty();}

/** Return the number of items in the priority queue */
size_t size() const {return the_data.size();}

private:

// Typedef to make life easier
typedef std::pair<int, Item_Type> Entry_Type;

/** Function to swap entries and their corresponding locators */
void swap(int a, int b) {
  // Swap the entries
  std::swap(the_data[a], the_data[b]);
  // Update the locator values
  locators[the_data[a].first] = a;
  locators[the_data[b].first] = b;
}

// Comparator for Entry_Types
struct Compare_Entries {
  Compare value_comp;
  bool operator()(const Entry_Type& left,
                  const Entry_Type& right) {
    return value_comp(left.second, right.second);
  }
};

/** The vector to hold the data */
std::vector<Entry_Type> the_data;

/** The vector to hold the locators */
std::vector<int> locators;

/** The comparator function object */
Compare_Entries comp;
```

```
      // For debugging
      public:
      void print_tables(const std::vector<int>& loc) {
        std::cout << "i\tloc\tlocators\tthe_data\n";
        for (size_t i = 0; i < loc.size(); i++) {
          std::cout << i << "\t" << loc[i]
                    << "\t" << locators[i]
                    << "\t" << the_data[i].first
                    << "\t" << the_data[i].second << std::endl;
      }
    }
  };

// Implementation of member functions

template<typename Item_Type, typename Compare>
  int Modifiable_Priority_Queue<Item_Type, Compare>::insert(
          const Item_Type& item) {
  Entry_Type the_pair(locators.size(), item);
  the_data.push_back(the_pair);
  locators.push_back(the_data.size() - 1);
  int child = size() - 1;
  int parent = (child - 1) / 2;
  // Reheap
  while (parent >= 0
          && comp(the_data[parent], the_data[child])) {
    swap(child, parent);
    child = parent;
    parent = (child - 1) / 2;
  }
  return locators.size() - 1;
}

template<typename Item_Type, typename Compare>
  void Modifiable_Priority_Queue<Item_Type, Compare>::pop() {
  if (size() == 1) {
    the_data.pop_back();
    return;
  }
  swap(0, size() - 1);
  the_data.pop_back();
  int parent = 0;
  while (true) {
    int left_child = 2 * parent + 1;
    if (left_child >= size())
      break; // out of heap
    int right_child = left_child + 1;
    int max_child = left_child;
    if (right_child < size()
        && comp(the_data[left_child], the_data[right_child]))
      max_child = right_child;
    // assert: max_child is the index of the larger child
    if (comp(the_data[parent], the_data[max_child])) {
      swap(max_child, parent);
      parent = max_child;
    }
```

```
        else
          break;
      }
    }


    /** Replace the item at the specified location.
        @param loc The locator value of the current item
        @param new_value The new value
    */
    template<typename Item_Type, typename Compare>
      void Modifiable_Priority_Queue<Item_Type, Compare>::
          replace_item(int loc, const Item_Type& new_value) {
      the_data[locators[loc]].second = new_value;
      // The new value should have a smaller value . . .
      int child = locators[loc];
      int parent = (child - 1) / 2; // Find child's parent.
      // Reheap
      while (parent >= 0
            && comp(the_data[parent], the_data[child])) {
        swap(parent, child);
        child = parent;
        parent = (child - 1) / 2;
      }
      // ... however, it is not required, so let's check that direction too
      parent = child;
      while (true) {
        int left_child = 2 * parent + 1;
        if (left_child >= the_data.size()) {
          break; // Out of heap.
        }
        int right_child = left_child + 1;
        int max_child = left_child; // Assume left_child is larger.
        // See whether right_child is smaller.
        if (right_child < the_data.size()
            && comp(the_data[left_child],
                    the_data[right_child]) > 0) {
          max_child = right_child;
        }
        // assert: min_child is the index of the smaller child.
        // Move smaller child up heap if necessary.
        if (comp(the_data[parent],
                the_data[max_child]) > 0) {
          swap(parent, max_child);
          parent = max_child;
        }
        else { // Heap property is restored.
          break;
        }
      }
      // Heap property is now restored either way
    }
} // End namespace KW

#endif
```

4. Implement Dijkstra's algorithm using the modifiable_priority_queue.

5. Implement Prim's algorithm using the modifiable_priorty_queue.

6. A maze can be constructed from a series of concentric circles. Between the circles there are walls placed, and around
the circles there are doors. The walls divide the areas
between the circles into chambers, and the doors permit
movement between chambers. The positions of the doors
and walls are given in degrees measured counterclockwise
from the horizontal. For example, the maze shown in the
figure can be described as follows:

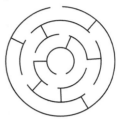

Number of circles	4	
Position of doors	Outer circle	90–95
	Next inner circle	26–40, 128–133, 198–215, 305–319
	Next inner circle	67–90, 161–180, 243–256, 342–360
	Innermost circle	251–288
Position of walls:	Outer ring	45, 135, 300
	Middle ring	0, 100, 255, 270
	Inner ring	65, 180

Write a program that inputs a description of a maze in this format and finds the shortest
path from the outside to the innermost circle. The shortest path is the one that goes
through the fewest number of chambers.

7. A rectangular maze can be represented as a sequence of lines consisting of 0s and 1s,
where a 0 represents an open square and a 1 represents a closed one. For example, the
maze shown in Figure 12.21 and reproduced here, has the following input file:

```
01111111111111111111111
00000000000000000000001
01111111111111011111101
01111110000000101111101
01111110111111011000001
00000000000000011011011
11011110110111101011011
11011110110111101011011
11011110110100001011011
11011110110111111011011
11011110110000000011011
11000001101111111111011
11110111110000000001011
11110111111111111101000
11110000000000000001110
11111111111111111111110
```

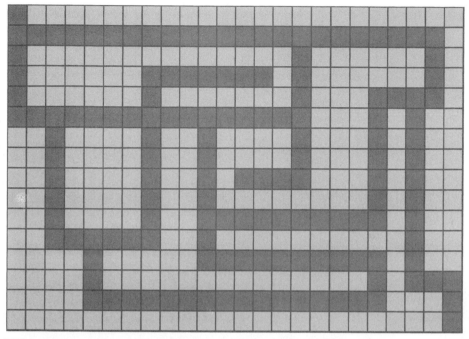

Write a program that reads input in this format and finds the shortest path, where the distance along a path is defined by the number of squares covered.

8. A third possible representation of a graph is to use the set class to contain the edges. By defining a comparator that first compares on the source vertex and then the destination vertex, we can use the lower_bound and upper_bound functions to obtain iterators that span the edges originating at a given vertex. Design and implement a class that meets the requirements of the Graph interface and uses a set to hold the edges.

Appendix **A**

Advanced C++ Topics

Advanced C++ Topics

A.1 Source Character Set, Trigraphs, Digraphs, and Alternate Keywords
A.2 The Allocator
A.3 Traits
A.4 Virtual Base Classes
A.5 Smart Pointers

A.1 Source Character Set, Trigraphs, Digraphs, and Alternate Keywords

C++ uses the United States subset of the 7-bit international character set (defined by ISO 646-1983), commonly called ASCII (American Standard Code for Information Interchange). This character set consists of the special characters space, horizontal tab, vertical tab, form feed, and newline, plus the following characters:

```
a b c d e f g h i j k l m n o p q r s t u v w x y z
A B C D E F G H I J K L M N O P Q R S T U V W X Y Z
0 1 2 3 4 5 6 7 8 9
_ { } [ ] # ( ) < > % : ; . ? * + - / ^ & | ~ = , \ " '
```

However, users in other countries do not have all of these characters available in the 7-bit subsets defined for their countries. For example, the Danish national character set uses Æ, æ, Ø, ø, Å, and å in place of [,], {, }, |, and \. A set of three-character sequences, known as *trigraphs*, have been defined to allow users to write C++ programs in a truly portable way using a minimum set of characters. These all begin with two question-marks (??) followed by a single character.

TABLE A.1
Trigraphs, Alternate Keywords, and Digraphs

Trigraph	Alternate Keyword	Digraph	Equivalent
??=		%:	#
		%:%:	##
??/			\
??'	xor		^
??(		<:	[
??)		:>	]
??!	bitor		|
	or		||
??<		<%	{
??>		%>	}
??-	compl		~
	and		&&
	bitand		&
	and_eq		&=
	or_eq		|=
	xor_eq		^=
	not		!
	not_eq		!=

In addition to the trigraphs, C++ provides alternate operator keywords and what are called *digraphs* for some of the special symbols. The trigraphs, alternate keywords, and digraphs are shown in Table A.1.

The distinction between the trigraphs and the alternate keywords and digraphs is that the trigraphs are replaced with their equivalents by the preprocessor, whereas the alternate keywords and digraphs are retained but treated as if they were the equivalent symbol. Therefore, the expression sqrt(x??(0??)) would be changed to sqrt(x[0]) but the expression sqrt(x<:0:>) would not be changed.

A.2 The Allocator

The container classes are defined in the standard library to take a second template parameter called an *allocator*. For example, the vector class is declared in the standard as:

```
template<typename Item_Type,
         typename Allocator = allocator<Item_Type> >
   class vector { . . . };
```

Normally you do not need to be concerned with the allocator. A default allocator is provided by the standard. However, if your program contains a syntax error that involves one of the standard containers, the error message generated by the compiler can be quite confusing. For example, an error made that involves a vector of strings will make reference to:

```
std::vector<std::basic_string<char, std::char_traits<char>,
std::allocator<char> >, std::allocator< std::basic_string<char,
std::char_traits<char>, std::allocator<char> > >
```

In this section we describe the allocator class and why you might want to replace the default one with your own.

The allocator encapsulates information about the memory allocation model, pointers, and pointer differences (the result of subtracting two pointers). At the time that the standard library was first proposed, there were a variety of memory models that depended on the underlying computer architecture. For example, on one architecture pointers were 16 bits in length, and far_pointers were 32 bits consisting of two 16-bit components. Also, the new and delete operations, as they were initially defined, were not sufficiently general to implement the standard library efficiently.

Today the ability to define your own allocator is still useful because the default allocation may be wasteful of memory. For example, an implementation may always allocate a minimum-size block of memory whenever the new operator is used. This minimum-size block could be much larger than required. With the g++ compiler,

```
double* pd = new double;
```

allocates space for three **double** values, and the statement

```
char* pc = new char;
```

allocates space for 24 **char** values.

If you defined your own allocator my_alloc, you could then declare a vector of **char** as

```
vector<char, my_alloc<char> > my_vector;
```

This vector would then use my_alloc to allocate memory in a more efficient manner.

The requirements for the allocator are summarized in Table A.2. We only need to implement the functions allocate and destroy. The other functions can either be copied from or delegated to the standard allocator. The Companion Web site for this book contains a case study discussion of the design of an allocator that allocates storage more efficiently for small objects or small arrays.

A.3 Traits

C++ uses what is known as a *traits class* to provide information to the compiler about types. This information is used by template classes and functions. This allows treating the built-in types and user-defined types (classes) in a uniform manner. If we only had user-defined types, we could define functions and data fields that would provide the necessary information. However, if we want the same information about a built-in type, we must provide it in some other way since we cannot define member functions or data fields for the built-in types.

In Chapter 10 we showed how the iterator_traits class can be used for both a built-in type (pointer) and a user-defined type (iterator).

TABLE A.2
Requirements for an Allocator Class

Typedefs	Purpose
pointer	Pointer to Item_Type
const_pointer	**const** pointer to Item_Type
reference	Reference to Item_Type
const_reference	**const** reference to Item_Type
value_type	Identical to Item_Type
size_type	An unsigned type that can hold the maximum number of items allocatable
difference_type	A signed type that can hold the difference between two pointers
typename template rebind<U>::other	Used by client templates to obtain an allocator for a different type using the same allocator implementation
Functions	**Behavior**
pointer address(Item_Type& r); const_pointer address(const Item_Type& r)	Returns a pointer to the argument.
pointer allocate(size_type n, allocator<void>::pointer hint = 0)	Allocates space for n objects of type Item_Type. The optional hint parameter may be used to keep objects together, but the implementation may ignore it. Note this only allocates space; it does not construct objects.
void construct(pointer p, const Item_Type& val)	Constructs a new object of type Item_Type at location p by making a copy of val.
void deallocate(pointer p, size_type n)	Returns the storage for n objects at location p to the free storage pool. The objects are assumed to have been destroyed.
void destroy(pointer p)	Destroys the object located at p.
size_type max_size()	Returns the maximum number of objects that can be allocated.
bool operator== bool operator!=	Two allocator objects are equal if storage allocated by one can be deallocated by the other. Allocators used with the standard library containers are all required to be equal to each other.

Basic Structure of a Traits Class

A traits class is a template class that declares types, data fields, and member functions. The template definition may or may not include actual definitions of its members. If definitions are provided, they access members of the template parameter. Thus, when instantiated with a class as the template argument, the traits member is defined in terms of the template argument. For example, the `iterator_traits` class contains the **typedef** member value_type, defined as follows:

```
template<typename Iterator>
  struct iterator_traits {
    typedef Iterator::value_type value_type;
    ...
};
```

To accommodate built-in types, specializations of the traits class are defined. In the case of `iterator_traits` an alternative definition is

```
template<typename Value_Type*>
  struct iterator_traits {
    typedef Value_Type value_type;
    ...
};
```

Thus when the class `iterator_traits` is instantiated with an `iterator` class type, the class member value_type will be defined to be the `iterator` member value_type, and when the class `iterator_traits` is instantiated with a pointer type, the class member value_type will be defined to be the type that the pointer points to.

The `char_traits` Class

The `char_traits` class is used to encapsulate operations on character values. Since the character types are build-in types (**char** and **wchar_t**), the `char_traits` template does not define any of its members. Specializations are provided for the standard character types (**char** and **wchar_t**). This class is used by the `basic_string`, `basic_istream`, and `basic_ostream` classes. The complete details of the `char_traits` class is beyond the scope of this text. However, the textbook Web site has a case study that shows how to use the `char_traits` to define a specialized version of the `string` class.

A.4 Virtual Base Classes

Refactoring the Employee and Student Classes

In Chapter 3 we briefly introduced multiple inheritance using the example of the Student_Worker class derived from the Employee and Student classes. We observed that the Employee and Student classes contain common information. Removing this common information and placing it into a separate class is known as *refactoring*, and is a common object-oriented design process.

FIGURE A.1
StudentWorker
Derived from **Student**
and **Employee** Using a
Common Base Class

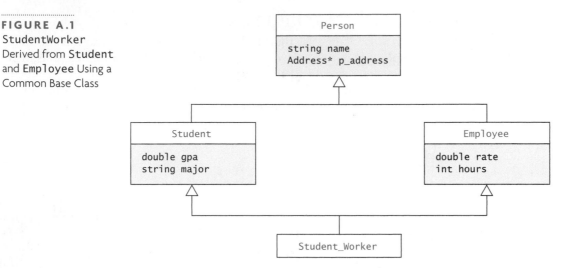

Both Employees and Students are people, thus we define the class Person to represent the common data about both Employees and Students. Figure A.1 shows the class diagram for our Student_Worker class. Listing A.1 shows the declaration and definition of Person.

LISTING A.1
Person.h

```
#ifndef PERSON_H_
#define PERSON_H_

#include "address.h"
#include <string>

class Person
{
  public:

  /** Create an empty Person. */
  Person() {}

  /** Create a person from the given parameters.
      @param the_name The person's name
      @param the_address A pointer to the person's address
  */
  explicit Person(const std::string& the_name,
                  Address* the_address) :
    name(the_name), p_address(the_address) {}

  /** The copy constructor */
  Person(const Person& other) :
    name(other.name), p_address(other.p_address->clone()) {}
```

```
    /** The assignment operator */
    Person& operator=(const Person& other);

    /** The destructor */
    virtual ~Person() { delete p_address; }

    /** Update Person's house number. */
    void set_house_number (std::string new_house_number) {
      p_address->set_house_number(new_house_number);
    }

    /** Swap the contents of this Person and the other Person. */
    void swap(Person& other) {
      std::swap(name, other.name);
      std::swap(p_address, other.p_address);
    }

    /** Return string representation of Person. */
    std::string to_string() const;

    protected:

    std::string name;
    Address* p_address;
};

inline
void swap(Person& p1, Person& p2) {
  p1.swap(p2);
}

#endif
```

LISTING A.2
Person.cpp

```
#include "Person.h"
#include <ostream>
#include <sstream>

/** Return string representation of Person. */
std::string Person::to_string() const {
  std::ostringstream result;
  result << name << '\n' << p_address->to_string();
  return result.str();
}

/** Assignment operator */
Person& Person::operator=(const Person& other) {
  Person temp(other);
  swap(temp);
  return *this;
}
```

The classes `Employee` and `Student` are now simplified to the following:

```cpp
#ifndef EMPLOYEE_H_
#define EMPLOYEE_H_

#include "Person.h"
#include <string>
#include <algorithm>
#include <iostream>
#include <ostream>

class Employee : public Person {

  public:

  /** Create an empty Employee. */
  Employee() {}

  /** Create an employee from the given parameters.
      @param the_name The employee's name
      @param the_address Pointer to employee's address
      @param the_rate The employee's hourly rate
  */
  Employee(const std::string& the_name,
           Address* the_address,
           double the_rate) :
    Person(the_name, the_address), rate(the_rate), hours(0.0) {}

  /** Update Employee's house number. */
  void set_house_number (std::string new_house_number) {
    p_address->set_house_number(new_house_number);
  }

  /** Return a string representation of Employee. */
  std::string to_string() const;

  protected:

  double rate;
  double hours;
};

#endif

#ifndef STUDENT_H_
#define STUDENT_H_

#include "Person.h"
#include <string>

class Student: public Person {

  public:

  /** Create an empty Student. */
  Student() {}
```

```
    /** Create a Student from the given parameters.
       @param the_name The student's name
       @param the_address A pointer to the student's address
       @param the_major The student's major
    */
    Student(const std::string& the_name,
            Address* the_address,
            const std::string& the_major) :
      Person(the_name, the_address), gpa(0.0), major(the_major) {}

    /** Update Student's house number. */
    void set_house_number (std::string new_house_number) {
      p_address->set_house_number(new_house_number);
    }

    /** Set Student's gpa. */
    void set_gpa(double new_gpa) { gpa = new_gpa; }

    /** Return string representation of Student. */
    std::string to_string();

    protected:

    double gpa;
    std::string major;
};

#endif
```

Class `Student_Worker.h` (Listing 3.9) would not change. However, we need to modify the `to_string` function as follows:

```
#include "Student_Worker.h"
#include <sstream>

/** Return String representation of student worker. */
std::string Student_Worker::to_string() const {
  std::ostringstream result;
  result << this->Person::to_string()
         << "Major: " << major << " GPA: "
         << gpa << " Rate: " << rate << " Hours: "
         << hours;
  return result.str();
}
```

However, we really haven't solved the problem yet. There are two `Person` components in the `Student_Worker` class: one inherited from `Employee` and the other inherited from `Student`. Some compilers will detect this and issue an error message, while other compilers arbitrarily pick one of the `Person` components, but it still has two `p_address` fields with duplicate values, and the destructor tries to delete them both, causing a run-time error.

Virtual Base Classes

C++ provides a solution to this problem, but not without its own pitfalls. The solution is to declare `Person` to be a **virtual** base class of both `Employee` and `Student`. This is done using the following syntax.

SYNTAX   Declaring a Virtual Base Class

FORM:

```
class derived-class : public virtual base-class { ... };
```

EXAMPLE:

```
class Student : public virtual Person { ... };
class Employee : public virtual Person { ... };
```

MEANING:

If a class is derived from two other classes that share a common **virtual** base class, then only one instance of the base class will be included in the derived class. To ensure that there is no inconsistency in the initialization process, the constructor(s) for the **virtual** base class(es) is(are) invoked before the constructors of the other base classes. Therefore, if initialization of a **virtual** base class is required, it must be specified by the constructor of the final derived class.

Using the syntax just described, we change the declaration of Employee and Student to make Person a virtual base class. The following constructor would replace the one shown in class Student_Worker.h (Listing 3.9).

```
    Student_Worker(const std::string& the_name,
                   Address* the_address,
                   double the_rate,
                   const std::string& the_major) :
  Person(the_name, the_address),
  Employee(the_name, the_address, the_rate) ,
  Student(the_name, the_address, the_major) {}
```

Notice that we need to initialize the Person base class explicitly as well as the Employee and Student classes. This is because a virtual base class must be explicitly initialized by a derived class.

The problem with multiple inheritance is that, to be used effectively or even correctly, the derived class must know the details of the base classes—specifically, whether there are common data fields or member functions, or if there is a common base class. Such commonality may be far removed in the inheritance chain when classes are selected from one or more libraries. However, when used with full knowledge of the base classes, multiple inheritance can be a very useful and powerful design tool.

A.5 Smart Pointers

A *smart pointer* is an object that acts like a pointer and also manages the memory allocated to the object pointed to. Several kinds of smart pointers have been proposed and implemented. The idea is that you construct a smart pointer object to hold a pointer to a dynamically allocated object. You can use the smart pointer just

> ⊘ **PITFALL**
>
> **Failure to Initialize a `virtual` Base Class**
>
> If a **`virtual`** base class needs to be initialized, and a derived class that multiply inherits it does not explicitly initialize it, it will remain uninitialized. For example, if our `Student_Worker` class had the following constructor:
>
> ```
> Student_Worker(const std::string& the_name,
>                Address* the_address,
>                double the_rate,
>                const std::string& the_major) :
>   Employee(the_name, the_address, the_rate) ,
>   Student(the_name, the_address, the_major) {}
> ```
>
> it would invoke the `Employee` and `Student` constructors. These constructors contain calls to the three-argument `Person` constructor. However, since `Person` is a **`virtual`** base class, the no-argument constructor for `Person` is invoked before the constructors for `Employee` and `Student`. When the `Employee` and `Student` constructors are invoked, their calls to the three-argument `Person` constructor are not performed.

as if it were a regular pointer by applying the dereferencing operators (* and ->). The advantage is that you do not need to delete the dynamically allocated object explicitly. When the smart pointer(s) are no longer used, the dynamically allocated object is automatically deleted.

The `auto_ptr`

The C++ standard library contains the template class `auto_ptr`, which is a fairly limited smart pointer. The design of the `auto_ptr` assumes that there is a one-to-one correspondence between the `auto_ptr` objects and the objects pointed to. When the `auto_ptr` object is destroyed, the pointed-to object is also destroyed.

Because the `auto_ptr` assumes a one-to-one correspondence between the `auto_ptr` object and the pointed-to object, when one `auto_ptr` value is copied or assigned to another `auto_ptr` object, the ownership of the pointed-to object is transferred. Thus, if an `auto_ptr` is copied to another `auto_ptr` (either via the copy constructor or via assignment), the ownership of the pointed-to object is transferred. When this second `auto_ptr` is destroyed, the pointed-to object will also be destroyed.

The `shared_ptr`

A more useful construct is the `shared_ptr`. With the `shared_ptr`, more than one `shared_ptr` object can point to a given dynamically allocated object. When all `shared_ptrs` have been destroyed, then the dynamically allocated object is deleted. There have been several proposed designs for a `shared_ptr` class, and a `shared_ptr` is proposed for the next revision to the C++ standard. In this section we will describe a simplified version of the proposed `shared_ptr` class.

FIGURE A.2
Example of a
`shared_ptr`

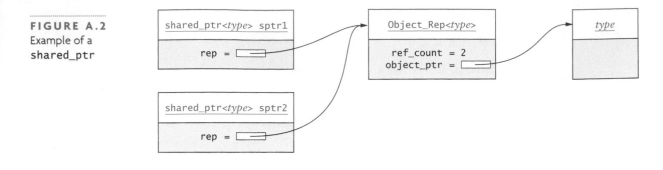

A robust implementation of the `shared_ptr` is quite tricky. A reference implementation of the proposed standard is available from www.boost.org. We will briefly describe the design. Table A.3 summarizes the design of a `shared_ptr` class that is similar to the proposed standard.

Overview of the Design

Figure A.2 illustrates the design of the `shared_ptr`. The `shared_ptr` contains a single data member, `rep`, that points to an `Object_Rep`. The `Object_Rep` contains two data fields: `object_ptr`, which is a pointer to the dynamically allocated object, and `ref_count`, which is the count of the number of `shared_ptrs` that point to this object. As shown in the figure, there are two `shared_ptrs` pointing to the same object, so the `ref_count` is 2. The first time a `shared_ptr` is created to point to a dynamically allocated object, an `Object_Rep` is allocated. When other `shared_ptrs` are assigned to point to the same object, the `ref_count` is incremented. When a `shared_ptr` is destroyed, the `ref_count` is decremented. If the `ref_count` goes to zero, both the `Object_Rep` and the pointed-to object are deleted.

TABLE A.3
Design of `shared_ptr`

Data Field	Attribute
`Object_Rep<Object_Type> rep`	A pointer to the `Object_Rep`
Member Functions	**Behavior**
`shared_ptr<Object_Type>(Object_Type* ptr = NULL)`	Creates a new `shared_ptr` that references a new `Object_Rep` that references the object pointed to by `ptr`. *Note:* The `ptr` parameter should be the result of the application of the **new** operator.
`template<typename Subclass_Type> shared_ptr<Object_Type>(Subclass_Type* ptr = NULL)`	Creates a new `shared_ptr` that references a new `Object_Rep` that references the object pointed to by `ptr`. *Note:* The `ptr` parameter should be the result of the application of the **new** operator and point to an object that is a subclass of `Object_Type`.
`shared_ptr(const shared_ptr& other)`	Makes a copy of a `shared_ptr`.

TABLE A.3 (cont.)

Member Functions	Behavior
`~shared_ptr()`	Destroys a `shared_ptr`. The reference count is decremented, and if it becomes zero, the referenced object and the object reference are deleted.
`void swap(shared_ptr& other)`	Swaps this `shared_ptr` with another.
`shared_ptr& operator=(const shared_ptr& other)`	Assigns one `shared_ptr` to another. After the assignment the target and the original point to the same object, and that object's reference count is incremented. The reference count of the object the target originally pointed to is decremented.
`Object_Type& operator*()`	Dereferences a `shared_ptr`.
`Object_Type& operator->()`	Dereferences a `shared_ptr` for member access.
`bool operator==(const shared_ptr* other) const;` `bool operator==(void*) const`	Tests for equality. The second form is provided for test with **NULL.**
`bool operator!=(const shared_ptr* other) const;` `bool operator!=(void*) const`	Tests for inequality. The second form is provided for test with **NULL.**
`long count()`	Returns the reference count. This is provided for testing.
`Object_Type* get()`	Returns a pointer to the referenced object. This is provided for testing.

Overview of UML

The Unified Modeling Language (UML) represents the unification of earlier object-oriented design modeling techniques. Specifically, notations developed by Grady Booch, Ivar Jacobson, and James Rumbaugh were adapted to form the initial version. This version was submitted to the Object Modeling Group for formal standardization. Since that initial submission, the UML standard has undergone several revisions and continues to be revised.

We call UML a modeling language much in the same way we call C++ a programming language. There is a formal definition of the syntax and semantics. There are software tools that are used both to draw the diagrams and to capture the underlying design information. These tools can then be used to analyze the resulting model, verify the model's consistency, and generate code.

UML defines twelve types of diagrams. In this text we use only two of them: the class diagram and the sequence diagram. Throughout the text, where we use these diagrams, we provide brief explanations of the diagram and the meaning of the notations used. The purpose of this appendix is to provide a more complete reference to the diagrams as they are used in this text.

In this text, we use a notation that has been adapted from the UML standard to match the syntax of C++ more closely. Other books may use slightly different versions of these diagrams that follow the standard syntax, but the principles are the same.

Overview of UML

B.1 The Class Diagram

The *class diagram* shows the classes and their relationships. It is a static diagram that represents the structure of the program. The classes are represented by rectangles, and lines between the classes represent the relationships. The style of a line, symbols on the ends of the lines, and text placed near the line are used to indicate the kind of relationship being modeled.

A large amount of information about the structure of a program can be represented in a class diagram. If all of the possible information were presented, the diagram would become quite cluttered. Therefore, the practice is to show only the essential information. For example, in a class diagram the complete method declaration can show the method's visibility, return type, name, and parameter types. Sometimes only the method's name is necessary, in which case you would elect to suppress the other information. Also, some methods may not be significant to the discussion, so those methods need not be shown. Sometimes only the class's name is the essential item, and thus the methods and attributes are not shown.

Representing Classes and Interfaces

FIGURE B.1
General Representation of a Class

ClassName
Attributes
Operations

A class is represented by a rectangle divided into three segments as shown in Figure B.1.

The Class Name

Every class has a name that distinguishes it from other classes. In C++ a class may be a member of a namespace, in which case we may show the complete name including the namespace name (for example, std::string). In other cases we just show the class name (for example, Node). Italics indicate abstract classes. The class name is centered in the box representing the class. For example, Figure B.2 shows the abstract class Address and the concrete classes derived from it.

FIGURE B.2
The Abstract Class **Address** and Concrete Derived Classes

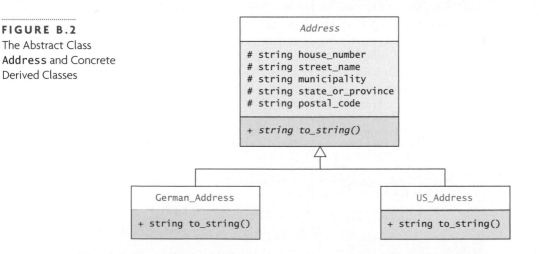

```
        «interface»
      Phone_Directory
  ────────────────────────
  load_data()
  add_or_change_entry()
  lookup_entry()
  remove_entry()
  save()
```

Interfaces

The word *interface* enclosed in double angle brackets (« and », called guillemets) placed before a class name indicates that the class is an interface. Unlike some other OO languages, C++ does not have a specific syntactic element called an interface. In this text we use the interface notation to represent an Abstract Data Type such as the `Phone_Directory`. Because interfaces, like abstract classes, cannot be instantiated, the name is shown in italics. See Figure B.3.

We also use the interface notation with the word *concept* to show that classes have common requirements. For example the `vector`, `deque`, and `list` all must meet the requirements for a *sequence*. Thus we show the *sequence* as a concept (See Figure B.8).

Alternative UML Syntax for Class Names

In other texts you may see the class name in a bold sans-serif font. Also, abstract classes may be indicated by {abstract}, as shown in Figure B.4.

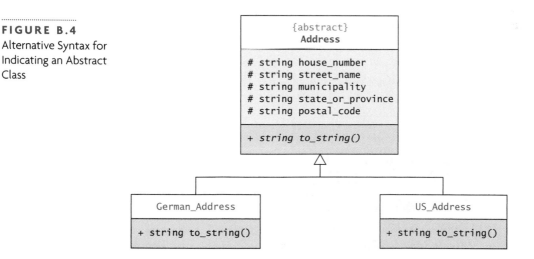

The Attributes

The attributes of a class are the data fields. As a minimum we show the name. Optionally we can also show the visibility and type. The visibility is indicated by the symbols shown in Table B.1.

TABLE B.1
Visibility Specifiers

Symbol	Visiblity
+	Public
–	Private
#	Protected

In this text we use the C++ language syntax to indicate the type of an attribute by placing the type name before the attribute name. For example, the class `Person` could have the attributes `family_name`, `given_name`, and `address`, as shown in the following figure.

```
        Person

  - string given_name
  - string family_name
  - Address address
```

Where they are not essential to the current discussion, we will omit the visibility indicator, the type, or both, as shown in the following figure.

```
        Person

  given_name
  family_name
  address
```

Static attributes are indicated by underlining their name. For example, the class `Lap_Top` has the static attribute `DEFAULT_LT_MAN`.

```
        Lap_Top

  string DEFAULT_LT_MAN
  double screen_size
  double weight
```

Standard UML Syntax for Attribute Types

In other texts you may see a different syntax for showing the attribute type. The UML standard specifies that the attribute type be specified following the name and separated by a colon.

```
        Person

  - given_name:string
  - family_name:string
  - address:Address
```

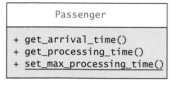

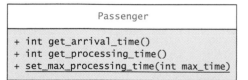

The Operations

The operations are the member functions of the class. At a minimum, we show the function name followed by a pair of parentheses. An empty set of parentheses does not necessarily indicate that this function takes no parameters. Italics are used to indicate an abstract function, and underlining is used to indicate a static function. For example, Figure B.5 shows the class `Passenger` with the static method `set_max_processing_time` and the nonstatic methods `get_arrival_time` and `get_processing_time`. The attributes are not shown.

We may also show the visibility, the parameter types, and the return type. The visibility is shown using the same symbols as used for the attributes (see Table B.1). In this text we use the C++ function declaration syntax, as shown in Figure B.6, to show the parameter types and return type. A return type of **void**, however, will not be shown.

Standard UML Syntax for Operations

In other texts you may see a different syntax for showing the parameter types and return type. The UML standard specifies that the parameter type be preceded by a colon and shown following the parameter name, and that the return type be shown following the operation name, also preceded by a colon. The class `Passenger` using this syntax is shown in the following figure.

```
                Computer
 ┌──────────────────────────────┐
 │ string manufacturer          │
 │ string processor             │
 │ int ram_size                 │
 │ int disk_size                │
 ├──────────────────────────────┤
 │ int get_ram_size()           │
 │ int get_disk_size()          │
 │ string to_string()           │
 └──────────────────────────────┘
               △
 ┌──────────────────────────────┐
 │          Lap_Top             │
 ├──────────────────────────────┤
 │ string DEFAULT_LT_MAN        │
 │ double screen_size           │
 │ double weight                │
 ├──────────────────────────────┤
 │ string to_string()           │
 └──────────────────────────────┘
```

```
                Passenger
 ┌──────────────────────────────────────────┐
 │ + get_arrival_time():int                  │
 │ + get_processing_time():int               │
 │ + set_max_processing_time(max_time:int)   │
 └──────────────────────────────────────────┘
```

Generalization

UML uses the term *generalization* to describe the relationship between a base class and its derived classes. Drawing a solid line with a large open arrowhead (Δ) pointing to the base class shows generalization. Figure B.7 shows the class `Lap_Top` as a subclass of `Computer`. A dashed line with a large open arrowhead is used to show that a class implements an interface.

FIGURE B.8

FIGURE B.8
The `container` Concept, Its Subconcepts, and the Classes That Implement Them

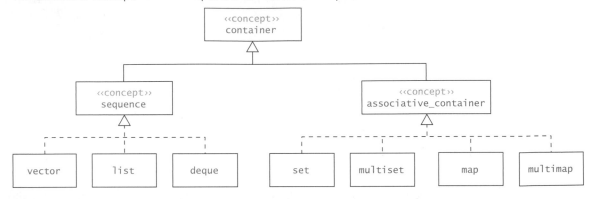

Figure B.8 shows that the concepts `sequence` and `associative_container` share common requirements defined by the concept `container`. The dashed lines from `vector`, `list`, and `deque` indicate that these classes implement these concepts.

Inner or Nested Classes

A class that is declared within the body of another class is called an inner class or nested class. In UML this relationship is indicated by a solid line between the two classes, with what the UML standard calls an *anchor* on the end connected to the enclosing class. The anchor is a cross inside a circle (⊕). For example, in Figure B.9 the class `Node` is declared as an inner class of the class `KW::list`.

Association

An association between classes represents a relationship between objects of those classes. In object-oriented terminology we say that "object A sends a message to object B." This statement implies two things:

1. There is a method in class B that will receive the message.

2. There must be a reference within class A that references object B.

An association indicates the presence of the reference required by condition 2. Thus, in the analysis process in which we examine a use case and determine the flow of information from one object to another, we identify the requirements for methods and associations. Note that the association may represent a data field, or it may represent a parameter.

Figure B.10 shows the UML notation for an association. The association name, multiplicities, and roles are all optional. The association name is a name given to the association. The multiplicity represents the number of objects of that class that participate in the association. Where the association is implemented as a data field, the role name is generally used as the name of the data field. Thus, in `ClassA` there would be a reference of type `ClassB` with the name `roleB`. The role name may have

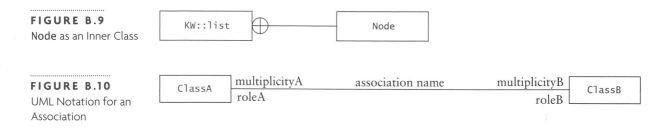

FIGURE B.9
Node as an Inner Class

FIGURE B.10
UML Notation for an
Association

a visibility specifier (see Table B.1). The role and multiplicity may be either above or below the line.

Multiplicity represents the number of objects of the class that are related to the other class. Thus, multiplicityB represents the number of objects of ClassB that are associated with an object of ClassA, and multiplicityA represents the number of objects of ClassA that are associated with an object of ClassB. Multiplicity may be either a single number or a range of numbers. The symbol * is used to indicate an indefinite number. A range of numbers is specified by a low bound followed by a high bound separated by two periods. Examples are shown in Table B.2.

TABLE B.2
Multiplicity Examples

Multiplicity	Meaning
1	There is only 1
1..5	There is at least 1, and there may be as many as 5
3..*	There are at least 3
*	There could be any number, including 0

In addition, an arrow can be placed at one or both ends of the line. The presence of an arrow indicates the navigation direction. Thus, if there is an arrow on the ClassB end, then objects of ClassA can send messages to objects of ClassB, but objects of ClassB cannot send messages to objects of ClassA. The absence of arrows generally represents that navigation in both directions is possible, but it may also mean that the navigation is not being shown. Generally, if navigation is possible from ClassA to ClassB, then ClassA will contain a pointer to ClassB.

Composition

In those cases where we wish to show that an association definitely is represented by a data field, we place a filled diamond on the end of the line next to the class that will contain the data field. This represents the has-a relationship. For example, an Airplane is composed of two wings, a body, and a tail, none of which would exist unless they were components of an Airplane. This would be modeled as shown in Figure B.11.

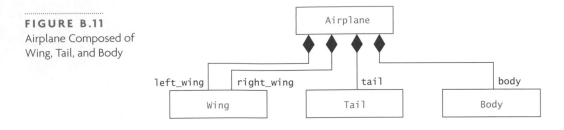

Generic (or Template) Classes

We will indicate a generic class by placing the generic parameter(s) in a dotted rectangle in the upper right corner of the rectangle that models the class. Thus the generic class vector is modeled by the diagram shown in Figure B.12.

An invocation of a generic class is indicated by including the actual parameters inside a pair of angle brackets (less-than and greater-than) symbols following the name. Thus a vector of strings would be written vector<string>.

B.2 Sequence Diagrams

Sequence diagrams are used to show the flow of information through the program. Sequence diagrams are generally developed on a use case basis and show the message sequence associated with a particular use case. The purpose of developing a sequence diagram is to identify the messages that are passed from one object to another. This then identifies the requirements for the corresponding classes. Recall that if object A sends a message to object B, then

1. Class B must have a method to process that message.
2. Class A must have a reference to an object of class B.

Thus, when you enter a message on a sequence diagram, you identify a requirement for an operation and an association to be entered on the class diagram. Many UML modeling software tools automate the process of keeping the sequence diagrams and class diagrams consistent.

Figure B.13 shows an example of a sequence diagram. This is a two-dimensional diagram with time running down the vertical axis and objects listed across the horizontal axis. The ordering across the horizontal axis is insignificant.

Time Axis

Time flows down the vertical axis. Generally the scale is not significant, but for some applications, where timing is critical, a precise timing scale can be used. The sequence along the time axis is always significant.

Objects

Objects are listed across the horizontal axis. Their order is insignificant. An object is represented by a rectangle with the name of the object underlined. For anonymous objects, the name of the class is given.

Objects are listed across the top of the sequence diagram unless they are created during the time period represented by the sequence diagram. If an object is created, then it is shown lower in the diagram, at the point at which it is created. As shown in Figure B.13, two Passenger objects are created during the sequence of events depicted.

FIGURE B.13
Sequence Diagram Example

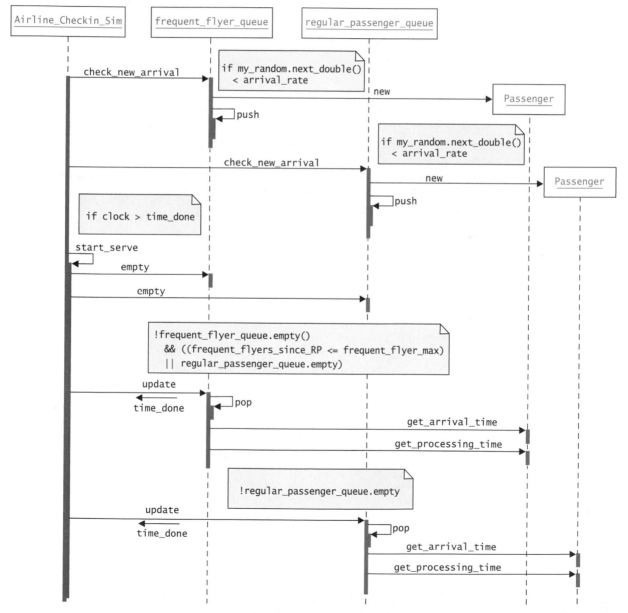

Life Lines

Flowing down from each object is its life line. This is a dashed line that begins when the object is created and ends when the object is destroyed.

Activation Bars

The thin long rectangles along the life line are *activation bars*. These represent the time during which the object is responding to a given message. Note that if a second message is received while a message is being processed, a second activation bar is drawn to the right of the first activation bar. This can be seen in Figure B.13, where the `Airline_Checkin_Sim` object sends itself the `start_serve` message, or where the `frequent_flyer_queue` and `regular_passenger_queue` objects send themselves the `push` message.

Messages

Messages are indicated by a horizontal arrow from the sending object to the receiving object. The name of the message is shown above the arrow. Optionally, the parameters may be shown in parentheses following the message name. Also, a small reverse direction arrow may be used to indicate a return value with the value shown below it. An example of this is shown in Figure B.13 where `time_done` is returned to the `Airline_Checkin_Sim` object in response to the `update` message sent to the `frequent_flyer_queue`.

Use of Notes

Notes may be used on any UML diagram. They are free-form text enclosed in a rectangle with the upper right corner folded down.

The purpose of the sequence diagram is to identify the sequence of messages that occur during a use case. For a given instance of a use case, not all messages will be sent. For example, as shown in Figure B.13, the `check_new_arrival` message to the `frequent_flyer_queue` may or may not result in the creation of a new `Passenger` object. Notes can be used to document the conditions for sending a message. For example, the `check_new_arrival` message is sent when the result of the random number generator is less than `arrival_rate`.

The CppUnit Test Framework

The test framework CppUnit can be configured to run with the Microsoft Visual Studio .NET development environment under Windows, or it can be configured to run under Linux and other UNIX platforms. Below we show a test suite for the Directory_Entry class constructed using the CppUnit framework. The class for the test suite must extend class TestFixture (defined in CppUnit). We explain about extending classes in Chapter 3. The setUp function is used to declare the test objects that are shared among test cases. We will not use it in this example, but it must be defined in the test suite.

```
#include <cppunit/extensions/HelperMacros.h>

class TestDirectoryEntry : public CppUnit::TestFixture {
  CPPUNIT_TEST_SUITE(TestDirectoryEntry);
  CPPUNIT_TEST(testTomCreate);
  CPPUNIT_TEST(testTomEqualsDick);
  CPPUNIT_TEST(testTomEqualsTom2);
  CPPUNIT_TEST(testSetNumber);
  CPPUNIT_TEST_SUITE_END();

  public:
  void setUp();
  void tearDown();
  void testTomCreate();
  void testTomEqualsDick();
  void testTomEqualsTom2();
  void testSetNumber();
};
```

We then write a series of test cases by writing functions named testXxxxx. For example to test that the object tom was created correctly, we write the function testTomCreate as follows:

```
void TestDirectoryEntry::testTomCreate() {
  string tomName = "Tom";
  string tomNumber = "123-456-7890";
  Directory_Entry tom(tomName, tomNumber);
  CPPUNIT_ASSERT_EQUAL(tom.get_name(), tomName);
  CPPUNIT_ASSERT_EQUAL(tom.get_number(), tomNumber);
}
```

The macro CPPUNIT_ASSERT_EQUAL will report an error if its arguments are not equal, indicating that the results of get_name or get_number are not as expected (tomName or tomNumber, respectively). The various CPPUNIT_ASSERT_xxxxx macros are specific to CppUnit. This should not be confused with the C++ assert macro, which we discuss in Section 2.4.

We can test the Directory_Entry::operator!= and Directory_Entry::operator== functions using the following methods:

```
void TestDirectoryEntry::testTomEqualsDick() {
  Directory_Entry tom("Tom", "123-456-7890");
  Directory_Entry dick("Dick", "908-765-4321");
  CPPUNIT_ASSERT(tom != dick);
  CPPUNIT_ASSERT(dick != tom);
}

void TestDirectoryEntry::testTomEqualsTom2() {
  Directory_Entry tom("Tom", "123-456-7890");
  Directory_Entry tom2("Tom", "111-222-3333");
  CPPUNIT_ASSERT(tom == tom2);
  CPPUNIT_ASSERT(tom2 == tom);
}
```

The CPPUNIT_ASSERT macro will report an error if its argument does not evaluate to **true**. We expect that tom is not equal to dick, so we use tom != dick as the argument for the first macro call in the first function, and we expect that tom and tom2 are equal, so we use tom == tom2 as the argument for the first macro call in the second function. (Recall that the == operator compares the name field only of directory entries.)

Finally, we write a test case for the set_number function.

```
void TestDirectoryEntry::testSetNumber() {
  string newNumber = "999-999-9999";
  Directory_Entry tom("Tom", "123-456-7890");
  tom.set_number(newNumber);
  CPPUNIT_ASSERT_EQUAL(tom.get_number(), newNumber);
}
```

To run the tests we also need to define a main program that invokes the test runner. The test runner is the function within CppUnit that runs the test and records the results. An example of such a main program follows.

```
#include <cppunit/CompilerOutputter.h>
#include <cppunit/extensions/TestFactoryRegistry.h>
#include <cppunit/ui/text/TestRunner.h>
```

```
int main() {
  // Get the test suite from the registry.
  CppUnit::Test* suite =
      CppUnit::TestFactoryRegistry::getRegistry().makeTest();

  // Add this test suite to the lists of test to run.
  CppUnit::TextUi::TestRunner runner;
  runner.addTest(suite);

  // Set the outputter.
  runner.setOutputter(new CppUnit::CompilerOutputter(
      &runner.result(), std::cerr));

  // Run the tests.
  bool wasSuccessful = runner.run();

  // Return error code.
  if (wasSuccessful)
    return 0;
  else
    return 1;
}
```

If all tests pass, the output is simply:

```
....

OK (4)
```

indicating that the four tests passed. On the other hand, if there is an error, the test that failed is indicated. For example, let us assume that we did not implement operator != correctly, and instead it reports the opposite of what it should. Then the results of our test are as follows:

```
..F..

TestDirectoryEntry.cpp:29:Assertion
Test name: TestDirectoryEntry::testTomEqualsDick
assertion failed
- Expression: tom != dick
```

Glossary

2-3 tree A search tree in which each node may have two or three children.

2-3-4 tree A search tree in which each node may have two, three, or four children.

2-node A node in a 2-3 or 2-3-4 tree with two children.

3-node A node in a 2-3 or 2-3-4 tree with three children.

4-node A node in a 2-3-4 tree with four children.

abstract class A class that contains at least one abstract member function. An abstract class cannot have instances.

abstract data type An implementation-independent specification of a set of data items and the operations performed on those data items.

abstract function A virtual function that is declared but not defined in a base class. It leaves its definition up to the derived classes. Sometimes also called a *pure virtual function*.

abstraction A model of a physical entity or activity.

acceptance testing A sequence of tests that demonstrates to the customer that a software product meets all of its requirements. Acceptance testing generally is observed by a customer representative.

access specifier One of the key words **public**, **protected**, or **private** that appears within a class definition that specifies the access rules of the members following it. All members following an access specifier have the specified access until the next access specifier or the end of the class definition.

accessor A member function that returns the current value of an instance variable of an object. The accessor should have no other effects. Also called a getter; it is recommended that the name of the accessor consist of the word get_ followed by the name of the instance variable.

activation bar The thick line along the life line in a sequence diagram that indicates the time that a function is executing in response to the receipt of a message.

activation frame An area of memory allocated to store the actual parameters and local variables for a particular call to a function. In C++, activation frames are stored on the run-time stack. When a function is called, a new activation frame is pushed onto the stack, and when a function exits, the activation frame is popped.

actor An entity that is external to a given software system. In many cases an actor is a human user of the software system, but an actor may be another system.

actual class A class for which objects can be instantiated. An actual class cannot have any abstract members. If an actual class is derived from an abstract class, it must implement all inherited abstract member functions. Also called a *concrete class*.

adapter class A class that provides the same or very similar functionality as another class but with different function signatures. The actual work is performed by delegation to the functions in the other class.

address A number that represents an object's location in memory.

address-of operator The operator &, which returns the address of the object whose identifier follows.

adjacency lists A representation of a graph in which the vertices (the destinations) adjacent to a given vertex (the source) are stored in a list associated with that vertex. The actual edge (source, destination, weight) from the source vertex to the destination may be stored.

adjacency matrix A representation of a graph in which the presence or absence of an edge is indicated by a value in a matrix that is indexed by the two vertices. The value stored is 0 for no edge, 1 for an edge in an unweighted graph, and the weight itself for a weighted graph.

adjacent (vertex) In a directed graph, a vertex, v, is adjacent to another vertex, u, if there is an edge, (u, v), from vertex u to vertex v. In an undirected graph v is adjacent to u if there is an edge $\{u, v\}$ between them.

aggregation An association between two classes in which one class is composed of a collection of objects of the other class.

alias An alternate name for the same thing. Aliases for types are declared using the keyword **typedef**. Many compilers simply replace the alias with the original type name. Aliases for variables are declared using references.

allocator A class that contains functions for allocating memory to be used by objects and deallocating it when no longer needed. A programmer may write a custom allocator and supply it as a parameter when instantiating a template class to replace the template class's default allocator.

amortized constant time The time taken by part of an operation, made to be constant on average by performing the part sufficiently infrequently. For example, expanding an array and copying the elements to the new array to make room for new elements takes $O(n)$ time. If the array is expanded by doubling each time, the expansion operation will not have to be performed again until another n

elements are added, so the expansion adds, on average, $O(1)$ to the time required to add an element.

analysis In the waterfall model, the phase of the software life cycle (or, in the Unified Model, the workflow) during which the requirements are clarified and the overall architecture of the solution is determined.

ancestor A node in a tree that is at a higher level than a given node and from which there is a path to that node (the descendant).

ancestor-descendant relationship A generalization of the parent-child relationship. (See *ancestor* and *descendant*).

anchor The symbol, $\oplus$, that is used in a UML class diagram to indicate that a class is an inner class of another class.

anonymous object An object for which there is no named reference. The C++ **new** operator returns a pointer to an anonymous object.

anonymous pointer A pointer not yet stored in a variable, generated by a dynamic cast.

argument The value specified for a parameter of a function when the function is called.

assertion A statement about the current value of one or more variables.

association A relationship between two classes.

associative array A container for key-value pairs in which an expression containing a key with the same syntax used for the index of an array returns the corresponding value.

associative container A container class in which the objects contained are not in a linear order and are accessed by value rather than by position.

assignment operator The operator operator=, used to give a class-type variable a value.

attributes The set of data values that determine the state of an object. Generally the attributes of a class are represented by data fields within the class.

AVL tree A self-balancing binary search tree (discovered by G. M. Adel'son-Vel'skii and E. M. Landis) in which the difference between the heights of the subtrees is stored in each tree node. The insertion and removal algorithms use rotations to maintain this difference within the range –1 to +1.

back edge An edge that is discovered during a depth-first search that leads to an ancestor in the depth-first search tree.

back end The part of an application program that interacts with data in persistent storage rather than with the user.

backtracking An approach to implementing a systematic trial-and-error search for a solution. When a dead end is reached, the algorithm follows a path back to the decision point that led to the dead end, then moves forward along a different path.

balanced binary search tree A binary search tree in which the height of each pair of subtrees is approximately the same.

base case The case in a recursive algorithm that can be solved directly.

base class A class from which another class is derived. Compare *derived class*. Also called a *superclass*.

batch processing A way of using a computer in which a series of jobs (individual programs) are collected together and then executed sequentially.

big-O notation The specification of a set of functions that represent the upper bound of a given function. Formally the function $f(n)$ is said to be $O(g(n))$ if there are constants $c > 0$ and $n_0 > 0$ such that for all $n > n_0$, $cg(n) \geq f(n)$.

binary search The process of searching a sorted sequence that begins by examining the middle element. If the middle element is greater than the target, then the search is applied recursively to the lower half; if it is less than the target, the search is applied recursively to the upper half.

binary search tree A binary tree in which the items in the left subtree of a node are all less than that node, and the items in the right subtree are all greater than that node.

binary tree A tree in which each node has 0, 1, or 2 children. The children are distinguished by the names left and right. If a node has one child, that child is distinguished as being a left child or a right child.

black-box testing A testing approach in which the internal structure of the item being tested is not known or taken into account in the design of the test cases. The test cases are based only on the functional requirements for the item being tested.

block A compound statement that may contain local variables and class declarations.

bottom-up design A design process in which the lower-level functions are designed first. A lowest-level function is one that does not depend on other functions to perform its task.

boundary condition A value of a variable that causes a different path to be taken. For example, in the statement if (x > C) { ... } else { ... }, the value of C is a boundary condition.

branch coverage A measure of testing thoroughness. Each alternative from a decision point (**if**, **switch**, or **while** statement) is considered a branch. If a test exercises a branch, then that branch is considered covered. The ratio of the covered branches to the total number of branches is the branch coverage. See also *path coverage* and *statement coverage*.

branch In a tree, the link between a parent node and one of its children.

breadth-first search A way of searching through a graph in which the vertices adjacent to a given vertex are all examined and placed into a queue. Once all the adjacent vertices are examined, the next vertex is removed from the queue. Thus vertices are examined in increasing distance (as measured by the number of edges) from the starting vertex.

breadth-first traversal See *breadth-first search.*

breakpoint A point in a program at which the debugger is instructed to suspend execution when it is reached. This allows for examination of the value of variables at a given point before execution is resumed.

B-tree A balanced search tree in which each node is a leaf or may have up to *n* children and *n* − 1 data items. The leaves are all at the bottom level. Each node (except for the root) is kept at least half full. That is, each node has between (*n* − 1)/2 and *n* − 1 data items. The root either is a single node (leaf) or has at least one data item and two children.

B+tree A variation of the B-tree in which the leaves contain keys and pointers to the associated data values, but the internal nodes contain keys and pointers to other nodes. The key of the parent is repeated as the first key in the child. Each node holds up to *n* pointers and *n* keys.

bubble sort A sort algorithm that makes several passes through the sequence being sorted. During each pass, adjacent items are examined and, if out of order, swapped. If there are no exchanges on a given pass, then the process is complete. The effect of each pass is that the largest item in the unsorted part of the sequence is moved to (bubbles to) the end of the sequence.

bucket The list of keys stored in a hash table entry that uses chaining. All the keys in the list map to the index of that table entry.

bucket hashing See *chaining.*

C-style cast An expression of the form (*type*)*value*. The kind of cast actually performed depends upon the type of the value and the target type. Use of an explicit type conversion or one of the cast operations is the preferred C++ programming practice.

call by reference A way of specifying a parameter for a function in which the function receives a reference to the object named by the corresponding argument. If the function changes the value of such a parameter, the object itself will be changed after the function exits. The parameter can be specified to be const to prevent the function from modifying it.

call by value A way of specifying a parameter to a function in which the function receives a copy of the object named by the corresponding argument. The function may change the value of the parameter, but only the copy will be affected. After the function exits, the original object remains unchanged.

casting The process of converting or reinterpreting the type of a value. C++ has several casting operators. The *explicit type conversion*, **dynamic_cast**, and **const_cast** operations are used in this text.

catch an exception See *handle an exception.*

catch block The specification of an exception type and the statements to be executed when an exception of that type is caught. One or more **catch** blocks follow a **try** block and will catch the exceptions thrown from that **try** block. Also called an *exception handler.*

chaining An approach to hashing in which all keys that are mapped to a given entry in the hash table are placed into a list. The list is called a bucket.

child A node in a tree that is the immediate descendant of another node.

class diagram A UML diagram that shows a number of classes and the relationships between them.

class A fundamental programming unit in C++. A class defines a particular kind of object. The class consists of a collection of zero or more pieces of information (data fields or instance variables) characteristic of an object of that kind (an instance of the class) as well as zero or more functions (or member functions) that specify actions that take place involving instances of the class.

class definition Code that identifies the name of a class, the types and access specifiers of its data members, and the signatures of its member functions. It is usually in a file with the .h extension.

class implementation Code that defines the member functions of a class. It is usually in a file with the .cpp extension.

class type A type of data whose definition is not built into the C++ language and therefore must be supplied as a class; it is built up of one or more data fields that may be of primitive type or class type.

client A class or function that uses a given class.

closed-box testing See *black-box testing.*

collision The mapping of two or more keys into the same position in a hash table.

compile To translate a program from a programming language such as C++ into machine language.

complete binary tree A binary tree in which the nodes at all but the deepest level contain two children. At the deepest level, all nodes that have two children are to the left of those that have no children, and there is at most one node with a left child that is between these two groups.

component testing The testing of an individual part of a program by itself. In a C++ program a component may be a function or a class.

component class A class whose objects are part of another object. See *composition.*

composition The association between two classes in which objects of one class are part of another class. The parts generally do not have an independent existence, but are created when the parent object is created. For example an Airplane object is composed of a Body object, two Wing objects, and a Tail object.

compound statement Zero or more statements enclosed within braces { ... }.

concept A common interface that a generic class must meet.

concrete class See *actual class*.

connected components A set of vertices within a graph for which there is a path between every pair of vertices.

connected graph A graph that consists of a single connected component.

construction phase The phase of the Unified Model of the software life cycle during which most of the activity is devoted to writing the software.

constructor A function that initializes an object when it is first created.

container A template class whose instances can contain one or more objects.

contract The specification of the pre- and postconditions of a function.

copy constructor A constructor used to make an independent copy of an object.

cost of a spanning tree The sum of the weights of the edges.

coverage testing Testing the performance of a function under all possible combinations of conditions for which it was programmed.

cycle A path in a graph in which the first and final vertices are the same.

constant casting A cast operation that can change the **const** attribute of a pointer or reference.

data abstraction The specification of the data items of a problem and the operations to be performed on these data items that does not specify how they (the data items) will be represented and stored in memory. See also *abstract data type*.

data field See *instance variable*.

data member See *instance variable*.

debugging The process of finding and removing defects ("bugs") from a program.

declaration A statement that informs the C++ compiler that a function, variable, or class is available for use and gives the compiler all the information necessary to use that item, such as its name, the type of a variable, the types of arguments and return value of a function, or the declarations of all the functions in a class.

deep copy A copy of an object in which data field values and pointers to immutable objects are simply duplicated, but each pointer to a mutable object references a copy of that object. If any object that is copied contains pointers to other mutable objects, the corresponding pointers in the copy reference copies of those objects. The effect is that you can change any value in a deep copy of an object without modifiying the original object.

default constructor The no-parameter constructor that is generated by the C++ compiler if no constructors are defined.

defensive programming An approach to designing a program that builds in statements to test the values of variables that might result in an exception or run-time error (to be sure that they are valid) before statements that use the variables are executed.

delegation The implementation of a function in one class by merely calling a function in another class.

delimiter characters Characters that are defined to separate a string into tokens.

dense graph A graph in which the number of edges, $|E|$, is close to the square of the number of vertices, $|V|$ — that is, one in which nearly every edge that could exist does exist.

depth (level) The number of nodes in a path from the root to a node.

depth-first search A method of searching a graph in which adjacent vertices are examined along a path until a dead end is reached. The search then backtracks until an unexamined vertex is found, and the search continues with that vertex.

depth-first traversal See *depth-first search*.

deque An abstract data type consisting of a structure in which elements may be inserted at either end, and removed from either end, combining the access capabilities of a stack and a queue.

dereference To obtain the object to which a pointer points.

derived class A class that extends one or more classes, known as *base classes*, inheriting the members of all of them. Particularly in discussion of object-oriented languages other than C++, such as Java, a derived class is also known as a *subclass*.

descendant In a tree, a lower node that can be reached by following a path from a given node.

design The process (workflow, in the Unified Model) by which classes and functions are identified and defined to create a program that satisfies a given set of requirements.

destination The vertex in a directed graph to which an edge is directed.

destructor A member function called when an object is no longer to be used, before the memory for the object is released to the operating system for use in allocating new objects. If the object has other objects as instance variables, the destructor should ensure that the memory for those objects is also relinquished in order to prevent memory leaks.

digraph See *directed graph*.

directed edge An edge in a directed graph.

directed acyclic graph A directed graph that contains no cycles.

directed graph A graph in which every edge is considered to have a direction. If u and v are vertices in a graph, then the presence of the edge (u, v) indicates that v is adjacent to u, but u may not be adjacent to v. Contrast with *undirected graph*.

discovery order The order in which vertices are discovered in a depth-first search.

dot notation Writing an object identifier followed by a dot followed by the name of a member function of the object's class to apply the member function to the object.

downcast A cast of a pointer to a base class to a pointer to a derived class. See *dynamic casting*.

driver A program whose purpose is to call a function being tested and provide it with appropriate argument values. Usually, the result of executing the function is displayed immediately to the user.

dynamic casting Conversion of a base-class pointer to a derived-class pointer, matching the type of the object actually pointed to, at run time.

edges In a graph, the links between pairs of vertices.

elaboration phase The phase in the Unified Model of the software life cycle during which the software architecture is defined.

encapsulate To combine the various pieces of information about an abstract data type into one module with which the outside world interacts through a specifically defined interface without having to be concerned with the details of implementation.

enumeration A data type that is declared as a list of permissible values and each instance of the type consists of one of those values.

escape sequence A sequence of characters beginning with the backslash (\) which is used to indicate another character that cannot be directly entered. For example the sequence \n represents the newline character.

Euler tour A path around a tree, starting and ending with the root. The tree is always kept to the left of the path when viewed from the direction of travel along the path.

event The occurrence of an external input or an internal state change.

exception An object that can be thrown when an error is encountered. By catching the exception, the program may be able to recover from the error.

exception handler See **catch** *block*.

extending The process of adding functionality by defining a new class that adds data fields and/or adds or overrides functions of an existing class.

external node See *leaf*.

explicit type conversion An expression of the form *type(value)*. If there is a conversion defined, the type of the value is converted to the target type.

Extreme Programming A software development process in which programmers work in pairs. One programmer writes functions while the other designs tests for those functions. The programmers alternate roles. The programmers also share a workstation so that when one programmer is using the workstation the other is observing.

factory function A function that is responsible for creating objects of a class. Generally a factory function will be associated with an abstract class and will choose an appropriate concrete class that extends the abstract class based upon parameters passed to the factory function, system parameters, or both. It returns a pointer to a new object of this concrete class.

finish order The order in which the vertices are finished in a depth-first search. A vertex is considered finished when all of the paths to adjacent vertices have been finished.

forest A collection of trees that may result from a depth-first search of a directed graph or an unconnected graph.

friend A class or function that another class allows to have access to the latter class's private data members.

front end The part of an application program that interacts with a user rather than with data in persistent storage.

full binary tree A binary tree in which each node is a leaf or has two children.

function The fundamental unit in C++ programming; a sequence of statements that performs a specific task, given all the information needed to perform the task, and possibly returns a value indicating the result.

functional testing Testing that concentrates on verifying that software meets its functional requirements. See also *black-box testing*.

function declaration The specification of the name, parameters, and return type of a function. See also *signature*.

function overloading The presence of multiple functions in a class with the same name but different signatures.

function overriding The replacement of an inherited virtual function with a different implementation in a subclass.

function class A class that overrides the function call operator, operator().

function object An instance of a function class.

generalization The relationship between two classes in which one class is the base class (or superclass) and the other is a derived class (or subclass). The base class is a generalization of the derived class.

generic class A class with type parameters that are specified when instances are created. These parameters specify the actual data type for the internal data fields of the object that is created. See also *template class*.

generic function A function whose arguments are not restricted as to type. Type parameters are used to represent the data types of its formal parameters. The type parameters are determined when the function is called and enable the function to process actual parameters of different data types. See also *template function*.

generic type See *generic class*.

getter See *accessor*.

glass-box testing See *white-box testing*.

global object An object declared outside the scope of any function or class.

graph A mathematical structure consisting of a set of vertices and edges. The edges represent a relationship between the vertices.

handle an exception To respond in a controlled way when a particular type of exception is thrown so that the program can recover from the error, clean up memory, or report the error intelligently.

has-a relationship The relationship between two classes, each instance of one of which is associated with zero or more instances of the other, but not necessarily the other way around. For example, an airplane may have wheels, but not all wheels belong to airplanes; furthermore, an airplane is not a wheel and a wheel is not an airplane. Object-oriented languages capture the has-a relationship by giving the possessing class data members whose type is the possessed class.

hash code A function that transforms an object into an integer value that may be used as an index into a hash table.

hash table A data structure in which items are accessed directly based on a computed hash code rather than through a search.

header A C++ file containing declarations of functions, classes, and variables to be included in every program that uses those functions, classes, and variables.

heap A binary tree in which the value in a node is beyond—greater than (in a max heap) or less than (in a min heap)—all the values in both subtrees.

heapsort A sort algorithm in which the items being sorted are inserted into a heap, then removed one at a time.

height of a node In a tree, the number of nodes in the longest path from the node to a leaf.

height of a tree The number of nodes in a path from the root to the deepest leaf.

Huffman code A varying length binary code in which each symbol is assigned a code whose length is inversely proportional to the frequency with which that symbol appears (or is expected to appear) in a message. The resulting coded message is the minimum possible length.

immutable A class that is immutable has no functions to change the value of its data fields. An immutable object can't be changed.

implement (an abstract data type) To provide in a class an implementation of all of the functions specified by the interface of an abstract data type.

implicit parameter The object to which a member function of that object's class is applied using the member access operator (. or ->) notation.

inception phase In the Unified model of the software life cycle, the initial phase of a project in which the requirements are first identified.

include file A file containing declarations of classes and functions (such as those in the C++ standard library) that can be used by a C++ program. See also *header*.

increment operator The operator that has the side effect of adding one to its operand.

independent copy An object that has been copied from another object and can be modified without modifying the original object.

index A value that specifies a position within an array.

infix notation Mathematical notation in which the operators are between the operands.

information hiding The design principle that states that the internal data representations of a class cannot be used or directly modified by clients.

inherit To receive from an ancestor. In an object-oriented language, a derived class inherits the member functions and data fields of its base classes. These inherited functions and data fields appear to clients of the derived class as if they were members specifically declared in that class.

inline function A function for which code is substituted for the function call during compilation, allowing more rapid execution. Functions whose bodies are defined within a class definition are compiled inline. Also a function may be declared inline by preceding its declaration with the keyword **inline**.

initializer list A list of values, enclosed in braces, that initializes the values in an array.

inner class A class that is defined within another class.

inorder predecessor For a binary search tree, the inorder predecessor of an item is the largest item that is less than this item. The node containing an item's inorder prececessor would be visited just prior to that item in an inorder traversal.

inorder traversal Processing a binary tree by traversing a node's left subtree, visiting the node itself, and then traversing the node's right subtree, beginning with the root node.

input stream A sequence of characters from some source, from which a program can obtain input.

insertion sort A sorting algorithm in which each item is inserted into its proper place in the sorted region.

instance See *object*.

instance function A function (member function) that is associated with an object. Contrast with *static function*.

instance variables A variable of a class that is associated with an object (i.e., a data field of an object). Contrast with *static variable*.

I/O manipulator A member function of the stream input/output classes that can be used to control the format of subsequent input or output.

integration testing Testing in which the interaction of the components or units of a software program is validated.

interface The external view of a class. In C++ the interface of a class is defined by its public members.

internal node A node in a tree that has one or more children. Contrast with *leaf*.

is-a relationship The relationship between two classes in which all the instances of one are also instances of the other, but not necessarily the other way around. For example, a jet airplane is an airplane, and a laptop computer is a computer, but not all airplanes are jets and not all computers are laptops. Object-oriented languages capture the is-a relationship by extending classes.

iteration In a loop, a complete execution of the loop body. In the Unified Model of the software life cycle, a sequence of activities that results in the release of a set of software artifacts.

iterator An object that accesses the objects contained in a sequence one at a time.

Javadoc In the Java system, a program that generates Web-compatible documentation from comments that follow specific conventions in a Java source program. Software is now available to do the same for C++ programs.

key A value or reference that is unique to a particular object and thereby identifies that object (e.g., a social security number). Keys are used to access elements in associative containers.

Last In, First Out (LIFO) An organization of data such that the most recently inserted item is the one that is removed first.

last-line recursion A recursive algorithm or function in which the recursive call is the last executable statement.

leaf (node) A node in a tree that has no children. Contrast with *internal node*.

left rotation The transformation of a binary search tree in which the right child of the current root becomes the new root, and the old root becomes the left child of the new root.

level of a node The number of nodes in a path from the root to this node.

life line The dotted vertical line in a UML sequence diagram that indicates the life time of an object.

linear probing A collision resolution method in which sequential locations in a hash table are searched to find the item sought or an empty location.

linear search A search algorithm in which items in a sequence are examined sequentially.

link A pointer from one node to another.

linker A program that takes one or more object files produced by the compiler and puts them together into a machine langage file that the computer can execute.

literal A constant value that appears directly in a statement.

load factor In a hash table, the proportion of total capacity that is filled.

logic error An error in the design of an algorithm or program that does not prevent the program from compiling or running but produces incorrect results. Contrast with *syntax error* and *run-time error*.

logical view A description of the data stored in an object that does not specify the physical layout of the data in memory.

loop invariant An assertion that is true before each execution of the loop body and is true when the loop exits.

l-value An expression that can have a value assigned to it; that is, it can be put on the left side of an assignment operator.

machine language The form of a computer program that the computer can execute directly.

many-to-one mapping An association among items in which more than one item (a key) is associated with a single item (a value).

max heap A heap in which the value at a node is greater than the values in the node's subtrees.

member A piece of information found in all objects belonging to a class (a data member) or a function that can be invoked on any object of the class (a member function).

member function A function that can be called on any object of a class. The identifier for the object is written followed by a dot followed by the name of the function. Within the function implementation, the identifier for a data member means the value of that data member for that object.

memory leak A condition in which a program allocates memory for objects but fails to give the memory back to the operating system when the objects go out of use. The computer's performance gradually degrades as the operating system has less and less memory available. Destructor functions must be coded correctly to prevent memory leaks.

merge The process of combining two sorted sequences into a single sorted sequence.

merge sort A sorting algorithm in which sorted subsequences are merged to form larger sorted sequences.

message In an object-oriented design, a message represents an occurrence of a function call.

message to self A message that is passed from an object to itself. It represents a function calling another function within the same class.

method A sequence of statements that can be invoked (or called) passing a fixed number of values as arguments and optionally returning a value. See also *member function*.

min heap A heap in which the value at a node is less than all the values in its subtrees.

minimum spanning tree A subset of the edges of a connected graph such that the graph remains connected and the sum of the weights of the edges is the minimum.

modifier A member function to enable a client to change the value of an instance variable. The modifier should not return any value. Also called a *mutator* or *setter*. The name of the modifier function should begin with the word set_ followed by the name of the instance variable.

multiple inheritance The ability of a class to inheriting from more than one base class.

multiplicity An indication of the number of objects in an association.

mutator See *modifier*.

namespace A collection of names that are all defined together and are all distinct from each other.

narrowing conversion A conversion from a type that has a larger range of values to a type that has a smaller one.

nested class See *inner class*.

network A system consisting of interconnected entities.

new operator The C++ operator that creates objects (or instances) of a class.

newline The special character that indicates the end of a line of input or output.

node An object to store data in a linked list or tree. This object will also contain pointers to other nodes.

null character A character whose value in seven-bit ASCII is zero. The null character, represented by '\0' in C++, is not the same as the printable zero character '0'.

null pointer A pointer value that indicates that the pointer does not reference any object.

object An example or instance of a class. Internally, it is an area of memory that is structured as defined by a class. The functions of that class operate on the values defined within this memory area.

object code A form of a program that has been mostly translated into machine language except for references to variables, functions, or classes defined outside of the original source file.

object-oriented design A design approach that identifies the entities, or objects, that participate in a problem or system and then designs classes to model these objects within a program.

offset A constant that can be added to a pointer.

onto mapping A mapping in which each value in the value set is mapped to by at least one member of the key set.

open addressing Resolving collisions in a hash table by inserting the new item in the first unoccupied position above the location of the collision. The item can then be found by linear probing.

open-box testing See *white-box testing*.

operations The functions (or methods) defined in a class.

operator For classes, operator is another name for *function*. For primitive types, it represents a pre-defined function on one or two values (for example, addition).

operator function A function whose name is in the form **operator@**, where @ is one of the operator symbols (e.g. +, *, =). These functions may be defined for classes so that they define the corresponding operator for that class.

order of a B-tree The maximum number of children in a node.

output buffer A memory area in which information written to an output stream is stored prior to being written to disk.

output stream A sequence of characters produced by a program for use by some other program or a user.

overload To define more than one member function or operator with the same name but different signatures so that they can be called with different sets and/or types of parameters.

override To define a virtual member function in a derived class that replaces the member function with the same signature inherited from the base class.

parameter An item of information for which a function needs a value when it is called in order to perform its task.

parent The node that is directly above a node within a tree.

partitioning The process of separating a sequence into two sequences; used in *quicksort*.

path In a graph, a sequence of vertices in which each vertex is adjacent to its predecessor.

path coverage A measure of testing thoroughness. If a test exercises a path through a function, then that path is considered covered. The ratio of the covered paths to the total number of paths is the path coverage. See also *branch coverage* and *statement coverage*.

peeking the stack Accessing the top element of a stack without removing it.

persistent storage Part of a computer system that keeps data even when the application program that works with that data is not running, such as a hard disk drive.

phase In the Unified Model of the software life cycle, the span of time between two major milestones.

physical view A view of an object that considers its actual representation in computer memory.

pivot In the *quicksort* algorithm, a value in the sequence being sorted that is used to partition the sequence. The sequence is partitioned into one subsequence of values that are less than or equal to the pivot and another subsequence of values that are greater than the pivot.

pointer An object that contains the memory address of another object.

polymorphism The ability to select the correct definition of a member function based on the type of the actual object being pointed to at run time, regardless of the type of the pointer variable. In C++ a member function has polymorphism if it is declared *virtual*.

pop Remove the top element of a stack.

postcondition An assertion that will be true after a function is executed assuming that the preconditions were true before the function is executed.

postfix increment The increment operator (e.g., i++) that has the side effect of incrementing the variable to which it is applied, but its current value is the value of the variable before the increment takes place (e.g., i).

postfix notation A mathematical notation in which the operators appear after their operands.

postorder traversal An approach to traversal of a tree in which the left and right subtrees of each node are traversed before the node itself is visited.

precedence The degree of binding of infix operators. Operators of higher precedence are evaluated before operators of lower precedence.

precondition An assertion that must be true before a function is executed for the function to perform as specified.

prefix increment The increment operator (e.g., ++i) that has the side effect of incrementing the variable to which it is applied, and its current value is the value of the variable after the increment takes place (e.g., i + 1).

preorder traversal An approach to traversal of a tree in which each node is visited before its subtrees are traversed.

preprocessor Part of the C++ compiler system that modifies a program before the compiler itself begins to translate the modified source code into machine language. The preprocessor is used to define constants and incorporate other source code files.

primitive type A type of data whose definition is built into the C++ language, such as a character or number.

priority queue A data structure in which the item with the highest priority is removed next, rather than the most recently added item (as in a stack) or the first item added (as in a queue).

private Of a class member, visible only to functions defined in the same class or to classes or functions declared to be friends.

procedural abstraction The philosophy that procedure (function) development should separate the concern of *what* is to be achieved by a procedure (or function) from the details of *how* it is to be achieved.

proof by induction A proof method which demonstrates that a proposition is true for a base case (usually 0) and then demonstrates that if the proposition is true for an arbitrary value (k) is it then true for the successor of that value ($k + 1$).

protected visibility A level of visibility whereby variables and functions are visible to functions defined in the same class, derived classes of that class, or friends of that class.

pseudocode A description of an algorithm that is structured like a programming language implementation, but lacks the formal syntax and notation of a programming language. Generally pseudocode will use common programming language decision and looping constructs.

pseudorandom numbers A computer-generated sequence of values that appear to be random because they pass various statistical tests that are consistent with those that would be produced by a truly random sequence.

public visibility Of a class member, visible to all functions.

pure virtual function See *abstract function*.

quadratic probing In a hash table, a collision resolution technique in which the sequence of locations that are examined increases as the square of the number of probes made.

queue An abstract data type consisting of a structure in which elements can be added at one end and removed at the other so that the first element added is the first element retrieved.

queuing theory The branch of mathematics developed to solve problems associated with queues by developing mathematical models for these problems.

quicksort A sorting algorithm in which a sequence is partitioned into two subsequences, one that is less than or equal to a pivot value and the other that is greater than the pivot value. The process is then recursively applied to the subsequences until a subsequence with one item is reached.

random access The ability to access any object in a sequence by means of an index.

recursion A programming technique in which a function solves a problem by calling itself to solve simpler versions of the problem.

recursive case A case in a recursive algorithm that is solved by applying the algorithm to a transformed version of its parameter.

recursive data structure A data structure that is defined in terms of itself.

recursive function A function that calls itself.

Red-Black tree A self balancing binary search tree that maintains balance by distinguishing the nodes by one of two states: "red" or "black". Algorithms for insertion and deletion maintain the balance by ensuring that the number of black nodes in any path from the root to a leaf is the same.

refactoring Reorganizing a class hierarchy so that members common to more than one class are grouped together in a class by themselves.

reference To contain the memory location of an object.

reference variable A variable that references an object. A reference is an alias for the referenced object.

regression testing Testing that ensures that changes to the item being tested do not invalidate previously verified functions.

rehashing The process of moving the items in one hash table to a larger hash table using hashing to find each item's new location.

relocatable Of object code, able to work correctly regardless of where it is placed in the computer's memory.

requirements specification A document that specifies what a program or system is to do without specifying how it is done.

reusable code Code written for one program that can be used in another.

right rotation The transformation of a binary search tree in which the left child of the current root becomes the new root, and the old root becomes the right child of the new root.

root The node in a tree that has no parent and is at the top level.

run-time error An error that is detected when the program executes.

r-value The expression to the right of an assignment operator. In a strongly typed language such as C++, the r-value must be of the same type as the l-value in that assignment.

seed The initial value in a pseudorandom number sequence. Changing the seed causes a different sequence to be generated by the pseudorandom number generator.

selection sort A sort algorithm in which the smallest item is selected from the unsorted portion of the sequence and placed into the next position in the sorted portion.

self-balancing search tree A search tree with insertion and removal algorithms that maintain the tree in balance. See *balanced binary search tree, AVL tree, Red-Black tree, 2-3 tree,* and *2-3-4 tree.*

sequence A data structure that contains one or more elements, within which elements can be inserted or deleted at any position.

sequence diagram A UML diagram that shows the sequence of messages between objects that are required to perform a given function or realize a use case.

sequential access Access to elements within a sequence in a specific order.

sequential container A container class in which the objects contained are in some linear order and can be accessed by position in that order (such as the vector element at a given index position, or the list element that precedes or follows a given one).

set difference For sets A and B, A–B is the subset of a set, A, that does not contain elements of some other set, B.

set intersection A set of the elements that are common to two sets.

setter See *modifier.*

set union A set of the elements that are in one set or the other.

shallow copy A copy of an object in which only the values of the data fields are copied. If a data field is a pointer, the original and the copy reference the same target object.

Shell sort A variation on insertion sort in which elements separated by a value known as the gap are sorted using the insertion sort algorithm. This process repeats using a decreasing sequence of values for the gap.

sibling One of two or more nodes in a tree that have a common parent.

signature A function's name and the types of its parameters. The return type is not part of the signature, because it is illegal to have two functions with the same signature and different return types.

simple path A path that contains no cycles.

simulation The process of modeling a physical system using a computer program.

single-step execution In debugging, the process of executing one statement at a time so that the user may examine the values of variables after each statement is executed.

smart pointer An object that acts like a pointer but deletes the object it points to when that object has no owner.

software life cycle The sequence of phases that a software product goes through as it is developed.

source The vertex from which an edge in a directed graph is directed.

spanning tree A subset of the vertices of a connected graph that contains no more than one edge between any two vertices but that still results in a connected graph.

sparse graph A graph in which the number of edges, |E|, is much less than the square of the number of vertices, |V|—that is, one in which most of the edges that could exist do not.

specialization An implementation of a template function (or class) specially written for a particular parameter type so that the compiler will use it rather than instantiate the general template function (or class) when called (or instantiated) on that type.

stack An abstract data type consisting of a structure in which elements are added and removed at one end so that only the most recently added element can be accessed or removed.

standard library A collection of classes and functions that is available to any C++ program.

Standard Template Library (STL) A collection of template classes that are incorporated into the standard library. The STL consists of the collection classes, iterators, and algorithm functions.

starter function See *wrapper function.*

state The current value of all of the data fields in an object.

statement coverage A measure of testing thoroughness. If a test exercises a statement, then the statement is considered covered. The ratio of the covered statements to the total number of statements is the statement coverage. See also *branch coverage,* and *path coverage.*

static function A member function defined within a class, but not associated with any particular object of that class. Contrast with *instance function*.

static variable A variable defined in a class that is not a member of any particular object, but shared by all objects of the class. Contrast with *instance variable*.

step into When debugging in single-step mode, setting the next statement to be executed to be the first statement of the function. Each individual statement in the function is executed in sequence.

step over When debugging in single-step mode, setting the function call to be treated as a single statement.

stepwise refinement The process of breaking a complicated problem into simpler problems. This process is repeated with the smaller problems until a problem of solvable size is reached.

strongly typed language A programming language in which the type of objects is verified when arguments are bound to parameters and when values are assigned to variables. A syntax error occurs if the types are not compatible.

structure chart A diagram that represents the relationship between problems and their subproblems.

structured walkthrough A design or code review following a defined process in which the author of a program leads the review team through the design and implementation, and the reviewers follow a check-list of common defects to verify that these defects are not present.

stub A dummy function that is used to test another function. A stub takes the place of a function that the function being tested calls. A stub will typically return a known result.

subclass See *derived class*.

subset A set that contains only elements that are in some other set. A subset may contain any or all of the elements of the other set or it may be the empty set.

subtree of a node The tree that consists of this node as its root.

superclass See *base class*.

syntax error An error that violates the syntax rules of the language, preventing successful compilation. Syntax errors are generally the result of a mistake in entering the program into the computer (typographical error) or a misunderstanding of the language syntax. Syntax errors are detected by the compiler.

system analyst A person who analyzes a problem to determine the requirements for a software program.

system testing Testing of a complete program or solution to a problem in the context (operating system, other applications) in which it will be used.

tail recursion See *last line recursion*.

template class A class that enables a programmer to create and manage pieces of information whose type is passed to the template class as a parameter when objects of the class are created. See also *generic class*.

template function A function in which the parameter types are given as template types and are replaced by actual parameter types at compile time. See also *generic function*.

test case An individual test.

test framework A set of classes and procedures used to design and conduct tests.

test harness A function that executes the individual test cases of a test suite and records the results.

test suite A collection of test cases.

throw an exception Indicate that the situation that causes an exception has been detected.

token A character or string extracted from a larger string. Tokens are separated by *delimiters*.

top-down design An approach to design that represents the solution to a higher module in terms of the solution to one or more lower-level modules.

topological sort An ordering of a sequence of items for which a partial order is defined that does not violate the partial order. For example, if a is defined to be before b (a is a prerequisite of b) by the partial order, then a will not appear later in the sequence than b. A partial order is defined by a directed acyclic graph.

transition phase In the Unified Model of the software life cycle, the phase in which the software product is turned over to the end users.

traverse a graph Visit all the vertices in the graph by advancing from vertex to vertex along edges.

tree A data structure consisting of nodes that have one or more successors (children) but no more than one predecessor (parent).

tree traversal The process of systematically visiting each node in a tree.

try block A compound statement preceded by the keyword **try** so that exceptions generated within that statement sequence can be handled by the exception handlers that follow.

type A property of an item of data that specifies what kind of information it contains. The type determines what values the item can have and what can and cannot be done with the information.

type cast The process of converting from one type to another.

undirected edge An edge in an undirected graph.

undirected graph A graph in which no edge has a direction. If u and v are vertices in a graph then the presence of the edge $\{u, v\}$ indicates that v is adjacent to u, and u is adjacent to v. Contrast with *directed graph*.

Unified Model A software development life cycle model that is defined in terms of a sequence of phases and workflows. The workflows are exercised during each iteration of each phase, but the distribution of the amount of effort for each workflow varies from iteration to iteration.

Unified Modeling Language (UML) A language to describe the modeling of an object-oriented design that is the unification of several previous modeling systems. Specifically, the modeling techniques developed by Booch, Jacobson, and Rumbaugh were combined to form the initial version. UML has since evolved and is defined by a standard issued by the Object Modeling Group.

unit testing Testing of an individual unit of a software program. In C++, a unit is generally a function or a class.

unnamed pointer See *anonymous pointer*.

unnamed reference See *anonymous reference*.

unwinding the recursion The process of returning from a sequence of function calls and forming the result.

use case The documentation of the sequences of interactions between a computer system and its user needed to accomplish a given process.

user interface (UI) The way in which the user and a program interact, or the class that provides this interaction.

using declaration A line that indicates that an identifier declared in another namespace can be used in this namespace without need of a qualifying prefix.

using directive A line that indicates that all identifiers declared in a given namespace can be used in this namespace without need of a qualifying prefix.

vector An indexed sequence into which elements may be inserted or deleted at any position and whose length can be changed.

version control The process of keeping track of the various changes that are made to a program as it is developed or maintained.

vertices The set of items that are part of a graph. The vertices are related to one another by edges.

virtual function A member function whose definition is to be selected at run time based on the type of the actual object on which it is called. If a member function is not declared virtual, the definition is determined when the class is compiled, and that definition will always be called when the function is invoked through a pointer to that class, even if the object pointed to actually belongs to a derived class that overrides the function.

visit a node In tree traversal, to process and consume the information in the node. Merely encountering the node and going on to a child of the node does not constitute visiting the node.

waterfall model A software development model in which all of the activities of one workflow are completed before the next one is started.

weight A value associated with an edge in a weighted graph.

weighted graph A graph in which each edge is assigned a value.

white-box testing Testing that takes into account the internal structure of the unit being tested. Also called *glass-box testing* or *open-box testing*. See also *coverage testing*.

widening conversion A conversion from a type that has a smaller set of values to one that has a larger set of values.

workflow In the Unified Model of the software life cycle, a sequence of activities performed by participating workers and the artifacts they produce.

wrapper class A class that encapsulates a primitive data type.

wrapper function A function whose only purpose is to call a recursive function, perhaps providing initial values for some parameters, and returning the result. Also called a *starter function*.

Index

Terms beginning with numbers, such as 2-3-4 trees, are indexed as if spelled out.

?: operator, 20*t*
*, *See* dereferencing operator
*, to represent indefinite number of multiplicities, 775
! operator, 12
!= operator, 20*t*
operator, 9
% operator, 20*t*
& operator, 24, 25
&& operator, 12
* operator, 19, 20*t*
+ operator, 19, 20*t*, 31
++ operator, *See* increment operator
- operator, 19, 20*t*, 31
-- operator, *See* decrement operator
-> operator, 20*t*
/ operator, 19, 20*t*
< operator, 20*t*
<< operator, 20*t*
<= operator, 20*t*
= operator, 20*t*
== operator, 20*t*
> operator, 20*t*
>= operator, 20*t*
>> operator, 20*t*
|| operator, 12
~ operator, 20*t*

A

abstract classes, 202–204, 771
abstract data types, 99–100
  interface notation to represent, 99, 771
  preconditions and postconditions, 100–101
abstract functions, 202–204
abstraction, 73–75
acceptance testing, 68*t*, 149
accessor member functions, 87
  inline definition, 88
access specifiers, 77

accumulate function, 301*t*
activation bars, in UML sequence diagrams, 778
activation frames, 409–411
actual classes, 204
adapter classes
  queue class as, 366
  stack class as, 326
addresses, displaying for different countries case study, 206–209
address function, allocator class, 758*t*
address-of operator (&), 24
  syntax, 25
adjacency list, graphs, 701–702
adjacency matrix, graphs, 701, 702–703
adjacent vertex, 694
airline passengers simulation case study, 381–397
algorithm library, 299–301
algorithms
  Dijkstra's, 734, 736–738
  efficiency, 170–178
  growth rates compared, 176, 177
  Prim's, 738–742
  recursive algorithms, 404–411
  using weighted graphs, 734–742
allocate function, allocator class, 757, 758*t*
allocator, 235–236, 756–757
allocator class, 757, 758*t*
alternate keywords, 756, 756*t*
amortized constant time, 246
analysis, in software life cycle, 65, 66, 69–70
ancestor-descendant relationship, 447
anchor, for inner or nested classes, 774
and_eq keyword, digraphs, trigraphs, or equivalents for, 756*t*
and keyword, digraphs, trigraphs, or equivalents for, 756*t*
and operator, 12, 20*t*
anonymous pointer, 205
app openmode flag, 55*t*
architectural design, 68*t*

arguments, 30
  arrays, 36
arithmetic operators, 19, 20*t*
array arguments, 36
array data fields, 94
array indexing, 34
array index out of bounds error, 132*t*, 132–135
array-pointer equivalence, 34–35
Array_Queue.tc, 370, 372, 374–375
arrays, 33–37
  crude nature of, 231
  disadvantages relative vectors, 233
  dynamically allocated, 34–35
  falling off either end, 613
  multidimensional, 36–37
  out-of-bound subscripts, 33
  performance of sorted compared to hash tables and binary search trees, 540
  recursive algorithm to search, 405
  returning failure before examining all elements, 119
  security holes associated with lack of range checking, 237
  selection sort using, 576
  for storage in queue, 370–374
  telephone directory case study, 108–113
array subscript operator, 20*t*
artificial intelligence (AI), 403
The Art of Computer Programming, Vol 3: Sorting and Searching (Knuth), 496, 539
ASCII (American Standard Code for Information Interchange), 17–18, 18*t*, 755
assertions, 166
assert macro, 168–169
assignment, 204
assignment operator, 20*t*, 250–251
  failure to define, 252
association, UML notation, 774–775
associative array, 523
associative container concept, 292
associative containers, 292, 511, 774